ISBN 978-1-5276-2873-1
PIBN 10876630

1 MONTH OF
FREE
READING

at

www.ForgottenBooks.com

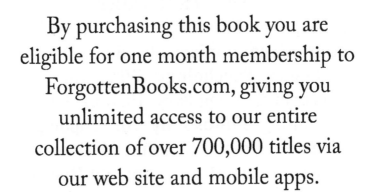

By purchasing this book you are eligible for one month membership to ForgottenBooks.com, giving you unlimited access to our entire collection of over 700,000 titles via our web site and mobile apps.

To claim your free month visit:

www.forgottenbooks.com/free876630

AGRICULTURE

IN SOME OF ITS RELATIONS WITH

CHEMISTRY

BY

F. H. STORER, S.B., A.M.

PROFESSOR OF AGRICULTURAL CHEMISTRY IN HARVARD UNIVERSITY

IN THREE VOLUMES

VOL. I.

SEVENTH EDITION
REVISED AND ENLARGED

NEW YORK
CHARLES SCRIBNER'S SONS
1897

S
555
. S7cx

V. 1

PRESS OF
Carl H. Heintzemann, Boston, Mass.

PREFACE.

Thɪs book has been written in the interest of persons fond of rural affairs, and of students of agriculture. It makes no special appeal to chemists or to students of chemistry. It is based upon lectures delivered annually by the author at the Bussey Institution during the years 1871 to 1897. These lectures, whɪch have been many times altered and revised, were addressed to small classes of students of two distinct types, viz.: young farmers, and sons of farmers, familiar with the manual practice of agricultural operations, who were desirous of studying some of the sciences which bear most immediately upon the art of farming; and, secondly, city-bred men, — often graduates of the academic department of the University, — who intended either to establish themselves upon farms, or to occupy country seats, or to become landscape gardeners. The purpose of the teaching was to familiarize the students with some of the scientific principles upon which the art of agriculture depends, and to illustrate and enforce these principles by examples drawn from the practical experience of farmers at home and abroad.

Until shortly before the publication of the first edition, in 1887, there had been no thought of ever printing any part of the matter of the lectures, and it was only because of the solicitations of students that the book was then issued. Naturally enough, more recent additions and interpolations have been made with an eye to their ultimate publication. It is hoped that the work as now enlarged may appeal, as the earlier editions have done, to many members of that large class of practical farmers, interested in scientific agriculture, who cannot possibly find time to leave home to study it.

The author desires to acknowledge his indebtedness to his teachers, Stoeckhardt and Boussingault, and to the books of Malaguti, Mulder, Gasparin, Bobierre, Wolff, A. Mayer, Sachs, Dehérain, and Muntz and Girard; and especially to those of

iii

Knop,[1] Heiden,[2] and Hellriegel.[3]   Like all other agricultural chemists, he owes a great debt of gratitude to the collaborators of the Jahresbericht and the Centralblatt der Agricultur-Chemie, which were established respectively by R. Hoffmann and R. Biedermann; the Journal of the Royal Agricultural Society of England has been helpful, and so also to a certain extent have been the Journal of the Highland and Agricultural Society of Scotland, and the recently established " Experiment Station Record " of the United States Department of Agriculture.   He is glad to be able to acknowledge his sense of indebtedness to Professors H. P. Armsby and F. H. King, and he regrets that he has been unable to refer explicitly to several matters in Professor King's book entitled " The Soil," since it was not published until some months after the manuscript of these volumes had been placed in the printer's hands.

Special mention needs to be made of the publications of his friend, Professor S. W. Johnson of New Haven, and of the important researches of Professors E. W. Hilgard of California, and Milton Whitney of Washington, D. C.   With regard to the books of Professor Johnson, notably those entitled " How Crops Grow," and " How Crops Feed," — which it is fair to presume are already in the hands of almost every student of agriculture, — the author would urge upon the reader, as he has been accustomed to urge upon his pupils, the great importance both of studying these treatises for their own sakes, and of consulting them freely in elucidation of many subjects which are treated of in the present work.   Not a few points have here been lightly touched upon, or even wholly omitted, simply because full explanations concerning them may be found in one or another of Johnson's books.

It will be noticed that numerous and important changes have been made in the text.   The book is printed in larger type and necessarily from new plates.   In fact, every page of the earlier book has been rewritten in the hope of elucidating the subject more clearly, and for the purpose of interpolating new matter which the progress of science has brought forward.

BUSSEY INSTITUTION OF HARVARD UNIVERSITY.
Jamaica Plain (Boston), Massachusetts.

---

[1] Lehrbuch der Agricultur-Chemie, 8vo, 2 vols.   [2] Lehrbuch der Düngerlehre, 3 vols.
[3] Beiträge zu den naturwissenschaftlichen Grundlagen des Ackerbaus.

CONTENTS OF VOLUME I.

PAGES.

AGRICULTURE.

CHAPTER I.

On considering the relations in which plants stand to the air and the soil which surround them, the questions naturally arise, What are the sources from which plants derive food? and, How is it that plants take in their food?

Suppose, for example, that a seed was buried in the earth some time since, that it has germinated there, and that the plant has begun to grow independently, of what significance for this plant are the soil and the air with which it is in contact?

Strange as it may seem on first sight, it is from air and from water that plants are chiefly derived. All the so-called carbonaceous matters in a plant are formed from carbonic acid which is taken into the plant through the leaves. From the air, too, comes no inconsiderable part of the oxygen which next to carbon is the predominant constituent of the dry matter in plants; though much oxygen comes to the plant in the form of water, whence the hydrogen also is derived. Boussingault found in a crop of 4,500 lb. of clover hay harvested from an acre of land

1680 lb. of carbon,	177 lb. of hydrogen, and
1340 lb. of oxygen,	74 lb. of nitrogen.

Plants contain much Water.

A fresh or living plant consists largely of mere water. Young grass, for example, is three fourths water, which may be dried out at 212° F. Potatoes also contain almost 75% of water, and the more succulent vegetables contain a still larger proportion. Beets and carrots contain 80 or 90% of water. A 2,000 lb. ton of turnips may contain more than 1,800 lb. of water. Even trees seldom contain less than one third their weight of it. Schuebler found that ash trees felled at the end of January contained 29% of water, a maple contained 34%, and a fir 53%. The same kinds of trees felled early in April had 39, 40, and 61% of water respectively. Gelesnoff, who made determinations for every month in the year, found that the average yearly amount of water in a pine tree was 61%, in a poplar 53%, in a birch 49%, and in a maple 42%.

This water comes from the soil, i. e. it is taken into the plant through the roots. From the soil also plants take in that small proportion of inorganic matter which is left as ashes when their carbonaceous parts are consumed. Every hundred pounds of the clover hay examined by Boussingault contained some six pounds of ashes. It is through their roots moreover that the ordinary plants of cultivation take in the nitrogenous compounds which are needed for their growth.

Water Culture.

It is quite possible to make plants grow tolerably well without the intervention of any soil, using the term soil of course in its ordinary acceptation.

Not only do we see parasitic plants, like the mistletoe, growing freely in mere air, but it is easy to make a great variety of plants grow in water. It has long been customary in domestic horticulture to grow hyacinths and other bulbs, as well as cuttings of rosebushes and of the so-called Wandering-Jew (*Tradescantia*), in glasses of water, and it is true that almost any of the ordinary grains may be made to grow and bear seeds in this way, Indian corn notably. It is only necessary that the water shall hold dissolved certain so-called inorganic, or ash-producing, constituents of the plant, and a small quantity of some compound of nitric acid, the very things, namely, which are ordinarily taken by the plant from the soil. Though these soil-derived substances are few in number, and though the quantity of each of them required by a plant is exceedingly small, they are none the less essential and indispensable.

In direct opposition to the idea of our forefathers that the ashes of plants may perhaps be useless or accidental, it is accounted one of the most important discoveries of the present century that it is impossible for plants of the higher orders to develop themselves in the absence of potash, lime, magnesia, iron, phosphoric acid, sulphuric acid, and hydrochloric acid, and some nitrogen compound, such as one of nitric acid or of ammonia.

We know thus much not only from the fact that the substances in question (excepting the nitrogen compounds) are always to be found in the ashes of plants; but, better, we know it from the results of manifold experiments made with factitious soils, in the compounding of which one or more of the substances enumerated were left out.

Even the parasitic plants, like the mistletoe, take food from the sap of the tree to which they are attached, or from the decaying wood itself in case they grow upon a lifeless branch.

History of Water Culture.

The method of " water culture," just now alluded to, has often been put to use by investigators as a means of testing methods of feeding plants. Many experiments of great value for the elucidation of questions in vegetable physiology have been tried by means of it. The idea itself is old. The Swiss naturalist Bonnet studied it long ago. So too, as early as 1758, the French chemist and botanist Duhamel grew beans in this way, and he produced chestnut, oak and almond trees. Some of his trees were six and eight years old when an accident destroyed them. Duhamel found that it was necessary to change the water frequently, and we now know that it is the matters in the water, the substances namely which are held dissolved in the water, that need to be renewed.

In experimenting in this way it is no longer customary to take spring water, but pure distilled water, in which can be dissolved whatever substances we may wish to experiment upon. The subject is described in some detail in Professor S. W. Johnson's book entitled " How Crops Grow," under the head of " Water Culture."

Sand Culture.

Instead of placing the clear aqueous solution to be experimented upon in a jar by itself, it might be poured into a vessel filled with pulverized quartz, or with any other inert substance incapable of yielding plant-food, such as beach-sand which has been leached with an acid. If this be done, it will be found that plants will grow in the mixture very much in the same way that they grow in the water without the sand, excepting that in the sand the plant provides for its own mechanical support.

The use of sand in this way is closely allied to a common method employed by gardeners in their propagating-houses, though the object of using sand in this case is to " start " cuttings

in a soil free from any putrescible matters charged with microscopic organisms, which might make the cuttings rot. So too, in
Holland, gardeners grow the bulbs of flowering plants on the
large scale, and very superior potatoes also, on the sand dunes of
that country, after having heavily manured them. The mobile
sand allows the roots and tubers to develop smoothly and symmetrically, i. e. an unusually large proportion of the sand-grown crop
is free from blemishes or irregularities of form.

Many experiments have been made in this way by scientific
men also. For example, the German chemists Wiegmann and
Polstorff, in order to obtain an absolutely inert sand, cut a quantity of platinum wire into small pieces; they put the fragments
in a platinum cup together with a definite number of seeds of
the common cress (*Lepidium sativum*) and they moistened the
wire with pure distilled water. The cup was then put under a
bell glass to protect its contents from dust, and the air of the
bell glass was kept fresh and proper for the growth of the seeds.

The seeds germinated, grew naturally during some days, and
even reached a height of three inches before they began to
droop and die. On igniting the cup and its contents so that the
plants were burned to ashes, these ashes were found to weigh
precisely as much as the ashes obtained from another lot of seeds,
equal in number to those sown upon the platinum. This experiment is here cited merely in illustration of the method of research.
The real object of the experiment was to determine precisely
what happens when a seed is made to sprout in a soil destitute of
plant-food. It helps to enforce the lesson, which has been learned
from many other observations, that, for continuous growth, food
must be supplied continually. If there had been dropped upon the
platinum sand a mixture of the needed ingredients, the plants
would have grown well enough, and would even have formed
perfect seeds.

Uses of the Soil.

It would appear that ordinary earthy soil is of use primarily
as standing room; the roots of plants spreading among the minute particles of which the soil is composed adhere to them in such
wise that the plant is held securely in the position proper to it.
The plant is braced and ballasted. The soil holds moisture also,
as a sponge would, and it is evident, that soils from which crops
are to be taken must contain in some shape the ash-producing
ingredients proper to those crops.

Assimilation of Plant-Food.

The questions still remain to be answered, In what state is the plant-food contained in the soil? and, How does the plant get at its food?

The weight of evidence thus far accumulated goes to show that the plant-food passes from the soil into the plant in the form of a solution. But it is by no means universally true that all the food consumed by a crop is in a state of solution in the soil, ready and waiting to flow towards the roots and to enter the plant when needed. Some plant-food — especially some particular kinds of plant-food — is undoubtedly held in solution in the moisture of the soil, so that the earth of cultivated fields is not wholly dissimilar to the moistened sand of the greenhouse men and of the scientific experimenters. But it would be highly erroneous to regard the soil as if it were nothing more than a sort of sponge charged with solutions of substances proper for the growth of plants. Really, the soil, beside being a storehouse from which plant-food is derived, is a laboratory in which solutions of plant-food are compounded; and, in addition to all this, it is known that the roots of plants, or rather matters exuded from the roots, play a very important part in dissolving substances out of the earth which mere water would be incapable of dissolving. The little hairs, in particular, upon the roots which cling so tightly to the soil, are active agents both for absorbing food from the soil-water and for dissolving food from the soil.

The earth serves also to arrest and retain many substances excluded by the plant which would do harm if they were suffered to remain dissolved so that they could accumulate about the roots. One of the chief difficulties inherent to the method of experimenting by water culture is precisely this accumulation of hurtful matters in the solutions used, as will be explained hereafter.

Diffusion and Osmose.

Nevertheless, for the sake of the argument, it may perhaps be well at first to consider the soil as if it were merely a source or reservoir of saline solutions — which indeed it most truly is as well as something more. This supposition will afford a convenient basis for the inquiry as to the manner in which the plant receives its food, and lead directly to a brief consideration of the laws of Osmose and of the diffusion of liquids, which control the admission of food to plants.

It is a matter of experience, that, if some salt be placed at the bottom of a tall jar, and the jar be then quietly filled with water and left at rest in a place of constant temperature, a perfectly homogeneous solution of salt and water will be obtained after the lapse of some time. No matter how carefully the vessel may be protected from mechanical agitation, the heavy brine which forms at the bottom of the jar when the salt and the water first come in contact with each other will gradually diffuse into the lighter water above it, until the entire mass of liquid has one uniform composition. This fact of diffusion pure and simple may readily be illustrated by placing a small quantity of a solution of a colored salt, such as potassium bichromate, at the bottom of a bottle of water, and allowing the latter to stand at rest for a day or two.

Even when brine and water are separated from each other by a porous membrane, like bladder or the outer covering of the minute cells of which plants and their roots are composed, this liquid diffusion will still go on, though the phenomenon is then found to be less simple than before.

On interposing the membrane between the brine and the water, phenomena depending upon capillary attraction, or the mechanical power of the membrane to absorb liquids as a sponge absorbs water, and upon chemical affinity of some ingredients of the membrane for those in the liquids, are liable to be manifested simultaneously with the movement of mere diffusion. That is to say, whatever force, whether of adhesion or of affinity, the matter of the membrane can exert upon the substance dissolved in the liquid, comes in to modify the simple diffusive force.

Thus, if a bladder full of brine be fastened to a narrow tube, best of glass, and then be sunk in a jar of water, it will be seen that water passes into the bladder more rapidly than the brine passes out, and so causes a rise of liquid in the narrow gauge tube. By analyzing the water in the jar, it would be found indeed, that a small quantity of salt has diffused out into the water; but it is apparent from the position of the water in the gauge tube that in this case water moves in through the membrane much faster than the salt moves out. Similar results can be obtained by substituting other dense liquids, such as syrup of sugar, for example, for the brine in this experiment. The quantity of water which passes in this way into a saline solution is often very much larger than would be introduced by mere liquid diffusion. It may even amount to several hundred times the weight of the saline matter displaced.

The movement or current of liquid inward (i. e. of the water in the supposed case) is called Endosmose, and the outward movement (of the salt in this case) is called Exosmose. The shorter word Osmose, or Osmosis (impulsion), which includes both the others, is used as a distinctive term for the phenomena of diffusion through membranes.

Now in the same way that the bladder acts in the experiment, so are the roots of plants supposed to act in the soil. The roots, and all other parts of plants as well, are composed of numberless minute bags or bladders, called cells, which lie close together and constitute the atoms, as it were, of which the tissues of the plant are built up. These cells are generally very small, and even of microscopic size, though in some plants they are large enough to be readily seen and experimented with. Since the liquids within the root-cells are of different composition from the liquids in the soil, the soil liquids are presumed to pass into the root-cells in much the same way that the water flows into the brine in the experiment just now cited.

Some Membranes specially Active.

It is to be observed that in all osmotic action very much depends upon the character of the membrane employed. Different kinds of membranes differ widely as to the amount of attraction, whether of adhesion or of affinity, which they exert upon the substances exposed to them. If, for example, the water and the brine in the cited experiment were separated by a membrane of such character that it could exert no action upon either of the liquids, the diffusion would proceed very much in the same way as if no membrane were present. Graham has, in fact, shown that common salt diffuses into water through a thin sheet of ox-bladder deprived of its outer membrane at about the same rate as when no membrane is interposed.

On the other hand, it has been proved by experiments of Schacht on the cell membranes of plants having single cells large enough for such observations, that the phenomena of osmose are well marked in the case of these plant membranes. A marine plant called *Caulerpa prolifera*, which has served for this purpose, is said to consist of a single cell that is often a foot in length.

Instead of an actual bladder, a convenient osmometer may be prepared by tying a piece of membrane (such as bladder, parchment paper or a collodion film) over the mouth of a glass funnel to the shank of which a narrow glass tube has been fastened. On filling the funnel with syrup or brine, and sinking it mouth downward in a glass of water, so that the membrane is kept wet, the liquid will rise high up in the narrow tube, and perhaps even flow over at the top of it.

Colloids and Crystalloids.

One other point needs to be mentioned as bearing upon the rapidity of the flow of liquids into plants. The character of the substances in solution, namely, has to be considered, as well as that of the membranes through which the solutions are to flow. It has been found by experiment that different substances diffuse through water, even, at very different rates. There is one class of bodies of very low diffusive power called colloids, which are characterized by a tendency to form jellies with water. And there is another class of comparatively high diffusive power, called crystalloids, most of which are capable of crystallizing when they assume the solid form.

Among colloids may be named glue (gelatin), the various gums and uncrystallizable albuminous substances, dextrin, pectin, and starch. Precisely those things which are formed within the living plant in abundance have small chance to leak out through the cell walls. Among the crystalloids, on the other hand, are sugar, many vegetable acids, such as citric, tartaric, and oxalic acids, and most of the ordinary salts.

Movements of Plant-Food.

On proceeding to inquire as to the bearings of the foregoing facts upon the theory of the growth of plants, it will be seen that active cells in the rootlets will naturally absorb saline matters from the soil, since the liquids in the root-cells (of a sprouted seed, for example) are of different composition from the liquids in the soil. Each root-cell is, so to say, charged with syrup or with brine as in the supposed experiment.

Diffusion and osmotic action must, moreover, go on from cell to cell, throughout the entire plant, so long as, from any cause, the unlike liquids in the various cells are prevented from coming to a state of equilibrium.

But, by virtue of the mere fact of its life, perpetual changes are occurring in every part of a growing plant, and there is consequently no lack of causes operating to prevent the attainment of any permanent equilibrium. Almost every change which occurs within the growing plant, no matter whether the alteration depends upon chemical or upon physical action, will tend to perpetuate this incessant diffusion of liquids.

If it be conceived, for example, that a portion of the contents of one cell have combined to form solid starch or some sluggish colloid substance, like albumen or dextrin, an osmotic vacuum, as it were, will be there established, and at the same time a movement of liquids will be started throughout the entire plant to try to fill this void space. A particle of lime coming in contact with oxalic acid to form the insoluble compound oxalate of lime would produce a similar effect. But changes analogous to these are constantly occurring throughout the entire plant. As the plant grows, new cells and new membranes are formed incessantly, and new quantities of soluble matter are continually brought into the plant.

In the foregoing brief sketch of the mode of introduction of food to plants through their roots, the subject is presented merely as witnessed from the chemist's point of view. It should be said, furthermore, that inside of the actual wall of the young vegetable cell, which is a true membrane composed of cellulose etc., there is a layer of mucilaginous or granulating matter, called protoplasm, which, beside lining the interior wall and often stretching across the cell from one side to the other in the form of stripes or bands, may actually reach through the walls from one cell to another in the form of fine threads, in such manner that special lines of communication are kept up by means of it between the several cells. This protoplasm is regarded by physiologists as the chief living constituent of the cell, i. e. as "the essential part of the cell, which carries out all the vital processes (Green)." The albuminoids in living protoplasm, moreover, are active chemical substances which doubtless do important service in exciting and regulating the osmotic functions of the cells. It should here be said that all the movements within the plant which are ordinarily spoken of as "osmotic" should really be regarded as dependent in some measure upon the vitality of the plant, i. e. on the vitality of the protoplasm in its cells and on the active character of the chemical substances of which the protoplasm consists.

Transpiration of Water.

It is necessary to distinguish carefully between the movements of mere water, by way of osmose, and the movements of plant-food. The evaporation, exhalation, or rather transpiration of water from the leaves of plants, undoubtedly exerts a highly important, and at times a paramount, influence on the osmotic movement of this particular liquid, while it may have nothing or next to nothing to do with the introduction of plant-food proper. In so far as mere water is concerned, it will naturally happen that, as fast as the contents of cells at the extremities of a plant become concentrated through loss of water that escapes as vapor into the air, fresh supplies of water will diffuse into them from the cells next adjacent, and so the movement of water will be transmitted from cell to cell until the store of moisture in the soil outside the plant has been reached. But it is plain at the first glance that this movement of liquid water through the plant is a fact to be considered by itself, and that the exhalation of vapor from foliage cannot be regarded as a prime motor in the matter of supplying saline food to plants. Indeed we often see vegetation assuming special luxuriance and vigor in atmospheres that are completely saturated with moisture, as in tropical forests, in some greenhouses and in the so-called Wardian case. That is to say, growth is most rapid under precisely those conditions where exhalation from the leaves is necessarily small.

Ward's Case.

The Wardian case, named from its inventor, Mr. Ward of London, is a piece of apparatus worthy of attentive consideration. It consists of a close box, provided with a glazed cover and charged with moistened earth for plants to grow in. In its original simplest form the Wardian case was merely a corked bottle half full of moist loam. Commonly it consists of a strong wooden box lined with zinc or lead. At the bottom of this box a porous stratum of gravel or broken earthenware is laid down; immediately upon the gravel a thin layer of turfy loam is placed to serve as subsoil, and finally the box is filled to its brim with loam proper. The loam is well moistened at the start, and a quantity of water is poured into the gravel to serve as a store or reservoir for supplying water continually. After plants have been set out in the earth, a closely fitting glazed cover is placed upon the box, and, if need were, this cover might be firmly cemented to the box.

The apparatus thus represents a little world by itself, in which one and the same quantity of water continues to be used over and over again for the support of the plants, while carbonic acid and nitrates are supplied to the plants by the decay of the humus in the earth. The moisture that evaporates from the loam, as well as that which is pumped up and exhaled by the plants, keeps the air in the apparatus saturated with vapor, and the excess of this vapor either condenses upon the inside of the glass cover, and thence trickles down upon the earth, or it is reabsorbed directly, as vapor, by the earth, whenever the temperature of the glass is too high to permit of condensation there. Thus it happens that the plants are maintained in an atmosphere saturated with moisture, and are so continually supplied with water that all the evils of capricious and irregular watering are done away with. So too the oxygen which is set free when the plants decompose carbonic acid or water, as will be explained directly, is returned to the air just as it is in the world at large, and this oxygen is thus used over and over again for the oxidation of humus.

Ordinarily, as employed in crowded cities where their chief purpose is to protect the plants from soot, dust, grime and foul air, the cases are not made absolutely air-tight, for it is a matter of convenience to be able to open them occasionally in order to pluck off dead leaves or to trim or readjust the plants. Thus it happens that small portions of the outer air do gain access to the plants, but it is not necessary that this should occur. One conspicuous merit of the Wardian case is that, practically speaking, it takes care of itself, both as regards water and air, and the maintenance of a considerable degree of regularity in respect to temperature. But when plants are to be carried long distances on shipboard, as when, for example, Mr. Fortune sent to Europe numerous living specimens of the florist's plants discovered by him in China, the cases are thoroughly closed. After having once been sealed up and placed in such positions that they are properly exposed to sunlight, they are left unopened for almost indefinite periods, sometimes for months. In smoky London, in particular, these cases were at one time largely used, both within doors and out of doors in yards and courts and on balconies.

Influence of Capillarity.

It need hardly be said that capillary action within the fibres of the plant is an important aid to liquid impulsion and to the osmotic movements of water in particular. But this capillary or rather conducting movement may be regarded in some sort as if it were outside the cells proper, between them, as it were, in the interspaces. It has been noticed by physiologists that water passes most readily through the fibrous, vascular parts of plants, and it is to be presumed that water drawn in at the roots by way of osmose may cling as a thin film to the walls of the conducting channels, and creep up these walls more rapidly than it could pass from cell to cell to make good the loss of water through exhalation from the leaves. It is evident, moreover, that water from the roots may be forced through the open channels by the pumping agencies which are constantly in action within the plant more readily than it could possibly be made to pass through a series of closed cells.

The significance of the capillary movement is shown by the familiar experiment in which children suck up water through a stick of rattan or the stem of a pond lily, and when they make the flexible lily stem serve as a syphon to drain water from a dish. The matter is well illustrated by the experience of the inventor Boucherie with his patent process for preserving timber. In some instances holes were bored at the base of the living tree while it was still standing, and the preservative liquid was led from a barrel into these holes by means of pipes. The ascent of the liquid into the tree through the porous sap-wood was found to be very rapid, but little or none of it went into the heart-wood at the centre of the trunk. In other cases, after the trees had been felled, and had had their tops lopped off, the preservative liquid was run into the trunks under a considerable head of pressure, which was obtained by elevating the reservoir cask. Under these conditions, the incoming liquid speedily forced out the sap from the channels in the wood, and took its place.

As regards evaporation from the leaves, it may be said yet again, that, although there are frequent times and seasons when the flow of water into and through the plant to supply the waste of water from the leaves is exceptionally rapid, this flow has little or nothing to do with the bringing in either of nitrogen or of ash ingredients from the soil for feeding the plant. Transpiration from the leaves, and the movements of water into and through the plant to that end, must be considered by themselves. They are of vast importance, doubtless, but should not be confounded with the normal movements of food and of organized matters downward as well as upward, into all parts of the plant, and which likewise appear to be due for the most part to the action of diffusion and osmose working slowly and constantly through the liquids with which the plant and its cells are charged.

Beside the fact just now alluded to, that plants in greenhouses and glass cases and in tropical forests grow exceptionally well in atmospheres saturated with moisture, we have the common experience that field crops often grow with astonishing rapidity in damp and rainy weather, when the air is so highly charged with moisture that all processes of simple evaporation wellnigh cease, and any loss of water from the leaves by mere evaporation must be decidedly slower than usual.

Transpiration a Physiological Process.

A clear distinction must be made, too, between the idea of mere evaporation, as of water from moist earth, and this special power of "exhalation" or "transpiration," i. e. the throwing off of vapor of water into the air, which is possessed by the leaves of living plants, and which goes on incessantly, to some extent even when the air which bathes the leaves is already saturated with moisture. Manifestly the exhalation depends in some way upon vital processes which work to that end.

Naturally enough, the escape of aqueous vapor from the leaves of a plant is most rapid in dry, hot, windy weather, especially when the soil as well as the air is warm; but there are experiments which go to show that the exhalation does not entirely cease when the plant is kept in a confined volume of air absolutely saturated with moisture, as in the Wardian case, for example.

Stomata, or Breathing Pores.

According to physiologists, the water transpired from plants escapes for the most part through myriads of minute openings or valves, called stomata or "mouths" which exist upon the surface of leaves and of young stems. These openings close in the dark, and they close partially when a leaf wilts, and, as a general rule, also when a leaf is wet with water. Transpiration is known to be much more rapid in direct sunlight than in darkness, and it is supposed that one reason why this is so is that the stomata or breathing pores are wide open in sunshine, while in the dark they close, and in diffused light they tend to close. For example, Wiesner found that a plant of Indian corn transpired in one hour from 100 square centimetres of surface:

In the dark . . . . . 97 milligrams of water.
In diffused daylight . . 114   "   "   "
In sunlight 785   "   "   "

But he casts a doubt as to whether the opening of the stomata can account for the whole of these differences, since he found the stomata of young maize plants closed at a time when much water was transpired by these plants.

The main point to be insisted on, however, in this place, is that the exhalation of water appears not to be essential for the feeding of the plant with nitrogenous matters and ash ingredients. Plants can live, and flourish, for a considerable time at least, in atmospheres so highly charged with moisture that exhalation is very feeble. And, on the other hand, no harm is done when exhalation is very rapid, provided the roots are supplied with water enough to make good what is lost from the leaves; otherwise the plant will wilt and droop and die. We find in nature plants exposed to the most varied conditions in this regard; while some kinds of plants actually live immersed in water, others are so constructed that they can get along with a very scanty supply of the liquid, and can retain water within their tissues with no little tenacity when once they have obtained it. Such plants are able, so to say, to resist transpiration, and to husband their water supply, although the water within them can doubtless move freely enough from one part of the plant to another, as occasion may require. There is a wide range between those aquatic plants which are constantly covered with water and the cactuses and sagebrush of the rainless deserts.

Yet the amount of water actually exhaled by ordinary agricultural plants is enormous; and it is certain that crops cannot be grown with full luxuriance unless the earth can continually supply to their roots enough water fully to compensate for all that goes off through the leaves. It is plain, not only that water is of the first importance as a means of maintaining plants in a succulent, juicy condition, so that food may move freely within them, and all the necessary physiological processes be favored, but that the exhalation of water acts as a great regulator, which, by absorbing and removing heat, keeps the plants within fit and proper limits of temperature. The importance of exhalation as a means of keeping plants cool is seen not only out of doors in hot summer weather, when water taken through the roots from the soil is thrown off by the leaves, and carries away, as it were, the excess of heat which would otherwise have destroyed the plant, but it is seen also only too frequently in greenhouses and hotbeds, when through deficient ventilation or inadequate protection from the sun's heat, plants are "blighted," by being unduly heated at a time when they are surrounded with air so completely saturated with vapor that the leaves are prevented from transpiring moisture fast enough to keep their tissues cool. So too, when young plants are transplanted in warm or dry weather, it is well to shield them somewhat from the sun at first, or until their roots have had time to become adjusted to the soil, and so made ready to perform their function of supplying moisture to the leaves.

In order to sound health, most crops need to have a constant and adequate supply of moisture at their roots, and that their leaves shall be surrounded with mobile air which is neither unduly moist nor excessively dry. It is important that the conditions shall permit transpiration to act freely, and preserve the plant from harm. Too much moisture, either in the soil or in the air, is hurtful. It is noticeable that gardeners are at pains to moderate their waterings when the air is damp, or even to abstain from watering altogether during periods of excessive dampness.

Examples of Transpiration.

There is a familiar illustration of the rapid exhalation of moisture from blades of grass, which has never been sufficiently dwelt upon. When the outer sashes of windows (double windows) are taken down or put up in spring or autumn, or when the sashes of cellar windows are removed, the workmen are apt to leave some of these glazed sashes for a time lying upon the grass about the house. But the moment the cool glass is thus exposed to the exhalation of moisture from the grass, it becomes cloudy and obscure through deposition of the moisture. So too, if a cold bell glass be placed over a bunch of growing grass, even in the driest season, water enough to trickle from the sides of the jar will be deposited in the course of two or three minutes.

The English observer, Watson, who first performed this experiment, was led to conclude from it that an acre of grass land might exhale more than 30 hogsheads of water in a day. Numerous experiments made by observers in different countries on various kinds of crops, show that, as a general rule, more than 300 pounds of water pass through a plant, and are transpired from its leaves for every pound of dry solid matter fixed or assimilated by the plant. Generally speaking, young plants and the younger parts of plants give off more water in this way than old ones.

In the old experiments of Hales a single cabbage plant of

moderate size exhaled 25 ounces of water in the course of 12 hours, and a sunflower plant 3.5 feet high gave off nearly 2 lb. of water in the course of 12 hours on a very warm, dry day. More recent experimenters have observed that grass-sod may give off as much as from 2 to 5 lb. of water for each and every square foot of surface in 24 hours. According to Knop, a grass plant in a hot, dry summer's day will exhale its own weight of water, while the experiments of Dehérain show that a young leaf of wheat or of rye, exposed to sunlight, may exhale its own weight of water in a single hour.

In experiments by Lawes and Gilbert certain plots of mowing land yielded, on an average of 15 years, 3 long tons of hay or 2.5 tons of dry substance per year and per acre. But, since at least 300 lb. of water are exhaled by grass for each lb. of dry matter assimilated, these hay crops must have exhaled about 750 long tons of water per acre during the growing season, which in this case lasted no later than the middle or end of June. So too in experimental fields of wheat which yielded 8 tons of total produce (grain and straw) to the acre, each year, there was harvested 2.5 tons of dry substance, which multiplied into 300 — the number of pounds of water exhaled for each pound of dry substance formed — gives 750 as the number of tons of water transpired from an acre of land by these wheat crops, which were harvested in late July or by the middle of August.

Hellriegel has taken a great deal of trouble to determine how many pounds of water were transpired by various plants which were thoroughly well fed, watered and cared for at Dahme, a village some miles south of Berlin, in Prussia. For barley, in particular, he found that in the course of its entire life 310 pounds of water were exhaled for every pound of dry matter which was produced, in the form of leaves, stem, and fruit, at that particular locality. For other plants, somewhat less carefully studied, he gives the following figures as the amount of water transpired for each pound of dry crop produced:—

	lb.		lb.		lb.
Summer wheat,	338	Horsebeans,	282	Buckwheat,	363
Summer rye,	353	Peas,	273	Summer rape,	329
Oats,	376	Red clover,	310		

The general result of the experiments is evidently that the various crops do not by any means differ so much from one another as to their relative powers of transpiring water as might have

been suspected from the differences which they exhibit as to
their outward forms or structure. It is of interest to observe in
particular that the leguminous plants tested seemed, on the whole,
to transpire less water than the cereals for each pound of dry crop
produced; and this conclusion was supported by measurements
of the transpiratory surfaces of barley, bean, and lupine plants,
taken at that particular stage of development of the plants, i. e.
that condition of maturity, when their lower leaves had begun to
die. It appeared, in fact, that these plants have very much the
same amounts of transpiratory surface for every pound of dry
substance which they contain. Thus the relations found for barley were 1 : 115 and 1 : 139; for the horse bean, 1 : 131; and for
the lupine, 1 : 136.

The figures in the table all refer to perfect plants, that grew
under the most favorable conditions possible. But it was noticed
that, when the yield of a crop is lessened by any circumstance
that hinders growth, the proportion of water transpired to crop
produced is always abnormally high.

Apparatus for exhibiting the Force of Osmose.

One prime purpose of roots is to keep plants full of water,
and, in order to this result, no small amount of power is expended. Ocular evidence of the great force with which the roots of
growing plants take in water from the soil may be had by arranging an experiment such as is depicted in the diagram on page 369
of "How Crops Grow." On fastening a pressure gauge to the
stump of a vigorous plant in the spring, water will be pumped up
by the plant from the soil into the gauge, and the mercury in the
latter will be forced up into the narrow tube until the column of
mercury in that tube is so high that its pressure has become equal
to the absorptive force which the roots of the plant are capable of
exerting.

By experimenting in this way, Hales found that a grapevine
was capable of supporting a column of mercury 32.5 inches high,
— which would be equal to a column of water 36.5 feet high.
Another experimenter, Hofmeister, found that a grapevine supported 29 inches of mercury, a nettle 14 inches, and a bean 6
inches. The flowing of sap in trees when excited by the return
of warmth in the spring, long before the appearance of any
leaves, as familiarly witnessed in the case of the sugar maple or
the "bleeding" of a grapevine that has been cut or injured in

the spring, illustrates the same thing precisely. If a glass tube be tied in a vertical position upon a bleeding branch, it is easy to collect a column of liquid that has been forced up by root-action in direct opposition to the force of gravitation.

Mention may here be made of another piece of apparatus,* devised by the German physiologist, Sachs, to illustrate the osmotic action of the root-cells. A short piece of wide glass tubing is closed at one end with a piece of pig's bladder; it is then filled with a solution of sugar, and closed at the other end with a piece of parchment paper. A caoutchouc cap carrying a narrow bent tube is then tied firmly over the parchment-paper end of the apparatus, and the latter is immersed in water.

The short, wide tube represents a root-cell, the outer or bladder-covered wall of which is less penetrable to liquids when exposed to pressure than the inner wall of parchment paper. But the water that passes into the cell by force of osmose soon exerts such a pressure on the parchment paper that a quantity of liquid is forced through this paper into the bent tube, in which it rises to a very considerable height above the surface of the water in the dish. The narrow bent tube may be regarded as representing the stem of a plant, or rather, as representing an open capillary channel within a plant-stem. This apparatus is readily prepared, and is highly efficient. It will sometimes continue to pump water actively during several days.

Solutions of Plant-Food may be highly Dilute.

The subject of osmose and the so-called selective power of plants for inorganic foods will naturally come up again for discussion under the head of manures. For the present, it will be sufficient to have indicated roughly the relation of the plant to the soil, if only the student has been led thereby to reflect upon the manner in which the food of plants is absorbed.

It is to be remembered that the water, or rather the moisture, within the soil, like much of the water which flows from the soil into wells and springs, is usually by no means highly charged with the substances which have been named above as essential to the growth of vegetation. But the plant has power to gather its food from exceedingly dilute solutions. It can collect phosphoric acid, for example, from waters which contain no more than one part of that substance in ten thousand or twenty thousand parts of

---

* Figured on page 400 of "How Crops Grow."

the liquid. It is no unusual thing for the chemist to find substances in the ashes of a plant which he cannot detect by his most delicate experiments, either in the soil in which the plant grew or in the water of that soil. It is a familiar fact, for that matter, that an abundance of iodine for use in medicine and in the arts is obtained from the ashes of sea-weeds, though we are wholly incompetent to obtain iodine directly from sea-water, or even to detect its presence there with certainty.

It may be remarked, in passing, that sea-plants well illustrate this capital principle of osmose. The floating sargasso, or gulf-weed, of the middle Atlantic; the kelp of our own coast,— growing often upon a loose stone or an old mussel-shell, from which no nourishment can be derived; the green slimes that flourish upon the surface both of salt and of fresh water, and all the other vegetations which have their being beneath the surface of water, are capital examples of the phenomena in question.

It should be understood, withal, that it is not from actual flowing water alone that plants are nourished. Most plants are supplied with food and with water also in good part from the mere dampness which is noticeable in loam that has been recently disturbed. The hairs upon the rootlets of plants cling to the damp loam and drink in the moisture from it. Young plants are apt to wilt when transplanted because their rootlets cannot immediately come into intimate contact with the earth, and they remain wilted until the rootlets have had time to adhere to the soil.

The significance of the dampness in loam is a matter of common observation. It is exemplified in some sense by an experiment of Sachs. Having grown a bean plant in a pot filled with stiff clay, this experimenter left the plant unwatered until it began to wilt. He then hung the pot in a close vessel full of air that was wellnigh saturated with moisture, but he left the plant proper projecting into the outer air. The wilted leaves soon revived, and the plant remained fresh during the two months devoted to the experiment, although it did not grow.

CHAPTER II.

THE ATMOSPHERE AS A SOURCE OF PLANT-FOOD.

As has been said already, a very large proportion of the dry matter of plants is derived from the air. A seed planted in mere sand may grow into a perfect plant if it be properly watered, and may produce a crop of new seeds, each as large and perfect as the first, although no particle of organic matter, of woody fibre, of starch, of oil, or of any other of the so-called proximate constituents of the plant, be contained in the sand or the water from which the plant has apparently been produced. In one word, there need not be any carbon in the soil, for this most important constituent of plants comes from the air.

Composition of the Air.

Concerning the chemical composition of the atmosphere, it needs to be insisted, first of all, that beside oxygen, nitrogen and argon, together with some vapor of water and a minute trace of ammonia, air always contains a certain small proportion of carbonic acid gas. The average composition of dry air, by volume, may be stated as follows :—

Oxygen	20.99
Nitrogen (and argon)	78.98
Carbonic acid	0.03

Since carbonic acid gas is 1.53 times as heavy as air, 3 volumes of it in 10,000 volumes of air means five ten-thousandths parts by weight.

The proportion of carbonic acid in the air varies somewhat in different places, and in any one place at different times, though, taking the whole world through, the amount of the gas is wonderfully uniform. In countries like the French province Auvergne, or the Eifel district on the western bank of the Rhine, where the gas is given off in very large quantities from fissures in the earth, and in the vicinity of active volcanoes, it is but natural that more carbonic acid than the usual proportion should be found in the air. The amount of this gas given off every day from volcanoes in South America is simply enormous. Even in a thick wood where the ground is covered with decaying leaves, twice as much carbonic acid may be found in the air as in that above open fields. Much carbonic acid is, however, evolved from the soil anyway, where it is formed by the oxidation of organic matters; much of it is formed also whenever wood, or coal, or peat is burned, and it is a constant product of the respiration of all kinds of animals.

The Carbon in Plants and Animals all comes from the Air.

It is this carbonic acid in the air that feeds the plant. In the absence of carbonic acid no green plant can grow. The foliage of young plants cannot even exist for any length of time when exposed to sunlight in air that is totally free from carbonic acid. De Saussure has shown this by enclosing the branches of plants in glass vessels charged with moistened lime, so that the carbonic acid might be absorbed by the lime, and thus be removed from about the leaves.

In view of its power of supporting plants, it would be difficult to overrate the importance of the carbonic acid which the air contains, even though at first sight the amount of it may seem to be but small. Inasmuch as animals either feed upon plants or upon other animals which have eaten plants, it follows that all living things in the world are nourished, either directly or indirectly, by carbonic acid. It is true in fact that life as it now exists on the globe is absolutely dependent upon the carbonic acid of the atmosphere. If the apparently trifling quantity of this gas which is found normally in the air were to be taken away, in an instant the whole surface of the earth would become a desolate waste without the possibility of vegetable life. (Draper.)

Decomposition of Carbonic Acid by Foliage.

The history of the discovery that the leaves of plants decompose carbonic acid is not a little curious, and some of the old experiments through which the knowledge of the fact was finally arrived at are highly instructive.

So long ago as 1752 the Swiss naturalist Bonnet observed that green leaves immersed in water and exposed to sunlight give off a gas. Methods of analyzing gases had not at that time been discovered, so that Bonnet's means of studying the phenomenon were limited. He observed, however, that leaves which were immersed in water that had been recently boiled developed no gas, whence he concluded, incorrectly, as we now know, that the gas ordinarily observed was nothing more than atmospheric air which had been dissolved by the water, and which collected upon the leaves when the latter were immersed in the water.

In 1771, Priestley, who had devised methods of analyzing gases, turned his attention to the subject. He found that the gas given off by the leaves of plants was sometimes carbonic acid and sometimes oxygen; sometimes he could not get any gas at all. He noticed however, that "plants reverse the effects of breathing, and tend to keep the atmosphere sweet and wholesome when it is

become noxious in consequence of animals either living and breathing or dying and putrefying in it." Franklin, also, who had an
opportunity to observe Priestley's experiment of the "plants in
a very flourishing state in highly noxious air," wrote of it as
follows: "That the vegetable creation should restore the air
which is spoiled by the animal part of it, looks like a rational system and seems to be of a piece with the rest. * * * * The strong
thriving state of your plant in putrid air seems to show that the
air is mended by taking something from it and not by adding to
it." Percival was the first observer who maintained that carbonic acid taken in at the leaves serves for the support of plants.

A few years after Priestley, in 1779 namely, Ingenhouss proved
that oxygen is given off only when the leaves and water are
exposed to sunlight. This was the key to the whole matter. He
found also that carbonic acid is given off in the dark, and that
those parts of the plant which are not green, such as flowers, roots
and fruit, never give off oxygen, but only carbonic acid. He
found, moreover, that in well water the plant evolved more oxygen
than in river water. We now know that the well water employed by
him probably contained more carbonic acid than the river water.

Our own countryman, Rumford, devoted some time to the study
of the question at this period, and his observations are not a
little interesting. But it was Senebier who first systematized the
matter by showing conclusively, in 1783, that the oxygen thus
given off from leaves comes from carbonic acid that was held
dissolved in the water in which the leaves were immersed. If
there is no carbonic acid in the water, no oxygen will be set free
when the mixture of water and leaves is exposed to sunlight.
Just so it is with sea-plants that live immersed in water, and so
it is with leaves that are in the air. Finally, at the beginning of
this century, De Saussure proved that, simultaneously with the
evolution of oxygen, the plant increases in weight through the
formation of organic matter; and it was shown by Draper, in
1843, that green leaves can not only decompose in sunlight carbonic acid which is held dissolved as such in water, but that they
readily decompose also the carbonic acid of alkaline carbonates
and bicarbonates when immersed in solutions of these substances.

Cloez in 1849 published a simple and effective method of exhibiting the fact of the decomposition of carbonic acid by green
leaves. His idea was to operate upon plants that naturally live

in water. He placed loosely in a large bottle four-fifths full of ordinary water a number of stalks of the plant known as water-pest (*Elodea Canadensis*), or some other aquatic plant, and then filled the bottle completely with soda water (water saturated with carbonic acid gas). The bottle was closed with a cork carrying an abduction tube full of water, and was put in connection with an inverted jar full of water, standing in a pneumatic trough. On placing the bottle in sunlight, bubbles of oxygen are given off from the submerged leaves, and this oxygen passes over into the collecting jar. When a manageable quantity of the gas has been collected it may be freed from any accidental impurity of carbonic acid by means of potash, and tested for oxygen with a glowing match, which will burst into flame when immersed in it.

It is to be remarked, however, that, in many cases, it would be more convenient nowadays to study this subject with plants or leaves kept in the air, and not in water. The foregoing statement is simply a fragment of history which may serve to indicate how one item of knowledge now familiar was first acquired. There is indeed no one fact relating to vegetable growth which can be more truly called fundamental than this,— that green leaves decompose carbonic acid in sunlight, and that the oxygen of the carbonic acid is set free while the carbon is retained in the plant.

Direct proof that carbonic acid is absorbed from the atmosphere by the leaves of plants is given by an experiment of Boussingault. This chemist thrust the branch of a living vine into one of the orifices of a three-necked glass globe, and fastened it there, air-tight. He made a current of air charged with a definite quantity of carbonic acid to flow into one of the orifices of the globe and out of the third orifice. But attached to the third orifice was an apparatus for collecting and weighing all the carbonic acid which was left undecomposed by the vine leaves. He found when the globe was exposed to sunlight that the foliage within it consumed three quarters of the carbonic acid which was admitted.

Osmose of Gases.

Carbonic acid doubtless enters the leaves of the plant by virtue of the forces of diffusion and osmose,— in a manner analogous to that in which liquids enter at the roots. It is true of gases even more emphatically than of liquids, that, when two or more of them are brought together in a confined space, they instantly begin to commingle, no matter how dissimilar their weights, nor what their relative positions may be. They continue thus to diffuse into one another until a perfectly homogeneous mixture is obtained.

As regards osmose also, it is with gases as with liquids; the rate of their passage through membranes depends only in part upon their relative diffusibilities, since the character and condition of the membrane, and the degree of adhesive force by which it can attract the various gases, come in to modify the mere diffusive force. Other things being equal, the gas which adheres to or is attracted by the membrane most strongly will soonest penetrate the partition. In this sense, a gas which is soluble in water may diffuse much more rapidly through a moist membrane than it can through the same membrane when dry. A wet bladder filled with carbonic acid will speedily collapse, while a dry bladder full of this gas remains tense.

A remarkable application of this osmotic action was suggested by Graham, who found that the oxygen of the air can be concentrated, as it were, by osmotic filtration. Thin films of caoutchouc, for example, as well as of other membranous substances, though impervious to air, as such, and devoid of porosity, in the ordinary sense of the term, are nevertheless capable of absorbing or liquefying the individual gases of which air is composed in such manner that the oxygen and nitrogen absorbed can pass through the membrane, just as ether or naphtha would, and can evaporate again in the form of gas into a vacuum upon the other side of the film.

It appears that in a given time oxygen can pass through a caoutchouc film two and a half times more abundantly than nitrogen,— so that the film may be used as a sieve, so to say, to sift out or exclude as much as one half of the nitrogen contained in ordinary air. Air that has been made to pass through such a film contains between 41 and 42 per cent of oxygen, instead of the 21 per cent which is normally present. A glowing splinter of wood will burst into flame in this concentrated air.

In order to perform the filtration, one side of a thin caoutchouc bag, kept distended by wire cloth or other proper mechanical appliance, is freely exposed to the outer air, while the atmosphere inside the bag is maintained in a state of partial rarefaction by means of an air-pump. It was thought at one time that air thus concentrated would be useful for smelting metals, but experience showed that it cost more to get the improved air than it was worth.

In the same way, Graham found that carbonic acid can pass through thin films of caoutchouc much more rapidly than air or than oxygen. The rapidity of passage of nitrogen being taken as 1,000,

That of oxygen is 2,556
That of atmospheric air 1,149
That of carbonic acid 13,558

Absorption of Gases by Plants.

The leaves of plants, or, more precisely, the membranous coverings of the cells which abut upon the numberless air-passages which pervade the plant, are permeable to gases, as other membranes are; they take in the carbonic acid of the air, and the green parts of the plant have power to decompose this carbonic acid in such wise that its carbon is retained by the plant, while the oxygen is allowed to return to the air.

There is no special attraction on the part of the leaves that should draw carbonic acid towards them, except that, as fast as one particle of the gas is decomposed at a given spot in the air, and so withdrawn from the air, another particle diffuses thither to fill the void space, and is naturally decomposed in its turn. As Pfeffer has well said, the movement of carbonic acid in the air towards the leaves of plants is similar in principle to the movement of this gas towards a lump of caustic potash that has been left exposed to the air. In a very short time this potash will absorb a great deal of carbonic acid, simply because, as fast as one particle of the gas is absorbed, another particle moves into its place to be in its turn held fast by the alkali.

In this way it happens that carbonic acid is continually taken in by plants out of the atmosphere, and transformed into the various components of vegetation. By force of the law of the diffusion of gases, supplemented as it is by the stirring action of winds and of currents of air which tend to pass up from the surface of the soil through foliage when it is heated by the sun's rays, new portions of carbonic acid are incessantly brought to the plant from without, and the wellnigh incessant movements of leaves and branches, caused by the aforesaid currents of air, of course act continually to bring the leaves into intimate contact with new layers of air.

Fixation of Carbon by Plants.

Very little is known as to the precise manner in which the decomposition of carbonic acid is effected within the plant. It has been found indeed that the volume of oxygen set free is very nearly equal to that of the carbonic acid decomposed; it has been proved that the decomposition is in some way intimately connected with the green chlorophyl grains to which the color of the leaves is due; and it is known that light is necessary in order that the decomposition may be brought about. But little has been learned as yet as to the details of the process of decomposition.

Boussingault long ago suggested the hypothesis, that carbonic acid and water may possibly be decomposed and deoxidized simultaneously, in accordance with the formula,

$$CO_2 + H_2O = COH_2 + O_2.$$

He urged that this idea is supported by the facts, observed by him, that water as well as carbonic acid is actually decomposed by the green parts of plants, and that carbonic oxide (CO) is not decomposed by them, as well as by the circumstance that the elements carbon, hydrogen and oxygen are combined in very nearly this proportion in the sugar, starch and cellulose which are known to be found in leaves. Thus, on multiplying the formula CH_2O by 6 we have $C_6H_{12}O_6$, which is the formula of several sugars found in plants. On multiplying by 12 and subtracting one molecule of water there will be obtained $C_{12}H_{22}O_{11}$, which represents the composition of cane sugar, and on subtracting another molecule of water there will be left $C_{12}H_{20}O_{10}$, which is the formula of starch and cellulose and dextrin.

With the advance of knowledge, this suggestion of Boussingault has come to be accepted as a highly probable theory. It is now recognized that the formula CH_2O is that of a well known substance, formic aldehyde, which may probably enough be formed in the leaves of plants. It is not difficult in the laboratory to transform formic aldehyde into a kind of sugar, and it may well be possible that such transformation can occur in leaves and lead to the production of sugar, starch and cellulose, and analogous substances. Microscopists are familiar with the fact that more or less starch can be seen in the chlorophyl grains of most plants when they are exposed to sunlight, and that this starch disappears completely when the leaves are kept for some time in the dark or in air that contains no carbonic acid, but that new quantities of starch speedily reappear when the plant is again exposed to light and to normal air so that the leaves may have opportunity to proceed with their proper work of decomposing carbonic acid. It is to be understood that the starch thus formed is continually dissolved and carried out from the leaves to be used in building up new leaves and other parts of the plant, and it is only the excess of it, so to say, that can be observed at any one moment.

Ordinarily starch is the first visible product formed by the decomposition of carbonic acid in the leaves of plants, and it is only in exceptional instances that other compounds of carbon, hydrogen and oxygen appear in the chlorophyl grains instead of starch, as when oil is detected, or mannite, or a kind of sugar (as in the onion). But it is none the less true that there are some good reasons for believing that the formation of sugar may precede the formation of starch, and that the starch in leaves is really a product of the transmutation of sugar.

As illustrating the conversion of the carbon of carbonic acid into organized matter, it is of interest to observe that the leaves of most agricultural plants normally contain more starch towards evening than they do in the early morning, simply because starch passes out from the leaves during the night, as well as by day, while it is formed only in sunlight. A. Mayer has suggested that profit may perhaps be gained in some cases by acting upon the knowledge of this fact. For example, where mulberry trees are grown for the purpose of feeding silkworms it might be good policy to pluck the leaves in the evening rather than in the morning. So too, tobacco leaves collected in the morning might perhaps be cured with less trouble than those gathered late in the afternoon, since they would contain about one fifth less starch, to be destroyed in the processes of drying and fermenting.

Whatever the details of the processes may be, the prominent facts to be held to are that the green chlorophyl grains assimilate a part of the carbonic acid of the air, and that the assimilated matter is digested by the plant cells and converted into the various components of the plant, somewhat in the same way that the food eaten by an animal is changed to bone and muscle by the stomach and the blood.

Some Plants feed upon Organic Matter.

The foregoing statement refers, of course, to the ordinary plants of cultivation which bear flowers and seeds. Mushrooms, toadstools, and the other fungi, assimilate food in a different way; most of them neither decompose carbonic acid nor give off oxygen. Generally speaking they have no power to produce organic matter out of carbonic acid and water; but, like animals, they are forced to feed upon vegetable or animal matters, or their remains, which they find ready formed. Not only do we see the larger fungi growing freely upon decaying matters, and parasites in great variety feeding upon living plants — notably those species which injure grasses and grain crops by causing them to rust, smut or mildew — but experimenters are accustomed to cultivate the smaller microscopic kinds of fungi in solutions that contain some soluble compound of carbon, such as sugar, or a tartrate, or an acetate, beside ash ingredients and a nitrogen compound. It is noticeable of those fungi which have no need to decompose carbonic acid, that many of them can grow freely in the dark. Large quantities of mushrooms, for example, are grown in cellars and caves in France, and it has been suggested in England that the arches of railway viaducts might be used for mushroom beds.

Unlike animals, which destroy organized matter, plants of the higher orders may be regarded as agents for accumulating power from inorganic materials, and for storing up power for future use in the form of food and fuel. All the heat and all the force developed by living things come from the food they eat, and food in the last analysis is all of vegetable origin. Much in the same way, heat is got by burning fuel, and power is obtained from the heat by means of appropriate machines. In this sense the prime object of agriculture is to collect, for purposes of human aggrandizement, as much as may be possible of the energy which comes to the world in the form of light and heat from the sun. Plants work constantly to counteract destructive agencies, such as combustion and animal life, which are continually resolving fuel and food into inorganic materials. All the wood, coal, and peat, and all the food in the world, have been formed in the last analysis from the action of sunlight on the chlorophyl grains in the leaves of plants, working to decompose the carbonic acid of the air. It has been well said that chlorophyl is the starting point and the foundation stone of life. Of course, every pound of carbon thus taken from the air and converted into vegetable matter represents an increase in the available energy of the world equal to the force which can be generated on burning this amount of carbon.

Kind of Light needed for the Fixation of Carbon.

With regard to the agency of light in the matter of decomposing carbonic acid, it is interesting to observe that the action is not due to the actinic or chemical rays, whose power of effecting chemical decomposition is familiarly seen in the processes of photography, and in the myriad instances of the " fading " of colors by sunlight. The actinic rays doubtless play an important part in the elaboration of some of the components of the plant, but they have very little if any influence in the process of decomposing carbonic acid. For this fundamental operation intense sunlight is essential.

Several observers have found that the decomposition of carbonic acid by leaves is most rapid in the yellow rays of the solar spectrum, and that in passing from the yellow part of the spectrum towards either of its ends the decomposition diminishes. Pfeffer has drawn up the following table to illustrate the rate of diminution, the maximum decomposition in the brightest yellow being taken at 100 :—

Red	25.4	Blue	22.1
Orange	63.0	Indigo	13.5
Yellow	100.0	Violet	7.1
Green	37.2		

In the invisible heat-rays that lie beyond the violet there was no decomposition at all. When the results as above given are depicted graphically, the curve resembles very nearly one which represents the brightness of the spectrum as it appears to the eye.

Plants need Abundant Light.

All experience teaches that the amount of carbonic acid decomposed at a given time depends on the intensity of the light; and, in general, it is known that the prosperity of plants depends largely upon the amount of light they receive. Indeed, the importance of abundant light, as distinguished from heat, for the rapid growth of plants, can hardly be overrated.

The marvellously rapid advance of vegetation which, as travellers report, is to be seen in Norway and Sweden in spite of the late spring and short and by no means hot summer of that northern clime, is to be explained by a reference to the very short nights, or rather to the long continued daylight, to which vegetation is there exposed. The plants grow continuously in the constant sunshine, and it is to be noted also that they and the surface soil are kept tolerably warm because there is comparatively little opportunity for cooling off during the short night. As Tisserand has well said, the progress of vegetation in these high northern latitudes bears comparison with that of an express train which is rapid because it is continuous and uninterrupted by stoppages at way stations.

The farther north grain is grown, so much the shorter is the term of its vegetation. Barley ripens 20 days earlier at Alten in 70° of north latitude, where on the average of years the mean summer temperature is only 54° F., than it does at Christiania in latitude 60°, where the mean summer temperature is 60°; and yet the plants are as well developed in the one place as in the other. Curiously enough, this power of ripening speedily becomes hereditary in the course of some generations, so that plants springing from seeds that have been brought from the far north to more southern localities grow as fast, at first, or almost as fast, as they would have grown at home.

It is because of the abundant light of the arctic summer that rye and wheat can be grown in Siberia as far north as latitude 65° or 66°, where, because of the long, cold winter, the mean annual temperature is no higher than 15° F., and where the ground is so nearly perpetually frozen that the soil never melts to a greater depth than two or three feet.

Plants grown by Artificial Light.

It was disputed at one time whether the normal processes of growth can be carried on at all in artificial light, and the question was complicated by results such as those obtained long since by Mr. Ward (the inventor of the closed case), who found that crocuses at least may be grown by gas-light. But here, of course, the motive force had been stored up in the crocus bulb the year before. In a similar category must be placed an old experiment of the botanist De Candolle. By confining a sensitive-plant in a dark place in the day-time, he found that the leaves soon closed; but on lighting the chamber with many lamps they opened again. Among other observations, it has been noticed that etiolated plants may become green in gas-light, and still more readily in the light of electric lamps.

The general conclusion seems to have been, that the light of oil lamps and gas burners is not strong enough to enable the leaves of plants to decompose carbonic acid; though the experiments of Hervé-Mangon in France, of Siemens in England, and of many other observers, have shown that the growth of many plants is possible in strong artificial light, such as that of the electric arc, much in the same way that it is possible in the dim light of a forest, or in any dense shade. Latterly, several market-gardeners have claimed that they find it profitable to grow lettuce with the help of the arc light, and there is no longer any doubt that many kinds of plants may be grown by artificial light, especially such plants as require but little light naturally.

Some Plants grow in Cool Weather.

It hardly needs to be said that a certain degree of cold checks the power of leaves to decompose carbonic acid. Cloez found that at 39° F. certain water-plants studied by him no longer evolved oxygen, and that none was given off until the temperature had reached 59° F. From this point the evolution increased until 86° had been reached, at which point it was at its maximum. When the temperature was allowed to fall, the decomposition of carbonic acid diminished, until at 50° it ceased entirely. On the other hand, Boussingault found that larch-needles decomposed carbonic acid at temperatures ranging from 33° to 36° F., and that the leaves of a kind of grass decomposed it at temperatures from 35° to 38°. It is probable that many kinds of plants which continue to grow in cool weather can assimilate carbonic acid perhaps even more readily than the larch, and it has been maintained by Jumelle that certain pines, junipers and lichens can still assimilate carbonic acid at a temperature 40° below zero.

Heinrich observed that Hottonia leaves can still decompose carbonic acid regularly at a temperature of 42° F., but hardly to an appreciable extent at 37°. The highest temperature at which these leaves still evolve oxygen lies between 122° and 133° F., and the best action occurs at about 88° F. In the case of Vallisneria, Sachs observed a slow evolution of oxygen at 50° F., but none at 45°. Indian corn and Mimosa pudica, he says, first begin to decompose carbonic acid at temperatures above 59° F.

Plants give off Carbonic Acid in the Dark.

It is to be observed that in the entire absence of light plants exhale no oxygen, but only carbonic acid. So far from the plants being able to decompose carbonic acid in the dark, this gas is then not only produced within the plant, by the action of oxygen upon some portion of it, but is actually given off from the plant into the air. This point will be referred to again directly, when the relations of the plant to oxygen are treated of.

In testing the significance of light, Boussingault found that a bean which weighed 0.922 grm. grew in 25 days, under normal conditions, to a plant which weighed when dry 1.293 grm. The increase of 0.371 grm. consisted of 0.1926 grm. carbon, 0.1591 grm. oxygen, and 0.02 grm. hydrogen. But another bean grown at the same time, under like conditions excepting that light was excluded from it, diminished in weight from 0.926 to 0.566 grm. This loss of 0.36 grm. consisted of 0.1598 grm. carbon, 0.1766 grm. oxygen, and 0.0232 grm. hydrogen.

Composition of the Air in Plants.

The importance of light in enabling the plant to decompose carbonic acid has been shown by still another method of research, somewhat different from either of those above alluded to. It has been shown, namely, by comparing air taken from the interior of plants which had been kept for some time in the dark with air taken from inside similar plants after exposure to sunlight.

To collect the air, the plants under examination were placed in glass vessels full of water, from which water all traces of air had been expelled by boiling. The vessels were then put into communication with a vacuum, in such wise that the air in the interior of the plants escaped therefrom into the vacuum, where it was collected for analysis. Separate pairs of bundles of the plants were kept in the dark for some time; one of the bundles was then exposed to sunlight for about 20 minutes, and both bundles were then subjected to the process of exhaustion which freed them from air.

Oat Plants kept	Date.	The Air in the Plants contained per cent of		
		Nitrogen.	Oxygen.	Carbonic Acid.
In the dark,	31 July	77.08	3.75	19.17
In sunlight,	"	68.69	24.93	6.38
In the dark,	2 Aug.	68.28	10.21	21.51
In sunlight,	"	67.86	25.95	6.89
In the dark,	"	76.87	8.14	14.99
In sunlight,	"	69.43	27.17	3.40

These experiments, which were made by Messrs. Lawes, Gilbert and Pugh, show, that atmospheric air does gain access to the interior of the plant; that, in the dark, the oxygen of the air acts upon portions of the plant to form carbonic acid; and that in sunlight carbonic acid is decomposed by the plant, and oxygen set free.

It is noticeable in the table, that the proportion of oxygen was in one instance reduced, in the dark, from the normal 21% to 4% of the volume of the air. Evidently most of the oxygen had been used up in combining with some carbonaceous portion of the plant.

Importance of Oxygen as Plant-Food.

It should be recognized clearly that this action of oxygen upon the growing plant is a matter of the first importance. Misconceptions as to this point are apt to arise in the minds of students, because of the fact that the subject is so complicated with that of the decomposition of carbonic acid that writers often allude to the evolved oxygen as if it were a subordinate or even trivial matter. This is not the case. To begin with, the amount of oxygen contained in vegetable matters is really very large. Boussingault weighed and analyzed all the crops produced in the courses of various rotations practised on his farm in Alsatia, and he found, for example, that the useful products harvested from a hectare (= 2.5 acres) of land during a six years' rotation of potatoes, wheat, clover, wheat and turnips, peas, and rye, weighed altogether 46,566 kilograms (1 kilo.= 2.2 lb.) in the fresh or air-dried condition, and that there was contained in all these products : [1]—

10950 kilos of carbon.	9405 kilos of oxygen.	1269 kilos of hydrogen.	354 kilos of nitrogen.	1353 kilos of ashes.

Furthermore, it may be said of plants as truly as it can be said of animals, that all the processes of life go on within them by day and by night by virtue of forces developed by the oxidation of organic matter. In the same way that animals die when placed in air which contains no oxygen, so do green plants die, except that the latter can (in the light) get enough oxygen to prolong their existence somewhat, by decomposing the carbonic acid which is formed within them. Some plants of the lower orders, such as the yeast-plant, for example, are exceptions to the rule only in so far as they are able to get the necessary oxygen from the organic substances on which they feed. It has been noticed even as regards mushrooms and lichens, that they absorb oxygen freely from the air for purposes of respiration and growth, and that they evolve carbonic acid.

In order that a plant may grow, new cells must be built up from the materials elaborated in the older cells, and oxygen plays an essential part in the chemical reactions which occur in these processes, while more or less carbonic acid is set free as one result of the reaction. As was just now said, oxygen is as necessary for plants as it is for animals, for the cells of plants respire constantly, and a plant may be suffocated, as an animal can, by depriving the cells of oxygen.

The respiration of plants is as real as that of animals; so much so

---

[1] Mémoires de l'Académie de France, 1842, xviii. 383.

indeed that in former days plants have sometimes been regarded as " animals turned inside out."

The old idea was that the leaves of plants correspond to the lungs of animals, and that the roots act somewhat similarly to the absorbent membranes of the intestines of animals. But it is to be remembered that the mouths (so to say) of plants are found both in the roots and in the leaves, and that unlike materials enter through these openings accordingly as they are situated above ground or below, and that the food taken in either by leaves or roots has to be elaborated and digested within the plant, by the cells proper. The respiration of plants occurs in the cells, and an abundance of oxygen is required for the support of the chemically active albuminoid matters which are contained in the protoplasm of the cells.

Large quantities of Oxygen are consumed by Germinating Seeds, and by Roots, Buds, Flowers, and Fruit.

Oxygen is essential, from the beginning, for the process of germination. Seeds do not germinate in the absence of oxygen. Even a seed that had sprouted would soon wither and perish if it were wholly deprived of oxygen. It has been noticed, however, that, while in pure oxygen germination is no quicker than in ordinary air, the process succeeds in air that contains from $\frac{1}{8}$ to $\frac{1}{16}$ of oxygen as well as if the air contained the normal proportion ($\frac{1}{5}$) of oxygen. Germination is still possible in air that contains no more than $\frac{1}{17}$ of oxygen, though in this case the process is very much retarded, and there is a risk of producing weak and unhealthy plants. In sowing seeds care has to be taken not to bury them too deeply, lest they should be too completely cut off from the oxygen of the air. So too seeds will putrefy and not germinate in soils saturated with water, simply because of the absence of available oxygen, though it is an easy matter to make seeds germinate beneath the surface of fresh water which naturally holds in solution a certain amount of free oxygen.

The opening buds of trees absorb oxygen from the air in considerable quantity, as was shown long ago by De Saussure, and in an atmosphere free from oxygen such buds soon decay. Some oxygen is taken up by the roots of plants also, and the presence of oxygen is essential for the life and activity of roots, though plants differ very much as to the amount of oxygen needed for this particular purpose. Most agricultural plants will not prosper unless the soil in which they stand contains numerous pores, which are filled more or less completely with air. Such plants are apt to suffer whenever the soil becomes water-soaked, and thereby freed from air. But many water-plants have access only to the oxygen which is held in solution by the water which surrounds them. Various rushes also, and other swamp-plants, grow freely in soils so saturated with water that very little air can come to their roots beside that which is dissolved in the water. Indeed, some swamp and marsh plants can withstand water which has been exposed to reducing agencies, and deprived of most of the oxygen that would naturally be dissolved in it. But it is never-theless true, generally speaking, that the roots of plants need oxygen in order that they may live, and it will be noticed even of swamp-plants that the clumps or hassocks which are formed by many of them are the results of efforts made by the plant to se-cure for itself, and for its roots also, standing ground to which air can gain access. It is to be observed that many kinds of trees can perfectly well bear to have their roots washed continually by running water, which is "living" and charged with oxygen, although they would soon sicken and die if their roots were to be immersed in stagnant water. Most plants speedily die when their roots are enveloped with an atmosphere that contains nothing but carbonic acid gas and nitrogen. Roots appear to be able to live, however, when immersed even in pure oxygen; and it has been noticed that while the roots take up oxygen they give out carbonic acid, though the amount of the latter exhaled is less than the quan-tity of oxygen absorbed.

Chaptal was surprised, in his day, on observing a practice of vine-dressers in the south of France. In a region where it rarely or never rains in the summer, he saw that it was customary to remove the earth from the foot of each vine-stock by digging around it a circular ditch large enough to lay bare the stock and the rootlets which cover it. He noticed that the mouth of this pit or ditch was speedily covered over by the leaves of vine-shoots which grew across it, and he argued that the roots were probably benefited by the vapor of water which came to them from the air. It is more probable, however, that the long and powerful roots of the vine got their supply of water from below, and that the merit of the pits consisted in supplying oxygen to the roots.

One objection to the establishment of too large an amount of asphaltum pavement in pleasure grounds or parks appears to be that the asphalt may hinder the tree-roots from gaining ready access to oxygen, though the vapors or liquids that come from the asphalt are likely to be directly hurtful in themselves.

Even in water culture it has been noticed that the roots grow better when air is made to bubble through the liquid, and that the formation of sulphide of iron which ordinarily occurs there may thus be wholly prevented.

Oxygen is taken up by ripening fruit also, and particularly by flowers, a corresponding quantity of carbonic acid being meanwhile produced, and even given off from those parts of the plants which have absorbed much oxygen.

Plants generate Heat.

It is notorious that in all chemical processes of oxidation, such as these, more or less heat is evolved, and it is found as a matter of fact that heat is actually generated by growing plants. It often happens that snow falling upon growing grass in early autumn or late spring may be seen to melt away rapidly, and continue to do so for a considerable period of time, while it may remain lying intact for a long while upon the adjacent ploughed fields and roadways. The aqueous vapor which the grass exhales is naturally warm enough to melt the damp snow. So too, when a leafy plant is placed in a confined volume of air that has been saturated with moisture, it will continue to throw off vapor of water from its leaves into that air, while the temperature of the air, and consequently its capacity for holding the vapor of water, will be increased by the heat which the plant emits.

Indeed, the mere act of evaporating water from the leaves into ordinary air must often depend in some part on warmth that has been generated within the plant by the chemical reactions which occur there. It is because of this chemical action that the temperature of plants is usually somewhat higher than that of the surrounding air, and that from plants, as from animals, aqueous vapor is constantly escaping in the form of insensible perspiration.

At the moment of flowering, so much heat is developed by plants that it is often easy to measure it with the thermometer. Garreau observed that a spike of the flowers of Arum italicum absorbed 28.5 times its own bulk of oxygen in one hour, and that its temperature was 15° F. higher than that of the surrounding air. Dutrochet noted an increase of temperature of 11 or 12° C. caused by Arum maculatum in the act of blossoming, and Poisson reports an increase of about 10° C. above the temperature of the room when Dioon edule flowered.

Oxygen is needed by Stored Fruits and Vegetables.

Fruits, such as apples, pears and oranges, absorb large quantities of oxygen, and give off corresponding amounts of carbonic acid, not only in ripening, but even when they are fully ripe, as the term is ; and this process of oxidation is manifestly necessary, both for the maturation and for the life of the fruit.   Interesting observations have been made by Heintz in respect to the evolution of carbonic acid from ripe beet-roots.   Even when stored for winter use, the " respiration " of sugar-beets goes on continually and a part of their sugar (as well as of other matters) is consumed while carbonic acid is given off.   Heintz found that as much as 10 cwt. of sugar were lost in two months' time from a store of beet-roots weighing 1000 cwt.   Air taken from within these roots contained from 30 to 35 % of carbonic acid, 0.2 to 0.6 % of oxygen and from 64 to 69% of nitrogen.

So too with germinating seeds. A seed that has been made to germinate in the dark, far from showing any increase of weight as the sprout grows, actually decreases in weight steadily, from loss of substance through oxidation. Carbonic acid is given off from it, as was just now stated. Oxygen seems, in short, to act for the most part upon matter which is already organized in the plant. By reacting upon the compounds in the cells, it takes conspicuous part in the changes by which these substances are transmuted into other organized forms ; as when portions of the plant are converted into flowers and fruit, or the matter of the germinating seed is made to nourish the young sprout. These are processes, it should be noticed, which go forward at the expense of the plant itself, both by night and by day. It is only in the green leaves and stalks of plants, not in their seeds and flowers, that the crude, unorganized materials taken in from the air and the soil are elaborated into new compounds. The flowers and fruits of plants correspond to the eggs and the young of animals in that they are nourished by the parent plant.

The Action of Oxygen is Incessant.

That oxygen has important functions to perform at all times might justly be inferred from the familiar fact that in the dark plants slowly but incessantly exhale carbonic acid derived from the oxidation of some part of them. Indeed it is now well known that the gas is really produced continually within the plant, both in the light and in darkness, by the action of oxygen upon certain components of the plant. It is known too that some of the substances in the plant, such as sugar or the like, are converted into other substances by the action of the living cells, and that carbonic acid is one of the products of this cell action. But in the light, much of the carbonic acid thus formed is decomposed again in due course by the green chlorophyl grains, so that it is never actually exhaled. Hence it is easier to detect the evolution of carbonic acid in the dark than in sunlight, though, as Garreau has suggested, the fact that carbonic acid is given off continually even in the light may be shown by putting a leafy branch in a bottle together with a thin layer of lime-water and shaking the air and the water together after some time. The liquid will become milky from the presence of carbonate of lime.

It has been found that plants exposed to the dull light of a cloudy day will sometimes exhale carbonic acid, and at other times oxygen, according to the intensity of the light and the age, or rather the state of development, of the plant. But in any event the quantity of oxygen absorbed by plants, as measured by the amount of carbonic acid given off in the dark, is vastly less than the quantity of carbonic acid fixed by the plant during the day.

From the experiments of Corenwinder, it appears that a plant will absorb and decompose as much carbonic acid in 15 or 20 minutes of direct sunlight as it would exhale in a whole night. Boussingault found, as the average of 31 trials on oleander leaves which were exposed to light from 8 A. M. to 5 P. M. on different days between May and October, under the most favorable conditions, in air rich in carbonic acid, that one square decimetre of leaf decomposed 5.28 c.c. of carbonic acid per hour, while in 5 trials where the leaves were kept in darkness in ordinary air no more than 0.33 c.c. of carbonic acid was given off per square centimetre of leaf-surface and per hour.

Chlorophyl is masked in some Colored Leaves.

It is to be remarked, that red, or dark, or purple leaves, as of the purple beech, for example, or colored algæ, decompose carbonic acid by means of chlorophyl grains which are masked or concealed by the dominant color. It has been noticed however by Jumelle, that the power of red leaves to assimilate carbon is decidedly less than that of green leaves. He found, for example, that under similar circumstances, leaves from red beech trees and red sycamore maples assimilated six times less carbon than the leaves of the ordinary varieties of the beech and the maple. All of which consists with the fact of observation that trees with green leaves commonly increase in size more rapidly than do those of their varieties which have colored leaves.

The relations of oxygen to the soil need not be considered here, since they can be discussed much more conveniently further on, in connection with the subject of tillage.

Relations of the Nitrogen in the Air to Crops.

There is abundant evidence that free nitrogen gas, such as exists in the air, has no direct action to promote the growth of agricultural plants. In order that grain crops, such as barley or oats, for example, may grow, it is necessary that their roots shall have access to certain compounds of nitrogen which are found in fertile soils, notably nitrates and ammonium salts; while for the prosperity of peas, clover, and other kinds of leguminous plants, it is essential either that nitrates shall be present in the soil or that there shall grow upon the roots of these plants certain bacteria which have power to abstract nitrogen from the air and convey it to the plants upon which they live.

As will be set forth in a subsequent chapter, it has been found that certain microscopic organisms having power to fix nitrogen from the air may live upon the roots of leguminous plants (though not upon those of the cereal grains), and that when this growth occurs the plant can feed upon the nitrogen which the microorganisms have accumulated.

It was long a matter of wonderment that plants should not feed directly upon the atmospheric nitrogen. It seemed strange indeed to most men that their crops should be bathed with air which contained nearly 80% of nitrogen and have no power to use any of this material. Hence much thought and labor have been expended by chemists in studying the question from various points of view. But all the trustworthy experiments which have been made hitherto, and there is no lack of them, point to the conclusion that free nitrogen cannot be assimilated directly by the leaves of the higher orders of plants.

Without going into any discussion of the extended researches which have been made upon this subject, it will be sufficient to describe briefly one of the methods of research employed by the distinguished French chemist Boussingault. He put into a number of glass carboys artificial soils made of washed and roasted pumice-stone admixed with the ashes of stable-manure. He moistened the soils with pure water, and sowed in them the seeds of various kinds of plants. After the seeds had germinated he inverted a small flask of carbonic acid gas in the mouth of the carboy, and fixed it there air-tight, the idea being to supply in this way the carbon needed for the growth of the plants. The apparatus was then set into the soil of a garden to keep it cool, and left to itself for several months. It was a Ward's case, except that the soil in which the seeds were sown contained neither nitrogen nor carbon.

Finally, the plants obtained were carefully analyzed for nitrogen; and, in the same way, an equal number of the seeds were analyzed, i. e. a number of seeds similar to that from which the plants had grown.

As the mean of many experiments, it appeared that the total amount of nitrogen in the dwarf plants obtained was a little less than that contained in the seeds from which they grew. Absolutely no nitrogen was gained from the air.

But plants have great need of nitrogen, and if any of that element had been put into the carboy in assimilable form (as a nitrate or an ammonium salt, for example) it would have been quickly taken in by the plants and have been detected when the plants were analyzed.

It is always hard to prove a negative; but in the present case so large a mass of adverse evidence has been accumulated that there would seem to be no longer any point left open for discussion, were it not for the discovery as just now mentioned, that certain microscopic organisms do actually fix free nitrogen from the air, as will be described more particularly under the head of Symbiosis. Although these microbes differ widely from most agricultural plants, their action suggests anew the inquiry whether the cells of some special kinds of cultivated plants may not perhaps be able to fix small quantities of free nitrogen in an analogous way. As has been said, there is much evidence which militates against this supposition.

An interesting account of several standard experiments made to test the significance of nitrogen gas as plant-food will be found in Johnson's " How Crops Feed," pp. 28-33. It is to be remarked that the investigation is beset with several palpable sources of error, which need to be specially guarded against.

1. The soil employed must be wholly freed from nitrogenous matters and from germs of micro-organisms, and no dust from the air should be allowed to gain access either to the soil or to the plants.

2. There are some small traces of ammonia and of nitrates in the air whose influence must be avoided

3. It is extremely difficult, if not impossible, to prepare water that is wholly free from ammonia; and in any method of experimentation, where much air or much water is used, the influence of the ammoniacal impurity tends to become cumulative, and greatly to increase the risk that it may vitiate the experiment.

4. Probably most plants, if not all plants, can on occasion obtain a little nitrogenous food from insects that die upon them, and it is assuredly possible that lupines (which are both hairy and sticky), and perhaps clover also, may really be carnivorous enough to profit to an appreciable extent from the nitrogen of insects which they may capture.

5. It is known that microscopic fungi which live upon the roots of some kinds of plants can absorb and "fix" free nitrogen gas and convert it into compounds upon which crops can feed.

From all of which it appears that that method of experimenting must be best which most fully excludes the various sources of error. Regarded in this light, the arrangement of Boussingault's apparatus will be seen to display an amount of common-sense which distinctly simulates genius. The merit of it has recently been illustrated anew by Hellriegel, who, on repeating the experiment of Boussingault and adding to the sand in the carboy a minute quantity of loam-water which contained the proper microscopic organisms, had no trouble in growing vigorous pea-plants which were found to contain an abundance of nitrogen that had been taken from the air. Oats and buckwheat, on the contrary, starved through lack of nitrogen in spite of the presence of the micro-organisms.

Leaves may absorb Ammonia Gas.

There can be no doubt that the carbonate of ammonia which exists in minute proportion as a gas in the air is absorbed by plants. But the amount of this atmospheric ammonia is so extremely small that it can have little direct effect upon vegetation. In fact, many experiments have proved that the ammonia normally present in the air has no appreciable influence on the growth of plants, although it has been found that the vapor either of am-monia or of carbonate of ammonia, added artificially to the air, greatly promotes the growth of plants that are standing in that air, whence it appears that the only trouble with the atmospheric ammonia is its extreme dilution. If there were but more of it, it would be valuable.

Very striking results are said to have been obtained by placing lumps of solid carbonate of ammonia upon the hot-water pipes of a conservatory, so that the ammonium salt could evaporate into the apartment in the proportion of from 2 to 4 parts for every 10,000 parts by weight of air.

It does not appear that light has any influence upon the absorp-tion of such atmospheric ammonia. It is likely, however, as Mulder has suggested, that the ammonia enters into chemical combination with the acids with which the juices of growing plants are almost always charged. Even before the elaborate experi-ments of Darwin showed that various fly-catching plants actually digest and feed upon the flesh of their prey, it might justly have been concluded that the pitcher-plant can gain nitrogenous food from the insects that are drowned in its reservoir of water. For in case the insects were not consumed directly by the plant, they would decay in the water, and ammonia would thus be formed, and by the absorption of this ammonia the plant would profit.

Absorption of Aqueous Vapor by the Leaves of Plants.

Ordinarily, air contains small quantities of invisible vapor of water; perhaps to the extent of 0.45% of the weight of the air on the average, though, since the capacity of air to hold moisture increases with the temperature, the amount of water thus held is of course subject to wide variations. It is possible for a given volume of air, at 32° F., to absorb moisture to the extent of the hundred and sixtieth part of its own weight, and this amount of moisture may be doubled for every 27 additional degrees of the thermometer. Thus at 32° air can absorb the 160th of its own weight of moisture, at 59° it can absorb the 80th part, at 86° the 40th, and at 113° the 20th part of its weight. It has been not a little disputed whether ordinary plants ever absorb directly for purposes of growth any of this vapor of water which so constantly exists in the air. That they can do so on occasion, at least in some cases, is familiarly shown by branches, or even logs, of willow or poplar, that have been detached from the parent stem or stump before the growing season, and left disconnected in the air. Such branches or boughs die hard. They may indeed live for several months, and continue to form occasional new leaves after all connection with the soil has ceased, and no liquid water has come to them. It is plain in this case that the vapor of water in the air must play an important part in keeping up the movement of sap by which the leaves upon these detached boughs are nourished. Such observations as these seem at first sight to be little consistent with the well-known fact that aqueous vapor is ordinarily given off continually and under all circumstances from the leaves of plants which are growing upon the land, even when the air that surrounds the leaves is saturated with moisture. But since neither of the facts can be discredited, the chief point to be insisted upon is that the quantity of water ordinarily absorbed by leaves must be very small. ` On the other hand, there can be no question that the amount of water taken in by roots is very large, and of overwhelming importance for the growth of crops.

Contrary to the commonly received opinion, it does not appear that the foliage of ordinary plants usually absorbs much of the liquid water that falls upon it as rain, or that is deposited as dew; although it is true, it has been shown by careful experiments, that small quantities of liquid water can be absorbed by leaves that are immersed in it, and brought into intimate contact with it. Mariotte taught, toward the close of the seventeenth century, that when wilted leafy twigs are placed in water with their tips downward so that the part where the twig has been cut or broken shall be left in the air, the leaves will gradually swell to their original condition. There are experiments by Chmielewsky also, in which one-half of the leaves on cut twigs were kept immersed in water while the other half of the leaves were left in the air, and the behavior of the leaves thus exposed was contrasted with that of leaves on similar twigs which were kept wholly in the air. It appeared, in most instances, that the leaves on twigs left wholly in the air wilted speedily, while during the same period none of the leaves wilted on those twigs which were partially immersed in water. In other words, the moisture naturally exhaled from the leaves above the water was constantly replaced by moisture imbibed by the leaves that were in the water. Indeed the rapidity with which plants that stand badly wilted in the field in hot weather are seen to revive when they are rained upon, would seem to indicate that some of the rain-water must be absorbed directly by the leaves, for it is not easy to believe that when leaves are cooled by rain the moisture previously lost from them by excessive exhalation can immediately be made good by water which is pumped into the plant by the roots. It would seem as if much more time would be required in order that water may pass from the roots to the leaves than does in fact elapse during the actual resuscitation.

Many Leaves Shed Water.

But, upon the other hand, it will be noticed, when the leaves and stalks of plants are covered with particles of rain or dew, that the liquid is usually prevented from coming into intimate contact with the absorbent surfaces of the plant, either by the waxy coating natural to the leaf or stem, or by the numberless little hairs which grow upon it, though as a matter of course the vapor which arises from, and as it were surrounds, the dew as it clings to a leaf will naturally tend to check transpiration and in that way refresh the leaf.

The foregoing statements all refer to ordinary leafy plants, but, as regards mosses and lichens, it is known that they can absorb moisture freely from damp air, and become soft and flexible; and that contrariwise they are made harsh and brittle by hot, dry air. After all has been said, it may be asserted without any hesitancy that the roots of plants are the true absorbents of water, and that practically speaking almost the whole of the water consumed by plants is taken in through the roots from the soil.

As has been explained already, it is a matter of familiar experience, that enormous quantities of water are taken in at the roots of plants and given off again into the air through the leaves. A certain part of the water thus taken in is undoubtedly assimilated by the plant, and made to combine chemically with carbon to form vegetable compounds; from the water thus fixed, so to say, comes the hydrogen which is an essential component of every organized substance. Some water, moreover, is always held mechanically in the pores of the plant.

As might be anticipated, all the experiments go to show that the amount of vapor given off by plants may vary greatly, accordingly as the external air and the soil also are hot or cold, moist or dry. Transpiration is peculiarly rapid in warm, dry air.

It is much more active in direct sunlight than in the shade, but it does not wholly cease even at night. Evergreen plants are said to transpire less than other kinds. In the intense heat of summer, plants wilt because moisture is given off by their leaves faster than the roots can supply moisture; but the revival of the wilted plants by a shower of rain appears to be due chiefly to the facts, that evaporation is checked when the plants are cooled by the rain-water, and that the air around the leaves becomes partially saturated with moisture.

Relation of the Soil to Heat.

There is little need of insisting that abundant heat is indispensable for the growth of crops. Other things being equal, the force and rapidity of vegetable growth is in proportion to the temperature of the air and the soil; and, as is well known, " it is the fertile season, rather than the artificial treatment of the land, that results in a maximum of produce." It is a familiar fact that the distribution of each particular kind of plant upon the earth's surface is determined primarily by climate. In the words of De Saussure, " We deceive ourselves exceedingly when we imagine that the fertility of any district depends wholly on the nature of the soil, because abundance and scarcity in crops arise principally from the degree of heat and humidity in the air." " I have seen," he says, " in Sicily and Calabria, arid and uncultivated rocks and gravel, such as in Switzerland would have been altogether barren, which there produced more vigorous plants than are to be seen on the richest and best cultivated lands among the Helvetic mountains."

Lord Bacon noticed that the training of fruit-trees "upon the back of a chimney where a fire is kept doth hasten their comming on and ripening. Nay more, the drawing of the boughes into the inside of a roome where a fire is continually kept worketh the same effect. Vines that have been drawne in at the window of a kitchen have sent forth grapes a moneth (at least) before others. Stoves at the backe of walls bring forth orenges here with us."

It is true, however, after fully allowing for the general climate of the locality, that the temperature of the soil of any particular field may be subject to a great variety of circumstances. It will be influenced not only by the quantity, quality and direction of the sun's rays which fall upon it, but by the temperature and amount of the air, the rain, and the ground-water which come in contact with it; by the amount of heat developed within it through oxidation of the organic or other oxidizable substances which it contains; by loss of heat through evaporation of water; by the capacity of the soil itself for absorbing and retaining, or for radiating and reflecting heat, and doubtless by other conditions, such, for example, as those dependent upon the presence or absence of vegetation, and of microscopic organisms.

Position of the Soil as regards Sunlight.

The importance of "aspect" or "exposure" need hardly be dwelt upon. Everybody recognizes the significance of the "lay of the land." In popular estimation, the morning sun is held to be specially auspicious for the growth of plants, and no doubt justly. In the words of an English writer (Marshall) : "A southeastern aspect collects a greater quantity of heat, enjoys a longer day, than any other. It is noon before a western aspect reflects a ray. In the morning it will frequently remain dewy and cold several hours after vegetation has been roused against an eastern inclination. The afternoon sun is no doubt more intense on the west than on the east side of a hill; but its duration is short. In the afternoon the air is everywhere warm; and a regular supply of warmth appears to be more genial to vegetation than a great and sudden transition from heat to cold. The coolness of evening comes on, and vegetation is probably checked as soon, or nearly as soon, in all aspects. Hence we may fairly conclude that the southeastern aspect enjoys more vegetative hours, and receives a more regular supply of heat, than any other."

Mr. Mitchell also speaks in terms of enthusiasm of "the gentle slope south or eastward which shall catch the first beams of the morning, and the first warmth of every recurring spring." He says : "In a mere economic point of view, such slope is commended in every northern latitude by the best of agricultural reasons. In all temperate zones two hours of morning are worth three of the afternoon. I do not know of a writer upon husbandry who does not affirm this choice, with respect to all temperate regions. If this be true of European countries, it must be doubly true of New England, where the most trying winds drive from the northwest." For some kinds of crops it may well be true that the best situation will be a hillside sloping boldly to the south, and yet not so steep as to hinder tillage or that the soil shall too easily be washed away by rains.

In Italy, the irrigated mowing-fields are made to slope from north to south, whenever practicable, while the irrigating and drainage ditches run across them from east to west. It is on high mountains, however, that the significance of exposure is best seen. It is known, for example, that on the southerly sides of some of the Alps both vegetation in general, and the cultivation of grain in particular, reach higher elevations than on the northerly sides. While rye and barley are grown at a height of 4,000 feet above the sea-level in Swiss valleys that face to the north, they attain to 5,000 feet in valleys that are exposed to the south. In Lapland also, and in Spitzbergen, the southern sides of hills are said to be sometimes covered with vegetation, while the northern slopes are buried in perpetual snow.

Lord Bacon in his " Sylva " says, " The planting of trees warme upon a wall, against the south or south-east sunne doth hasten their comming on and ripening, and the south-east is found to be better than the south-west, though the south-west be the hotter coast. But the same is chiefly, for that the heat of the morning succeedeth the cold of the night, and partly because (many times) the south-west sunne is too parching."

Houghton, writing in 1693 of land laid up in ridges, in England, states that " Most ridges are ploughed east and west, that the sun may come most to them." The steeper the slope, so much the more strongly will the soil be heated by the sun's rays. Gasparin has urged that it is often highly advantageous to plant flower-seeds on the sunny sides of sloping beds in order that the sun's heat may be put to profit. If on a parterre running from east to west, the north side of a bed is built up to a height of six inches while the southern edge is sunk to a depth of six inches, the bed will have a slope of a foot looking toward the south, and all kinds of early seeds sown upon it in the spring will start several days sooner than they would if sown on a flat bed. Similar results may be got on beds that are less elevated and even on slopes made by the passing of a hoe.

Southern exposures not always the best.

It must not be forgotten however that, as Evelyn has set forth, a place " is eligible according to the purposes you would employ it for; some plants affecting hotter, others colder exposures. Some delight to dwell on the hills, others in the vallies and closer seats ; and some again are indifferent to either; but generally speaking most of them choose the warm and more benign." Here in Massachusetts, it is noticed that peach orchards are apt to succeed best when set out in sandy or gravelly loam upon the northerly slopes of hills, because the ground in such situations remains so cold during the warm days which occur occasionally in late autumn, that the sap of the trees is not set in motion and the fruit-buds on their branches are left in a state of repose which is highly conducive to their welfare. Whenever it happens that peach-trees in Massachusetts are unduly warmed in October or November many of the fruit-buds upon them will swell to such an extent that the outer covering which should protect them from the winter's cold will be loosened and the buds will subsequently perish when exposed to no more than moderately cold weather. For success with peaches in this region, it is essential that the new wood shall ripen completely and the buds be well-developed and be kept quiet until the next spring. In so cold a locality, the peach-crop can neither bear forcing manures or forcing exposures. (E. Hersey.)

The question of aspect has been studied methodically by Kerner, and afterwards by Wollny at Munich, who threw up for his experiments an artificial mound, in the soil of which were planted numerous thermometers. These instruments were sunk six inches deep in the sandy soil, which contained a little humus and which lay sloping at an angle of 15°. It appeared plainly that the maximum temperature of the soil in the winter, i. e. from November to April, was on the slope that faced southwest; in the summer, it was on the southeast slope; at the beginning of autumn, on the south; and in late autumn, on the southwest. So too, in beds running in various directions, thermometers sunk six inches deep showed in summer that the southerly sides were warmest; next came the flat land, then the east and west sides of the beds, while the northerly slopes were coldest. Hence crops cultivated in beds running from north to south will be more equably warmed than if the beds ran east and west, although the latter may sometimes attain a higher temperature by day. It was noticed, however, that flat cultivation insured a more equable temperature than any of the beds, and indeed a higher average temperature than the best of them.

Wollny concludes that, of the several exposures, the south, southwest, and southeast are the warmest; that east and west come next in order, then northeast and northwest, and last north, which shows the lowest temperature of all. Generally speaking, variations of temperature in the soil are widest on southerly exposures, and they are smaller in proportion as the slope approaches towards the north.

Spring crops may be grown on hillsides.

The steepness of a slope is not without its influence. The sun's rays will strike most powerfully upon a hillside inclined towards the south at an angle of 25° or 30°. In northern countries a declivity thus exposed to the sun, and sheltered against cold winds, may enjoy a local climate as different from that of the surrounding region as if the field had been transported through several degrees of latitude. In Arctic regions vegetation occurs occasionally at high elevations where the slopes of hills that are favorably situated receive the sun's rays nearly vertically; for in high latitudes the sun is always near the horizon; moreover, there would be comparatively little cooling by night in localities where clouds and mists prevail and prevent radiation. (Pansch.)

In the vicinity of Boston farmers choose the southern slopes of hills, even where the soil seems to be poor and gravelly, for growing early vegetables. So it is with regard to the placing of dwelling-houses, as well as with the planting of crops. As the city expands, many houses are built upon the "right sides" of the suburban hills long before any one thinks of erecting buildings upon the "wrong side." As Marshall has put it, "A hill dipping to the south partakes of the nature of a south wall. The atmosphere, a few feet from the ground, is probably many degrees hotter on the south than on the north side of a regular hill; and the richness and flavor of fruit depends much on the heat of the atmosphere it matures in. The fruit on a branch of a grape-vine, for instance, which is introduced into a greenhouse is (in England) much richer and more highly flavored than that on the other branches of the same vine which remain in the outer air." It is to be remembered, however, that a light, permeable soil on the southerly slope of a hill might become so dry in midsummer that any crop growing upon it would be liable to suffer extremely, while the same kind of land on the northerly side of the hill would be less apt to be overheated.

Reflected Heat.

The significance of reflected heat is illustrated by the common European custom of ripening delicate fruits upon the sunny sides of walls. Pears and plums are ripened in this way in the north of England every year, even in the least favorable seasons, in a climate which even a New Englander would call horrible. In the words of Lord Bacon, " It is usually practised [in England] to set trees that require much sunne upon walls against the south, as apricots, peaches, plums, vines, figs, and the like. It hath a double commoditie: The one, the heat of the wall by reflexion; the other, the taking away of the shade; for when a tree groweth round, the upper boughes overshadow the lower, but when it is spread upon a wall the sunne cometh alike upon the upper and lower branches. . . . . Musk melons are sowen upon a hot bed, dunged below, upon a bank turned upon the south sunne to give heat by reflexion, laid upon tiles which increaseth the heat, and covered with straw to keepe them from cold. . . . And by these helps they become as good in England as in Italy or Provence."

It often happens that a wall must be credited with the protection against harsh winds which it affords to tender plants; but as Gasparin has suggested, when the student is speculating as to how great the heating effect of a south wall or the southern slope of a hill may really be, it is well enough to call to mind the opposite fact, that the northern side of the wall is extremely cold and most unfriendly to vegetation. In Tuscany, grapes grown on trellised walls are shielded from night-frosts by mats which are rolled up by day and can be let down by night, on occasion.

Absorption and Radiation of Heat.— Significance of Color.

The capacity of walls and soils for absorbing and radiating heat is another item of importance; and with this point the color of the soil is more or less intimately connected. As a general rule, it may be said that dark-colored soils absorb heat most rapidly, and radiate it most freely. According to Gasparin there may be as much as 12 or 14° difference of temperature between two parcels of soil similarly exposed to sunlight, if one of the soils were made white by covering it with a thin layer of magnesia and the other were to be strewn with lampblack.

The experiments of Franklin are familiar, in which bits of cloth of different colors were laid on the surface of snow. After a while it was found that the snow had melted most beneath the darkest cloths. Other things being equal, it is the frozen ridges of black soil in the ploughed fields which are first seen to emerge from beneath the snow in early spring. Light-colored soils can be made warm in this sense by strewing dark-colored substances upon them; and it may occasionally be economically possible to improve such soils by putting upon them coal-slack or refuse lignite or shale.

There is an old experiment of Professor Lampadius, of Frei-berg, who was able to ripen melons in that inclement town by covering the soil with coal-dust to the depth of about an inch. So, too, Hanney leached a quantity of soot with water to remove its fertilizing constituents, and strewed it in alternate stripes upon half the soil of a potato-field. Before the vines had grown large enough to shade the ground, the temperature of the soil on sunny days, as the mean of ten observations, was :—

At a Depth of 2 Inches.		At a Depth of 8 Inches.	
Soot.	No Soot.	Soot.	No Soot.
62° F.	60°	60°	58.5°

The potatoes sprouted sooner beneath the soot, and the vines grew faster and more vigorously there; that is to say, the soot gave the plants a good start.

On the Rhine, grapes are said to mature best where the soil has been covered with fragments of black slate; though it is not im-possible, as some writers have urged, that a part of the useful effect may depend upon the fertilizing power of potash that is con-tained in the crumbly shale. It is true withal that the fragments of slate act as a mulch to hold water in the soil.

The geologist Bakewell, when travelling in Switzerland, in pass-ing by a ravine near Tour, noticed a deep section made in a bed of very dark schist, that was covered on many parts of its surface with a saline efflorescence, which, as his guide informed him, was often licked off by chamois that descended for the purpose. "It is from this bed," he says, "that the inhabitants procure the black earth which they sprinkle over the snow to accelerate its solution in the spring. As the summers in this elevated situation are of short duration, it is of great importance to save time in get-ting their seed into the ground, and it was probably accident which first discovered to them a fact now well known in natural philosophy, that dark surfaces are sooner heated by the sun's rays than white ones. It was proved by the experiments of Franklin, that black cloth laid upon snow caused it to melt faster than where it was uncovered, by absorbing the sun's rays, which are in a great measure reflected from the surface of the snow itself. The simple process of sprinkling the surface of their fields with this black earth makes the snow melt many days sooner than it would otherwise do; but our guide informed us, it was sometimes a tedious labor, for if any fresh snow should fall, or be drifted over the black earth, the operation must be repeated. We saw several heaps of this black earth collected near the cottages, to be ready for the following spring."

Of course, such practices as the foregoing are of special importance only in cold countries. In hot climates, on the other hand, it is customary to take pains to provide a light shade for certain crops, such as the coffee-tree. Even in New England it is well to shade somewhat several kinds of fruit-bearing bushes, notably the currant. (E. Hersey.)

In a series of experiments upon potatoes, the French chemist Girardin found that the times at which the crop ripened varied from 8 to 14 days, according to the character of the soil. At a given date (the 25th of August) he found 26 varieties of his potatoes ripe in a very dark soil charged with much organic matter, while upon sandy soil there were but 20 varieties ripe; in clay 19 varieties, and on a white limestone soil only 16.

According to Gasparin, it is a matter of familiar observation in the spring at the South of France that chalk soils are cold and late because of their white color. It is also noticeable there that fields and vineyards which are of reddish or yellowish color are warmer than white fields or vineyards similarly situated and equally well supplied with moisture. Gasparin tells of a white clay soil the temperature of which rose to 106° F., when exposed to sunshine in air of 77°, while on blackening the clay its temperature rose to 120° F. He suggests that beside the other advantages gained by burning clayey soils it may sometimes happen that the land is benefited by the changed color of the burnt clay. Oemler has tested a variety of air-dried soils of different colors, as to their power of absorbing heat when exposed to the sun's rays. His results are given in the following table:

	Average Absorption of Heat.	Percentage Absorption.
Moor earth	24.40	100.00
Fine dark brown humus	23.25	95.29
Sandy humus (50% humus)	22.75	93.24
Dark reddish brown sand	22.65	92.87
Loam rich in humus (20% humus)	22.10	90.57
Clay " " " "	21.40	87.70
Reddish yellow loam	21.00	86.07
Light grey clay	20.00	81.97
Fine sand, containing a little loam	20.75	85.04
Limestone colored with blue phosphate of iron	20.70	84.83
Coarse sand	20.50	84.02
Pure chalk	19.77	77.90

Schuebler long ago examined a variety of soils as to the influence of color upon their temperature. A table of his results is given in " How Crops Feed," p. 196.

Wollny also found, from the results of numerous experiments, that a dry soil is generally warmer in proportion as the color of its surface is darker; and that as a rule, at least as regards soils that are tolerably nearly alike in respect to their condition, color has no inconsiderable influence on the temperature of the soil, even at appreciable depths. This influence of color varies, of course, according to the time of year and the time of day, and as the sky is clear or cloudy. The greatest differences were found when the temperature of the soils were highest. At times when the earth attains a daily maximum of temperature, in summer sunshine, a soil will be decidedly warmer in proportion as its color is darker. But during the colder seasons the differences in temperature between dark and light colored soils are less emphatic, and they are less noticeable below the surface. Both elevation and depression of temperature are more rapid in dark than in light soils, and dark-colored soils are consequently liable to wider daily variations of temperature than soils of lighter color. The dark soils cool off more rapidly by night than the light-colored soils, although the temperature falls no lower in one than in the other. By the time the temperature of the twenty-four hours has fallen to its lowest point, it appears that all differences between the temperatures of soils of different colors have disappeared.

For the experiments in question, boxes were filled with dry white quartz sand, upon the surface of which was sifted a thin layer of the coloring matter, in the same way that Schuebler had done previously. For one set of experiments the coloring matter consisted of mixtures of lamp-black and marble-powder in the proportions of $\frac{3}{4}$: $\frac{1}{4}$, $\frac{1}{2}$: $\frac{1}{2}$, and $\frac{1}{4}$: $\frac{3}{4}$; while for another set of trials hydrated oxide of iron and marble-powder were mixed in similar proportions. One box was strewn with pure lamp-black and one with the iron oxide. All of the boxes were shielded from rain, and two thermometers were sunk in the earth of each box. The bulb of one of the thermometers was placed four inches below the surface, while that of the other was just covered with earth. The thermometers were observed every two hours during the twenty-four, and the figures in the table represent the means of all the readings by day and by night. The lamp-black experiments are given in the first part of the following table, and those with iron oxide in the second. The figures denote degrees of the centigrade thermometer.

		At Surface.			Four Inches deep.			
	Black.	Dark gray.	Med. gray.	Light gray.	Black.	Dark gray.	Med. gray.	Light gray.
28, 29 June, 1879,	32.82	32.39	31.98	30.94	28.33	28.46	27.83	27.20
Variations . .	34.55	32.90	32.45	30.10	15.20	14.25	12.50	11.85
	Dark brown.	Med. brown.	Light brown.	Faint brown.	Dark brown.	Med. brown.	Light brown.	Faint brown.
28, 29 June, 1879,	31.76	31.65	30.93	30.70	27.29	27.19	27.34	26.40
Variations . .	31.95	31.75	29.90	27.65	12.30	12.15	11.80	10.75

It is interesting to observe, in all such experiments, that a mere superficial layer of the coloring matter imparts its character to the soil beneath it; and that the whole of the soil behaves as if it were as capable as the matter which covers it of absorbing the sun's heat.

Both Reflected and Radiated Heat may be Useful.

It should be borne in mind, that the question of the absorption and radiation of heat is usually complicated with that of reflection, and that in many instances the reflective power of a soil may be as important for the crop as its power of absorbing and radiating heat. Almost any smooth surface will reflect a good part of the sun's heat, especially if the substance is white or light-colored, instead of absorbing and radiating the heat, as a rough or dark-colored body would do. A white, smooth, calcareous or micaceous sand, for example, would reflect at once much heat that a dark-colored shaly gravel would absorb and subsequently radiate. In some accounts of the Rhine vineyards it is reported that the vines are kept low and as near the soil as possible, in order that the heat of the sun may be reflected back upon them from the ground during the day, and that the process of ripening may go on through the night by virtue of the heat radiated from the earth. Here both reflection and radiation are sought for, and it might perhaps be possible to profit from both by strewing two kinds of stones, or say black coal and bright tin. A similar idea was suggested long ago by Gasparin, who speculated as to whether blackened walls might not be better than whitewashed walls for ripening fruit in some localities, especially at the south. White walls will naturally be best in countries which, like England, are moderately warm though not overburdened by sunshine.

As was just now said, smoothly polished surfaces reflect heat more completely, while they absorb and radiate it less easily, than substances which are rough,—all this quite independent of color. Sand, for example, reflects a large proportion of the sun's heat, vastly more than dry humus would; but what heat the sand does absorb it holds comparatively well. In walking over a dark or a white soil in hot sunshine a great difference will be perceived in respect to reflected heat. From the light-colored soil much heat will be reflected, while the dark soil absorbs so much of the heat which reaches it that the air above this land seems cool by comparison. Substances differ widely withal in their capacities for absorbing heat of different degrees of intensity. Some things, like lamp-black, absorb and radiate all kinds of heat equally well; but there are other substances, such as white-lead and snow, which, while they can readily absorb heat of low intensity, such as is radiated from a can of hot water, or from earth or stones that have been heated, have comparatively little power to absorb intense heat, such as comes from a lamp, or fire, or from the sun. It is noteworthy that green leaves absorb and radiate heat as readily as lamp-black does. (Maquenne.)

Loose, incoherent sands, especially if they are dark-colored, may become hotter in sunshine than other soils. Even in temperate climates, Arago found that the temperature of sand on the surface might occasionally be as high as 122 F°.; and at the Cape of Good Hope, Herschel observed temperatures as high as 159°.

Gravel Retains Heat better than Sand.

As a rule, soils that become warm the quickest cool off most rapidly and are subject to the widest variations of temperature. The greater the weight of a given bulk of soil,—in other words,

the larger and denser its particles, — so much the longer will it
retain heat. Gravel cools much more slowly than sand. It remains warm much later in the night. Hence gravelly soils are
esteemed to be "early" by market-gardeners, and are known to
be well suited for the ripening of grapes; not to say of potatoes,
in cold, dank latitudes. It is precisely in the matter of spring
vegetables and delicate fruits that considerations like the foregoing have their application; they are comparatively unimportant,
however, with regard to many crops. Evidently they can have
little bearing in the case of crops whose foliage covers the surface
of the ground; their influence will then be limited to the time
during which the soil remains bare after the seed is sown. Malaguti and Durocher have shown in fact that land covered with
grass-sod is cooler (in summer) than bare land. A thermometer
bulb sunk four inches deep under greensward showed the same
temperature as one sunk seven inches in the same soil when bare.
In South America it has been observed that a bare granite rock
marked 118° F., while an adjacent rock that was covered with
grass marked 86°.

In general, it is to be said that the amount of shade cast upon
the soil of any given field by the growing crop, from spring to
autumn, has a paramount influence upon the temperature of the
surface-soil; and it is to be remembered that the amount of shade
cast by a crop will depend not wholly upon its habit of growth
and more or less vigorous development, and upon the length of
time it remains upon the land, but largely also upon the manner
in which the crop has been planted, and upon the amount of seed
sown. When plants are grown in rows and when the spaces
between the rows are kept free from weeds, the sun's heat will
manifestly have better access to the soil and will continue to
warm it for a longer time than if the crop had been sown thickly,
broadcast. In the same sense, the surface-soil of a bare fallow-
field will usually be much warmer during the summer months than
the soil of contiguous fields which are covered with vegetation.
(Wollny.)

The warmth of gravel may be illustrated by that of rocks and
masses of masonry. The following paragraph is quoted from Dr.
Hooker's "Himalayan Journals": —

"We encountered a group of Tibetans encamped to leeward of
an immense boulder of gneiss, against which they had raised a

shelter with salt-bags. . . . They were crouched round a small fire of juniper wood. . . . A resting-house was in sight across the stream,— a loose stone hut, to which we repaired. I wondered why these Tibetans had not taken possession of the hut before we arrived, not being then aware of the value they attach to a rock on account of the great warmth which it imbibes from the sun's rays during the day, and retains at night. This invaluable property of otherwise inhospitable granite I had afterwards many opportunities of proving."

The same thing is shown very emphatically in cities, where masses of brickwork cool off but slowly by night. So also, when, in winter weather, a heated brick or piece of soapstone is made to serve for hours to warm the feet or hands of female travelers. This device was by no means unimportant in former days, before methods had been invented for warming the meeting-houses of New England.

Oemler determined the time required by different soils to cool down to 59° F. after they had all been equally heated to 122° F. His results are given in the following table :—

	Minutes consumed in Cooling.	Comparative Power of retaining Heat, Coarse Sand being taken as 100.
Coarse sand	192	100.0
Fine sand	175	91.2
Loam	166	86.5
Pure Clay	161	83.9
" chalk	158	82.3
Loamy humus	156	81.3
Clayey humus	152	79.2
Sandy humus	142	74.0
Fine humus	127	66.2
Moor-earth	120	62.5

Moisture keeps Soils cool.

The influence of moisture in the soil upon its temperature will be treated of under Draining. It need only be said here, that the presence of varying quantities of moisture in the soil makes it difficult to experiment satisfactorily upon points like those of the absorption, radiation, and reflection of heat, to which reference has just been made. It is a very difficult matter in the field to eliminate this disturbing element of moisture, so that the amount of heat really due to absorption can be accurately measured, in any given case. Thus, one very prominent reason why sandy soils are "warm" is that they are permeable and do not so readily retain moisture as loam and clays. A vast amount of heat, which would be spent in evaporating water from a moist soil, penetrates and pervades the sand and warms it so thoroughly that seeds sown upon it can germinate quickly in the spring, and the young crop can grow rapidly so long as there is a fair supply of moisture left in the land. Crops will naturally ripen early on such land. In England grain is often harvested from 10 to 14 days earlier on sandy than on clayey soils, and the fact is regarded as one of no small importance in a country where there is commonly no lack of moisture during the growing season, and where the weather is apt to be uncertain at the time of harvest.

A sloping field which permits water to flow away, and to drain away from the soil, will naturally be warmer in the spring than flat land from which water has no ready means of escape other than by way of evaporation. So too, a clayey soil, even when well drained and cultivated, will remain cool as compared with sand, while clays that are undrained may be kept actually cold by the constant evaporation of water from them. Practically, loamy and sandy soils are warm because of their porosity and dryness, though chalk and limestones are cooler, in that their light color makes them good reflectors and bad absorbents of heat. Agriculturally speaking, dry soils are never regarded as cold.

Cobbett, in urging that the soil best fitted for a garden is a loam several feet in depth, with a bed of limestone, sandstone or sand below, has said: "If we have a choice, we ought to reject [for our garden] clay and gravel, not only as a top soil but as a bottom soil. . . If there be clay within even six feet of the surface there will be a coldness in the land which will in spite of all you can do keep your spring crops a week or ten days behind those upon land which has not a bottom of clay. Gravel is warm, and it would be very desirable if you could exchange it for some other soil early in June; but since you cannot do this, you must submit to be burnt up in summer if you have the benefit of a gravelly bottom in the spring."

When speaking of making soils warm by means of dark-colored matters placed upon them, it is important to insist that neither swamp-mud nor black loam is at all suitable for the purpose, because such muds and peats have an enormous capacity for holding water in their pores, and when the sun shines upon them this water absorbs the heat of the sun, and is thereby changed to vapor, which flies off and carries the heat with it, so that the effect of the peat may really be to make the land cool in spite of its black color. It is much as when a man sits in damp clothing in a breezy place. Lampadius's black coal-dust, and the black slate of the Swiss mountaineers, are true examples of the significance of dark-colored materials. Neither of these things would be likely to absorb enough moisture to interfere with their proper action as absorbers of heat. Dr. Hooker's rock also was a compact mass practically free from moisture.

Within the Arctic Circle, where the ground is permanently frozen, and where the surface soil never melts to a depth greater than a few feet, it is noticed that the influence of the sun's heat in summer is much more pronounced on gravelly and sandy soils than on those composed of peat or clay. According to Seemann, while peat or clay may not be thawed, even at the close of summer, in Northern Alaska, to a depth of more than 2 feet, porous gravel or sand may be free from frost to a depth of six feet.

From what has been said already, it follows as a matter of course that under like conditions, where the supply of moisture is limited, a light-colored soil will retain more water than a dark-colored soil can retain, simply because under a given amount of sunlight more heat will be absorbed by the dark-colored soil and more water will be carried off from that soil by way of evaporation.

One highly important fact in respect to the transmission of heat is, that, while the sun's rays can readily pass through the air, without sensibly heating it, to warm the earth by their impact, heat such as is radiated back from the earth to the air cannot so easily pass through it. Hence atmospheric air, and particularly the vapor of water in the air, acts as a cloak or screen to hinder the escape of heat which the earth has recieved from the sun.

Influence of Hedges and Shelter-Belts.

In horticulture, it is a common practice to improve the climate of special yards or gardens by means of hedges, fences or "shelter-belts" of trees placed across the direction of the prevailing winds of the locality in such a manner that the sheltered spot may be kept warmer than it would be if cold winds could freely blow across it. A subsidiary advantage is found in the fact that high winds cannot molest the plants. It has been observed in several European localities that the mean annual temperature of a gar den may be increased by this device to the extent of one or two degrees. But there is danger, too, on clear nights in the spring, that plants standing in the calm, tranquil air of fields thus sheltered may be more subject to injury from frosts than if they were in an open field where the wind could blow upon them. According to Gasparin, writing of the valley of the Rhone, where early vegetables need to be sheltered from the violence of the winds as well as against their coldness, the protecting influence of a hedge 5 feet high is felt to a distance of 60 feet to the leeward of it.

" *Turn of the Year.*"

In discussing the influence of light and heat upon the growth of crops the time of year needs to be kept in view. In other words, due allowance must be made for those obscure causes which induce some crops to grow at one time or season and other crops at another. We are ignorant, for example, as to the reasons why the true dandelion blossoms and forms seeds in the spring, while the hawkbit thrives in the autumn. We are unable to explain, as yet, why it is that winter wheat sown in the spring " only grows leaves and stems and does not form ears."

We can only surmise that through inheritance plants have gradually acquired properties which harmonize with the conditions in which they live and which conduce to the prosperity and the permanence of the species. It is a familiar fact, for example, that roots and tubers harvested in the autumn, in cold or temperate countries, do habitually and persistently lie dormant for a season, and it is evident that they are " adapted " to this method of hibernation. It is no easy matter to make potatoes, " roots," onions, or the like, germinate normally in late autumn or early winter even under seemingly favorable conditions as to warmth and moisture, though in late winter or early spring they can be made to grow readily enough. Gardeners are familiar with the fact, that many kinds of plants grow better in greenhouses at some times and seasons than at others. In general it is thought by green-house men to be well to delay sowing many kinds of seeds until the " turn of the year." That is to say, they prefer to sow seeds in January rather than in December. Vilmorin, in calling attention to the dissimilarity of behavior of various plants in this respect, has stated that, while the term of growth of strawberries, melons and grapes may be much shortened in a heated greenhouse, that of wheat, rye, oats, and turnips remains very much the same as it is naturally out of doors. As he puts it, strawberries, melons, and grapes seem to be wellnigh indifferent to the season. They can readily be forced to grow fast at any time when constantly exposed to high temperatures.

CHAPTER III.

RELATIONS OF WATER TO THE SOIL.

THE importance of water for the plant, and its uses also, in some part, will have appeared from what has already been set forth; but there is still much to be said concerning the water in the soil.

The most familiar source from which any soil derives water is rain, and it is certain that the agriculture of a country, and indeed the power of a country to support inhabitants, must depend upon the amount of rain that falls within or near its limits.

The first question to be considered is, What becomes of the rain-water that has fallen upon the earth and has soaked into it? And this question can perhaps best be answered by considering some special instances where the conditions are not complex.

Between the large islands Nantucket and Martha's Vineyard, off the southern coast of Massachusetts, there is a little sand-island called Muskeget, which, like thousands of other similar islands, well illustrates the subject now under consideration. Muskeget is a mere sand-heap, a mile or so across, elevated a few feet above the surface of the ocean, and kept from blowing away by a scanty growth of beach-grass. But on digging down two or three feet anywhere into this sand, which was brought there by ocean currents, and is kept there by conflicting tides, a well of fresh water may be obtained. Whence comes this water? Manifestly from the rain that falls upon the island; for modern investigations have clearly shown that particles of mere silicious sand have no such power of removing saline matters from solutions as would serve to make sea-water fresh.

In the well-holes on the island now in question, the fresh water falls and rises slightly as the tide of the ocean ebbs and flows; and so it should, to accord with our theory. The water of the wells is nothing but rain-water which, falling upon the sand, has been absorbed by it, as by a sponge; and the supply of fresh water in the island is kept up by the rainfall.

No doubt the sea-water outside tends incessantly to diffuse into the fresh water, and to percolate through the sand towards the heart of the island; but this process of diffusion takes time, and, as things now are, it can never be completed. No doubt thorough diffusion and penetration would ensue if there should happen to be at Muskeget a long series of years without rain. But as matters really stand, every new rainfall pushes outward the line of brackish water about the shore, and a state of equilibrium is maintained which enables the fishermen to get fresh water by digging only a few feet back from the sea-beach.

We have in the foregoing illustration an exceedingly simple instance of a state of things which exists everywhere in rainy counries in all kinds of soils. Rain falling from the clouds soaks into the earth and remains there as "ground-water," at a height determined by the head of water around it. The surrounding water may be that of the sea immediately, as at Muskeget, or more commonly, it may be other ground-water in the soil of adjacent fields, dependent finally for the most part upon the back-action of brook- or river- or sea-water for the height at which it stands. An instance has been noticed where the back-pressure of the river Rhine at high water affected the height of water in a well 1670 feet distant from the river's edge; and Chaumont has noticed also in Hampshire, England, that a well 83 feet deep and 140 feet above mean water-level was affected by tides in the Hamble River at a distance of 2240 feet.

In studying this subject, it will be instructive to reflect upon what must happen to the rain-water which falls upon a narrow, isolated ridge of gravel, and to consider how the draining away of water from the gravel, which is now rapidly accomplished, would be retarded if the ridge were to be sunk in the sea almost to the level of its summit; or if, instead of water, the ridge were to be completely surrounded with earth of one kind or another. Whenever water gets enclosed between impervious beds or layers of soil, a flowing spring may often be had by pricking the superimposed layer. From causes like this fresh water sometimes spouts up from beneath the sea. It did so formerly in Boston Harbor, at a point now covered by Long Wharf. Were there no sea around Muskeget, if that island could be left in the air high and dry as a hill of sand, most of the water would soon drain out of it, and holes might be dug in the sand in vain.

Pumping May Lower Ground-Water.

So too, if numerous powerful pumps were set in action to draw water from the wells in the sand, sea-water would eventually soak into them. Roberts has described a condition of things at Liverpool which consists very nearly with the last named supposition. He says that beneath the buildings and pavements of that city there are pebble-beds, in the so-called Bunter sandstone, which are overlaid by a thick layer of impervious boulder-clay. Every day several millions of gallons of water are pumped out from wells sunk in the pebble-beds, though from the circumstances above stated it is improbable that much, if any, of this water can have percolated directly down from the surface into the sandstone. Manifestly this large supply of water must come from some distant source; and, from the observed fact that the water of the wells becomes more and more brackish with the course of years, it is evident that, ever since the wells have been established and drawn from, sea-water from the river Mersey has been continually percolating in towards the wells; that is to say, experience shows that the ground-water proper to the locality is not in sufficient quantity both to push back the sea-water, as of old, and to supply the new drain occasioned by the continual pumping from the wells.

As one example among several, Roberts gives analyses of water taken from a well situated 850 yards from the river Mersey and 500 yards from the nearest dock:—

Salts in Solution in the Well-water.	Grains per Gallon.			In the River Mersey.
	In 1867.	In 1871.	In 1878.	
Chloride of Sodium	. . . . –	133.44	208.64	. . .
Chloride of Magnesium	. . .	49.01	63.49	. . .
Chloride of Calcium	. . .	51.45	69.26	. . .
Total chlorides	. . .	233.90	341.39	1334.9
Sulphate of Lime	. . .	26.55	37.38	. . .
Carbonate of Magnesia	. . .	2.22	1.16	. . .
Carbonate of Lime	. . .	8.68	6.58	. . .
Nitrate of Soda	. . .	. . .	2.15	. . .
Total solids	231.00	271.35	388.66	1505.0

Between the years 1867 and 1871 the salts increased 19.63%, and between 1871 and 1878 they further increased 40.64%. The rate of increase during the first period was almost 5% per annum, while during the second period it was nearly 6%. This difference consists with the fact that much more water was pumped from the well during the second period. Since 1871, 295,200 gallons daily have been taken from the well, or very nearly 90,000,000 gallons per annum. There are several such wells within a mile of the river, yielding daily many million gallons of water. The yield has been continuous for many years, but the water has become more brackish each year, so that in some cases it is now half as salt as sea-water.

The Soil a Moistened Sponge.

The soil upon the earth's surface, with much of the rock also in those parts of the world which are well moistened and naturally adapted to agriculture, may be regarded as if, like the cited sand-island, it were a great sponge full of water up to a certain height. Near the surface, it usually happens that this sponge of earth is merely damp, and not actually wet. Here its pores are full of air, and only some comparatively speaking small quantities of moisture cling to the solid portions of the earth by force of capillary attraction. But at and below a certain small depth all the interstices of the sponge of earth are filled with water, so that there would be a continuous sheet of this liquid were it not for the fact that the fluid particles are separated from one another by the solid particles of soil. Out from the lower, i. e. the wet portion of the sponge of earth, there is everywhere a constant slow draining away of ground-water into and towards the sea.

It was simply this fact which was affirmed by Julius Cæsar when he answered his soldiers at Alexandria, that "they might easily find fresh water by digging wells, since all sea-coasts naturally abound with fresh springs." By sinking pits, in accordance with this idea, the Roman army obtained fresh water in abundance, and was saved from the destruction the Egyptians had thought to bring upon it when, by pouring sea-water into the aqueducts, they had spoiled the drinking-water with which the Romans had previously been supplied.

Even from so small an island as Muskeget some water must drain away whenever showers of rain have made the head of water within the island greater than the head of water in the sea outside; and, as has been said, the water in the wells on this island sinks and rises accordingly as the fall or rise of the tide decreases or increases the external head.

This draining away of the ground-water is of course impeded

here and there by the presence of ledges of rocks and beds or bars of clay, and in general by any impervious layers of soil or rock, such as were just now alluded to; but these hindrances are of exceptional character, and their existence does not in any way invalidate the general argument.

The growth of trees upon places like the Milldam in Boston, and the little oases of upland which occur frequently upon some of the salt marshes of the New England coast, point out, as well as the sand-island, the presence and the source of ground-water. It is to be presumed, of course, in the case of a small island like Muskeget, that at a moderate depth the sand must everywhere be saturated with sea-water, and that the fresh water which flows into the wells must lie as a mere layer above the saline bottom water. These conditions have been observed to exist at James Island, near Charleston, S. C., by Professor M. Whitney, who says: " The surface of the water in the wells is generally five or six feet below the surface of the ground, and the water is quite fresh even if the well is near the shore; but if the well is much deeper than five or six feet, the water is salt, even in the centre of the island." So, too, at Akabah, in the Arabian Desert, at the head of the Gulf of that name, Colonel Warren's party noticed that " The drainage from the hills percolates through the sandy soil, and runs on to the beach just above the level of the sea, so that by digging down a few feet abundant fresh water can be obtained; but if the hole is made too deep, the water is quite salt."

Movements of the Ground-water.

Yet another illustration may here be given, which is perhaps even more striking than either of the foregoing, inasmuch as some of the conditions of the experiment were artificial.

It is but a few years, comparatively speaking, since the large tract of land in Boston known as the Back Bay district was covered to no small depth with salt water. The Back Bay, which formerly lay behind the city, has been filled up, since 1858, with clean sandy gravel, so that the surface of the soil, on which houses are now built, is elevated a considerable number of feet above the salt-water level. At the beginning of the operation of filling, a railway was run across the middle of the bay on piles, and the gravel was dumped into the water by car-loads in such manner that every load of the gravel was thoroughly soaked with salt water, excepting that very small proportion of the whole which went to form the uppermost layer or surface of the land.

In 1870, when the outer edge of a part of the filling was just beyond Dartmouth Street at the west, and at the line of the Providence Railroad at the south, as it had been then for five or six years, there was still — at the point where the Albany and Providence railways intersect — a little pool of water that was separated but a few feet from the salt water of the unfilled bay by a low, narrow strip of gravel. On noticing that frogs lived in this pool, I had some of the water from it analyzed, to see how much saltness the creatures could withstand. To my surprise, it appeared that the water was fresh water.

Following up the inquiry, analyses were made of ground-water taken from several different points upon the filled land, the samples having been collected at a comparatively dry time from holes that had been dug for the purpose of sawing off the heads of piles upon which buildings were to be erected. The results of the analyses [1] are given in the following table:

		grm.
1.	One litre of water taken from frog-puddle at the intersection of the railways contained of common salt	0.3699
2.	One litre from a well-hole at corner of Berkeley and Boylston Streets (Hotel Berkeley)	0.3363
3.	One litre from a well-hole, then not far from the unfilled bay, on Dartmouth Street, opposite the Museum of Fine Arts .	0.6604
4.	One litre dipped from the still open bay, between the two railways	17.2196
5.	One litre dipped from the open bay, half-way between Dartmouth and Parker Streets	18.1428
6.	One litre dipped from the open bay at another point, nearer Charles River	20.1459

At the time these analyses were made there was a narrow line or ditch of fresh water on the south side of the Providence Railroad, filled with rushes and flags and other fresh-water plants, although the land where the ditch then was had been filled in but a few years, and was separated from salt water by nothing but the low railroad bed. From all these facts it appears that, in the course of the few years which had elapsed since the land had been made, the ground-water of the soil had pushed out almost the whole of the salt water with which the gravel must have been saturated at the time of the filling in.

In so far as the water in it is concerned, the whole territory

---

[1] These analyses were made by my lamented friend, William Ripley Nichols, subsequently widely known as an authority on the chemistry of waters, who was at that time my assistant in the laboratory of the Massachusetts Institute of Technology. — F. H. S.

had in fact arrived at the condition proper to a normal soil. Fresh water could be had upon it anywhere, as it can now, by digging wells of very few feet in depth. It was noticeable, furthermore, in 1870, as it has been in more recent years, that in the spring-time the ground-water stands at a much higher level in the excavations that are made in this land for laying the foundations of houses than it does in midsummer or early autumn, after time has been afforded for the water derived from the rains of winter and spring to drain away into the sea. One conclusion to be drawn from this fact, which seems indeed to have been fully impressed upon the minds of builders, is that piles had better be driven in late summer or early autumn, so that their heads may be sawn off without any such expense for pumping out the foundation trenches as has to be incurred whenever the level of the ground-water has been brought somewhat nearer the surface by the rains of late autumn, winter and spring.

The Water-Table.

It is this ground- or bottom-water — subsoil-water, or underground water, as it is often called — which supplies wells and springs, and for that matter brooks and rivers, at all times excepting those when rain or snow-water is flowing off the surface of the ground. It is impossible to insist too strongly upon the enormous importance of it for the growth of crops.

Engineers call the upper surface of ground-water the " water-table," and they are familiar with the fact that it lies at very different depths in different soils and places, and at different seasons of the year. Sometimes the water-table is at the very surface of the ground, or at a depth of no more than a few inches or a few feet, while in other situations it may lie perhaps hundreds of feet below the surface of the land. Much depends on the amount of the yearly rainfall and on the times or seasons at which it occurs; and on the condition of the soil, as to whether it is porous or compact, whether or not the upper soil is underlaid by impermeable strata, and whether or not there is ready opportunity for the water to flow out sideways and so escape from the soil.

The position of the water-table, i. e. the height of the ground-water, is continually changing, and the rate of change naturally varies very much in different places. Generally speaking, in regions of moderately abundant rains, the distance between the

highest and lowest points reached by the water-table in the course
of a year amounts to several feet at the least. At Munich, for
example, the distance is estimated at ten feet. But in some
places the rise and fall of the ground-water may be no more than
a few inches in the course of the year. At Saugor, in Central
India, the water-table is but a few inches below the surface of
the land in the rainy season, while it is 17 feet deep in May. At
Jubbulpoor it is 2 feet from the surface in the wet season, and
12 or 15 feet in the dry season.

The rate at which the ground-water drains away may depend
not only on the character of the soil or rock, i. e., whether it is
permeable or impervious, compact or full of veins or fissures, on
the amount of the rainfall and of the back-pressure from brooks
and rivers or from the sea, but also in some instances, on the
amount of water that flows in from behind, as it were. It has
sometimes been noticed that rains occurring in distant places may
cause the ground-water to rise, notably on plains which lie at the
foot of hills. Occasionally in such situations the effect of rains
may not be felt until several weeks, or even months, have elapsed
since they fell. In Northern India a great stretch of country lying
at the foot of the Himalayas is underlaid by a water-bearing stratum which is fed by the heavy rains that fall upon the mountains.
In ordinary years, the ground-water lies so near the surface of the
soil throughout this region that even sugar-cane can be grown
there with little or no irrigation.   (Caird.)

It is to be noted that, in the lack of any such exceptional
source of supply as this, it must follow as a matter of course in
arid regions where rain seldom falls, or where it falls only in hot
weather, — i. e., at a time when the moisture evaporates into the
air almost as soon as it has fallen, — there can be no hope of finding a water-table excepting at very great depths. So, too, in
regions not actually arid, but of uncertain rainfall, when several
droughty years succeed one another, it may happen that the
land dries out so thoroughly that when abundant rains do fall only
the low-lying land is saturated at first, thanks to the water which
flows down to it from the surface of higher land as well as to the
rain which falls directly upon it. Hence the water-table, which
had sunk to a great depth during the drought, may now actually
rise to a higher level in the low land than in the soil beneath fields
which are more elevated. It may justly be said of such cases

that the moisture which soaks sideways into the dry soil tends to move up hill.

Wells and Ponds.

An ordinary well is nothing but a hole sunk to a depth lower than the level at which ground-water habitually remains in the soil. It is a hole made large enough to contain an amount of water somewhat greater than is likely to be consumed at any one moment or hour, and deep enough that it may draw water from a considerable space; that is to say, that the ground-water may be led to flow into and towards it from distances sufficient to ensure a constant and an adequate supply. A pond is often nothing but a large well. An Artesian well is a boring driven until an abundance of water is reached, usually supplied from some distant source. Sometimes the Artesian boring reaches water confined under pressure, which may be due simply to a head of water or to pent up "natural gas," and then a fountain or "flowing well" is obtained. Years ago, water was obtained for several manufacturing establishments on the Cambridge marshes by boring down through the peat into the water-bearing subsoil below the lowest depth of the salt water of the river. From these wells the fresh water had to be lifted, of course, with pumps.

There is a simple device for reaching the ground-water that finds much favor in this country, which consists simply in driving narrow iron tubes into the ground to a point below the level of the water-table, and then pumping the water through the tubes. The first length of tube is closed at the very end, but has many small holes bored through its sides near the end. This first tube is driven into the soil with sledge-hammers; a second length of tube is then screwed to it, and driven down as before; then a third length is screwed on and driven; and the process is continued until the level of the water is reached. On attaching a pump to the tube, and working it, quantities of sand and fine earth are brought up with the water at first, so that a sort of reservoir to collect and hold a supply of water is soon washed out around the bottom of the tube.

This method can hardly be applicable in stiff clays, or where there are rocks or boulders in the soil; but for many loamy, sandy, and gravelly regions it has great merit. It is readily applicable on low-lying, sandy plains, and has often been found invaluable by armies of invasion, as in the war of the rebellion, when it was invented, and more recently by the English armies in Abyssinia and Egypt.

Height of Ground-Water Variable.

As was just now said, the height of the ground-water, that is to say, its distance from the surface of the earth, varies greatly at different times in any given soil, according to the permeability of the soil, and to the time which has elapsed since heavy rains. According to King, it may be admitted as an average result in humid regions, that one inch of rainfall will cause the water-table to rise 0.42 of a foot. More or less ground-water will naturally be present according as a season is wet or dry, and as less or more time has been allowed for it to drain away. Its movements are usually slow after the first flush of water caused by the rains of spring has subsided.

When people speak of wells and springs as being "full" or "low," their meaning is that the ground-water is up or down. So, too, a "never-failing well" is one that has been sunk so deeply into the domain of the ground-water that the store of water in the soil is ample, even in late summer, for the demands that are made upon it. It happens constantly, of course, in many places, that before the supplies of such a well are wholly exhausted by the natural draining away of the ground-water and by pumpings they are replenished more or less completely by new falls of rain.

Many interesting observations upon the flow, or rather the percolation of ground-water, have been made by engineers in various localities when studying the question of supplying potable water to towns,— notably in connection with the water supply of Brooklyn, N. Y., as well as that of Munich and that of Berlin.[1]

Grading and Excavating may do Harm by changing the Position of the Ground-Water.

In the vicinity of a growing city the significance of the ground-water for the support of vegetation is constantly brought to notice by the sufferings of large trees near places where the land has been considerably disturbed, either by excavating or filling, as where banks of gravel are dug down, or roads and avenues are built. It will constantly be seen in such cases, even where no roots have been laid bare, that trees pine away or die simply because their relations with the ground-water have been disturbed. A tree may suffer from this cause either because water can now

---

[1] Compare W. R. Nichols in his book on "Water Supply," New York, 1883, p. 105.

drain out from the land so much more quickly and completely than was possible before, that the tree is no longer adequately supplied with moisture at all times; or because, conversely, the building up of a new bank of earth has put a check upon the old system of drainage, and compelled the ground-water to remain so long upon the roots of the tree that they are smothered or "drowned out." The explanation is similar to that of an instance cited by Marshall, where the trees of an orchard were " greatly injured" by leading upon the land " the washings of the street and yards of a neighboring village."

Even in cities, highly interesting effects are often produced by processes of grading or excavating. In Boston, for example, there is a district lying around Church Street which was originally low land that sloped gently down to the water's edge. This declivity was built upon many years ago, long before there was any thought that the Back Bay just now spoken of would ever be filled up. But as soon as the Back Bay had been filled with gravel to its present high level, the Church Street district, lying behind it, so to say, and at a lower level, became undrainable, and as good as uninhabitable, not only because the water proper to it could no longer find an outlet, but because ground-water from the comparatively high new land soaked out continually upon the lower tract which lay beside it. To obviate this trouble all the houses upon the older land had to be raised up by means of screws, and gravel was thrown in beneath them until the surface of the land was almost as high as that of the adjoining new tract. But one of the results of this operation was to make a new stretch of table-land behind houses facing the Public Garden, and into the cellars of some of these houses ground-water immediately proceeded to flow, to the great annoyance of the occupants.

Several other similar instances that have occurred in Boston might be mentioned. One set of men will build houses just above the marsh-level; but directly another set of men will fill in the land next adjoining to a proper height, and from this higher land the ground-water will inevitably flow towards the lower. Next the city authorities step in, and raise, at great expense, the houses on the low tract, and in so doing usually cause the difficulty to pass along to a new place. The houses upon the region about Dover Street in Boston, for example, have been lifted twice during the last fifty years at the cost of the city, and gravel has been thrown in beneath them to raise the grade of the land.

To Determine the Height of the Ground-water.

An approximate estimate of the height of the ground-water in a flat field may often be got by noting the height at which water is standing in any well or ditch or hole upon the field; though it is to be observed that ordinarily the surface of the water in the well or ditch will be a little lower than that of the water in the soil, because the movement of the water is retarded both by obstacles which the soil puts in the way of flowing water and by the actual adhesion of the water to the particles of the soil. For the same reason the water-table tends to correspond in some measure with the configuration of the surface of the land. It can seldom be represented in any given case by a horizontal line drawn across a field or domain of irregular contour. In experiments made near a lake in Wisconsin, King found that the ground-water stood everywhere at a higher level in the soil than the water at the surface of the lake. Thus, at a distance of 130 feet from the lake the ground-water stood about two feet higher than the lake level, but further back from the shore the difference of level was nearly ten feet, and similar differences were noticed in other localities.

In the case of clayey soils, special regard must be had to the impermeable character of clay. In stiff clays the wells are commonly "over-shot wells," as the term is; i. e. they are mere pits to receive and hold the surface water, which flows into them at the top, and in many soils that contain clay much water is apt to run in, at the top of the well, out from the tillable surface-soil, which is often much more permeable than the subsoil. It may even happen during or immediately after rain that the water in such a well will stand at a higher level than the water-table.

Best Height for Ground-water.

The proper height at which ground-water should stand in order best to conduce to the prosperity of the growing plant is a question of no little complexity. There are numberless swamp-plants which prefer to have their roots constantly immersed in ground-water. Rice also, and the cranberry, and ribbon-grass, and a few other useful grasses, flourish with their roots actually wet. But as a general rule the plants of cultivation cannot bear such an excess of this kind of moisture; it is with them much as it is with greenhouse plants, there must be a hole in the bottom of the pot or the plant will drown. Many plants having powerful roots do indeed send some of them down to the bottom-water. There are innumerable examples upon record, for that matter, of the choking of drains, in which water was standing or flowing, by the roots of various kinds of clover, and of turnips, grape-vines, and the like. As has been shown withal, under the head of Water Culture, it is possible to grow a great variety of plants in mere water. But in spite of all this, it is notorious that winter grain often succeeds best in soils where the ground-water is several feet distant from the surface of the land. In the cultivation of moors and bogs in Europe, it is held as one essential condition of success that the ground-water must be kept at least three feet below the surface of the land in summer, and as much as two feet below the surface in winter.

Much depends of course on the kinds of crops which are to be grown. As Gasparin has said, dry soils are fit only for the crops — such as cereals and pulse — in which fructification occurs by the end of the spring; they are not well adapted for the support of plants which vegetate in midsummer. As regards forage crops, in hot countries, it is notorious that dry soils will not yield half as much fodder as soils which are fairly moist; while in many cases no aftermath can be expected on the dry fields. In many situations, however, trees of various kinds,— thanks to their wide-reaching roots — do well on soils which are apt to dry out at the surface.

The comparatively low temperature of ground-water is undoubtedly one reason why the too close proximity of such water is obnoxious to plants, but it must sometimes happen, in the case of non-aerated waters, that harmful soluble products of reduction may be present. A distinction must always be carefully made between running water like that of a brook, or of an open drain even, and the cold, sluggish ground-water. A noteworthy example of the distinction to be made in this case is to be seen in the floating islands of the old Mexicans, as well as those still to be seen in China and in Cashmere. These islands were great flats of basket-work made strong enough to carry a layer of earth, which was of course kept continually moist by the water of the lake on which the island floated. But the ground-water in the earth of these islands was really the surface-water of the lake, i. e. a warm, living water, in every way fit to be used for irrigation. The roots of the maize and of the various kinds of vegetables that were grown upon

these floating islands must have been continually immersed in the
ground-water; but precisely as in the case of the experiments in
water-culture, the ground-water was of a kind that did the roots
no harm.

For northern countries and for some important crops — notably
for winter grain — it is held that where the soil, even though it be
light and friable, is in good heart, the ground-water should be
from four to eight feet distant from the surface. The good results obtained by laying tile-drains deep in clayey soils enforce
the justice of the idea. King has observed in Wisconsin that
Indian corn growing on a deep loam overlying a subsoil of rather
coarse sand, was able to draw upon the permanent water in the
ground when this water lay at a depth at least as great as 7.5
feet. But he remarks that it is commonly observed in seasons of
drought that vegetation is apt to suffer from lack of moisture even
when the water-table lies within five feet of the surface, whence
the conclusion that the rate at which the capillary action can carry
water towards the surface is not great enough to meet at all times
the demands of all kinds of crops. It is true, withal, of many
grasses and of not a few vegetables — notably squashes — that
they succeed well in certain soils where the ground-water is much
higher than has here been stated.

Most vegetables indeed grow best in soils where a not too cold
ground-water is very near the surface of the land, and since garden
vegetables are summer crops for the most part, there is small need
of considering on their account what the winter height of the
ground-water in any given case may be. But it would be highly
imprudent to sow wheat in the autumn on land liable to become
water-soaked. It happened, indeed, formerly, in many districts
in Europe, where soil and climate (and tariffs) compelled the
farmers to grow wheat in positions not really suited to it, that
clayey soils were thrown up into ridges which should shed the
surface-water from the fields and serve to keep the roots of
the young crop high enough above the ground-water to prevent
them from dying. But it was always recognized that this mode
of cultivation was a make-shift and that wheat prefers a much
drier situation. As regards vegetables, there is of course always
the risk in low-lying fields that late frosts in the spring and early
frosts in the autumn may injure tender plants; and this practical
consideration is one of vast importance, which must be duly

weighed, though it should not be allowed to obscure the question now in debate.

Fleischer has reported of moorland near Bremen that the best crops of rye and potatoes are got when the ditches are from 20 to 30 inches deep, and that the yield of rye diminished to the extent of 12 to 34% and the yield of potatoes from 8 to 23% when the ditches were deepened. The pea-crop was less sensitive in respect to varying amounts of water in the soil, in so far as the yield of grain was concerned, though the vines grew more freely when the ditches were not deeper than 20 or 30 inches.

Almost any one can recall from his own observation plots of grass-land where the ground-water is at just the right height for this kind of vegetation. At the banks of brooks it might perhaps be said that the influence of flowing water is felt, and that the observed luxuriance is due to irrigation from the brook rather than to the presence of ground-water. Usually, however, this conception would not be true; for in the generality of such cases it is ground-water percolating towards the brook that supplies moisture to the grass. Just so it is on the bottom lands of rivers (intervales), and in reclaimed bogs. Very much depends, of course, on the texture of the soil. Clayey soils retain their ground-water with great tenacity, and are often, on that account, unfit for general culture until drained by artificial means.

Water in Sand-Dunes.

Some interesting examples, where the presence of ground-water at just the right height makes the cultivation of mere sands possible, are recorded by Boussingault. In a certain district in Spain there were a number of sand-dunes composed of sand so loose and dry that it drifted hither and thither with the wind But since the lower portions of these hills are kept continually moist by the infiltration of water from the Guadalquivir, it was only necessary to remove the loose sand from above the moistened layer, in places where no great amount of labor was required, in order to obtain some very fertile land; i. e. a soil which united in the highest degree two essential conditions of fertility, porosity and a constant supply of moisture. The climate, moreover, was specially well suited for land thus moistened, and it was found in fact that the levelled dunes yielded abundant crops, particularly when the sand was manured. This instance is closely related to the so-called method of sand-culture, which has been successfully employed in many scientific experiments.   One great merit of the method, as has been urged by Hellriegel, depends on the remarkably complete manner in which the roots of plants develop in the incoherent sand.   A perfectly developed system of roots occupying every part of the soil proper to it must manifestly be particularly well fitted for taking nourishment from that soil, and from the water that comes to it.

I have myself noticed an instance somewhat analogous to the foregoing, on the bank of the Merrimac River, on the line of the railway, not far from Concord, N. H., where mere sand lying upon high bluffs upon the river's bank yields crops in spite of the very unpromising appearance of the land.   The explanation in this case appears to be that the sand is fine enough to be capillary, and that the ground-water is continually percolating through the bluff towards the river, at a depth from the surface not too great to put it out of reach of the crops.   Indeed, the history of the improvement of sand-dunes by plantations of trees is full of instances of the advantages to be derived from the ground-water when it is near enough to be accessible to the roots.   The idea is simply that, where there is ground-water within reach, trees can be started, and whenever this can be done the action of wind upon the loose sand in the vicinity can be checked, and the dunes thus be kept quiet enough to admit of grass, and finally useful trees, being grown upon them.   In Holland, the best possible potatoes are grown on sand-dunes, thanks to the presence of ground-water and the free use of manure.

In some localities, the presence of beds of clayey loam, at a depth of a few feet beneath the surface, permits profitable crops to be grown continually, although nothing but sand is to be seen where the plants are standing.   It is manifest, in such cases, that the capacity of the subsoil to hold a store of moisture is the salvation of the farmer.

Low-lying Slopes may be moist.

Upon the slopes of hills there is generally a strong probability that somewhere, i. e. on some part of the slope, ground-water may be found at a good height.   It is for this reason, doubtless, as much as on account of the soil which has been washed down from above, that so many of the hill-farms of New England are situated near the bases of sloping hills.   Indeed it might almost be urged as a general rule, that the positions of homesteads and of farms in Northern New England have been determined by the position and character of the ground-water as much or more than by the quality of the soil. The house was put where water could be got handily; but where water can be got handily, crops will flourish. Of course, as the country has dried up through the destruction of woodland,— or rather of the mossy humus which the wood protected,— the relations of the ground-water to the surface soil have been greatly changed in many places. In the beginning, even the roads had to be carried along the high ridges in order that they should be moderately dry during the rainy seasons, and that they should dry off after rain.

It is very noticeable that the most successful market-gardeners in the vicinity of Boston keep near the ground-water. That is to say, they cultivate low-lying land for the most part,— often that which is very low. And it is true, in general, that the differences noticed in the fertility of fields or districts depend as often, or perhaps even more frequently, upon the presence in the soil of good supplies of moisture, as upon the stores of plant-food of other kinds than water.

In exceptionally dry seasons, indeed, access to the ground-water may become an absolute necessity for the success of crops, as may be seen from the following experiments by Wilhelm. It happened that an unusually small amount of rain fell in Germany during the autumn of 1865 and the following winter, while from March to July, 1866, the rainfall was very nearly equal to the average for that season. But, because of the previous lack of rain, all kinds of crops were seen to be suffering from drought during the spring of 1866, excepting those grown upon fields low enough to be within reach of the ground-water.

In order to determine how large the deficiency of water really was, samples of soil were collected at different depths in March and June, and examined as to how much moisture was contained in them.

I. *From low-lying fields, moistened by the ground-water.*

SAMPLES OF MARCH 2.

At Depth in feet.	Kind of Soil.	Amount of Water in 100 Parts of the Fresh Earth.	Amount of Water for every 100 Parts of Dry Earth.
$\frac{1}{2}$	Loamy marl running to	16.92 — 18.84	20.37 — 23.22
$1\frac{1}{2}$	sandy marl and to sand,	18.01 — 20.81	21.96 — 26.28
$2\frac{1}{2}$	according to the depth,	21.61 — 24.26	27.57 — 32.03

SAMPLES OF JUNE 18.

At Depth in Feet.	Kind of Soil.	Amount of Water in 100 Parts of the Fresh Earth.	for every 100 Parts of Dry Earth.
⅓		18.86	23.25
1⅓	[As above.]	21.19	26.88
2⅓		21.56	27.44

II. *From upland fields, above the influence of the ground-water.*

SAMPLES OF MARCH 6.

⅓	Sandy marl	7.20 — 10.96	7.76 — 12.31
1⅓	Quicksand	2.32 — 5.09	2.38 — 5.37
2⅓	Sand and gravel	0.65 — 1.07	0.66 — 1.09

SAMPLES OF JUNE 18.

⅓		9.74	10.79
1⅓	[As above.]	4.92	5.17
2⅓		0.66	0.66

It will be noticed that the foregoing remarks apply more particularly to rainy regions such as New England and Northern Europe. In countries of scanty rainfall, or of deep-lying ground-water, special pains are sometimes taken to put the crops into connection with what little moisture there is in the soil. Thus, on the rainless table-lands of the higher Colorado, where the sandy soil is subjected to intense heat in the summer, the Moqui Indians are said to plant the seeds of Indian corn at a depth of 12 or 14 inches in order that they may germinate and that the roots of the crop may be within reach of the moisture which soaked into the ground on the melting of the winter snows. (Newberry, in Johnson's "How Crops Grow.") In the African desert, the date-palm — for the sake of keeping its roots within reach of moisture — is sometimes, in extreme cases, planted in pits as much as twelve feet in depth, from which the crown ultimately emerges. The method of growing maize in Kansas, known as "listing" appear to be based in part on a similar idea. In this case, the seeds are planted in the bottom of little trenches which subsequently become filled up with soil when the crop comes to be "cultivated" for the purpose of hindering the evaporation of moisture.

Importance of an Abundant Rainfall.

The dependence of any country on the amount of its rainfall is illustrated by the following table given in the census report of 1890 to show the distribution of the population of the United States as related to the mean annual rainfall in different sections of the country.

Inches of Rainfall.	Population per Square mile.			Increase of the Population per Square mile.	
	1870.	1880.	1890	1870–'80	1880–'90
Below 10	0.3	0.6	0.8	0.3	0.2
10 to 20	0.4	0.8	1.8	0.4	1.0
20 to 30	1.6	4.7	8.1	3.1	3.4
30 to 40	28.6	35.5	43.1	6.9	7.6
40 to 50	39.4	49.2	59.0	9.8	9.8
50 to 60	15.5	20.9	25.1	5.4	4.2
60 to 70	11.9	14.5	18.1	2.6	3.6
Above 70	0.8	2.1	4.1	1.3	2.0

According to J. D. Whitney, nearly three-fourths of the population of the United States inhabit a region over which the rainfall is between 30 and 50 inches in amount, and on either side of the area thus favored the number of persons to the square mile diminishes very rapidly, although it is not true that the scantiness of the population in the regions with more than 50 inches of rainfall is solely due to the excessive precipitation. In this case, local causes are of paramount importance in hindering the settlement of the country viz., the great difficulty of draining much of the lowlying swamp-land of southern Florida and of the delta of the Mississippi and the great labor involved in clearing the forest in the mountainous and inaccessible parts of Oregon and Washington. Many large areas of the earth's surface are densely inhabited where the precipitation is much larger than it is in any part of the United States.

It is a matter of familiar knowledge that the amount of rain which falls upon the land varies widely in different regions. Of some countries, such as Peru and a part of Egypt, as well as of the deserts of Africa and Central Asia, it is practically true that there is never any rain there. Upon the table-land of Mexico, and in many other localities, rains are very rare. Speaking in general terms, the most abundant rainfall is in regions near the equator, where there are usually regular wet and dry seasons; though in certain localities, as in some parts of Guiana, it rains wellnigh continually. Nevertheless, taking the year through, there are commonly fewer rainy days in the tropics than in the temperate zones. While as many as 95 inches of rain may fall at the equator in 80 days, there are some 170 rainy days at St. Petersburg, although no more than 17 inches of rain falls there in a year. On the eastern coast of Ireland it rains 208 days in a year, in England about 150 days, at Kazan 90, and in Siberia 60 days. In the northern portions of the United States there may be some 130-odd rainy days in the year against perhaps rather more than 100 in the Southern States. The average rainfall in the temperate zone is something like 35 inches, though there are wide variations in different countries. Some 25 inches of rain fall in a year at London, and nearly 280 inches at Vera Cruz. Thanks to the Gulf-stream and the frequency with which south-west winds blow over them, the westernmost countries of Europe are well moistened by rains and enjoy a favorable mean annual temperature; but on passing inland towards the east of Europe the number of rainy days diminishes, the rainfall is less, and the mean annual temperature lower.

Soakage of Rain-water.

Beside the question of the amount of the rainfall, there is another point of primary importance, classed by engineers as " percolation of rainfall," which demands the farmer's attention, especially in so far as it relates to the soils of his own fields, for few of the conditions which determine the success of crops are of more importance than the capacity of a soil to absorb and hold a good store of the water that soaks into it from the surface. It would certainly be well for every farmer to know, if he could, about how much rain-water will soak into and pass out from the soil of each of his fields in the course of a year, and how much at each season of the year. Many experiments have been made, indeed, in various localities, in order to ascertain what proportion of the rainwater that falls on a given field passes into or through the soil.

The rapidity of percolation will, of course, depend upon the character of the soil. Thus, Gasparin, on testing the rate of flow of water through wet soils of different kinds, found that a layer of water 20 inches thick (50 centim.) passed through a layer of the soil 12 inches thick (30 centim.) and saturated with water in the times stated in the following table : —

	Hours.
Coarse sand, somewhat calcareous	1.54
Ditto, after removal of the lime	1.20
Fine quartz sand from a porcelain factory . .	1.57
Sand from Hartz forest	6.25
Limestone soil with 11% of humus	7.94
Magnesite, from Salinelles	12.00
Sand No. 1, ground extremely fine	33.33
Powdered blue-white marble	88.11
Whiting (Spanish white).	201.60

Kaolin, from Biscay 603.27
Tile-maker's clay 252.00
Refractory clay from a field 168.00
Crucible clay (water would not pass through this
specimen) . . . . ———

As Lawes and Gilbert have put it, the amount of percolation-water passing through any soil depends, first, on the amount of the rainfall; secondly, on the physical condition of the soil, i. e. its permeability and water-holding power; and, thirdly, on the amount of evaporation that is taking place. This evaporation, which depends largely on the temperature of the soil and of the air, and upon the capillary power of the soil, is often greatly increased when crops are growing upon the land, both because the foliage presents a large surface for the evaporation of rain-water which collects upon it and clings to it, as is seen very conspicuously in woodland, and because the crops pump up much water from the soil and transpire it as vapor from their leaves into the air.

Evaporation from hot Sand.

Evaporation must often be very large, even where no crops are growing, as is shown conspicuously when rain falls upon hot sand. At the extremity of Cape Cod a brisk summer shower falling upon the shingled roof of a house will be seen to add several barrels of water to the contents of the cistern which supplies the needs of the family, but the water from such a shower that falls upon the bare sand which surrounds the house simply causes the particles of sand to cling together for a moment, at the very surface of the land, and almost immediately passes off into the air, in the form of vapor. Under the supposed conditions, none of the water soaks downward and, when the brief shower has ceased, the sand will be found dry as ashes just below the moistened surface-film. On the other hand the amount of evaporation from cool sand may be very small, and almost the entire rainfall may pass down into the sand. Mr. Greaves, at Lee Bridge, in England, who made observations during 14 years on the amounts of water that evaporated and percolated from a gauge filled with sand, found that most of the rainfall passed through the sand without hindrance and that comparatively little water evaporated from the surface even in the height of summer. The average yearly rainfall of the locality was 25.7 inches, but only 4.2 inches of water per annum evaporated from the sanded gauge.

Wollny has noticed that even the color of a soil may have some influence on the amount of water which soaks into it, for inasmuch as dark-colored soils absorb heat more readily than those of lighter color, more water will evaporate from soils of dark color. Hence it may happen that, of a given rainfall, a larger proportion of the water will percolate into light-colored land than can be absorbed by contiguous land of dark color.

According to J. D. Whitney, very much the same condition of things in regard to evaporation prevails in the arid region of Colorado as in the case of the hot sand just now alluded to. During July and August, he says, rain falls copiously almost every afternoon, heavy showers often continuing for several hours, yet in his experience the ground was never wet to a depth of more than a few inches and not a particle of water penetrated so deep as to be retained permanently. An examination of the soil showed that nearly every drop of the rain which reached the earth was returned to the atmosphere within a few hours after it had fallen. The small amount of moisture which does percolate the soil in this region must come from the winter's rain or snow, and since the amount of snow is as a rule exceedingly small, and since most of the year's rain comes at a time when the conditions are best suited for its rapid evaporation, it is evident that the total percolation in this region must be very trifling.

The following experiments by Nessler bear upon the question of permeability: Three tubes, each one foot high by two inches wide, were closed at one end with a strip of thin linen and were filled with loam. Into tube A the loam was loosely shaken, in B it was packed and pressed throughout the entire length of the tube, and in C only the uppermost inch and a half of the loam was compressed, while the remainder of the loam, beneath the packed layer, was left loose. Equal amounts of water were allowed to drop slowly into each of the tubes, which were then covered with plates of glass and left at rest for six days. On examination it was found that the water had moved about in the loam as is stated in the following table: —

Percentage amounts of water in the	Uppermost 1½ inches.	Just below Packed layer.	4 inches from top.
A. Loose loam	15.6	——	12.6
B. Packed loam	13.9	——	8.8
C. Packed on top but loose below	20.0	15.0	3.9

It will be noticed that in C the layer of compressed loam at the top of the tube remained wellnigh saturated with water, while beneath the compressed layer, at a depth of 4 inches from the surface, the loam was comparatively dry. The downward percolation of water was at its best in the tube where all the loam had been left loose.

Drain-Gauges.

The usual method of studying the question of the percolation of rain-water is to establish drain-gauges in the soil of the field which is to be examined. So long ago as 1796–98, the English chemist Dalton sunk a cylinder three feet deep and ten inches in diameter into the soil, filled it with earth, made it level with the surface of the land, and after the first year grew grass upon it. By collecting the water at the bottom of this cylinder, he found that 25% of the yearly rainfall had percolated through the earth in it. The difference he attributed to evaporation.

Simultaneously with Dalton, Maurice at Geneva, using an iron cylinder filled with earth, found that the percolation was equal to 39% of a rainfall amounting to 26 inches per annum. Gasparin, operating at the south of France, in a rather hot country subject to spring and summer droughts, observed that the yearly percolation amounted to no more than 18% of the annual rainfall of 28 inches.

Dickinson, in England (in 1836–43), at a locality where the average rainfall was 26.6 inches, used a Dalton drain-gauge 3 feet deep and 12 inches wide, filled with gravelly loam and grass-grown at the surface. He found, as the average of eight year's observations, that 11.3 inches percolated in a year, or about 42.5% of the rainfall, while 57.5% either evaporated or remained in the soil. In round numbers $\frac{2}{5}$ of the rainfall in this case would pass out from the land through the drains, though very considerable variations were noticed, ranging from 33 to 57%, in the course of the experiments. Or, stated, in other terms, while the annual rainfall ranged from 21 to 32 inches and amounted to from 2,137 to 3,139 long tons to the acre, the annual evaporation was from 43 to 67% of the rainfall. The mean winter rain of the eight years, i. e. from October to March inclusive, was 13.95 inches, of which 10.39 inches percolated, or 74.5%; while the mean summer rain of the same years, viz., between April and September, was 12.67 inches, of which only 0.9 inch percolated, or 7.1% of the rainfall of these summer months. During the warmer months of the years 1840 and 1841 absolutely no water percolated through the drain-gauge.

Dickinson's experiments were continued by Evans. He found the average rainfall of 15 years (1860–75) to be 25.6 inches, and the annual percolation through 3 feet of grass-covered loam 5.6 inches. During summer the amount of percolation averaged only

0.35 inch. In another gauge, filled with chalk, and turfed, the average annual percolation was 8.8 inches. Of course, in a poor soil, where the grass grew less vigorously, percolation would be larger and evaporation less than where the stand of grass was heavy.

Greaves, at Lee Bridge, in England, whose gauges were 3 feet deep, found as the averages of 14 years (1860–73), that while the rainfall was 25.7 inches the percolation through a gauge filled with a mixture of soft loam, gravel and sand, trodden in and turfed, was 7.6 inches. Through a gauge filled with sand 21.5 inches of rain-water percolated annually, as was just now said. During the growing season (April to Sept.) practically no drainage took place from the turfed gauge, nearly the whole of the rainfall being transpired by the grass.

Risler in Switzerland (1867–78), by gauging drains that had been laid 4 feet deep in a compact, impervious soil, which bore crops at the time of the experiment, found that 30% of the average annual rainfall of 41 inches percolated, while 70% of it evaporated.

Pfaff in Erlangen, and Woldrich at Salzburg and at Vienna, found that only $\frac{1}{4}$ of the yearly rainfall percolated through 2 feet of bare soil when evaporation was greater than the rainfall; that almost $\frac{1}{3}$ percolated when evaporation was equal to the rainfall; and that rather more than $\frac{1}{2}$ percolated when evaporation was somewhat less than the rainfall. Woldrich found invariably that less water percolated 2 feet in soil upon which grass was growing than in a bare soil. Very light rains were wholly lost by evaporation from the grass, because the drops clung to the leaves until they evaporated. During late autumn and winter the differences between the percolation in bare land and that which was grass-grown were less than they were from May to September. In January they were least, and it was noticed, when the ground was frozen and covered with snow, that the soil-water in the bare land continued to sink to a greater depth than it did in the grass-covered earth. When the snow melted in spring, the water from it passed into the bare land much quicker and in larger quantity than it did into the soil that was grass-covered.

With the first awakening of vegetation in the spring, the differences between the bare and the grass land became more prominent, both because of evaporation of water that had clung to the blades of grass and because of the transpiration of water by the plants. The greatest differences were noticed in hot summer weather, viz., in June and July. In May not quite half as much water percolated through the grass-land as through the bare earth; and during the last fortnight of June, at Salzburg, 23.16 lines of water passed through the bare soil against only 0.23 line that passed through the grass-covered earth. A similar contrast was observed in July also. The monthly differences between the bare and the grass-covered land were as follows: May, 25 %; June, 53 %; July, 23 %; August 29 %; September, 12 %. At Vienna in the winter 7½ % less water percolated 2 feet in grass-land than in land that was bare, while for the spring months the figures were 22¼ %; or 15%, taking winter and spring together. At Salzburg 35¼ % less water percolated through grass-land in summer than passed through the bare land.

The Bavarian Experiments.

Some of the results of percolation experiments made in woodlands by Bavarian observers will be found on a subsequent page under the head of Mulching. In these Bavarian experiments it was found that in winter and spring rather more water dropped from drain-gauges that were 4 feet deep than from those 1 foot deep; i. e. within these limits of depth there was less water in the upper layers of the soil at that time of the year than in the lower layers. In autumn and summer, on the contrary, the percolation-water diminished as the depth of the gauges was greater. In summer, indeed, there was less than half as much water at a depth of 4 feet as at 1 foot. All of which illustrates the well-known importance of the store of water which accumulates in the land from the rains of late autumn, winter, and early spring.

From a rainfall of any given amount, more water will soak into the ground when it comes in the form of moderate persistent rain than when it falls in short, heavy showers, and the fact is specially true, of course, as regards hillsides or any sloping land. But it has been found to be true, in Central Europe, that, excepting short, sharp showers, more water will soak into level ground at a given time from a heavy rain than from two lighter rains yielding the same amount of water to a rain-gauge, manifestly because of the better chance for evaporation in the second case. In any event, percolation of rain-water is greatly modified by evaporation; and since evaporation is much more rapid from the upper layers of the

soil than from the lower layers, it sometimes happens when the
surface of the soil appears to be dry, that water may still be dropping from a drain-gauge, even at a depth no greater than one
foot, some considerable time after the last rain has fallen.

In Bavaria, much more of the water from a given amount of
rainfall percolates in winter than in summer, because of the small
amount of evaporation in winter; and for a similar reason much
more of the rain that falls on a drain-gauge kept in the shade of a
wood during the summer months will percolate, than can at that
season pass through a drain-gauge kept in an open field.

In general, it appeared that, with the rapid increase of evaporation from May to the end of September the moisture in the soil
diminished, while with the diminution of evaporation in October
and the later months the moisture in the soil increased. So that,
even if the amount of rainfall in late autumn and winter were to
be considerably smaller than it is in summer, the amount of
water in the soil would still be larger during the cold months than
during those which are warm. In other words, the amount of
water in the soil stands in no direct proportion to the rainfall of
the several months.

Matted Roots hinder Percolation.

It is to be remembered that while tillage may promote percolation, by loosening and lightening the soil, so that water can
freely enter it, a thick mat of vegetation will hinder the admission of water. Any crop that stands thick, and fills the soil with
roots that are entwined one with another, hinders the percolation
of rain-water. Much less water will soak through grass-sod than
into bare earth, and European foresters have noticed a similar
hindrance when the soil is covered with the matted roots of heath
plants. On this account, it has been urged that, when young
trees are to be planted, it will be best to remove heath, grass, or
the like, and to cover the land with a layer of loose litter, such as
will permit water to pass through it. On the same account, it has
been urged that large trees growing in a wood so situated that
they get no other water than the rain which falls upon them may
perhaps do better in case there is a growth of underbrush beneath
them instead of a sod of grass; but in this case the water taken
by the shrubs for their own support might perhaps more than
counterbalance the increased soakage. The trouble with the grass
sod, or similar mat, is not only that the plants use water and hold

it upon their leaves to be evaporated, but that the felted roots offer a serious mechanical obstruction to the admission of water.

None of the water of light summer showers penetrates far into the soil in any event, because it evaporates from the upper layers of soil, and from the causes just now enumerated, it may happen that such showers will be as good as lost on soils closely covered with vegetation. At some of the Bavarian stations, drain-gauges 2 and 4 feet deep, that were kept in open fields, gave out no drop of water during July, August, and September, and in two of the localities water ceased to drop from the one-foot gauge even in July.

As will be shown more in detail on a subsequent page, percolation may be greatly increased by hindering evaporation and facilitating the admission of water to the soil, as happens when leaf-covered drain-gauges are kept in the woods.

Wollny found that a calcareous loam which permitted 38% of the rainfall from April 14 to November 18 to soak through it, when it was bare of vegetation, percolated no more than 20% of the rainfall when grass or clover was growing upon it. In other trials, lasting from May to October inclusive, three different soils, viz., sand, peat, and clay, were compared side by side in three conditions; i. e., bare of vegetation; with grass growing upon them; and covered with a layer of horse-manure $2\frac{1}{2}$ inches deep. The percolation was as follows, in per cent. of the rainfall: sand, peat, and clay, when bare, 64, 44 and 32, respectively; when grassed, 14, 9, and 1; when mulched, 45, 39, and 49. The superiority of clay and peat as absorbents of water is manifest, as well as the pumping power of vigorous plants. The heavy mulch lessened the amount of percolation as regards sand and peat, i. e. as compared with the bare soils, but increased it in the case of clay. On repeating the mulching trials with a layer of horse-manure only $\frac{6}{10}$ inch deep, the percolation was somewhat larger than through the bare soil, and evaporation was less. A coating of gravel had the same effect as the thin layer of manure in lessening evaporation and increasing percolation.

Lawes's Drain-Gauge.

No one has taken more trouble to study the subject of percolation than Lawes and Gilbert, who built elaborate rectangular drain-gauges 6 feet by 7 feet 3 inches in area ($= \frac{1}{1000}$ of an acre). These gauges had depths respectively of 20, 40, and 60 inches.

Care was taken to keep the soil in a perfectly natural condition of consolidation, so that it should neither be more porous nor more compact than ordinary field-soil, and the surfaces of the gauges were kept bare of vegetation. The results of these trials have been tabulated for each of the several depths above mentioned, and for each month of each year during a period of many years. From 1870 to 1881 the average rainfall of the locality was 31.5 inches per annum, and the mean yearly percolation through the drain-gauge that was 20 inches deep amounted to 14 inches; through the gauge that was 40 inches deep, the percolation was 14.9 inches and through the 60-inch gauge it was 13¼ inches.

As tabulated by Lawes and Gilbert, the percentages were as follows :—

During the	Mean Rainfall. Inches.	Per cent. of Rainfall that went through the Gauge.		
		20-inch.	40-inch.	60-inch.
4 years, 1871–74	27.3	35.4	34.7	28.4
6 " 1875–80	34.2	49.6	54.2	49.4
10 " 1871–80	31.5	44.6	47.4	42.1

During the 13 years, 1877 to 1890, the annual rainfall was 30.21 inches, and the mean annual percolation through the 20-inch gauge was 15.45 inches, and through the 60-inch gauge 15.05 inches. Evaporation from the soil was found to be greatest in July, and in this month 100 parts of rain give on the average 24 parts of drainage, while in December 100 parts of rain yield 80 parts of drainage. The principal amount of drainage occurs there in the five months, October to February, when some 63% of the total percolation of the year takes place.

American Experience.

Naturally enough, some of these European experiences may not be directly applicable to a country the surface soil of which remains so long frozen as does that of the Northern United States, or to regions where the air is so dry as ours is, and which are subject to showers so violent as those we not infrequently experience. Moreover, rain falling upon our superheated soils in midsummer will be exposed to excessive loss through evaporation. Hence the special importance for us of American experiments. Dr. Sturtevant, at South Framingham, Mass., found that of the annual rainfall of 47.15 inches, 8.7 inches, or 17.9%, percolated through the 25 inches of grass-covered sandy soil in his drain-gauge. Stockbridge, at Amherst, observing during the seven growing months of the year, found that 5.14 inches of the 25.7 inches of rain that fell during these seven months percolated through 36 inches of a very leachy soil; that is to say, he noticed a summer percolation of 20%. During the same period, $27\frac{9}{10}$ inches of rain fell upon Dr. Sturtevant's drain-gauge, and $14\frac{7}{10}\%$ of the water percolated through it.

S. W. Johnson has called attention to the fact that, while the percentage of percolation is larger in England than in this country, the total amounts of water that penetrate the soil, as measured in inches, are not very different in the different countries. He cites the English results of Dickinson, Greaves, and Lawes, $11\frac{1}{10}$, $6\frac{9}{10}$, and 10 inches respectively; the Swiss results of Maurice and Risler, $10\frac{1}{2}$ and $12\frac{3}{10}$; the French of Gasparin, $5\frac{9}{10}$; and the American of Sturtevant ($5\frac{7}{10}$ in 1876 and $11\frac{4}{10}$ in 1877) and Stockbridge ($5\frac{44}{100}$ for seven months of 1877), in illustration of this view, and argues that the filtration of water through drain-gauges amounts to from 5 to 10 inches annually with a rainfall of 26 to 44 inches. Heavier rainfalls are evidently compensated by greater and more rapid evaporation; and evaporation and rainfall vary within much wider limits than percolation, which is relatively constant. Warington has said of the percolation experiments of Lawes and Gilbert, that the average annual drainage through bare, uncropped soil during 13 years was about 15 inches, or one-half the rainfall; but the drainage bears no fixed proportion to the rainfall. The drainage in any year is merely the excess of rainfall over evaporation, and the quantity of water annually evaporated from a bare soil at Rothamsted is a fairly constant quantity.

The quantity of water which soaks into the soil at any given locality in the course of a year will naturally depend in no small measure upon the season at which the rain falls. Thus in the region east of the base of the Rocky Mountains, where the precipitation is almost exclusively limited to the spring and summer months, that of the winter months amounting to almost nothing, there can be very little percolation, because the rate of evaporation during the summer is excessive, as has already been explained. (J. D. Whitney.)

As a matter of course, water can percolate more rapidly through sand than through clay or humus, or, stated more precisely, "the relative rate of movement of water through soils will depend upon how much space there is in the soil, and upon how much this space is subdivided, i. e., upon how many grains of sand and clay there are in the soil, upon how these grains are arranged, and upon how this skeleton structure is filled in and modified by organic matter." (M. Whitney.)

Where there are actual cracks and crevices in a soil, water will naturally run down such conduits without check, and this fact may explain statements which have been made to the effect that water has been seen to permeate sand to a depth of 18 inches in one hour. But ordinarily the movement of water is much less rapid. The following examples are taken from a mass of results obtained by Milton Whitney in his examinations of typical subsoils from Maryland. He found that an inch in depth of water passed in 8 minutes through sand (from pine barrens) that contained about 4% of clay and had 40% of empty space; while 100 minutes were required for this amount of water to pass through a calcareous clayey soil that contained nearly 44 % of clay and had 65% of empty space. Through the subsoil of typical wheat-land of the locality, which contained 23 % of clay and had 55 % of empty space, an inch of water passed in 45 minutes.

Rocks retain Moisture.

Even rocks can usually retain some of the rain-water that falls upon them. The coarser the grain of the rock or of the sand, so much the more freely can water pass into it and through it; while in the case of compact rocks most of the rain that falls upon them flows off from the surface so quickly that very little percolation can occur. It is said that a rainfall of one inch in 10 or 12 hours will run off well nigh completely from a hill of compact rock or of clay almost as quickly as it falls, while on a steep hill of chalk or porous limestone even as much as two inches of rain per hour might all soak into the ground.

In England it has been stated of regions where the geological formations are of recent origin, that percolation is so considerable, except in the case of clays, that there is scarcely any flow off the surface. The flow of the rivers in these districts is nearly constant, while floods are rare and occur only under exceptional circumstances. In the region of red sandstone, for example, rain-water is absorbed almost as fast as it reaches the ground and there is always an abundant supply of water in the wells.

The French geologist Belgrand long ago insisted that the soils of some regions are permeable and those of others impermeable because of differences in the geological structure of the countries. Not only may water be discharged more or less rapidly from some districts than from others because of differences in the mode of stratification and the jointing of the rocks, but the character of the rocks themselves has no little influence on the permeability of their soils. He classed among impermeable formations, the granites, the lias, greensand, and many tertiary formations, while oölite, the true chalks and some tertiary deposits are permeable. In France, it has been noted as an agricultural feature of the impermeable formations, that mowing fields are maintained on the slopes and sides of the valleys as well as at their bottoms, while in permeable districts grass-fields are seen only on the borders of water-courses, i. e., on the bottom-lands. A consequence of this distribution of green herbage is that in the impermeable districts the eye rests on a smiling landscape which presents a semblance of fertility even where the soil is really poor, while the permeable regions may seem to be sterile, although their soils are often very fertile. In the damp climate of Ireland, on the contrary, and on some parts of the coast of England, constant mists keep the grass on the chalk-downs exquisitely green.

Chalk is highly Absorbent.

Laboratory experiments show that dry silicious sand can imbibe as much water as will amount to 20 or 25 % of its weight. Engineers have noticed in the field that loose sands may hold two gallons of water to the cubic foot, and that ordinary sandstone may hold one gallon of water to the cubic foot. Chalk is said to be as absorbent as loose sand, and the capacity of chalk soils to retain rain-water is easily accounted for when it is considered that a cubic foot of dry chalk will absorb from 2 to 2.5 gallons of water, or from 33 to 40% of its bulk, equal to 56,000,000 gallons for every foot in depth per square mile, or about 4 inches of rainfall. (Ansted.) Even some magnesian limestones have been found to retain 1.5 gallons of water to the cubic foot.

So strong is the power of chalk to absorb water that, as engineers have urged, the distribution of chalk in England may be traced on a map by noting the absence of streams and rivers. It has been remarked also, as another item of evidence, that in chalk districts the openings of bridges and culverts across streams are habitually made smaller than they are made in regions of clay.

Cobbett, in describing the downs of Southern England, has said:
"There are no downs without a chalk bottom. . . . Here
there is never any drought to cause inconvenience. The chalk is
at bottom and it takes care of all. . . . [In this locality],
a chalk bottom does not suffer the surface to burn, however shallow the top soil may be. It seems to me to absorb and to retain
the water, and to keep it ready to be drawn up by the heat of the
sun. · At any rate, the fact is that the surface above it does not
burn, for there never yet was a summer when the downs did not
retain their greenness to a certain degree while the rich pastures
and even the meadows were burnt so as to be as brown as the
bare earth."

So too, Banister wrote long ago as follows: "Chalky soils
possess a very material advantage over gravels in their power of
resisting longer the heat of the summer. The crops on chalky
soils often recover after a kindly rain when those on the gravels,
unable to withstand the preceding drought, are burnt up."

But as Gasparin has urged, while the foregoing statements are true
enough of a country of frequent showers — which serve to re-
plenish from time to time the reservoir of water in the chalk — a
very different state of things is found in the hot, dry climate of
Southern France, where chalk soils are apt to be completely arid
and to be bare and wholly devoid of vegetation excepting in the
spring and the autumn. In that region, the chalk dries out so
completely in midsummer that no perennial plant can be grown
upon it.

Rankine has given the following figures as a guide to the proportion of available to total rainfall which may be counted upon
by English engineers: On chalk 0; in flat, cultivated districts,
0.5 to 0.4; on moorland and hilly pastures, 0.8 to 0.6; and on
steep surfaces of granite, gneiss and slate, nearly 1. Deep-seated
springs and wells may give from 0.3 to 0.4 of the total rainfall.
The famous blue-grass pastures of Kentucky are upon limestone soils, and it has been said that the finest grazing lands,
both in Kentucky and Ohio, are confined to limestone moulds
which have a peculiar power of absorbing and retaining moisture.

It is said that Liverpool sandstone, when saturated with water,
can take up $\frac{1}{27}$ of its own weight of the liquid, and that $\frac{1}{16}$ will
drain away by force of gravity, while $\frac{1}{12}$ remains fixed in the
cavities of the stone by capillary attraction. According to Rob-

erts, each cubic foot of this sandstone can store 0.733 gallons of water. Even the driest granites and marbles may contain from 0.4 to 4.0% of water, or perhaps as much as a pint in each cubic yard. Looking from the geological point of view, it has been argued in England, that, on an average, about 25% of the rainfall in that country penetrates into the chalk, and from 60 to 96% into the loose sands, while the remainder either runs off the surface of the land or evaporates.

CHAPTER IV.

MOVEMENTS OF WATER IN THE SOIL.

THERE are two kinds of movements of water in the soil. First, the movement of percolation of the ground-water towards the sea, which is, on the whole, a downward movement; and, secondly, a movement by force of capillarity, which is, or may be, a movement in all directions in those parts of the soil which are above the ground-water proper.

The movement of percolation, caused by the ground-water seeking its level, is usually slow. It is retarded by a great variety of circumstances. Witness, for example, how much more slowly water drains away from a wooded country — covered with moss and leaves and vegetable mould — than it does from the same region when cleared. Even the roots of trees have been found to retard its movements.

Sometimes, as in a stiff, retentive clay, the movement seems to be as good as annihilated. Its sluggishness, in almost any soil, is made manifest when a deep well into which some impurity has fallen is left for a time to itself. It often happens in this event, that the water will long remain foul, so slow is the current that flows through or across the well. At Munich, Pettenkofer reckons the rate of the lateral flow of the ground-water at fifteen feet daily, while in the rather dense chalks of England engineers have supposed that the water moves three feet downward in the course of a year.

Rate of Percolation of Ground-water.

An interesting example of the rate at which water percolates through soil is afforded by the Natron Ponds between Cairo and Alexandria in Egypt. These so-called ponds are a series of rock-walled basins about thirty-five miles west from the Rosetta branch of the Nile. They are fed by infiltration from the Nile, whose waters take three months or more to percolate through the interjacent desert of sand and rock. Thus the annual rise of the Nile culminates in the third or fourth week of September, after which the water of the river begins to fall gradually; but the annual rise of the water in the Natron Ponds begins only about the end of December, and continues till the middle of March, when the fall commences.

The water that percolates through the desert dissolves out from it a quantity of carbonate of soda and common salt, and carries them into the ponds; and when the water evaporates during the summer, these saline matters crystallize out, and are collected and sold, as they have been time out of mind.

Professor Gregory of Edinburgh many years ago called attention to an interesting illustration of the movement of ground-water. He found that the carcass of a pig, buried on the slope of a hill which was moist and undrained, had in the course of 14 years shrunk into a flat cake, composed entirely of fatty acids, from the fat of the animal. Not only had the muscles and membranes, nerves and vessels, all putrefied and disappeared, but no trace of bone-earth was to be found. The whole of it had been dissolved — probably in much less time than the 14 years — by water percolating through the body of the animal. Gregory found that the water of the locality contained considerable carbonic acid, and it was evident that this carbonic acid had helped to dissolve the bone. But the fact that percolation must have occurred was manifest. In general, it may be said that so long as springs and rivers flow there can be no doubt as to the movement of the upper layers of the ground-water.

Deep-lying Water.

It is evident that, generally speaking, deep-lying ground-water can have comparatively little movement. Those portions of the ground-water, namely, which lie at a lower level than that of the brooks or ponds or wells into which the upper layers of the ground-water flow, cannot possibly find any easy outlet. To take again the example of the isolated gravel-ridge with a brook flowing at its base, it is evident that the great mass of the ground-water that results from the rainfall will drain out from the ridge into the brook; but how is it with the water that lies deeper than the brook? Why, that will slowly drain away towards the sea, beneath the brook. It will drain away in the same general direction as the brook flows, both beneath the line of the brook and beneath the plane of the brook. There is no longer any ready escape for it.

It follows, of course, that in a great number of instances deep ground-water must be more or less stagnant; and in fact it is found on boring or digging into such water, that it is apt to be either somewhat highly charged with saline matters which have been dissolved out from the rocks and gravel that are continually soaked by the water; or it is apt to be somewhat "sulphuretted," as the term is. That is to say, it tastes and smells feebly of sulphuretted hydrogen which has resulted from the decomposition of gypsum (or other sulphates) and organic matter, reacting one upon the other, in the stagnant water. Of the two most prominent artesian wells in Boston, one, at the gas-works, yields water which is decidedly saline, while the other, near the Providence Railway station, gives a somewhat sulphuretted water. But the soil of Boston rests in a great cup or depression, against one side of which, or rather against the front of which, the deep sea presses and so prevents the lower ground-water from draining out. It has been noticed in England that the water of most wells and springs in chalk districts contains in solution comparatively large quantities of chlorides, and the suggestion has been thrown out by Warington, that the highly retentive chalk may still hold in its deeper strata some of the common salt which was in the sea-water with which the chalk was saturated when it first emerged from the ocean.

As a general rule — to which there are some noteworthy exceptions — the waters of artesian wells are apt to be more or less highly charged with saline matters, often to such an extent that they are unfit for household use and for purposes of irrigation. It has been noticed moreover that the waters of artesian wells commonly contain no oxygen in solution, and that even the water of deep ordinary wells may contain next to no oxygen. So too, in ponds with muddy or peaty bottoms it often happens that no oxygen can be detected during the summer months at depths of 20 or 30 feet or more from the surface, i. e. in the lower layers of water which have lain for some time undisturbed by the wind.

Where to dig Wells.

The power possessed by some men of selecting places where wells may be dug with success depends upon a just appreciation of the conditions which control the percolative movements of ground-water. There was a French Abbé years ago, named Paramelle, who became noted for his power of discovering subterranean water. Many powerful springs were opened by him, — ten thousand or more, of one kind or another, as the story goes. He was called to all parts of France to exercise his art, and, after practising it with great success, he published a book which describes his methods of procedure. The gist of his narration is simply that water tends to flow, i. e. it tends to percolate, most freely beneath the lowest part of valleys, ravines, furrows, gutters, slopes, and depressions of all kinds; that is to say, water stands or flows at precisely those places beneath the surface where it would stand or flow most readily on the surface if there were enough of it to reach the surface.

In like manner Prestwick, in England, has insisted that subterranean water is governed in its movement by the same laws which regulate the flow of surface streams. The greatest elevation of the subterranean water above sea-level is usually found under the highest lands, and the least elevation under the lands having the lowest level. The flow of water laterally is from the hills to the valleys, and longitudinally down the valley-lines. In general the flow of subterranean water conforms to the surface-falls of a country, though exceptions to this rule are occasionally met with.

Illustrations of the Capillary Movement.

It is a familiar experiment that if one end of a fine tube of glass, or of any other substance, be touched to water, the liquid will be drawn into the tube to a considerable height, which will be the greater according as the tube is finer. In like manner, water will be sucked up by the soil, or by the wick of a lamp, or by blotting-paper, or by a sponge, or by any other porous substance. The soil (or the lamp-wick, etc.) may be regarded as consisting of a number of tubes of irregular shape, the walls of which are formed by the particles of soil, while the open spaces between these particles correspond to the bore of the tube. The actual movement of the water from below upwards is effected by the adhesion or surface attraction of the soil and the water, one for the other. The water tends to stick to the soil. A dry soil, like an empty sponge, drinks up, absorbs, and actually lifts the water; and beside all this there will be a movement of water through any soil that is moistened, even no more than very slightly, to make good whatever waste of water has occurred by way of evaporation from the contiguous parcels of soil.

There are two prominent facts to be held to: first, that the particles and pores of the soil absorb and hold rain-water that comes to them from above, so that not only the rain of spring and summer is retained for the use of crops, but an actual reservoir or store of water is accumulated from the rain which falls in autumn and in winter upon unfrozen ground; secondly, that the particles of soil and the pores of the soil above the ground-water proper suck up moisture from it precisely as a wick draws up oil in a lamp. Hence it happens, not only that moisture is left adhering to every soil to a considerable height above the ground-water after the draining away of the latter from any cause, and after every fall of rain, but that new portions of moisture taken from the ground-water are incessantly though slowly lifted through the soil, even to its surface, if not too distant, by force of capillarity, there to supply the place of the moisture which has been taken up by plants, or in any way evaporated from the surface.

The gradual upward soaking of moisture into dry earth is well shown by an experiment of Liebenberg, in which four tubes filled with a capillary marl were placed with their lower ends in water and tests made at intervals of an hour and a half, one day, one week, and five weeks, as to the amounts of water that were contained in the earth at various heights. The results of these trials are given in the following table:

Percentage of water in the marl after				At height in the tube of c.m.
1.5 Hours.	1 Day.	1 Week.	5 Weeks.	
——	——	——	6.23	78
——	——	——	7.72	75
——	——	——	8.44	70
——	——	1.42	——	66
——	——	——	9.61	65
——	——	7.85	——	64
——	——	9.55	10.59	60
——	——	10.27	11.17	55
——	6.94	10.94	11.75	50
——	8.23	11.73	12.77	45
——	12.99	13.16	14.05	40
——	15.62	14.83	15.23	35
——	16.60	17.01	19.52	30
17.39	19.39	17.48	19.45	25
18.68	18.73	20.06	20.69	20
17.67	18.90	20.05	20.43	15
18.75	19.34	20.59	18.88	10
18.82	18.90	20.64	22.21	5
20.21	18.47	20.70	20.01	1

In experiments such as these, the moisture in the lower layers of the earth will still continue to creep upward in case the tubes are lifted out of the water before time enough has been allowed for the whole of the earth to become saturated. Thus, Nessler charged two tubes with air-dried loam, the one loosely, while the other was tightly packed, he set them in water for a while and then took them out. The following table gives the heights in inches to which water rose in these tubes under the varying conditions of the experiment :—

Water rose to a height in inches,	In the Compact Earth.	In the Loose Earth.
In 3 days while the tubes stood in water,	11.00	7.80
In 24 hours after tubes were taken from the water,	0.65	0.58
Next 24 hours " " "	0.65	0.54
Next 24 hours " " "	0.54	0.39
In 24 days " ". "	5.50	2.80

That the superior lifting power of the compacted earth, as stated in the table, did not depend upon the amount of water contained in this earth is shown by the fact that at the close of the experiment there was found in the case of the compact earth 10.2 % of water in the uppermost inch-and-a-half of the column to which moisture had visibly been lifted, and in the case of the loose earth 13.5 %. At the same time there was found 20.18% of water in the lowest inch of the column of compact earth and 20.78% in the corresponding layer of the loose earth.

In the packed earth water rose in 27 days 7.34 inches and in the loose earth 4.21 inches after the tubes had been removed from the dish of water. Manifestly there were finer capillary tubes in the packed earth, than in that which lay loose. Generally speaking, however, the capillary movement is favored by bringing the soil into a fine, porous, mellow condition by frequent tillage. As Professor Johnson has said, just as the strands of wicking in a lamp must neither fit too tightly nor too loosely in the socket in order to the best capillary action, so in the soil there is a certain degree of porosity which is best suited to the lifting of water.

The Capillary Movement may be very slow.

. It needs to be insisted, however, while considering the question of capillary action in soils, that practically in many instances when a soil, lying in the field, has once become dry the capillary movement of moisture from the ground-water upward is by no means rapid. Thus, King filled a number of tinware cylinders (1 foot long by 6 inches wide) with dried earth from a field of Indian corn and stood them up in water in such manner that the lowest inch of soil was saturated with water. But even after 36 days the earth had not yet sucked up all the moisture it was really capable of holding. Indeed the fact of familiar observation that, in seasons of drought, crops may suffer from lack of moisture even when permanent water exists in the ground within a few feet of the surface, is conclusive evidence that the normal rate of the capillary movement cannot be very rapid. In other experiments, King determined, on October 23 and again on December 13, the per-cent of water down to a depth of 3 feet in the soil of a field on which Indian corn had grown during the summer. At the time of these examinations, the water-table lay at a depth of 7.5 feet beneath the surface, yet it appeared that the third foot of soil, which was only 4.5 feet from the permanent ground-water, had gained from below, by way of capillarity, in 51 days only about 0.025 lb. of water.

But even if it be admitted that the upward capillary movement of moisture is seldom if ever really rapid, it is none the less true that it is a constant quantity. It is incessant, so long as there is any outgo of water from the upper layers of the soil either through mere evaporation or by force of the exhalation of water by growing plants. It acts with equal intensity by night and by day; while the evaporation of water from the surface of the land will usually be largest during the day when the sun is shining on the soil and on the plants that are growing in it. But when this evaporation is checked at night the capillary movement within the soil still goes on and has in so far better opportunity to supply moisture from below to make good what has been lost from the surface during the preceding day. In the course of a summer's day there are in fact 24 hours of capillary lifting to offset 10 or 12 hours of excessive evaporation.

It is noticeable that occasionally the force of gravitation may act in harmony with the capillary movement and tend to accelerate it. Thus when rain falls upon the earth, or when snow melts upon it, those portions of water which soak into the soil are speedily subjected to the influence of capillarity, and dragged downward. Even in the heaviest showers the rain does not penetrate as such to the depth of an inch. It is only when the capillary pores at the surface of the soil have become full that water passes downward into the pores which lie below the surface, and it is only when all the pores of the soil have become saturated by the capillary movement that percolation proper, due to hydrostatic pressure, can occur.

But at times when no water is coming to the land, either as rain or snow, the capillary movement is upward rather than downward, and it is occasioned, or rather kept up, by evaporation of moisture from the surface of the ground; and this evaporation may be due either to exhalation of moisture by plants, or to the direct action of sun and wind upon the land.

As regards permeability, Hellriegel has shown that, while rain-water will soak into a soil so much the faster in proportion as the particles of the soil are coarser, it is still true that where there are layers of coarse and fine particles the latter will take up and hold the largest amount of water. The fine earth may even suck water out from the layer of coarser materials, and, in general, it will not give up water to the coarser layers until it has itself become surcharged.

Saline Incrustations upon Soils.

It is by this capillary movement of the soil-water that saline matters are brought to the surface in many dry climates in such quantity as to incrust the surface of the ground throughout the summer season; and in this way, also, soluble matters necessary to the growth of the plant may be brought up out of the depths of the soil to the roots which feed upon them.

It is said that in some parts of Greece, after the rainy season has ended, and rapid evaporation of water from the soil has set in, saline matters rise to the surface in such abundance that the more tender herbage is gradually killed by them, and only very robust plants continue to grow. Even the growth of grass is prevented, although abundant wheat crops can be ripened every year, apparently because the more important part of the life of the wheat-plant is finished before the land has become salter than the crop can bear. It is known withal that wheat can resist, better than some other crops, the destructive action of salt. Gasparin tells of saline soils at the south of France where superb crops of wheat are grown in favorable years when there is a sufficient supply of moisture, though the crop may come to nothing in years when the weather is droughty in the spring.

In some parts of India much land is made barren by saline

efflorescences, and they are common also on the plains of central Asia. They occur occasionally in our own Western States, as on "the alkali desert." It is well known, however, to practical men, that land which is even somewhat highly charged with saline matters may still be made to bear crops if pains are taken to check evaporation from the surface of the land. By so doing, the saline matters are hindered from accumulating on and corroding the root-crowns of the plants. For some crops, this purpose may be accomplished by deep and thorough tillage persistently maintained throughout the season, while for other crops mulches of straw or rushes will serve a good purpose. Yet another method of procedure is to keep the land pretty constantly shaded by growing upon it deep-rooted, leafy, free-growing forage crops. Underdrainage also, when combined with irrigation, will effect a radical cure. (Gasparin: Hilgard.)

Darwin has described in the following terms the incrustations of sulphate of soda admixed with common salt which he met with frequently in Patagonia and other parts of South America. As long as the ground remains moist, he says, nothing is to be seen but an extensive plain composed of black muddy soil, supporting scattered tufts of succulent plants. On returning through one of these tracts, after a week of hot weather, one is surprised to see square miles of the plain white, as if from a slight fall of snow, here and there heaped up by the winds into little drifts. This latter appearance is chiefly caused by the salts being drawn up during the slow evaporation of the moisture around blades of dead grass, stumps of wood, and pieces of broken earth, instead of being crystallized at the bottoms of the puddles of water.

In certain districts of India sesqui-carbonate of soda which has been brought to the surface of the soil by force of capillarity is methodically purified by the same means. To this end, a quantity of earth charged with the alkaline matter is scraped from the surface of the soil and thrown into the form of a circular bed or saucer, which is filled first with water and subsequently to the brim with the alkaline earth. The surface of this earth having been made smooth, the bed is left exposed to the sun during two days of hot, dry summer weather. The sodium carbonate is brought to the surface by the water as it rises and evaporates and is collected, in the form of a crust, in a condition of purity which admits of its being used for glass-making.

Movement of Saline Matters.

It is a familiar observation that the soil in an ordinary flower-pot may be moistened, even to the surface, by pouring a sufficiency of water into the saucer of the pot, in the same way that the surface soil of fields tends to be kept moist by water drawn up from below. To illustrate this lifting action of loam, experiments have been made in ordinary earthen flowerpots by cementing into the hole at the bottom of the pot a tube a foot or so in length, and filling both pot and tube with loam. The pot is then placed upon a rack in such a manner that the lower end of the tube may dip into a fertilizing solution, such as barn-yard liquor, for example, or a solution of nitrate of potash: It is easy to see in this way that the plants in those pots whose tubes have access to plant-food grow much better than those so situated that the tubes dip into mere water. Moreover, by putting saline solutions at the bottoms of the tubes, and occasionally analyzing these solutions, it will be seen how rapidly the saline matter is drawn up into the earth.

Nessler has illustrated the matter by experiments made to test the question whether moisture evaporates chiefly from the surface of the soil, or whether any considerable quantity of it can exhale directly into the air, as vapor which has formed in lower layers of the soil. He filled two cylinders with loam that contained 14% of moisture, and sunk them in the earth so that their tops were level with the surface of the ground. The loam in one of these cylinders was pretty firmly compressed, while that in the other was made to lie as loosely as possible in order that evaporation from its interior pores might be favored. Both of the cylinders were shielded from rain. In the course of six weeks 510 grm. of water evaporated per square foot of surface from the loosely packed loam, and 1680 grm. from the loam which had been compressed. Samples were collected for analysis, to the depth of about one line from the surface of the original soil, and of the loams in the two cylinders, and there was found in 1,000 parts of the

	Original Earth.	Loose Earth.	Compressed Earth.
Total soluble matters . . .	0.14	0.19	1.00
Organic " "	0.06	0.08	0.32
Inorganic " "	0.08	0.11	0.68
Potash	——	0.03	0.19

Whence it appeared that the evaporation of water was chiefly from the surface of the soil; that too much loosening of the earth diminished evaporation; and that substances such as potash, which tend to be fixed and held by the soil, as will be explained hereafter, do nevertheless move towards the surface in the current of the capillary water. But since, as a general rule, more water evaporates from soils during the summer months than comes to their surfaces as rain, more soluble substances will be brought to the surface in summer than will be carried down from the surface into or towards the subsoil.

In the field, when everything is favorable for the growth of plants, there is between the ground-water and the surface of the land a gradation of moisture ranging from the soil that is saturated or absolutely wet with moisture by mere force of capillarity to that which is nearly or quite "air-dried." It is capillary water which is seen when, on digging a few inches below the surface of the soil, even in midsummer, we find the earth to be, not dry and dusty, but somewhat moist.

Frost in the Ground.

So too, when, as the saying is, the soil freezes in the winter, it is the capillary moisture in the soil that congeals to a greater or less depth accordingly as the soil is bare and exposed, or shielded from the cold, as when covered with a mat of sod. Leslie noticed near Edinburgh, at a time when the frost had penetrated to a depth of 13 inches in ploughed land, that it had reached only to a depth of 8 inches in one pasture and to 4 inches in another. Any covering of loose materials, as of snow, or straw, or leaves, or branches of evergreen trees, will greatly hinder the penetration of the frost; while in case the soil is firmly compacted, as on a well-worn or macadamized road, it may freeze to a great depth. A neat application of this knowledge is seen when excavations are made in cold autumn weather, and the workmen take care at nightfall to loosen a layer of the soil with their pickaxes, and to leave it lying until next morning as a mulch to hinder the soil beneath it from freezing.

In the spring, on the other hand, after extreme cold weather has ceased, and the frozen soil begins to melt, the moisture in the soil beneath the frozen layers often exerts a very marked influence to accelerate the process of melting. That is to say, the comparatively warm ground-water and the capillary water that is lifted from it help to "draw the frost"; or, to state the matter in the language of the farm, when "frost is coming out of the ground," the moisture beneath the frost often assists very materially to hasten the process. Instances have fallen under my own observation in Boston where firmly frozen ground, that had been covered with a thick bed of gravel towards the end of winter, thawed out completely before the advent of spring. The land in question was coarse, loose gravel, and the original surface of it was no more than three feet or so above the ground-water.

As was said before, it is the almost invisible moisture held by capillary action in the soil, which in the main supplies both water and saline nourishment to the roots of cultivated plants. The little hairs with which the rootlets are covered (see "How Crops Grow," p. 265) cling tightly to the particles of soil, and extract therefrom the capillary water and whatever of plant-food this water holds in solution.

Capillary Power of Soils.

From the following table drawn up by Zenger, it appears that the capillary power of soils is greater in proportion as their pores are finer; but fineness of pores must not be confounded with fineness of particles. It is true enough that up to a certain point a soil will have more capillary power in proportion as its particles are more finely divided; but the moment this limit is passed, fineness is disadvantageous for capillarity, since the minute particles of earth are apt to cohere and cling together so closely that few if any open spaces are left between them for the admission of water. Practically, it is observed that fine soils usually retain moisture longer than coarse soils.

The figures in column I. of the table represent the percentage amounts of water that were imbibed by the soils which had been screened to a tolerably uniform state of moderate fineness, while in column II. are given the percentage amounts of water imbibed by the same soils after they had been finely pulverized. It will be noticed that there is but little difference between the second column and the first in the case of soils which are naturally porous.

Other experiments have confirmed these results by Zenger. Thus, Wilhelm noticed, for example, that a garden-loam that naturally imbibed 114% of water could absorb only 62% after it had been pulverized.

	I.	II.
Quartz sand	26	54
Marl	30	55
"Marl" from beneath a peat-bed	39	49

Brick-clay	.	.	.	.	.	.	66	58
Moor-earth	.	.	.	.	.	.	105	101
Calcareous sinter	.	.	.	.	.	108	70
Soil from a moor-meadow		.	.	.	.	178	103
Peat-dust	.	.	.	.	.	.	377	269
Garden-loam	.	.	.	.	.	.	123	——

The chemical character of a soil, though far less important than its porosity, may nevertheless have some influence upon the rapidity of the capillary movement, as may be seen on contrasting quartz and kaolin that have been reduced to powders of equal fineness. The quartz will absorb water considerably quicker than the kaolin. Schuebler noticed in his day that calcareous sand could hold rather more water than silicious sand of the same degree of fineness. Hilgard insists that there is a marked difference between mineral powders, however fine, and colloidal plastic clay, which, as he says, may in some respects be compared with glue. " The finest particle of quartz or feldspar," he says, " remains of the same size when wetted; while the dry clay particle on wetting enlarges to 20 or more times its original size, and on drying again contracts to a greater or less degree, according to the moisture condition. Moreover, it is glutinous and has the very important and critical quality of plasticity, of which the rest of the soil constituents are totally destitute."

The following table gives the water-holding power of a variety of soils as determined by different observers. The figures represent percentages of liquid water absorbed and held by the dry soils, as determined by soaking the weighed soils in water, throwing the wet mass on a filter, allowing the excess of liquid to drain away, and again weighing the wet earth. It is to be remarked that while useful comparative results may undoubtedly be obtained in this way, the method is apt to convey an exaggerated idea of the water-holding power of soils, since the moisture held in a mass of wet earth lying upon a filter can only drip away incompletely, so that even the larger interstices between the particles of earth will remain filled with water. In the field, on the contrary, any excess of water which might be held momentarily in this way near the surface after a fall of rain would speedily be dragged away by capillary action into the contiguous portions of non-saturated earth. In order to determine practically how much water is really held by a soil, samples of the wet earth may be taken from different depths in the field soon after rain, and the water may be dried out from them after they have been weighed. By operating in this way, Schloesing found that many good soils contained from 30 to 45% of water, while in coarse sands there was sometimes ten times less than these quantities.

	Schue-bler.	Trom-mer.	Chap-tal.	S. W. Johnson.	Heid-en.
Quartz sand, coarse, sometimes	20	....	....	....	....
" " very fine	30	....	....	....	....
" " with rounded edges	25	26	....	....	....
" " " flakes of mica	....	32	....	....	....
" " blowing sand, capable of yielding 9 bushels of rye to the acre once in 2 or 3 years	....	....	....	34	....
Mica sand	60	....	....	....	....
Silicic acid,* as prepared from silicate of potash	280	241	25—	....	....
Alumina, pure, precipitated and heated	....	....	250	....	....
Oxide of iron, pure precipitated	23	....	....	....	....
Limestone sand	29	29	....	....	....
Carbonate of lime, precipitated	47	....	....	....	....
" " in powder	....	80	80	....	....
Thoroughly air-slaked lime	85	....	....	....	....
Carbonate of magnesia	456†	....	....	....	....
Gypsum, native, unburned, finely powdered	27	....	....	....	....
A clay, which contained 60% of clay and 40% of fine sand	40	....	....	—....	....
A loamy clay which contained about 76% of clay and 24% of fine sand	50	....	....	....	....
A fat clay (about 89% clay and 11% sand)	61	....	....	....	....
Clay freed from sand but still containing 58% silica, 36% alumina and 6% iron oxide	70	....	....	....	....
Potter's clay	...	40.	....	....	....
Loamy clay	....	50	....	....	....
Pure, gray clay	....	70	....	....	....
Yellow clay	....	68	....	....	....
Heavy, sticky clay	....	61	....	....	....
White clay	....	74	....	....	....
Elutriated feldspar	....	54	....	....	....
Prairie soil from Illinois, yielding 80 bushels of maize to the acre	....	....	....	57	....
Loam from a garden (54% clay, 37% quartz sand, 2% calcareous sand, 2% lime, and 7% humus	96	....	....	....	....
Loam from a field (51% clay, 43% quartz sand, 0.4% calcareous sand, 2.3% lime, and 3.4% humus),	52	....	....	....	....
Loam from a mountain valley (64% quartz sand, 33% clay, 1.2% calcareous sand, 1.2% lime, and 1.2% humus)	47	....	....	....	....
Wheat soil	....	58	....	....	....
Fertile marly loam	....	59	....	....	....
Barley soil of second quality	....	47	....	....	....
Strong wheat land with 8% carbonate of lime	....	61	....	....	....
Loam ‡	....	....	....	....	40
Peat ‡	....	....	....	309	201
Vegetable mould §, such as occurs in ordinary loam	190	180	....	.	....
Humus § (not acid), prepared from peat	....	....	....	....	645
Humic acid, from peat	....	....	....	....	1200

[For foot-notes * to §, see next page.]

See also Meister's experiments in Hoffmann's Jahresbericht der Agrikulturchemie, II. 39.

From his figures, as given in the foregoing table, which refer of course to small samples of the soils, no more than a few inches in depth, Johnson has calculated, for the sake of the argument, that an acre of surface-soil one foot deep might hold the following quantities of water, viz.: the sand, 1,197,900 lb.; the prairie soil, 1,524,600 lb.; and the peat 2,047,300 lb. But in New England there falls on the average 40 inches of rain in the course of a year, or 9,075,000 lb., to the acre of land, and at the given rates of absorption the whole of this water would be held in 7.5 feet in depth of the sand; in 6 feet in depth of the prairie soil, and in 4.5 feet in depth of the peat."

"But," as Johnson says, "while a thin layer or a little depth of sand or coarse loam will remain with its pores full of water, in a deep mass of such soil the water will sink downward, leaving the larger of the pores near the surface, and for a certain depth, not full but simply lined with water. It may thus happen that a sand contains but 10% of water at the surface, while a foot or two down it holds 20%. . . . In an actual trial made at New Haven with a column 40 inches in depth of (another) sandy soil, screened for masons' use, it was found, after pouring upon the soil more water than it could hold and letting it stand until dripping ceased, that the uppermost 13 inches retained water corresponding to 15.75 lb. per cubic foot, the middle 13 inches 25.4 lb., and the bottom 14 inches 26.6 lb. per cubic foot. This sandy soil taken to a depth of 40 inches held 22.6 lb. of water to the cubic foot, and a solid mass of this soil one foot square at

---

* The difference between the figures relating to silicic acid may perhaps be due to the hydrated or anhydrous condition of the specimens examined.

† "Burger gives the water-holding power of carbonate of magnesia as 546. I find by new trials that much depends on the fineness of the samples, and something also on the quantity of earth which is taken for an experiment. When quantities of magnesium carbonate no larger than 100 grains are operated upon, a comparatively larger amount of water will be retained than when 400 or 500 grains are taken. My practice is to operate upon 400 grain samples." (Schuebler, 1823.)

‡ Gasparin remarks that he has observed in practice soils (loams) that could hold 93% of water and others that could hold no more than 25%; he studied many varieties which gave results ranging from 43 to 50%.

§ With regards to humus, Trommer remarks that the water-holding power of different varieties depends largely upon the proportion of incompletely decayed vegetable matters which they contain, and upon the physical structure of these materials. Those peats which contain much vegetable fibre will naturally hold more water than those which consist for the most part of humic acids, and the remark is particularly true of peats which are still mossy. To illustrate this point, Trommer tested the water-holding power of unsized papers made from flax and from cotton, and he found that the linen paper, which consists of solid bast cells, took up 330% of water, while the paper made from cotton, which consists of long, delicate, tubular cells, took up 440% of water.

the surface and 40 inches deep would hold 94 lb. of water, equal to a rainfall of 18.7 inches.   In case of a finely-porous material like peat or clay, the amount of water retained near the surface much more nearly approaches that found at a depth. Thus, in trials with a mass of peat 30 inches deep, the surface held about the same as the deeper-lying portions, averaging 47 lb. of water per cubic foot, so that a mass one foot square at the surface and 40 inches deep would hold in its pores 156 lb., equal to a rainfall of 30 inches."

In Maryland, where the annual rainfall of 43 inches is on the whole fairly well distributed, since there are commonly 2 or 3 consecutive days of rain after a week or ten days of dry weather, and there are on the average 4 inches of rain a month, Milton Whitney has studied the capacity of different kinds of soils to retain the rain water during the terms of dry weather.   He finds that the finer the texture of the soil and in general the more clay it contains, the greater is the resistance offered to the escape of the rainwater.   A limestone soil containing 45% of clay will maintain, on an average, from 18 to 22% of water, or about 400 tons of water per acre one foot deep, which corresponds to 4 inches of rain-fall; while a light sandy soil, containing 5% of clay, such as is highly esteemed for growing early garden truck, is so porous that water passes through it freely and there is maintained for the use of crops no more than 5 or 6% of moisture, or say 100 tons per acre one foot deep, which amounts to one inch of rainfall, i. e. about one quarter of the amount retained by the limestone soil.   It is because of these differences that wheat can be grown with success in Maryland on the limestone soil, but not upon the sandy loam.

Water-holding Power of Mixtures.

Experiments have been made by Treutler to test the question whether or not the water-holding power of mixtures of different kinds of soils is equal to the sum of the water-holding powers of the substances when unmixed.   It appears from his results, as given in the following table, that with few exceptions the power of mixtures to imbibe and hold water is less than that of their components taken separately.   It is reasonable to suppose that, if the particles of each of the substances to be mixed were of equal size, the mixture would hold water about as well as its components, as appears indeed to be the case with some of the mixtures of fine earth and whiting or magnesia, in the table.   But when the particles are of unlike sizes, the smaller ones fall into the spaces between the larger, and prevent water from occupying these spaces. Compare the mixtures of sand with whiting and magnesia. Schuebler observed long ago that the weight of any given volume of artificial mixtures, in varying proportions, of sands, clays and marl, is not the arithmetical mean of the weights of the components, but is always somewhat larger than the mean weight.

In Treutler's experiments, 100 cc. of water and 50 grams of the substance to be tested were placed in a glass funnel, at the apex of which there was a small moistened filter which permitted the water that was not held by the earth to drain away. Each trial lasted 24 hours, excepting those with magnesia, which required 2 or 3 days. In column A of the table are given the number of cubic centimeters of water which were held by the earth, while column B gives the sums of the absorptive powers of the components of the mixtures. Fifty grams of the substances named absorbed and held respectively the following quantities of water : —

Substances.	A. Found. cc.	B. Calculated. cc.	Difference. cc.
Fine earth	34.2	——	——
Quartz sand	14.0	——	——
Caustic lime	61.0	——	——
Whiting	25.0	——	——
Magnesia	230.0	——	——
40 grm. fine earth and 10 grm. lime . .	44.0	39.6	—4.4
30 " " " " 20 " " . .	49.0	45.0	—4.0
25 " " " " 25 " " . .	51.6	47.6	—4.0
40 " " " " 10 " whiting	32.0	32.4	+0.4
30 " " " " 20 " "	27.0	30.5	+3.5
25 " " " " 25 " "	26.0	29.6	+3.6
40 " " " " 10 " magnesia	73.5	73.4	—0.1
30 " " " " 20 " "	112.0	112.5	+0.5
25 " " " " 25 " "	133.5	132.1	—1.4
40 " " " " 10 " quartz sand	28.5	30.2	+1.7
30 " " " " 20 " "	23.0	26.1	+3.1
40 " quartz sand " 10 " lime	19.0	23.4	+4.4
30 " " " " 20 " "	29.0	32.8	+3.8
25 " " " " 25 " "	34.5	37.5	+3.0
40 " " " " 10 " whiting	12.0	16.2	+4.2
30 " " " " 20 " "	12.0	18.4	+6.4
25 " " " " 25 " "	14.0	19.5	+5.5
40 " " " " 10 " magnesia	53.5	57.5	+4.0
30 " " " " 20 " "	96.5	100.4	+3.9
25 " " " " 25 " "	113.5	122.0	+8.5
40 " " " " 10 " fine earth	15.0	18.0	+3.0
30 " " " " 20 " "	18.5	22.1	+3.6
25 " " " " 25 " "	21.0	24.1	+3.1

The increased absorptive power exhibited by the mixtures of fine loam and caustic lime is probably due to granulation or "flocculation" of the earth by the lime, as will be stated more explicitly under the head of Tillage, though possibly it may depend on chemical combination, i. e. on the formation of a hydrated silicate of lime.

Detmer also, experimenting with mixtures of sand and peat, found that by a mixture containing : —

Per-cent of Sand.	Per-cent of Peat.	There were absorbed Grams of Water	If Sand = 1, the observed Absorptive Power =
100	—	12.2	1
80	20	24.0	2
60	40	42.0	3.5
40	60	71.7	6
20	80	99.1	8
—	100	114.4	9.3

The Capillary Force Hinders Evaporation.

Naturally enough, the power of a soil to hold water tends to retard evaporation from the soil. Chaptal found that finely ground, pure silicic acid, which absorbed hardly a quarter of its weight of water, allowed this water to evaporate twice as fast as carbonate of lime, equally finely divided, which absorbed 80%, of water; and five times as fast as pure, dry alumina, in the same state of division, which absorbed two and a half times its own weight of water. The question was studied long ago by Schuebler, whose results are given in the following table : —

Kind of Soil.	There evaporated in 4 hours at 66° F., from 100 lbs. of water in the wet earths, Lb. of water.	Equal weights of the wet earths became niue-tenths dry (at 66° F.) in	
		Hours.	Minutes.
Quartz sand	88.4	4	4
Calcareous sand	75.9	4	44
Clay, containing 60% clay and 40% fine sand	52.0		55
Loamy clay (76% clay and 24% fine sand)	45.7	7	52
Fat clay (89% clay and 11% fine sand)	34.9	10	19
Clay free from fine sand (58% silica, 36.2 % clay, and 5.8 % iron oxide .	31.3	11	17
Carbonate of lime, fine	28.0	12	51
Vegetable mould	20.5	17	33
Carbonate of magnesia	10.8	33	20
Gypsum, native unburned, finely powdered	71.7	5	1
Garden loam	24.5	14	49
Loam from a ploughed field . .	32.0	11	15
Sandy loam from mountain valley	40.1	8	58

See also Meister's results in Hoffmann's Jahresbericht, II., 41.

It will be noticed that, in proportion as a soil absorbs more water by imbibition, so much the less water does it give off through evaporation. The powerfully absorptive soils not only lose comparatively little water through evaporation in a given time, but, from having a larger store of moisture, they can continue to meet the demands of evaporation through a much longer period than the soils which are, comparatively speaking, non-absorptive.

From some experiments of Sachs, it appears that plants cannot exhaust the retentive soils so completely of their water as they can the soils which are non-retentive. Thus, in a loam capable of holding 52% of capillary water, a tobacco plant wilted at night, when the soil contained 8% of moisture. In a mixture of humus and sand competent to absorb 46% of moisture, another tobacco plant wilted when the moisture had been reduced to 12%; and in coarse sand which could hold 21% of moisture, a third plant wilted when the proportion had fallen to $1\frac{1}{2}$%. Here the plant was able to pump the soil almost absolutely dry. In these experiments 44%, 34% and 19% of water, respectively, were more or less available for the plant.

Different kinds of plants appear to resemble one another more closely than would have been expected in respect to this power of exhausting soils of their moisture, and experiments by Hellriegel have shown that any soil can supply plants with all the water they need, and as fast as they need it, so long as the moisture within the soil is not reduced below one-third of the whole amount that it can hold.

Influence of Humus and Clay on Capillarity.

From the tables above given it appears, as would be anticipated, that the best soils possess a medium absorptive power. According to Trommer, writing of North Germany, it may be admitted that soils suitable for grain-growing there, will be found to have water-holding powers laying somewhat between 40 and 70%. The lack of this power in coarse sandy soils is doubtless one prominent cause of their sterility.

It is to be remembered always that in actual farm practice soils of one or another degree of capillarity will be preferred according to the situation of a field, as regards the ground-water, and according to the climate of the locality. Those soils which are capable of holding much water can hardly be the best in very rainy seasons or in regions where rains are frequent, and it is almost always desirable that the conditions which obtain in high, dry fields shall be different from those in low-lying lands. In hot, dry climates sandy soils are apt to be arid deserts, while in moist and temperate regions they are not infrequently fruitful. Everywhere, however, it is recognized that sandy soils which are not fine enough to be capillary are commonly highly uncertain as to the crops they bear, because they have so little power to hold moisture. When well manured in moist climates, as in Holland, they may often be cultivated with profit. They bear good crops also in many situations where there is ground-water within reach of the plants; but as a general rule coarse sands suffer extremely in times of drought, and there is always a risk that the crops may "burn off" them in hot weather. Instances have been reported in Belgium where certain sands could not be covered with soil by mere irrigation until after the land had been improved by addition of humus and barnyard manure.

Some coarse limestone soils also have so little coherence that they cannot retain water enough for the use of crops in times of drought. It has been noticed in England that in regions of frequent rains the limestone soils are often remarkably fertile, while in districts that are comparatively dry such soils are often poor and readily affected by drought.

It has long been recognized, moreover, as a general rule, true of light and loamy soils, that the power of a soil to hold water is much greater when the soil has been well manured than it was before the manure had been applied to it. (Gasparin.) In the vicinity of Boston, formerly, when the farmers found it profitable to apply abundant dressings of stable-manure to crops of maize and potatoes on upland soils, a much heavier burden of hay was obtained when grass was grown after the hoed crops than is got habitually from the same land nowadays, because, economically speaking, it is no longer so easy as it once was to charge these light, droughty soils thoroughly with manure.

In very many instances, the value of humus and of clay as components of loam must depend in great measure on the power of these substances to imbibe and retain moisture. The presence of too much either of sand or of clay will naturally be hurtful. It is a matter of familiar observation that soils rich in clay greatly impede the circulation of water and are apt to retain moisture too forcibly. In northern countries, many undrained clays remain so long wet and cold that the crops harvested upon them are apt to be late and small. It is true also that in some places where rains are infrequent, a clayey soil may be as estimable as it is objectionable in regions that are wet and cold. In Bohemia, winter wheat and horse-beans are habitually grown upon strong clays, and the farmers are accustomed to grow nothing but rye upon their sandy soils, such as on the rainy west coast of England. continually give good crops of wheat and beans. (Kodym.) The names, hot, cold, dry, wet, leachy, and the like, used by practical men to designate the characters of soils, depend in good part on the power of the soils to hold water and upon the rapidity with which the water is lost which has fallen upon them as rain. (Schuebler.)

Very Fine Sand is Capillary.

It is true of some soils, such as fine sands, that they are at once highly capillary and readily permeable. Such soils can drink in water readily, lift it rapidly and hold it forcibly; it is an easy matter to moisten them equally and thoroughly. But this remark is by no means true of all soils, for some are very little permeable, though highly capillary, and others are not capillary though permeable to a fault. Humus, for example, is highly capillary though not particularly permeable, while clay is but slightly permeable though it has considerable capillary power. It has often been remarked that the application of very heavy dressings of farm-yard manure to some kinds of clayey loams will increase their fertility out of all proportion to the amount of plant-food which the manure has brought to the land, and it is to be inferred that the mechanical condition of the soil must have been improved by the manure so that moisture can now move about among the particles of clay more freely than was possible before. (Gasparin.)

In general it may be said, that the larger the proportion of clay or of humus, or of very fine sand in a soil, so much the more power will that soil have of holding water; while the water-holding power will be so much the smaller in proportion as ordinary coarse sand is more abundant in the soil. "The fine particles of clay not only make the spaces within the soil exceedingly small, so that the rainfall must pass downward very slowly through the soil, but by increasing the area of the water-surface they enable the soil to draw up water to the plant to supply the loss from evaporation and

to replace that which has been used by the plant." (M. Whitney.)
While coarse gravel can be seen to suck up the ground-water to no
greater height than an inch or two, good capillary loam may visibly
lift it to a height of six feet.   On the other hand, a small amount
of rain-water falling upon the land may moisten a large volume of
coarse sand, perhaps as much as twenty times its own bulk, while
the same amount of rain-water might not moisten more than three
. times its bulk of cohesive clay. Numerous experiments by Meister
upon the power of air-dried soils to suck up water from moist
earth are recorded in Hoffmann's Jahresbericht, II., 42; those of
Gasparin are in Vol. VI., pp. 271–274 of his "Cours d'Agriculture," and those of Nessler and Liebenberg have already been cited.

As an example of such experiments, the results obtained by
Trommer are given in the following table.   He tied pieces of
muslin across the ends of glass tubes half an inch in diameter,
filled the tubes carefully with the materials to be tested and hung
up the tubes with their lower ends dipping in water.   After five
hours, there was found in 100 parts of the earths the following
quantities of water, viz., in

	Per cent.
Quartz sand, fine grained	30
" " somewhat coarser	32
" " size of pepper-corns	4.6
Calcareous sand, size of pins' heads	23
" " somewhat finer	27
" " very fine	28
White clay	59
Loam, marly	48
" wheat-land	41

In the fine-grained sand, it could be seen that the water had
risen to a height of two feet.   One merit of the ploughing in of
green crops upon sandy soils is that humus is thus supplied to
increase the capillary and the retentive power of the soil.   In case
this had been done with the third soil of Sachs, above-mentioned, it might perhaps have been made equal to the first soil.

It has long been recognized by practical men that a certain degree of solidity in the soil is requisite for the successful growth of
most kinds of grain, and especially for the growth of wheat; and
the use of marl and clay has been upheld as a means of correcting
undue looseness.   It has been urged that these substances may
act both to cement the particles of the soil and to interpose new
matter between the original particles of the too coarse earth.

Merit of Mellow Humus.

The significance of mellow humus as a means of storing and of lifting water is shown very emphatically in some parts of India where irrigation is practised extensively. It is noticed there that, in years of average rainfall, certain deep black fertile soils yield large crops without irrigation for the simple reason that soils rich in good humus hold water forcibly, and lift it also rapidly on occasion from the subsoil. The power of these black soils to support drought is so well marked that many persons have believed that much moisture is absorbed by them from the atmosphere, even when rain does not fall. Soils thus naturally retentive of moisture do not need the same arrangements for artificial irrigation that are required by the ordinary dry soils of India, and grave mistakes have been made in several instances in that country by English engineers who, in planning canals for irrigation, erroneously estimated that income could be counted on from the sale of water to the cultivators of the black cotton soils as well as from the ordinary soils of the locality.

Dry Peat may Shed Water.

It is noticed not infrequently of soils too highly charged with some kinds of organic matter — as in the case of recently reclaimed, muddy peat-bogs which have not yet had time to become mellow through decay — that, though capable of holding much water when wet, they have only a comparatively feeble power of absorbing water when once thoroughly dried. Such soils, though wet and cold in the spring, may become so dry in summer as wellnigh to lose all power of absorbing moisture. Rain-water may even stand upon the surface of such soil for a considerable time without being absorbed to any appreciable degree. In most cases this behavior manifestly depends on an actual alteration of the physical texture of the peat, i. e. upon a loss of porosity brought about by the muddy peat-particles sticking together and becoming consolidated to hard, compact lumps. The gummy "colloidal" character of the wet peat is so changed by the act of drying that a multitude of small, hard, non-absorbent clods are formed at the surface of the land, which is thus left covered with a loose, incoherent, non-capillary coating — a sort of light gravel — which is far enough from being suitable for the support of crops. It has been noticed in reclaiming peat-bogs in Scotland, that "while it is desirable that the furrow of peat or moss should be partially dried before it is broken up, it will not do to let the drying be continued long enough to produce a dry turf fit for burning; for if once thoroughly dried, the peat will resist the action of the atmosphere and remain hard for several seasons."

It is not impossible in some instances that the peculiar repellent power of dried peat may be due to the presence in it of waxy, resinous, and fatty matters, which coat the surfaces of the particles of peat and make them greasy enough to hinder water from adhering to them. It has been noticed by Reinsch and others that appreciable quantities of matters soluble in ether and in alcohol can be detected in most soils that are rich in organic matter, and there is no improbability in the idea that some soils may contain such things in considerable quantity. Fatty matters may be produced in the soil by the action of microscopic organisms, such as the butyric ferment; wax may come from the chlorophyl of decayed plants, and resinous matters from pine needles or the like.

The Values of Soils Vary with Climates.

In view of the self-evident truth that a soil of any one special degree of capillarity may practically be more or less fertile in different localities according as the climates differ and as the rainfall is more or less abundant, it is not at all strange that the ideas of farmers should differ widely as to what constitutes a good capillary soil according as they are inhabitants of the rainy coast of Western England or of the dry region at the centre of Europe. It is true also that in many localities, as in the vicinity of Boston, most farmers would rightly prefer a good depth of loam upon the surface of their upland fields, even if this loam were of no more than moderate capillary power, rather than a thin layer of loam of exceptionally good character. Moreover, a soil of one and the same degree of capillary power may be more or less valuable on different fields in case it is reposing on an impermeable or on an open subsoil. A thin layer of loam, no matter how good, which reposes on a porous subsoil, can have but little value in dry seasons, unless indeed it can be irrigated. So too, one or another degree of capillarity may be preferable in a field according as the surface of that field slopes more or less steeply and so favors or hinders the flowing away of the rain-water which falls on it, and according as the field is so situated that it can or cannot receive water which has flowed off from other fields.

Best Amount of Capillary Water.

As regards clay and humus, it should be said that it is bad to have too large a proportion of either of them in a soil because of their liability to make the soil too wet. The fact that mere bog-earth can hold enormous quantities of water makes it difficult to have crops standing on such land during the winter unless indeed the texture of the humus has been changed by mixing it with sand or gravel, for when wet bog-earth freezes, the particles of earth are pushed up so forcibly, and so far apart withal, by the great masses of ice which form beneath and between them, that the roots of almost any crop would be torn asunder, and the crop be " thrown out." Afterward, when the ice within it melts, the earth is apt to be left as a loose, coarse, incoherent powder, wholly unfit for supporting the roots of plants. By serving to correct this physical fault, dressings of sand, or coal-ashes, or street sweepings, may often be more useful upon reclaimed bog-land than manure, though manure itself is useful on this very account. In spring and summer, on the other hand, at least in all northern climates, wet land is always cold land. It cannot be warmed rapidly by the sun, because water needs to absorb a peculiarly large amount of heat in order that its temperature may be increased, and because water carries away much heat when it evaporates. Many wet soils cannot be ploughed or tilled early in the spring, for reasons that will be set forth under Tillage, nor can air gain access to them when their pores are full of water.

In the climate of Massachusetts, it is highly desirable that a soil should be able to retain during the growing season, moisture enough to enable crops to endure short terms of drought, and yet be porous enough to allow liquid water to drain away freely, so that any undue excess of rain which falls upon the land may soon pass off by way of percolation and permit an abundance of air to permeate the soil. In case a soil is so constituted that it is apt to retain too much water, it will often enough be found to be necessary or advisable to provide means for the escape of the surplus.

It is a fact of observation, that plants are liable to sicken and die on soils that are too wet, the more readily, no doubt, in case the water becomes stagnant, and so occasions reducing chemical action such as leads to the formation of ferrous and sulphuretted compounds that are poisonous to most agricultural plants. Hellriegel finds that as much water as may amount to 80% (or more) of what the soil can hold is hurtful to ordinary agricultural plants, and that a soil charged with water to the extent of 50 or 60% of its capacity offers the best possible conditions for the growth of crops, when other circumstances are favorable. Gasparin observed long ago that annual plants suffer in the field when the soil at the depth of one foot contains no more than 10% of moisture, and that they prosper when there is present 15 or 20% of moisture.

Plants need so much water, and it is in general so important that the capillary and water-holding power of a soil shall be large, that it might be thought at first sight that the best soils would be those which can offer the largest amounts of water to crops. But, as has just been indicated, this conclusion can only be true for cases where the stores of moisture are not excessive. The living water of the Spanish sand-dunes, before mentioned, and that of the floating gardens, is a very different thing from cold or stagnant water, such as might clog or poison soils that are too rich in humus or clay. Examples of good capillary soils may be seen in many of the mixtures of peat, sand, leaf-mould, rotted sod, etc., which greenhouse gardeners prepare for the growth of ferns and certain other plants.

Ameliorants, so called.

The results recorded in the table above given explain at once the good effects which are often seen to follow the application of various other substances beside humus, which alter the texture of a soil. It is a practical maxim, however, that while a small proportion of clay will greatly improve a light sand, a large quantity of sand is needed to correct the tenacity of a stiff clay. Other examples of the "amelioration" of soils are seen in the application of lime to clay, and in the burning of clay. The particles of burnt clay are no longer plastic and sticky, like those of the crude earth. In this sense, coal-ashes are often valuable as an application to stiff clays. Walz was accustomed to urge that while the physical character of soils is, generally speaking, determined by the fineness of their particles, and by the amounts of sand, clay, lime and humus which are contained in them, it is very noticeable that in order to the best results the proportions of these ingredients should vary in different localities according to the climate. In a region of much moisture the proportion of mere silicious sand or gravel may well be large; in cold regions, soils rich in calcareous sand may perhaps be the best, while a tolerably large proportion of clay may make the best soil in countries dry enough to permit the clay land to receive suitable tillage.

Very much the same idea is expressed in the maxims that clays may be made drier, lighter and warmer by means of sand and lime; that sands may be made more compact, moister and cooler by means of clay, or compact and moist by means of clay and lime; and that compactness, moisture and coolness may be imparted to calcareous soils by means of clay. In England, where chalk has been used to an enormous extent for improving land, it is said that this material "makes heavy (clay) lands mellow and easy to plough, and gravels less liable to burn."

It is true no doubt that ameliorants are no longer so much employed as they have been occasionally in times that are past, for the improved methods of communication which now enable farmers all over the world to send their produce to distant markets have greatly diminished the incentive to improve farms situated not far from markets, such as could formerly repay freely the costs of generous treatment.

In England at one time the texture of many sandy and peaty soils was greatly improved by means of chalk, marl and clay. It has been said, indeed, that the admixture of chalky and marly subsoils with the surface earth contributed more than any other single circumstance toward putting the cultivation of the light lands of Norfolk and Suffolk counties in the front rank of successful farming. So too, in the fen country of England, where the staple products towards the close of the last century were oats and rape, the application of clay completely changed the character of the soil and permitted the adoption of courses of rotation in which wheat and horsebeans found conspicuous place.

In several regions the character of considerable tracts of sandy or peaty soil has been permanently improved by bringing on muddy freshet water in such manner that the matters held in suspension by the water should be deposited on the surface of the land, as will be explained under the head of Warping. But under the non-lucrative systems of farming which prevail nowadays, the use of amendments is restricted to the occasional improvement of a small garden-patch, or a reclaimed bog-meadow, or to operations of the landscape architect where the question of the cost of an improvement may not be much considered.

The question was sometimes propounded, long ago, " Is clay any better than dung ? " But, as was remarked by Pusey, the answer to it in some cases may well be Yes! For on very light land, even dung may not bring a crop of wheat where a dressing of clay will.

Improvement of Sands.

Interesting results have been obtained by Adolf Mayer in field experiments made in Holland upon a barren sand-waste where it was found that the improvement of the physical character of the sand by means of peat was more important than mere additions of plant-food. The following table relates to rye which was grown upon the sandy field in question after a crop of lupines (which failed) and of spurry had been ploughed under. It will be noticed that plots Nos. 7 and 8 differ from the others in that the rye was here sown directly upon sand that had borne neither lupines, nor spurry nor any other green crop.

No. of Plot.	Fertilizer used per hectare.	Crop per hectare Grain (kilo.)	Straw (kilo.)
I.	Nothing	1.2	40
II.	1000 kg. bone meal and 300 kg. muriate of potash	222	720
III.	100 cubic metres of peat dust	124	560
IV.	100 cm. peat dust and 100 kg. bone meal and 300 kg. muriate of potash . . .	472	1120
V.	300 kg. muriate of potash	6	170
VI.	1000 kg. bone meal	309	660
VII.	300 kg. muriate of potash, without any green manuring	2	90
VIII.	1000 kg. bone meal, without any green manuring	180	480

It will be observed that while bone meal, did some good by itself, it did much more good when used in conjunction with peat. The influence of the green manuring is well marked also.

After the rye, potatoes were grown upon the land (in 1880) with the results stated in the following table.

No. of Plot.	Fertilizer used per hectare in the year 1878.	1879.	1880.	Crop of Potatoes. Kilos, per hectare.
I.	Nothing.	750 kg. bone meal.	200 kg. sulphate of ammonia.	1041
II.	1000 kg. bone meal and 300 kg. muriate of potash.	Nothing.	200 kg. sulphate of ammonia.	2470

No. of Plot.	1878.	Fertilizer used per hectare in the year 1879.	1890.	Crop of Potatoes. Kilos, per hectare.
III.	100 cubm. peat dust.	{ 750 kg. bone meal. 200 kg. muriate of potash.	{ 200 kg. sulphate of ammonia.	6938
IV.	100 cm. peat dust. 1000 kg. bone meal. 300 kg. muriate of potash.	} Nothing.	{ 200 kg. sulphate of ammonia.	4966
V.	300 kg. muriate of potash.	{ 750 kg. bone meal. 200 kg. muriate of potash.	{ 200 kg. sulphate of ammonia.	3877
VI.	000 kg. bone meal.	{ 200 kg. lime. 200 kg. muriate of potash.	{ 200 kg. sulphate of ammonia.	3171
VII.	300 kg. muriate of potash.	{ 200 kg. lime. 750 kg. bone meal.	{ 200 kg. sulphate of ammonia. 200 kg. muriate of potash. 200 kg. lime.	3063
VIII.	1600 kg. bone meal.	Nothing.	Same as No. 7.	3358

Here again the peat did good service, and the crops obtained by means of it may, unlike the others, perhaps have repaid the cost of the artificial fertilizers which were put upon them. But the main point to be insisted upon is that the peat permanently improved the land by increasing its capacity to hold water. This improvement was brought out most clearly subsequently when lupines and serradella were grown upon the land (in 1881). After the lupines had died out it appeared that the serradella was growing most luxuriantly on plots Nos. 3 and 4. Among the other plots No. 6 was the best, and after that Nos. 5, 2, 7, 8, and last of all No. 1.

A just conception of the mode of action of the capillary force may be got by considering a process of butter-making that was patented at Washington some years since. It is perhaps the more instructive because of its economic absurdity. It has long been believed by many agricultural populations, that cream wrapped in close cloths and buried in the earth over night may be changed to solid butter by morning. All the watery portions of the cream, with whatever the water may have held in solution, will be absorbed by the earth by virtue of capillary attraction, which drags the buttermilk first into the porous napkins and then into the soil. Acting on this idea the patentee buries his bag of sweet cream in a vessel filled with slightly moistened bran or with meal, and leaves it there for twenty-four hours. He then finds butter inside the bag, while outside the bag he has meal charged with buttermilk which he proposes to feed to hogs, or to other animals, as a most nourishing and fattening food.

Capillarity as modified by Hygroscopicity.

The main facts as to capillarity are evident enough, but some of the details [1] are sufficiently complex, as may be seen, for example, on seeking to explain the manner in which moisture rises through the soil to or towards the surface of a high gravelly ridge. Here processes of evaporation and condensation within the soil come in to help the capillary movement, i. e. vapor exhales from that part of the soil which is moistened by simple capillarity, and this vapor is absorbed by the overlying soil. But when once the soil has become damp in this way, it is better able than it was before to lift water from the adjacent layers of soil, and the scope of the capillary movement is thereby extended.

Experimenters operating upon tubes standing in water, and filled with dry earth so arranged that samples of it could be taken out at different heights for examination, have found that the proportion of moisture in the columns of soil diminishes so gradually from below upward that it is wellnigh impossible to distinguish between simple capillary and hygroscopic movements, or to detect any limit of height at which water ceases to be absorbed. As evidence of the constancy with which the hygroscopic dampening precedes the capillary lifting, Wollny reports a trial where four tubes full of earth were made to stand up in a dish of water and were subsequently examined as to the amount of water that had disseminated itself in the earth. One of the tubes was examined at the end of an hour and a half, another after it had stood for a day, the third at the end of a week, and the fourth after five weeks. It appeared that the soil gradually took up more and more water, and continually lifted it to higher elevations, in such manner that it was evident that at any given height the soil must have passed through various stages or degrees of moistness before it finally acquired the full amount of water that it was capable of holding under the conditions of the experiments.

Speaking generally, it is plain enough that up to a certain height above the actual ground-water the pores of the soil will be completely filled with liquid, just as the pores of a lamp-wick are filled with oil, by force of capillary adhesion. But above this

---

[1] The agricultural student will do well to study the experiments of Johnson and Armsby in the Reports of the Connecticut Agricultural Experiment Station for 1877 and 1878; and those of Nessler in Hoffman's Jahresbericht der Agrikulturchemie, 1873-74, I.

real or conceivable limit of absolute saturation there must be in multitudes of cases layers of soil that are only partially saturated by the capillary movement, and, above these, there will be other layers still less completely saturated; and so we may readily conceive of passing to heights quite beyond the scope of capillarity, in so far as it relates immediately to the ground-water, and come to layers of soil so elevated that, if no rains were to fall, the soil might soon become nearly or quite air-dried between the uppermost limit of capillary action and the surface of the land. In the case here supposed, slow evaporation would naturally occur at the top of the uppermost layer of moistened earth, even when, as was just suggested, it is situated at some distance beneath the surface, and the vapor thus generated would slowly escape into and towards the air.

Soils are moistened from above and below.

Practically, however, that is to say in countries where rains are not infrequent, the earth is moistened by rain-water from above, as well as by water lifted from the permanent store below; and whenever liquid water sinks downward through the soil, very considerable quantities of it will be retained by the soil, no matter at how great a distance above the ground-water the surface soil may be situated. That is to say, much water will be retained both by soaking into the actual particles of the soil, and by clinging to the surfaces of the particles, especially at the points where the particles touch or nearly touch one another. The finer the soil, up to a certain point, so much the larger will be its power of thus retaining water, because of the great extent of surface presented by its particles; and a similar remark will apply to the condition of looseness, or rather compactness, in which a soil happens to be. In order to the best results, the soil must neither be too hard and compact, nor yet too loose. As Johnson and Armsby have urged, the tendency in the field is simply to preserve the original distribution of the water by a motion through the already filled or partly filled interstices of the soil toward the point from which water is being abstracted, — generally the surface. Nevertheless it is true as a general rule, in countries not actually arid, that there is a well-nigh continuous movement of capillary water from below upward tending to replace that wasted at the surface, and, excepting times of actual rain, this movement is doubtless very extended, since it is naturally transmitted from one particle to another even to considerable depths. A soil that will permit both rain-water and capillary water to move freely and rapidly within it, to supply a deficiency at any point, is said to be in good mechanical condition.

For soils that lie high above the ground-water, it is important that their texture and the crops may be such that the amount of water evaporated into the air shall not be too largely in excess of the supply of rain-water which can be held in the soil by virtue of capillary adhesion. Some crops indeed thrive best when they are placed very near to ground-water. For success with timothy, squashes, and other thirsty crops, it is well-nigh essential that the amount of water sent out into the air from the land shall be no greater than what can rise daily through the soil. It is noteworthy withal, that even coarse soils may often serve perfectly well for transmitting water upward, to supply that wasted by evaporation, in cases where the ground-water is high, i. e. near the surface of the soil. Here, mere permeability is all important.

Hygroscopic Moisture.

In connection with the retention of liquid water may be mentioned the power of the soil to draw in and hold small portions of the invisible aqueous vapor, which, as is well known, forms a constituent part of the atmosphere. That moisture can really be absorbed and held in this way is proved by the fact that a soil to all appearance dry, as it lies in contact with the air, will still lose weight when heated to 212°, the point at which water boils. It is found in practice that ordinary air-dried soils heated in this way during several hours invariably suffer an appreciable loss of weight which may range from less than 1% to 10% or more. Even the driest dust of the highway is by no means wholly free from moisture. When once within the soil, the hygroscopic water that has been absorbed from the air is not to be distinguished from the capillary water with which it may be said to mix.

The power of the soil to absorb atmospheric moisture is of course nothing more than a particular instance of a very general law. There are hosts of things far more hygroscopic than any soil; wool and hair, for example, of which hygrometers are sometimes made. In selling silk in France, it is customary to make an allowance for the hygroscopic moisture. At the same time that a lot of silk is weighed for sale, a small sample is weighed out by itself, and the proportion of moisture contained in it is determined by drying. The amount of water thus found is then subtracted from the weight of the undried portion of the silk. According to Lord Bacon, " In the countrey they use many times, in deceit, when their wooll is new shorne, to set some pailes of water by, in the same roome to increase the weight of the wooll." Bacon tried the following experiment: "A quantitie of wooll tyed loose together being let downe into a deepe well, and hanging in the middle some three fathome from the water for a night in the winter time, increased in weight to a fifth part." He says also " we see that wood, lute strings, and the like doe swell in moist seasons ; as appeareth by the breaking of the strings, the hard turning of the pegs, and the hard drawing forth of boxes, and the opening of wainscot doores."

As a rule, vegetable matters, such as the more delicate parts of plants and plant-roots, even when they are partially decayed, can absorb more moisture from the air than most soils can absorb. Thus, Trommer has insisted that, in general, vegetable fibres are more hygroscopic than the humus which results from their decay, and that the hygroscopic power of soils often depends in some part on the vegetable matter which is contained in them. Hay, straw, corn-stalks, and most other air-dried vegetable matters — even grain — usually contain some 10 or 12% of hygroscopic moisture, and when exposed to damp air they contain much more than these amounts. Cross and Bevan have noticed that jute under normal atmospheric conditions may hold from 9 to 12% of hygroscopic moisture, while from air saturated with aqueous vapor at ordinary temperatures it may take up 23 %. Trommer found that the following number of pounds of water were absorbed from moist air by

	In 12 hours.	In 24 hours.	In 48 hours.	In 72 hours.
100 lb. rasped or grated barley straw	15	24	35	45
100 lb. rasped or grated rye straw	12	20	27	29
200 lb. rasped or grated white unsized paper . .	8	12	18	20

Perhaps the most familiar instance of all is charcoal, which freely absorbs aqueous vapor from the air, as well as many other gases, to the extent sometimes of a quarter of its own weight. Charcoal that has been recently burned, or heated to expel the absorbed vapor, kindles very easily ; whereas, in case it has been kept

for some time in a damp place, it kindles with difficulty and snaps
and smokes while burning. After having had occasion to use a
charcoal fire, chemists sometimes throw any live coals that are left
into an iron pot, which they cover tightly, in order to have a
store of perfectly dry coal wherewith to kindle the next fire. After
having long been stored in a damp cellar, charcoal and even fire-
wood do not kindle readily.

Aqueous Vapor sometimes all-important.

It is evident from what sometimes happens in the closed glass
cases of Mr. Ward that vapor absorbed from the air by the soil
may occasionally — when all the conditions are favorable — be of
very great importance for the support of plants. In the Wardian
case, as was explained before, the soil is left to itself, after
having once been watered, so that vegetation is subsequently supported by the water which the soil drinks in continually, as vapor,
out of the air, as well as by condensed water, which in temperate
climates trickles down from the roof and sides of the case. But
at sea within the tropics where the temperature of air and water,
and of things upon the water, is continually the same (almost
85° F.), there can be comparatively little condensation of vapor
on those parts of the Wardian case which are above the soil. Here
at least the atmosphere of the case is kept charged with vapor by
the natural exhalation from the plants, and the soil must drink in
much of the vapor, as such. Once in the soil, the roots of the
plants will again pump the moisture up to be again exhaled.

So too in the field-cultivation of broad-leaved plants, — such
as the whole tribe of turnips and cabbages, clover, Indian corn,
squashes and the like, — the ground doubtless reabsorbs a part of
the aqueous vapor which is exhaled by the leaves, though this
illustration is of course much less emphatic than the previous one.
It is complicated, moreover, to a slight extent, by the consideration that the plants in question shade the ground, and so hinder
somewhat the evaporation from the surface which would naturally
be due to the action of sun and wind upon the soil; and by the fact
that much dew condenses upon the great leaves by night, so that
liquid water dribbles from them into the ground. In the tropics, in
particular, where the nocturnal radiation of heat occasions very
considerable differences of temperature between night and day, so
much dew is deposited that in some localities it goes far to supply
plants with all the moisture they need. It is said that in some

tropical forests so much dew condenses by night, that it may often be heard dripping from the leaves of the trees even at daybreak.

Surface Soil often very Hot.

The absorption of moisture by the soil from the air naturally tends to increase by night and to diminish by day. Doubtless at some seasons of the year dry soils exposed to moist air may gather in this way appreciable quantities of moisture, even when no dew is deposited. But it must be remembered that in droughty summer weather the surface of a dry soil may become very hot. Herschel observed at the Cape of Good Hope that the soil attained a temperature of 150° F., when the air was 120°; and Humboldt says that in the tropics the temperature of the soil often rises to from 124° to 136°. But a soil once thoroughly heated, even in temperate climates, will often remain so warm throughout the night that it cannot be in a condition to absorb much hygroscopic water. On the contrary, soils thus heated must often give off by night vapor that may perhaps have come from considerable depths, where supplies of moisture are held in store.

Nessler has observed in late summer, when the days are hot and the nights cool, that on placing an inverted glass funnel on the ground by night, much water will be deposited upon the inside of the glass; thus showing that a part of the moisture which, on such nights, condenses as dew upon plants or other matters at the surface of the ground, has come, not out of the air, but out of the soil. Indeed, the moisture that in times of drought evaporates within the soil from those layers which are still moist, and passes up as vapor into the dry surface-soil, is presumably much more important for vegetation than any vapor that is absorbed by the soil from the outer air. This subterranean evaporation must be strongest at times when the soil is most thoroughly heated in dry weather, and much of the vapor must condense near the surface, whenever, as of an autumn night, this part of the soil becomes cooler than the layers of earth immediately below it. It is true, in general, that the air contained in the pores of the soil is decidedly damp, even if it is not actually saturated with aqueous vapor, at no great distance below the surface. This fact is familiarly illustrated in every-day life by the sensation of dampness which we feel on descending into cellars in midsummer. But whenever the surface-soil is not too strongly heated, some part of the subterranean vapor which reaches it will be absorbed and held, to the advantage of any crop which may be growing upon the land.

It has sometimes been argued that the utility of the time-honored practice of frequently stirring the surface-soil in the dry season, by means of hoes or the cultivator, in order that the crop may not suffer from drought, is to be attributed to the increased power of the loosened soil to absorb the vapor of water from the air; but this explanation can no longer be accepted as a true one, as will be seen in the chapter on Tillage where the purpose of summer cultivation is discussed.

Estimations of Amount of Hygroscopic Moisture.

Several investigators have been at pains to estimate the quantities of aqueous vapor which can be absorbed from moist air by different kinds of soils. The observations of Davy, Schuebler, Trommer, Meister and Knop in particular have often been cited, though, according to Hilgard, most of them lack precision in that not enough pains were taken to saturate thoroughly with moisture the air which was operated upon, and that the absorptive power of the soils was impaired by heating and drying them before they were exposed to the vapor of water. Hilgard finds that in order to obtain a rigorously saturated atmosphere it is necessary not only to have the bottom of the absorption-box covered with water, but to line the sides and even the cover of this box with sheets of wet blotting-paper. A failure to moisten the top of the absorption-box is especially productive of inaccuracy, and should it be found dry or nearly so on opening the box the experiment must be rejected. Hilgard insists also that the soil should not be heated, in order to dry it, before testing its hygroscopic power, for few soils absorb as much moisture after they have been heated to 212° F., as they do when tested in their natural condition. In the case of soils rich in humus, the power of absorbing aqueous vapor is materially diminished if the soil is dried by heating it.

Hygroscopic Constituents in Soils.

According to Hilgard, the power of ordinary soils to absorb aqueous vapor depends upon the presence of one or more of four substances, viz., humus, ferric hydrate, clay and lime, which are here set down in the order of their efficiency. The amount of hygroscopic moisture that can be taken up and held by cultivated soils at ordinary temperatures when they are exposed to air thoroughly saturated with moisture, varies from about 1.5% to 23%, according to the character of the soil. Pure clays can rarely absorb more than 12% of their weight of the vapor of water, though ferruginous clays and some calcareous clays can hold from 15 to 21%. Peaty soils may hold as much as 23% of hygroscopic moisture or even more. This result had already been arrived at by Voelcker who cites the case of two soils which he powdered and kept in a heated room until they were completely air-dry, and had ceased to show either any loss or gain of water when weighed from day to day. It appeared that one of these soils taken from a wheat-field contained 6% of organic matter, and retained 4.7% of moisture which could be driven off at the temperature of boiling water, while the other soil, from a permanent pasture, had 22% of organic matter and held 22.35% of moisture.

As regards ferric hydrate, it was noticed by Hilgard that its efficacy depends essentially on a state of fine division; it exerts little or no influence when it exists in a soil as a mere incrustation on grains of sand or when it occurs aggregated into grains of bog-ore, although analysis may show a high percentage of it. Some highly-colored soils showing but a small percentage of iron are nevertheless strongly hygroscopic because the ferric hydrate is in good condition and thoroughly diffused in them.

Influence of Heat on Hygroscopicity.

Contrary to an opinion expressed by Knop, Hilgard finds that the quantity of aqueous vapor absorbed by soils from thoroughly saturated air, far from increasing with diminution of temperature, as Knop had urged, increases decidedly as the temperature is increased. Hilgard had been led by his earlier experiments to the conclusion that for practical purposes the amount of absorption in most soils, and especially in soils poor in humus, might be considered as very nearly constant for temperatures between 45° and 77° F. But he found subsequently that in saturated air the quantity of vapor absorbed by soils increases appreciably as the temperature is increased. In some soils this increase may amount to nearly 0.1% for each degree centigrade, between 14° and 35°. For example, in the case of a fine droughty alluvial silt, which contained little clay or humus, it was observed that while it absorbed 2.13% of moisture from saturated air at 61° F., it absorbed 4.21% at 95°. At 84°, the absorption was 3.4%, and at 77°, it was 2.98%.

Since under natural conditions, the atmosphere is only partially saturated with moisture, results obtained with saturated air as above cannot be accepted as showing the actual state of things in the fields, and it was found in fact that from half-saturated air absorption decreased as the temperature rose though "only to a very small extent, and not nearly enough to satisfy the requirement's of Knop's supposed law." It is to be inferred from these observations that somewhere between the conditions of half-saturation and total saturation there must be a state of saturation which will permit absorption to be independent of temperature, i. e., between the limits commonly experienced. Ordinarily, the air in non-arid regions, during the growing season, may be assumed to be nearly three-fourths saturated. In some of the experiments above mentioned, it was observed that the absolute amounts of vapor absorbed from half-saturated air approximated roughly to one-half of those taken up from air saturated with moisture.

Schloesing also has observed that the absorption of hygroscopic moisture by a soil from partially saturated air may be practically independent of changes of temperature. His experiments go to show that at temperatures between 48° and 95° F., a soil will absorb very nearly the same amount of hygroscopic moisture from air which contains a given amount of aqueous vapor, no matter how widely the temperature may vary between these limits.

Real Importance of Hygroscopic Moisture.

From his study of the subject in the dry climate of California, Hilgard has convinced himself that the agricultural value of a soil may depend not infrequently in some part on the power of that soil to absorb the vapor of water from the air, i. e., either from atmospheric air or from ground air which has been charged with moisture as it lay in contact with lower layers of soil. All soils, he says, which can absorb no more than 2 % of moisture at 59° F. when placed under the most favorable conditions are in practice droughty soils. Ordinary upland soils not easily damaged by drought can absorb at the best from 4 to 8%. Soils more hygroscopic than this are mostly heavy clays, whose resistance to drought is great when they are well tilled.

Furthermore, while admitting freely that crops naturally obtain their supplies of moisture through those roots which lie buried deeply enough to be nourished from the store of capillary moisture, he calls attention to the fact that the evaporation of the hygroscopic water from a soil in times of extreme heat may act as a safeguard to keep the soil cool; i. e. it may hinder the soil from becoming so hot that the surface roots of crops may be destroyed. This consideration must be of especial importance in those arid countries where rain falls only in winter, to be succeeded by long-continued dry weather, and where the success of crops is dependent upon the power of the soil to husband the supply of water within it until such time as the crop has completed its term of growth. In California it is observed in fact that very small differences in the hygroscopic power of soils will manifest themselves in adjacent plots of grain by the total burning off of the crop in the one case and the maintenance of growth in others. In critical cases the presence of a single per cent of hygroscopic moisture may be a saving clause to prevent the surface roots of the crop from being overcome at a time of scorching heat. (Hilgard.)

The importance of Hilgard's observations is the more conspicuous, inasmuch as they indicate the limitations of other experiments which have been made in mere pots of earth; i. e. under conditions where there are not any deep-lying roots to supply the plants with water, and where there can be no damp air continually rising from the subsoil to supplement and protect the capillary water, and to eke out the supply available for the crops. For example, Heinrich and A. Mayer have found that most plants wilt when the soil in which they are growing still contains considerably more moisture than it has the power to absorb when dry from moist air. Thus Heinrich, experimenting with oats and maize, found that the plants

Wilted when 100 Parts of the dry Earth contained Parts of Moisture	But 100 Parts of the dry Soil could absorb from moist Air no more Moisture than Parts	Kind of Soil.
1.5	1.15	Coarse sandy soil.
4.6	3.00	Sandy garden loam.
6.2	3.98	Fine sandy humus.
7.8	5.74	Sandy loam.
9.8	5.20	Calcareous soil.
49.7	42.30	Peaty soil.

Numerous other experiments with grasses and leguminous plants showed that in a calcareous soil capable of holding 5.2% of hygroscopic moisture the minimum of moisture for grasses was 9.85%, and for legumes 10.95. In a peaty soil competent to hold 42.3 of hygroscopic moisture, the figures were 50.79 and 52.87 respectively.

A. Mayer's experiments with peas showed that the plants

Wilted when Hyg. Moisture was	The dry Soil could absorb % of Moisture	Kind of Soil.
1.3	0.3	Sand.
33.3	16.3	Sawdust.
4.7	1.9	Marl.

Liebenberg, also, who experimented with beans, gives the following table : —

Percent by Volume of Moisture in Soil when the Plants wilted.	Percent by Volume of Hyg. Water absorbable at 59° F.	Kind of Soil.
6.91	3.40	Marl.
10.02	7.46	Loam.
10.32	3.43	Granitic soil.
12.49	6.18	Sandy moor-earth.
9.15	5.89	Calcareous soil.
1.20	0.46	Coarse sand.
0.51	0.19	Moderately fine sand.

Similar experiments had been published by Hellriegel in his turn which seemed to enforce the conclusion that the amount of aqueous vapor ordinarily absorbed by soils from the air cannot be of much practical importance for the growth of crops. For in his trials the water thus absorbed by garden-loam amounted to less than 2% of the weight of the dry earth, and to no more than 3 or 4% of the water that the soil was capable of holding, while plants could not grow at all in such soil unless it contained more water than amounted to 5% of its water-holding power, and even 10% was inadequate for the support of crops.

Frost is Frozen Vapor.

An exaggerated view of the influence of moisture derived from the air may be had by considering what happens during frosty nights, i. e. when the temperature of the soil is decidedly below the dew-point of the air, for then actual liquid water will condense in and upon the soil, and soak into it or freeze upon it. A small thermometer laid upon grass-land by night, when all the conditions are favorable for radiation, may mark some 6 or 8 or 10°, or even as much as 15 or 16° lower than the temperature of the surrounding air. Jourdanet has stated that certain marshes in Mexico cool so decidedly at night that they cease to be malarious for the time being, i. e. they are not dangerous by night. He reports that a thermometer there indicated 32° F. at the surface of the ground, and 50° when hung 16 feet above the ground.

That vapor thus deposited may occasionally be of some impor-

tance to crops is indicated by the fact that drain-gauges sometimes discharge more water than has come to them in the form
of rain. Thus, Ebermayer, experimenting with gauges one yard
deep found when they were filled with retentive soils, such as
loams and peats, that the quantity of water flowing from the
bottom of the gauge was always considerably smaller than the
rainfall,—thanks of course to the better opportunity for the evaporation of water when no rain is falling which the capillary soils
afford. But different results were obtained with gauges that had
been filled with non-retentive and so to say granular soils.
Thus, as the mean of 4 years' observations, a gauge one yard
deep filled with fine quartz sand gave out in winter 29%, in summer
and autumn 4%, and as the mean of the whole year 7%, more
water than came to the surface of the gauge as rain. In gauges
filled with fine-grained, calcareous sand, the excess of drip was
noticed only in winter, but it amounted to 25%. So too in
gauges charged with coarse quartz sand an excess of drip was
occasionally noticed in winter. In one season it amounted to
10% and in another to 14% of the total percolate.

As has been insisted already, it is to be presumed from the
observations of Hilgard that, practically, in the fields, the
absorption of hygroscopic moisture by soils that are no more
than half dried, or even by soils which have but just begun to
become dry, must serve constantly to compensate in some measure for the loss of water by way of evaporation and must tend
to postpone somewhat the time of unbearable dryness when the
crop would perish. It is to be noted that the justice of Hilgard's view had already been indicated by the experiment
of Sachs, mentioned on a previous page, in which a wilted bean
plant, standing in air-dried loam, quickly revived and remained
fresh and green and turgid during June and July when the flower-
pot which contained it was hung up in air that was saturated or
nearly saturated with aqueous vapor. The bean plant did not
actually grow under these conditions, but it remained healthy in
spite of the meagre supply of moisture. Like the plants of the
desert during the dry season, it held its own and waited patiently
for the coming of seasonable rains. A tobacco plant with three
leaves, standing in mellow humus, was subjected by Sachs to the
same test as the bean, and a similar result was obtained, though
it was not quite so favorable.

As bearing upon the subject now under discussion, it is of interest to note that the observations of physicists have shown that air can take up and hold the

160th part of its own weight of aqueous vapor at					32° F.
80th "	"	"	"	"	59°
40th "	"	"	"	"	86°
20th "	"	"	"	"	113°;

whence it appears that the capacity of air to retain moisture increases so rapidly with the temperature that this capacity is doubled for every 27° of increase of temperature above 32° F. The remark applies of course to air which is completely saturated with moisture, i. e., to air which contains as much invisible aqueous vapor as it is capable of holding at any given temperature.

Fertility Dependent on Moisture.

From all that has been said hitherto, it is evident that the fertility of any soil must depend in no small measure upon the behavior of the soil towards water, and upon its position or situation with regard to the ground-water. It has been urged indeed by some writers that vegetation depends absolutely on temperature and moisture. If the earth be of such quality that it can imbibe moisture freely, and retain it tolerably forcibly, without impeding that capillary movement which is essential to the proper transfer and circulation of the water in the soil, and if at the same time the ground-water be at such a height that it favors the capillary movement, there will be little risk that tillage and manure will fail of producing good effects. With an open sand or a close clay it is often difficult to fulfil these conditions. Through coarse sand, rain-water runs away quickly, carrying with it mechanically some of the fertilizers which may have been applied, while into clay the rain-water can hardly penetrate at all. Unless it be improved by green manuring, or by the application of peat or clay, coarse sand has comparatively little power to lift water by capillary action, or to hold it against evaporation. And, on the other hand, clays are apt to be so dense that they materially hinder the capillary movement.

Paramount Importance of Moisture.

It is interesting to observe in agricultural practice the enormous influence which may be exerted by the amount of available moisture in any given soil in determining the practical value of that soil, and to note how differently the several kinds of soils are managed by farmers, both as regards the quantities of manure which are applied to the land and the crops that are grown upon it. Upon clayey soils it is customary to grow such crops as grass and winter-wheat, which feed slowly, as it were, and which remain upon the land a comparatively long time, and get but little cultivation. Such land is thought to be specially well adapted to hold the goodness of farmyard manure, and as a general rule manure is applied to it only at infrequent intervals. Each application of manure is expected to produce useful effects on such land during several years.

But for quick-growing vegetables, such as are supplied by market gardeners, light soils are esteemed, and the inability of these soils to retain manure is not regarded as an objection, since it is customary to apply manure to them in very large quantities and often, in order to force the crops. The frequent cultivation which vegetables require is easily and cheaply performed on the light land, and the weeds which might interfere with the growth of the young crops are there easily kept down.

It is essential, however, for success with these garden crops, that the light land shall be adequately supplied with moisture, and it is noticeable that this desideratum may be obtained in several ways. Upon upland fields, the store of water that has come from the winter's rain will be sufficient for growing early vegetables, such as peas, for example, especially in view of the fact that the capillary condition of the soil is greatly improved by the heavy applications of manure; while the crops of mid-summer will be grown either by way of irrigation or upon low-lying fields well supplied with ground-water. It happens not infrequently, as has been said already, that mere sand which is fine enough to be capillary is found to serve excellently well for growing vegetables even when the surface of the sand lies at a considerable distance above the level of the ground-water.

The Rain that falls on a Field is insufficient for Large Crops.

The importance of the ground-water for agricultural crops, and the futility of trying to grow all kinds of plants — unless it should be by way of irrigation — in places where the ground-water lies at so great a distance beneath the surface soil that it can have but little direct influence on the growth of crops, may be shown very emphatically by carefully considering the question, is the rain-water that falls upon a crop during the period of its growth sufficient for the support of that crop? Many European investigators have studied this question, and they have frequently found that it must be answered in the negative.

For most temperate regions it may be laid down as a rule that the ground does not receive, during the growing season, enough rain-water for the support of really good crops. In many places there is not nearly enough rain-water. If any different conclusion from this could be reached, it would follow that a much larger proportion of the earth's surface could be profitably cultivated than is now found to be possible. As bearing upon this question Lawes and Gilbert have called attention to the fact that a good crop of hay, wheat, or barley will exhale rather more than 700 long tons of water to the acre during the period of growth, or about seven inches of rain, since one inch of rain represents 101 tons of water to an acre. In a year (1870) of extreme drought in England they found that all the rain which fell during April, May, and June amounted to no more than 2.79 inches, or 282 tons to the acre. But from a mowing field which had been dressed for many years with a mixture of artificial fertilizers, there was harvested in 1870 rather more than 56 cwt. of hay, so that some 700 tons of water to the acre must have been exhaled by the grass, on the assumption that no more than 300 lb. of water had passed through the plants for each pound of dry substance produced. In this case it is evident that little more than one-third the water actually transpired by the crop could have been supplied by the rain which fell during the period of growth.

The contrast between the amount of water needed by crops, and that supplied directly to a field by rain, is all the more striking when we reflect how small a proportion of the yearly rain falls during the growing season, in most localities, how much of it runs off the land anyway, or soaks away from the crop into the depths of the earth, and how much of it evaporates directly without passing through the crop. It has been thought in Germany that hardly one-half of all the rain-water that falls in a year upon an acre of land can possibly be of any direct use to the crop that is standing upon the land. In the vicinity of Boston much more rain comes to the land than in North Germany, for the annual rainfall amounts to more than forty inches. But our storms and showers are so very unevenly distributed that even here the water supply cannot be regarded as particularly favorable for vegetation. Nevertheless, very much depends upon the time of year when the rain falls. Thus, in California, in the valleys of the Sacramento and San Joaquin, where the annual rainfall rarely exceeds twenty inches, and is often very much less than this, abundant crops of grain are obtained, provided as much as twelve or fifteen inches of rain fall in late winter and early spring; for much of the water is absorbed by the soil, and held in store during the spring months; i. e., long enough to nourish the crops, and to enable them to ripen off before the dry season. In central Nebraska, on the other hand, where nearly 24 inches of rain fall annually, the seasonal distribution of the rain is admitted to be favorable on the whole to agriculture, although it is very irregular. From October to March the rainfall there amounts to less than one-quarter of the yearly amount, and the spring is a period of almost drought. The maximum amount of rain falls in June, July and August and diminishes somewhat regularly after the middle of August until November, when the minimum is reached. Naturally enough, no small advantage can be got in this locality by irrigating the land in the spring where it is possible to do so.

Most crops stand in special need of an abundant supply of water at that period of development when growth is most vigorous, i. e. when the largest amount of water is transpired from their leaves. As regards grain and pulse, it has been found that the best crops are obtained when the plants have a copious supply of water from the time when their stems begin to shoot up until they have finished blossoming, and that the worst crops are got when the plants suffer from drought at this particular stage of development.

Young crops can better bear a somewhat scanty supply of water than those in full vigor of growth, because plants that are young and small really transpire in the aggregate a much smaller quantity of water than plants which are of middle age. It is to be remembered that in non-arid regions most soils naturally hold in their pores very considerable quantities of water. Observations made in Germany have shown that a layer 25 feet thick even of fine sand can hold as much water as would amount to the yearly rainfall of the locality.

Evaporation versus Rainfall.

Extremely interesting tables, showing the differences that have

been observed at various localities between the rainfall and the
amounts of water that evaporate from open reservoirs, are given
in the books that relate to hydraulic engineering. Naturally
enough there are very considerable variations, at any given
locality, from year to year accordingly as the seasons are hot and
dry or cold and rainy. At Tübingen, Schuebler observed that in
the course of the years 1826, 1827 and 1828 there evaporated
from vessels of water kept in the shade, 20.45, 28.05 and 26.18
inches, respectively, or as the mean of three years 24.87 inches;
while the numbers of inches of water that fell as rain and snow in
these years were 1826, 21.81 inches, in 1827, 27.92 inches, and
in 1828, 22.91 inches, or in the mean 24.21 inches.

At London, it has sometimes been said that evaporation from
the surface of an open reservoir is very nearly equal in a year to
the rainfall which occurs there, though according to Daniell the
mean annual rainfall at London is only 22 inches, while nearly 24
inches of water evaporate there annually from open reservoirs.
As he states the matter, one and three-quarters inches more water
evaporate than fall at London. At Birmingham, in 1843, 26.72
inches of rain fell and 31.98 inches of water evaporated, i. e. the
evaporation was 5.27 inches more than the rainfall. Howard at
Plaistow found, as the average of three years, that 21 inches of
water evaporated from the surface of a vessel in a year, while 23
inches were caught in an adjacent rain-gauge. Dividing the year
into terms of four months, he found on the average,

	Rainfall.	Evaporation.
For the winter period	7.28	3.66
" spring "	7.79	10.41
" summer "	8.08	7.06

Greaves at Lee Bridge in England, found as the average of 14
years, that the annual rainfall was 25.7 inches and that the
amount of evaporation from a water-surface was 20.7 inches. It
is to be remarked that in Greaves's experiments the gauge for
measuring evaporation was kept afloat in a flowing stream. The
average evaporation from the water-surface during summer was
15.9 inches and during winter 4.8 inches. Very considerable
variations were noticed from year to year. Thus, in 1862 the
annual evaporation was 17.3 inches, while the hot season of 1868
brought it up to 26.9 inches. According to Burnell, the mean
daily evaporation from the surface of a reservoir or other body of

water in England is considered to vary from the 12th to the 16th of an inch.

Vallé at Dijon, as the mean of seven years, found that 26 inches of water evaporated from a reservoir per annum, while the rainfall was 27 inches. Hoffmann at Giessen observed that from May to September 457 tenths of cubic inches of rain fell, while 559 tenths of cubic inches evaporated from an open vessel that was charged daily with water. This evaporating-dish was placed in a garden six feet from the ground; it was somewhat shielded from wind, but not from rain or from the sun. Golding at Copenhagen, as the mean of twelve years' observations, noted that the rainfall was 22 inches, and that the evaporation from a dish of water was 28 inches. He found also that 44 inches of water were exhaled in a year from long grass grown in soil kept saturated with water in a vessel that had no outlet, and that 30 inches were exhaled from a second plot similarly moistened where the grass was kept short.

Meister in Bavaria, and Grouven in North Germany, observed in the year 1863 that the amount of evaporation from the surface of water kept in the shade was larger than all the water that fell as rain, snow, dew, etc., during the year. Grouven found even that there were but two months in the year (March and November) when the rainfall of the month was larger than the evaporation from the surface of a dish of water. Schuebler claimed in his day that the average evaporation of water per diem during the growing season, from one square foot of surface, was, from water, 1 line; from sod, 2–3 lines; from bare soil, 0.6 line; and from woodland, 0.25 line.

At Palermo, experiments made by Tacchini indicated that temperature is the prime productive cause of evaporation, and that this action is promoted by the force of the wind and impeded by humidity in the air. Tacchini observed the amount of evaporation both from vessels of water that were freely exposed to the sun and outside air, and that from vessels which were shielded from the direct action of the sun and the wind. It appeared in the course of a year that 2.25 times as much water evaporated from the sheltered vessel as fell in the form of rain, while from the exposed vessel the annual evaporation was very nearly thrice as large as the rainfall. Reckoning by months, evaporation from the sheltered vessel was nearly equal to the rainfall in January,

February, March and December, and it was much larger than the rainfall in all the other months of the year. From the exposed vessel evaporation was about equal to the rainfall only in January and December; it was much larger than the rainfall in all the other months.

Evaporation from the Soil.

The foregoing experiments, it will be noticed, refer merely to the evaporation of water from vessels artificially charged therewith; and it will be observed how very different the results are from those of the experiments, made with drain-gauges, on the percolation of rainfall. Thus of the 26.6 inches of rain that fell in a year on Dickinson's three-foot gauge only 15.3 inches were restored directly to the atmosphere, while 11.3 inches passed away through the soil to the rivers.

But it is none the less true that more water may evaporate from a soil which is very wet, than can evaporate from a sheet of mere water. That is to say, in case a soil saturated with water is so situated that the liquid cannot escape by draining away, evaporation may be more rapid from this soil than it could be from water by itself. This fact may be due in part to asperities of the soil which increase the evaporative surface, and in part perhaps to the color of the soil. It consists at all events with Wollny's observation that the heat absorbed by dark-colored wet soils accelerates the evaporation of water from them. Wilhelm urges that the evaporation from wet earth is more rapid in proportion as the surface is more uneven. When he separated the coarse from the fine portions of a soil and moistened both, he found that the coarse material lost water by evaporation much faster than the fine earth because it exposed a much larger surface to the air.

He suggests that in dry regions, in order to retain in the soil the water that has been brought to it by the winter's rains, it will be well not to plough the land in the spring, or at the least, not to leave it lying in rough furrows at that season for any length of time. This idea has long been familiar to English farmers, some of whom have insisted that on light soils in dry climates, where drought is the most serious obstacle that has to be contended with, special care should be taken to retain the moisture in the land. For growing turnips in such cases they direct that the land should not be ploughed in the spring, because evaporation from the loosened earth would be too rapid. In the spring, they say, the land should be worked entirely with cultivators, harrows and rollers, in order that the moisture in the soil may be kept there, and that a good start may be secured for the turnip-plants.

Schulze found at Rostock on the Baltic, during the six months May to October, 1859, that 596,000 grm. of water, or, in other words, a layer of water nearly 21½ inches thick, evaporated from an open vessel one square metre in area that was daily filled with this liquid. The vessel was kept on a stand three feet from the ground, in the middle of a garden that was somewhat sheltered from north winds, but was uncovered, and not shielded in any way from sun or air.

In contrast with the evaporation from mere water, a variety of experiments were made in similar vessels, upon soils both in their natural state, and when kept more or less saturated with water. In the cases where the earths were kept wet, the bottoms of the vessels were perforated, so that rain-water might flow through into a trap below. One set of vessels were charged with so-called dry earths as follows: white sea-sand, with a water-holding power of 26%, that contained 19% of water; garden-loam, with a capacity to hold 94% of water, that contained 11%; and moor-earth, the capacity of which for water was 170%, and which contained 49%. The mean daily evaporation of water from these dry earths, during the months stated, is given in the following table, together with the rainfall, comparative force of the wind, etc. The area of surface in each case was one square metre.

	Loam. grm.	Sand. grm.	Moor-Earth. grm	Water. grm.	Rain. grm.	Moisture of Air, %	Temp. ° C.	Wind.
May,	630	965	751	4760	8864	67.5	13.7	20
June,	1041	1082	1160	4543	25927	76.6	16.9	14
July,	864	915	859	3563	32526	77.6	19.0	5
August,	1076	1093	1136	3245	69138	77.2	19.5	4

The rains of July were at the end of the month, and show their influence upon the increased evaporation of August.

Other experiments were made with loam that was kept half wet, i. e. half as much water was added to it as it could hold; and in other experiments both the loam and the moor-earth were kept saturated to ⅔ their capacity. Finally, experiments were made with fully saturated earths. From the fully saturated loam and moor-earth the mean daily evaporation from a square metre of surface for the several months was as follows, rainy days being excluded from the account :—

	Saturated Loam. grm.	Saturated Moor-Earth. grm.
June 25–30	7600	7783
July	4680	4935
August	4433	4600
September	2640	2713
October	972	1076

Whence it appears that the wet moor-earth gave off water rather more freely than the wet loam.

The behavior of the partially saturated loam will appear from the following table, which gives the average daily evaporation, as before.

	¼ wet Loam. grm.	½ wet Loam. grm.	Saturated Loam. grm.	Water. grm.
June 25–30 . . .	6248	....	7600	5587
July	4116	....	4856	3847
August	3137	....	4405	3448
September . . .	2722	2965	3025	2569
October	1113	1181	1026	907

Influence of Shade on Evaporation.

In numerous experiments made in Bavaria, as reported by Ebermayer, it was found, in general, that during the summer months rather more water evaporates from a layer of earth half a foot deep that is kept saturated with moisture, than will evaporate from an equally large surface of water, though occasionally the reverse of this is true, since much depends upon the amount of wind that blows. In woodland, where the movements of air are comparatively feeble, evaporation of water from the saturated earth is almost always larger than that from mere water similarly sheltered from wind.

Naturally enough the evaporation of water from saturated woodland soil, even that which is bare of leaves, is less than from saturated soil in the open. It was in fact from 61 to 63% less. From saturated woodland soil covered with leaves the evaporation was still less (22% less); i. e. both trees and leaves upon the ground beneath trees work to hinder the evaporation of water from the surface of the ground. In general, the evaporation of water from soil covered with litter and kept in woodland was 6¼ times smaller than the evaporation from bare saturated soil in open fields.

At most of the Bavarian stations the yearly rainfall was larger than the amount of evaporation from the surface of water that

was shaded from the sun's rays and shielded from rain, but
kept in open fields; while in the close forests the evaporation
from dishes of water was so small as to be very much less than
the rain and snow that came to the ground in such situations in
the course of the year.   During the summer months more water
was almost always lost by evaporation from the dishes kept in
fields than fell as rain, as had been noticed before by Hoffmann,
Dufour and others, while in the woods the rainfall exceeded the
evaporation even in summer.   In winter, when the evaporation
was small anyway, there was a great excess of rainfall both in the
woods and in the open.

In the course of the year, 36 cubic inches of water evaporated
on the average from dishes kept in the woods for every 100 c. in.
that evaporated from dishes in the fields; i. e. evaporation from
a sheet of water in the woods was 2.8 times less, i. e. 64% less
than in the fields.   In summer, evaporation from dishes of
water was four times more rapid than in winter, and it was nearly
three times less rapid in the woods than in the fields.   429 c. in.
evaporated in the woods in summer, and 111 c. in. in winter,
while in the fields the quantities were 1223 c. in. in summer, and
314 c. in. in winter.   It was noticed that by night evaporation
was $\frac{1}{4}$ to $\frac{1}{2}$ less than by day.

Wollny found that water evaporated most rapidly from sand
that was saturated with water, and least rapidly from peat thus
saturated, while Haberlandt found that both sand and loam, even
when they are not completely saturated with moisture, lose more
water by evaporation than is lost from an actual sheet of water.
According to Eser, the amount of evaporation from any soil depends first of all on the amount of water contained in the soil, i. e.
the moister the soil, the larger the evaporation.   Even from soils
of unlike physical character, very nearly equal amounts of water
will evaporate provided all the soils are thoroughly wet.   So too,
when other conditions are equal, the amount of evaporation from
a soil will depend upon the capacity of that soil to hold water,
and upon the amount of water which comes to the soil either from
above or from below.   Masure found that from a soil which
is tolerably, but not excessively wet, water may evaporate
just about as rapidly as from mere water; but from drier soils
evaporation is not so rapid as from water by itself.   He urges
that the evaporation is less rapid in proportion as the soil is drier.

Evaporation from Arable land less than the Rainfall.

It is plain from all this, that the yearly evaporation from a field wholly bare of vegetation must generally be less than the rainfall. In actual farm practice there must be wide variations in this regard, according to the character of the soil, the contour of the district, and the kind of vegetation, as well as the amount and the distribution of the rainfall. On a light soil bare of vegetation and fully exposed to sun and wind, evaporation will often be rapid immediately after rain; but when once the surface soil has become dry, the rate of evaporation may be greatly diminished. On the other hand, where crops are growing, the evaporation will be more constant on the whole, though sometimes less conspicuous immediately after rain. From woodland in particular, there is always continuous and rapid exhalation of water from the foliage during the spring and summer months, although the surface of the ground is shielded so that comparatively little evaporation can occur there. Light showers, even though frequent, may be of little use to crops because of the rapid evaporation of the water which they have brought.

It appears that even frozen water, or rather melting ice, may serve as a useful store of moisture, at least in certain situations and for some crops. Mr. Barneby reports of Assinobia, on the line of the Canada Pacific Railroad, that even in late July some of the soil still holds the winter's frost at a depth of several feet below the surface. He says: "This underground layer of frozen earth is believed to explain the wonderful fertility of the soil; as the frost, in gradually coming to the surface during the summer months, creates a moisture which, meeting the warmth from above, forms a kind of natural hot-bed. This moisture counteracts the scarcity of rain during the spring and summer, and accounts for the grain being forced with such amazing rapidity after the late sowing; for in point of fact grain crops are not usually sown until early in May, and yet they are harvested at the end of August."

Modes of controlling the Ground-water.

It has been shown already in treating of the capillary power of soils and of the percolation of rainfall, that many soils rich in clay or in humus retain water so forcibly that it is often a matter of the utmost practical importance that means should be provided artificially for the hastening of percolation, in order that the excess of moisture may quickly be removed and that by means of tillage the land may be brought to a good capillary condition.

The remark is true both of situations where the supply of water is renewed constantly or frequently—either by rains, or by flowing or percolating from higher levels—and where the land in its natural condition is unable to discharge the water rapidly enough to permit of the soil's being brought into a fit condition for the growth of crops, and it is also true of fields which, though surcharged with water during the rainy season, may dry out utterly at a time even of moderate drought. It will be instructive therefore to consider briefly what steps have been taken by farmers, at one time and another, to put the soils of their fields into proper relations with water.

The open ditch seen so often in bog-meadows is one simple example. Instances are abundant where the level of the ground-water has been reduced by means of such ditches to a point which permits the cultivation of English grasses, potatoes, squashes, or the like; particularly when the excessively high capillary power of the bog earth is mitigated by a dressing of sand or gravel.

The method employed on the sunken polders of Holland is not dissimilar, though, in the lack of any natural outfall there, the ditches have to be pumped out continually in order that the ground-water may drain into them. In case a drought occurs, the pumps are stopped, and the ground-water is left in the land to support the crops.

Trees as Pumping Engines.

The planting of willows and poplars, that is to say, of trees that love water, is another device for drying over-wet pastures, or even meadows so that sweet grasses may work in. Inasmuch, as has been shown, the exhalation of moisture from mere grass sod can bedew and obscure glass in the twinkling of an eye, it is manifest that the great mass of foliage which is concentrated into the space occupied by a single tree must be an engine of no small power. In point of fact, trees do pump off and evaporate enormous quantities of water, and they thus hinder the stagnation of it beneath the soil.

Some idea of the efficacy of this method may be got by considering the amount of leaf surface which is presented by a good-sized tree. Professor Asa Gray computed, some years ago, that

the Washington Elm at Cambridge, which, though a fine tree
when in its prime, was never extraordinarily large, must produce
every year some seven millions of leaves, equal to 200,000
square feet of surface, or about five acres.   But since the crown
of this tree is no more than about seventy feet in diameter it
cannot cover as much as one-tenth of an acre of land.

It is to the enormous extent of leaf surface thus presented to
the air that the drying effect of trees must be attributed, for it is
known that less water can evaporate from any limited area of
leaf surface than evaporates from a similar surface of water.
Unger found that, in general, about three times as much water
evaporates from a measured surface of water as from a similar
surface of leaves, and this conclusion has been corroborated by
the experiments of Sachs.   Occasionally, indeed, Unger found
that the evaporation from water was five or six times larger than
from leaves.

But it is none the less true, that, when vigorous plants are
grown upon a given surface of soil, they will evaporate much
more water than would evaporate either from the soil or from a
water-surface of similar area, because the evaporation from the
leaf surface is added to that from the soil-surface.   Thus, in the
experiments of Schulze, at Rostock, barley was sown in June
upon garden-earth contained in a vessel one square metre in area,
and duckweed was floated on a square metre of water.   Grass-sod
also, and other plants, were set out in garden-earth contained in
similar vessels, and all were copiously watered, and kept in a
garden.   Though some of the plants suffered from exposure to
rain, and perhaps from improper transplanting also, they gave
off very large quantities of water, as will appear from the following table, which gives the mean daily evaporation in lines from
water in a dish, and from the several kinds of plants, as well as
the rainfall, the humidity of the air, the temperature, and the
force of the wind.

	Water. Lines.	Nightshade (Solanum ni-gram).	Grass (Poa annua.)	Barley.	Houseleek (Sempervivum tectorum.)
June	2.05	3.13	2.92	2.08	——
July	1.60	3.27	2.74	2.58	——
Aug.	1.41	2.50	1.95	1.70	0.63
Sept.	0.81	——	1.44	——	0.35
Oct.	0.36	——	0.60	——	0.39

	Duckweed (Lemna minor).	Rainfall.	Moisture of Air, per Cent.	Temp. °C.	Force of Wind.
June	——	11.6	76.6	16.9	14
July	——	14.5	77.6	19.0	5
Aug.	1.54	7.2	77.2	19.5	4
Sept.	0.60	31.2	85.1	14.1	7
Oct.	0.30	6.4	92.9	9.5	5

On comparing the evaporative power of the plant Xeranthemum bracteatum with the evaporation from an exposed surface of water, Masure found that three times as much water was transpired by the plant as evaporated from the water-surface. Pfaff, at Erlangen, in Germany, studied in detail the power of an oak-tree to transpire water. He found that his tree had 700,000 and more leaves, which between the 18th of May and the 24th of October, that is to say, from the time the leaves appeared until they fell, transpired 264,000 lb. of water into the air during the daytime. But this amount of water was $8\frac{1}{5}$ times more than fell as rain upon an area equal in circumference to the tree-top. In addition to this, it is known that about one-quarter of the summer rainfall may cling to the leaves of trees and evaporate therefrom. In a similar way, Vaillant observed that an oak-tree, 69 feet high and $8\frac{2}{3}$ feet in circumference at $3\frac{1}{4}$ feet from the ground, transpired of a fine summer's day 4,400 lb. of water.

European foresters have often noticed that clay lands are apt to become wet, and gradually to get into a springy or swampy condition after trees have been cut off from them; and that conversely, such lands dry out when new trees have been planted upon them, and have attained to some size. In this country, N. P. Willis long ago wrote of the upper Susquehanna, "There is a curious fact I have learned for the first time in this wild country, that as the forest is cleared, new springs rise to the surface of the ground, as if at the touch of the sunshine." It is well known indeed to foresters that, in many situations, groves of trees, and especially those which are evergreeen, act to dry out land which might be soggy or swampy if it were left bare.

"Root-Ditches."

In some districts in England where the enclosures are small and there are numerous hedgerows beset with pollards and timber trees, so much harm is done by the tree-roots that a practice known as root-ditching is prevalent. A ditch or drain, some 20 inches deep, is dug around the edge of the field, parallel with and about 10 feet distant from the hedges. By this means, the roots of the trees are cut off and prevented from invading the field proper. It is said that were it not for these root-ditches an incredible amount of damage would be done to the crops by the trees, particularly in dry seasons. It is the stealing of water by such trees as ashes, elms and poplars which explains in good part the detestation in which these trees are held by most farmers and gardeners. Each of these trees has been thought to be specially apt to suck the land dry; though it is not wholly improbable that the fungi which grow upon the roots of trees may take so much and such kinds of food from the soil as to render it unsuitable for the growth of many crops.

In studying this question of the drying out of land by trees, Risler dug up samples of earth from contiguous fields, on which different kinds of plants had been grown, or were growing, and determined how much water was contained in the earth in each instance. The soil of the locality was a stiff clay, and the conditions to which the several fields were exposed were similar, excepting the differences due to unlike crops. The pieces of woodland were some 25 or 30 acres in extent.

Date.	The samples of Earth were taken from	Per Cent of Water in the Soil, at a Depth of		
		6 to 8 in.	16 to 18 in.	Mean.
Aug. 25.	An unplanted part of a garden not far from fruit-trees	15.00	17.00	16.0
" 26.	A field that had borne winter vetches, and had been ploughed after the harvest in July. . . .	11.00	18.20	14.6
" 26.	A stubble-field, not touched since the oats were harvested	7.57	17.38	12.5
" 26.	Woodland, oaks 9 years old . . .	10.57	13.95	12.3
" 26.	Woodland, oaks 35 to 40 years old .	9.53 .	7.54	8.5
" 26.	Woodland, spruces 20 years old . .	12.85	4.46	8.6
" 24.	Vineyard	9.25	10.41	9.8

Not only did it appear that towards the end of August the woodland soils had become drier than those of the garden and fields, but it was noticed that in the subsequent months the forest soils became drier still, for the rains of early autumn happened to be light, and a large part of the water that fell upon the tree-tops was caught there and evaporated without ever coming to the ground.

Surface-Drains.

The running of simple water-furrows with a plough across those parts of a field that are liable to suffer from moisture is another device of merit, and the system of furrows may, of course, be made as simple or elaborate as the case demands. Many fields which might be injured if water were left to stand upon them may be greatly benefited by providing means to prevent such stagnation. Some little trouble must naturally be taken to clear the furrows at their points of intersection, and wherever earth has clogged them through imperfect action of the plough. It is to be noted, however, that the purpose of the water-furrow, like its construction, is superficial. It is useful to remove any excess of water that may fall in a violent shower, and may consequently, sometimes be almost as important on land that is tile-drained as on that which has no artificial drainage. It has been observed in some parts of England, after the soil has been well opened by several years of deep cultivation with steam ploughs, that the necessity of having open water-furrows has been very much lessened. Some farmers have been enabled to dispense with them altogether, while others now use them only occasionally on heavy land in order to relieve the surface as quickly as possible during very heavy rainstorms.

It should be noted that in many districts of light soils, water-furrows are often drawn upon cultivated hillsides for the purpose of affording a ready outlet for the rain-water, so that the soil shall not be gullied or washed away bodily. The crops are planted in rows also, which are drawn in harmony with the water-furrows and suitably connected with them. As a general rule these hillside ditches should be made broad and shallow rather than narrow and deep, because water moving slowly over a considerable breadth of surface will be less apt to scour out the soil than would be the case if it were to run rapidly through a single furrow. It is no very difficult matter to construct shallow ditches, with shoulders on the side towards the base of the hill, by simply ploughing (best with a swivel plough) a number of furrows across the slope of the hill, or at the point where the ditch is to be, and turning these selfsame furrows again and again with the ploughshare — always in one and the same direction — until the furrow slices have been heaped up to a rough bank on the one side while a wide shallow ditch has been opened on the other.

Land-Beds.

The throwing up of beds or ridges upon moist or springy land is another method, used not infrequently upon the somewhat sloping banks of brooks and ponds, and upon level clay-lands also. Indeed, there are to be found in practice numerous gradations between the merest water-furrow and the most pronounced land-bed; the same general idea that the surface of the field shall be made water below drawn from the hedges. By this means the roots of the trees are cut off and prevented from draining the soil proper. It is said, that were it not for these precautions as an ... the amount of damage would be done to the crops by the trees, particularly in dry seasons. It is the sucking of water by such trees as ashes, elms and poplars which explains in good part the detestation in which these trees are held by most farmers and gardeners. Each of these trees has been thought to be specially apt to suck the land dry; though it is not wholly improbable that the fungi, which grow upon the roots of trees may take so much and such kinds of food from the soil as to render it unsuitable for the growth of many crops.

In studying the question of the drying out of land by trees, ... dug up samples of earth from contiguous fields, on which different kinds of plants had been grown, or were growing, and determined how much water was contained in the earth in each instance. The soil of the locality was a stiff clay, and the conditions to which the several fields were exposed were similar, excepting the differences due to unlike crops. The pieces of woodland were some 25 or 30 acres in extent.

Date.	The samples of Earth were taken from	Per Cent of Water in the Soil, at a Depth of		
		6 to 8 in.	16 to 18 in.	Mean.
Aug. 25.	An unplanted part of a garden not far from fruit-trees	15.00	17.00	16.0
" 25.	A field that had borne winter vetches, and had been ploughed after the harvest in July. . . .	11.00	18.20	14.6
" 25.	A stubble field, not touched since the oats were harvested	7.57	17.38	12.5
" 25.	Woodland, oaks 9 years old . . .	10.57	13.95	12.2
" 25.	Woodland, oaks 35 to 40 years old .	9.53	7.54	8.5
" 25.	Woodland, spruces 20 years old . .	12.85	4.44	8.6
" 24.	Vineyard	9.25	10.41	

Not only did it appear that towards the end of Aug... woodland soils had become drier than those of the ... fields, but it was noticed that in the subsequent mon... soils became drier still, for the rains of early aut... be light, and a large part of the water that ... was caught there and evaporated without ...

Surface-Drain...

The running of simple water-furrow... parts of a field that are liable to su...

device of merit, and the system of furrows may, of course, be made as simple or elaborate as the case demands. Many fields which might be injured if water were left to stand upon them may be greatly benefited by providing means to prevent such stagnation. Some little trouble must naturally be taken to clear the furrows at their points of intersection, and wherever earth has clogged them through imperfect action of the plough. It is to be noted, however, that the purpose of the water-furrow, like its construction, is superficial. It is useful to remove any excess of water that may fall in a violent shower, and may consequently, sometimes be almost as important on land that is tile-drained as on that which has no artificial drainage. It has been observed in some parts of England, after the soil has been well opened by several years of deep cultivation with steam ploughs, that the necessity of having open water-furrows has been very much lessened. Some farmers have been enabled to dispense with them altogether, while others now use them only occasionally on heavy land in order to relieve the surface as quickly as possible during very heavy rainstorms.

It should be noted that in many districts of light soils, water-furrows are often drawn upon cultivated hillsides for the purpose of affording a ready outlet for the rain-water, so that the soil may not be gullied or washed away bodily. The crops are planted in rows also, which are drawn in harmony with the water-furrows and suitably connected with them. As a general rule these hillside ditches should be made broad and shallow rather than narrow and deep, because water moving slowly over a considerable breadth of surface will be to slope sufficiently that no water can remain standing upon the land having led to the construction of many varieties of ridges.

As a rule it would appear that on stiff, level, retentive soils in England the ridges are made narrower according as the soil is stiffer, and that they are laid up in somewhat different shapes according to the crops which the land is to bear. For winter wheat, ridges which are comparatively high and narrow have been commended, while for grass they may be made low and wide. Marshall, in his day, suggested that beds half a rod wide might be best for wheat, and that for grass two rods might be a good width.

On the clay farms of Norfolk and Suffolk in England it is said to be customary to plough up the land into " stiches " of such width that they are adapted to the size of the drills which are there habitually in use. Thus the beds may be laid up two yards wide for a bout of the drill, or sometimes they are made one yard wide for one stroke of the drill. Another account says that the beds are made 7.5 or 9 feet wide, and that the drills are constructed to sow either a whole or a half stich at once, leaving, for wheat, about one foot in the furrows unsown.

A whole drill, to cover a stich, was drawn by four horses for wheat-sowing, two horses in each furrow. Sometimes 6 horses were used in very large drills that covered a 9-foot stich. Commonly, however, on such large beds, half-drills were used that sowed only half the bed at once. For such drills the shafts were " quartered," so that the two horses walked in one furrow and were followed by one of the wheels, while the other wheel ran upon the top of the bed ; or the half-drill was fitted with a slip-axle which could be lengthened out and adjusted so that the wheel most distant from the horses could run in the further furrow.

The other implements of tillage also, such as harrows, rollers, and horse-hoes, were, in like manner, constructed to fit the beds so that the horses should walk in the furrows, and quarter-carts were used for removing the crops in some cases, such as roots and cabbages. In these carts, the shafts are so placed that the horse walks before the right-hand wheel in one furrow, while the other wheel runs in the other furrow, and the body of the cart passes over the land-bed. By means of these devices both hoofs and wheels are kept off the tilled land and always in the furrows, so that after the land has once been ploughed, the risk of injuring its tilth by poaching, trampling, and rolling is practically done away with.

Need of Ridges on Wet Clay.

Such ridges as the foregoing are in some sort a necessity on heavy clays in wet climates. In some parts of England when wheat was to be grown on clayey land it has always been deemed indispensably necessary that the fields should be laid up in sharp ridges as a means of maintaining tilth. Experience had taught that if the land were to be laid down flat, or even if the tops of the land-beds were made too flat, the surface soil would be converted to liquid mud by the first rain which might fall after the wheat had been sown, and that this sea of mud would form so hard a crust on drying that the wheat would be smothered. But considerable labor and trouble are necessarily involved in the making of the ridges, and no crop is grown on that part of the land where the ditches or interspaces are, unless, indeed, the land is in grass. As will be explained in another chapter, stiff clay lands are much less frequently cultivated nowadays than they were formerly.

It is noticeable that on low-lying meadows the purpose of land-beds, like that of open ditches, is to lower the level of the ground-water slightly, so as to permit the better kinds of grasses to grow. The idea differs in the two cases only that by the ditch water is taken from the land, while in building a land-bed, an effort is made to take the land from the water.

It is noteworthy also, that this idea of raising the level of the soil, without lowering the original level of the water, is a thoroughly natural one. The process is to be seen in every wild swamp or bog where the height of the soil has been increased by the growth and slow deposition of water-plants, and of the products of their partial decay. Many of the numerous patches of bog-land which have been brought under cultivation in New England are to all intents and purposes land-beds, which have been built up naturally through the growth of aquatic plants. That drains have to be cut after all to depress the level of the water in these natural land-beds is due mainly to the exceedingly retentive character of the vegetable matter with which they have been built.

Beds across Slopes.

Land-beds were formerly a favorite device of the English farmers. They doubtless mark one stage in the progress of a country towards civilization. Thus Tull, writing in 1733, argues as a matter of practical experience, that for improving cold, poachy hillsides, land-beds should be ploughed up in pairs across the slope of the hill. He says: " The two sorts of land most liable to be over-glutted with water are hills whereof the upper stratum or staple is mould lying upon a stratum of clay ; and generally all strong, deep land. Hills are made wet and spewy by the rain-water which falls upon and soaks into them, but being stopped by the clay lying beneath the surface or staple, cannot enter the clay, and for want of entrance spreads itself upon it.

" As water naturally tends downwards, it is, by the incumbent mould, partly stopped in its descent from the upper towards the lower side of the hill ; and being followed and pressed upon by more water from above, it is forced to rise up into the mould, which it fills as a cistern does a fountain. The land of such a hill is not the less wet or spewy for being laid up in ridges, if they be made from the higher to the lower part of the field, for the force of the water's weight continued will raise it so as to cause it to issue out at the very tops of those ridges. The earth becomes a sort of pap or batter, and being like a quagmire, the feet of men or cattle in going over it will sink in till they come to the clay.

"Therefore it is a better method to plough the ridges across the hill almost horizontally, that their parting furrows lying open, may each serve as a drain to the ridge next below it. When the plough has made the bottom of these horizontal furrows a few inches deeper than the surface of the clay, the water will run to their ends very securely without rising into the mould, provided no part of the furrows be lower than their ends. These parting furrows and their ridges must be made more or less oblique according to the form and declivity of the hill, but the more horizontal they are, the sooner the rain-water will run off the lands, for in that case it will run to the furrows by the shortest possible course. . . I find upon trial that narrow ridges, no more than six feet wide — doubtless those no more than four or five feet wide would answer — are as effectual as any other for carrying the water off from any clayey hill. . . After wet weather the ridges will be fit to be ploughed much sooner than level ground."

Half a century later, Marshall urged a similar plan. If the beds are thrown across a slope, he says, taking care merely to give descent enough that water may find its way along the interfurrows, none of the rain-water that falls upon the beds will ever have to run any farther than the width of a single bed before it is caught by an interfurrow, even supposing that it falls upon the upper edge of the bed. But where the beds run up and down the hillside, much of the rain-water which falls upon them will flow over their entire length, from the top to the bottom of the hill, without finding its way into the parallel furrows. Unless the up and down beds be crowned tolerably high at their centres, there will be comparatively little tendency for water to run off sideways into or towards the open furrows.

Making of Land-Beds.

Land-beds, such as are made in this country for the sake of growing grass, have the merit that they can be cheaply constructed. The making of them is a mere matter of ploughing and harrowing. An approved method is to measure off the land and plough a furrow at the place which is to be the middle of the bed. Then plough deep furrows on either side of the first furrow so as to "shut it," as the term is, i. e. so as to bury the first furrow; and so go on ploughing the land up towards the centre until the edge of the plot is reached, where open furrows will be left on either side to serve as ditches. The bed is then harrowed and left to itself for the earth to settle, after which the operation of ploughing may be repeated. It happens ordinarily that the beds are ploughed in the same way, year after year, whenever the land needs to be ploughed, and that they are thus kept in shape or even made higher with the lapse of time. Of course, the dead furrows at the edge of the bed need to be cleared out and made to dip so that water may flow in them. One very old plan was to drag a log of wood through the open furrows to make them smooth for the easy passage of the surface-water. It would be well, however, nowadays, when practicable, to make the ditches wide with edges sloping so gradually that the mowing machine could be driven through them.

Celtic Land-Beds or Ridges.

Beside the comparatively shallow land-beds proper, such as are still used, much higher beds or ridges were formerly in vogue. Until a comparatively recent period, the soil of many districts in England, no matter what the crop, was kept permanently laid up in broad high ridges, which had existed from time immemorial, and the purpose of which had even been forgotten. During a very long period the tendency was to make these ridges continually higher and higher, by always ploughing the land in one and the same direction, and it is not improbable that many of them must still exist, since it is not easy to destroy one of them all at once without turning up an undue quantity of unproductive subsoil.

These ridges are said to have prevailed particularly in the countries which had been brought under the influence of the Roman civilization. In other words, they were most common in districts that had been longest settled, for the Romans were accustomed to overrun and occupy inhabited places.

As to the size of the ridges, Marshall, writing in 1796 of the Vale of Gloucester, says that the usual ridge of that period and locality was about 8 yards wide and from 2 to 2½ feet high. Some ridges that he measured were 15 yards wide, by 4 feet or more high; others were 20 and 25 yards wide, and high in proportion, — so high, indeed, that a horseman riding in one ditch could hardly see his companion riding in the ditch at the other edge of the bed.

There can be no doubt that the original idea of heaping up the soil in this way was to render some portion of it dry and warm, by removing it from the influence of ground-water; though in the course of centuries the reasons of the practice were so far lost sight of that ridges were built, not only upon clays and the other fine soils which are liable to become muddy and impervious when soaked with rain, but upon all kinds of soils, even in elevated positions and upon porous subsoils. The ditches between the ridges, moreover, were neglected and suffered to become clogged, often to such an extent that they stood full of stagnant water in wet seasons. Towards the close of the last century, instances were described where the tops of the ridges for 6 or 8 feet across had come to be the only profitable part of the soil, while the furrows and the land adjacent to them were mere pools and reservoirs of water.

" Lazy-Beds."

It needs to be said, however, that at the beginning and on poor land one subsidiary motive for heaping up the soil in beds was to obtain a sufficient depth of loam in which to grow crops. In Ireland, potatoes and other crops are still often grown on so-called lazy-beds which are beds or ridges made with earth taken from ditches or alleys that are left between the beds ; and it is noticed that not only the depth but the breadth also of the alleys is regulated by the character of the soil. When the original soil is of good depth the alleys are made narrow and deep, i. e. they are true ditches which serve as outlets for ground-water from the bottoms of the beds, but in case the soil is naturally shallow, wide alleys are made in order that earth enough may be got to cover the potato sets and to "mould" the young plants. These shallow alleys act of course only as surface-drains. Unlike the deeper ditches, they can have but little direct influence upon the ground-water. Considered as a method of husbandry, the making of lazy-beds is undoubtedly an efficient means of reclaiming rough land, and especially land which needs draining, though it is manifest that the system is specially adapted to the circumstances of primitive or backward races, so situated that they cannot maintain cattle for purposes of draught. Gasparin says, however, that this method has been employed with great success for reclaiming certain fens on the River Rhone which were formerly subject to inundation. Great ditches were dug at intervals wide enough and deep enough to supply earth for raising the intervening land-beds to a height sufficient to permit of the growing upon them of agricultural plants.

Ridging augments Surface.

Until a comparatively recent period there was a popular belief in England that the soil of the old, high ridges had been heaped up merely to increase the amount of surface. Tull insisted strongly that the amount of surface gained by ridges may perhaps be worthy of some consideration. "If," as he says, "a flat piece be ploughed into ridges, and if in each sixteen feet breadth there be an empty furrow of two feet, and yet by the height and roundness of the ridges they have eighteen feet of surface capable of producing grain equally to eighteen feet whilst the piece was flat, there will be one-eighth part of profitable ground or surface gained more than it had when level; and this, I believe, experience will prove if the thing were well examined into. . . Vegetables being fed by the earth require much more of its surface to nourish them than is necessary for them to stand on. . . It is to be observed that all vegetables have horizontal roots and roots parallel to the earth's surface or superficies, and unless those roots have a sufficient superficies of earth to range in for nourishment of a plant, the stems and branches cannot prosper. . . . Where a plain is ploughed up into moderate ridges, their height being in proportion to the depth of the staple, below which the plough must take nothing into the ridges, the soil is equally rich whether it be ploughed plain or ridged up, and as the surface is increased in the ridges there is nothing . . . that shows why this increased surface should not produce more vegetables than the same earth could do whilst it was level."

As Marshall has intimated, this reasoning applies with special force to the case where the ridges are used for pasturage, and it is evident enough that the high ridges must have had no little merit upon retentive soils, and for pasture-land in countries liable to much rain. In a field thus laid up there was always a variety of herbage suited to every season, just as there was a variety of soil and of moisture. In a wet season some portion of the ridge would still afford sweet pasturage and dry land for the stock to rest upon, while even in the driest seasons the furrows still remained green. In Brittany, Rieffel noticed instances where the vegetation of crops growing on ridges was a fortnight earlier than that of similar crops on adjacent flat land, and it is manifest that in flat, wet countries ridges must be well suited for such crops as are to remain on the land during the winter. There can be no doubt that ridges enabled the earlier inhabitants of Europe to grow wheat in many situations where this crop could not have been grown before the invention of them.

A capital illustration of the utility of ridges has been noticed by Milton Whitney on the cotton-growing islands of South Carolina. He says, " When Sea Island cotton was first introduced into South Carolina, about 100 years ago, it failed to mature before frost, and for this reason the crop was lost. The crop ripens now very much earlier, so that there is no danger from frost. The planters have evolved a very peculiar system of cultivation, the plants are grown on very high beds or ridges from 12 to 18 inches high, and from 4 to 5 feet broad, . . . to keep the roots of the plant in thoroughly drained and comparatively dry soil. The subsoil is never disturbed, and soft salt mud from the adjacent marshes, and salt marsh-grass and litter of all kinds are placed in the bottom of the bed, effectually keeping the roots from developing down into the moist subsoil. The bed itself is very highly manured. . . In the interior of the island the land is not so well drained, and does not yield as productive crops of cotton nor as fine staple, though the planters themselves believe that under-drainage and high beds with heavy applications of salt mud to keep the roots from developing down into the subsoil, will check the growth of the plant and enable as good crops to be grown here as elsewhere, but as these lands are inland, both the mud and drainage are costly and difficult to apply."

In Europe, the old high ridges have been wholly superseded by systems of underground drains. Their insufficiency was clearly seen by Arthur Young, who, writing in 1769, urged that the ridges should everywhere be ploughed down, and the whole field be hollow-drained. Practically, it has turned out to be a costly matter to throw down the ridges; yet this must be done before drains are laid, for in case lines of tiles are buried beneath the furrows without lowering the crests of the ridges, the action of the drains will be local rather than general, much of the land will fail to be benefited, and some of it, at the crowns of the ridges, will be made too dry. (Hoskyns, Roy. Ag. Soc. Jour., 1856, 17, 327).

It is now recognized that the ridges are a characteristic of the husbandry of the Celts, who preceded the present races as occupiers of the soil of Europe. Indeed, the history of the ridges is not a little interesting, as indicating the strenuous and long-continued fight that had to be waged against water in the days when Europe was a mere swamp covered with forests. Some remnants of this style of farming may be seen to-day in the tendency to operate upon wet lands, to dig ditches, to throw up beds, and to handle spades rather than hold ploughs, which is exhibited by Irishmen, both in their own country and in many other localities where they have happened to settle down. Historically considered, the term " bog-trotter " is seen to depend upon truths which might not be fully evident at the first glance.

" Hilling " versus Flat Cultivation.

In like manner, the practice, still common in many localities, of " hilling up " around Indian corn and potatoes, is a device for keeping the soil dry and warm; so that, even when much water is near at hand, some portion of the roots of the crop may stand in earth that is dry enough to permit air freely to penetrate its pores. While it is true of certain kinds of potatoes that they may need to be hilled because they are apt to form tubers at the surface of the soil or even above the surface, it may, nevertheless, be said, in general, of the practice of hilling, that it is a relic which has been handed down to us from times and lands of more abundant moisture.

In wet countries the gutters or valleys between the hills may have served sometimes as water-courses to carry off the excess of actual running water, while during intervals of dry weather the earth of the hills would occasionally be found to be in a state fit to be hoed. There can be little doubt that in the moist climate of Ireland, for example, hills and ridges may be useful devices for increasing the yield of crops, for it must be well-nigh impossible to "cultivate" flat land in a wet country without running the risk of puddling it; but in dry climates, very little can be said in defence of the system of hilling. The ability to use cultivators and other implements of tillage where "flat cultivation" is practised is one advantage to be counted in favor of that system, and it is coming to be recognized that this method is to be preferred on land dry enough to admit of it. Excepting as a temporary device for enabling the seeds of Indian corn to start readily when first planted — and for covering some kinds of potatoes as was said — hills and ridges may well be discarded unless the soil is wet or cold. Actually, many good practitioners do now resort to "flat culture," and some writers have urged that hills should be wholly discarded. It is evident at all events that in dry situations more moisture may be retained in the soil by resorting to flat cultivation.

In an experiment, made by the editor of the "Rural New Yorker" (1884, p. 182), in which Indian corn was grown in drills upon a field of strong clayey loam which had been in grass for several years, flat culture was practised with the exception of ten rows. When dry weather set in, in August, these ten "hilled" rows were the first to suffer, and as the drought continued, the stalks of the corn in these rows turned yellow, while the plants upon the remainder of the field were still green and growing.

Wollny, who has studied the question in no little detail, found, on good open loams, that the system of hilling is, on the whole, inferior to flat cultivation, though his results varied not a little, both according to the kinds of plants operated upon, and accordingly as the season happened to be more or less dry. Some kinds of plants, such as horse-beans, vetches, soy-beans and kohl-rabi, were usually benefited by hilling, both in respect to quantity and quality of the crops obtained. Other plants, such as rape, rye, beets and turnips were benefited by hilling in some years, and injured in others.

Indian corn and carrots got no good from hilling as a general rule, and they were often harmed by it, while upon potatoes the effect of hilling varied according as the sets had been more or less deeply buried at the time of planting ; the more shallow the planting, so much the more good was done by hilling, and the deeper the planting, so much the less need was there of hilling up around the plants. In some years, deep-planted potatoes, that were not hilled, gave the largest crops, and in other years the maximum yield was from shallow-planted potatoes that were cultivated by hilling.   But it was found to be an easy matter to injure the potato crop by hilling it too strongly, and the rule seems to be well founded, that the deeper the sets have been buried, so much the smaller should the hills be made.

Beside the influence which hilling may exert upon the moisture of the soil, Wollny thinks that good may be done in some cases through the throwing out of new roots by those parts of the plants which are more nearly in contact with the heaped-up earth.   He urges that the formation of these lateral roots is encouraged by the fact that the temperature of the earth in the hills is higher and less subject to variations by day than that of flat land, and he states his belief that in general, only those kinds of plants can be hilled with profit which readily throw out these side-roots.

As for the time at which to make the hills, the plants should be rather young and still capable of throwing out new roots freely, but not too young lest too many of their leaves be buried, and a check be thus put upon growth.   Since earth heaped up in hills is specially apt to become dry, it follows that the process of hilling is really necessary only in moist climates and on stiff, close soils rich in humus, such as hold water tenaciously, and that it is unsuitable for dry climates and for all soils that dry out easily.

According to Wollny, the rows of hills had better be made to run north and south, as will be explained directly, because in this case the soil will attain to a higher and a more equable temperature than if the rows ran east and west, and the chances of getting good crops will be improved.   In his experiments, potatoes did in fact give larger crops when grown in north and south rows, and Marek found that beets grown in such rows gave more sugar, although the weight of the crop was no larger than that grown on east and west rows.

Experiments by Gabler as to the comparative merits of hills or no hills were continued for a term of years and many different varieties of potatoes were tested.   On the whole, it appeared that larger crops were obtained by hilling than by flat cultivation, though some varietes of potatoes profited much more than others from being hilled.   The results differed from year to year, according to the character of the seasons, and they were complicated by the fact that the earth heaped upon the hilled tubers tended to protect them from rot and from other diseases.   These trials led to no very definite conclusions as to the significance of hilling as a means of regulating water supply, but they teach the lesson that the potato is a crop not well adapted for studying the question, because of its liability to suffer from disease.   Horsky noticed, as long ago as when the potato-rot first ravaged Europe, that upon his estates, potatoes grown in ridges were much less liable to suffer from the disease than those grown on contiguous fields without ridging.   Both the dryness of the hills or ridges and the thick layer of earth which covers the tubers tend to hinder the action of the rot-fungus.

With regard to potatoes, it has been said by some writers that it is well not to hill them until the vines have attained a considerable size, and it has even been argued that a proper time for hilling is shortly before the moment of blossoming, when the plants have nearly attained their growth, and are ready to devote themselves to the work of developing tubers. If the hills were to be made much later than this period, the young tubers might be buried too deeply and the growth of new tubers encouraged while the older tubers might remain small.

It is said that no matter at what depth the sets may have been planted, each kind of potato is apt — under favorable circumstances — to develop its tubers at a depth peculiar to itself, and it is certainly true that some varieties of potatoes are apt to develop many tubers so close together, in a bunch, that some individuals may even be pushed up to the very surface of the soil; while other varieties habitually form their tubers so far apart one from the other that there is little or no crowding. One merit of hilling potatoes is that, in case cold weather should set in just after the young shoots have begun to appear above ground, the crop may readily be shielded from frost by running a plough between the rows in such manner that a light covering of earth may be thrown upon the plants to cover them.

In order to determine what influence hilling may exert upon the temperature of a soil, and upon the amount of water retained by it, Wollny made a number of hills, each of them a foot high and twenty inches broad, with soils of various kinds, and contrasted the temperature of these hills with that of contiguous flat land that was similarly exposed to sun and air. Observations for temperature were made by day and by night, at regular and frequent intervals during the growing season, upon thermometers whose bulbs had been sunk four and eight inches in the earth.

It was found that the earth in the hills retained decidedly less water than was held by the contiguous flat land, especially in the case of soils of good capillary power and of small capacity for heat; and that, in general, during the growing period, the earth in the hills was warmer than that of the flat land. The difference between the two situations was greatest at the season when the daily mean temperature of the soil was at its highest, and it was least noticeable when the daily mean temperature of the soil was at its lowest. But it was only in the summer and in warm weather that the temperature of the hilled earth was higher than that of the flat land. In cold weather, viz. in spring and autumn, and whenever cool weather occurred in summer, the temperature of the hilled earth was lower than that of the flat earth.

It was noticed furthermore, during the growing season, that in warm weather, the earth in the hills was decidedly warmer by day and usually cooler by night than that of the flat land, and that the variations in temperature in the hilled earth were much wider than those in the flat earth. The high day temperature of the hilled

earth, as compared with that of the flat earth, is said to have been
specially evident on contrasting the average mean temperature of
day (6 A. M. to 6 P. M.) with that of night, reckoning from 8 P. M. to
6 A. M. By night, however, except in peaty soils, the temperature of
the hilled earth was correspondingly low.

In the morning, the earth of the hills was, in warm weather, usually cooler than that of the flat land ; but in the evening it was
warmer. Other experiments made to test the influence of varying
exposures to sunlight, showed that hills running from east to west
were warmer by day and cooler by night, and were subject to wider
variations of temperature than those ranging from north to south.

Covered Drains.

Beside open ditches, the employment of which is as old as agriculture itself, covered drains of one kind or another have long
been used occasionally, and their use has become extremely common of late years in many districts. They were, in fact, not unknown to the ancients, and in England, as long ago as 1650, a
work was published by W. Bligh in which he recommended that
drains should be made by putting fagots or pebbles at the bottom
of a trench and covering them with earth.

Marshall, the old English agricultural writer, has much to say
of covered drains. He describes several varieties. The oldest
consisted of three alder poles or larch poles, laid one upon two, so
as to form a kind of pipe. Others were formed of bundles of
fagots : these lasted a dozen or fifteen years. An excellent
drain, said to be more durable than the fagot drains, was made
of sods, by scooping out a narrow trench so as to leave a shoulder
upon which, and across the water-way, sods were laid grass side
downwards, and then trodden firm and close, after which operation the trench was filled with the excavated soil. In case the soil
was not firm enough for the shoulder, an artificial shoulder was
formed with sods cut square and set firmly on each side of the
bottom of the trench, so as to leave a channel 3 or 4 inches wide
between them. A simpler plan, recently practised in some parts
of England, is to make the trench perfectly wedge-shaped, even to
the bottom, and to insert, at some little distance from the bottom,
a plug or wedge of sod in such manner that an open space is left
beneath this sod-wedge, at the bottom of the trench. The sod-
wedge is rammed firmly into the trench so that it shall bear closely against the earth on both sides, small pebbles are filled in
above the sod and earth above the pebbles. In wet land, the sod-
wedge is said not to moulder but to become "greasy." Mar-

shall commended pebble drains, but he directs that sods should be laid upon the pebbles to cover them before the earth is shovelled in.

A modification of the old pole drain has recently been described as in use in British Columbia. Trees are split edgeways, and the sections are placed with their narrower part downward at the bottom of a narrow, three-foot-deep trench. Water runs freely beneath the wood, i. e. between the point of the wedge-shaped rail and the sides of the trench, and, if good hearty timber is selected, the drain will continue to work for years.

Arthur Young, in his "Six Months' Tour," describes at some length the very extensive drainage operations of Lord Rockingham, which consisted in first digging numerous open ditches of suitable depths, and of width proportionate to the original wetness of the land. The larger ditches were left permanently open, but all the smaller ones were converted into covered drains. In some of them, capacious rectangular drains were built of flagging stone set against the sides of the ditch, and covered on top with broad, flat stones laid across and resting upon the tops of the upright flags. In ditches that were still smaller, oblong flags were set with their lower edges on the bottom of the ditch, and their upper edges resting against each other so as to form an inverted Λ. Pebbles were thrown in upon these stone conduits, and finally a good depth of earth. Though costly, such drains were doubtless effective and durable. Young says of them: "The improvement by these drains, which last forever, is almost immediately manifest. The summer succeeding the first winter totally eradicates in grass lands all those weeds which proceed from too much water, and leaves the surface in the depth of winter perfectly dry and sound, insomuch that the same land which before poached with the weight of a man, will now bear without damage the tread of an ox. In arable lands the effect is equally striking, for upon land that used to be flowed with rain, and quite poisoned by it during winter and spring, grain now lies perfectly dry throughout the year. In the tillage of such land a prodigious benefit accrues from this excellent practice, for the drained fields are ready in the spring for the plough before the others can be touched. It is well known how pernicious it is to any land to plough or harrow it while wet."

This example is interesting, as showing what strenuous efforts were sometimes made to drain land before drain-tiles were invented. So too, Fellenberg at Hoffwyl drained his entire estate with fagot or pebble drains in the year 1804.

Drainage by Pricking.

Still another system applicable in certain cases was to bore into moist places with a boring tool, so that the confined water might well up through the opening and flow away. The same boring implement was used also for pricking retentive subsoils, so that the ground-water might drain away into the underlying gravel or sand. Both these operations, however, were of extremely limited applicability; and good judgment, as well as an accurate practical knowledge of the geological structure of the locality, was required in order that they should succeed. It appears that in some districts in England, where stiff clays happen to repose on chalk rock, the surface soil may readily be drained by boring through the clay into the chalk. Indeed it may happen occasionally where a retentive soil rests upon a porous one, that deep tillage alone may be sufficient to drain the land.

Instances have actually been met with in England where land that seemed to require tile-drains has been made dry by deep cultivation. One case has been described, of a field of stiff clay overlying chalk to a depth of 3 or 4 feet, where water was often seen standing in the furrows when the land had been ploughed by means of horses, but a single deep cultivation by means of steam-power so stirred the first 12 inches and shook the clay below that the land was thoroughly drained and permanently improved. Other cases have been recorded of beds of stiff clay 2 or 3 feet thick, which formerly became water-logged in wet seasons, having been made dry and manageable by steam cultivation; the explanation being that when once the clay had been well stirred and shaken, water could pass through it into deposits of marl or gravel beneath.

Many instances are upon record where the drainage of basins has been effected by sinking shafts known as dumb-wells in clay, until an underlying stratum of chalk, porous limestone or sandstone has been reached. In one English instance dumb-wells were dug through clay 18 feet thick in order to reach the chalk, and they were finally filled up with flint-stones to ensure permanent percolation. In another case the tile-drains on several hundred acres of land were made to discharge into a shaft 3 feet in diameter, sunk 20 or 30 feet deep into the oolite, which readily disposed of all the water that came to it. Similar effects occur naturally in many localities where streams disappear from the surface and are absorbed by swallow-holes.

Another method of merit in some special cases, as where an isolated flat or saucer-shaped field is surcharged with moisture, is to dig a simple well or pond-hole, and pump water from it continually, or as often as need be, with wind, or steam, or water power. In this way, a considerable area of land may be drained when the circumstances are favorable.

Drain-Tiles.

An enormous impetus was given to the practice of thorough draining, by the substitution of bent roofing-tiles for the poles and fagots and stones previously employed. A horse-shoe tile was laid at the bottom of a trench with the convexity upward, like an inverted Ω. An improvement on this idea was to put a flat tile or a piece of slate beneath the horse-shoe, thus Ω; or, sometimes the tile was laid with its opening turned upward, and a slate or a peat-sod was placed upon it as a cover. In either case the earth was shovelled back into the trench to bury the tiles.

Short earthen tubes made expressly as "drain-tiles" were soon substituted for the clumsy roofing-tiles. Taken in section, the commonest form of drain-tile resembles the letter O. Such tiles have now for many years been in familiar use in most countries where agriculture is in an advanced condition. In several districts of this country, enormous numbers of them have been laid down, notably in some parts of the Mississippi Valley.

Ordinarily, the drain-pipes are simply placed end to end at the bottom of the narrow ditch which has been scooped out to receive them, and the earth is packed down hard above them. The pipes thus constitute a continuous tube, which is laid at such inclination, and so connected with cross or main drains, that the water can flow in it freely, and find ready discharge.

Water will run freely in a hollow pipe like this even when the fall is very slight. It is said that, when carefully laid, such drains will still discharge water where the fall is not more than at the rate of three feet to the mile, though in actual farm-practice the fall is of course much greater than this. The ground-water slowly sinks in at the joints of the pipes, and quickly flows through the hollow tube.

It is noticeable in records of methodical observations which have been made in England upon the rates at which water is discharged from drains, that as a general rule the flow does not begin until the autumnal rains have thoroughly saturated the land. As soon, however, as the soil has once become filled with water, a large proportion of every shower that falls is immediately discharged through the pipes. First of all, the store of water which the soil is able to hold in its pores, and which has been expended during the summer by way of evaporation and percolation and for feeding plants, must be completely replenished before the drain-tiles can begin to act freely.

In other words, the soil must become so charged with water that the water-table — i. e. liquid ground-water — shall rise to the level of the drains, in order that the excess of moisture shall flow through them. In one instance, reported by Denton, where lines of tiles had been laid 4 feet deep and 25 feet apart " in a most forbidding clay," it was observed that 1.645 inches of rain fell during the month of October and 1.630 inches in November, or, together, more than 74,000 gallons or 330 long tons of water to the acre. The drains began to trickle on Nov. 27, after a fall of half an inch of rain, and test-holes dug in the land showed that the water-table was rising, but had not yet reached the level of the drains. On Dec. 12, the drains were discharging 160 gallons per day and per acre, after frequent small rains in the early part of the month. On Dec. 13, nearly half an inch of rain fell, and the drains increased their discharge from 160 to 975 gallons. On Jan. 9, the rate of discharge was 125 gallons per diem, but on Jan. 10, rather more than half an inch of rain fell, and the discharge from the drains rose to 5,150 gallons per day and per acre.

Ordinarily, the purpose of tile-drains is to keep down the water-table to an appropriate height at those times and seasons when, were it not for the drains, there might be more water in the land than crops could bear ; but in some special cases where the soil lies upon porous materials, — as in the experimental fields of Lawes and Gilbert, which repose upon chalk — the water-table can never rise to the level of the tiles. At Rothamsted the water which flows from the drains is said to come from the saturated soil above and around the pipes, with what may have come directly from the surface, through cracks in the soil. These drains stop running a few hours after rain has ceased. (Warington.)

Experience teaches that even the stiffest clays may be dried and made mellow in the course of a few seasons by drain-tiles laid at a depth of 3 or 4 feet, in frequent rows, from 15 to 30 feet apart, as is the custom in Europe ; while on the porous prairie soils of this country, lines of tiles three feet deep will do good service when laid 100 feet apart. In consonance with these wider distances, comparatively large tiles are more commonly used in this country than abroad.

Instead of the 2-inch tiles of former days, modern western practice prefers tiles of from 3 to 6 inches in diameter, and still larger sizes are used for mains and for the lower sections of any long line of pipes. With regard to the soaking of the ground-water into the pipes, it may be observed that it is an exceedingly difficult matter to keep water out of any earthen-ware construction sunk in the ground. The sewers in cities, for example, though built of hard-burnt bricks laid in cement, are apt to drain off the ground-water from the territory through which they pass, though no intentional cracks or openings are left in them. Aqueducts built of masonry often act in precisely the same way. Great trouble is commonly experienced when a village grows to be a town, and proceeds to have sewers laid in its streets; for the sewers almost invariably drain many of the wells completely dry, from which the water supply of the inhabitants had been procured. And the trouble is one that cannot readily be avoided, since it is important that sewers should always be laid before aqueducts, lest the increased use of water, due to its presence in unwonted abundance, cause the old cesspools to overflow, and occasion epidemics of disease.

Drought often mitigated by Draining.

Far better results have been obtained by the use of hollow drains on clayey soils than could have been anticipated. It is plain enough that great advantage will be gained when wet lands are drained, in that they can now be ploughed and harrowed much earlier in the spring than was possible before, and with far greater ease to the laboring animals, and that, in consequence of this power of tillage, the farmer will have much greater freedom on the drained land for planting crops at appropriate seasons, and in respect to the cultivating of them at his convenience throughout the summer. It is evident, moreover, that it might easily happen that, through unfavorable weather, undrained land could not be planted at all until after the proper time for planting had gone by; or, supposing that the land had been planted, rains might set in, either in spring or autumn, and so clog the pores of the soil that seeds could not germinate, or young plants continue to live in it. In enumerating the diseases and "ill accidents" of grain, Lord Bacon tells us that "Another ill accident is over wet at sowing time, which with us breedeth much dearth, insomuch as the corne never commeth up; and many times they are forced to re-sow summer-corne where they sowed winter-corne."

It could hardly have been foreseen, however, though now found to be true of many clayey soils, that the ground, beside being made warm and sweet and mellow when thoroughly drained, is actually much less liable to suffer from drought than it was before. It is only the superfluous water which flows away through the drains, that is to say, the liquid water which was in excess of what the soil could hold naturally, by capillary attraction, and which is really useful for the support of crops. Thus it happens, that the depth of soil fit for roots to penetrate is so much greater in drained land than in that which is undrained, that the plant provides itself with better apparatus for taking up water. More than this, the capillary movement of water is freer in the drained soil; and the power of such soil to absorb rain and dew is increased.

Into undrained land rain can only penetrate slowly and with difficulty. Much water flows off from the surface of such land sideways. But it is desirable that a great store of water shall sink into and through the land, and that it shall accumulate in the soil, there to be held in such condition, and in such quantities as may be most useful for crops. In well-drained, mellow land, the movements of capillary moisture are comparatively free, and the demands of crops can be supplied readily, while in a crude, undrained clay, the movement of moisture may be so extremely slow that crops may suffer — even when there is a considerable store of moisture almost within reach — very much as they would in a sandy soil that could hold but little water. There is no need to say that drains should always be laid deep enough to admit the plough to pass freely and deeply above them in order that the capillary condition of the soil may be maintained.

For temperate climates, it may be laid down as a general rule, that the best soils are those naturally possessing moderate tenacity which are ploughed deeply to ensure an adequate and gradually diminishing store of moisture, and which have been thoroughly drained to protect them against periods of undue wetness. (Gasparin.) The fact that drained land quickly becomes dry at the surface after a summer-shower is advantageous in that it permits the farmer to stir the soil almost immediately with the cultivator or the hoe for the purpose of husbanding the store of moisture beneath the surface, as will be explained directly in the chapter on Tillage.

The admission of air to the land through the pores formerly

filled with water, enables manure to ferment or decay there in a useful way, and to be put to better profit by the crops than was possible before the drains were laid. The whole subject of aeration of the soil can be conveniently discussed under the head of Tillage.

Tile-Drains better than Pebble-Drains.

Tile-drains are almost always much to be preferred to the rough pebble-drains which are still clung to in some parts of New England. In view of the fact that a comparatively narrow trench is all sufficient for the reception of the pipe, tile-drains are often very much cheaper than the other kind, and they are vastly more efficient. The open pipes offer a ready flow and outlet for the ground-water, as if they were a natural brook, while in drains full of stones the flow is hindered and checked at every turn. Moreover, the soil immediately above the narrow tile-drain has access to water, and does not fail to draw up an abundant supply of it by force of capillary attraction. Above the broad ditch of stones, on the contrary, there is apt to be an arid strip, where the plants, being cut off from water, might suffer from thirst. On this account, it would manifestly be improper to put layers of pebbles above the tiles, as was proposed by several persons when tile-drains first came into use. Heiden has shown that a layer of gravel one inch in thickness has power to cut off capillary movements when placed between layers of loam.

The argument so often heard in favor of the pebble-drains, that the farmer must in some way disembarrass himself of the stones upon the surface of his fields, is apt to be a specious argument. Such pebbles had better be thrown away, or into heaps, or into bog-holes, for the chief cost of a tile-drain must always be the labor of excavating for it. It is worthy of remark, however, that the stone walls so prevalent in New England were often laid upon trenches filled with small stones, in order to preserve the wall from the lifting action of frost. But these "trench-walls" naturally served in many instances as pebble-drains for removing water from the fields. They have doubtless exerted an appreciable influence in some localities for drying out the soil.

Tiles not proper for Bogs.

One word needs specially to be said to New Englanders with regard to the inapplicability of tile-drains in soggy peat-meadows. When the water is drained out from such spongy lands, the earth

settles upon itself to an enormous extent, and so tends to bring
near to the surface any tiles which may have been laid in the bog,
no matter how deeply.   But when thus raised up, as it were, the
tiles can no longer do efficient service, and they are liable withal
to be struck by the ploughshare.   In the fen districts of England,
the subsidence of embanked and drained land has been found to
amount ordinarily to as much as 2 or 3 feet, and even in extreme
cases to 7 or 8 feet in the course of 18 or 20 years.   Arthur
Young tells of an instance in Ireland where a bog, on being
drained, subsided from 15 to 20 feet in the course of 10 years.
From being extremely wet and impassable, it became firm enough
to bear a loaded cart.

As a rule, the process of draining wet, boggy peat-lands should
be gradual, and care has to be taken that the spongy peat shall
not dry out too completely in droughty summers.   To prevent
this accident, check-boards to hold back the water in the open
ditches may sometimes do good service.   Usually, frequent open
ditches, that may occasionally be deepened in the course of years
as the land subsides, should precede the tiles, which may eventually be put in deeply beneath the bottoms of the ditches when the
land has become consolidated.   It is in such soft and mucky
places as this that " collars," (i. e. rings which encircle the joints
of the drain) have significance, as a means of holding the pipes
in place.   But collars are usually quite unnecessary when tiles
are laid in stiff clays.

In cases where there is no risk of the soil's settling unduly, tile-
drains may do excellent service by tending to counteract the
harm which may be done to crops of grass, clover, or grain, standing on very wet land, by the alternate freezing and thawing of
the excess of water in the soil.   The smaller the opportunity a
soil may have to become unduly wet, the less the chance that the
heaving action of frost will do harm.   One difficulty which might
be encountered in some low-lying fields liable to be overflowed by
brooks or rivers, is that the tiles may be clogged by silt, when the
water which backs up into the drains holds much solid matter in
suspension.

Drain-Tiles are not stopped up by Roots.

Nothing illustrates better the mode of action of tile-drains than
the fact that, when properly laid without " dips " or depressions,
the roots of crops rarely stop them.   But why is this?   Simply

because the roots of agricultural plants have absolutely no inducement to enter the hollow pipes. At the times when water is actually flowing through the drains, the soil around them is surcharged with moisture, and the crop has more water at its disposal than it can use. But when the drain is not flowing, there is no water inside it, and nothing to attract the roots. The moisture is all now outside the pipes, — below them indeed, — and there, in point of fact, the roots go in search of it.

A mat of rootlets outside the tiles is common enough, but they have no call to enter the pipes, unless perchance the pipes have been laid improperly, so that there are depressions in them filled with water or with moist silt. Of course, in case one of the lines of pipes should serve as an outlet for some actual spring, then it would be an aqueduct, and might contain water when the soil around the pipe was comparatively dry. In this event roots would be liable to enter the pipe, but instances such as this are exceptional. Cases are on record, however, where the fibrous roots of turnips and mangolds have completely filled up and stopped such aqueduct pipes laid two or three feet beneath the surface of the soil.

Drains warm the Land.

The influence of drains in warming the soil is very decided, particularly in the spring of the year. The large amount of water which then drains away from the land through the pipes, instead of evaporating, represents an amount of heat equal to that which would have been consumed in effecting the evaporation. The moment an attempt is made to calculate the quantity of heat which would be required to evaporate the surplus water from an acre of land, figures are encountered which are simply enormous. Beside the immense amount of heat required for evaporating water, that is to say, for changing liquid water to the vapor of water, there is another reason, as was said before, why wet land must always be cold land; viz., because the caloric capacity or specific heat of water itself is larger than that of any other solid or liquid substance. More heat is required in order to warm up a given weight of water than would be needed to warm a similar weight of soil. More heat is used up, so to say, in raising the temperature of the water from one thermometric degree to another, than would suffice similarly to increase the temperature of the soil itself. Oemler has determined the specific heats of several kinds of soils as follows. All the samples of soils were completely dry.

	Specific Heat.			Specific Heat.
Water	1.0000	Loam		0.1496
Moor-earth	0.2215	Pure clay		0.1373
Humus	0.2086	Fine sand		0.1048
Sandy humus	0.1414	Coarse sand		0.0968
Loam rich in humus	0.1662	Pure chalk		0.1848
Clayey humus	0.1579			

Some of these figures are specially interesting, notably those which show how small a capacity for heat is possessed by sandy soils, and how much greater is the power of clay and humus and chalk. It is always to be remembered, however, that all soils as they lie in the fields contain more or less moisture, and that this moisture works very emphatically to modify the relations of the soil to heat. Sandy soils are called hot soils, while soils rich in clay and in humus are often enough called cold, simply because sand has but little power to hold moisture, as compared with the amounts constantly held by clays and loams. In so far as agricultural soils are concerned, it does not help matters much that water, when once it has been warmed, holds heat forcibly, as is seen familiarly in the comparatively slow cooling of the water of the ocean and of lakes at the close of summer.

It may here be said that the great capacity of water for absorbing heat is familiarly illustrated by the action of the summer's heat and the winter's cold on large masses of water. As everybody knows, enormous amounts of heat have to be absorbed, in order that a large body of water may become warm, while equally enormous amounts of heat are given off in case the water is exposed to cooling influences.

Many countries that border on the ocean are distinguished by mild autumns and harsh, cold springs, as well as by the occasional mitigation of the heats of summer and the frosts of winter. While the sea-water is absorbing a vast amount of heat during the early summer, the adjacent lands naturally remain cold and backward; and conversely, when this heat is given off from the sea in autumn and winter, the climate of the neighboring lands will be mitigated. So too, when early frosts occur in the autumn, the store of heat contained in any considerable body of water, as in a ditch or pool, will be given off so slowly that no ice can form there, except, perhaps, at the edges of the water.

Water conducts Heat badly.

An excess of water in the soil may hinder the absorption of heat in another way, viz., because water is a very poor conductor of heat. When water is warmed at its surface, only very little, if any, of the heat can be transmitted downward. The soaking of warm rain-water into a drained soil has, however, a marked effect in elevating the temperature of the soil. It is evident that, in soils naturally so porous that rain can readily soak into them, the warmth brought from the air by this water and that taken by it from the surface of the land will be imparted to lower layers of the soil, often to the great advantage of the crops; and the same thing has been found to be true of soils that have been made porous by draining them.

The English engineer Parkes observed that a natural bog had a constant temperature of 46° F. at depths between 12 inches and 30 feet, and a constant temperature of 47° at a depth of 7 inches; whereas in a portion of the bog that was drained and tilled a thermometer sunk to a depth of 31 inches indicated a maximum temperature of 48¼°. In the tilled land the temperature rose to 66° at a depth of 7 inches after a thunder-storm, and on the average the temperature was 10° higher at a depth of 7 inches than it was in the natural bog. By a rain in the middle of June, the temperature of the tilled land at a depth of 7 inches was raised 3¼°, though it fell again half an hour after the rain had ceased, because of the rapid evaporation of water from the surface of the soil.

Warmth of Drained Land.

Practical men justly attach much importance to all processes of culture which tend to make soils warm and mellow. It is not alone the warmth of the air, but that of the soil also, which promotes the growth of crops. It is a fact of familiar observation that the advance of vegetation is peculiarly rapid upon drained land, and the result of an official inquiry made in Prussia many years ago indicated that the winter's snow disappears in that country a week earlier, on the average, from drained land than from undrained land similarly situated. Neither of these facts is in the least surprising, if account be taken of the cooling effects which are known to be produced by the evaporation of water. Experiments have shown that the heat evolved by the combustion of one pound of coal of average quality can evaporate no more than about 9 lb. of water. Hence something like 222 lb. of coal would be needed to evaporate one ton of water. But a single inch of rainfall brings to an acre of land 113 tons of water (of 2,000 lb. each),[1] and to evaporate this quantity of water there will be required $222 \times 113 = 25,086$ lb. or 12.5 tons of the coal.

---

[1] In terms of U. S. gallons, one inch of rain falling on an acre of land will deliver 27,154 gallons or 862 barrels, or rather more than 113 tons of 2,000 lb. each.

In localities where as much as 40 inches of rain fall in a year, that would amount to more than 4,500 tons of water to the acre of land, and in order to evaporate so large an amount of water there would have to be burned 1,003,440 lb. or more than 500 tons of the coal. If the evaporation were continuous, 2,750 lb. of the coal would have to be burned every day throughout the year, or some 115 lb. every hour.

Gasparin, in France, taking into account not so much the total rainfall as that part of it which evaporates from the land, noted that 82% of the water which falls upon an acre in his locality, goes off by way of evaporation, or 5,326,000 lb. of water in the course of a year. But to evaporate this much water, an amount of heat would be required equal to that disengaged by burning 295 tons of coal, of the quality above-mentioned.

Wet Soils are cold.

The amount of water actually present in a soil has often a preponderant influence on the temperature of that soil; and the different kinds of soils, when once thoroughly wet, will naturally be very much alike as to their power of absorbing and retaining heat, for the absorption of heat by the water, as it passes from the liquid to the gaseous state in the process of evaporation, will be the chief cause of refrigeration. Schuebler found constantly that soils were 10 or 12 degrees (F.) cooler when wet than when they were dry.

The importance of having the land dry out and become warm in the spring is seen conspicuously enough in the case of those tropical plants such as melons, squashes and Indian corn which are cultivated in temperate climates. The seeds of such plants may germinate readily enough on drained land at the very time when they might fail and decay on an adjacent field that remained wet and cold.

The cooling influence of water is shown very distinctly in experiments made to test the effect of dark-colored substances upon the temperature of soils. Wollny found in effect that the influence of color on temperature diminished in proportion as the amount of water in a soil was larger, and that it might be entirely overpowered in cases where the presence of an abundance of humus, or some other circumstance, was favorable for the accumulation of large quantities of water. The darker the soil, however, so much the more strongly may water depress its temperature, since the heat absorbed by the colored material enables just so much more water to evaporate in a given time.

Although there are hundreds of thousands of acres in this country that could be improved by means of tile-drains, the fact must not be lost sight of that current statements regarding the general or universal good effects of draining apply far more forcibly to damp countries, like England and North Germany, than they do to most parts of the United States. They apply also to districts where the soil is extremely fine, as in some of the Western States, as well as to stiff clay soils. Since the main province of drains is not to carry off a sudden fall of rain, but to relieve the land from any excess of water which may soak into it from any source, and to promote the circulation of air and moisture in the soil, their purpose will naturally be better accomplished in countries where light drizzling rains abound, than in our own land of heavy showers.

In countries where the land is liable to be frequently moistened at seasons when the operations of tillage and seeding need to be attended to, drains are often indispensable. But in this country rains are not particularly frequent. They are apt to be heavy, and are often of such character that much of their water flows off the surface of the land. It is true that a larger number of inches of rain falls here in New England in the course of a year than in England and Germany, but the character of our showers is very different from that of theirs. The fact must be remembered also, though often lost sight of by over-strenuous advocates of drainage, that many of our leachy, hungry uplands of " drift " gravel are far too thoroughly drained already. It is true withal, that in America much land is so cheap that it might often be better policy to buy an additional new field rather than to spend money in improving an old one. For sanitary reasons the draining of fields about houses is not infrequently a matter of importance everywhere.

CHAPTER V.

TILLAGE.

THE purposes of tillage are twofold. First, to improve the texture of the soil, in the mere mechanical sense. That is to say, to stir and loosen the soil so that the roots of plants may readily pass through it; that air and water may freely enter it; and that water may move through it easily, while at the same time a certain amount of moisture may be retained, and indeed be rather firmly held by it. Secondly, so to alter the position and condition of the particles of which the soil is made up, that changes in the chemical composition of these particles may be brought about by the action of air and water, and the microscopic organisms which act as ferments.

Some soils are so stiff and heavy that neither roots nor water can freely penetrate them. Others are too light and open; and the particles of some are so very finely divided that special care must be taken lest they run to mere mud at every fall of rain, and thereafter bake hard. In all these cases great improvement may be made by tillage, through mere alteration of the mechanical condition of the land.

But it is manifestly impossible to disturb the soil in any way without bringing its particles into new relations with the air, and commingling anew the various substances proper to the soil, together with whatever fertilizing or alterative materials may have been added to the soil or have been grown upon it. Hence, as a matter of course, chemical changes are induced in all operations of tillage as will be insisted more in detail hereafter.

It is true, also, that biological changes are induced by the operations of tillage; for, as is now well known, a variety of microscopic organisms, some of them useful and others hurtful in respect to the growth of plants, have their being in agricultural soils. It is known, too, that the growth of some of the useful kinds of these microdemes is most rapid in soils that have been brought into a good condition of porosity, so that air and moisture may have free access to all their particles. "There is a fermentation that takes place in soils immediately after they have been dug over or moved, and a dew arises in the soil which did not arise before. These greatly exceed, in power of causing the plant to strike, anything to be obtained by rain on the plants at the time of planting or by planting in wet earth." (Cobbett.)

Importance of Good Tilth.

It will be proper first of all to describe some of the essential conditions in respect to standing room which plants require, and to dwell upon the enormous influence which good tilth must necessarily exert upon the growth of crops.

A soil should be firm enough to afford proper support to the plants that grow in it, and yet be loose enough to allow the most delicate rootlets to grow without hindrance. Its condition should be such that air may freely enter the pores, and that any undue excess of water may drain away readily, and yet the texture should be so close that much of the rain-water which falls upon the land may be retained and held permanently, or until the growing crops have put it to use. Nothing illustrates more forcibly the sentiments of practical men upon this point than the care they take to prepare mellow seed-beds for the growth of many delicate crops. There are in fact very good reasons why the soil with which seeds are to be put into immediate contact should be made mellow before seeds are sown in it. For not only is it necessary that some air shall gain access to a germinating seed, but the points of the roots of young plants that are just starting into life are so soft and feeble that they can only make progress in those directions where they find pores in the soil. Every hard obstacle which such roots encounter tends to distress the plant: it is a hindrance to proper growth and may even cause the young plant to perish in case the roots cannot find a way of working around it.

So too with more mature plants. The soft points of growing roots do not habitually bore through solid clods or firmly impacted earth, but they push into any open spaces which they may happen to encounter between the lumps and particles of which the soil is made up. Hence the importance of tilling the soil to increase the number of these interspaces. A soil that is in good tilth, and mellow, presents innumerable openings and channels for the passage of rootlets in this way.

Roots must have ample Room and Freedom of Motion.

Practical men lay special stress also upon the importance of thorough tillage for "root-crops," such as beets, carrots and rutabagas. They direct that, in preparing for these crops, the land should be ploughed and harrowed repeatedly to make it mellow and friable, and urge that it is useless to try to grow roots unless the land can be well prepared beforehand. It is said indeed that for the production of beets rich in sugar deep cultivation is indispensable. In badly worked land a considerable portion of the beet-root is apt to grow above the surface of the soil, and experience has shown that this projecting part of the root is much poorer in sugar than the lower part, which is covered with earth. For this reason, in the case of beets grown for sugar-making, it is well to draw up earth around the crowns of the roots, when the crop is hoed or cultivated. It is well understood, for instance, in England, that beets do not prosper upon stiff clays, and that it is unwise to try to grow them on any land which is in a bad state of cultivation.

A familiar illustration of the importance for rootlets of open spaces, which they may enter,— of air, moisture and good drainage,— is seen in American greenhouses in the use of very small flower-pots for growing cuttings after they have been "started" in a propagating bed. As compared with the amount of earth that is contained in these little pots, there is presented a very large inner surface of porous earthenware, and the roots insinuate themselves between the earth and the inside of the pot, where they find room for their development, while an abundance of air comes to the roots through the porous ware, either directly or to replace the water exhaled from it. There is little chance withal that so small a volume of soil can become much impacted.

Roots are developed by Young Plants.

The natural tendency of roots is to grow downwards, when the soil is in fit condition to receive them, and to grow with surprising rapidity so long as the plant is young. Hellriegel found upon barley plants that had but a single leaf some roots that were 9 or 10 inches long; on plants whose second leaf had begun to unfold there were single roots 20 inches long. On a barley plant one month old he found some roots that were 3 feet long.

So too, buckwheat a fortnight old that was beginning to develop its second leaf had roots nearly a foot long, and so had clover plants that were showing their fifth leaf. Pea plants a month old that were 10 to 16 inches high had some roots that were 13 to 17 inches long. These figures, it will be noticed, have no reference to the total length of the roots, as obtained by adding together the lengths of all the roots of a plant. They refer only to single roots, which had attained the lengths above stated in garden-loam under favorable conditions.

Hellriegel found that barley plants ten days old in their third leaf had 42 lb. of dry matter in their roots for every 58 lb. of dry matter in the leaves and stem. In plants a month old, at the time of shooting, the relations were 29 in the roots to 71 in the leaves and stem; while in ripe barley plants there were less than 8 lb. of dry matter in the roots for 92 in the leaves and stalks. With oats, the relations were 24½ : 76, 17 : 83, and 13 : 87 of dry matter in the roots to that in the stem and leaves when the plants were shooting, in blossom, and ripe, respectively.

In the chapter relating to Rotation of Crops examples will be given of the distribution of the roots of various crops in soils of different characters.

Roots strive to develop Symmetrical Forms.

In general, it may be said that just as any obstruction above ground that interfered with the symmetrical development of the branches of a tree would hinder the profitable growth of the tree, so any impediment or injury to the roots of plants that impairs their useful development will lessen the amount of crop to be harvested. The analogy is specially close in respect to the crowding of one plant by its fellows, as when too many plants are permitted to grow in a given space. In such case, the roots of the different individuals interfere with one another very seriously, and the growth of the crop is apt to receive even a more emphatic check than would be occasioned by the crowding of its leaves and branches above ground. But the better the land has been tilled, so much the more useful root space will it contain, and so much the larger will be the number of plants that can be grown upon a given area without distressing one another.

It is to be observed that the leaves and branches of plants have naturally a much better opportunity to unfold than the roots can have. For the air offers no resistance to their development in any direction, while the soil must necessarily present obstacles at every turn to interfere with the progress of the rootlets.

The power of obstructions to hinder the growth of roots is well illustrated by some experiments of Hellriegel, where peas and beans were grown in moistened sawdust, some samples of which had been impacted and others not. When the sawdust had been strongly compressed, it was noticed that the development of the roots of many of the plants was greatly impeded, and that many of the tap-roots in particular were arrested, or even destroyed. One prime purpose of tillage is to diminish such interference of the roots of crowded plants, in so far as it can be done economically. Both deep tillage and drainage must manifestly help to increase the amount of room useful for the growth of roots.

Many Kinds of Plants need abundant Standing-Room.

The importance of abundant standing room is familiarly illustrated by root crops, such as beets, carrots and rutabagas. These crops are seldom or never sown excepting on well-tilled land, and it is noticeable, when care is taken to thin out the rows properly soon after the young plants have started, so that plenty of room shall be left between each individual plant, that the crop will prosper, and that fine large roots will be secured. But if the plants are not thinned, i. e. if they are permitted to crowd one another unduly, they suffer very much, and few of them will grow to a large size.

In illustration of this matter Tull suggested long ago a neat experiment. He directs that a wedge-shaped plot — 20 yards long, 12 feet wide at the broad end and 2 feet wide at the narrow end — shall be staked out in the midst of some " whole, hard ground," and that the earth of the plot shall be spaded to a fine tilth. In a row at the middle of this plot 20 turnips are to be sown early and the soil about them kept well stirred during their term of growth. At first, as he says, dig near the plants with a spade, and each time afterwards a foot further distance, till all the earth be once well dug. If weeds appear where it has been so dug, hoe them out shallow with a hand-hoe.

But dig all the piece next the outer lines deep every time, that the soil may be the finer for the roots to enter when they are permitted to come thither. If these turnips are all gradually bigger as they stand nearer the broad end of the plot, it is a proof that their roots all extend to the outer edge of the spaded land, and the 20th turnip will appear to draw nourishment from a distance of 6 feet on either side. But if the turnips numbered 16, 17, 18, 19 and 20 grow no larger than No. 15, it will be clear that their roots extend no further than those of turnip No. 15, which is but about 4 feet on either hand.

Generally speaking, the better the soil, the closer may roots be allowed to grow. There are certain cases, however, where it is not desirable to produce very large roots, and where it is specially advantageous to avoid actual crowding on the one hand and too great luxuriance of growth on the other. Thus, when beets are grown for making sugar, if the plants are set very wide apart on good land, their roots grow to a great size indeed, but they contain less sugar than roots which have been planted nearer together, and which have not grown so large. According to Voelcker, the distance between the rows and from plant to plant should not be less, generally speaking, than 12 inches, nor greater than 18 inches.

Petermann, who tried many experiments to determine how far

apart sugar-beets should stand in order to get the best crops and the best juice, concluded that the distance commonly allowed in Belgium (18 x 12 inches) is too large. He commends a distance of 16 x 10 inches, which would allow some 40,000 plants to grow on an acre instead of a scant 30,000, as in the other case. When large kinds of beets were allowed to grow closer together than 16 x 10, the yield was diminished, though smaller varieties of beets, and those which do not project much above the soil, may be set as near together as 14 x 7 inches.

Boussingault measured the amounts of space that are habitually allotted to various plants by practical men in the garden-culture of Alsatia. He found that each bean plant has at its disposal 57 lb. of earth, a potato plant 190 lb., a tobacco plant 470 lb., and a hop plant 2,900 lb. These weights correspond very nearly with 1, 3, 7 and 50 cubic feet respectively.   As contrasted with the results of scientific experiments made under conditions which permitted the soil to be kept constantly in good tilth, the measurements go to show how very far from theoretic perfection the operations of field-tillage must be, even at their best.

Experiments to test Need of Space.

This question of standing-room, or rather the influence exerted by varying amounts of soil on the growth of plants, has been carefully studied by Hellriegel in two distinct ways, and some of his results may well be cited as illustrating the vast importance of tillage for the success of crops. They fully support the common conception that all things are possible in a deep soil kept in good tilth and well watered. He first filled a large number of glass jars of four different sizes with sifted garden-loam of good quality, and grew pairs of plants of various kinds in these jars in such wise that each kind of plant could be tested as to the freedom of its growth in jars of all the sizes. The idea was that the amounts of earth in the jars should be to one another as 1 : 2 : 4 : 6, and that the absolute weights of soil should be 7, 14, 28 and 42 lb. respectively.   The soil used was known to be rich enough for the growth of maximum crops ; it was kept constantly moistened to good advantage, and all the jars were kept out of doors in fair spring and summer weather, being set on a railway carriage which could be run under cover in case of storms.

In the course of three or four weeks after the beginning of the experiment, it could be seen that all the plants in the larger jars prospered better than those in the smaller, and that the plants the root-room of which was restricted could not keep pace with those which had an abundance of earth at their disposal.

It was found to be true of clover, barley, buckwheat, peas, horse-beans and lupines, that the plants formed regular series or grada-tions in consonance with the varying sizes of the jars in which they were growing. That is to say, each individual plant was larger in accordance with the amount of ground which had been allotted for its own exclusive use. It was found also that the weights of the crops harvested varied much in the same proportion as the amounts of earth in which they had grown.

As Hellriegel puts it, it could truly be said that the amount of crop harvested was practically in inverse proportion to the sum of the mechanical hindrances to their development which the roots had encountered. He urges that the roots of plants do not natur-ally form a chaotic tangle, but strive always to grow in harmony with a symmetrical plan, which is just as definite and well propor-tioned, and as characteristic for each particular kind of plant, as are the forms exhibited by the stems, boughs and leaves of the plant, above ground. Anything which works seriously to prevent the original plan as to root-structure from being carried out will be seen to affect the development of the crop as well. It is as true of earth as of air that, " all things that grow, will grow as they finde roome." (Bacon.)

In the case of the pot experiments just now cited, it was found that the mass of roots was much larger in the larger jars than in the smaller, though it was somewhat less compact.

The Weight of a Crop may depend on the Amount of Standing-Room.

Some curious parallelisms between the amounts of standing-room and the weights of crops produced were noticed. Thus, with red clover, while the amounts of earth in the jars were as $1:2:6$, the dry crops were $1:2.4:5.7$. In the case of peas, quantities of earth related to one another as $1:2$ gave dry crops equal to 1 and to 1.6 respectively, and similar coincidences were noticed in re-spect to beans and barley.

Even in volumes of earth so small as those employed in these experiments, it was easy to destroy the tilth of the soil by improper treatment. For example, in case air-dried loam was poured into the jars and left to lie loose until after the time of planting, the mechanical condition of the soil was damaged to such an extent when water was then poured upon it that the crops were seen to suffer. This effect was more conspicuous in the larger jars, and seems to have been due to a partial puddling of the earth. The trouble was avoided in subsequent experiments by compressing the dry soil slightly, layer by layer, when it was placed in the jars.

Harm done by Crowding.

By another and still more interesting series of experiments, Hellriegel proved that any considerable number of plants grown together in large jars did no better, individually, than one or two plants grown in a small jar. Indeed, generally speaking, they did not grow as well. That is to say, the bad effects of crowding may be shown as conspicuously by growing an undue number of plants together in a large volume of earth, as by allotting a small volume of earth to a single plant, or to a pair of plants.

In these trials 1, 2, 3, 4, 6, 8, 12, 16 and 24 barley plants were grown in jars of three different sizes containing respectively about 4, 11 and 28 lb. of garden-earth. The plants were fed and watered, and cared for as before. It was calculated that in the large jars that carried 3 and 4 plants, in the medium jars that had 3 plants, and the small jars that had 2 plants, the crop stood about as thickly as barley does usually in field culture; but that the larger jars, with 8 or 12 or more plants, were crowded. So were the small jars that carried 4, 6 and 8 plants, while the jars which had only a single plant, and most of those that had two, supplied from two to four times as much space as is ordinarily allowed to barley plants in the field.

The effects of the crowding were soon seen in the smaller size of the plants both in the small jars and in the jars that contained many individuals, and these differences were more and more clearly defined as the plants became more fully developed. The growth of the single plant in the largest jar is said to have been marvellous. There seemed to be no limit to its power of stooling. When the first ears of grain were ripening, young shoots were still being thrown up from below. This plant produced no less than fifteen stalks that bore ears, and some of the ears were of gigantic size, filled with superb grain.[1] In the large jar that had two plants, the

---

[1] It is of interest to compare Hellriegel's results with some of the best which have been obtained in field experience. Thus, Houghton reported in 1692 an experiment with wheat where the grains were set out at distances of 10 inches from one another, and were freely fertilized. In several instances 60 or 70 stalks grew from a single seed, and in one instance there was produced from one seed 80 stalks with very large ears full of large

luxuriance was already less marked, though one of the plants had eight stalks that bore ears and the other had six. In the other jars the tendency of the plants to stool decreased according as they were more crowded ; the large jar that had 24 plants showed hardly a trace of it. The crowded plants ripened also sooner than the others.

Evils of Rank Growth.

It was noticed long ago by Cobbett, as an objection to the application of Tull's drill husbandry to wheat, " that the plants keep on growing to too late a season. . . . The tillage makes the plants keep on growing to a much later period than when they stand thickly all over the ground and have no tillage while growing. This late growth and the juiciness of the stalks and leaves expose the plants to that sort of blight which makes the straw speckled, and sometimes gives it a dark line all over; and whenever this blight lays hold, the grain is thin and light."

" The grains of the drilled wheat are much larger than those from fields sown broadcast, but if the blight lay hold, they are not so heavy, nor anything like it. In hot countries, where this blight is unknown, the drilled wheat would always exceed the broadcast, but in the chilly and backward climate of England you must on the average of years expect this blight unless you sow very early. My land did not permit me to sow early, and though I had in 1814 on a 5-acre field 32 bushels to the acre of white Essex wheat, sown on 4-foot ridges, a single row upon a ridge, I found so much blight generally that I was obliged to discontinue the system as to wheat, though with regard to Swedish turnips I found it excellent."

" If you can sow your wheat in August, five times out of six you may escape the blight in the straw. But even then you must not sow too thin, always bearing in mind that the thinner the plants stand, the later the wheat is in getting ripe, and the greater the

---

grains. Many of these ears were 6 inches long, and some of them had more than 60 grains to the ear ; altogether there were more than 4,000 grains obtained from the one seed. It was noticed that the plants had ample room to grow when the seeds were sown 10 inches apart. Barley treated in a similar way to the wheat produced in some instances 60 ears from a single seed.

Tull, in commenting on the foregoing experiment, remarked that he had himself never found above 40 ears from a single plant in his fields, " Yet there is no doubt," he says, " but that every plant would produce as many as Mr. Houghton's of the same sort with the same nourishment. But I should not desire any to be so prolific in stalks, lest they should fail of bringing such a multitude of ears to perfection. . . . I have numbered 109 grains in one ear of my grey cone-wheat that had been drilled and horse-hoed ; and one ear of my Lammas wheat has been measured to be 8 inches long, which is double to those of wheat sown broadcast."

Cobbett viewed a crop of white cone-wheat that had been sown in rows, by Mr. Budd, on ridges with very wide intervals, and ploughed all summer according to Tull's plan. " If he reckoned that ground only which the wheat grew upon, he had 130 bushels to the acre, and even if he reckoned the whole of the ground, he had 28 bushels to the acre, all but 2 gallons. But the best wheat he grew this year was dibbled in between rows of Swedish turnips in November, 4 rows upon a ridge with an 18-inch interval between each 2 rows, and a 5-foot interval between the outside rows on each ridge. He had ears with 130 grains in each."

chance of blight. . . . Beside the early sowing, care must be taken not to sow too thin. By thick sowing along the drills you get the plants to stave one another a little, and the wheat ripens at an earlier period."

It may well have been true, however, that Cobbett's results were complicated by the formation of nitrates in the soil. Thus, he says: —"The nearer you go to the plants with the plough, the more gross they will be, and the later they will continue to grow. This grossness, produced by the tillage, does, however, fully show the truth of the grand principle of Tull, namely, that tillage and tillage alone will create and supply the food of plants, and will in many cases render manure wholly unnecessary."

As illustrating the impropriety of sowing grain too thinly upon fertile land, the story is told of a Yorkshire farm that had gained a bad name because oats would not ripen on it. A new tenant corrected the evil at once by sowing two bushels more oats to the acre than his predecessors had been accustomed to sow. The farm came to be one of the most productive in the county.

In England it has been noticed, as regards wheat, that larger amounts of seed to the acre are sown upon light soils than on those which are heavy. On rich loams comparatively small quantities of seed are sown, but care is taken to sow late in the season, lest the crop should become " winter-proud " and run too much to straw.

Sizes of Hellriegel's Barley Plants.

In contrast with the enormous single plant in Hellriegel's large jar that contained about 28 lb. of earth, the 24 plants in the medium-sized jar which contained 11 lb. of earth were noteworthy. The crowded plants were perfectly healthy, and to all appearance normal, though comparatively small. Each of these mature plants weighed when dry from 600 to 1,200 milligrams, and bore from 10 to 22 seeds, while the single plant of the large jar weighed over 33,000 milligrams and bore 636 seeds.

All the experiments went to show that it is easy to determine beforehand how large a well-fed and well-watered plant shall grow by limiting the volume of earth which stands at its sole disposal. It is noticeable withal, that, where the supplies of food and water are ample, an undue excess of standing-room may lead to a not wholly advantageous luxurious habit of growth, somewhat in the same way that an excess of manure might. Hence it may be said that a certain amount of crowding is necessary in order to the best utilization of the space which has been devoted to a crop.

Indeed, the significance of tillage might be very well illustrated by a reference to the different numbers of plants that are grown to the acre of land in new and in old countries. Washington wrote long ago, in a letter to Arthur Young, "An English farmer must

have a very indifferent opinion of our American soil when he hears
that an acre of it produces no more than from 8 to 10 bushels of
wheat; but he must not forget that in all countries where land is
cheap and labor is dear the people prefer cultivating much to cultivating well."

In the same sense, Boussingault tells of a field near Pampeluna
where he saw wheat growing in isolated tufts, all extremely vigorous and very heavy in the ear, though the ground had had very
little preparation. A yield of from 60 to 80 times the seed was
expected, and the crop was regarded as a profitable one, though
it could not have amounted to more than 7 or 8 bushels to the acre.
Whence it appears that a large area of ill-tilled standing-room
may suit each individual plant as well as a much smaller area that
has been subjected to tillage.

Some of the results obtained by Hellriegel are given in very
condensed form in the following table :—

No. of Plants in a Jar.	LARGE JAR. (12½ kilos earth.)			MEDIUM JAR. (5 kilos earth.)			SMALL JAR. (1.7 kilos earth.)		
	No. of Ears.	Weight of Crop. Grain. grm.	Total. grm.	No. of Ears.	Weight of Crop. Grain. grm.	Total. grm.	No. of Ears.	Weight of Crop. Grain. grm.	Total. grm.
1	867	14.82	33.16	381	9.11	17.27	228	4.05	7.70
2	723	15.12	31.31	465	10.13	19.69	228	4.65	9.34
3	765	13.78	31.22	453	10.64	19.86	246	4.44	8.54
4	984	18.79	39.50	480	10.96	20.42	291	4.35	9.40
6	1050	18.53	38.93	480	11.87	21.78	177	4.50	8.55
8	1170	20.23	41.82	466	12.77	22.53	246	5.32	10.03
12	1101	20.81	41.56	471	11.96	21.37	...	...	...
16	978	20.50	41.18	546	11.92	22.32	...	...	...
24	1062	21.07	41.65	591	12.41	24.42	...	...	...

It is very remarkable how little difference there is, in one and
the same kind of jar, between the crops obtained from different
numbers of seeds. It will be noticed in each of the three series
that there is a point beyond which the crop tends to diminish when
the number of plants is larger, and that the total yield is not increased to any great extent on increasing the number of plants.
Thus, in the series of large jars, 8 plants gave a crop as large
as that obtained from 24 plants; but the 8 plants gave little more
crop than 4 plants, and each of the 8 plants was only about half as
large as the plants in the 4-seed pot. In other words, the volume
of earth in the large jars (some 28 lb.) can be utilized as completely by 8 plants as by 24, but cannot be fully utilized by less
than 6 or 8 plants; whence the inference that a given volume of

the earth could afford to a plant only a certain definite amount of useful space, and that, when this space is once fully occupied, the growth of the roots must cease. But since the production of stalks and leaves and grain stands in a definite relation to the number of roots, and depends upon this number or quantity, the crop will naturally suffer whenever it is diminished.

In the medium-sized jars that contained 11 lb. of earth, 4 to 6 plants made about as good use of the soil as any larger number; and in the small jars containing about 4 lb. of earth, 1 or 2 plants gave almost as large a yield as any larger number.

All these experiments enforce the lesson, that one fundamental advantage derivable from tillage is the removal of mechanical impediments to the symmetrical development of the roots of crops, and they go to show that an abundance of root-space provided with a proper supply of water may often be more important on the whole than heavy manuring. Hellriegel found, in fact, that, no matter how much or how many fertilizing substances were applied to the soil, it was impossible for plants to make proper use of these materials unless they had adequate standing-room. Whenever the volume of earth was restricted, he soon came to a limit beyond which it was impossible to increase the crop by giving it more food: the thing then necessary to be done was to provide more room for the roots, and so remove or avoid the impediments which had previously hindered their proper development.

The Old Belief that Tillage may serve instead of Manure.

So important is thorough tillage for the growth of good crops that it has sometimes been argued that manure might be dispensed with if the operations of tillage could but be made perfect. A noteworthy instance of this belief is recorded in the history of English agriculture, in respect to the famous system of horse-shoeing husbandry, specially advocated by Tull (1680-1740), and repeatedly illustrated, even in recent times, by his disciples. Tull noticed that the growth of plants is greatly favored by cultivating them in rows, and frequently stirring the soil between and around them, even when this soil has been left unmanured, whence he jumped to the conclusion that manures are not really necessary; that finely pulverized earth and moisture are all-sufficient, and that mechanical operations competent to effect the stirring may be substituted in all cases for manures and systems of rotation.

It is to be said that Tull's hypothesis was in so far supported
by his practice that he was enabled to obtain twelve successive
remunerative crops of wheat from the same land without manure
by repeatedly ploughing and cultivating it.   But the soil of his
farm was a fairly good, deep loam, free from wet, on a bottom of
chalk.   It was such land as is often found in countries that have
long been cultivated.   Doubtless the limitations of the method
would have been speedily discovered by an experimenter operating upon a New England gravel.

Tull no doubt held erroneous theoretical views in respect to the
kinds of benefits derivable from tillage, and he may have argued
somewhat too strongly, from the observation of a limited number
of experiments, in favor of the general applicability of his system.
But there can be no question that he was a man of genius, or that
his system of drill husbandry has exerted a highly important influence on the development of practical agriculture, especially as regards methods of cultivating root-crops, potatoes and Indian corn.
Scientifically speaking, it may be said that Tull's labors have led
to the diffusion of much clearer conceptions as to the real significance of tillage, and even as to the action of manures, than had
been held previously to his time.

It is still customary to speak of Tull's experience as of a failure
which must necessarily have come to pass sooner or later if his conception had been persisted in and carried out practically ; and it is
doubtless true that some part of the influence which Tull's teachings have exerted upon the progress of agriculture depends upon the
limitations to which his conception is really subject.   But it has
nevertheless been proved repeatedly that tillage may be of paramount
importance on certain soils, and notably on such as were operated
upon by Tull.

Practice of Tull's Successors.

Soon after the death of Tull, Hunter, in England, put in practice
a modification of his system as follows: The fields were laid out in
strips 9 feet wide, and every other one of these strips were sown,
while the intermediate strips were kept bare of all vegetation, and
were ploughed repeatedly at appropriate moments.   In the autumn
the bare strips were sown, while the others which had carried a crop
were ploughed up, and were repeatedly ploughed during the next
year to fit them for being sown in the autumn.

Hunter stated, "In this alternate way I manage weak arable lands,
and I have the satisfaction to find that very little manure is required;
which is a most agreeable circumstance, as such lands are generally
remote from a large town.   I dare venture to say that the same field
managed in this alternate way for a few years will be found to produce one-third part more profit than when cultivated in the usual

manner. . . . The same grain may be cultivated as long as we please on land managed in this manner. . . . In the cultivation of wheat, however, the utmost attention must be paid to the cleanness of the fallow lands."

It should be said that a method of cultivating and manuring land in alternate strips has long been practised in Japan, especially upon new land which is in process of reclamation. Manure is applied to those strips on which crops are grown, while the bare strips are tilled frequently. It is said that experience teaches that better results are got in this way than if the crop were to be grown upon an undivided half of the field, while the other half was left bare.

The system of growing wheat on strips of land has occasionally found strong supporters in England, and was at one time practised with remarkable success by the Rev. Mr. Smith at Lois-Weedon in Northamptonshire. By operating in this way on a clayey soil well charged with nitrogenous humus, and upon gravel that reposed on clay, Mr. Smith was able to produce large crops of wheat on the same land year after year without manure, by simply laying out his fields in strips, and growing the crop on alternate strips in successive years. His plan was to sow the wheat, at the rate of but little more than a peck to the acre, by dropping the grains 3 inches from each other in triple rows. Each of the rows was one foot distant from the others, and an unoccupied interval 3 feet in width was left between each triple row. In the autumn, when the wheat plants had become large enough to be distinctly visible, he trenched the intervals, in preparation for the next crop, taking care to bring up 6 inches of the subsoil, and to cast the overlying 7 inches of loam into the bottom of the trenches. In the spring the rows of wheat were well hoed and hand-weeded, and the intervals of unoccupied land between the rows were stirred with a one-horse scarifier 3 or 4 times up to the period when the grain blossomed in June.

By this abundant tillage, thorough aeration, nitrification and disintegration of the soil was ensured, and a supply of food provided for the crop to be grown next year. Mr. Smith claimed that he concentrated the natural yield of two years into one, and that he raised the produce of an acre from 17 bushels to 34. The ears of wheat were large, compact, and enormously heavy, and the straw was " reed-like." In some cases the half portion of each acre which carried the crop yielded from 36 to 40 bushels.

Mr. Smith appears to have been somewhat more advantageously situated than Tull, in that his soil admitted of being ploughed more deeply. That Tull would have been glad to do so, he has distinctly stated, as follows: "We not only plough a deep furrow, but also plough to the depth of two furrows; that is, we trench-plough where the land will allow it. . . . Or, if the staple of the land be too thin or shallow, we can help it by raising the ridges, prepared for the rows, the higher above the level. Very little of my land will admit the plough to go to the depth of two common furrows without reaching the chalk, but deep land may be easily thus trench-ploughed with great advantage, and even when there is only the depth of a single furrow that may sometimes be advantageously ploughed twice."

Tillage and Manure are Best.

The foregoing experiments show clearly what may be done by tillage alone on good land in cases where a proper relation is maintained between the amount of crop and the area of land devoted to the crop. As a general rule, however, it will be found more advantageous, on the whole, to combine abundant tillage with the free use of appropriate fertilizers, and this conclusion was speedily reached in England, where the drill husbandry has long been extensively applied for the growing of Swedish turnips. Mr. Smith himself was accustomed to apply to root-crops all the manure that was made upon his farm, and to practise his deep cultivation in addition. In this way he grew "splendid specimens of mangolds and swedes."

The following experiment, made by Cobbett in 1813, may be classed with those previously cited in illustration of the importance of tillage and standing-room. On a plot 9 feet wide and 13 rods long, consisting of land in very good condition and well suited to the crop, spring wheat was sown broadcast in April, at the rate of 3 bushels to the acre. On each side of this plot, and close to it, 3 ridges were made running lengthwise with the field and 3 feet asunder. At the top of each of these ridges a single row or drill of the wheat was sown, at the rate of 5 gallons to the acre. The broadcast wheat was weeded and kept in very good order, while the spaces between the ridges were carefully ploughed and the rows themselves weeded. "Many persons saw this wheat while growing, and though all were struck with the superior strength of straw, and length and size of ear in the drilled wheat, it appeared to every one impossible that a plot 9 feet wide, having only 3 rows of wheat upon it, should bear as much as a like quantity of land covered all over with wheat-plants."

When the wheat was harvested in August, there was obtained from the broadcast plot 2 bushels 7.5 gallons of grain, i. e. at the rate of 36 bushels and 0.5 gallon to the acre ; while one-half of the wheat from the drilled land amounted to 2 bushels 5.75 gallons, or say 33 bushels 6 gallons to the acre. On deducting the seeds sown, it appears that the clear produce was at the rate of a trifle more than 33 bushels to the acre in both instances. As Cobbett has suggested, such drilled wheat might well be grown by peasant proprietors upon their little plots of land. "They might grow 30 bushels of wheat to the acre, and have crops of cabbages in the intervals at the same time; or of potatoes if they liked them better."

Conditions under which Crops can grow.

It is now very well known that there are several conditions necessary for the growth of crops, such, for example, as an abundance of fit food, an adequate supply of moisture, and proper standing-room, and that each one of these requirements is as necessary as either of the others ; though it is true enough that one or another of them may sometimes be supplied naturally upon a given field in such fulness that the farmer feels no need of taking thought for it, and is at liberty to devote himself more particularly to the task of supplying whatever may be most conspicuously lacking.

The system of tilling wide interspaces deeply, though specially interesting as an illustration of the advantage of giving plants an abundance of standing-room, well prepared for the development of roots and for the storage of moisture, has in addition enough resemblance to the old method of " summer fallows " to be mentioned in connection with them. As will be explained under Rotation of Crops, a fallow field was a field left bare and without any crop. But evidently such a field is much the same thing for a whole farm that the vacant strips of Mr. Smith are for a single field. The fallow fields, like the vacant interspaces at Lois-Weedon, were repeatedly ploughed and harrowed to fit them for the crops of the next year. That is to say, they were thus ploughed and harrowed by the best farmers, so that various processes of decay and disintegration within the soil were hastened, and many constituents of the earth that were previously lying there inert and useless became available for feeding crops.

It should be said that Lawes and Gilbert grew wheat on Mr. Smith's plan during several successive years at Rothamsted, and were by no means encouraged by the results of their labors. The Rothamsted soil appeared to be well suited for the purpose, for " without being of high, it is still of good average quality and capable of growing good wheat-crops. The natural drainage is good. The surface soil is a heavy loam, with a subsoil of stiff reddish-yellow clay, which rests upon chalk at a depth of never less than 6 or 7 feet, and frequently twice this depth."

Yet the wheat-crops obtained on this land by tilling in the Lois-Weedon manner were small, — they were no better than those got by the ordinary system of fallowing, and not even as good. Analysis showed that in the soil at Rothamsted there was less nitrogen than in the soil at Lois-Weedon, whence the conclusion that nitrification must have played a very important part for the success of Mr. Smith's own operations. Like Cobbett, Lawes and Gilbert noticed that the crops on the constantly tilled land were specially apt to suffer from blight.

Disintegration of Rocks as related to Processes of Tillage.

Having in mind the vast importance of the disintegration of rocks for supplying plant food, some writers have argued that tillage may justly be regarded as an extension and continuation of the natural processes by which soils are produced out of the original rocks. Undoubtedly it is interesting and instructive to look upon this side of the matter, though it can only present a partial and limited view of the subject.

As is well known, most soils are composed of more or less minute fragments of rock, broken and corroded beyond all hope of recognition. If the original rock were limestone, a calcareous soil will naturally result from its disintegration, and if the rock happened to be rich in fossil remains a specially fertile soil may be formed; from feldspathic rocks clays are derived; while from silicious rocks come sands and gravels in infinite variety. Both sands and gravels sometimes consist of grains of nearly pure silica, though usually they contain many fragments of broken rocks and minerals which are very far from being wholly silicious.

Speaking in general terms, it may be said of cultivable soils that they consist essentially of sand and clay, often admixed indeed with some small portions of the remains of organic matters. The sand may have come directly from the disintegration of rocks where it lies, though throughout the Northern United States, as in the vicinity of Boston, for example, it has almost always been transported by water, if not by ice. Clay is usually a product of those kinds of disintegration which are accompanied with or succeeded by processes of washing with water, whereby the fine particles of clay are floated off as mud to be deposited as such in due course in special beds or layers; though sometimes clayey soils are formed from the decay of limestones and dolomites, and the actual solution of the carbonates of lime and magnesia in these rocks, in such wise that whatever of insoluble clay or other matters they may have contained is simply left as a residue. One variety of clay, the so-called till or boulder-clay, consists of great masses of mud and disintegrated rock which have been pushed forward by the ice of glaciers, and left as ridges or hillocks which not infrequently yield fairly fertile soils since the clay in this case is apt to be well admixed with other rock materials.

It is a familiar observation that when the rocks upon a mountain's side decay, no matter how slowly, some of the products of the disintegration — and especially the clay — are carried off by rain-water to be deposited in valleys and lowlands. Much of the finest of the earthy matter is carried away bodily by the waters of rivers, especially in seasons of freshets, to be deposited at the bottoms of lakes and seas. Even the stones which rub against one another as they roll down a mountain brook add no small amount of sand-dust for the subsequent building-up of soils.

"Truck-land."

Generally speaking, mixtures of sand with a moderate amount of clay and a due proportion of humus are well fitted for agricultural purposes. When the proportion of sand or gravel is unduly large, the soil may still have merit in that it is easily tilled, and that it admits of being tilled at almost any time when it is not actually frozen. Crops grown upon such soils can readily be kept clean and free from weeds.

Here in Massachusetts it is found indeed that micaceous sands so fine that they can hold much water by capillary attraction are often particularly well fitted for growing some kinds of vegetables. In the Middle States many light sandy soils are devoted to the growing of early vegetables ("truck"), and are highly esteemed because of their superiority over other land for this particular purpose. Since such soils are warm and dry even in the spring, they are specially well adapted for forcing plants to mature early, and the fact that vegetables grown on the sandy land can be marketed 2 or 3 weeks sooner than those grown on heavier soils permits of their being sold at comparatively high prices, and much more than counterbalances any advantage that might be got from heavier crops grown more slowly on moister land. But unless they happen to be particularly favorably situated as regards the ground-water, gravels or sands that are coarse enough to be non-capillary can hardly ever be suitable for the generality of crops in dry climates, because they cannot hold rainwater in sufficient quantity or long enough either to supply the needs of summer crops, or to enable such crops to profit fully from the manures which are applied to them.

As regards grain and the other heavy agricultural crops, it may be said that the chief reason why light sandy soils are cultivated is that the cost of ploughing and working them is extremely small, comparatively speaking. It has been said, for example, that the area of land habitually cultivated on the chalky soils of Champagne is "immense," as compared with the small amount of land that can be worked by the same number of animals in any region of clays.

Practical men in Germany have sometimes suggested that for

general use the best soils of all are those of medium character —
neither light nor heavy — which contain clay and sand in nearly
equal proportions, together with several per cent of lime and an
abundance of mellow humus. In that country, such soils are not
apt to dry out too quickly, like sand, nor are they liable to be
beaten by rain to mud — and crusts (and clods) — as clay is. A
soil containing more than 50% of clay is regarded as "heavy," and
in some parts of Europe is called wheat land (winter wheat). So
too, soils containing from 30 to 50% of clay are spoken of as
barley land, and those with 20 to 30% of clay as barley and oat
land. Soils with 10 to 20% of clay are called oat and rye land,
and those with less than 10% of clay simply rye land.

Here, in America, M. Whitney has concluded from numerous
experiments that under the climatic conditions of Maryland, "The
subsoil of good grass-land should contain not less than 30% of
clay, or about 12,000 million grains per gramme, good wheat-land
not less than 20% of clay, or about 9,000 million grains per
gramme, and early truck-land not over 10% of clay, or about
4,000 million grains per gramme; provided these grains have a
certain mean arrangement, and that this skeleton structure contains an average amount of organic matter."

Stiff Clays are Troublesome.

When clay is in excess, the soil is difficult to till at any time,
even when it is dry, and especially when it is wet. Not only has
the ploughshare to overcome the adherence of the clay to the iron,
but also the very great resistance which is presented by the cohesive attraction of the particles of clay for one another. Moreover,
there are special reasons why clays can only be tilled with advantage at those times and seasons when they are "in fit condition,"
as will be explained directly. In a wet season it may happen that
there will be very few days when clay can be properly worked. It
has been said in England, that while two horses may till 80 acres
or more of light land in a year, they can seldom do the tillage of
60 acres of clay. Hence the clays, though often fertile and very
productive when well managed, and devoted to the comparatively
few crops for which they are adapted, are less generally esteemed
than the loams proper.

It is said that at Stockholm clay lands are never in fit condition
to be ploughed, excepting at the end of May and during June,
while at Orange, in southern France, the land is too wet to be

ploughed during February and March, and too dry during June, July, August and 20 days in September. It is in condition there during March, April, May, 10 days in September, October, November and December. At Paris, clayey soils cannot be ploughed in January, February, November and December because of wetness, nor in June, July, August and September because of dryness. It is only in March, April, May and October that such land is in fit condition to be tilled. (Gasparin.)

It is noteworthy that some finely divided calcareous soils are apt to form clods if they are ploughed when wet, but that — unlike clay clods — these calcareous clods have comparatively little endurance, and admit of being crumbled with the harrow after a few days. As Gasparin has insisted, it is in many instances by no means easy to judge as to the character of the mechanical ingredients of a soil by mere inspection, for the fine pulverulent particles in the soil are apt to cling so closely to the other particles that the whole mass may assume a somewhat homogeneous appearance. But on stirring up a given quantity of the sifted soil repeatedly with fresh portions of water, and pouring off the muddy liquids, and allowing them to settle in separate jars, it is possible to effect a rough " mechanical analysis " ; and by inspecting the different deposits with a lens a good general idea of their character may sometimes be obtained.

Light and Heavy Soils.

It is to be remembered that the terms "light" and "heavy" as applied to soils have usually no reference whatever to weight; they refer solely to the amount of force which has to be exerted in tilling the land, and this will depend upon the adhesiveness of the soil particles, and not upon their weight. Excepting peaty soils, which are usually light in both senses of the word, most so-called "light soils" actually weigh more than the "heavy soils."

Any given bulk of sand, for example, or of a sandy soil, will weigh more than the same bulk of clay. According to Schuebler's determinations, a cubic foot of quartz sand dried for half an hour at temperatures ranging from 100° to 122° F. weighed 100 lb. avoirdupois, while a cubic foot of clay similarly treated weighed no more than 68 lb. Hence, a plant growing in a cubic foot of sand might have access to more food than another plant standing in an equal bulk of clay, simply because, in the case of the sand, the absolute weight of soil to which the roots of the plant have access is almost half as large again as it is in the case of the clay.

Other determinations by Schuebler are as follows : 1 cubic foot of arable loam from a field (51% clay, 43% quartz sand, 3% calcareous sand, and 3% humus) weighed 76 lb. ; and a garden-loam also (52% clay, 37% quartz sand, 4% calcareous sand, and 7% humus) weighed 76 lb. ; while a cubic foot of clayey loam (60% clay and 40% fine sand) weighed 88 lb. ; and 1 cubic foot of vegetable mould such as occurs in fertile loams weighed 31 lb.[1] Since there are 43,560 square feet in an acre of land, this number multiplied into either of the foregoing figures will give the weight of an acre of such land taken to the depth of one foot.

It is noteworthy that if the air which is enclosed in them be thrown out of the account, most soils, excepting only those which contain a large proportion of humus, have nearly the same density. As a general rule, soils are rather more than $2\frac{1}{2}$ times as heavy as water, one cubic foot of which weighs 62.5 lb. The specific gravity of sandy and clayey soils ranges from 2.65 to 2.69, and the extreme limits noticed by Schoene in 14 soils were 2.53 and 2.71, the last figure representing the specific gravity of a certain calcareous soil, and the other that of a soil rich in humus.

The Volume of Empty Space in Soils.

The amount of empty space in a soil may be measured by weighing a known volume of the soil, then saturating the soil with water and again weighing, for the quantity of water absorbed by the soil represents the sum of the interspaces in that soil which had been open or " empty," i. e. merely filled with air. According to Pettenkofer's teachings, the volume of the pores does not vary much in different soils, and may be considered to occupy one-third of the whole, though the dimensions of each pore may vary considerably in different soils. Through soils which contain large pores water percolates rapidly, while the compact soils with very fine pores are extremely hygrometric or retentive of moisture. Milton Whitney, however, found that on the average the amount of empty space in soils is about 50% by volume, though there are considerable variations. Thus he found 35% by volume of empty space in the undisturbed subsoil of a coarse sandy land, and 65 to 70% in the subsoil of a strong clay.

He says, " However compact and close-textured a soil or subsoil may look, there is still about 50% by volume of empty space between

---

[1] When wet, i. e. at the moment when water ceased to drop from the water-soaked earths as they lay upon filters, the weights were as follows : one cubic foot of the wet sand weighed 122 lb., of the clay 104 lb., of the arable loam 107 lb., of the garden-loam 92 lb., of the clayey loam 117 lb., and of the humus 70 lb.

the solid particles; i.e. a cubic foot of soil will hold half a cubic foot of water if all the space is filled. Clay soils have more empty space than sandy soils. We have found on the average about 45 % by volume of empty space in sandy soils and 55 % in clay lands. . . . A soil having 40 % by volume of empty space will hold 20 % by weight of water when all the space within the soil is filled, and a soil having 55 % by volume of empty space will hold 31.5 % by weight of water. The amount of empty space in the soil is an important factor in the movement of water through the soil and in the drainage of land; for the water of the soil has to move in this empty space, and the relative rate of the movement will depend upon how many particles there are in the soil, for this will determine the number and size of the spaces between the particles in which the water will have to move. . . .

" The plasticity of moist clay and the hardness of dry clay in mass, as distinguished from the looseness and incoherency of sand, are due to the fact that the clay has a vastly larger number of particles in a unit mass than sand has, and as each grain touches the surface of 6 or 8 adjacent grains, there are many more points of contact for surface attraction to act and bind the mass of clay together. . . . If we assume that there is the same amount of empty space in a clay soil as in a sandy soil, there are at least 10 times the number of spaces in the clay soil for water to move through, and the movement is practically very much slower than in a sandy soil. Clay has no inherent property of absorbing and holding moisture not possessed by sand, the difference being due entirely to the number of particles per unit mass. . . .

" When saturated with water, sandy land has a capacity of holding only about two-thirds or one-half the amount of water which clay soils can hold, and when fresh portions of water are added to soils already saturated, the water will move off through the clay more easily and more rapidly (provided there is an outlet for it) because of the larger aggregate amount of space for it to flow through, notwithstanding the smaller size of the separate spaces. This fact may very likely account for the matter of very common experience that crops suffer more in exceedingly wet seasons in light lands than they do on heavier soils. . . . But where the soils are short of saturation, the conditions are reversed, as the size of the separate spaces very largely determines the rate of flow, and the spaces within the sandy land being larger, water flows through more readily. . . . If the half cubic foot of empty space in a cubic foot of soil formed one large cylinder, it is evident that a large body of water would flow through with great rapidity, but it is also evident that water will flow through this space more and more slowly the more it is subdivided."

Decomposition of Rocks in Place.

In New England, where a large proportion of the surface of the country is covered with the deposit of loose water-worn and ice-worn stones, — which the older geologists called " drift," and which has been brought by moving ice from a more northern posi-

tion,— and where even the clays have been accumulated and transported by glacial action, it is not often that there is any good
opportunity to recognize that gradation from soil to rock which is
the general rule in the formation of soils all over the world, and
which may be observed abundantly in central Europe and in many
other countries.

In many localities a tolerably accurate opinion as to the character and fertility of any given soil may be formed by noting the
source from which the soil has been derived and the manner of
the derivation; i. e. the character of the parent rock, the degree
of its disintegration or erosion, and the distance to which some of
the products of disintegration have been transported. A soil that
has resulted from the disintegration of a feldspathic rock in place
may fairly be expected to be a fertile soil, at least in respect to
potash; and so may a clay which has manifestly been derived
from neighboring granite. In both these cases the soils would
naturally be expected to be "strong," and to have considerable
power of holding water. Alluvial lands which have been formed
by the washing down or deposition of finely divided products of
disintegration from a variety of rocks are often particularly fertile
and well balanced as to their chemical composition. The remark
applies also to sandy loams, such as are not infrequently met with
in the valleys of sandy districts. It often happens in such situations that clay enough to mitigate the sand has been commingled
with it, and in cases where limestone also and organic matters
have been added, very fertile soils may be found.

*Evidences of Disintegration are specially Strong in some Hot
Climates.*

In the Southern States of this country soils are common enough
which have resulted from the decomposition of rocks in place;
and it is noteworthy that the decomposition of the rocks in southern latitudes seems to have proceeded much farther than is the
case at the North, and that the soils are consequently deeper. In
Alabama, for example, in the region of granite and other primitive rocks, it is said to be not uncommon to find, in railway cuttings and wells, soils of disintegration 30, 50, or even 70 or 80 feet
thick. Von Bibra (Reise in Süd-Amerika, 1854, vol. I., pp. 118,
136) was much impressed by similar appearances in the vicinity
of Rio Janeiro. The warmer climate of the South seems to
favor this deep-seated disintegration, and it is true that compara-

tively warm water there percolates the soil throughout the year, and that acids of one kind or another must be generated continually through the decay of organic matter. That is to say, some of the agents which work for disintegration are incessantly active.

Mr. Belt, writing of Nicaragua, says, "The decomposition of the rocks (dolerites) is very great, and extends from the tops of the hills to a depth, as proved in the mines, of at least 200 feet. Next the surface, they are often as soft as alluvial clay, and might be cut with a spade. This decomposition of rocks near the surface prevails in many parts of tropical America, and is principally, if not always, confined to the forest regions. It has been ascribed, and probably with reason, to the percolation through the rocks of rain-water charged with a little acid from the decomposing vegetation." It is possible, of course, as some geologists have urged, that the comparative absence of glacial action at the South has left many examples of old disintegrated rocks in place, while at the North the rotten hills have been planed off by ice or swept away by water. It is notorious, for that matter, that the causes of deep-seated disintegration, such as is often exhibited by great masses of rocks that contain ferrous silicates, are not clearly understood. Boussingault in one instance traced such disintegration to a depth of more than 300 feet in a mine worked in syenitic porphyry.

Soils of Disintegration are often " Residual Soils."

The deep Southern soils just mentioned, resulting from the decomposition of granite on which they repose, are commonly of excellent quality; but it needs to be said of them that the decayed rocks have been subjected, for the most part, to processes of leaching and of straining as well as to those of disintegration and decomposition. It is said of many of the soils which have been formed where they lie through the disintegration of granitic rocks, that, although they have never been subjected to denudation in the ordinary meaning of the term, they have nevertheless been changed superficially to a very considerable extent by the long-continued action of rain-water which has floated away from the surface-soil the particles of clay which were originally contained in it.

Thus the land has finally become covered with a layer of very sandy soil, to the depth of 1 or 2 feet, or more, while immediately beneath the sand there is found the true clayey soil which resulted from the disintegration and decay of the rock. Since this clay subsoil is retentive of moisture, and is usually fairly fertile, good crops are grown upon the land in many localities where the superficial layer of sand is not too deep, in spite of the highly unpromising appearance of the sand.

Another common class of residual soils is found in regions where disintegrated limestones or dolomites have been exposed to the long-continued solvent action of water. Thus in some parts of Virginia, "The surface of the country is covered to a depth sometimes exceeding 50 feet with a red clay which has resulted almost entirely from the decay of limestone. It is a residual deposit that accumulated at

the surface as the limestone in which it once formed an impurity
was slowly dissolved away." (J. C. Russell.)

Disintegration in Arid Regions.

As Hilgard has taught, the processes of disintegration in dry
countries differ materially from those familiar to Europeans and to
residents of our Atlantic States. A great difference is to be seen, for
example, on comparing the granitic rocks of the southern Alleghan-
ies with the corresponding rocks in the arid plateau region west of
the Rocky Mountains, as well as in California and Arizona. "The
sharpness of the ridges of the Sierra Madre, and the roughness of
the hard granitic surfaces, contrasts strikingly with the rounded
ranges formed by the 'rotten' granites of the Atlantic Slope." A
corresponding difference is seen, even on the most cursory observation, to exist in the character of the soils formed under the influence
of these diverse climatic conditions.

While the soils of the Atlantic Slope are prevalently loams, containing a considerable proportion of plastic clay which serves to
make the soil coherent, or even "heavy" when the clay is in excess,
the soils of arid regions are predominantly sandy or silty, with but a
small proportion of plastic clay, unless, indeed, they have been derived from pre-existing formations of clay or clay-shales. "This inco-
herence of the soil-material in arid climates, resulting from the
scarcity of plastic clay, becomes obvious to the traveller in the sand
and dust storms that sometimes annoy him while traversing what
has been conventionally known as the Great American Desert,
which is a desert only so long as the life-giving influence of water is
withheld from it."

"Droughts may render the surface of the country in the Atlantic
States, or in Europe, as dry as the great plains themselves; yet away
from the highways or cultivated fields little or no dust will ordinarily
be raised by the strongest wind, because of the coherence of the
soil, which will generally be found covered by a hard-baked crust.
In the arid region, under the same conditions, a mere puff of wind
may raise a cloud of dust, and a wind-storm becomes almost unavoid-
ably a sand or dust storm also. The same general facts are known
of the other arid regions of the globe, whether in Asia, Africa or
Australia." Mechanical analysis of such "dust-soils" shows that
they contain very little plastic clay, though a good deal of extremely
fine silt. Chemical analysis shows that, other things being equal,
the "residue insoluble in acids," that is to say, the proportion of
inert sand, is decidedly larger in the soils of humid districts than in
those of arid regions, because the latter—never having been exposed to the leaching action of rain—have retained so large a proportion of soluble matters that the insoluble ingredients have had no
opportunity to become particularly prominent.

The results of many analyses show that while good soils from the
humid regions of the United States contain on the average as much as
84 % of sand and other matters insoluble in acids, those from the arid
States contain no more than about 70 % of "insoluble residue." In
consonance with this result it appears also that the quantity of mineral
plant-food in the arid soils is by no means small, and practical experi-

ence teaches that such soils are extremely productive when watered. "But so generally has the idea of inherent fertility been associated, in humid regions, with soils of more or less clayey character, that the terms " strong," " substantial," " durable " are habitually applied to them in contradistinction from "light" and "unsubstantial" soils of the sandy or silty type. Hence the newcomer will frequently be suspicious of the productiveness and durability of soils in the arid region that experience has proved to be of the highest type in both respects."

The great depth to which disintegration extends in arid regions and the remarkable uniformity of the resulting material are not a little extraordinary. "The difference between soil and subsoil, which is so striking and important in regions of abundant rainfall, is largely obliterated in arid climates. Very commonly, hardly a perceptible change of tint or texture is found for depths of several feet; and what is more important, material from such depths, when thrown on the surface, oftentimes subserves the agricultural uses of a soil nearly or quite as well as the original surface-soil. The unconcern with which irrigators proceed to level or otherwise grade their land, even though this may involve covering up large areas of surface-soil with subsoil that has been taken from a depth of several feet, and the rapidity with which the natural forest-growth of the region recovers the red loam of the placer mines of the Sierra Nevada foot-hills, are examples of the fact familiar to the residents, but surprising to newcomers who are accustomed to dread the upturning of the subsoil as likely to deprive them of remunerative crops for several years, or until the ' raw ' subsoil has had time to be ' vitalized ' by the fallowing effect of the atmosphere."

Hilgard attributes the difference between soil and subsoil in humid climates to the fact that the soils of humid regions contain plastic clay which in times of abundant rains becomes partially diffused in the rain-water and percolates the soil in that condition, and tends to accumulate in the subsoil, the result being that the subsoils in humid regions are very decidedly more clayey than the corresponding surface-soils. Moreover, as was just now said, the rain-water often floats away much finely divided clay from surface-soils, and thus tends to leave the surface-soil poorer in respect to clay than the subsoil is.

Other Examples of Rock Disintegration.

In the fertile hilly region of Saxony, where the soil proper is a fine deep loam, wellnigh free from tangible stones, there will often be found a subsoil of angular fragments of gneiss or schist resting undisturbed upon the rocks of which they were once a part. At the mouths of mine-pits in the still higher Saxon hills great heaps of artificial fragments of the same kinds of stones may be seen, in all stages of disintegration and decomposition.

Many of the older heaps, which date by centuries, have become covered with soil enough to support grasses and other conspicuous plants, — sometimes even small trees, — while patches of moss are only just beginning to grow upon the rock-heaps of recent years.

The soil of the famous Constantia vineyards, near Cape Town, at the Cape of Good Hope, is a coarse feldspathic gravel resting immediately upon the granite, through the disintegration of which it has been formed.

Similar effects are conspicuous in the volcanic regions of many hot countries. After a hardened stream of lava has been exposed to the weather for years, it may become corroded sufficiently for lichens and mosses to gain a foothold, and upon the ruins of the mosses other plants will take root, so that, in spite of the denuding action of wind and rain, the lava becomes covered, in the course of years, with a film of soil proper for the growth of many plants. This process of disintegration never stops. It goes on incessantly, even when the rock has become covered with a deep fertile soil bearing a dense forest. At Vesuvius, in 1787, Goethe was impressed by the contrast between the " bare repulsive spaces where rocks of slag defied vegetable life and the luxuriant vegetation which finally overran and possessed itself of these fields of death, and even maintained a grove of stately oaks on the sides of an ancient crater." On walking across the lava of the year 1771, he noticed that "a fine but compact moss was already growing upon it." The same agencies are at work all around us, upon every kind of rock, and upon every soil, though in a country so recently devastated by fires as New England it is easier to observe the beginning of the process of disintegration than to trace its results. The fires of the early settlers have left many of the New England hills almost as bleak and bare as if nature had never been at the pains to cover them with soil and forest.

Influence of Vegetation on Rock Disintegration.

Vegetation, when once established, aids materially in the formation of a soil. It not only does so by holding in place the particles of soil already formed, so that they shall not be carried away by rain and wind, but it tends to collect and retain moisture occasionally, and thus enables water and acids in the water to act upon the rock, as will be explained directly. Moreover, the substance of the dead plants serves to increase the bulk of the soil, and to hold water upon the rock.

Plants contain withal various substances competent to corrode rocks, which must necessarily be brought into contact with the rock after the death of the plants, and which may also reach the rock while the plant is living through the diffusion and osmose of liquids from its roots.

Mechanical Disintegration by Roots.

Several plants are conspicuous from the power their roots possess of mechanically splitting rocks. Livingstone has dwelt on this fact in the following terms: " In passing along near Rapesh [in South-central Africa] we see everywhere the power of vegetation in breaking up the outer crust of tufa. A moponé tree (Bauhinia) growing in a small chink, as it increases in size rends and lifts up large fragments of the rock all around it, subjecting them to the disintegrating influence of the atmosphere."

So too, it is said that in Sicily the lava beds of Ætna are sometimes purposely planted with the prickly-pear; and although it seems probable that, in the ordinary course of events, several centuries might pass before even the surface of the hard lava could disintegrate into soil, the roots of the cactus soon crack it, and in a few years break it up to a sufficient depth to allow of vineyards being planted. On the great pyramids of old Mexico, likewise, the same cactus has broken the porous amygdaloid rock with which the pyramids were faced, and has cut up the surface to a lamentable extent. But the vegetation which now covers these pyramids does good, in that it tends to protect their sides from the washing action of rains.

The action of roots as here described is akin to a mode of cultivation practised by Trappist monks in the elevated part of the Roman Campagna. They bore into the hard volcanic subsoil, blast it with dynamite, and find that seedling Eucalyptus trees planted in the mixture of shattered rock and earth succeed extremely well.

Chemical Disintegration by Roots and other Vegetable Matter.

The chemical action of roots, or rather of matters exuded from the roots, is undoubtedly of vast importance, both for the corrosion of rocks and as a means of enabling plants to take in food from the soil, as will be explained more in detail under the head of Manures. It will be enough to say here, that the juices of living plants often contain acid salts of one kind or another, and that it is known that some of these acid substances have power to dissolve and bring into the plant various useful matters that were previously lying outside the roots insoluble in water.

Several observers have called attention to the softened condition of the surface of rocks at spots where lichens are growing, as contrasted with the bare portions of the same rock. It is noticed that beneath the lichens a small quantity of the rock can often be cut or scraped away without much difficulty, while the adjacent uncovered surface is so hard that the knife makes no impression upon it. Some lichens have been found to contain as much as half their weight of oxalate of lime, and oxalate of lime is a substance that would slowly corrode many rocks. Beside all this, the acid and ammoniacal products which result from the decomposition, i. e. the fermentation and decay, of the dead plants, are all efficient agents for the disintegration of rocks.

It has been noticed by geologists, that sands originally very strongly colored with oxide of iron sometimes become white at points where they happen to be in contact with dead roots, as white indeed as if they had been soaked in an acid. The action of a root an eighth of an inch in thickness may extend to a distance of one or two inches. The same thing is often seen in woods and gardens, where sand has lain beneath rotting leaves. The sand is decolorized.

So, too, under moor-earth in some situations. Not far northward from Boston, on the tops of the higher hills of New Hampshire, and on the coast of Maine also, a cold, sour, black earth will often be noticed at the surface of the ground, immediately beneath which is sometimes a layer of remarkably white earth. The whiteness is due to the solvent action of acids that soak out from the black humus, and which leach out from the underlying clay and sand the oxides of iron that formerly colored them, leaving only the insoluble pure clay or sand.

The disintegrating action of decaying vegetation is sometimes specially noticeable in warm climates. Thus in the soft calcareous rock of the Bahama Islands numerous holes — like pot-holes — are formed by decaying leaves. Some of these so-called "banana-holes" are no larger than a pint cup, while others resemble great cisterns, but all of them contain large quantities of leaves or other vegetable refuse, which is kept wet either by the heavy rains of the country, or by ground-water which is forced up from below through the porous rock by each rising tide. The acids formed by the fermentation of the leaves corrode and gradually dissolve the limestone. (Dolley.)

Agents that convert Rock to Soil.

It is to be remembered always that the "weathering" of rocks and of soils also goes on incessantly everywhere through all time. It is less conspicuous, it is true, in temperate climates, than in those which are warmer, but the effects of it may nevertheless be seen even in the most rigorous climates.

It will be well, perhaps, to distinguish rather more carefully than has been done hitherto between those kinds of disintegration which may be regarded as simply mechanical, and those which depend upon chemical action. A rock may be reduced to gravel and sand by purely mechanical means, while it is by the solvent or oxidizing action of chemical substances that the surfaces of gravel or sand are corroded, and made fit to be classed as soil. It should be said, moreover, that various animals and plants — both microscopic and visible — have much to do with the formation of soils and the bringing of them to conditions of fertility. But none the less does it remain true that the prime agents for the conversion of rock to soil are the corrosive action of air and water; the chemical action of matters dissolved by water; the growth of plants, particularly of those hardy mosses and lichens which find nourishment in the rock itself; and especially, in all cold climates at least, the disruptive force of ice.

Less emphatic than the visible crumbling caused by the formation of ice within the rock, but still appreciable, is the slow disorganization of rocks through ordinary changes of temperature. As a rule, all substances expand on being heated, and contract again when they cool. Many of the cracks and joints to be seen in quarries and ledges were formed during the cooling of rocks at times when their temperatures were higher than they are now. But even under the conditions which now prevail it constantly happens that a part of a rock — say its surface — when heated by the sun's rays, tends to tear itself away from those portions which have remained cool. So, too, in rocks composed of several different minerals, one of the minerals may become heated somewhat more quickly than the others in such wise that it may finally work loose from its connections after it has been warmed and cooled very many times. As a matter of course any loosening of a rock in this way will give better opportunity for the entrance of air and water, and for disruption by ice.

Attrition by Wind and Water.

The attrition of particles of gravel and sand, moved by ice, or water, or wind, is another powerful means of disintegration. Witness, for example, the eroded trap-dikes at Nahant and Cohasset and Newport, the drift-scratches and planed surfaces upon the puddingstone of the vicinity of Boston, and the grinding up of the stones upon any shingle beach where surf is breaking.

Many sand-bearing rivers remove vast quantities of disintegrated rock, and grind it continually until it has become fine enough to form soil. Livingstone noticed long ago, that, in most rivers where much wearing is going on, a person diving to the bottom may hear thousands of stones knocking against each other. He adds that this attrition, being carried on for hundreds of miles in different rivers, must have an effect greater than if all the pestles and mortars and mills of the world were grinding and wearing away the rocks.

Even the force of the wind is by no means despicable in this regard. Before the governmental planting of beach grass at Provincetown, on Cape Cod, the window-panes in the houses of the fishermen there were quickly converted to the state of ground glass, and finally the glass was bored through and through, actually honey-combed, by the drifting sand.

Disruptive Force of Ice.

Of all the sources of action above mentioned, that of freezing water is the most conspicuous in northern countries. A stone absorbs moisture; this moisture freezes, and since water in freezing expands to the extent of $\frac{1}{11}$ its bulk, the stone is either split into fragments, or shaken and made " crazy," or particles of dust or sand are scaled off from it.

It is through this agency that enormous heaps of broken rocks have accumulated at the bottoms of cliffs and mountains in every country where the winters are cold. But this frost-action occurs as well with the smallest pebbles, and in every kind of soil. When marl is strewn in England as a fertilizer, the water that freezes within it is said often to cause the fragments of marl to crumble and fall to powder in a highly satisfactory way. So, too, upon ploughed land, it may often be noticed when the earth thaws in the spring that the coarser lumps and clods fall apart when the cementing ice within them has melted, because that ice in forming forced the particles of the clods asunder, displaced these particles from their original positions, and destroyed their connection one with another.

The disruptive force of ice has sometimes been applied methodically for splitting rocks in quarries, water being poured into holes and seams in the rock and confined there, and then allowed to freeze. Methodical experiments also have been made in this way with bomb-shells, and with thick globes of brass having small cavities at their centres, the brass being burst by pouring water into the cavities and freezing it. An instance is recorded where an amount of force estimated at 27,720 lb. was exerted in bursting a globe whose cavity was no more than an inch in diameter.

A familiar example of the expansive force of ice is seen in the so-called "heaving" of the soil in winter, whereby walls are often overthrown, and crops, as well as the posts of gates and fences, lifted from their proper positions. As the common term is, the posts are "thrown out." In many districts in northern countries, farmers are annoyed by the continual rising of loose stones to the surface of ploughed land, year after year, no matter how often they may be picked off. It is plain in this instance that the stones are lifted up together with the earth when it freezes, and that, whenever the earth thaws, more or less of the muddy loam falls or runs in under the stone before it can settle back to its old position. In this way earth enough is deposited beneath the stone to hold it up, and by the frequent repetition of these processes the pebble is finally thrown out upon the surface of the land.

Disposal of River Sand and Silt.

With regard to the mud or other finely divided matter which results from the grinding together of stones by the action of rapid rivers, or of surf, or of glaciers, as well as that washed out as such by rain from the soil proper, or cut out from the land by brooks, or rivers, or surf, it is to be noted that much of it has been deposited in past ages as alluvial land, particularly at the edges of brooks and rivers, to form the fringes of low-lying fertile soil that are known as intervales in New England and river-bottoms at the West. Indeed, vast tracts of the most fertile farming land in the world have been formed in this way, by the gradual filling up of lakes and seas.

Fine mud is continually being deposited to-day at the mouths of rivers the moment they reach the sea; for by the action of the saline matters in sea-water the mud is made ready to settle, as will be explained more fully under the head of Sodium Compounds. Mud proper tends to subside in moderately shallow water at the mouths of rivers and in quiet bays, and in general in places that are not exposed to the action of breaking waves or sweeping currents. During the process of settling from moving water, it is but natural that materials of similar kinds, i. e. of nearly identical weights and shapes, will be deposited together, in special beds or layers. Mud will subside by itself and sand by itself, while gravel will be strewn in yet other strata according to the different degrees of coarseness of the material. Thus it happens that some beaches are covered with pebbles and others with coarse sand, while fine micaceous sands are seen to accumulate by themselves in special coves or pockets.

Clay accumulates in great mud-flats, such as are left bare by the lowest tides; while in many cases much of the finest mud and silt is caught and held entangled by marine or marsh plants, new generations of which subsequently grow upon it, so that in many situations dry land finally results. When such marsh lands are embanked and drained, as in Holland, highly fertile soils are obtained. So, too, by slow geological processes of upheaval, matters which have been deposited at the bottoms of lakes and oceans are lifted up to form banks and shoals and finally cultivable soils. Mud-flats are often seen to be in process of change to marshes, while marshes, in their turn, may become dry land. In many swamps and ponds, also, mud accumulates slowly to fill them, and the process is often hastened by the growth of mosses and other water-plants which hold the mud and grow upon it.

Disintegrating Action of Water.

The decomposing action of water upon rocks is very great, even if the water be regarded as perfectly pure, and no heed be taken of the chemical action exerted by carbonic acid and the various saline substances with which water that has been in contact with the earth is always charged. It is easy to satisfy one's self of this truth by an experiment suggested by the brothers Rogers. If a fragment of almost any kind of rock be ground to very fine powder, and the powder be moistened with pure water, it will be found after a while, on pressing red litmus paper against the moist powder, that it exhibits a distinct alkaline reaction. A portion of the silicate of potash, of soda, or of lime, contained in the minerals of which the rock was composed, is actually dissolved by the water.

By digesting powdered feldspar, hornblende, and various other minerals, with water for a week, the Messrs. Rogers found that from a third of 1 per cent to 1 per cent of the mineral was dissolved out by the water. If, for the sake of the argument, the lowest of these estimates be taken, — namely, that one-third of a pound of mineral is dissolved out of every 100 lb. of the rock,— and this quantity be multiplied into the 3,500,000 lb. of material which go to make up an acre of ordinary soil, taken to the depth of one foot, it will be found that 10,000 lb. and more might be dissolved upon an acre of land. But it is known from the analyses of Voelcker that 15 tons of good half-rotted stable manure will supply to an acre of land no more than about 150 lb. of potash and 140 lb. of phosphoric acid; whence it may be inferred that the solvent action of water upon fertilizing matters proper to the soil must be a power of real importance for the support of plants.

Significance of Pulverization.

The solvent action of water is of course exerted upon the solid rock, as well as upon that which is powdered. The only use in powdering the mineral is to enable the experimenter to present an enormous surface of it to be acted upon by a small quantity of water.

There is an instructive experiment of the French chemist Pelouze, which bears upon this point. After he had kept water constantly boiling for five days in a bottle of about 500 cc. capacity, he found that the dry phial had scarcely lost 0.1 grm., say a grain and a half, in weight. He then cut off the neck of the phial, ground this thick, heavy neck to powder, and boiled the powder with water in the body of the phial during another term of five days. But in this case the decomposition and solution was so great that fully one-third the weight of the original phial was lost, i. e. dissolved by the water. So great is the influence of comminution that a glass vessel in which water might be kept for years without any very great loss of weight will give up as much as 2 or 3% of its weight if it be ground to powder and left even for a few minutes in contact with cold water.

The French geologist Daubrée put fragments of feldspar in cylinders of stoneware and of iron together with water, and made the cylinders revolve by machinery at such a rate that the fragments should be moved something like a mile and a half in an hour; i. e. they were made to travel about as rapidly as they might have done in a brawling brook. In stoneware cylinders enough silicate of potash was dissolved from the feldspar to make the water alkaline, while much mud was formed from the rubbing down of the mineral; while in the iron cylinders the water was made alkaline by the presence of potash itself, since the silica dissolved at first from the feldspar combined with oxide of iron from the cylinder.

On agitating 6½ lb. of feldspar with 5½ quarts of water 192 hours in an iron cylinder, i. e. long enough for the fragments to have been moved some 280-odd miles, nearly 6 lb. of mud were formed, while the water contained 193 grains of potash, or nearly 40 grains to the quart. The dissolved potash amounted to 2 or 3% of the potash contained in the original feldspar, but to no more than from 3 to 5 thousandths of the mud that was formed by the friction. The amount of dissolved potash was proportional to the amount of mud. In case the feldspar was "crazed" by being thrown into cold water while it was hot, and then subjected to the friction, much more dissolved potash and much more mud also were obtained in a given time.

Solvent Action of Carbonic Acid.

The solvent power of the waters found in nature, even that of rain-water, is usually more pronounced than that of the chemically pure water employed in the experiments above mentioned.

Carbonic acid, for example, is a powerful solvent of many minerals which are wellnigh insoluble in mere water, and this carbonic acid is found very generally in natural waters, usually in combination with lime as a soluble bi- or sesqui-carbonate. Hence it may be said that carbonic acid plays a very important part in the formation and alteration of soils, not only by acting upon rocks directly, when exuded from the roots of plants and when formed through the decay of organic matter, but by bringing other chemical agents to act upon them.

The older, original, or so-called primitive rocks which are composed of silicates of alumina, iron, lime, magnesia, potash and soda, give up to carbonic-acid water some of their constituents much more readily than others. The tendency always is that soda, potash, magnesia and lime will dissolve and be removed from the rock, while disintegrated material consisting of free silica and silicate of alumina or silicate of iron — i. e. sand and clay —

will remain behind in the insoluble condition. This sand and clay are spread out in their turn, and relegated to separate beds by the mechanical action of water, as has been said, while the dissolved matters enter into new combinations in the soil, as will be explained in another chapter. Much of the carbonate of lime, in particular, is carried far away from the parent rock to be finally deposited in great beds of limestone of numerous kinds and varieties. It is noticeable as one result of this method of disintegrating rocks, that from the beginning of time vast quantities of carbonic acid have been removed from the air and stored away in the earth, in combination with lime and magnesia, in the form of enormous beds of limestone and dolomite which are met with on every hand.

This disintegrating power of carbonic acid must be of direct and immediate importance for the growth of plants, since it enables water to dissolve and convey to the plants many fertilizing substances which are hardly at all soluble in pure water. The air in the pores of cultivated soils is highly charged with carbonic acid, as has been shown by the investigations of numerous observers, and the formation of it is no doubt promoted by all those operations of tillage which tend to lighten the soil or to introduce air into it.

The waters of springs and rivers are far from being pure. They are in reality exceedingly dilute solutions of saline substances, such as the chlorides, the sulphates, the carbonates and the nitrates of soda, lime and magnesia, and they are consequently better fitted than mere water to promote the decomposition of rocks and the formation of soils. Phosphate of lime, for example, that is to say bone-earth, though scarcely at all soluble in pure water, is taken up in considerable quantity by water which contains carbonic acid, or even a salt of ammonia or soda. Pierre has shown that even the phosphate of iron, which is known to form in the soil from the action of iron salts upon solutions of the lime phosphate, is by no means absolutely insoluble in water charged with carbonic acid.

The beneficial effects resulting from the application of lime to stiff clayey soils have been attributed by some observers to the solvent, or rather to the decomposing, action of the lime upon fragments of feldspar in the clay. In this case water and carbonic acid are the vehicles which bring the lime to the feldspar.

In regions where granitic rocks prevail it often happens that the waters of springs and wells are faintly alkaline from the presence of traces of the carbonates and silicates of soda and potash. Such waters are particularly " soft," and they have a considerable solvent power. They are highly esteemed for household use, and it is noticeable that, thanks to their alkalinity, they may even become colored, by dissolving humus, when they are put in contact with some kinds of soils.

Rocks are not Homogeneous.

One fact to be noted is that most rocks are composed of mixtures of several different minerals, some of which are much more readily acted upon by the solvents and other agents that work for corrosion than the others are. Hence it happens that great masses of rock may become crumbly and honey-combed, or even fall down to the condition of gravel, though only a comparatively small portion of the rock has really been acted upon directly. By the action of oxygen, for example, upon the protoxides and sulphides of iron, which are wholly absent from very few rocks, and upon manganous compounds also, in some cases, the integrity of the rock is impaired and the crumbling process hastened. Not only may the action of freezing water be specially emphatic upon rocks thus corroded in spots and streaks, but even the alternating action of heat and cold must in some cases help to break up rocks which are not homogeneous enough to expand and contract equably.

Aeration of the Soil favors Nitrification.

The action of oxygen in producing carbonic acid from organic matter in the soil has already been alluded to. There remains to be noticed, however, the agency of air in the production of nitrates, the so-called process of nitrification, which is one of the most im- . portant subjects in the chemistry of agriculture.

Until a comparatively recent period almost the whole of the saltpetre (nitrate of potash) used in Europe was produced in that country by artificial means. A mixture of loam, manure, marl, and leached ashes was thrown into shallow heaps or beds, which were kept loose and open, sometimes even by means of racks and gratings. These heaps were moistened occasionally with barnyard liquor or with urine, and they were shovelled over at frequent intervals, pains being taken that air should be freely admitted to the interior of the heap. After some months of exposure to the air in this way the earth was leached methodically with water, and there was obtained a quantity of nitrate of potash and nitrate of lime.

Now, precisely as the process of nitrification went on in these artificial heaps, so must it also go on in every cultivated field to a certain extent; and it is well to insist upon this obsolete process of saltpetre-making for the sake of impressing the lesson that one prime object of tillage, and of draining also, is the admission of air to the soil. Every well-tilled field, or better yet, every well-tilled field provided with tile-drains, is in some sort a saltpetre-yard. In such a field, much of the manure and of the remains of plants, and of the humus in the soil, will readily be converted into saltpetre; and all experience teaches the great value of this substance considered as a manure. Indeed, when the soil is merely stirred as with the hoe, or harrow, or cultivator, it must often happen that the formation of nitrates will be promoted, and some part of the significance of the summer tillage of crops may fairly be attributed to an actual increase of fertility through changes gradually brought about by the action of oxygen on organic matters in the soil.

Manure may decay slowly in the Soil.

But even if saltpetre be left out of consideration, it will still be true that the good effects produced by frequently ploughing, harrowing and hoeing, and by draining also, result not merely from an alteration in the mechanical condition of the soil, but largely from the admission of air and moisture, which not only go to feed the plants directly, but so act upon various substances in the soil as to fit them to be taken up by plants. It is not sufficient, in order to the best results, to bury a seed and throw upon it some manure. Care must be taken that the soil around the seed, and about the manure also, is in such condition that air and moisture may come in to act their parts in the elaboration and conveyance of food from the soil to the plant. Indeed nothing illustrates better the significance of tillage than the behavior of farm-yard manure when simply buried in land which has never been properly worked. Though much will depend, of course, on the physical character of the soil, manure thus roughly buried will usually decay but slowly. To ensure the thorough rotting of any animal or vegetable matter it is essential that air and moisture should have easy access to it. Manure thus crudely buried can hardly be put to use so fully by the first crop that is sown upon it as if the land had been lightened and the manure thoroughly worked in by repeated ploughings and harrowings.

It happens not infrequently when manure has simply been ploughed under on heavy land that the original shape of the fragments of manure is retained for many months, as is seen on again ploughing the field after harvesting the crop for which the manure was applied. So, too, when stubble has been ploughed under and a crop sown immediately upon the furrow, the vegetable remains are often found undecomposed after the lapse of a year or more. Walz has reported an instance where the stubble of clover growing on sandy loam was ploughed under 6 inches deep in early autumn and spelt was sown. After harvesting this crop, the land was left to lie fallow for 3 years, yet on breaking up the fallow field the form of the old clover stubble was still plainly visible, that is to say, 4 full years after it had been buried. In speaking of manure in this way, it must naturally be conceived of as if it were a part of the soil. It is in fact wellnigh impossible to draw any clear line of demarcation between fertilizers added to the soil and those derived from it. The idea of Tull would be realized if a soil could but be brought to such a degree of fertility that the yearly disintegration and oxidation of its particles, as induced by tillage, should supply an amount of fertilizing material equal to that needed by the annual crop. It was precisely this result which Mr. Smith attained.

CHAPTER VI.

IMPLEMENTS AND OPERATIONS OF TILLAGE.

It would be quite out of place in this book to describe in any detail the manifold implements which are used, or which have been used, for purposes of tillage. But it is noteworthy that, when considered from the chemical point of view, the dissimilarity of the tools used for tillage is much less conspicuous than the fundamental points of resemblance which stamp them all as members of a single family. The wild Indian squaw used a pointed stick hardened by fire. It served her as plough and spade, as rake and hoe. More civilized nations, like the Hindoos, learned in the course of time to set their stick plough-wise, and to drag it through the soil by means of ox or horse power, and the later nations, Americans included, have labored in many ways to perfect this simple implement. But while the stick grew into a plough, or a spade, or a hoe, on the one side, it grew into a rake or a harrow upon the other. And among and between these various implements there may be found all shades and degrees of differences and connecting links; witness the cultivator as one, the so-called "horse-hoe" of the earlier English writers.

Trenching.

Perhaps the most thorough-going tillage of any is to be seen in the so-called process of trenching, which is in one sense much the same thing as digging with a spade, in spite of the fact that, in trenching, the earth is loosened and admixed to a depth of several feet; for in either case every spadeful of earth that is lifted is turned upside down at the same time that it is broken and loosened, not to say pulverized, and more or less admixed.

The main difference is that, by the act of trenching, the surface soil is methodically buried, while the subsoil is brought to the surface. To this end a ditch or trench 3 or 4 feet wide and 2 or 3 feet deep is excavated across one end of the field that is to be operated upon, and the earth from this first trench is thrown out upon the land. The first trench is then filled by throwing into it the earth that is dug out from a second trench, and the second trench is filled in its turn on digging out the third, and so on until the entire field has been dug over.

The chief peculiarity of the process consists in the fact that the surface soil from the second and from each successive trench is thrown into the bottom of the trench that preceded it. Upon this first or bottom layer is thrown the earth that was originally next beneath the surface soil, and so the soil is inverted, layer by layer, in such manner that the gravel or other subsoil that has been dug from the bottom of each of the trenches is finally left at the surface of the land.

Practically, the different layers of earth are much more thoroughly mixed than might be thought from the foregoing statement, for care is taken so to throw the earth from each new trench that the face of the heap of moved soil shall always slope towards the operator. Hence it happens that each spadeful of earth tends to run down the slant, instead of being left where it fell to form a horizontal layer. It is enjoined, moreover, in order to promote admixture, that pains should be taken to keep open a clear space 2 or 3 feet wide between the unbroken land and the heap of loosened soil, so that the workman can readily pick down the earth from the face of the solid side, and let it fall to the bottom of the open trench before he throws it upon the slope of the soil that has already been moved. Thus it happens that each of the trenches is filled with soil that has really been pretty thoroughly mixed, as well as loosened; although, as a general fact, what was before at the top of the land is now deeply buried at the bottom of the loosened earth.

In case there were any special reason for wishing to keep a good surface soil at the surface, the mode of procedure might be modified in that the loam taken from the top of the first and second trenches should be thrown aside by itself at the beginning, and the subsequent operations be conducted in such wise that each new portion of loam would be tossed on top of the loosened earth in a trench that had just been filled with subsoil. As a general rule, however, subsoil and surface soil are mixed, and the operation then affords a capital example of the amelioration or amendment of a soil by bringing another soil to it, for it will seldom happen that subsoil and surface soil are much alike; usually one will be more sandy or more loamy than the other.

Different Modes of Ploughing.

Looking at the plough alone, which is perhaps the most variable of all agricultural implements, it will be perceived that after all not many different kinds of results are obtained by means of it. It is easy, however, to distinguish four kinds of effects which are sought to be produced in different instances. The first is the throwing up of the soil in high, narrow ridges, so as to expose the largest possible amount of rough surface to the action of frost and air. In this operation all the lower fertile portion of the soil is thrown up, together perhaps with a very little of the subsoil, in case the farmer wishes to deepen his land gradually. When left exposed in this way to the frosts of winter, even the stiffest and closest clays may be reduced to a friable condition such as could not be produced by any amount of mere ploughing or harrowing; though, as will be explained directly, clay land which has been thus improved must not be meddled with so long as it remains wet. Of course it is always by the expansion of freezing water in the clay that the crumbling is brought about. Even the coldest weather would have no power to disintegrate lumps of clay which were absolutely dry. According to Gasparin, it has happened occasionally at the South of France in dry winters that the frost has failed to act upon furrows of clay, so that ploughed fields have remained covered with great clods not only through the winter and spring, but through the entire summer also, until they were softened by the abundant rains of autumn. On mellow soils, one conspicuous merit of the ridged furrows is that earth thus laid up can be harrowed down to a fine tilth much more readily than could be done in case the furrow-slices had been laid over one another flat and smooth.

Oxidation and Reduction in Soils.

Not only will earth which has been exposed in rough furrows to severe cold and to alternate freezings and thawings during the winter and early spring undergo no small amount of disintegration in the mere mechanical sense, but beside disintegration, thorough oxidation of the components of the soil will be insured.

As has been insisted already, roots need to be supplied with oxygen, and one important purpose of tillage is to make the earth friable and porous, so that air may freely enter it. But beside its influence upon roots, the action of air upon the soil itself needs to be considered. It was observed long ago by Humboldt, Schuebler, and others, that large quantities of oxygen are continually absorbed by moistened soils, at all times when they are not actually frozen, and it is easy to see nowadays how important this consumption of oxygen must be for keeping land in good condition. It happens, in situations where there is no proper drainage, that land becomes not only soggy, but "sour," because the oxygen of the air cannot gain proper access to it; and even in the best of soils the lower layers are often very inadequately aerated.

As has already been intimated, there are in most soils numberless microscopic organisms which act as ferments to bring about the chemical changes which occur there. It is known that the kinds and character of these micro-organisms may differ widely according as the soil is or is not well aerated; some of the most useful of these ferments can thrive only in the presence of abundant supplies of air, while others act in the absence of air. When organic matters decay in well-drained, permeable soils, the action of the micro-organisms leads to the union of oxygen with the organic matter and with other constituents of the soil, and to the formation of fertile, mellow humus well suited for the growth of agricultural crops, whereas in soils so wet or so closely impacted that air cannot penetrate them, it is observed that reducing actions may predominate. In other words, water-soaked soils are apt to be inhabited by micro-organisms which can take oxygen away from decaying vegetable matter and from some other of the constituents of the soil which contain oxygen. As a result of this reduction a variety of substances are formed which contain either no oxygen or comparatively little oxygen. Ferric oxide may thus be reduced to ferrous oxide, and ferrous sulphate to black sulphide of iron or to sulphuretted hydrogen, while sour humus is formed, so that the land often becomes improper for the growth of useful plants, and can support nothing but bulrushes, sedges, mosses, or other swamp vegetation.

That the reducing action in non-aerated soils is really very powerful is evidenced by the facts that chlorates may thus be reduced to chlorides, bromates to bromides, and iodates to iodides, as well as sulphates to sulphides, and nitrates to nitrites or to ammonia, or even to free nitrogen gas in some cases. (Muntz.) In some boggy places the reducing and oxidizing actions may alternate in such wise that iron pyrites (bi-sulphide of iron) and ferrous sulphate (copperas) will be formed alternately according as less or more air has access to the soil. But ferrous sulphate is a compound which is actually poisonous to plants. According to Voelcker, the presence even of so small a proportion of it as half of one per cent will render a soil almost barren, and on land that contains little more than one per cent nothing whatever can grow. By draining and ploughing such soils, or even by ploughing alone when the conditions are not too bad, air is brought into contact with the noxious constituents, and they are destroyed, either by mere oxidation, or by the action of certain microscopic organisms which prosper in presence of air. Wherever drains have been established, it happens that, as fast as the water with which the pores of the soil were clogged soaks away, air enters the pores to take the place of the water, and speedily brings about an entirely new set of chemical reactions. The soil now becomes a fit residence for quite another class of microdemes from those which infested it before.

Hoppe-Seyler suggests that some idea of these matters may be got by putting a quantity of mud from a barn-yard ditch or house drain into an open glass vessel, together with enough water to cover it, and noting how a brown film forms after a while at the surface of the black mud through oxidation of sulphide of iron to ferric oxide. Numberless microscopic organisms can be detected in the brown film, as well as compounds of nitrous acid. But neither nitrites nor nitrates can exist in the lower black non-aerated mud, and in case a little nitrite or nitrate of lime or soda should be mixed with such mud it would speedily be reduced to carbonate of ammonia. On removing the layer of water from above the mud, i. e. by diminishing the height of the ground-water, the depth of the brown surface layer will increase, and a much larger part of the mud become inhabitable by the micro-organisms which prosper in presence of air.

Subsoils not fully Aerated.

Of course the amount of air in the pores of any soil will fluctu-ate, both with the varying barometric pressure and according as more or less liquid water comes in to occupy the pores, either from rain or any other source. When rain-water soaks into the land, much of the air which the soil contained when it was dry will be pushed out; and, on the other hand, as fast as the moist-ure drains away, new quantities of air will enter the soil and fill the emptied spaces. The looser and the more porous the soil is, so much the more air can pass into it, and so much the more quickly can the air and the water change places. It may be said that, by facilitating the admission of air, ploughing, like draining, checks the tendency towards reducing chemical actions in the soil, and thus in many instances prevents good land from falling out of condition. As a rule, yellow subsoils are yellow because of the presence in them of ferrous silicate, which will speedily change to red ferric silicate when brought to the surface of the ground and put into full contact with the air. In consonance with the lack of oxygen, microscopists have noticed that comparatively few living organisms are to be found in subsoils. Micro-organisms appear to be seldom met with in soils at depths greater than 3 feet.

On the other hand, many surface soils are seen to be red from the presence of ferric silicate, especially when they have been worked continuously for many years, or until so much of the dark humus has been used up that the color of the ferric com-pound can no longer be wholly concealed by it. According to Hilgard, however, the common impression that strongly ferrugin-ous soils are usually poor in humus is a delusion due to the ob-scuration of the dark humus tint by that of the ferric compound.

Any good surface soil which has been for months exposed to sun and air becomes more or less highly charged with products of oxidation, such as the ferric silicate just now mentioned, and when turned under by the ploughshare it carries these compounds into a lower layer of the soil, where they slowly give up some part of their oxygen while they are themselves reduced to a lower stage of oxidation. In this way compounds of the oxides of iron, in particular, act as carriers of oxygen, and they modify not a little the organic matters with which they come into contact. It thus appears that by the act of ploughing oxidation is brought about, both in the soil which is freshly turned up, and in the lower layers also by means of the soil which is turned under, so that a very general freshening of the soil results. In the words of Voelcker, "Many unproductive soils contain protoxide of iron in considerable quantities, and scarcely any red peroxide — a sure indication of poor cultivation. In many instances these conditions may be greatly improved by better drainage, subsoiling, grubbing and other mechanical operations tending to admit air more freely into the soil. In such cases, protoxide of iron manifests itself by the bluish-gray or dark green color which may be noticed in many clay subsoils and stiff, tenacious soils improperly cultivated. A change of color from blue to reddish-brown is justly regarded as a sure sign of improved condition, for it indicates the transformation of protoxide into peroxide of iron, and tells of the free admission of air into the land. . . . Abundance of protoxide of iron, and absence of peroxide, indicates a bad physical condition of the land."

Experiments on aerating Land.

It has often been insisted that one prime advantage derivable from tile-drains is that they admit a draught of air to the soil, and it has been urged occasionally that profit may be got in some cases by arranging the tile-drains of a field in such manner that a current or draught of air shall continually flow through them. To obtain this result, the uppermost ends of the lines of drains are carried out into the air by means of head drains or "air-drains," which act merely as chimneys through which air from the drains proper may escape into the atmosphere. Experiments made in England on heavy clay land, to test this idea, showed that during windy or breezy weather a draught of air through the drains was always perceptible at the outlets; and at other times, after water had ceased to be discharged, a hazy vapor was frequently visible. It was observed that the land above the aired drains dried out more rapidly after rain, and got into good condition sooner than the adjacent land where the drains had no chimneys, and that better crops grew on the aerated land.

The idea may well have merit in some situations, and there would be little danger in testing it, since it would not be difficult to close the chimneys in case of drought or whenever this aeration might seem to be doing harm. Sometimes in permanent mowing-fields and pastures the heads of the lines of tile-drains have been brought to the surface on a slant, i. e. the lines of tiles have been so laid that they shall have their beginnings at the surface of the ground. The merit of thus thoroughly aerating the soil is illustrated by the following experiment of Stoeckhardt. A level field of sandy loam rich in humus, overlying stony gravel at a depth of 20 inches, was divided into three plots, each one square rod in area. In one plot (No. I.) rows of drain tiles (1 inch in diameter) were laid 1½ feet apart. No collars were used to join the tiles, but they were laid loosely, with a straw's breadth of open space between their ends and a shard above this open space to keep out the earth. The drains were laid sloping, in such manner that, while their lower ends were 20 inches below the surface, their upper ends were only buried 10 inches deep. The upper ends of the drains were carried out to the open air by means of knee-shaped zinc pipes, and their lower ends were carried into open pits, so that air could at all times freely circulate through the pipes. At no time during the experiment did rain-water enough fall to cause the drains to flow.

The drained plot No. I. was spaded 20″ deep. Neither plot No. II. or No. III. was drained; but one of them was spaded 10″ deep, and the other 20″. No fertilizer was put upon either of the plots. On May 17th, barley was sown. It came up well upon all the plots, but the plants on the aerated land immediately took the lead. They were noticeably more luxuriant, taller, and deeper-colored than the others. It seemed as if plot No. I. had been manured and the others not. At the time of blossoming a long drought set in, which greatly distressed the plants on the undrained land, and caused them to become yellow and sickly. The plants of plot I. retained their green color through the drought, though they were finally badly lodged by a heavy shower. All the plants were gathered on August 12th, and the yield per Morgen (= 0.631 acre) was as follows:—

	Lb. Grain.	Total Crop.
Plot No. I. Aerated and spaded 20 inches	672	2772
" II. Spaded 10 inches	504	2072
" III. Spaded 20 inches	476	1964

On investigation, it appeared that the soil of the drained plot was really better supplied with water than the soil of the other plots, as will be seen from the following table, which gives the per cent of water in the soil.

	On July 8.		On July 22.	
	4″ deep.	8″ deep.	4″ deep.	8″ deep.
I. Drained and spaded 20 inches	11.95	11.94	9.85	12.10
II. Spaded 10 inches deep . . .	5.87	6.07	6.15	6.20
III. Spaded 20 inches deep . . .	4.95	6.05	5.90	5.40

It was shown furthermore, by thermometric observations, that during the hot months July and August the soil of the aerated plot was constantly somewhat cooler than that of the other plots. In view of the fact that the utility of aeration must be attributed in some part to fermentations of the humus in the soil which are promoted by the presence of air, it may well be questioned whether the advantage gained by such excessive aeration as the foregoing would persist after the first or second year. Unless the humus were particularly abundant, it might be oxidized so rapidly and completely that the soil would be permanently injured.

Ploughing to bury Sods.

As a second method of ploughing may be cited the mere turning over and burying of sods, in such manner that the old grass and roots may decay in a position favorable for the nourishment of the next crop. This sod-turning is a favorable device in New England.

Ploughing for Tilth.

A third method of ploughing consists in turning over, loosening, mixing, stirring, and pulverizing the soil, as by a spade or hoe. This result is effected not only by the so-called trench-ploughs, designed to break up and mix intimately the under soil and surface soil to the depth of 2 or 3 feet, but is produced in the majority of instances where an old tilled field or stubble-land is ploughed immediately before the introduction of a crop. For this purpose ploughs are preferred which cut a wide furrow and leave the furrow-slice in a crumbly condition, almost ready for the reception of seeds.

Where the soil is rich and mellow, a field ploughed in this way will differ but little from a garden dug over with a spade. By this kind of ploughing a part of the soil previously in contact with the air will be turned under, to freshen the lower soil, while there is brought towards the surface new portions of soil which from having been deeply buried have had perhaps comparatively little share in nourishing the preceding crop. One highly important result is that those portions of soil which, from having been in actual contact with the roots of the previous crop, have been deprived more or less completely of their store of available plant-food will now be mixed with the better earth and commingled therewith to form a tolerably uniform and homogeneous material.

An effect similar in kind, though less in degree, is produced by the so-called moulding-ploughs, used for throwing up earth against plants grown in rows. It is produced in some part by cultivators and harrows; also when manure is ploughed under, or the land is ploughed across former furrows, or merely stirred to receive seeds.

Subsoil Ploughing.

A fourth method of ploughing consists in stirring the subsoil, the object being in this case merely to loosen the subsoil so as to permit the passage through it of air and moisture, without bringing any of the barren earth to the surface.

The significance of subsoil ploughing has already been hinted at when speaking of the capillary water of the soil. It is a method of tillage the merit of which cannot be too strongly insisted upon when applied understandingly in fit situations. The result of subsoiling is much as if, in the operation of trenching, when the ground has been dug out to the utmost depth meant to be reached, the workmen should loosen the entire sole of the trench by means of pickaxes and spading forks, and then shovel the soil from the next trench upon this loosened sole.

It is an important point to have the texture of the soil homogeneous, or so to say, continuous, in so far as may be practicable. For example, in the case of a soil of good capillary power lying on top of a coarse, loose subsoil, it might happen that the capillary connection between the two layers would be so poor and insufficient that the surface soil would be less thoroughly drained in wet weather than if the subsoil were as fine, and of the same texture, as the soil above it; while in dry weather the surface soil would suffer from drought for a precisely similar reason. That is to say, during and after rains, water falling upon such land might be held too long near its surface because of inadequate capillary suction to drag it downward; and whenever continuous dry weather should set in to evaporate off the water from the surface soil, new supplies could not come up from below quickly enough to supply the waste. For this particular case trenching would doubtless work a more certain cure than subsoiling, because it is better fitted to establish uniformity of tilth. So it would be also in the case of a layer of gravel reposing upon earth of good capillary character; for moisture could not readily be lifted by the gravel.

In some places where steam-ploughs are used, it is noticeable that a system of ploughing and subsoiling by means of tines — fastened behind the plough — which scratch deeply into the earth, is preferred to the drawing of very deep furrows. For example, where the plough has been run 7 inches deep, the subsoiling attachment may be made to stir 7 inches more, so that the land is loosened to a depth of 14 inches. In our New England practice, it might perhaps be well sometimes to apply this idea to supplement the turning over of a shallow grass sod. If a narrow cultivator drawn by a second team were to follow the plough and stir the sole of its furrow, the capacity of the soil to hold rain-water might in many instances be improved.

Cases occur infrequently here in Massachusetts where excellent crops of vegetables are grown by means of fertilizers, on soils which are conspicuously light and sandy, and which lie high above the water-table. The explanation of the matter appears to be that these micaceous sands are so fine that they are highly capillary and capable of holding much rain-water, and that the particles of sand are so nearly of a size that water is readily lifted through them from very considerable depths by force of capillarity. In England, it is a matter of observation that permanent fertility is usually found in those deep loams which repose upon somewhat permeable subsoils or upon chalk or limestone rocks that are porous enough to permit of good natural drainage.

Plough-Pan.

In soils which contain much plastic clay there are in rainy regions several agencies which act to remove the clay from the surface soil rather than the sandy or gravelly constituents. Not only are vast quantities of clay floated away in the muddy water which flows from the surface of the ground during heavy rains, but the water which percolates through the soil carries with it into the subsoil much finely divided clay, so that subsoils almost invariably contain more clay than do the loams which overlie them. Thus it happens that many a clay or clayey loam may at the surface appear to be dry enough to be ploughed, at times when the subsoil is still full of moisture and unfit for tillage. Hence a great risk that the sole of the plough may form a layer of puddled clay as it slips across the wet subsoil. In point of fact, it has been noticed in many localities in Europe that a so-called plough-pan is apt to form after a while when the land has been ploughed frequently to a uniform depth, and especially in regions of tenacious soils where 4 or 5 large horses are commonly made to walk in line in the furrows to drag the plough. What with the trampling of the animals on the moist soil, and the compression which the sole of the plough exerts upon the land beneath it, a hard bed is formed into which neither roots, nor air, nor water can readily penetrate. In cases where the surface soil does not overlie hungry gravel or sand, an occasional subsoiling would destroy the pan and permit the farmer thereafter to plough as deeply as he might please.

According to Gasparin, it was noticed at the South of France, after the introduction of madder, which requires deep tillage, that many soils which had previously been regarded as unduly wet were cured of this defect the moment the old pan was broken by deeper ploughing, so that any excess of rain-water in the surface soil might drain away downward and subsequently be brought up again by capillary attraction when needed. He noticed that the soils of many fields which had not been adequately drained by the ditches or water-furrows formerly provided, now became fit to bear lucern, which could not have been grown on them before, and that they were now really excellent in respect to the amount of moisture which they held in store. But the improvement was not a permanent one. After a few years, the condition of the land fell away again, and in order to regain what was thus lost, it was found to be advantageous to repeat the deep ploughing as often as once in 12 years.

A clayey hard pan closely related to the plough-pan above described sometimes forms on heavy alkali soils in California and other arid regions as a compacted, impermeable, puddled layer, but in this case the pan will gradually yield to applications of gypsum, which neutralizes the carbonate of soda which caused the excessive plasticity, and the clay finally becomes porous enough to permit water and rootlets to penetrate it. (Hilgard.)

In some rare instances a plough-pan may perhaps serve a useful purpose, for examples have occasionally been noticed where the soil immediately beneath a plough-pan was so open and porous that water could run through it much too readily when the pan was broken. Thus, Marshall, writing of Norfolk county (England), says, "It is a fact well established that breaking up the pan, by ploughing below the accustomed depth, is [in this locality] very injurious to succeeding crops. * * * The firm, close contexture of the pan renders it in a degree water-tight. It is at least a check to the rain-water, which sinks through the soil, prolonging its stay in the sphere of vegetation. But the pan being broken, the rain which is not immediately retained by the soil escapes irretrievably into an insatiable bed of sand, or some other absorbent subsoil."

Tillage increases the Capacity of Soils to store Rain-water.

One of the most important results of trenching, of trench-ploughing, of steam-ploughing, and of ordinary ploughing also, is to improve the storage capacity of the soil as regards water. Into the loosened earth of the trenches rain-water will soak readily all the way, instead of running off from the surface of the soil, or soaking out sideways from the upper layers, as it would if the earth were compact and hard. The deeper the cultivation, so much the larger will be the sponge for holding water. But from this wet sponge, that is to say, from the store of moisture held in the trenched earth, plants can easily supply themselves, and the surface soil can readily pump up its supply of moisture by means of capillary action. Deep soils are apt to be particularly fertile soils, both because of their power to hold moisture in store, and because the roots of plants have access in them to abundant supplies of plant-food.

Gasparin has computed that the weight of a square yard of calcareous, clayey soil of medium capillary power, such as would weigh 2,859 lb. to the cubic yard, would amount to 1,076 lb., reckoning that the earth is taken to a depth of 13 inches. Hence, if the soil is capable of holding 48 % of its weight of water, a square yard of the land will retain 495 lb. of water so forcibly that it will not drain out of the soil by way of percolation. For water does not begin to percolate from a soil until that soil is saturated or, rather, supersaturated with moisture. Some of the water would escape, of course, by capillary attraction if the land were in contact with a drier soil, but the natural outlet is by way of evaporation, and by transpiration from the leaves of plants. It will be seen subsequently, in the chapter on Irrigation, that the quantity of water naturally held, as above stated, by a single foot of moderately retentive land, is very much larger than the quantity of water which ordinarily falls as rain in temperate climates in the course of a month.

King, in Wisconsin, has determined by experiment that the upper 5 feet of soil in a field of Indian corn were able to store 21.24 inches of water, or three-fifths of the total annual rainfall of the locality. It appeared also that this soil when thoroughly filled with water, as might be the case after heavy rains, could contain 24.48 inches of water to each square foot of surface, or more than two-thirds of the average annual rainfall. It is manifest, that in soils which have not been trenched, but only subsoiled, or even merely ploughed, there may be obtained an approximation to the moist sponge which is so great a desideratum.

Generally speaking, soils which are stiff through the presence of clay have the power to hold considerable quantities of water, although, as has been said already, it may happen that capillary water will have no little difficulty in moving about in harsh, crude clays before they have been made mellow by drainage, by manuring or by judicious cultivation; while soils which are naturally loose and open are almost always "dry." By referring to the tables relating to capillarity, which have been given on a previous page, it will be seen that while 100 lb. of clay may have the power to retain some 70 lb. of water, 100 lb. of quartz sand can often hold no more than 25 lb. Moreover, a soil that is too loose will give plants no proper chance to support themselves. The best soils will clearly be those which are neither too close nor too open, and it is the business of the farmer so to till and manure his fields that both these extremes may be avoided. When the tilth is good and deep, water will be held and supplied advantageously, and the roots of crops can penetrate as far and develop as freely as they will, without hindrance.

Paramount Importance of Tillage.

In the great majority of cases the quality of upland fields will be found to depend upon the depth and the mechanical condition of the soil; and of two soils of good and similar texture the one which is deepest will naturally be the best. Wherever a surface soil is shallow and bottomed by a dry, infertile subsoil, whether of stiff clay or of sharp sand or gravel, the land will necessarily be poor. The prime essentials for fertility are that the soil shall be deep enough and of good mechanical texture, and be properly drained, either naturally by a porous subsoil or by the aid of art. On land thus thoroughly drained, it is, generally speaking, desirable that a very large proportion or even the whole of the rain which falls may pass into and through the soil. As Voelcker has suggested, it is possible to conceive that the mechanical condition even of a high-lying, stiff clay-soil might be so much improved by deep and thorough tillage with steam implements, that the land should become capable of absorbing, and holding for the use of crops, every inch of rain that falls upon it (in England).

In this sense, it may often be well to plough land in the autumn for the sake of loosening it, for the freer admission of rain-water. Everyone admits, for that matter, the merit of deep beds of fertile, well-drained loam, such as occur naturally in some favored localities. It is notorious that such soils, though dry enough for early and constant cultivation, rarely suffer much from drought because of their excellent capillary condition; on the other hand, heavy rains do not drown such land, because the water can readily distribute itself.

Cobbett, in speaking of the rich meadows and pastures on the very tops of the North Hamphire Hills in England, says, "The soil is a stiff loam, in some places 20 feet deep, on a bottom of chalk. Though the grass grows so finely, there is no apparent wetness in the land. The wells are more than 300 feet deep. The main part of the water, for all uses, comes from the clouds, and indeed these are pretty constant companions of these chalk hills, which are very often enveloped in clouds and wet when it is sunshine below." That is to say, fertility may be counted upon when frequent rains fall upon soils that are in fit condition to hold the rain-water in the capillary state.

As an example of the advantages derivable from deep tillage, the cultivation of hops may be cited. Trenching, trench-ploughing and, in more recent years, subsoiling have all been found highly meritorious by the hop-farmers of England. In very many instances it is important that ploughing shall be done in the autumn. Indeed, in many localities it is an accepted rule that preparations for next year's crops shall be made in the autumn, so that the least possible amount of ploughing shall be left to be done in the spring. For, if the land is light, much moisture will dry out from it if it is made loose in the spring, while in respect to heavy land there is a risk that spring ploughing may not give a mellower tilth than has been imparted to the soil already by the action of the winter's frost. Moreover, as was just now said, when the earth has been loosened by autumnal ploughing, it will become thoroughly saturated with moisture by the rains of autumn and of the early spring. It is to be remarked, however, that in the northern United States, wherever maize is the standard crop, spring ploughing is very commonly practised, even on light land, because the soil is made warm by the ploughing, and the germination of the seed corn is hastened.

Different Cultivation of Sand and Clay.

It need hardly be said that the methods of cultivating sands and clays differ widely in accordance with the natural characters of the two classes of soils. With clays, it is a matter of great importance to loosen the soil and to make it friable. To this end it is ploughed repeatedly, and it is dressed with long manure, or with lime, and in some cases even it is partially burned to ashes to help destroy its tenacity; while upon sandy soils the plough is used sparingly, seeds are sown immediately after ploughing in order to get the benefit of the moisture in the furrows, and pains are taken also to roll or trample the land for the purpose of controlling whatever moisture it may contain. Much will depend, of course, on the climate of the locality and on the character of the rainfall. In regions where rains are frequent during the spring and summer, good crops may be got, even with careless cultivation, from soils that have comparatively little power to hold water; while stiff clays could hardly be cultivated at all under such conditions.

As Milton Whitney insists, it commonly happens in this country that the growth of crops on upland fields may depend more intimately on the texture and the physical properties of the soil than upon the amount of plant-food contained in it. A good upland soil is one able to hold in store so large a proportion of the rain-water which falls upon it that abundant crops may be grown without suffering much from lack of moisture, except in droughty years. As everyone knows, the summer rainfall in this country is usually distributed very unequally, since it comes as heavy showers with considerable intervals of sunny weather between the rains. Under these conditions, soils differ widely as to their power of holding the rain-water and making it available for the support of crops.

It may be assumed that, on the average, all soils contain about half as much open space into which water may enter, as they contain of solid particles, but soils differ extremely as to the manner in which this open space is distributed between the solid particles.

In a heavy clay soil, the particles of earth are extremely small; there is a vast number of them in a cubic foot, and the open spaces between the particles are so minute that water can only move through them very slowly, and it has great difficulty in escaping downward out of the soil. Such land as this will maintain a relatively large and abundant supply of water throughout the season, and the crops grown upon it will be apt to be leafy and to continue to grow for a considerable period, so that they will mature late; while in a coarse, sandy soil the solid particles are comparatively large in size and few in number, and the spaces between the particles are so large that water will easily run through them and pass downward out of the soil, and not enough of the water can be retained to supply a large crop. On such land as this crops ripen earlier than on clays, and the plants are lighter in weight and of a more delicate structure. A really good soil should be able to absorb and hold a large proportion of the water that falls in showers, and subsequently it should give up this moisture to the crop steadily and continuously during the rainless periods.

Sometimes, in what are known as "good growing years," soaking rains fall tolerably regularly, at intervals of a week or ten days, and there are terms of warm sunny days between the storms. Under these conditions, many soils that would be worthless in droughty years can maintain, during the week or so of sunshine, a sufficient amount of water for the needs of the plants best adapted to them, and then the supply of water is replenished so that a good crop is finally obtained.

Water-holding Power of Loose and Compact Loam contrasted.

Hellriegel divided a quantity of garden-loam into two parts of equal weight, and compressed one part firmly while the other part was left loose. On determining the water-holding power of each, it appeared that the loose earth could retain 42% of its weight of water, while the compacted earth could only hold about 26%. That is to say, the water-holding power of the loose earth was almost one-third larger than that of the compact earth.

So, too, Heiden took up samples of loam to a depth of 10 inches from 7 different plots, and placed them in tubes 2 inches wide by 10 inches deep, across the bottoms of which strips of linen had been tied. These loams were all of similar origin, and differed only according as the physical character of the land had been changed by different styles of manuring during a term of 10 years. Into one set of the tubes the loams were loosely shaken, while they were firmly pressed and packed into the tubes of the other set. Water was sprinkled upon each of these columns of loam, in the form of a fine rain, until the first drop of percolate had collected upon and fallen from the linen at the bottom of the tube. The following table shows the rates at which water passed into these soils, and the amounts of water which were held by them.

			Loose loam.	Packed loam.
Surface Soil.	{	Minutes before a drop of water fell from	85 to 202	355 to 501
	(	Per cent of water held by	41.25 to 43.37	30.53 to 33.06
Subsoil.	{	Minutes before a drop of water fell from . . .	145 to 209	416 to 624
	(	Per cent of water held by	41.70 to 42.76	30.08 to 30.74

Mr. Wilson, near Edinburgh, operating on land that had been tile-drained, ploughed a field 8 inches deep and subsoiled a part of it to a depth of 18 inches. The differences in the crop grown the first year after these operations are given in the table.

	Turnips.		Barley.		Potatoes.	
			Grain.	Straw.		
	Tons.	cwt.	Bushels.	cwt.	Tons.	cwt.
Ploughed to 8 inches	20	7	60	28	6	14¼
Subsoiled to 18 "	26	17	70	36½	7	9¼
Differences	6	10	10	8½	—	15¼

Mr. Maclean, in the same vicinity, made a similar experiment with the following result.

	Turnips.		Barley.	
			Grain.	Straw.
	Tons.	cwt.	Bushels.	Stone.
Ploughed 8 inches deep	19	15	54	168½
Subsoiled 15 " "	23	17	62	206½
Differences	4	2	8	38

In another case, where accurate accounts of the produce were kept, the good effects of subsoiling were seen for five successive years after the operation.

In this country Sanborn ploughed two plots of land, each of $\frac{1}{10}$ acre, seven inches deep, and then subsoiled one of them to a depth of nine inches more, so that this plot was stirred to a depth of 16 inches in all. After drought had become severe, he drove gas-pipes into the earth so that samples of the soil could be taken up from both plots to a depth of 15 inches. In the earth from the subsoiled plot he found 10.1% of moisture, while in that from the other plot there was only 8½%. The subsoiled plot yielded corn at the rate of 70 bushels to the acre, and the other plot yielded only 49 bushels to the acre.

Contrast between a Hard Road-bed and a Tilled Field.

In order to gain a clear conception of the significance of such tillage as relates to the formation and maintenance of a deep bed of soil to hold rain-water, one needs only to observe a hard, dusty, macadamized road in the spring after a few days of dry weather; and to contrast the surface of the road with that of any well-tilled garden that abuts upon the road, that is to say, which is at the same level with it. To judge from the dusty road, one might suppose there was a drought, and the drivers are in fact all wishing for rain to " lay the dust " ; but from the agricultural point of view there may not be the least need of rain, for the tilled land is moist and fresh even to the surface, and the ground is full of moisture. The road-bed has been built hard and compact, on purpose to exclude water. Rain-water cannot soak into it from above, nor can ground-water be sucked up by it from below. It is a hard pan at the surface of the ground. But in the arable land all the conditions should be as different from these of the turnpike as they can well be made. The same lesson may be enforced in the autumn when a worn and dusty road is seen to be covered with mud, after heavy rain, while the adjacent ploughland is dry enough to walk upon; for all the rain-water has been absorbed and disseminated in the plough-land, while it has " puddled " and been retained by the dust on the road. The soil of the fields needs to be mellow, and not compact. If the earth is too stiff and its texture too close, seeds have great difficulty in germinating in it, and many of them perish because not enough air can come to them, young plants have a hard struggle to establish themselves, and even older plants cannot grow freely and vigorously. It is easy to show all this by the experiment of trying to grow plants in jars of pure clay. The plants languish and soon die, and their roots are found to be clogged with minute particles of the adhesive clay.

It is observed by geologists that beds of clay often restrain the percolative flow of ground-water even more completely than beds of rock can restrain it. According to Chamberlin, the nearest approximation in Nature to beds of soil or rock which are completely impervious to water is furnished by a thick layer of fine, unhardened clay. It has even been noticed, in cases where clay has been solidified to the condition of rock by heat and pressure, that so many fissures form in this rock that it is usually less impervious than the original clay. As has been said already, puddled clay is peculiarly impermeable, and so is any soil — devoid of saline or other constituents which work for flocculation — whose particles are so fine that they readily cling together and form mud when they are moistened and stirred. Such muds hold much water, since the water cannot readily.drip or drain away from them.

Risk that the Rain-water Store may be drained by Trees.

Another illustration of the advantage of having a bed of porous earth in the subsoil, which shall act as a moist sponge, is seen in a somewhat different way by the suffering of crops in times of drought in those parts of a field where the water is drawn out from the soil by special pumping engines such as trees or great weeds. It is said that in some of the Western States, where wood is scarce, poplars, i. e. cottonwood trees, are sometimes grown on the arable land much as fruit-trees are grown elsewhere. But when maize is planted in the same field with the trees, it is noticed that the crop grows well enough until a drought sets in, when the leaves of the plants near the trees soon wilt, and the plants fall behind those upon the other parts of the field.

The first thought naturally is, that the shade of the trees has hurt the corn; but a very little attention shows that the corn suffers most on the south side of the trees, where there is little or no shade. The fact is, that the trees pump up so much moisture out of the land that there is but little left for the corn. It is to be noticed in this case, that, if there were much moisture absorbed as vapor from the air, the corn near the trees would profit by it as much as the rest of the corn. In reality, it is subsoil moisture that the trees steal from the corn-crop, and unless the rain-water bed can be made deep enough to supply both the corn and the trees, one or the other of these crops should be omitted. In seeming contradiction to the foregoing statement, it is said that in the valley of California wheat is often grown among the scattered oak-trees which constitute the natural growth of the country, and that the crop succeeds as well or better beneath the trees than in the open spaces. But in this case it is evident that the roots of the trees lie deep in the arid soil, and that they obtain their supplies of moisture from a different layer of soil than that whence the roots of the grain-plants get their nourishment. The grain depends on the limited store of water which has soaked into the surface soil during the winter rains, and the light shade which the oaks cast may do good rather than harm by shielding the grain-plants from the too intense heat of the sun. (Hilgard.)

It has been noticed in Algeria that the eucalyptus tree may pump out from the soil as much water as would amount to twelve times the annual rainfall. Both in that country and in Italy extremely malarious places have been made healthy in four or five years' time by establishing plantations of this tree, which grows very rapidly and dries out the unhealthy locality. In New England quantities of gigantic sunflowers may often be seen growing around farmhouses. They have been planted for a double purpose, sanitary and economic; i. e. they serve to keep the soil dry outside the kitchen sink, and they supply a crop of seeds to be used as food for poultry.

Water transpired by Sunflowers and other Plants.

Experiments have been made by Sachs to measure the amount of water transpired by the leaves of sunflowers, as well as by those of other plants. It appears that, while much less water is evaporated from any given square inch or square foot of the leaf surface than would evaporate from the same surface of water during the given time and under like conditions of temperature, yet the leaves of a plant present such an enormous extent of surface to the air as compared with the surface of the soil in which the plant is standing, that plants have practically the effect of evaporating much more water from the soil they occupy than would be evaporated from that soil if it were bare of vegetation.

Sachs found that a sunflower-plant which had been cut off close to the roots when it was 4 feet high and in blossom, and set in a jar of water, transpired 1.2 quarts of water in 118 hours; and since the plant had an amount of leaf surface equal to 763 square inches, the amount of water transpired by it was equivalent to a layer 0.09 inch thick spread over the entire leaf-surface. But during these same 118 hours 0.21 inch of water evaporated from the surface of a body of water equal in extent to the leaf-surface, as above stated.

As a matter of physiological interest, Sachs urges that the water is not really transpired from the mere superficies of the leaves, but from the walls of intercellular spaces, which in the sunflower represent a much larger surface than that of the outsides of the leaves, — perhaps ten times larger. But since the air within these spaces is wellnigh saturated with moisture, water can only transpire into them rather slowly. It appears, indeed, that the amount of water transpired from a given surface of these intercellular walls in the sunflower cannot amount to more than $\frac{1}{15}$ the quantity of water that evaporates from an equal surface of water.

Cooling Effect of Transpiration from Plants

It is notorious that the enormous quantity of moisture exhaled by trees has a very considerable influence in cooling the air in the immediate vicinity of the leaves; for a great amount of heat must of course be used up, or made latent, wherever liquid water is changed to the gaseous form. The temperature of a place may in fact be perceptibly lowered by the evaporation of water from vegetation.

The freshness of a grove or forest does not depend alone upon the circumstance that the trees shade the ground, and so keep it cool, but that the evaporation of vast quantities of water into the air takes heat from that air. Methodical experiments have shown that in any given locality the air of forests during the growing season is both moister and cooler than the air of open fields. Even the soil and the trees in a forest are decidedly cooler in summer than the air of the open fields. Just so it is that greensward feels cool because of the transpiration of water by the blades of grass.

A noteworthy example of the influence of the exhalation of water upon the temperature of the air has been afforded by the cutting of the canal at Suez. The climate of the Isthmus has been sensibly modified by the opening of the canal, and the extension of cultivation along it, the summers being now perceptibly cooler than they were before. This improvement in the temperature is attributed to the infiltration of water into the desert soil, and in part to evaporation therefrom, but largely to exhalation from the vegetation which has sprung up near the banks of the canal, upon a broad belt of reclaimed land that is irrigated by the fresh-water canal.

In so far as woodland is concerned, the shade and the litter of course lessen evaporation from the very surface of the ground, though the amount of water abstracted from the whole of the ground by the pumping action is enormously larger than could possibly be removed by mere evaporation from the ground itself by sun or wind.

Too loose a Subsoil objectionable.

Manifestly, if the subsoil were already too loose and open, trenching and subsoiling in it might sometimes do harm, by letting the rain-water run to waste more rapidly even than before. There may be danger too, in some special cases, in breaking through the sole, as it were, upon which the soil proper rests. It might even happen in some cases, where the surface soil is fine, that it would run away mechanically with the rain-water into the depths of the earth if the sole were broken. As has been said already, Marshall noticed such soils as these in some parts of England; but, as a general rule, even gravelly subsoils are tolerably compact.

Excepting coarse sands, which are wellnigh incorrigible, the natural tendency is for gravel, as well as clay and loam, to become compact and bound together. As time rolls on, the particles of gravel settle down one upon another into close contact. They are beaten together by rain, and the finer particles continually tend to fall or float into the interstices between the larger particles. Hence, excepting the case of coarse sand, as was said, where the particles are pretty much all of one size, there are comparatively few subsoils that would not be benefited by trenching, or subsoiling, or by any other method of loosening.

It is to be noticed, however, that in many cases it is important to let the soil settle somewhat after it has been ploughed, in order that it may get into the best possible capillary condition before seeds are sown upon it. As will be seen on a subsequent page, it is a familiar maxim of English farmers that wheat should be sown on a stale furrow, and in some northern regions where winter rye has to be sown in midsummer, it is said that this crop will not succeed unless the land is allowed to get stale before seed-time. In Sweden a common practice is to take no crop from the land the year the rye is sown, but to plough under manure in late June or early July, and to harrow the land so that the preparation of the seed-bed shall be finished by the middle or end of July. The land is then allowed to settle, so as to be fit for rye-sowing by the beginning or middle of August, or for wheat-sowing about a fortnight later. Just before sowing, the surface of the land is stirred by means of a heavy harrow.

Rain compacts Surface Soils.

The influence of rain in impacting soils is well seen upon lanes and avenues that have been covered with sharp, non-binding gravel, i. e. in cases where no clay is present to cement the particles of gravel together. In the spring, after the frosts of winter have loosened the impaction which was brought about by the autumnal rains, the surface of such roadways is loose and incoherent; but the rains of spring soon beat the particles of gravel together, and make the surface of the road firm and hard.

This remark is as true of the soil of tilled fields as it is of the gravel of avenues. The frosts of winter and the tillage of spring loosen the surface soil, but the beating rains soon form a compact crust at the surface, which has to be broken up with hoes and cultivators.

It is to be noticed that, when particles of gravel are moist, they readily slip and slide upon one another, until they become firmly wedged in the chinks. It is because of this circumstance that avenues are rolled after rain, and that road-makers take care to sprinkle newly spread gravel with water before ramming or rolling it. Both the ramming and the rolling are mere extensions or exaggerations of the beating action of rain.

Hard Pan.

Beside the mere mechanical impaction of soil, it must be remembered that there is often a tendency towards the chemical binding of the particles of gravel and soil. As Professor Johnson has set forth in "How Crops Feed," p. 332, there are chemical forces, opposed to disintegration, which tend continually to make rocks out of soils by binding the particles of the soil together.

Sandstones, conglomerates, slates, shales, and many other kinds of rocks, were once soils which have been cemented or solidified by chemical action and pressure. Similar changes occur continually, though they are commonly slow, and hardly noticeable while in progress. In the vicinity of Boston, partially disintegrated pebbles of dolerite or trap may often be seen incrusted with a newly formed layer of rock that has resulted from the oxidation of the disintegrated material, and perhaps from its combination with silicates from the soil. These crusts are strictly analogous to "hard pan," which is, properly speaking, a true rock, which has been formed beneath the surface soil by the cementation of the sand or gravel of the subsoil by means of humate of iron, or of silicate of iron, or of silicate of lime, or the like.

In Europe, one of the chief difficulties foresters have had to contend with in planting wild heaths and moorlands is to break through a thin, hard, impervious pan of rock, which commonly underlies the moor-earth at no great depth. Nowadays they break through this pan at intervals, either by picking with pickaxes, or by running lines with a strong subsoil plough at distances of 8, 10 or 12 feet, so that rain-water may soak away from above, and that some capillary water can find its way up from below on occasion, and that the roots of the trees may go down the cracks. So, too, in the old "pricking" system of drainage, the idea was to break through a pan. Gasparin mentions a French instance where, by breaking up an impermeable clay layer or pan, no more than a foot in thickness, which lay upon a gravelly subsoil moistened with living water, the value of the land was enhanced eight-fold; for the surface soil having thus been brought into just relations with the ground-water became fit to bear madder which was at the time so profitable a crop that the value of the land rose from $93 to $730 the hectare.

It may even happen, in some situations, if holes are bored or dug through an impermeable layer, lying between the soil proper and the subsoil which contains the ground-water, that water will rise in the holes and moisten the surface soil either by actual percolation upward, when the water was confined under pressure beneath the pan, or perhaps, sometimes, merely by way of capillarity.

Capital illustrations of the formation of rock similar to one kind of hard pan may often be seen where fragments of metallic iron are left in contact with silicious sand under sea-water.[1] The oxide formed on the surface of the iron by the action of the salt water speedily unites with silica, not merely to cement the particles of sand, but to form an intimate chemical compound which completely incrusts the iron with a layer of hard, smooth stone, and if perchance a corner of this incrusting stone be broken off, the iron beneath it will slowly rust away and be washed out as rust, leaving a hollow shell of the same shape as the original fragment of metal.

Reversion of Soils to Rock as important as Disintegration.

The tendency of soils and of constituents in the soil to revert to rocks, and indeed all the chemical changes which occur in soils, need to be kept in view as constantly as those which relate to mere disintegration. Some idea of the state of things which must actually exist in soils may be got by considering the phenomena of pseudomorphism and petrifaction, which are familiar to mineralogists and geologists.

Pseudomorphs are minerals presenting definite crystalline forms which do not belong to the chemical substances of which these

---

[1] As at Old Point Comfort in Virginia.

minerals now consist, but to other substances which have disappeared, either wholly or in good part, out of the crystals, and been replaced by the present materials. Pseudomorphs, consequently, are not really crystals, although they occur in crystalline shapes. They are merely aggregates of substances which have been deposited little by little, as fast as the contents of the original crystal have been removed. Petrifications and fossils in great variety have been formed in the same way. But precisely such alterations must continually occur in soils, and in the particles and pebbles that are contained in soils, as well as in the rocks from which soils are formed.

The Forms of Ploughs differ with Localities.

In ordinary ploughing, the kind of implement employed and of furrow turned must of course depend in great measure upon the soil one has to deal with. The drift gravel of New England manifestly calls for a very different instrument from that which has been used from time immemorial to stir the soft river-mud of eastern countries.

Some writers have held, in general terms, that a deep, stiff soil can never be ploughed too deep, and can hardly be ploughed too often, provided the land is not too wet nor too dry at the moment of ploughing. But with soils so thin and poor as most of those in New England, this dictum would be utterly untenable. Care and judgment must be exercised always to avoid waste of vegetable remains, and to avoid loss of water, as well as to leave the infertile subsoil where it belongs, and not to bring too much of it to the surface at any one time. It is important in many cases that a soil must not be made too light and loose. As practical men well know, the too frequent ploughing of light land may diminish rather than increase its fertility.

Moreover, the character of the winters in any given locality may determine the times and seasons at which ploughing should be practised there. Thus, in places where the land remains constantly firmly frozen throughout the winter, autumn ploughing may be highly commendable, whereas in localities where the winters are open at intervals, and heavy falls of rain are apt to occur frequently at that season, it may ordinarily be the part of wisdom to break up sod or stubble-land in the spring rather than in the autumn, both for the sake of preventing the soil from being washed away bodily, and for hindering the leaching out of fertilizing matters. A distinction must always be made, too, between rough, stiff and, so to say, crude land, that needs to be worked pretty thoroughly in order that it may be manured with profit, and land which is already in good tilth and good heart. In the case of the latter, too much ploughing might do harm, especially if the land had been recently manured, both by exposing the soil (and the manure) too freely to the air, and by tending to pulverize the earth too finely.

In general, stiff land will profit from being ploughed in autumn. In many cases indeed success upon such land may depend upon the avoidance of spring ploughing. But practical men hold that, for land already fertile, any undue stirring, aeration or pulverization is to be deprecated. As bearing upon this belief, it is to be noted that land left for some time untilled, as in the case of old pastures and grass-fields, is not infrequently found to be in very fair condition.

Ploughing of Light Land.

It was said long ago in England, of Norfolk County, that light lands should be ploughed as little as possible, because experience has taught that the less weak soils are exposed to the action of the air in dry weather, the smaller is the risk that their power of supporting crops will be exhausted. In consonance with this view, a practice, at one time prevalent in some parts of England, of ploughing even light land 3 or 4 times in preparation for turnips has been discarded by many farmers who hold that one ploughing — in the spring — is amply sufficient for turnips on light soils. Subsequently, the crop is "cultivated" freely as a matter of course. The old idea of ploughing repeatedly was to pulverize the soil and make it work well, but experience has taught that light soils thus deeply and frequently stirred dry out too quickly. They are much more liable to suffer from drought in this case than when stirred only at the surface. When light turnip-land has to be ploughed in dry weather, it is thought to be good practice to roll it the same day in order to retain the moisture. After the rolling, it should be lightly harrowed.

It has even been said of the light chalky soils of Norfolk (England), that on some farms of great extent cultivators are used entirely for cleaning the fallow fields. For the reason that, "When these light lands are clean, autumnal cultivation does more harm than good. They are sufficiently friable by nature, and do not need to be finely pulverized or constantly stirred. . . . The idea has become very prevalent in Norfolk that if the land is clean the constant inversion of it by repeated ploughings in the spring is unnecessary, and there can be no doubt of the truth of this view,

on light lands. The sun is not required to extract every particle of
moisture before the turnips are planted, but a good, deep and finely
pulverized seed-bed can be obtained by the cultivator, and the
moisture still retained."

So, too, in some parts of Scotland, where, in preparing for turnips
after oats, " one deep ploughing in autumn and one or two cross-
ploughings in the spring were formerly habitually practised, cultivators and light harrows now take the place of the plough in
the spring, because frequent spring ploughings in dry seasons dis-
sipate the moisture of the soil." The farmer will naturally strive
to bring sandy and gravelly soils into such condition that they may
ultimately be ploughed deep, and fitted to absorb and retain moisture, whenever it is possible to do so, economically speaking; but
in order to do this by mere surface ploughing, long-continued
attention to the kinds of crops taken and of manures employed
will be as necessary as judicious tillage.

It is worthy of note that, while admitting fully the idea that land
needs to be moderately loose and open, to a considerable depth, some
practical farmers have none the less insisted that it may often be
well to have the ploughshare turn only a shallow furrow. Thus,
Horsky, in Austria — a life-long advocate of the importance of
cultivating farms as if they were gardens — after having practised
deep ploughing for many years, finally convinced himself that as a
general rule the utmost economic advantage can be gained by turning a furrow no more than 3 or 4 inches deep, and at the same time
stirring the subsoil to a further depth of 7 or 8 inches. His idea
was that it is best to loosen the soil to a depth of 10 or 12 inches,
for the free admission of air and rain and plant-roots, but not to
dilute the loam proper by mixing it with the subsoil. He urged
that the good loam and the manure should remain undiluted, at the
surface of the land; and claimed that this result could be got with
a saving of from one-quarter to one-third the power that would
have to be expended if the land were ploughed deep. There is
certainly much to be said in favor of Horsky's practice now that
the great importance of fostering useful micro-organisms in the
soil is beginning to be understood.

Application of the various Methods of Ploughing.

In case mere disintegration is sought for, the kind of furrow
first alluded to, viz. the sharp, high ridge, would be appropriate.
It is often drawn to that end in various localities. It has sometimes been urged that American farmers might often do well to
imitate this European practice, and it may be true that this should
be done in the case of soils naturally strong, that need to be thoroughly worked. But in New England there are comparatively
speaking few soils where disintegration can be counted upon as a
direct, speedy and available resource.

The hard polished gravel which composes the substratum of so many New England soils is little prone to decomposition. Of course it does decompose slowly, and the plants which grow upon it seek out those portions of the decomposed matters which are fit food for them, and bring them to the surface. It is by this process of slow decomposition, and the accumulation of the decomposed matters by plants, rather than by any rapid and easily appreciable disintegration, that New England soils appear to have been formed for the most part. Herein apparently lies the justification of the very common practice of ploughing a shallow furrow so as merely to invert the sod.

The growing of Indian corn, potatoes, oats, rye and grass upon inverted sods seems in fact to be a sort of specialty of New England farming; and it does not appear probable that the results now obtained with these crops can be much improved upon by merely changing the style of ploughing, unless indeed the subsoil plough be used more frequently than it is now. But in the case of clay soils, and of deep soils, after the inverted sod has rotted, it may be true that our farmers pay too little heed to the special requirements of such soils, and continue to plough them too much in their usual way.

A rough furrow laid up expressly to " take the frost" and to promote disintegration would seem to be appropriate occasionally upon many deep soils that have been long in tillage, and upon all soils which decompose readily, such as rotten gravels and clays, and in general upon all deep soils that rest directly upon their native rocks. In some parts of Scotland it is customary to plough stiff, strong land in autumn and winter, in order "to share-in the frost of winter so that the soil may be more easily pulverized in the spring"; though in the very same localities it is thought to be best to defer the ploughing of light sandy loams until spring, when oats or barley are to be sown.

Many farmers, even in fertile regions, have urged that it is important occasionally to plough land deeply in autumn, for the sake of bringing up a quantity of the lower soil to improve the texture of the soil at the surface, as well as for the purpose of bringing the inert lower soil to the air. There can be no doubt that, in many situations, this argument must have much force, especially in cases where the surface soil is of such character that frequent tillage of it alone is apt to injure the tilth. After the deep plough-

ing, some non-fastidious crop, such as oats or potatoes, would
naturally be grown first upon the dead earth. One merit of potatoes would be, that in hoeing them the crude earth would be
mixed with the old surface soil, and be the better prepared for
bearing winter grain.

It should always be remembered, that the disintegrating and
nitrifying action of air were the points specially sought for in the
old system of letting land lie fallow for a season. The destruction of weeds during the fallow was a merely incidental gain. So
far from the fallow land being left at rest, it was, in the old English practice, really ploughed and stirred frequently. Nevertheless, it should clearly be understood that in the great majority of
instances where land is ploughed or fallowed the objects sought
for are "condition" and "tilth" rather than the disintegration of
rock particles. The farmer seeks to bring his land into such
shape that certain ferment-organisms may prosper in it, that roots
may freely penetrate it and be properly supported by it, that
abundant supplies of air and water may enter it, and that moisture may be retained by it in adequate quantity and with a sufficient degree of force.

Derivation of the Word Manure.

Nothing illustrates better the high repute in which tillage has
always been held among practical men than the fact that the original meaning of the word *manure* was *manœuvre*. That is to say,
the man who worked his land manured his land. Fallow land
meant originally red land, as in the term *fallow deer;* for much
land that is thoroughly worked and exposed to the oxidizing action of the air will show red by contrast with ordinary land, because of the large proportion of ferric oxide that forms in or
upon it.

Circumstances modify Tillage.

Of course the method of tilling a soil of any given kind will be
influenced materially by the character of the subsoil, and the
height of the ground-water, as well as by the climate of the country in which the soil is found. The style of tillage will be different in different countries, according as the average heat and
moisture of the localities are different. The requirements of Italy
and of Scotland, for example, or of Old England and of New
England, or of the Eastern States and of California, are manifestly dissimilar.

After all is said and done, the relation of the soil to water will still remain the most important consideration. No matter how rich a soil may be in itself, it can hardly be made productive in a region subject to rains and droughts, if it happens to rest immediately upon an undrained, stiff clay, or if there be only a thin layer of it covering a deep bed of coarse dry gravel. But by draining in the case of the clay, or by gradually deepening the loam in the second case until it has become a foot or more deep, then crops may be grown in spite of the unfriendly subsoil. Some of the best grazing lands in England are said to be composed of stiff clay soil resting upon permeable gravel. It is evident that if the subsoil in these fields were as stiff as the surface soil is, the land would be stiff and cold; and it is equally plain that the land would be poor and hungry if the gravel came near the surface. In other parts of England where clays rest upon chalk rock, it is noticed that the soil, though wet and miry in rainy weather, soon becomes dry by giving its water to the chalk below. It is said that up to a certain point these clays are fertile in proportion as they contain more sand. Where sand is deficient they are apt to be cold and infertile, though they have often been much improved by sinking pits into the chalk, and bringing up this material to be mixed with the clay.

Even in the climate of New England, a bed of underlying gravel is not wholly to be deprecated; for if the upper soil be only deep enough to absorb and hold moisture, the open subsoil below it has the merit of acting much in the same way that a series of tile-drains would act. It is only when a thin soil reposes on a smooth ledge of rock that the case is really hopeless. In this event, irrigation is the sole resource. Attention to this truth might sometimes hinder the New Englander from putting in practice his much too familiar custom of burying large stones, in the fields where they lie, by digging pits under them deep enough to drop the stone below the scope of the plough. In situations where the ground-water is within the reach of crops, a stone thus buried may do but little harm, but on high-lying land it would necessarily interfere with the storage and the movements of water, and it might do much harm on this account particularly in dry seasons.

In speaking of tillage, it is to be remembered that one of the most important effects of thorough drainage consists in preventing the occurrence of wide extremes of wetness or dryness, of heat or cold. A drained soil is not only drier in a wet season than one which is undrained, but it is moister in dry seasons, — is warmer in cold weather and cooler in hot weather. And the same remark would be true of a deep soil overlying sharp gravel.

But, as has been said, the upper soil must be tolerably deep in order to good results. So long as the rootlets of the plant have abundant room for growth, and plenty of space from which to collect the capillary moisture of the soil, they can withstand many vicissitudes; as when, for example, the loosened surface soil dries out to the depth of several inches under the influence of a protracted drought. But with only a thin layer of soil, such an experience as this would be fatal to the crop.

Soils are not crushed, but crumble, by Tillage.

It would be of interest, if space permitted, to discuss in some detail the practical question what methods of tillage are best suited to the various kinds of soils. Much might be said on this topic. In any event, there are 2 or 3 points of general significance relating to it which need to be dwelt upon. It is noteworthy, for instance, how little there is, comparatively speaking, of any crushing action in most of the processes of tillage. The plough, for example, does not grind the soil to powder, but merely throws it up in such wise that it may fall into a looser condition than it was in before. The ploughshare works to counteract the continual settling together and impaction of the earth which occur when a field is left to itself. When earth which is slightly moist is thrown up into little ridges, i. e. furrows, the mere act of drying makes the earth crumble and fall down to a loose, light, porous powder; while in winter, through the action of frost, the particles of earth are loosened and torn asunder.

The merit of ploughing loams in spring, when the land is still rather moist, is not merely that the ploughshare slips easily through the soil without distressing the animals, but that the furrow-slice as it dries falls down of itself to the condition of loose earth. Of course the soil must not be too wet at the time of ploughing. There is a proper and an improper degree of moisture, as practical men well know.

Arthur Young has said, in speaking of preparing land for barley and clover seeds, " There is a variation of conduct founded on circumstances not easy fully to describe ; which is ploughing once, twice or thrice for barley. The soil must be dry, loose and friable for that grain, and it must be fine for the clover; but if the first ploughing is hit in proper time and weather, the land will be in finer order on many soils than after successive ploughings. The farmer in his field must be the judge of this : suffice it to say, that the right moment to send the ploughs into a field is one of the most difficult points to be learned in tillage, and which no instructions can teach. It is practice alone that can do it."

In hot countries, as in Southern France, farming operations are apt to be hampered by the extreme shortness of the season during which non-irrigated land is moist enough to admit of being ploughed. The farmer has often to wait until late autumn before the land is moistened, and is then embarrassed by the necessity of trying to crowd 2 or 3 months' work into one month. In many northern countries, however, the chief trouble is that much land is apt to remain too long wet. As has been said already, the general rule in northern countries, subject to summer droughts, is — exception being made occasionally for potatoes, Indian corn, Hungarian grass, or some other tropical plant — that ploughing had better be done in the autumn and not in the spring, for the reasons that stiff or hard land will be better able to absorb and retain the water of the winter's rains after it has been ploughed; that light land ploughed in the spring may easily become too dry through evaporation of the moisture with which the snows and rains of winter have charged the land ; and that the spring ploughing of clays will be apt to destroy the mellowness and tilth which have been brought about by the action of frost during the winter. The cultivator, or the harrow, used at a proper moment, in the spring, upon land that has been ploughed in the autumn, will ordinarily be fully competent to prepare the soil for the reception of seeds, and to aerate it sufficiently to promote vigorous nitrification.

Clays are hard to till.

If the soil when ploughed is wet enough to be plastic, and particularly if it be a clayey soil, then the furrow will dry either to a hard mass, or to hard clods such as the harrow cannot break, and the ploughing will likely enough do more harm than good. It is for the purpose of breaking up these hard clods, which are so difficult to avoid in clay soils, that the toothed rollers called " clod-crushers " are used in Europe. Indeed, the trouble and cost of working clay lands is so great, that, in spite of the fact that they are generally by no means lacking in respect to fertility, there is said to be a noticeable tendency almost everywhere to keep them in grass ; i. e. wherever there are other kinds of land available for cultivation and the farmer has a choice. As has been pointed out by Gasparin, the Roman writers on husbandry were familiar with the risk of "spoiling" land by ploughing it at improper moments. Thus, Columella (about 42 A. D.) enjoined that land should never be ploughed when it is muddy or when it has been half wetted by a light rain, lest it should be made sterile and remain sterile for 3 years. The peasants, he says, call such land speckled, or streaked, or "rotten." At a still earlier period, Cato (234 B. C. to 149 B. C.) had written, "Never plough rotten land, or allow animals or vehicles to go upon it. If this precept is neglected, no crop can be got from the land during the next 3 years." The risk of spoiling land in this way will, on some accounts, naturally be greater in hot, dry southern countries than in more temperate regions, because of the more rapid drying out of the wet clods; but it is a risk to be guarded against everywhere, especially on undrained wet land.

Some clays can hardly be managed anyway. Thus, Cobbett has told of two fields near Sutton (England), "Of as stiff land, I think, as I ever saw in my life. In summer time this land bakes so hard that they cannot plough it unless it be wet. When you have ploughed it, and the sun comes again, it bakes again. One of these fields had been thus ploughed and cross-ploughed in the month of June, and I saw the ground when it was lying in lumps of the size of portmanteaus, and not very small ones either. It would have been impossible to reduce this ground to small particles, except by means of sledge-hammers."

As with clay, so it is with almost any soil the particles of which are too finely divided. Schuebler noticed long ago that by the mere act of pulverization the character of a dry, loose, hot marl was changed to such an extent that the resulting soil had to be classed as wet and cold. So, too, in pot experiments, where plants are made to grow in powdered rocks, it has been found essential that the rock must not be ground to a very fine powder; for when such fine powder is moistened, its particles cling together and form a compact mass, which is eminently unfavorable for the growth of plant-roots. Moreover, when the mud thus formed by moistening finely powdered rock with water is allowed to dry, it may form hard lumps, wellnigh impenetrable by plant-roots or by air. But in more coarsely powdered rock, i. e. in powder whose particles are not fine enough to "cake," it is easy to grow plants by merely adding whatever elements of plant-food the rock may happen to lack, notably nitrogen. (Compare Dietrich, Hoffmann's Jahresbericht, 1863-64, p. 57.)

Practical men, in speaking of very stiff clays in England, have sometimes said that more rain will be needed in summer by wheat, growing upon such land, in proportion as the preceding winter has been wet. The argument is that the winter rains destroy the tilth to which the land had previously been brought by ploughing it, and that, when the water evaporates from the soil, a close, compact clay is left which is impermeable alike to summer showers and to the roots of plants, and which has but a small capacity for absorbing and holding capillary moisture. As Pusey has urged, there is a perpetual struggle going on between the ploughman on the one side, who endeavors to reduce the stubborn clay to mould, and the rains which render it solid again.

Processes of Kneading are to be avoided.

The practical difficulty of cultivating wet clay enforces a point of the utmost importance, and of great scientific interest; viz., the necessity of avoiding kneading and "puddling" in all operations of tillage. As is well known, when engineers wish to make a water-tight reservoir, they spread a quantity of clay upon the bottom, mix it with water, and "puddle" the mixture by long-continued harrowing, raking, and hoeing of it; that is to say, they knead it to and fro, much as in the mixing of lime and sand for mortar, but more thoroughly.

This puddling process has the effect both of removing particles of air from the clay, and of breaking down all granules or compound particles, so that there is finally nothing but an impalpable clay dust, which settles upon itself most compactly, and clings together as a whole with great tenacity, so that neither water nor anything else can pass through it.

In the kneading of clay by the potter's hands or feet, and in the process called "tamping," the same result is arrived at; that is to say, there is destruction of that friability and granulation of the particles of soil, which constitutes good tilth, while there is produced an increased plasticity of the material, and a capacity of forming masses of stony hardness when dry, i. e. clods.

A familiar example of tamping is seen in the process of filling holes in rocks that are to be blasted with gunpowder. Some fine earthy material is beaten down upon and above the powder by means of a copper tool called a tamping-iron. So, too, either tamping or puddling came into play in the making of earthen floors for barns or for threshing grounds, according to Old World methods.

In some places these floors were made with wet materials, i. e. they were puddled; but in other localities, which afforded fit kinds of earth, the materials were not moistened at all, but were worked dry. According to Marshall, the sifted earth was spread level upon a firm basis of stones and gravel, the several materials being used in such quantities that the whole bed was about one foot thick. The earth was then beaten continually with a flat wooden maul, such as gardeners use for beating sods. Under this treatment, the surface of the floor becomes as hard as stone, and rings like metal at every stroke. Unlike floors made by way of wet puddling, which require some months in order that they may become dry enough to be used, and which are liable to crack as they dry, the tamped floors are ready for use as soon as they are finished. In certain districts in England, tamped floors were preferred at one time to those of stone or of any other material, excepting sound oak plank. When properly made they lasted for years and were proof against flails and brooms.

Where the tillage of a soil is good, — that is to say, where the soil is ploughed and worked at just the right time, when it is neither too wet nor too dry, — the gentle stirring and loosening tend to undo the tamping and puddling which have been brought about by rain. As a result of the wholesome tillage, many of the minute particles of the clay will coalesce or "flocculate," as the term is, into granules or compound particles fit for the roots of plants to live and grow in, although it is true enough that the inherent plasticity of the clay when once fully brought out by illtimed tillage might render the soil refractory and almost useless for years. (Hilgard.)

Extremely fine Soils are hard to till.

The foregoing remarks, though particularly true of clay, apply in some degree to all extremely fine soils, such as river silts, marsh silts, bog-meadow mud, and pond mud, and to the very finest portions of all soils. They appear to apply in some degree to much of the prairie soil at the West. Knop mentions the case of a reclaimed bog that bore excellent crops for nearly fifty years without any addition of manure, and then got into such condition that complaints were made that the peat dust killed the crops in times of drought. Analysis showed that the soil contained an abundance of plant-food and no hurtful chemical substance. The trouble was, that the tilth of the humus had suffered, and that the soil now fell easily to too fine a powder. The embanked lands at the mouth of the river Elbe, though of inexhaustible fertility, are said to be difficult to cultivate because they are greasy and adhesive when wet, and hard and tough when dry. In order to succeed with such soil, it must be tilled at the critical moment when it is neither wet nor dry. According to Hilgard, "the presence of even 2% of plastic clay in certain fine, silty soils transforms them from a loose-textured, incoherent, chalky mass into a magma resembling nothing so much as putty, when worked wet, forming the most difficult class of soils to till."

The farmer must strive always to avoid kneading, and must seek to bring about crumbling. A loosely granulated or flocculated condition of the particles of the soil constitutes good tilth, while kneaded or puddled soils are unfit for the growth of plants.

Practice consists with Theory.

The reasons of some of the practical rules that have been laid down by agricultural writers in respect to the ploughing or working of heavy land become plain enough when viewed as devices for avoiding puddling. Thus Marshall, writing in 1785 of the old three-course rotation, as then practised on common fields in Leicestershire, says : " The manure is set on the fallow field, generally on the first or second ploughing, and in a long, strawy state ; raw as it rises out of the dung-yard. . . . The strawiness may serve to keep the fallowy soil in an open, porous state ; preventing its being run together by heavy rains ; a principal danger, perhaps, incident to fallow-field lands." And again, when speaking of the usual practices of the district, he says: "It is common, though not universal, to set the manure upon the land in a raw, long, strawy state ; carrying it immediately from the yard to the field, without having been previously turned up and digested. This is probably a dreg of the common field husbandry, in which the yard muck was perhaps judiciously left unmoved, with the intent that its strawiness might prevent the too fallowy mould — of land summer-fallowed every third year — from being run together by heavy rains."

In some parts of Great Britain, and in Germany also, it has long been customary to plough and prepare heavy clay land in the autumn for the reception of spring crops. For example, when root crops are to be grown on heavy land, it has been thought to be out of the question to postpone the ploughing until the spring, because of the necessity of preparing a good seed-bed for these crops. It is known that one of the greatest difficulties in growing roots on heavy land is to bring the soil to a proper tilth, and it is even said that it is seldom well to sow the seeds of roots (or of barley) immediately after ploughing the land. For these crops, there is an advantage in ploughing in the autumn, and in so preparing the land at that time that the seeds can be drilled in in the spring after a light harrowing, or after a turn of the cultivator; care being taken, in either case, not to bury the well weathered surface soil. Clays ploughed deeply in the autumn and left to the action of the winter's frost will often be made looser and mellower by this agency than they could be by any process of mere tillage, and it is noticeable that, generally speaking, comparatively little harm will be done in the autumn in case the clay is ploughed while it is wet. Nothing can be gained, however, by ploughing bare clay land when it is wet in the spring, for such ploughing would produce clods rather than mould.

Though much must depend, of course, upon the season, it has often been said in England that wet land which has been ploughed in autumn and left exposed during an open and rainy winter will be apt to work badly if it is again ploughed in the spring. Probably it will be much more difficult to work·such land in a wet spring than if it had been left unbroken in the autumn, because it is an easy matter to puddle clay if it be stirred soon after it has been frozen. According to one English writer, the drill is preceded by the cultivator or by harrows only in case the land is free from deep-rooted weeds. Spring ploughing, which was formerly thought to be essential to good farming, is now avoided, for the success of the crop is seen to depend on keeping the weathered surface soil at the top and in performing all the spring operations in dry weather. If heavy rain were to fall on a fresh furrow or before the land had become dry (and granulated), a hard surface crust would form to the great injury of the young plant.

Morton, in his Cyclopædia of Agriculture, says of English practice: " When barley or oats follow a bare fallow, the old practice was to lay on the manure in winter during frost, to spread it on the surface, and to allow it to lie there until the first good weather in spring, when it was ploughed under, and the seed was drilled in. But now many farmers endeavor to get the manure laid on in the autumn immediately after harvest, and to plough it in at once. The winter frost mellows the surface of the land, so that it will be found loose and friable in the spring, when the seed is easily drilled in, and a fine tilth obtained."

And again: " In summer-fallowing, on several of the varieties of English clays, the harrow and roller are used very sparingly. The land is never broken down to a fine mould, but is allowed to remain in a rough, cloddy state. The reasons why this practice is persisted in are as follows: If the land were worked fine, after a stirring furrow, the first heavy shower of rain would cause it to run to a solid mass (of mud), completely impervious to sun and wind, and if, while the land was in this state, drought should suddenly recur, no ploughshare could penetrate the soil."

In a description of certain strong soils based on a plastic clay, like bird-lime, which occur in Hampshire, England, it is said that they are utterly intractable until improved by drainage and chalking, and that even then their cultivation is a work of great difficulty, requiring much patience and perseverance. In sowing a crop on this land, " the processes of cultivation must be completed within the day. Plough a bit and harrow a bit, and then sow before night falls, or rain may come and ' set ' it all."

Another writer, in dwelling upon the fact that the wet winters of the West of England are apt to do much harm to wheat on undrained clay soils, has said, " Not only are the interstices of the soil so choked with water that no air can get to the roots of the plants, but the heavy winter rain beats the surface of the soil into a paste which on the return of dry weather is baked into a hard crust, hermetically sealing the land to atmospheric influence, and so injuring the wheat that a scanty crop invariably follows. The best husbandmen are therefore desirous of not working the wheatland down to a fine tilth, but to leave it in a rough state ; the clods are broken by a roller in the spring, and a light harrow opens the soil. The wheat wonderfully revives and flourishes after this treatment. By the access thus given to atmospheric agency, the act of lightly breaking the face of the soil has a beneficial influence to a much greater depth than the harrow penetrates."

In the county of Suffolk, England, the farmers who occupy heavy land insist upon the importance of sowing certain crops on a stale furrow as a means of avoiding spring-ploughing. Land which is to carry barley after beets is ploughed as soon as the roots are off, in preparation for the next year. So, too, barley stubble which is intended for peas and horsebeans is dressed with from 15 to 20 loads of manure to the acre, and ploughed before frosts set in.

Wet Land is unfit to be seeded.

Cobbett, in his Treatise on Gardening, says," Never sow when the ground is wet ; nor, indeed, if it can be avoided, perform any other act with or on the ground of a garden. If you dig ground in wet weather you make a sort of mortar of it ; it binds when the sun and wind dries it. The fermentation does not take place, and the land becomes unfavorable to vegetation, especially if it is in the smallest degree stiff in its nature. It is even desirable that wet should not come for some days after ground has been moved, for if the wet come before the ground be dry at top the earth will run together, and will become bound at top. Sow, therefore, if possible, in dry weather, but in freshly moved ground. . . . The weather for transplanting is the same as that for sowing. If you do this work in wet weather, or when the ground is wet, it cannot be well done. It has been observed as to seeds that they like the earth to touch them in every part and to lie close about them. It is the same with roots. The earth should be fine and free from clods, for if it is not, part of the roots will remain untouched by the earth. Make sure also that the earth be well pressed about the point of the root of the plant.

If the ground be wet, it cannot be fine; and if mixed wet, it will remain in a sort of mortar and will cling and bind together, and will leave more or less of cracks when it becomes dry. . . . If possible, therefore, transplant when the ground is not wet; but here again, as in the case of sowing, let it be dug or deeply moved and well broken immediately before you transplant into it. . . . I have proved in innumerable instances that cabbages and rutabagas planted in freshly moved earth, even under a burning sun, will be a great deal finer than those planted in wet ground or during rain. There never was a greater, though a most popular, error, than that of waiting for a shower in order to set about the work of transplanting. . . . If you plant in wet, that wet must be followed by dry; the earth, from being moved in wet, contracts the mortary nature; hardens first and then cracks, and the plants will stand in a stunted state till the ground be moved about them in dry weather. . . . In planting out robust kinds of vegetables I would find the ground perfectly dry at top; I would have it dug deeply, moved, plant immediately, and have no rain for three or four days. I would prefer [in England] no rain for a month to rain at the time of transplanting."

There is a story current in New England of a farmer who, having been called to dinner when his onion-bed was but half sown, got no good from that part of the bed which was seeded after he had finished his meal. The seed sown before dinner vegetated freely, while that sown after dinner never came up. The trouble was, that a slight fall of rain during the meal time had destroyed the tilth of the seed-bed. The argument is the same as that of an English farmer who has told of the loss he once suffered from being a single day too late in drilling a field of barley. On a part of this field the seed was drilled in early on a dry tilth, but wet weather set in before the whole of the field had been sown, and two or three weeks elapsed before the task could be completed. When the grain was harvested, the early sown portion was more productive by 16 bushels to the acre than the remainder of the field. "By sowing in wet is little to get," says Tusser.

It has been said of Scotland that on very heavy soils root crops are rarely attempted, because of the difficulty of obtaining a sufficiently fine tilth for the seed-bed, not to mention the risk of trouble in getting the crop off the land in case bad weather should set in early in the autumn.

The familiar observation, that land on which crops are growing often appears to be mellower and in better tilth than adjacent bare land, depends in part upon the fact that the surface of the bare land is liable to be frequently puddled and beaten together by showers, while the leaves of growing crops shield the soil beneath them from the direct action of rain, to a very considerable extent.

Instances are upon record where good, strong loams have been seriously injured by turning up upon them from the subsoil 2 or 3 inches of yellowish clay which was immediately puddled by rain, and baked hard by the sun, to the very great detriment of crops. Even light loams have sometimes been damaged in this way when an unfriendly subsoil has been brought up by ploughing too deeply.

Perhaps one reason why snow has been called " the poor man's manure " may depend upon the fact that when it falls in the spring upon land recently seeded, or prepared for seeding, it moistens the soil gently and gradually without impacting the particles by pounding them, and without floating up any clayey mud to the surface to encrust the land on drying. The influence of snow as a protection against extreme cold will be discussed in another chapter.

The significance of mulches for preserving tilth will be explained on a subsequent page. As will there be stated, even stones may sometimes serve a useful purpose both by mulching and by loosening the soil. Upon this point, Evelyn, writing in 1675, has expressed himself as follows : — " Here I take notice that husbandmen observe a too clean and accurate gathering of stones from off those grounds which lie almost covered with them, rather impoverishes than improves the land, especially where grain is sown, by exposing it to heat and cold. Certain it is that where the stones are not too gross and plentiful, a moderate interspersion of the smaller gravel preserves the earth both warm and loose, and keeps it from too sudden exhalation; whilst the over-fine grain, or too nice a sifting, makes it apt to constipate and grow stiff upon wetting, so as the tender seedlings can hardly issue through; and this is a document for ignorant gardeners, who, when they have a fine flower, think they can never make the ground fine enough about it." According to Shaw, winter wheat sown upon clay soils in Canada resists the action of bleak winds when some small clods have been left upon the surface of the land.

Freezing may help Puddling.

Although, as was said before, the freezing of a soil tends naturally to loosen it, and is really of the utmost importance in this respect, freezing may nevertheless help the puddling process unless care is taken to prevent such action.

Suppose, for example, that a well-granulated soil, such as commends itself, freezes in winter weather, i. e. that the water within the granules congeals. By the act of expansion due to the freezing, each granule may be more or less completely torn to pieces, and be reduced to a number of separate particles of dust, held asunder by particles of ice. If such land were to be ploughed immediately after the ice in it had thawed, it would be an easy matter to puddle the particles of wet dust, which need only to be stirred, in order that they may stick together. But if, on the contrary, the soil is left at rest after the thaw long enough for the dust particles to cohere into granules, as they will naturally do if left undisturbed, and if care be taken to plough only at that condition as to moisture which experience has shown to be fit for this particular soil, then the new-formed granules or flocks will be looser than ever.

As has been said, clays had better be ploughed in the autumn and left to dry out in the spring. When treated in this way, a well-drained clay will suffer comparatively little from the beating action of rain; but care should be taken neither to till nor to cart over clay land when it is wet, and it should not be trodden upon then by men or animals, lest many particles of the clay be compressed into hard lumps, and the land be " poached " also, to its great detriment.

Steam-Ploughs.

One prime merit of the steam-ploughs which have been used in England of late years is that they avoid this pounding or tamping of the land. Moreover, with the steam-plough, there is much less compression of the soil at the bottoms of the furrows, such as occurs when the sole of a plough slides there, and when horses are made to walk in the furrows. The steam-plough is usually supported by wheels in such manner that it cannot slide along with its whole weight resting on the subsoil, there to form a hard, impervious pan or floor. By doing away with this plough-pan, the upper and the subsoil are put into excellent relations with each other, rain-water, which soaks in at the surface of the field, has ample opportunity to percolate, and the risk of the land's becoming unduly sodden or choked with water is greatly diminished.

Even the consolidation of the soil which is caused by the pressure of the wheels of the steam-plough may be corrected by a grubbing-tine which is made to follow behind. Another great advantage of the steam-plough is found in the increased depth to which the soil can readily be worked, for ploughs moved by steam-power are vastly more efficient implements than those drawn by oxen or horses. Indeed, deep working might of itself often be sufficient to counteract the disadvantage of a plough-pan, i. e. the impaction of the soil at the bottom of the furrow would not be likely to do so much harm in case the land were ploughed occasionally to a depth of 14 inches, as might be done on land ploughed only 8 or 9 inches deep.

A great deal of time withal is gained by using steam, for a steam, plough capable of ploughing 10 acres a day will do the work of 10 men and 20 horses. It is said that sometimes these ploughs have performed day by day the work of 12, or 20, or even 30 horses. Of a long day a steam-plough may even do the work of 40 horses, and it is not unusual to work overtime on moonlight nights, on pressing occasions, for, unlike a team of horses, the engine is not subject to fatigue. In some cases it is possible to begin to work before the land is dry enough to bear the trampling of horses. And in any event, whenever the land is ready for the plough the whole of it can be finished in the course of a few days. On heavy land and in large fields, especially in localities where coal is cheap and water can be procured readily, many English farmers regard steam-ploughs as economical, effective, and expeditious.

It is admitted nowadays that the porosity and permeability of stiff clays may be greatly increased by tilling them with implements moved by steam-power, and that deeper and better tilth can be obtained in this way than can possibly be got by ploughing the land with animals. These points have often been illustrated in the case of fields of irregular shapes, where some portions of the land had to be ploughed with horses, while the main body of the field was ploughed with steam. Thus, it has been noticed, during the autumn months, immediately after ploughing, that after heavy falls of rain some water might remain standing for 48 hours on the surface of that part of the field where horses had done the work, while on the adjacent steam-ploughed land no standing water could be seen 24 hours after the rain had ceased to fall. In the spring, land previously ploughed with horses has remained wet so much longer than adjacent land ploughed with steam, that — after the latter has been seeded — the sowing of grain upon the other part of the field has had to be deferred during periods ranging from 1 to 4 weeks.

Some years since, a Committee of the Royal Agricultural Society of England reported as follows: " Upon medium and heavy soils, the benefits obtained by the application of steam-power to tillage operations are undeniable. A culture deeper than it is possible for horses to effect works a highly beneficial change in the texture of the soil, imparts additional efficiency to drainage works, augments the value

of the manure applied, and brings into operation certain latent properties of the soil, which much increases its fertility.   It fits land,
formerly unfit, for the growth of turnips, and allows of their being
fed off by sheep upon the land, whereby the operations of the field
are economized and the growth of subsequent crops is stimulated. . . .
Upon lighter land it has generally been considered that steam has no
locus standi whatever; and its progress hitherto in such districts is
apparently very small.   It seems to have been assumed somewhat
hastily, that land which can be ploughed easily by a pair of horses is
no place for steam.   Those light-land farmers, however, who have
tried steam, even with the apparatus adapted to heavy land, have
arrived at a different opinion.   Deep culture, which relieves a wet
soil in a rainy season, relieves a light burning soil in a dry season.
Though a light soil may not be benefited by inversion, it generally is
by deep stirring," — which fits it to absorb and hold more rain-water
than it could hold before.

Mending of Roads.

In the mending of roads and avenues, ready application may be
made of the ideas above set forth.   I have myself observed repeatedly, on placing fresh, coarse, non-binding gravel in the ruts
of a narrow lane during the first thawing days in the spring, and
leaving the gravel to soak, and freeze and thaw during the next
week of freezing and thawing weather, that a hard, compact road
was formed at once; for the gravel was thoroughly tamped and
puddled by the action of the frost, combined as it was with rolling
and pressing by the wheels of passing vehicles.   But in case the
gravel was put upon the road a day too late, it remained loose and
incoherent during the entire season.

The rule is, then, to roll avenues as soon as the frost will permit,
in order to make them hard, and, if fresh gravel is to be put upon
a road, it should be spread before the last freezing weather of
spring.   But fields, on the other hand, should not be ploughed in
the spring after frost, until time enough has been allowed for the
soil-dust to granulate.   It is well known to farmers, that ploughing land, when it is too wet after a freeze, is worse than ploughing too soon when the land has been wet with rain, though the
latter is bad enough.

An instance of puddled earth specially familiar to men bred in
cities is seen in the street-mud which is scraped off the pavement
with hoes in the spring after the ice has thawed.   On drying, this
material forms a hard cake, most unfriendly to vegetation.   During the winter the mud has frozen and thawed many times, and it
has been stirred and rolled by hoofs and wheels.   It is fine earth,
which has been thoroughly puddled.

Attempts have often been made in Boston to employ this material, instead of loam, for filling in the front yards of dwelling-houses, which are to be sodded in due course. When applied in this way, the dried mud often fails signally to serve any useful purpose, because of ignorance on the part of the people using it as to its peculiar qualities. Plants cannot thrive in puddled earth, i. e. they cannot grow in a thick layer of it, nor can water penetrate it. When employed to improve gravel, the true way of dealing with the street-mud would be to use but little of it on any one spot, and to harrow or rake this little into the gravel methodically, layer by layer, instead of leaving a bed of it by itself at the surface of the land. When thoroughly commingled with gravel, the street-mud would probably soon form a useful soil. It is a matter of experience, at all events, that if ordinary street-sweepings, which contain more or less horse-dung, are left to lie in great heaps for half a year, and are then forked over, moistened and left to themselves during another half-year, a friable, homogeneous earth is obtained which is suitable to be mixed with loam, or even to be used instead of loam.

Other Examples of Puddled Earths.

It will be noticed that dust or mud swept or scraped from a macadamized road, or, for that matter, from any unpaved highway, will cohere firmly when left to itself, or when thrown upon the side of the road to form a walk. Another substance easy to puddle is fine coal-ashes. I have seen most admirable, hard, compact sidewalks made by spreading, one above the other, repeated thin layers of sifted coal-ashes, and wetting, raking pertinaciously, and rolling each layer. This job requires patient toil, but the results of it are surprising.

Still another familiar example of puddled earth is seen in the layers of slime which are left whenever puddles of water upon the highway dry up. Indeed, the particles of clay or fine earth, which so obstinately refuse to settle from a mud-puddle, and which give the puddle its name, are not at all " flocculated " or " granulated," they are dust-like. Mud or slime such as this is peculiarly obnoxious both to the soil and to plants. When water comes into contact with it, it floats into the soil to clog the pores of the soil, and the cells of plant-roots also.

This trouble might readily be produced by the injudicious watering of earth in which seeds or young plants have recently been

placed.   Evelyn said long ago, "Whatsoever you sow or plant,
water not over-hastily, nor with too great a stream, for it hardens
the ground without penetrating. . . . Never cast water on things
newly planted, but at convenient distance, so as rather to moisten
the ground without sobbing the leaves of the plant, which ends in
scorching."   It is an old device of gardeners to sink an empty
flower-pot to its brim in the soil of the garden, near plants that
are to be watered, and to pour water freely into this pot so that
the liquid may soak into the earth in all directions without puddling the surface of the land.

On trying to grow plants in pure pipe-clay admixed with sand,
it will readily be seen how easily the roots are distressed by this
clogging of their cells.   When such "colloid clay" is floated by
water up to the surface of the land, it encrusts it speedily, and it
is to be noted that this kind of encrustation — though less emphatic and less troublesome than that which results from the beating action of rain — might be produced by irrigation-water as
well as by rain-water.

Pond-Mud and Harbor-Mud.

Some pond-muds are, to all intents and purposes, puddled earth,
and the diversity of action noticed when such muds are used as
fertilizers doubtless depends in some part on differences in the
mechanical condition of the different samples.   Some of these
muds must be excellently well suited for use upon sandy soils,
though perhaps they might be distinctly hurtful to some loams.
Discretion needs to be exercised in using such materials.   According to Evelyn, writing in 1675, "For earth which is too light,
there is nothing better than pond-mud, after a winter has passed
over it."   And again, he says, "Marsh-mud and churlish earth
will be civilized by the rigor and discipline of two winters; bis
frigora is the old method to make the stubborn clod relent; and
with the mixture of a little sand, if it be too close of body, it will
become excellent mould."

In Holland, mud taken from the harbors of several Dutch and
German seaports is largely used even now for fertilizing peaty
soils that are in process of reclamation, especially such as have
been mixed with sand.   The fresh mud is left in heaps some 4 to 8
months, to weather, and is forked over to hasten the aeration.   It
is applied, at a dry time, at the rate of 60 or 70 tons to the acre,
and the good effects of it are said to be felt during 20 or even 30

years. It is evident enough that such mud must bring in considerable quantities of fertilizing matters as well as exert a very decided mechanical effect. It may be accepted indeed, as a matter of practical experience, that the fine mud of bays, harbors and marshes may often be made to serve a good purpose when applied in large quantity to light, permeable soils which are neither wet nor too dry. But it is held to be essential that the (salt) mud must not be spread immediately after it has been dug. It had better be left in small heaps exposed to the action of frost, rain and sun until it has fallen to a dry powder.

Fleischer reports instances of the speedy recuperation by means of sea-mud of moorland which had been "exhausted" by repeatedly burning and cropping it. During the first year after applying the sea-mud satisfactory crops of oats were grown, while in the second year the clover, which succeeded the oats, yielded 3.4 tons of hay to the acre where 4.5 tons of sea-mud had been applied, and more than 4 tons of hay to the acre where 9 tons of the mud were used. The last-named crop was nearly 5 times larger than that got from similar land that had been manured but not dressed with the sea-mud.

On the continent of Europe there are many artificial fish-ponds, and in some localities it has long been customary to drain these ponds occasionally, and to grow crops for a series of years upon the land which had previously been covered with water. But if, after the water has been drained off, the winter happens to be so mild that the mud does not freeze hard, it is said to be a very difficult matter to prepare the land for seeding in the spring. The surface of the slimy mud is apt to dry out to a firm crust, as hard as a threshing-floor, though full of cracks, while the mud beneath this crust remains soft and greasy, and in a condition utterly unfit for harrowing or cultivating. Horsky once, on encountering this difficulty, got a good crop of oats by sweeping the seed with brooms into the cracks of the hard surface crust.

It is to be noted that by the action of frost the tilth of plastic, adhesive silts and clays is improved in two ways: not only are the particles of earth forced asunder mechanically by the particles of ice which form among them, and thus left in a condition which permits of their gradually cohering into granules, but it is true also that the, so to say, external sliminess of the clay or silt is destroyed by the act of freezing. It is noticeable, for example, when a mud-puddle freezes, that the particles of slimy clay in it cohere into flocks or granules, which settle readily enough when the ice melts. Similar appearances were observed by chemists long ago on freezing certain "pseudo-solutions," such, for example, as water which has been made opalescent by stirring into it a little thin starch paste. When such water freezes, the particles of starch in it cohere, and they settle out from the water in the form of visible lumps, as soon as the ice has melted. In the words of Professor Johnson, "When water, turbid from suspended clay that would remain without settling for weeks together, is frozen, the clay particles, before so attenuated as to be invisible under the microscope, are precipitated in distinct flocky masses, which, under the microscope, transmit much light, and have a granular or cellular appearance; and the water may be poured off quite clear and free from milkiness."

Earth-worms are sometimes Pernicious.

Gardeners are familiar with the fact that the presence of earth-worms in the soil of plant-pots is highly detrimental to the health and growth of the plants. The trouble appears to be, that worm-casts consist of thoroughly puddled earth, i. e. of earth which has been completely deflocculated by passing through the bodies of the worms. When water is poured upon the soil in the pots, the worm-casts pass into the condition of slimy mud, which soaks into the earth to clog its pores and those of the roots as well. So, too, it has been said by farmers in England that no grass land which is subject to worm-casts can be of good quality. And surprise has been expressed that this should be true by men who have noticed that the size of the worms in a field is an excellent criterion of the state of the land, and of its fitness to grow crops. "Where you have no worms," they say, "you will have no wheat." But in point of fact, it is in good, moist, rich land that earth-worms specially abound and wax fat. They affect land which is full of manure and of mellow organic matter, i. e. land where many of the conditions of fertility are so exceptionally favorable for the growth of plants, that crops can prosper in spite of the worms.

It is not improbable that worms feed upon and destroy many of the useful micro-organisms with which fertile soils are charged, and there can be little question that, in temperate climates at least, they may often be harmful in the narrow agricultural sense, though, as is well known, Darwin proved that earth-worms have no small geologic importance, in that they work continually in many localities to bring fine earth to the surface of the land, and do thus deepen the layer of loam upon many fields. In some hot, damp countries vast quantities of loam are said to be turned over by gigantic worms with astonishing rapidity.

Amelioration of Clays.

From what has been said above, it appears that the trouble with strong clay soils depends, not merely on the difficulty of finding appropriate moments in which to till them without forming clods, but also upon the risk that the pores in the soil, and even the cells of the roots of the crops, may be clogged by the muddy liquors which are formed in such soils by rains.

By the use of long manure, marl, lime, calcareous sand, burnt clay, coal-ashes, or even silicious sand or gravel, it is possible to correct in some measure both these faults of clayey soils, particularly when the clay is not too plastic and pure to begin with. Tile-drains especially may do excellent service, and it will be found in some localities that thoroughly drained clays are the most profitable of all soils for cultivation.

In the chapter on Paring and Burning it will be seen that the physical effect of fire on stiff clays is so marked that burning may be regarded as a means of tillage. Even the burning in hot summer weather of tall grain-stubble as it stands on a dry, clayey soil may greatly improve the texture of the surface soil, and make it mellow enough to permit the harrowing-in of seeds in due course. (Gasparin.) By means of steam-ploughs, also, enormous improvements in cultivating clay soils have been made in England. With the steam-plough the land can be broken up with a rapidity and thoroughness which was impossible before, so that the farmer can now take full advantage of moments when such soils are dry and in proper condition to be worked.

Some Soils not to be tilled when Dry.

It is not alone when soils are wet that it is wrong to try to till them. Few soils can be ploughed with advantage when they are completely dry. To say nothing of the great amount of force which must be expended in dragging the ploughshare through the hard ground, the dry furrows would not be so apt to crumble kindly after rain as they would if the land had been wetted before ploughing it. In many cases the plough would break a dry soil into mere clods of highly refractory character. It has been found, moreover, that some fine soils, composed of minute particles of uniform fineness, such as certain river-deposits, suffer very much on being ploughed when they are very dry. They are soils whose granules or flocks have so little coherence that, on drying, they fall to dust of their own weight, or on the least shock or movement to which the earth is subjected. (Hilgard.)

In ordinary soils, the beating and floating action of water which falls as rain destroys the floccules at the surface merely, by a process of mechanical puddling, though it may be that the surface crust is somewhat deepened by the infiltration of clay-water to the layer of soil next below the surface; but on stirring the fine silts now in question, the tamping process may go on to an appreciable depth, i. e. as far as the soil dries.

In some southern countries where irrigation is practised, it is a common custom to lead water upon the ground after a crop has been harvested in midsummer, for the purpose of softening it sufficiently to admit of its being ploughed, after a day or two, instead of having to wait two or three months for the advent of the autumnal rains. In general, the soils which permit the greatest freedom of tillage are those whose particles are not of uniform size, — good garden-loams, for instance.

Very Fine Soils are apt to need Tile-Drains.

It is said that many prairie-soils which had sufficient natural drainage at first get into such a condition, after years of cultivation, that it becomes almost absolutely necessary to tile-drain them. It appears that the continued cultivation of such finely divided soil tends to dry-puddle it somewhat,— to such an extent, namely, that water finds no easy passage through it.

To show how antagonistic puddling is to draining, instances might be cited from experiences in the Western States relating to the mud-roads of the prairie country. It would be an enormous gain if these loam-built roads could be kept dry enough and hard enough to bear wagons in soft winter weather; and it was thought at one time that tile-drains laid beneath the surface of the road would help to keep the earth dry. But on trying the experiment, the operators got no good for their trouble. The mud in winter and spring was just as deep on the tiled roads as upon the others.

A moment's reflection teaches that the soil at the surface of the road is so tamped and puddled, all through the year, by passing vehicles, that water cannot pass through it. It might almost be said that the puddled surface-soil has no connection with the subsoil in which the tiles were laid. Of course, in wet weather some of the puddled earth is softened and stirred up to the condition of mud by passing vehicles. But water cannot flow through such mud, and in so far as the mud is ground into the soil below it, so is the depth of the puddled earth increased.

Risk of Puddling in Subsoil Ploughing.

In view of what is known about the puddling of soils, it is now easier than it was formerly to understand one very important point in respect to the use of the subsoil plough, viz. the risk there is of puddling a clayey subsoil when this instrument is used upon it at an improper season.

A soil may be in excellent condition for tilling at the surface, and yet be too wet below; so wet below that the action of a subsoil plough would be simply to knead and pack the earth to a firm, tenacious dough, impervious to roots and to capillary moisture. In this event, subsoiling would do far more harm than good.

The question when best to subsoil is really a perplexing one; for with land of the supposed quality, it would not be easy to hit upon a time when the soil is fit to plough both at the surface and beneath. All is, the farmer must think about the matter, and must try to get as near the desired point as may be practicable.

It is evident enough that late summer or early autumn would be the natural time to approach the subject, for in spring the moisture dries out from the land slowly. But the objection has sometimes been raised that, if the subsoiling be done in autumn, the ground will subsequently settle in the course of the winter, to a certain extent, and there will thus be lost a considerable part of the effect which in the case of spring ploughing would have served to benefit a crop. Hence it has been urged, that in some cases it might perhaps be well to wait in the spring until the condition of the land has become fit, and then to put in some late crop, after subsoiling, such as fodder corn, millet, or any late soiling or ensilage crop, — perhaps even buckwheat; but it might readily happen in this case that the crop would actually have access to a smaller supply of moisture than if the subsoiling had been done in the autumn, and the soil made fit for holding a fair share of the winter's rain. It is probable that this tendency to puddle the land has done more than any other one thing to throw the subsoil plough into disrepute.

Summer or Surface Tillage.

Another point of prime importance is the question of surface tillage, — that is to say, summer tillage, — such as is performed with the hoe and the cultivator. The proper conduct of this surface loosening of the soil has an enormous influence upon the husbanding of the store of capillary water in the lower soil; and it is from this store of moisture that most crops have to depend in good part in dry summer weather.

For the sake of the argument, let it be supposed that a soil has been trenched, that the trenched earth has been charged by the spring rains with as much water as it can hold, and that dry weather has now set in. It is manifest that the more such a soil as this is ploughed or stirred, the more quickly will water evaporate out from it, particularly from the surfaces of the stirred portions; and it is plain that any soil made loose by stirring will expose a far larger surface to the atmosphere than a compact soil can.

Evaporation will naturally be proportionally rapid accordingly as the surface exposed to dry air is larger. But it is none the less true, upon the other hand, that the processes of surface-stirring may hinder the waste of water from the layers of soil immediately below that which is actually disturbed; and it is a fact that, by judiciously tilling the surface soil, the waste of water from the standing-room of the crop may be lessened.

To return for a moment to the bed of trenched soil charged with moisture, let it be supposed that no tillage has been practised since the crop was planted, some time since. The surface soil will naturally have settled down upon itself, after having been disturbed in preparation for planting, and there will now be found a more or less perfect capillary connection between the surface and the underlying soil in which the water is stored. So long as this good capillary connection is maintained, much water will be rapidly drawn up to the surface, and will there be evaporated off into the air, without serving any useful purpose for the maintenance of the crop. But if the dry surface soil be scratched or stirred, and made loose and light, the capillary connection with the underlying soil will be impaired, and the power of the soil to bring up water to the very surface will be greatly lessened. Hence the importance of the practical rules that the ground where crops are standing should be hoed as often as the mould begins to grow hard, and that " poor and stiff soils require more frequent hoeings than those which are fat and fruitful."

The real desideratum is to maintain the best possible capillary connection between the lower layers of soil, where the store of water is, and those layers in which the plant-roots are growing. More than this is not wanted, and pains must consequently be taken to break up continually the capillary connection between the surface and the root-bed. It is desirable that water shall rise freely into the root-bed; but when it has got there, it had much better go out through the plants, and not by way of mere evaporation from any part of the soil.

Importance of thorough Stirring.

In actual practice, the soil should be stirred to such a depth that there shall be formed a tolerably thick layer of dry, loose earth. Thus King, in Wisconsin, operating on a corn-field of clay-loam, tile-drained at a depth of 4 feet, where the water-table was about 4 feet from the surface when the seed was planted, and from 5 to 6 feet when the crop was cut, found more moisture in the soil throughout the entire season in those parts of the field which were cultivated to a depth of 3 inches, than in those parts which were cultivated to a depth somewhat less than one inch. It appears that when the layer of stirred soil at the surface is too thin, the loss of water by evaporation from the soil proper may not be sufficiently checked. Moreover, the soil beneath the thin layer of loose earth would be heated by the sun's rays more quickly than if the layers were thick, and water would then be lost both by way of evaporation and by actually moving downward away from the surface, for it has been noticed that when a soil becomes warm, its power of holding water decreases.

In a hot soil there is an appreciable diminution of the force of capillary attraction, and a part of the water previously held up in the soil passes downward out of the reach of some of the roots of the crop. It is manifest, however, that the surface soil should not be disturbed to so great a depth that the roots of the crop would be interfered with, or forced to go down in search of water to depths below those where the best soil and the most manure are situated. It is often an easy matter to dry out high-lying land by stirring it too deeply and freely, particularly when the land has never been brought to a good tilth. Even of the extremely moist climate of Northwestern Scotland, the case has been reported of a large field of wild land which was broken up with steam-ploughs and limed, and in the succeeding year worked with a very large and heavy disk-harrow, in the month of April, as a preparation for grass and oats. The summer happened to be unusually dry, and it was noticed that the crop was good on that part of the field which had been disked early in April, while both the oats and the grass failed from drought on the land which had been stirred by the disk-harrow late in the month.

Another point to be noted in favor of summer tillage is that, by admitting air freely to the soil, it may specially favor nitrification. This fact should be borne in mind, and perhaps worked for in cases where there is water enough in the soil both for the support of the crop and for the success of nitrification. Dehérain found, in laboratory experiments, that, by repeatedly stirring various samples of soils, the formation of nitrates in these soils was greatly promoted. In fact, 25 times as much nitrate-nitrogen was produced on the average in soils which were stirred as in those which were left undisturbed. It was noticed, too, that the influence of the stirring was more conspicuous in the autumn than in the spring. Doubtless, surface tillage of any kind is useful, in that it permits air to enter the soil more freely than it could before, not only to promote nitrification, but in order that oxygen may act upon the soil and upon the roots of the crops.

Spring Droughts show the Value of Deep Tillage.

The importance of having a deep bed of loam to hold rain-water, and of maintaining the best possible capillary connection between all parts of this rain-water bed and the roots of the crop, is illustrated occasionally here in Massachusetts by the sufferings of grass-fields in years when there happens to be a long-continued spell of dry weather in the spring. It is a peculiarity of those droughts which occur in May and in early June, that the nights are cool and the days moderately warm, though seldom very hot, and that the water in springs and wells is by no means low, i. e. the ground-water is all the while at a comparatively high level, and those crops which have ready access to it continue to grow well. It may be said in general of such seasons that crops may suffer very much on newly broken sod-land, while they may not suffer materially on land which has long been tilled, for in well-tilled land more water would be held, and it could be lifted much more readily by the capillary force than would be possible in a less homogeneous soil. From the beginning the well-tilled land, if other things are equal, will have been much more nearly in the condition of a moist sponge than the other.

It is noticeable in such years that white-weed (Leucanthemum), butter-cups (Ranunculus) and "rib-grass" (Plantago) take possession for the time being of old fields, while the grass proper is at a standstill from lack of moisture, and there can be no question in such years that some system of keeping the soil beneath grass-sods in a good capillary state would be of no little value to any farmer fortunate enough to have practised it. Light crops of "cow-hay" may be got of course by mowing the weeds above mentioned while they are in flower, but nothing like so good a harvest is obtained as would naturally have been grown but for the lack of moisture. On the occasion of a drought of this sort which occurred in Sweden, in 1868, A. Müller determined the amounts of moisture that were contained in a variety of soils at different depths, and clearly showed the importance of tilth as a means of supplying water to crops. See his paper in "Die landw. Versuchs-Stationen," 1869, XI, 168.

Summer Tillage should not be too deep.

Some persons seem to find a difficulty in grasping the two conceptions, that while judicious tillage helps crops to withstand droughts, too deep tillage in midsummer may heighten the bad effect of drought, and so do harm, particularly on light land in dry seasons. A writer in the "Country Gentleman" of Dec. 4, 1879, gives a good illustration of the harm of working soil too deeply, in the following words: "Contrary to orders, a field of sweet-corn in light, sandy loam was ploughed, instead of being cultivated with the horse-hoe. The plough was run very deeply, and the corn was well earthed up in a hot, dry time. From that day the corn stopped growing. It gradually dried up, and the incipient ears, and even those half grown, withered away." Manifestly, by the act of ploughing, the capillary connection in this particular soil had been most unhappily broken at an improper depth. Whereas, if only the surface of the land had been stirred with a cultivator, moisture would still have been lifted from below to supply the wants of the corn-crop, while comparatively little moisture could have escaped into the air by way of wasteful evaporation.

A sensible person would naturally take care not to stir the soil to any undue depth, in order to avoid injuring too many of the roots of the crop; for although the roots and rootlets of young plants are very abundant, and much more abundant than the leaves and stems, they all have work to do; and although new rootlets form speedily to replace those which have been injured, such act of replacement calls for the expenditure by the plant of both matter and force which had much better have been devoted to the perfecting of the merchantable part of the crop.

It should be said that some confusion seems to have arisen as to the true significance of summer tillage, from the fact that when applied to crops which are growing in hills or ridges, the cultivator may sometimes rake away so much earth from immediately about the plants as to distress them in dry weather. But when land has been worked "flat" from the beginning, the more frequently it is stirred at the surface during dry weather, so much the less will be the liability that the crop will suffer from drought. The idea is that the self-same dry, loose surface earth shall be continually stirred and prevented from becoming impacted without disturbing any of the soil from which the roots of the crop are getting their food and drink. It is a sound maxim of English farmers that, in dry weather, "the more the irons are among the turnips till the leaves spread across the rows, the better."

That multitudes of weeds are killed by the processes of summer tillage is a great advantage for the crop, and the more particularly because weeds are apt to steal much water. Gasparin has maintained that there is no better way of destroying couch-grass, for example, than by continually tearing out its root-stalks during a couple of months of the dryest summer weather, by passing the cultivator through the surface soil as often as may be practicable. But with the exception of this extreme case and of cases where weeds might smother a slow-growing young crop of onions, carrots, or other feeble plants, the purpose of surface tillage in New England is primarily to husband the water in the soil by checking evaporation, both from the soil directly and from weeds growing on the soil.

As was just now intimated, surface tillage must often do good by hindering the soil from being over-heated. A soil covered with loose earth could hardly be heated so deeply by the sun's rays in dry summer weather, as it would be if the earth were compact.

Harrowing of Crops in the Spring.

In many localities it is still customary, as it has been from a very early period, to harrow winter wheat lightly in the spring, after the surface soil has become dry enough. Even wheat which has been sown broadcast may be harrowed in this way, and it is found in many places that much good may thus be done, especially on heavy land. Clayey loams when thus harrowed may be made appreciably warmer and more dry at a time when warmth and dryness are important. At the same time air is admitted to the soil, and many weeds, which had started to grow together with the grain, are combed out and destroyed, while the crop itself suffers little harm, even when harrowed after it has reached a height of 4 or 5 inches. Under some conditions of weather, as Marshall observed, it may happen nevertheless that the crop is made foul by the harrowing, because the loosening of the soil incites the seeds of charlock, poppies and some other kinds of weeds to germinate. Though excellent for wheat, the harrow should not be applied to rye in the spring. (Gasparin.)

Many farmers harrow over fields of Indian corn also, plants and all, and the process may be repeated if need be until the crop has grown to a height of 3 or 4 inches. Clover, too, may be harrowed with advantage in the spring, and it bears the operation extremely well. In like manner, potatoes may often be helped very much by harrowing the land lightly at the moment when the young plants are about ready to come to the surface. The harrowing is highly beneficial provided no great number of the sprouts are broken. Nowadays, light harrows with reversed teeth, known as smoothing harrows, are used for this combing of growing crops, but it is noteworthy that there is a very old instrument, known as the Brabant harrow, which did the same kind of work in a similar way.

Tusser, in his day, urged that peas and horse-beans harrowed in February (in England) will flourish, while those left unharrowed may die from being " buried in clay." It is to be remembered, however, that for actual summer tillage an implement which, like the cultivator, stirs the surface of the land and forms a layer of loose earth upon it, will do better service than those harrows which act as mere rakes, for much earth may be left unbroken between the scratches made by a harrow, and the capillary connection between the surface and sub-surface in these undisturbed stripes may remain much as it was before the harrowing.

The Moisture in Arid Soils.

Interesting examples of the significance of summer tillage are to be seen in arid regions, as in some parts of California. In the San Joaquin valley, for instance, the farmers are said to be hopeful of securing a crop of grain whenever the quantity of rain which falls in the winter is sufficient to moisten the soil to a depth where the descending capillary moisture will meet that rising from below. And since the depth at which moisture is found at the end of the dry season will depend primarily on the amount of rainfall during the previous season, it makes a material difference whether a droughty winter has been preceded by a wet one, or whether a scanty rainfall preceded a deficient one. In the middle portion of the valley the summer drought will reach to a depth of from 3 to 5 feet, on untilled fields, according to the nature of the soil, and the whole mass of earth has to be remoistened to that depth in order that the successful growing of field-crops may be ensured. But in case the soil were to be left unplanted, and subjected to summer (surface) tillage, i. e. if it were summer-fallowed, moisture would be found in it at a much less depth in the autumn, and it would be remoistened comparatively quickly by

the autumnal rains, so that the chances of subsequently getting a
good crop would be materially increased. (Hilgard.)

Rolling moistens the Surface Soil.

The absolute opposite of surface tillage is seen in the use of the
roller upon grass-seeds and grain, or when the gardener pats
down and "firms" the earth with his hoe, or spade, or foot, or
thumb, after planting seeds. The object of this compression of
the surface soil is manifestly to bring moisture to the seeds. To
this end, a good capillary connection must be established between
that part of the soil where the seeds have been sown and the underlying soil which contains a store of moisture. In some parts
of California, where the success of the grain crop is dependent on
the scanty supply of rain which falls in the winter and is held by
the soil, it is said to be the universal practice to roll the grain-
fields as late as it can be done without injury to the growing grain,
in order to hinder the surface soil from becoming too dry and
that enough moisture may be maintained in those layers of the
soil where it will best serve to promote the growth of the young
crop. According to Hilgard this rolling can there hardly be over-
done on sandy soils, but harm would be done in case clayey land
were to be rolled when too wet.

An ideal condition of things, which might perhaps be sometimes realized in practice in the case of seeds large enough to bear
tolerably deep burying, would be to roll the land firmly after seeding it, and then to scratch the surface slightly with a light harrow
or rake; for the rolling would enable capillary water to be lifted
to the seeds, while the subsequent harrowing would diminish the
waste of water from the land by the evaporation which would
occur if the surface were to remain compressed as it was left by
the roller. This idea has occasionally been put in practice. Thus,
Arthur Young recommends that light land on which potatoes have
been planted should be rolled with a light roller, and that the
roller should be followed with a light harrow. There was an old
Belgian method of sowing winter rye which has been described as
follows: After ploughing, the land was rolled and left to settle
during 3 or 4 weeks, during which time it became green from the
growth of weeds — "the greener the better, excepting as regards
couch-grass." The seed-rye was then strewn upon the land at a
dry time, and harrowed in and rolled. Finally the land was
again harrowed.

The significance of compression is well shown by the footmarks which careless workmen leave in hoeing summer crops. Unless a man hoes in such a manner that his tracks are covered, that is to say, in case he first stirs the soil and then treads upon the loosened earth, his footprints can readily be traced in dry weather by the weeds that continue to live in these compressed and so moistened places.

As bearing upon the foregoing statements, it may be said that the old notion that wet or showery weather is necessary for success in transplanting field-crops should be taken with many grains of allowance. As Cobbett has insisted, " Finely broken earth is what ought to be placed about the roots of transplanted plants, and this cannot be had if we transplant in the wet." So, too, " In transplanting trees, you will take care that the earth shall be finely broken, that it lie close to the roots, that it be not tumbled into the hole in clods," and that after the soil has been duly compressed it shall be scratched at the surface or covered with straw, or the like, to hinder evaporation.

As illustrating the great waste of water that may occur from land when the surface is compressed, attention may again be called to the experiments cited on a previous page, which show that under favorable conditions more water may evaporate from wet earth than from a body of actual water.

A clear idea of the effects produced by the roller and the cultivator may be got by referring to the fundamental proposition of the physicists that the height to which water rises in a capillary tube is inversely as the diameter of the tube. That is to say, the finer the tube so much the higher will water rise in it. If water were to pass from a fine tube into a wider one, it could not rise so high as would have been the case if the whole tube had been left narrow; and, conversely, if water passes from a wide tube into a narrower one, it will be lifted higher than it could have been lifted by the original wide tube. Now when a loose surface soil is rolled, the tubes in it (so to say) are made narrower than they were before, and water rises in these tubes more freely than it could rise in the previous wider tubes. Conversely, when a rolled or otherwise impacted field is hoed or harrowed, the tubes in the soil are made wider and the capillary power of the soil is in so far lessened.

It may be said further that, by looking from this point of view, some useful ideas may be got as to the influence which layers of different kinds of soils may exert upon one another as to capillary action.

From the considerations thus far presented, it is evident enough

that in most of the operations of tillage the chief purpose is to
control the moisture of the soil, and that to this end the operations
must be varied in different cases· according as different kinds of
crops are to be grown, and as the soils differ as to their power of
holding water.　In subsequent chapters it will be seen that manures, and even saline fertilizers, may act as regulators of the
soil moisture, and it may be said that the process known as
" mulching" is of great importance in this respect.　Indeed it
would be impossible to treat justly either of the storage of capillary water in the soil, or of surface tillage, without insisting upon
the merit of mulches.

Mulching.

A mulch is anything laid upon the surface of the soil in such
wise that the evaporation of water from the surface is hindered.
Manure, straw, leaves, sawdust, chips, spent tan-bark, old boards,
and stones — especially if they are flat, like slates — are all used
for mulching.　The significance of the process is seen on turning
over any old log or stone in a field or pasture, and noting the
moist earth beneath it, with its manifold slugs and worms, and
all manner of insects that affect moisture.　In the words of Lord
Bacon, " It is an assured experience that an heape of flint or
stone laid about the bottome of a wilde tree (as an oake, elme,
ash, &c.), upon the first planting, doth make it prosper double as
much as without it.　The cause is for that it retaineth the moisture and suffereth it not to be exhaled by the sunne."

In experiments reported by Ebermayer, it was found, as the
average of several trials made in open fields during the summer
months, that 22% more water evaporated from a bed of soil half
a foot deep that was kept constantly saturated with water, than
from a similar bed of earth that was covered with leaves or moss,
such as would naturally collect beneath trees in a forest.

By mulching, a good capillary connection is maintained up to
the very surface of the soil, and there the movement of the water
is stopped; that is to say, evaporation of water from the surface of
the land is checked.　The thin surface layer of loosened earth, obtained by hoeing or cultivating, is to all intents and purposes a kind
of mulch, imperfect, it is true, but tolerably effective nevertheless.

Mulches prevent Puddling.

One very important effect of mulching proper is that it prevents
the puddling of the soil by rain, and so retains or preserves what-

ever of good tilth may have been imparted to the land. There are very few soils that do not become hard and close after having been repeatedly rained upon, unless pains are taken to prevent or destroy the incrustment. As Townsend put it long ago: "If soon after wheat or barley has been sown on what is called a running sand there falls a dashing rain, the sand runs together, that is, it forms a crust, which in a great measure is impervious to air, and scarcely a grain of the corn will grow. Or if, on clay land, during a time of drought, a garden plot is watered and left exposed to the scorching beams of the sun, the ground will bake; that is, the surface will be hardened, and, being thus rendered impervious to air, vegetation ceases. But if the surface has been previously covered with fern leaves, as practised by skilful and attentive gardeners, no such effect will be produced. The plot may be watered, and vegetation will be rapid."

A farmer in Scotland once remarked: "I have always observed, that, where land has been covered during winter with anything, even with stones, it raises a larger crop than that which has been exposed to the weather." He was arguing in favor of top-dressing land with farmyard manure, and justly insisted on the benefit of such a mulch. The old English practice of leaving manure spread upon clay land in winter is a special instance of the same general idea. On the sides of chalk hills in certain localities of Southeastern England, there are dry valleys, so called, in which streams of water flow for a short time only in very wet seasons when rain enough has fallen to supersaturate the chalk. At the bottoms of these valleys there are beds of flints, often of considerable thickness, intermixed with chalky loam which forms an excellent soil in spite of the fact that at first sight the field appears to be covered with nothing but flints. These flints manifestly serve a useful purpose by warming the land in the spring, and by mulching it in the summer, for experience has shown that the land is liable to be impoverished if the flints are removed. "So thick is the flint-drift, spread like a coverlet on the bed of chalk in some of the dry hollows, that cultivation would seem as little profitable there as on the shingle of a sea-beach. But you are reassured when told of the costly experience of a new-comer, who having picked off the flints and carted them away, and thereby lost his crops, acknowledged his error by restoring them." (Dickenson.)

It has been said, however, that the foregoing statement would not be true of hot climates where gravelly soils are notoriously apt to dry out at the surface, because the compact pebbles absorb much heat, and hold it and transmit it to the adjacent earth. According to Gasparin, gravelly soils become very hot in the summer at the South of France, and the practice of picking off stones from the surface of arable land which prevails there is fully justified on this account. And yet, as Pliny has told us, there is an old story to the effect that in the territory of Syracuse a husbandman, who was a stranger to the place, cleared the land of all the stones, and the consequence was that he lost his crops from the accumulation of mud; so that at last he was obliged to carry the stones back again.

Mulching of Saline Soils.

Another curious instance of the good effects of mulching is seen on the saline soils of the South of France, where wheat can be grown with success when rushes are strewn upon the land at the time of seeding. This mulch serves to keep the soil from drying out at the surface at a period when the formation of saline incrustations might ruin the crop, and it acts also to hinder the land from being puddled by rain. In this region the ability of a farmer to get rushes is a matter of great importance to him. (Gasparin.)

No doubt, mulching is a more effective method of controlling the water supply than surface tillage; though, generally speaking, mulching would cost too much for ordinary farm practice. Of course each farmer must decide for himself anew, in a great variety of cases, what is best to be done. For example, if in the vicinity of Boston anyone should wish to grow such thirsty crops as melons or squashes on dry, high-lying land, there would assuredly be better hope of success if the vines were mulched freely with manure. But of this case, as of most others, it may be said that mulches are employed in horticultural rather than in agricultural practice. All that a teacher can urge upon the student is that he should bear in mind the principles upon which tillage depends, and consider well his aims, and the best ways of reaching them, in each special instance that may happen to present itself to him in actual field-practice.

It should be said, perhaps, that mulches are occasionally made to serve other subsidiary purposes beside the retention of moisture in the soil. Strawberries, for example, growing upon sandy loam, may be hindered from becoming gritty by mulching the vines with tan-bark. It is said that both peas and gooseberries may be shielded to a considerable extent from mildew by mulches that are competent to protect the fruit from the damps of earth. It is true, of course, that such partial protection from the dampness of the soil can serve only as a palliative measure; for the germs of the mildew fungus come from the air, and the air often supplies moisture enough for their rapid development. It would be of interest to determine whether the fungus might not be repelled from gooseberries by supplementing the mulch with small quantities of the vapor of tar or petroleum, or some other appropriate germicide agent.

Another merit of mulches on good land is that they may promote the formation of nitrates in the soil, as will appear from considerations to be set forth in a subsequent chapter. Gurney noticed long ago not only that mulched grass grows more rapidly than that around it, but that it takes on a darker green color. He placed on moveable frames thin screens of long straw, a few inches above sod-land, and noticed that the grass grew rapidly and became of a deep green color when it was kept covered by day and uncovered by night (from 6 P.M. to 6 A.M.), but that when covered by night and uncovered by day it became yellow and sickly.

Significance of Natural Mulches in Woodland.

Some of the good effects of mulching are exhibited very conspicuously by the beds of leaves and moss which collect naturally in woodland. This covering of loose materials aids greatly in helping rain-water to soak into the earth where it falls; for not only is the rain caught and held temporarily by the bed of leaves and the moss, and hindered by them in various ways from flowing off the land, but on passing through the bed of litter the water finds at all times ready opportunity to soak into the soil beneath, because of its open, unpuddled, and uncrusted condition.

Another important advantage in keeping land covered, either by mulches, crops, grass, or trees, is that rains cannot wash the soil away, as would necessarily occur, and with great rapidity in many situations, if the land were bare.

In a series of Bavarian experiments reported by Ebermayer, it was found that a covering of loose litter permitted much more

water to soak into the soil than could pass through grass-sod; and
it is evident that, as regards the reception of rain-water, leaves,
moss, straw, sawdust, tan-bark or eel-grass will serve a much
better purpose when used for mulching, than can be served by
inverted sods or boards or stones, although either of these last
might perhaps be a more potent agent than the loose litter for preventing the drying out of water from the land.

But it was noticed when a bed of spongy litter thicker than $1\frac{1}{2}$
or 2 feet was used, such as sometimes collects in woodland under
coniferous trees, that most of the rain-water was held by this
thick layer of loose materials, and evaporated off from it in due
course; it was only in heavy rains that a part of the water soaked
through so thick a bed of litter into the soil proper. An observation of Lawes and Gilbert, which will be mentioned more particularly under the head of Manure, bears upon this question of
the retention of water by wood litter. It was found, namely, after
14 tons of farmyard manure to the acre had been applied annually during 30 years to a wheat-field, that the land had become
spongy enough to hold all the rain that fell upon it. Although
the mean annual rainfall at Rothamsted amounts to some 30
inches, it was only in exceptionally rainy years at seasons of very
heavy rains that any water escaped through the tile-drains of the
field thus heavily manured.

Wetness of the Soil in Forests.

In the forest, in the spring, when the great masses of snow which
have collected there slowly melt, large quantities of water soak
into the earth and saturate it completely, and this result is favored
by the fact that the soil has been not a little protected from freezing during winter by the layer of leaves upon its surface.

Speaking in general terms, comparatively little water flows off
from the surface of the land in wooded districts, while enormous
quantities of water soak into and through the soil slowly. Thus
it happens that land covered with forests may be kept continually
moist simply by its power of catching and holding rain-water,
and of retarding the movements of water in divers ways. In
dry summer weather, moreover, a loose covering of leaves or pine
needles will greatly hinder evaporation from the surface soil.

In spite of the enormous quantities of water which must be
pumped out of the soil by trees and transpired as vapor from their
leaves, it is seen to be true, generally speaking, that the power

of soils covered with forest to receive and hold water is so great, that, wherever considerable tracts of land are covered with trees, the whole region may be moister than it would be if the trees were absent.

In the wooded portions of northern New England, it is evident enough that both the abundance and the coldness of the ground-water have no inconsiderable influence on the coolness of the summers, especially on the coolness of the nights. The country becomes drier and hotter when cleared, not only because much water now drains away from it at once, but because the ground-water tends to dry out of the surface soil rapidly, and because the temperature of the ground-water naturally increases somewhat in proportion as woods are more completely removed from the land, and the soil is left exposed to the direct action of heat from the sun.

From the Bavarian experiments, it appears that a considerably smaller portion of the yearly rainfall actually comes to the ground in a forest than falls upon an open field, because much of the water, particularly when the showers are light, evaporates from the tree-tops to which it has clung. But in case the soil of the forest is strewn with leaves, this mulch, taken in connection with the shelter afforded by the trees, so lessens the evaporation from the soil that the water which never came to the earth because of the tree-tops is more than compensated for by the increased soakage into the earth. It appeared that, while on the average 26% less water reached drain-gauges that were kept in the Bavarian forests than fell upon open fields,[1] absolutely more water could percolate through leaf-covered soil situated in a forest, than percolated into the soils of fields.

In general, the difference between percolation through columns of soil placed in fields and forests was most marked at a depth of 2 feet. Of the water that fell on the fields, 50% percolated to a depth of 2 feet, while 77% of the water which fell on leaf-covered soil kept in a forest percolated to that depth. At a depth of one foot the figures were 54% and 74% respectively, and in case the soil kept in the forest was not leaf-strewn the percolation was 67% at the depth of one foot. This is to say, 20 and 27%, or a mean of 24%, more of the precipitated

---

[1] The amount of the evaporation from foliage naturally varied considerably, according to the kinds of trees, and whether they stood more or less thickly. In one instance where the rain-gauge was purposely put beneath a particularly thick grove of pines only 59% of the yearly rain-water reached the gauge. These trials are far from conclusive, however, since no account was taken of water that may reach the ground by running down the tree-trunks.

water percolated in leaf-strewn soil kept in woodland than in soils kept in fields, in spite of the great general fact that 26 % less water reached the earth in the forest than in the field.

In consonance with this approximate balancing of evaporation in the fields and soakage in the woods, it appeared that there was no great difference between the absolute amounts of water that percolated in a year at a depth of 4 feet in drain-gauges that were kept in the fields and in the woods. The figures were 2,623 c. in. and 2,235 c. in. respectively for gauges exposing a surface one square foot in area.

In general, it was found that the shade and shelter due to the trees themselves, together with the protecting influence of the bed of leaves or moss beneath the trees, work effectively to diminish loss of water by evaporation from the surface soil of a forest; though in wet years and in times of rain the influence of the leaf-bed in hindering evaporation was much less marked than it was in dry seasons. On the average, it was found that during the summer months evaporation from beds of earth that were kept saturated with moisture in a forest was 84 to 86 % less than evaporation from beds of uncovered saturated soil in open fields.

The shade and shelter cast by the trees themselves were competent to make the evaporation from the saturated soil 62 % less than it was in open fields, and the leaf-bed diminished the evaporation 22 % more. From leaf-covered saturated soil kept in woodland, it was found that evaporation was 60 % less than from a bed similarly situated but not covered with leaves.

Like the experiments on evaporation, these Bavarian experiments on percolation were made with great care at several different stations, at each of which the influence of field and forest and that of mulch and no mulch were contrasted. The drain-gauges employed were rectangular, and each of them was one Parisian square foot in area. They were made of sheet zinc, and were so constructed and arranged that observations were made at 1, 2 and 4 feet (Parisian). The gauges were filled with earth, and sunk in the ground almost, but not quite, to their topmost rims, i. e. they were fixed so that no surface water could flow into them from the surrounding land.

It is to be noticed particularly, however, that in no instance was the earth in these gauges subjected to the conditions which really exist in the soil of a forest, since no roots of trees had access to the soil in the gauges. Unlike many of the experiments upon sod-land such as have been reported on a previous page, the Bavarian drain-gauges were wholly shielded from the pumping action of the roots of plants. [This remark applies to the matter on the next pages, as well as to the preceding statements. But it needs to be said that special trials made subsequently by the Bavarian observers did but corroborate the well-known fact that the roots of forest-trees pump out vast quantities of water from the soil. In forests — especially in those of spruce and of pine, where the leaves transpire water the whole year through — it was found to be true at a depth of 1.5 to 3 feet, where the roots of the trees are thickest, that the soil was several per cent drier throughout the year than the corresponding soil of bare open fields, although the soil above the roots contained all the while more water than was held by similar land in fields where no trees were growing. In consonance with these facts, it was noticed that while the natural leaf-mulch in woodlands had a very decided influence in keeping the upper layers of soil moist, this influence was no longer appreciable, in summer, at depths where the roots of the trees were abundant.]

Through drain-gauges sunk in open fields the largest amounts of water percolated in winter. Indeed, thanks to the low rate of evaporation at this season, almost the whole of the rainfall passed through the drain-gauges. At this season the soil of the fields was more highly charged with water than at any other time; then followed in order spring, autumn and summer. But the differences between summer and winter were very large.

Taking the six colder months of the year, the percentage of percolation water at the depth of 4 feet in the open fields was about 3 times larger than it was in the six warmer months; while in woodland gauges covered with litter only $\frac{1}{4}$ more of the rainfall percolated 1 and 2 feet, and $\frac{1}{8}$ more percolated 4 feet, in the six winter months than in the six summer months. In woodland gauges not covered with litter about $\frac{1}{2}$ more of the rainfall percolated 1 foot in winter than in summer. Again, while in the winter half-year $\frac{1}{4}$ of the rainfall percolated 2 feet in open fields, and almost $\frac{7}{10}$ in woodland gauges covered with litter, only $\frac{1}{8}$ of the rainfall percolated to this depth in summer in the fields, and rather more than $\frac{7}{10}$ in the woodland.

In summer, properly so called, the quantities of water that percolated in the fields 1, 2 and 4 feet were, respectively, $3\frac{1}{2}$ $4\frac{1}{2}$ and $7\frac{1}{2}$ times smaller than in winter, because of the more abundant evaporation from the surface soil in summer.

Inasmuch as, both in winter and summer, the amounts of rain-water that fell upon the drain-gauges in the open fields were absolutely larger than those which fell upon the woodland gauges, more water naturally percolated through the deep gauges in the open fields during the winter months than passed through those in the woodland, because at this time of year the influence of the trees and the litter in checking evaporation is of very little importance. It appeared in winter, indeed, that beds of litter placed upon the drain-gauges had little or no influence upon the amount of percolation.

In spring, the increased rate of evaporation in the open fields was speedily felt at the drain-gauges in the diminished rate of percolation. But through the woodland gauges, on the contrary, the largest amount of percolation was in spring, when the snow was slowly melting. At this season the differences between the field and forest gauges were least clearly marked. But it was noticeable that in spring more water, both absolutely and relatively speaking, passed through the 4-feet gauges that were kept in the woods than passed through them during the winter months.

In summer, when evaporation from the surface soil is most rapid, percolation through drain-gauges kept in the woods was absolutely much larger than through gauges placed in open fields. The shel-

tering influence of the woodland was more marked at this season than
at any other. From May to September (inclusive) there percolated
to depths of 1, 2 and 4 feet, respectively, the following per cent of
the rainfall, through drain-gauges kept

	1 ft.	2 ft.	4 ft.
Covered with litter in the woods	73	74	58
Without litter " "	53	..	..
" " in open fields	17	16	17

That is to say, during these warm months 3 times as much water
percolated 1 foot through the unmulched woodland drain-gauges; 4½
times as much water percolated 1 and 2 feet, and 3½ times as much
percolated 4 feet, through mulched woodland gauges, as passed
through unmulched gauges in the open fields. In July, August and
September, evaporation was so rapid in the open fields that at several
of the stations no water, or next to none, passed through the field
drain-gauges, while in the woodland gauges percolation did not
cease, — not even in July. In this month enormous differences were
observed in the rates of percolation in the field and forest gauges.
The quantities of water that percolated through the woodland gauges
at depths of 1, 2 and 4 feet were respectively 5 times, 10 times and
5 times larger than those which percolated in the open fields.

In summer more than half the rain which fell on the bare woodland gauges percolated 1 foot; and in the gauges that were covered
with litter ½ of the rainfall percolated 1 foot, ⅔ percolated 2 feet, and
¼ percolated 4 feet, while through gauges in the open fields hardly ⅓,
¼ and $\frac{1}{15}$ part of the rainfall percolated at depths of 1, 2 and 4 feet
respectively.

When no plants are allowed to grow upon the gauges, it appears
that so large a part of the summer rainfall evaporates out of the upper
layers of the soil of the field gauges, that there is very little left to
percolate downward; whereas, when the surface soil is mulched and
shaded, as in woodland, a very considerable portion of the rainfall
can soak into the lower layers of the earth.

Though less water percolated through the woodland gauges from
May to September than during the other months of the year, the
differences were not so well marked as in the case of the field gauges.
More water percolated at a depth of one foot in the woodland gauges
from April to September, both when they were and were not mulched,
than passed through the field gauges. But from October to March
(inclusive) the reverse of this was true, and the field gauges percolated more freely than those in the woods. Taking the whole year,
more water percolated through the gauges that were covered with
litter than through those which were bare, though the advantage of
the mulch was most conspicuous in hot summer weather. Almost
as much again water passed through the woodland gauges that were
covered with litter, during the growing season, — i. e. during the
warmer part of the year, — as passed through the field gauges; and
20 % more of the rainfall percolated at a depth of one foot during the
growing summer months through the litter-covered woodland gauges
than through those which were bare.

During most months of the year less water dropped at a depth of

2 feet than at a depth of 1 foot from gauges in open fields, while in the mulched woodland gauges the soil held more water at 2 feet than at 1 foot during most months. As a general average, the earth in the bare field gauges was drier at a depth of 4 feet than at a depth of 1 foot; and in the mulched woodland gauges, also, during most months in the year, less water dropped from the soil at a depth of 4 feet than dropped at lesser depths. Usually, the woodland gauges held most water at a depth of 2 feet.

In autumn the percolation was found to be somewhat similar to what it was in the spring, though, since evaporation is rather stronger in autumn, percolation is proportionally weaker.

In the following table are given the average amounts of percolation at the different seasons of the year, as determined by the Bavarian observers. The statements are in terms of per cent of the water which came to the ground, as rain or snow, at the several seasons. There passed through drain-gauges that were

	Placed in open Fields, uncovered.			Placed in Woodlands. No Leaves.	Covered with Leaves.		
	1 foot.	2 feet.	4 feet.	1 foot.	1 foot.	2 feet.	4 feet.
Winter (Dec., Jan. and Feb.) .	94	89	99	91	94	97	63
Spring	55	56	64	70	81	81	83
Summer	19	14	11	52	72	65	36
July, by itself	11	6	7	..	58	61	34
Autumn	54	51	49	60	60	68	54
Winter half-year (Oct. to March, inclusive)	72	67	76	80	86	87	73
Summer half-year (Apr. to Sept., inclusive)	23	24	24	57	75	76	62
Difference	49	43	52	23	11	11	11

CHAPTER VII.

PRELIMINARY CONSIDERATIONS RELATING TO MANURES.

THERE is an experiment made many years ago by the French chemist Boussingault that is well worth considering. Boussingault washed three flower-pots carefully; he heated them to redness in a fire, and filled each of them with a mixture of fragments of recently burnt bricks and quartz sand. Both the brick and the sand were thoroughly washed with distilled water, and then calcined before being put in the pot.

To the soil in Pot 1, or rather to the contents of Pot 1, nothing was added but two seeds of the small sunflower (Helianthus argophyllus), and distilled water, from time to time, as the plants needed watering. Into the soil of Pot 2 small quantities of phosphate of lime (bone-ashes in fact), of the ashes of hay, and of nitrate of potash, were stirred. Pot 3 received the same dose of salts as the second pot, excepting that, instead of nitrate of potash, there was added enough bicarbonate of potash to bring in precisely as much potash as was contained in the nitrate of potash of the second pot.

Two seeds of the sunflower were planted in each of the pots on the 5th of July; the pots were placed in the open air under a glass roof to protect them from rain, and were carefully watered with distilled water, free from ammonia, but containing about $\frac{1}{4}$ part of its volume of carbonic acid.

On the 20th of September the plants ceased to grow, and on the 30th of that month their heights were to one another as the lengths of the lines here printed:

No. 1. ▬▬▬▬▬

" 3. ▬▬▬▬▬

" 2. ▬▬▬▬▬▬▬▬▬▬▬▬▬▬▬▬

Figures of the plants are given in "How Crops Feed," p. 271, from which it appears that, while the plants in Pot 2 grew luxuriantly, the plants in Pot 1 and 3 were miserable dwarfs. Each of these dwarf plants weighed no more than 4 or 5 times as much as the seed from which it sprung, while the vigorous crop obtained from the soil that had been fully manured weighed almost 200 times as much as the seed.

In 86 Days the Plants gained Grams of		Weight of the dry Crop, the Seeds being taken as 1.	Vegetable Matter formed, in Grams.	In the Pot which received
Carbon.	Nitrogen.			
0.114	0.0023	3.6	0.285	No manure.
8.444	0.1666	198.3	21.111	Ashes and nitrate of potash.
0.156	0.0027	4.6	0.391	Ashes and carbonate of potash.

This simple experiment is really a compendious treatise on the theory and practice of manuring. To make the illustration complete, there is needed only one other pot, to the soil of which nitrate of potash alone has been added, without any ashes or bone-earth. Boussingault did in fact subsequently perform this very experiment as a supplement to the other trials. He charged a flower-pot with calcined quartz sand, to which nothing but a small quantity of nitrate of potash had been added, and observed that the dry crop of sunflower plants grown in this fourth pot weighed 1.175 grams; that 0.42 grams of carbon was gained by the plants in 72 days, and that the dry crop weighed 10 times as much as the seeds. It is now known that the plants in this fourth pot must have found some traces of phosphates, etc., in the sand itself. It is in fact a very difficult matter to obtain sand which is absolutely free from ash ingredients; and it is true also that growing plants can put such food to use when they are adequately watered and supplied with nitrate of potash. Numberless experiments made by scientific observers in recent years have shown that Boussingault's Pot No. 4 would not have given a better crop than Pot 1 or Pot 8, if the sand and the brick-dust used by him had been absolutely free from assimilable ash ingredients. It is but fair to say, that the experiment just described was made merely to show the power of nitrates to supply nitrogen to plants; but it so well illustrates the subject of feeding plants, that the general significance of it cannot be too strongly insisted upon.

Plants need to be supplied with all Kinds of Food.

Whenever a seed germinates, as in Pots 1 and 8, or in the suppositious Pot 4, in a soil totally destitute either of any one or of all the ash ingredients and of the nitrogen compounds which are essential for vegetable growth, the plant will grow only at the expense of the substances contained in the seeds, or afterwards at its own expense for a brief period. It will soon cease to increase in weight, and after a while it will die. In order that any plant shall flourish, it must have continual access to all kinds of food, as in Pot No. 2.

It is impossible to lay too much stress on this fundamental conception, that in order that crops may succeed they must be fully supplied with ash ingredients, and with nitrogen compounds from the soil. And it is desirable that the student should immediately seek to apply this knowledge to the explanation of certain familiar facts in agricultural and horticultural practice.

Ordinary Loams contain all Kinds of Plant-Food.

If the sunflower seeds of Pots 1 and 8 had been sown in ordinary soil and then watered with rain-water, or, better, with spring or river water, the plants would have continued to grow well enough after the matter of the seed was exhausted, and would have come to maturity somewhat like those in Pot 2, though perhaps less completely.

Indeed, it is a matter of common observation and experience, that a plant left to itself in the field can obtain food from almost any cultivable soil that is duly supplied with air and water, whence it appears that ordinary soils, like the artificial mixture in Bous-

singault's Pot 2, contain naturally more or less of all the constituents of plant-food; and that the points specially in need of being
studied as to soils relate to the amounts of this natural food which
may occur in them, to the state in which it exists, and to the
means by which plants are enabled to obtain it.

It is evident, moreover, from the experiment above cited, that
by putting certain chemical substances upon a soil, its character
may readily be changed, and its power of feeding crops increased.
In like manner, it is easy to control or modify to a very considerable extent the action of water in or upon a soil, although as
regards the atmosphere in which a field-plant grows we have as yet
little or no power to check or control its action in any way.

There are upon record many striking instances where soils naturally sterile have suddenly been made fertile by the application to
them of plant-food.   In the Spanish province of Catalonia, more
especially in the vicinity of Barcelona, the soil is said to be principally quartz sand, which is rendered exceedingly productive by
means of moderate dressings of dung and copious irrigation.
Thanks also to the bright sun and hot climate of the locality,
abundant crops of all kinds are grown upon the sand as a result
of the treatment above mentioned.   So also, in the Belgian Cam-
pine, hundreds of acres of sterile sand have been brought into a
condition of high fertility by the application of guano and water.
Just below the city of Edinburgh there is an astonishingly fertile
tract of mowing-land, the soil of which is mere coal ashes and
sand; but over this soil the sewage of a part of the city is made
to flow.   There are many other such cases where mere irrigation
with water has produced permanent fertility, as will be explained
hereafter; it is a common remark indeed, of wide tracts of
country in various rainless regions — notably in Central Asia, and
in some of our own Western States — that it is not the land which
has value in such places, but only the water which can be brought
to the land.

Soils contain much Inert Matter.

All soils consist for the most part of substances which have no
direct or immediate use in feeding the plant.   Just as in Boussingault's experiment, so in natural soils there is a mass of inert
sand, gravel and clay, which last is often worse than so much
brick-dust, with some small portion of fertilizing matters scattered
among the other materials.   It is not probable that so much as

one part in a hundred of a good dried soil ever contributes directly to the feeding of the plants which are grown upon it. The influence of the inert portions of the soil upon the plant depends chiefly upon their relations to moisture and to heat, as has already been explained, and upon the facility with which they disintegrate and change into substances chemically active.

As has been said, soils and rocks are not wholly insoluble in water, particularly not in water such as is found in nature. Indeed, soils ordinarily contain so large a proportion of constituents that are not absolutely insoluble, but only difficultly soluble, as the term is, that it is quite impossible to determine accurately and precisely how much of a given sample of soil is soluble in water, for new portions of the soil continue to dissolve as long as new quantities of water are poured upon it. It is true, that much more matter is dissolved from the soil during the earlier stages of this leaching process than afterwards, and that by percolating a soil with small definite volumes of water it is possible to push out and collect the matters that dissolve easiest, as well as whatever was actually in solution in the soil at the beginning. It may be said of such solutions, obtained by leaching loam with comparatively small volumes of water, that they contain the matters which were unquestionably at the service of plants at the moment when the earth was experimented upon; and, in point of fact, everything needed for the growth of plants has been found in such solutions, though naturally enough some of the constituents of plant-food were present in them in extremely small proportion.

Extracts of Earth.

Several different methods of experimenting have been resorted to in order to determine what matters can be dissolved from the soil by water, and for the purpose of gaining an idea as to whether the soil-water is or is not capable of supplying plants with food.

One way of obtaining knowledge upon this point is, to soak a quantity of the soil for several hours in distilled water, to pour off the water from time to time into a special dish, and to replace it with fresh portions of water that are mixed with the earth. Verdeil and Risler experimented long ago in this way, and their experiments have been tabulated by Johnson in "How Crops Feed," p. 310. By evaporating to dryness the solutions obtained from various kinds of loams, these investigators got residues that contained from 30 to 67% of ash ingredients, and from 33 to 70% of organic and volatile matters. In the ashes they found varying quantities, often large, of sulphate, carbonate, and phosphate of lime, together with compounds of potash, soda and iron, and sometimes magnesia and alumina. The very considerable quantities of organic matter, as well as of ash ingredients, which were obtained by this method of research are noteworthy.

A better way of proceeding is to place in a percolator a considerable quantity of the soil to be tested, and gradually to pour enough water upon the top of the column of earth to push out or displace the water which was originally held in the soil. By operating in this manner, true samples of the soil-water — that is to say, of everything which this soil-water is holding in solution — may readily be obtained; for it is a well-established fact that in the process of percolation the pure water poured upon the top of the column has but little tendency to mix with the water previously in the soil. The upper layers of water simply push downward the lower layers without much diluting them. In all speculations relating to the action of the rain-water which falls upon and soaks into the soil, it is important to bear in mind the fact that the first action of percolating water is to push forward and displace the dissolved matters already in the soil, rather than to dilute or weaken their solution.

Osmosis in Soils.

Other experimenters have endeavored to study the soluble matters in soils by way of osmose. They have put on one side of a membrane a quantity of the soil to be tested, and have made the other side rest upon or against pure water, and have noted what kinds and amounts of materials diffuse out from the soil through the membrane into the water. Thus Sestini sunk cylinders of porous earthenware in the soil, filled them with distilled water, and found in this water, after a time, lime, magnesia, iron, potash, soda and sulphates. Petermann, working more carefully and using parchment paper, as the membrane, was able to detect in solutions from a large number of soils all the substances noticed by Sestini, as well as silicates, phosphates, nitrates, chlorides, and very considerable amounts of organic matter.

Experiments made in yet another way by putting a soil in an open cylinder of zinc or tin-ware, and placing the lower end of the cylinder in distilled water in such manner that capillary moisture may pass upward through the soil, have shown that comparatively large quantities of mineral matter are dissolved and carried up to the surface of the soil, in the form of carbonates, sulphates, chlorides and nitrates. To collect these dissolved matters, pads of purified, porous filter-paper were placed upon the top of the column of earth. (Sostegni.) This experiment is a refinement of one that is made every day in the flower-pots of domestic horticulture. The incrustations of lime-carbonate and other matters often to be seen on the rims of flower-pots have been formed from soluble salts dragged up out of the soil in the current of the capillary water.

In general, it appears that 1,000 parts of pure water can dissolve out of ordinary soils from $\frac{1}{2}$ to $1\frac{1}{2}$ parts of mixed organic and mineral matters. Poor sandy soils generally yield the minimum quantity, while very rich soils, especially if they have been recently and heavily manured, sometimes give the maximum amount. Usually these solutions contain a considerable proportion of organic matter, viz., as much as will amount to $\frac{1}{3}$ or $\frac{1}{2}$ the weight of all the material that has been dissolved. From peats and peaty soils taken from wet places 1,000 parts of water may dissolve as much as from 4 to 14 parts of matter, but it is chiefly organic, and is poor in respect to several important kinds of plant-food, notably phosphoric acid.

Several experimenters have been at pains to determine how much of each of the matters needed by plants can be extracted from a soil by water, as may be seen in the tables of analyses given on page 311 of "How Crops Feed."

Water from Wells and Field-Drains.

Another way of investigating the problem is to collect and analyze the waters of wells and of field-drains, and that which has soaked out from drain-gauges. Highly interesting results have been obtained in this way, for it appears that, with the exception of nitrates and lime, only very small quantities of the really useful constituents of plant-food pass off in the drain-water. See "How Crops Feed," pp. 313–315.[1] From $\frac{1}{4}$ to $\frac{1}{2}$ lb. of matter is usually found dissolved in each 1,000 parts of drain-water. The proportions of some of the more prominent substances in 1,000 parts of the water may be stated as follows: organic matter, 0.01 to 0.10; nitric acid, 0.05 to 0.20; lime, 0.02 to 0.10; potash,

---

[1] Compare Heiden's tables, in his "Düngerlehre," I. 294, 295.

phosphoric acid, and ammonia, traces; sulphuric acid, 0.02 to 0.07; soda, 0.01 to 0.03; magnesia, 0.001 to 0.03. Here, again, it was noticed by Frankland that even the clearest drain-waters may contain small quantities of highly nitrogenous organic matter. As obtained from drains in unmanured land, he observed that the ratio of carbon to nitrogen in this substance was as 1 to 2.6 in one case, and as 1 to 3 in another. In turbid drain-water, part of which had manifestly come directly from the surface soil through open channels, the proportion of organic matter was larger, and it was considerably richer in carbon.

But, as Mulder has suggested, the solutions that pass out from a drain-gauge contain only those things which can be carried down now and then by the excess of rain when it has fallen in quantities larger than the soil can hold. Such solutions do not really represent the dissolved matters which are offered to crops by the soil-water during the growing season. Most of the substances carried down by the percolation of rain-water towards the bottom of the drain-gauge in wet weather do not actually escape from the soil; and they are drawn up again towards the surface of the land by capillary action after the rain-water has ceased to soak downward.

The results of these numerous investigations lead to the conviction that water is capable of dissolving from the soil minute quantities of everything which plants need. Indeed, Eichhorn asserted at one time that capillary water left during 10 days in contact with undunged garden-loam contained as much matter in solution as would suffice for the requirements of a good crop; though Wunder, on repeating the experiment, denied that enough matter is thus dissolved to support an agricultural crop. It is true that in some of the experiments which have been reported the quantities of certain constituents of the soil-water, notably phosphoric acid, were present in so extremely small proportion, that they seemed to elude the analyst; but none the less it may be said that there is every reason to believe that these substances could always have been detected, as they have been usually, if only a larger quantity of soil had been leached, or if a larger portion of the solution, or of the drain-water, had been evaporated before applying the tests. The diversity of the results actually obtained hitherto by different experimenters points clearly to this conclusion. Indeed, it is well known that in the case of certain substances, such as iron and manganese — which are for the most part readily fixed and held by the soil — minute quantities are often or even usually dissolved in the soil-water, whence they are frequently taken in by plants and whereby they are continually carried to the ocean.

Plants can be grown in Well-water.

There is another item of experimental evidence which supports or indeed proves the idea that the soil-water contains a little of each and every kind of plant-food,— the fact, namely, that plants can be grown in the waters of wells and springs; as has been shown not only by scientific experiments in water-culture, but by the familiar practice in domestic horticulture of growing seeds and cuttings of various plants in jars of water.

Heinrich filled boxes that were 42½ centimetres deep and 1,000 square centimetres in superficial area with gravel and sterile sand, in which were sown seeds of various grasses, clovers and vegetables, and he watered the plants with spring-water applied in various quantities. Generally speaking, the crops were larger in proportion as more water had been given to them, as will appear from the following table: —

No. of cc. Water poured upon the Land each Day.	Average Weight of the Crops harvested, in Grams.
100	35
200	44
300	57
400	84
500	110
600	138
700	148
800	161
900	156
1,000	170

Birner and Lucanus grew an excellent crop of oats by way of water-culture in water taken from an ordinary well, and supplied at the rate of a quart a week to each of the plants. As compared with oats grown by them in garden-loam, and in ordinary field culture, the results of the experiment were as follows : —

Grown in	Weight in Grams of an average Plant dried.	Weight of the dry Grain.	The Seed being taken as 1, the dry Crop weighed
Garden-loam	5.27	1.23	193
Field	1.75	0.63	64
Well-water	2.91	1.25	106

It appeared that as much grain was got on the plant grown in well-water as from that grown in the garden-loam, and twice as

much as was got from the field-grown plant.   The plants grown
in water were larger and heavier than those grown in the field.

Heiden makes the capital point, that it cannot be strictly correct
to regard the water of wells and field drains as comparable, in
respect to chemical composition, with the water in the soil proper;
i. e. the loam at the surface of the field, for that portion of the
rain-water that finally escapes from the drains has to pass through
several feet of subsoil after it has soaked out of the surface loam,
and — in accordance with the laws that regulate the retention of
fertilizing matters, as will be explained directly — the subsoil
stands ready to absorb and fix potash, ammonia, phosphoric acid,
etc., to say nothing of the speedy absorption by plant-roots of
matters from the water, as it passes by them.

Soil Extracts rise less readily than Pure Water, by way of
Capillarity.

It has been noticed by M. Whitney that the surface tension of
the moisture naturally held in the pores of soils is lower than that
of pure water; that is to say, the soil has less power to lift up,
by capillarity, the moisture ordinarily contained in it than it has
of lifting pure water.   Thus, while the surface tension of pure
water is expressed by the figures 7.532, that of several soil
extracts examined by Whitney varied from 7.089 to 7.244.   To
this cause Whitney attributes the fact, observed at several localities in Southern States, that the wells in certain sandy formations
are at their fullest during extreme dry weather, but immediately
begin to fall when a soaking rain has followed a long spell of dry
weather.   He argues that as the soil becomes drier the tension of
the moisture in it is reduced to such an extent that this moisture
cannot maintain itself at the same height as formerly.   The water
of the lower depths of the subsoil is consequently let down into
the well when the surface soil becomes drier and the moisture in
it more concentrated.   With the advent of a soaking rain, the
moisture of the upper soil is diluted and its surface tension increased to such an extent that water is drawn up from below, or,
at the least, does not flow down so readily into the well.

Whitney has cited another example, as follows: " It is a matter
of common experience with gardeners that if a plant or piece of
lawn is watered in a very dry season, by applying water to the
surface of the ground, the watering has to be continued thereafter
during all the dry season, as the result of a single watering is to

leave the ground drier than it would otherwise have been. For this reason, they usually put off watering as long as possible, and when once they begin they continue it. King has proved this fact experimentally by watering a piece of ground and letting it stand for 24 hours. He then found by direct determinations that the upper foot was wetter than it had been immediately before the watering, but that the lower depths of the soil, down to 36 inches deep, were drier than before the watering. It would seem in this case that the higher surface tension of the pure water, or of the more dilute soil moisture in the surface soil, had pulled up water from below, where the surface tension is less, and the danger would be that this water being brought near the surface would then evaporate quickly, so that more of the original soil moisture would be lost by evaporation than if the water had not been applied to the surface.''

Rain-water changes the texture of Soils.

It will be shown in subsequent chapters that the extremely dilute saline solutions naturally contained in soils exert a powerful influence upon the tilth of the land and upon the solubility of the organic matters contained in it. Attention may here be called to one consequence of rinsing away the saline moisture, viz. to the fact of observation that on percolating a soil with successive quantities of pure water the rate of flow of this water becomes slower and slower. In one instance reported by M. Whitney, of a soil containing 47% by volume of empty space, the rate of flow decreased from 57 minutes to 169 minutes when 8 successive 100 cc. portions of water had been passed through it. In the case of another soil with 50% by volume of empty space, the rate of flow decreased from 36 minutes to 265 minutes when 18 successive 100 cc. portions of water had been passed through it.

Soils of Arid Regions.

It needs to be said that the preceding statements refer more particularly to Europe and the Eastern United States, i. e. to regions where the rainfall is abundant enough to thoroughly wash out the soil occasionally during the course of each and every year. As will be explained in the next chapter, some salts — notably those of sodium, of magnesium and of lime — are leached out more readily than compounds of potash are. But it is none the less a general fact that, thanks to the copious rains of Europe and our Atlantic States, only a comparatively small proportion of soluble matters is to be found in the soils which have been studied most frequently. It is impossible indeed that any large quantity of easily soluble salts, such as the chlorides and sulphates of sodium, calcium and magnesium, can be retained in the soils of rainy regions, for they will inevitably be dissolved by the rainfall, and thus be leached out from the soil and carried away into brooks, rivers and the sea.

But in arid regions, such as occur in some parts of Asia, Africa, Australia, and in several of our Western States, very considerable quantities of the above-mentioned soluble matters are retained in the soils, and it is a matter of familiar experience that soils thus charged with plant-food are extremely fertile when irrigated, unless indeed the saline matters happen to be present in too great excess. By comparing many analyses of good soils taken from arid and from humid regions, respectively, Hilgard has shown that while the soils of humid regions contain on the average something like 0.216% of potash (K_2O), the soils of arid regions contain 0.729%, i. e. the proportion is about as 3 to 1 in favor of the arid soils. For soda Hilgard finds the figures 0.091% in the soils of humid regions and 0.264% in arid soils; for magnesia he finds 0.225% and 1.411%, and for lime (in the case of non-calcareous soils) he finds 0.108% and 1.362%. Naturally enough, it happens in arid countries that a considerable part of the soluble matters is dissolved by the occasional rains which fall there, and is carried down in the water towards the lower grounds, where on the evaporation of the water saline matters often accumulate to an injurious extent.

Selective Power of Plants.

Attention has already been called to the fact, that the food which enters the plant from the soil probably does so in the form of an aqueous solution, and that the solution is moved by the forces of liquid diffusion and osmose. There remains to be considered, at somewhat greater length than was convenient before, the so-called "selective power" of the plant for special kinds of food. For although the manner in which the plant takes from the soil-water the things it needs may admit of a tolerably satisfactory explanation, it is not so plain at first sight how the plant can reject matters which it does not need; and yet it is extremely probable that the power of exclusion is nothing more than a simple consequence of the law of liquid diffusion.

If a solution of nitre, for example, be brought in contact with a solution of sugar, the two substances will diffuse until they are mixed equally throughout the entire liquid, and then the movement will come to rest; and it may be supposed that the same thing would happen in two contiguous plant-cells, if one were charged with the solution of nitre and the other with that of the sugar.

In this view of the matter, nitrate of potash or any other substance dissolved in the soil-water must necessarily diffuse into the root cells of a plant so long as the liquid in the root cells contains less of the nitrate than the soil-water contains. But the moment the liquid in the root cells comes to contain as much of the nitrate of potash as there is in the soil-water no more of that special substance can enter the cell, unless indeed a portion of it should be transferred to the adjacent cells, and room thus made for the admission of a new quantity. Naturally enough, the diffusion of any substance from cell to cell within the plant may be conceived of as going on in the same way as that of the soil-water into a single root cell.

In one word, whenever two miscible solutions of unlike composition are brought into contact, there diffusion will set in and proceed until an equilibrium has been established. Hence any harmless soluble substance not needed by the plant will enter freely until the sap contains just as much of it as the soil-water contains, and then matters will come to a standstill, so far as that particular substance is concerned. But with substances such as potash or phosphoric acid, for example, which are really put to use by the plant and incorporated into its structure, new quantities must constantly diffuse into the plant to take the place of those which have been removed from the sap.

As Pfeiffer has suggested, the matter may be illustrated by supposing that a bladder full of water has been immersed in a dilute solution of sulphate of copper, in which event the water and the copper solution will diffuse into one another until an equilibrium has been reached, and the solution is equally strong inside and outside the bladder. But in case a piece of metallic zinc were placed in the water of the bladder, then metallic copper would be precipitated upon the zinc as soon as any of the solution of the copper salt reached the zinc, and would consequently be withdrawn from the solution. This precipitation of copper would continue as long as any of the zinc remained undissolved, and room would in this way continually be made for the admission into the bladder of new supplies of the copper salt. Meanwhile sulphate of zinc would be formed continually, and would diffuse outward until all the copper had been precipitated upon the zinc, and the solution of sulphate of zinc had reached the same degree of concentration inside and outside the bladder walls. This reaction would go forward withal, no matter how dilute the solution of the copper salt might be, so that in the course of time much copper might accumulate in one spot, by precipitation upon the zinc, in case a continuous supply of the dilute cupric solution were maintained outside the bladder.

Some Plants take in Silica.

A familiar illustration of osmotic exclusion, as well as of osmotic entrance, of a useless substance, is seen in the case of silica, which is kept out by some kinds of plants and admitted by other kinds. It is found that the grasses and grain-bearing plants take in much more silica than clover and other leguminous plants do. But when the two kinds of plants grow side by side, so that their roots commingle in the same soil-water, it is fair enough to suppose that silica may at first enter both kinds of plants alike, and that the sap of both may soon be brought to the same state of saturation (as regards silica) that exists in the soil-water.

But the grasses deposit a part of this silica in their leaves and stems so that new portions of it can come into the sap from the soil. The clover, on the other hand, does not dispose of silica in this way, and the sap simply remains saturated, so to say, with that substance, from first to last, and no new portion of it is received from without. Practically it is found that while 1,000 lb. of grass may contain 7 lb. of silica, 1,000 lb. of red clover contain less than half a pound.

Here, as elsewhere, demand, or rather consumption, creates supply. Thus, while on the one hand the water of the soil will diffuse rapidly into the sap of the clover-plant to make good the loss of the large quantities of that liquid which are incessantly exhaled from the leaves into the air, the diffusion of silica will necessarily be slow since only a little of it is consumed. Other instances of similar import are seen in parasitic plants, the ashes of which may differ very considerably from the ashes of the plants on which they grow. The mistletoe, for example, while drawing its nourishment from the sap of the tree to which it is attached, will manifestly absorb freely only those constituents of this sap which it can put to use or which can somehow be deposited within it.

In the same way that a plant can select its food in this sense, so can it reject any saline or other soluble crystalloid substance for which it has no use, and which may have been formed within it in excess of the amount contained in the soil-water. It was in fact observed by chemists long ago, that potash, lime and phosphoric acid are ordinarily taken up by plants in much larger proportion than sulphuric acid and chlorine are taken, and Boussingault pointed out that the proportions in which sodium and chlorine are found in plants are so out of relation one with the other that it is to be presumed that the two elements must have entered the plant separately.

It is to be observed, furthermore, that even in the soil itself fertilizing matters will naturally move from one place to another by way of diffusion — quite independently of the movements of water due to percolation or to capillarity — in case there should happen to be a stronger solution of any soluble matter at one spot than at another.

Chemical Substances decomposed by Plant Roots.

It is now well known, from experiments made by way of water-culture, that plants vegetating in dilute solutions of various salts readily decompose them. Nitrate of potash, for example, is often broken up in this way, in such wise that, while the whole of the nitrogen goes into the plant, a part of the potash is left behind in the liquid. So, too, chloride of ammonium is split up, some of its chlorine remaining in the liquid in the form of hydrochloric acid.

There is nothing particularly strange in this fact, since solutions of many salts — such, for example, as alum and acid sulphate of potassium — may be decomposed by mere diffusion in water, and still more readily by osmose through porous films.

But it is evident that active chemical agents like caustic potash and muriatic acid cannot thus be set free in the soil without acting in some way upon it. It is altogether probable that the chemicals excluded by the plant in this way conduce to its growth, by dissolving food for it from the earth immediately around the roots. It is well to remember that one of the chief difficulties with which the method of experimenting by water-culture has to contend is this exclusion of corrosive substances by the roots of plants; and that, where there is no soil to absorb and neutralize the excluded matters, the roots themselves are often acted on and destroyed.

Roots corrode Rocks.

An important set of experiments by Dietrich, bearing upon the question of exclusion, were conducted as follows. The idea was to see how much soluble matter could finally be extracted from two samples of powdered rock, one sample being kept free from any vegetation while the other was made to support a crop of plants.

Samples of crushed basalt and of coarsely powdered sandstone were thoroughly washed with distilled water, and divided into 10-lb. portions. These weighed portions of the crushed rocks were put into separate series of pots, and 7 pots in each of the 2 series were planted with weighed quantities of seeds of various plants, such as peas, buckwheat, lupines, etc., while 2 pots of the basalt and 2 of the sandstone were left unplanted for the sake of comparison. The composition of each of the kinds of seeds employed was determined by analysis. Dust was excluded from the pots by means of paper covers, and by layers of cotton batting. All the samples of rock were watered alike with distilled water, and kept moist during the entire experiment. After its close the vegetable remains were removed, and the contents of all the pots were leached methodically with water that contained a hundredth part of nitric acid, in such manner that 2 litres of the acidulated water were used to a pot.

As the result of these tests, it appeared that more soluble matter was obtained in every instance from the samples of rock upon which plants had grown, than from those which were left unplanted, and this in spite of the fact that considerable quantities of mineral matter had been consumed by the plants themselves, and been removed in the plants when they were taken away from the pots. The amount of matter made soluble by the action of the roots of the following plants was : —

	In the Sandstone. grm.	In the Basalt. grm.
3 lupine plants	0.6080	0.7492
3 pea	0.4807	0.7132
20 spurry.	0.2678	0.3649
10 buckwheat	0.2322	0.3274
4 vetch	0.2212	0.2514
8 wheat	0.0272	0.1958
8 rye	0.0137	0.1316

Although the basalt was more freely acted upon than the sandstone, it was nevertheless true that the latter bore rather better plants, and plants that contained a larger percentage of mineral matters.

It appeared plainly enough that the roots of the leguminous plants, especially those of the lupine, exerted a more powerful solving influence than those of grain-bearing plants like wheat and rye; but in every case the decomposing power of the roots was distinct and unquestionable. It is interesting to observe, as one result of this corrosion of the soil by acids exuded from the roots, that the constituents of the soil must be set free directly in contact with the roots; that is to say, at the very places where they can be most readily absorbed and utilized by the plant.

Experiments to illustrate Corrosion by Roots.

Several different experimenters have studied in the laboratory the action of slightly acidulated water, kept on one side of a membrane, upon solid matters that were lying outside the membrane and in contact with it. First among them, Schumacher noticed that carbonate of lime, when separated from carbonic acid water by a membrane, could still be dissolved by the liquid, and so brought through the membrane by means of osmotic action. Then Zöller, having filled several glass vessels with distilled water, to which he had added enough acid of one kind or another to impart an acid reaction, tied pieces of bladder across the mouths of the vases in such manner that one side of the membrane should be in close contact with the acidulated liquid, and he strewed upon the upper side of the membrane a number of particles of phosphate of lime and of the insoluble double phosphate of magnesia and ammonia. Even after a very short time he was able to detect phosphoric acid, lime, magnesia and ammonia in the liquid, i. e. all the constituents of the insoluble matters upon which he was experimenting.

Heiden repeated these trials and obtained similar results. Among other things he tried phosphate and carbonate of lime against water acidulated with acetic acid, and for the sake of comparison he tried at the same time sulphate of lime against pure water. In all these instances the action was similar; i. e. enough of the acid liquid passed continually through the membranes to dissolve the matters that had been laid upon them, and the dissolved matters diffused back in their turn through the membrane into the store of liquid.

It is a familiar fact that the juices of many plants are highly
acid. Knop and Stohmann observed long ago that fresh rootlets
pressed against litmus paper give an acid reaction; and Dyer —
who made quantitative determinations of the acidity of the rootlets of many different kinds of plants — has estimated that on the
average there is as much acid in the sap of rootlets as would be
equivalent to about one per cent of crystallized citric acid, so that
it is certain that, beside the carbonic acid which roots are known
to exude, there are within the plant agents fully competent to dissolve food from the soil in the manner indicated by the experiments just cited, and to the extent shown by the experiments
of Dietrich. Several chemists, operating by way of water-culture, have noticed that the roots of plants can obtain phosphoric
acid from ferric phosphate, which is a compound practically insoluble in water; and Petersen has grown large and vigorous oat-
plants in a liquid that contained no soluble phosphoric acid, but
in which a quantity of ferric phosphate was suspended. In this case
the plants not only obtained some phosphoric acid from the insoluble material, but they obtained an abundance of it, i. e. enough
for their perfect development. Meanwhile it could be seen that
the color of the phosphate of iron underwent change, because
much phosphoric acid was removed from it.

A neat illustration of the acidity of roots has been suggested by
Cohn, who laid grains of barley to germinate on moistened litmus
paper, and noticed that, wherever the rootlets cling to the paper,
the color of it is changed from blue to red. On looking at the
other side of the sheet of paper the course of the rootlets may be
seen plainly traced in red lines upon the blue ground. It is to be
remembered that this action by chemical corrosion through the
roots is incessant and continuous.

This matter has been tested in still another way. Several chemists have grown plants successfully in soils naturally sterile, that
had been purposely saturated with the various substances needed
as plant-food and afterwards very thoroughly washed in order to
remove everything that was soluble in mere water. For example,
Stohmann, having soaked some peat in barnyard liquor during several hours, subsequently washed the peat with water for three weeks,
until the washings no longer contained anything appreciable in
solution. In one portion of this saturated, washed peat he grew
Indian corn directly, as contrasted with the growth of corn in the

original barren peat, and for the sake of still greater certainty he prepared two mixtures by commingling some of the saturated with the simple peat, and he grew corn in these mixtures also. The following weights of air-dried plants were harvested: —

	Simple Peat.	Saturated Peat.	⅓ Saturated and ⅔ Simple.	⅔ Saturated and ⅓ Simple.
Total weight of crop	17.5	836	282.0	368.0
Weight of grain	0.0	153	1.5	15.5

Whence it appears, again, that matters exuded from plant-roots must have power to dissolve from the soil many kinds of food that are insoluble in mere water.

Yet again, it is to the acid juices that are exuded from the roots of plants that must be accredited the lines and furrows which are often to be seen upon bones, and upon pebbles of limestone and other rocks with which roots have been in contact in the soil. A common way of exhibiting this action is to sow seeds in a small heap of sand or sawdust placed upon a slab of marble. After the seeds have germinated, their roots will cling to the marble, and corrode it so that, on removing the sand and roots after a time, the imprint of the latter will be found plainly visible etched upon the slab.

Roots develop rapidly when in Contact with Food.

It does not appear that plants have any selective power, in the sense that they can take in food in any other way than by osmotic action. Nor is it true that the roots of plants can start off at will, like the legs of animals, in the direction of any given mass of nourishment. But it is most distinctly true, that, when the rootlets come in contact with earth or water in which there is an abundance of plant-food, they will be developed there with far greater rapidity than in the neighboring portions of earth in which less food is to be found. The roots of a plant thus often get a distinct bias in one direction, almost as if they had intentionally proceeded in that direction from the first.

Thus it is that the roots of sainfoin are said to burrow for lime, and the roots of grape-vines and of many trees, such as willows, alders, poplars, elms, and ashes, and even the roots of ordinary plants, such as turnips and clover, are found running at large in sewers and house-drains. Drains have been found stopped with grass-roots at a depth of 2 feet, with beet-roots at depths of 4 and even 5 feet, with horseradish-roots at a depth of 7 feet, with the roots of gorse at 14 feet, and with those of an elm-tree at a depth of 9 feet, 50 yards distant from the tree. In all these cases it is to be presumed that the drains contained constantly more or less water. Probably they were conduits of water, and constantly in operation.

Experiments showing how Roots develop when fed.

Coranwinder planted a number of young beets in a circle two feet in diameter, and pushed down a bit of oil-cake an inch or so into the soil at the centre of the circle. Some months afterward he found that several of the beets had sent out horizontal roots as far as the oil-cake, which was covered with a complete mat of capillary roots. One or two of these side-roots had passed through a course of 16 inches before reaching the oil-cake.

Sprengel experimented upon this subject long ago as follows. By means of thin boards he made six tight compartments in a tub 18 inches high and 14 inches in diameter, and filled them all with garden-earth. No addition was made to the earth of one of the compartments; but in one he placed a mixture of potash, gypsum, and bone-meal; in another, some carbonate of lime; and in the others, bone-meal, gypsum, and common salt respectively. Upon the middle of this first tub he placed another, 12 inches high and 10 inches in diameter, that had no bottom. This second tub was filled with garden earth, in which were set out a number of clover plants that had roots six inches long. These plants were watered with rain-water until they were fully grown, when it was found that the largest and most abundant roots had grown in the compartments that contained bone-meal, while the smallest and feeblest were in the compartment that contained the common salt.

Somewhat similar experiments have been tried by Nobbe. A large quantity of a heavy clay-soil was sifted and divided into two equal portions. One of these portions was treated with various saline solutions, used in such quantities that the earth should be $\frac{1}{10}$ saturated with potash, soda, and phosphoric acid, and $\frac{1}{4}$ saturated with ammonia. Four large boxes, $2\frac{3}{4}$ feet deep, were filled in such wise that

No. I. contained nothing but the fertilized earth.
 " II. contained a $\frac{1}{2}$-foot layer of the fertilized earth above a deep layer of crude earth.
 " III. had 2 feet of fertilized earth at the bottom of the box, and crude earth above.
 " IV. contained nothing but the crude earth.

Red-clover seeds were sown in May, and at the end of a year the plants were thinned out so that 48 were left in each box. During the subsequent 14 months some of the plants died, especially in the unmanured soils, but there were harvested by several instalments the following quantities of dry hay, and finally of dry roots, in grams : —

		Hay.	Dry Roots.
I.	Wholly fertilized	592	60
II.	Fertilized on top	615	31
III.	Fertilized below	439	26
IV.	No fertilization	431	30

The roots from the different boxes differed very much in appearance. Both the unmanured and the fully manured earths were filled throughout with young, vigorous roots, though, naturally enough, the roots were more abundant in the fertilized earth. In box No. II, which had been fertilized at the surface, there was a great preponderance of roots near the surface; while in No. III, which was fertilized below, the roots were below also, and it was hard to find any new roots in the upper layer of the soil. From these experiments, Nobbe concludes that the clover-plant practically accommodates itself to circumstances, and that even in the third year of its life, — which was the year in which the roots were observed as above stated — clover takes most of its food from those layers of the soil where food is to be had most readily, no matter whether the layer be near the surface or deep down in the soil.

Stohmann also, having saturated a quantity of peat with dung liquor to which some superphosphate and potash salt had been added, rinsed away the excess of soluble matters, and spread the product layer by layer with crude peat in frames or boxes without bottoms, which were sunk in the earth.

No. I. had 9 inches of fertilized peat on top and 9 inches of crude peat below.
" II. had 9 inches of crude peat on top and 9 inches of fertilized peat below.
" III. had 6 inches of fertilized peat on top, then 6 inches of crude peat, and below that 6 inches of fertilized peat.
" IV. had 6 inches of crude, 4 inches of fertilized, and again 8 inches of crude peat.

Three grains of Indian corn were planted in each of the boxes. The young plants grew normally and vigorously from the very first, in boxes Nos. I and III; but in Nos. II and IV two of the seedlings soon died, and the surviving plants had a hard struggle until they reached the layer of fertilized earth, when they suddenly began to grow vigorously. The plant in No. IV soon fell away, however, while that in No. II prospered until it was ripe.

When the plants had ceased to grow, their roots were examined, and thick mats of fine tender roots were found wherever the fertilized peat had been reached. But in the layers of crude peat there was nothing but a few thick ligneous roots, which seemed to have died in all cases where they had not soon come into contact with a layer of the fertilized peat.

In box No. I the whole surface layer of soil was filled with a mat of roots, while below the surface layer there was nothing but some remains of roots which had perished in trying to penetrate the layer of crude peat. In No. III there was a thick mass of roots above, while below, especially at the sides of the box, there were a few individual roots which had reached the third layer, and had developed there so freely that the whole of the fertile earth was filled with a mat of them. In No. II a few ligneous roots had reached the fertile soil and had developed there freely. In No. IV also, a few strong roots had passed through the crude peat to the thin layer of fertile peat, and had completely filled it with fine fibres, but all the roots soon died on trying to penetrate the lower infertile layer.

Why some Plants grow on Special Soils.

The familiar fact that some plants prefer to grow on one kind of land, while other kinds are commonly found growing on soils of different character, has often been insisted upon as a means of distinguishing between soils and of judging as to their values. There are plants and classes of plants which are, so to say, characteristic of calcareous soils, and others which affect clays ; some kinds are found on sandy soils, and others on soils that are rich in humus, and the latter fall naturally into different classes according as the humus is "mild" or "sour," and as to whether it is of the nature of bog-mud or of moor-earth. It is evident at the first glance that a great variety of circumstances may be of influence in determining whether one or another kind of plant shall be left in possession of the soil of a given field. Wetness and dryness, heat and cold, are unquestionably of prime importance in this regard, and so is the texture of the soil according as it is mellow or plastic, hard and compact or open and friable. The chemical composition of the soil may be of influence also, in that the soil may or may not contain small quantities of an ingredient which is helpful or hurtful, or may be highly charged with some one peculiarly useful or detrimental constituent, such, for example, as limestone, sand, or sour humus.

It is true at all events that the habits of many wild plants, as well as the experience of greenhouse gardeners, show that not every kind of plant can be grown on every soil. Why is it, for example, that plantains, mallows, may-weed, goose-grass, etc., grow naturally around farm-houses, while such plants as the huckleberry, for instance, are impatient of domesticity? It is to be noted, however, that the questions here raised are somewhat different from those which bear directly upon selective power in the sense of the previous discussion. Moreover, it is evident enough that in many instances the power of a plant to bear hardship better than other plants may be the determining cause of the prevalence of that particular plant in a given locality. Just as sea-plants are adapted to the conditions in which they live, so strand-plants and the plants of the alkali desert are adapted to the conditions and circumstances in which they are found. Familiar examples of this sort are seen in the use of salt on asparagus beds, whereby many weeds are killed, but not the asparagus plants. So, too, the cocoanut palm can resist sea-water surprisingly; and many plants are so constructed that they can support dry climates, and even live on arid deserts. Witness the pitch-pine trees (Pinus rigida) of the sand-hills of the Atlantic States.

It would be a very interesting study, for its own sake, to ascertain more clearly than has been done hitherto the laws which determine the localization of species upon special soils. Among other instances of such localization is the so-called " shoe-string," or lead-plant, which in the galena-bearing region of Missouri and Illinois has been thought to indicate the presence of lead-ore. Many agricultural writers have remarked upon the luxuriant vegetation of calcareous soils and upon the peculiar character of this vegetation. It is said that many pernicious weeds, such as sheep-sorrel, wood-sorrel and feverfew, are seldom to be seen on limestone soils, where they seem to be replaced as it were by clovers and other leguminous plants.

With regard to non-corrosive soluble poisons, like barium chlo-

ride, for example, it is found, in consonance with the facts just
now stated, that plants take in small quantities of these matters
by way of osmose, and then die. On burning the plants thus killed,
no large quantities of the poisonous matters are found within
them, such as would assuredly have been sucked up in case the
roots had been corroded and access had thus been opened to the
capillary tubes in the plant.

Importance of the Chemical Matters excluded by Plants.

It is customary nowadays wholly to discard the crude notion of
Tull and of other old-time farmers, that plants are capable of feeding directly upon the finer particles of soil. There is not, in fact,
any evidence to support this view, though from the analogy of
animal tissues it is perhaps not impossible that minute mobile cells,
or even other minute solid particles, may pass, as such, from one
part of a plant to another.

Of late years, attention has been directed more particularly to
the power possessed by vegetation of decomposing the inert portions of soils by means of chemicals excluded or exuded by the
roots of plants, as was just now described. This fact is manifestly
one of great importance, and worthy of far more careful and extended study than has been accorded to it hitherto. Enough knowledge has been gained already, however, to release chemists from
the not wholly profitable discussion whether the soil-water, such
as is found running from drains, contains enough matter in solution to feed the crops upon the land. Much has been said, at one
time or another, upon this point by different observers, for it is
one involving so many obscure conditions that it is not by any
means easy to arrive at definite conclusions with regard to it. The
experiments of Dietrich, in particular, have shown that the consideration of this question may safely be dropped for the present.

Plants take Food from highly Dilute Solutions.

It is still true, however, that plants can derive food from exceedingly dilute solutions. Indeed, the experiments on water-culture go
to show that dilute solutions are essential for the well-being of the
plant. Nobbe, for example, found that the vigor of vegetation in
his experiments diminished both when the proportion of solid matter in the solution was reduced below 0.5 part to 1,000 parts of
water, or was increased to 2 parts in 1,000. In general, the proportion 1 to 1,000 may be remembered as one fit to be used under
almost any circumstances. Practical experience with saline fer-

tilizers, such as common salt, muriate of potash, or nitrate of
soda, teaches that these substances should seldom be applied to
the land in large quantities or under such conditions that the solutions of them which might come into contact with plants or seeds
can be other than extremely dilute.

As Mayer has remarked, the roots of most agricultural plants
through long-continued cultivation in mellow soils have become
well adapted to the highly dilute solutions of plant-food which
these soils contain. In the course of numberless generations,
the organization of the roots has become particularly well fitted
for the taking-in of food from dilute liquids, but not at all adapted
for withstanding the action of strong saline solutions.

The power of plants to extract food from exceedingly dilute
solutions is shown very emphatically in the case of seaweeds.
That is to say, of plants which live in the midst of water which
holds dissolved only very minute traces of matters so important
as phosphoric acid or even potash. The iodine also which sea-plants
contain must evidently be taken by them from the water in which
they grow; but, as Otto has shown, there cannot be as much as
one part of iodine in thirty million parts of the water. The absorption of phosphoric acid by land-plants is hardly less surprising,
though in this case it cannot be positively asserted that the acid
is always taken from solutions so dilute as the soil-water is, because of the known fact that the roots of plants may dissolve out
matters from the soil itself. That phosphoric acid is sometimes
actually taken from highly dilute solutions appears plainly enough
from the experiments of Birner and Lucanus on well-water, as
mentioned on a previous page. Ten million pounds of the water
in question contained no more than $1\frac{1}{4}$ lb. of phosphoric acid, and
yet this water supported a crop that bore twice as much grain as
was got from plants grown in an ordinary field for the sake of
comparison.

In all such speculations as this, it is to be remembered that the
contents of the soil-water may be continually renewed as fast as
the plants remove them. The soil is not only a great storehouse,
more or less filled with plant-food, but it is likewise a workshop in
which food is incessantly undergoing change and transformation.

It might be argued, for instance, that the good effects obtained
by irrigating a mowing-field with brook-water are due solely to
the fact that the grass-plants absorb the almost infinitesimally

minute proportion of phosphoric acid and other ingredients which the water has brought to the land; or it might be urged that the water, after having given up its original phosphoric acid, etc., to the grass, immediately acts upon the soil to dissolve out new quantities of plant-food and to carry them to the plants. In this way it might be possible for one and the same store of water to act over and over again upon the soil, and to carry much food from it to the crop.

But it may equally well be true, that the influence of matters dissolved in the original brook-water has been exerted indirectly to promote the growth of the grass. The chief part of the phosphoric acid, for example, found in the irrigated crop, may perhaps have come from the soil, whence it has been brought out by substances held dissolved in the water, or excluded by the plant, acting upon inert compounds in the soil.

Probably all these supposed methods of supplying plant-food may and do occur simultaneously, and it is to such complex considerations as these that must be referred the modes of action of many, if not of most manures. Hence the necessity of considering carefully what kinds of chemical action occur naturally in soils, before proceeding to discuss any one special kind of fertilizer, or trying to explain the causes of the benefits which are commonly obtained on applying it to the land for the use of crops.

CHAPTER VIII.

SOILS AS CHEMICAL AGENTS.

ALL kinds of soils, not even excepting drifting sands, possess much chemical activity. This fact may readily be illustrated by the simple experiment of digesting ammonia-water with clay, and searching for ammonia in the filtrate. Little or none of it will be found there. One way of trying the experiment would be to cut off the bottom of a large bottle, which could then be secured in a vertical position, mouth downward, and loosely plugged at the mouth by pushing down a tuft of cotton into the throat. On filling the body of the bottle loosely with clayey loam that has been slightly dampened, but not wet, and pouring small quantities of dilute ammonia-water upon the earth until liquid begins to drip from the mouth of the bottle, it will be found that this liquid is little more than mere water. By operating in this way, it has been proved that considerable quantities of ammonia may be retained by clay, and that ordinary agricultural soils do, in an analogous way, act chemically upon a great variety of compound substances.

The apparatus just described is well suited for studying the subject in detail. For example, if a number of inverted bottomless bottles were to be charged nearly full with sifted loam, and if there were to be poured upon the loam highly dilute solutions of various soluble salts, such as might occur in small quantity in any good soil, — such, for instance, as Epsom salt, Glauber's salt, and saltpetre, — it would be found on examining the first portions of the filtrates, that they contained, respectively, not sulphate of magnesia, but the sulphates of soda, lime, and potash; not sulphate of soda, but the sulphates of magnesia, lime, and potash; not nitrate of potash, but the nitrates of lime, magnesia, and soda.

Bases are fixed and held by the Soil.

In each of the cases specified, the bases of the salts which were employed would be retained by the loam, i. e. by chemical agents which lurk in it, while lime, or some other base, would be removed from the loam, in combination with the sulphuric or the nitric acid of the salts that were contained in the original solutions.

If the experiment were to be varied by pouring a solution of phosphate of potash or silicate of potash upon the earth, it would be found that both the phosphoric and the silicic acids would be retained in the soil, as well as the base potash, because these particular acids form insoluble compounds by uniting with certain substances with which they come in contact in the earth.

One good way of trying experiments upon the fixing power of soils is to put a known weight of dry soil in a bottle together with a measured quantity of a solution of known strength of the substance to be examined, — sulphate of potash, for example; to shake the mixture at intervals for hours, or days, or weeks; and finally to subject to analysis a measured fraction of the clear liquid. The analysis will show, not only how much of the potash of the salt taken has been absorbed and " fixed " by that amount of earth, but what kinds and amounts of bases have been set free or pushed out from the soil by the potash which has taken their place.

As the result of many experiments, it has been proved that all good soils can and do decompose, to a certain point, the solutions

of potash, soda, lime, and magnesia salts, in such wise that the
metals or bases, together with phosphoric and silicic acids if they
be present, are retained in the soil, while nitric, hydrochloric,
and sulphuric acids remain dissolved in the form of compounds
of lime or soda, or some other base or bases which they have taken
from the soil.

It is to be observed that the absorption of one base is always
attended by the liberation of an equivalent quantity of some other
base or bases; and any base which has been absorbed may be set
free again by the action of any other.   Of course, the capacity of
a given soil to effect the decomposition is limited by the quantity
of active chemical agents within it.   If we persist in pouring either
of the solutions upon the soil after it has become saturated with
that special ingredient, the liquid will soon run through unchanged.

Although this fixing power is specially pronounced in loams, —
i. e. in soils, properly so called, — it is still true that it may be
exhibited distinctly enough in fragments of some kinds of rocks,
notably in such as have been somewhat weathered superficially.
Ullik has noticed fixation of potash and of phosphoric acid in pieces
of compact basalt, and of certain marls and shales.

Fixation is seldom Complete.

For the sake of emphasis, the general fact of fixation has been
stated above in terms so brief that the inference might perhaps
be drawn that the whole of the potash is absorbed by the soil from
the saltpetre, the whole of the magnesia from the Epsom salt, and
so on.   But no such inference would be correct, since in point of
fact a certain small proportion of the potash, or other base, always
escapes fixation.

Chemists are familiar with the fact, that, in complex reactions,
such as the foregoing must undoubtedly be, and in general whenever several compounds act upon one another in presence of water,
the substances are apt to decompose each other mutually in such
wise that a certain part of the matter which would naturally,
under simpler conditions, have become insoluble, does, nevertheless, remain dissolved in the water.   It is not specially surprising,
therefore, if some small part of almost any substance, naturally
" insoluble," which is formed in presence of mixtures so complex
as the soil and the soil-water are known to be, should be found to
remain dissolved in the water of the soil.   Conversely, from the
very fact that fixation is never quite complete, it is to be presumed

that water can dissolve out from a soil a part of the potash or other base that has been fixed in it. It is true, also, as a general rule, that the larger the number of bases that can be fixed in a soil, within certain limits, so much the stronger will be the power of that soil to fix other kinds of bases that may be brought to it.

Bases thus fixed by Loam are accessible to Crops.

The enormous importance of the foregoing facts will be perceived on reflecting that those portions of the soil-water which have been partially or wholly deprived of soluble matters by the action of the roots of plants can immediately obtain new supplies of plant-food by dissolving the substances which the soil has fixed. One and the same quantity of water might, in this sense, act over and over again upon the soil, and serve for a long time as a carrier of food from the soil to the plant. It is to be observed, however, that at the best the fixed matters are not readily soluble, and that the quantity of water needed in order to redissolve them is not only large, but much larger than the amount of water from which they were originally absorbed. That is to say, the power of the soil to hold the fixable matters is, on the whole, much greater than the power of water to dissolve them.

There is no difficulty, however, in conceiving of such continuous solvent action as that just indicated, if only the fact be held to that each of the several substances which the soil-water contains dissolved can diffuse into the root-cells quite independently of the water, and of every other substance.

What causes Fixation?

The seat of the fixing power, above described, is found to reside in certain hydrated double silicates of alumina (or iron), lime, and an alkali metal, which are contained in the soil. The first intimation of this fact appeared from the researches of the English chemist Way, in 1850.

Way prepared artificially a double silicate of alumina and soda, by dissolving some silica and some alumina in separate portions of caustic soda, and mixing the two solutions. The precipitated highly basic double silicate of alumina and soda was then washed with water and subjected to treatment with various saline solutions. By means of a salt of lime, Way found that he could remove almost the whole of the soda, and obtain a silicate of alumina and lime. By means of a potash salt he could remove the soda, and obtain a silicate of alumina and potash. By means of magnesia salts, also, and of ammonia salts, double silicates containing these bases were obtained. But with the ammonia salt it was not possible to replace more than one-third of the soda, or other soluble base, by ammonia.

Way's results were severely criticised by Liebig, — very unjustly, as it then appeared to most chemists interested in the subject, and very unwisely, as has since been proved. The great merit of Way's research has been made only the more conspicuous in proportion as the subject has been more closely investigated.

Natural Double Silicates fix Bases as well as Artificial Silicates.

Instead of the artificial silicates of Way, several chemists, notably Eichhorn and Mulder, have operated upon a number of natural hydrated silicates, such as occur in the minerals known as Zeolites.[1] It is found that these zeolitic minerals are decomposed more or less rapidly by solutions of salts of the alkalies (including salts of ammonia), and by those of the alkaline earths, and that lime is dissolved out from the zeolite, while the other base or bases are retained in its place. It appears that the bases of alkali metals are fixed in this way more readily than those of the alkaline earthy metals.

By reversing the experiment, and treating the factitious double silicate of alumina and soda, for example, or the changed zeolite, with the solution of a lime salt, the soda will be eliminated and lime fixed again; — and so with the other bases, any of them may be made to replace the others if time enough be allowed for the liquids to act.

The Fixation of Bases is Speedy.

Generally speaking, the process of absorption and fixation of bases by the soil is rather rapid. Way found that the fixation of ammonia was often completed in half an hour, and Mulder has stated that one hour was sufficient for the fixation of bases in his experiments; though Peters observed that for the saturation of a soil with potash 48 hours were required. In an experiment made on one of the plots of Lawes and Gilbert's wheat-field, which was dressed every year with a mixture of all the ash ingredients needed by crops, a mixture of equal weights of sulphate and chloride of ammonium was ploughed into the soil, at the rate of 400 lb. to the acre, on October 25. It rained so heavily on the night of October 26, that the tile-drains laid at a depth of 2.5 feet dis-

[1] Described in "How Crops Feed," p. 114.

charged water on the morning of the 27th, and rain occurred afterward at frequent intervals so that a series of specimens of drainage was collected, the earliest of which was taken about 40 hours after the application of the ammonium salts. In the following table the amounts of nitrogen and of chlorine found in these waters are compared with those found in a sample of drainage taken on October 10, before the application of the ammonia. It will be noticed that although the sudden heavy rain washed out from the soil some undecomposed ammonia salt, it is none the less evident, from the enormous amount of chlorine in the first runnings, that most of the salt was decomposed at once, and its ammonia retained, to be subsequently changed to nitrates which were washed out in due course. The amount of chlorine steadily diminishes as it is washed out from the soil, while the quantity of nitrate is partially maintained through the nitrification of the fixed ammonia.

	In 1,000,000 parts of the drain-water there were parts of nitrogen :			
Date of collection.	As ammonia.	As nitrates.	Parts of chlorine.	Parts of nitrate-nitrogen to 100 parts of chlorine.
10 October	0.0	8.2	22.7	3.70
27 " 6.30 A.M.	9.0	13.5	146.4	9.2
27 " 1 P.M.	6.5	12.9	116.6	11.1
28 "	2.5	16.7	95.3	17.5
29 "	1.5	16.9	80.8	20.9
15, 16 November	0.0	50.8	54.2	93.7
19, 26 "	0.0	34.6	47.6	72.7
22, 29, 30 December	0.0	21.7	23.2	93.5
2, 8, 10 February	0.0	22.9	19.4	118.0

Henneberg and Stohmann noticed that phosphoric acid continued to be fixed after the lapse of 24 hours, and several observers have urged that phosphoric acid is often fixed rather slowly. Indeed, Voelcker has found in some instances that the process was not entirely completed at the end of three weeks. But it is hardly proper to discuss the fixation of phosphoric acid in this particular place, since it is known to depend upon different reactions from those which control the fixation of bases such as potash and ammonia.

It has been observed that the bases are absorbed more rapidly from solutions of some of their salts than from others. Potash, for example, is absorbed in least proportion from solutions of chloride of potassium, and in largest proportion from solutions of the phosphate, hydrate, and carbonate. Moreover, the bases are absorbed by the soil from strong solutions more rapidly and more completely than they are from dilute solutions. Still, although much depends upon the strength of the solutions used and upon the quantities employed in any given experiment, it is true, gener- ally speaking, that potash, lime and ammonia are fixed rather easily and firmly, while the fixation of soda and magnesia is apt to be somewhat less pronounced.

Soils vary as to their Fixing Power.

Naturally enough, soils vary widely as to their absorptive power. Thus Voelcker, on mixing dung liquor with loams of various kinds, found that from 0.49 to 0.74 parts of ammonia were fixed by 1,000 parts of earth. 1,000 parts of a sterile sandy loam fixed 0.121 part of ammonia; while, from a much weaker dung liquor, 1,000 parts of a clayey soil absorbed no more than 0.0905 part.

In experiments where diluted ammonia water and solutions of am- monium salts were used, instead of dung liquor, Voelcker obtained the results given in the following table. He prepared solutions of ammonia water, 1,000 grains of which contained respectively 0.673 and 0.332 grain of ammonia (NH_3); a solution of sulphate of am- monia, 1,000 grains of which contained 0.288 grain of ammonia; and a solution of chloride of ammonium, 1,000 grains of which contained 0.36 grain of ammonia. The figures in the table represent the amounts of ammonia, in grains, which were absorbed in the course of three days by 1,000 grains of the soils specified.

Kinds of soils.	Stronger am- monia water.	Weaker am- monia water.	Sulphate of ammonia.	Chloride of ammonium.
Calcareous clay	1.5193	0.882	0.608	0.68
Fertile loam	1.5363	0.804	0.640	0.76
Stiff clay	1.1240	0.754	0.576	0.80
Sterile sand	1.5220	0.868	0.256	0.16
Pasture earth	1.5217	0.576	0.448	0.64

In order to verify the fact that ammonia is absorbed more readily from strong solutions than from weak, experiments were made with liquids which contained respectively, in 1,000 grains, 0.634, 0.304, 0.176, and 0.088 grains of ammonia. There was absorbed from these solutions by 1,000-grain portions of a calcareous soil 1.32, 0.64, 0.26, and 0.10 grains of ammonia, respectively; and by pouring one of the stronger solutions on a soil already charged with ammonia from a weak solution, new portions of ammonia were immediately absorbed.

It will be noticed in the table that the sterile sandy soil absorbed as much ammonia from ammonia water as the clays did. But in no instance was the ammonia completely removed from the solutions no matter how weak they were; and in no instance was the ammonia so permanently fixed that water could not wash out appreciable quan- tities of it, though the proportion of ammonia removed by several washings was small in comparison with that retained by the soil.

Rautenberg found that 10,000 parts of different kinds of soils tested by him absorbed from a given solution quantities of am- monia ranging from 7 parts to 25. Variations such as these are readily explained, by assuming that more or less of the active double silicates are contained in one soil than in another, and it is found in fact that, if a soil be thoroughly washed with acids to remove the bases which it holds or has absorbed, its fixing power will be greatly diminished, manifestly through the destruction of the effective silicates which were contained in it. By adding a quantity of a zeolitic mineral to an ordinary soil, it is found that the power of the soil to absorb and fix bases is increased.

Are there Zeolites in ordinary Soils?

It would practically be impossible to detect zeolites in ordinary soils by mere inspection, but there are good reasons for presuming that these compounds are often formèd within the soil, and it is easy by means of certain chemical reactions to prove their absence, or exhibit their probable presence, as the case may be. It has been found in fact that the fixing power of a soil is intimately connected with the quantity of alumina which the soil yields to diluted hydrochloric acid, as well as with the amount of silica set free from the soil by the action of such acid ; and both these items of evidence go to show the probability of the soil's containing zeolites, for these minerals would act in this way with acids if they were there.

To estimate the amount of this zeolitic or so-called soluble silica, it is necessary to leach the soil with a hot solution of carbonate of soda, both before and after the treatment with the diluted acid. The amount of silica dissolved by the soda, after the acid has acted upon the soil, will indicate the amount of zeolitic silica which has been decomposed by the acid. Heiden has in this way determined the amount of soluble silica, such as occurs in zeolites, that is contained in various soils, and he finds from 2 to 7%, or more. He urges that considerable quantities of the zeolitic silica are really present in ordinary loams, and that it must be regarded as a normal constituent of loams. It is to be presumed that it is with the alumina and iron of these hydrated silicates that phosphoric acid unites when it is finally fixed in the earth, no matter whether it may have been applied as farmyard manure, as superphosphate, or in the form of some other variety of phosphate of lime.

The Soils of Arid Regions usually contain much Zeolitic Silica.

Hilgard has called attention to the fact that, in the United States, " the general average of soluble silica is very much larger in the soils of the arid regions than in those of the humid, approximating one to two in favor of the arid division." The averages of many analyses were 4.212% of soluble silica in the soils of humid regions, and 7.266% in the soils of arid regions. He observes that in the soils of regions where summer rains are insignificant or wanting, any soluble matters which may result from processes of disintegration not only remain in the soil, but their solutions are concentrated by evaporation to a degree which can never be reached in humid climates. "Prominent among these soluble ingredients are the silicates and carbonates of potash and soda. The former, when filtered through a soil containing the carbonates of lime and magnesia, will soon be transformed into complex silicates." The carbonates, in their turn, when in the concentrated form, are effective in decomposing silicate minerals which are refractory to milder agencies, such as solutions of calcic carbonate, and on this ground alone the more decomposed state of the soil minerals of the arid regions becomes intelligible. Moreover, it must not be forgotten that solutions of bicarbonate of lime may slowly bring about decompositions analogous to those produced by the alkaline carbonates. It is noticeable indeed, on contrasting analyses of calcareous and non-calcareous clays from humid regions, that the proportions of dissolved silica and alumina in the former are almost invariably larger than in the latter. "It is but rarely that even the heaviest non-calcareous soils yield to the acid usually used in soil analysis more than 10% of alumina, while heavy calcareous, prairie clays commonly yield between 13 and 20%." (Hilgard.)

Mulder's Experiments.

In connection with his experiments on natural zeolitic minerals, Mulder prepared artificially a substance of analogous composition, by dissolving hydraulic cement in muriatic acid, and adding to the solution enough ammonia water to neutralize the acid. The gelatinous precipitate thus formed, after having been washed with water, was found to contain a certain quantity of a double silicate of alumina, iron, and lime, beside hydrate of iron, alumina, and free silicic acid. On drenching the precipitate with dilute saline solutions of one kind or another, in order to test its fixing power, it was found that, like the artificial silicates of Way, this substance was competent to fix potash, magnesia, ammonia, and soda, while lime went into solution and was removed. Mulder proved also that silicates which contain ferric oxide (Fe_2O_3) instead of alumina (Al_2O_3) can serve to fix bases of the alkali metals and the alkaline earths.

In general, hydrated double silicates exhibit much more fixing power than silicates from which the water of hydration has been expelled. Way showed in his original research, that by burning or calcining a soil its absorptive power is diminished, or even destroyed; though he noticed at the same time that pipe-stems exhibited a considerable power of fixing bases. On exposing his artificial precipitated silicates to strong heat, he practically destroyed their ability to react upon saline solutions so as to fix or absorb the bases. But many of Way's calcined soils were still fairly active, and it is now recognized that, although the absorptive power of soils is greatly diminished by calcining them, it is not necessarily wholly destroyed by the calcination.

Even coal-ashes have a certain small absorptive power, and Eichhorn has shown that some anhydrous mineral silicates are acted upon by saline solutions, though slowly, and that the bases of the salts are absorbed. In one case recorded by Peters, 0.1841 grm. of potash was absorbed by a natural loam from a solution of potassium chloride, while 0.12 grm. was absorbed by the same loam after it had been burned to ashes.

Incessant Chemical Action in Soils.

It is evident enough from the foregoing statements that important changes, and changes almost infinite in variety, must be continually occurring in the soil by virtue of reactions in which the double silicates take part. With the exception perhaps of midwinter, when everything is frozen stiff, it is certain that chemical changes are constantly occurring in every soil. From the chemical point of view, nothing like rest can be conceived of in a mixture so complex as the loam of an ordinary field.

On the contrary, it is known that the constituents of such earth are subjected to incessant action, counter action, and change. If crops are growing on the land there will be many special changes, due to the activities of the plant-roots, that would not occur if the field were lying fallow; but although the changes which the soil undergoes will be different in the two cases, there is small reason to believe that there will be any fewer of them in the one case than in the other. With regard to the fixation of bases by zeolites, it is important to observe, that, although the compounds formed

by such fixation give up a part of their alkali to pure water, and
are consequently capable of feeding plants directly, the fixed matters must be still more readily soluble in carbonic-acid water, and
in the acids exuded or excluded by the roots of plants.

As will be shown in another place, certain double humates of
lime, or what not, have the power of fixing potash, ammonia, etc.,
in the soil in a manner analogous to that exhibited by the double
silicates. This result might naturally have been expected, since
the humic acids resemble silica in that they are weak acids and
polybasic acids; a single molecule of either of them is apt to combine with a large excess of base, or with several different bases,
which may be held more or less forcibly according to circumstances. Special stress is commonly laid by teachers upon the
action of the silicates, because, taking the world through, the efficient silicates are much more abundant than the humates.

Fixation by Colloids.

Several observers have noticed that neither lime, by itself, nor
magnesia, alumina, phosphate of alumina, gelatinous silica, quartz
sand, kaolin, chalk, humus from decaying wood, or the hydrates of
iron or alumina — no matter whether they are taken singly or admixed — have the power to decompose salts of the stronger acids,
and fix their bases in the manner above described. But Van Bemmelen, on the contrary, insists that several of the substances enumerated, provided they are in the colloid state, have the power to
absorb and fix alkalies and alkaline earths from saline solutions,
especially from hydrates, carbonates and phosphates, i. e. from
salts with weak acids. The action now in question is evidently
similar to that witnessed so often in the analytical laboratory when
no inconsiderable quantities of alkali or alkaline earth are firmly
held by colloid precipitates such as those of the hydrates and phosphates of alumina and iron, the hydrates of manganese, chromium,
tin, glucina and the like. According to Van Bemmelen, ordinary
soils contain colloid silicates and colloid humus, as well as colloid
silica and colloid iron oxide, and he argues that the power of soils
to fix fertilizers may depend chiefly on the activity of these substances, especially on the action of colloid silicates. Hilgard,
while admitting the importance of Van Bemmelen's observations,
remarks that he has himself found hydrous hydrate of alumina
to be a not infrequent constituent of soils. The visible occurrence
of the mineral gibbsite in modern formations, he says, also points
directly to this conclusion.

Fixation in Field Experiments.

The great practical importance of the fixation of fertilizers, considered as a means of enabling the soil to become a reservoir of plant-food, is well illustrated by some of the field experiments of Lawes and Gilbert, in which land which had been purposely charged with ash ingredients was made to bear wheat continuously during many successive years. In the year 1844 two plots of land were dressed with a mixture of mineral fertilizers, without any addition of nitrogen, and each plot yielded a crop of wheat at the rate of 15.5 bushels to the acre. In the next year (1845) both the plots were dressed with ammonium salts, and the yield of wheat was 32 bushels to the acre. Thenceforth the two fields were treated differently, as will appear from the following statement. One of the plots received no manure whatever in 1846 and 1847, while in 1848 it received both mineral manures and ammonium salts ; in 1849 it got ammonium salts alone, in 1850 minerals alone, and afterwards ammonium salts alone every year during 33 years. Meanwhile, the other plot was dressed with ammonium salts in 1846, and in each succeeding year for a period of 38 years.

The essential difference in treatment between the two plots was that one received only one dressing of mineral manures, followed by 39 dressings of ammonium salts ; while the other plot received 3 dressings of minerals, in the course of 7 years, followed by 33 dressings of ammonium salts. During the last 33 years of the experiment the two plots received precisely the same kinds and amounts of fertilizers. In the following table the crops obtained from the two plots are given in full for each of the first 8 years, but as regards the subsequent years, the average annual yield is stated for periods of 8 years.

	Minerals once. Grain, Bush.	Minerals thrice. Grain, Bush.	Minerals once. Total Grain and Straw, lb	Minerals thrice. Total Grain and Straw, lb
1844	15.5	15.5	2,120	2,120
1845	31.9	31.9	6,246	6,246
1846	27.4	17.6	4,094	2,671
1847	25.4	25.4	4,593	4,579
1848	19.3	25.1	3,701	4,530
1849	32.6	32.4	4,992	5,117
1850	27.0	18.0	4,810	3,120
1851	28.9	28.6	5,036	4,985
8 years, 1852–59	22.8	27.5	4,055	4,885
8 years, 1860–67	24.0	27.3	4,076	4,563
8 years, 1868–75	19.0	20.1	3,060	3,264
8 years, 1876–83	16.4	18.1	2,618	2,935
32 years, 1852–83	20.5	23.3	3,452	3,912

It appears from the figures of the table that — even 33 years after their application to the land — the phosphoric acid and potash which the soil had fixed were still exerting an appreciable influence upon the yield of wheat. Thanks to the more abundant store of plant-food in the land dressed with minerals, the crops of the 8 years' periods were always larger on that land than on the other, though, as time rolled on, the difference was a declining one. Nevertheless,

as regards the earlier years, when both the plots were adequately
charged with ash ingredients, it will be noticed that applications of
the nitrogenous fertilizers did more good than the application of
minerals.

Physical Fixation, as distinguished from Chemical.

Beside the chemical absorptive power due to the action of double
silicates or double humates, as above set forth, and the fixation
by means of colloid substances — which may perhaps be regarded
as dependent in some part on weak chemical action, as well as
upon physical adhesion — soils have yet another purely physical
power of holding some traces of saline matter by mere force of
adhesion or surface attraction, much in the same way that charcoal can absorb and hold them.   It is to be presumed, generally
speaking, that the larger part of the matters fixed by soils is fixed
by chemical means, though the fixation by colloids may sometimes
be of importance. It is certain at all events that the quantity of any
ordinary soluble salt, which can be held as such by mere force of
adhesion in a soil which is subjected to the leaching action of
water, is by no means large.   It is a quantity not to be compared
for a' moment with that of the base which could be taken from
that salt by a double silicate or a double humate, or even by a colloid, and thenceforth retained in the soil in spite of long-continued
washing.

According to Van Bemmelen, the colloids have but little power
to fix and hold saline matters as such, but it is probable that they
may play an important part in some familiar phenomena of fixation, as, for example, in the case where a colored liquid is clarified
by filtration through loam.

Examples of physical absorption by soils were noticed much
earlier than those which depend upon chemical action. Naturally
enough, practical men have long observed how readily barnyard
liquor and other colored waters are made clear and odorless when
put in contact with fresh loam or clay.   Several writers at one
time or another have called attention to the fact, and have dwelt
upon its importance, — notably Sir Humphry Davy in 1813, Gazzeri in 1819, Lambruschini in 1830, Bronner in 1836, Huxtable
in 1848, Bernays in 1849, and Thompson and Way in 1850.
Manifestly this fixation of coloring matters, etc., by the soil is
closely analogous to the fixing of such things by charcoal and
by vegetable tissues. There is an adage current in New England,
that clothes upon which the fetor of the skunk has fallen may be

" sweetened " by burying them in earth. The Indians are said to purify the carcass even of the skunk in this way, so as to fit it to be eaten; and in like manner the bones buried by dogs remain comparatively free from offensive odor. The practice of leaving the blade of a knife in the ground to remove the smell of onions is another case in point. (Way.) Other applications of the same principle are seen in the "earth-closet" system of deodorizing human excrements, and sometimes in the use of loam and peat upon manure-heaps, both of which points will need to be discussed in another chapter.

Not only are coloring matters and vapors, i. e. fetid exhalations, thus absorbed by the soil, but many soluble chemical substances also. It is an instructive experiment to put a quantity of half-dried garden-loam in a bottle together with some liquor that has drained from a dung-heap, to shake the two together, and finally to filter the mixture. If a proper proportion has been maintained between the amounts of loam and of liquid, the filtrate will be found to be mere water, almost completely colorless, devoid of odor, and well-nigh tasteless. This experiment is going on incessantly in nature. Drinking water as it flows from springs or is drawn from wells is a filtrate not much unlike that of the experiment. The experiment itself is similar in kind to the process employed in sugar refineries, where the brown color of raw sugar is removed by filtering solutions of the sugar through bone-black. The coloring matter adheres to the innumerable surfaces of the particles of bone-black in the one case, and to those of the porous soil in the other, and is thus held fast.

Saline Matters fixed by Adhesion.

As was just now said, it is well known that, beside coloring matters, small quantities of soluble saline substances can adhere to the soil. Even in the use of bone-charcoal for purifying syrup, some sugar adheres to the coal; and when other crystalline chemicals are purified by means of this agent, it usually happens that small portions of them are lost through adhesion to the coal.

Numerous observations of facts of this character even as regards soils are upon record, and a considerable number of them have been collected and published by Way. Thus Lord Bacon remembers " to have somewhere read that trial hath been made of salt-water passed through earth through ten vessels one within another, and yet it hath not lost its saltness as to become potable; but when drayned through twenty vessels, hath become fresh."

Hales, in 1739, mentions, on the authority of Boyle Godfrey, that "sea-water, being filtered through stone cisterns, the first pint that runs through will be pure water having no taste of salt, but the next pint will be salt as usual." Some allowance must be made in crude experiments such as these for the fresh water originally held in the pores of the stones, which would be pushed out by the salt water in such wise that the first drops of the filtrate would be fresh. Berzelius found, on filtering solutions of common salt through sand, that the first portions of the filtrate were free from salt, and Matteucci observed the same thing as regards other salts beside chloride of sodium. Wagemann found, on filtering acetic acid and diluted alcohol through pure sand, that the first fractions of the filtrate were almost pure water.

In the year 1819, the Italian chemist Gazzeri wrote as follows: "Loam and especially clay take possession of soluble matters which are intrusted to the soil, and retain them in order to give them by degrees to plants, conformably with their needs." Yet another Italian, Lambruschini, suggested, in 1830, that it might perhaps be well to apply the name "incorporation" to the act of combining dung-liquor and soil. We can readily recognize, he said, that fertilizing liquids and the constituents of a well-prepared soil enter into a peculiar combination, by virtue of a special affinity. This combination is not weak enough to allow any very easy loss of the fertilizing constituents, or to permit plants to consume them too rapidly, and yet the combination is not so strong, but that the vital action of growing plants can gradually overcome it. The German horticulturist Bronner, in 1836, in speaking of the clarifying of dung-liquor by earth, insisted that even the soluble salts in the dung-liquor are absorbed by the earth, and held so strongly by it that they are only washed out to a small extent by new quantities of water.

As recently as 1878, Roberts has maintained that a sandstone at Liverpool, through which sea-water slowly percolates, exerts an appreciable influence to hold back the salt. To test the matter, he prepared cubes of the sandstone, 12 inches square, dished out on top so as to hold water, and varnished on the sides to prevent leakage. He dried these cubes thoroughly in the air, placed them one above another in a frame, and poured sea-water upon the top of the uppermost. Matters were so arranged that the water which passed through the upper cube should drop into the cup at the top of the lower one, while that which dropped from the bottom of the lower cube was received in a bottle, for analysis.

Clear sea-water from the river Mersey was added by small portions to the dish of the upper cube until drops began to fall from the bottom of the stone, and when two fluid ounces of liquid had passed through, the amount of chlorides contained in it was determined. It appeared on this first trial that almost 81% of the chlorides of the original sea-water had been removed by the sandstone.

New quantities of the salt water were allowed to filter through the first cube and to drop upon the second, until the liquid passed through without any change from its original condition. The second cube was thus partially saturated with the filtrate from the first cube, and sea-water was added continuously till it began to drop from the bottom of the second cube, where it was collected and analyzed. The results of these trials are given in the following table.

Filtrates from 2 c. ft. of Sandstone.	Quantity of Liquid, in Fluid oz.	Percentage of Chlorides removed.
1st filtrate	3½	80.8
2d "	4	76.6
3d "	4	71.3
4th "	4	64.9
5th "	4	57.4
6th "	4	53.2
7th "	4	46.8
8th "	8	44.7
9th "	8	31.9
10th "	8	25.5
11th "	8	21.3
12th "	8	10.6
13th "	8	10.6
14th "	18	8.5

The last drops of the 14th filtrate had the same composition as the sea-water, showing that the absorptive power of the stones was exhausted. It appeared that 93½ fluid ounces of the sea-water passed through the two cubic feet of sandstone before they became inoperative, and that nearly the whole of the salts were removed from the water that first passed through.

In order to determine whether this fixation of chlorides was a mechanical or a chemical process, Roberts allowed one of the cubes of stone which had become saturated as above to dry in the air for a month, and then poured spring-water into the dished part, as he had done before with the sea-water. The results obtained in this way are given in the table.

Filtrates from 1 c. ft. of Sandstone.	Quantity of Liquid, in Fluid oz.	Percentage of Chlorides washed out.	
1st filtrate	24	157.77	
2d "	45	1k2.22	in 101 fluid oz.
3d "	32	102.22	
4th "	40	55.55	
5th "	40	4.44	in 92 fluid oz.
6th "	12	2.22	

Taking sea-water at 100 of the standard for comparison, it appeared that in the 1st filtrate of 24 fluid ounces there was an increase of 57.77 of the chlorides; and the 3d filtrate shows that it required 101 fluid ounces of water to reduce the salts that had accumulated in the pores of the sandstone during the previous filtration of the sea-water to the standard of the original sea-water. The 6th filtrate shows that the 92 additional fluid ounces of spring-water washed out all the remaining chlorides. The last drops of the 6th filtrate showed only a trace of salts remaining. It appears, therefore, that the fixation of salt by the sandstone was purely mechanical, and not dependent upon any chemical action of the sandstone upon sea-water.

Action of Loams on Liquid Manure.

Some of the changes which occur when liquid manure comes in contact with loam have been studied by Voelcker. In this research, definite quantities of the soil to be tested and of liquid manures of known composition were shaken together during terms of 1 or 3 days, and the clear liquid which was left when the loam had settled was subjected to analysis. By comparing the several columns of figures in the table on page 321, it will be seen that some of the loams exhibited a very remarkable power of absorbing fertilizing matters. The following list gives descriptions of the soils operated upon.

I. A calcareous clay from Cirencester; very stiff and sticky in wet weather. When worked in dry weather, it breaks up in hard clods. This soil contained 11 % organic matter, 11 % carbonate of lime, 52 % clay and 25 % sand.

II. A moderately stiff vegetable mould — taken from a permanent pasture — which held much more sand and much less lime than No. I. It contained 12 % organic matter, less than 2 % carbonate of lime, 48 % clay and 36 % sand.

III. An infertile red, sandy, non-calcareous soil, which contained 5 % organic matter, a quarter of one per cent of carbonate of lime, 5 % clay and 90 % sand.

IV. A soil of moderately retentive character and naturally very fertile. The surface soil was a friable sandy loam; the subsoil stiffer, containing less sand and more clay. Equal parts of the surface soil and subsoil were taken for the experiment, and were left in contact with the liquid manure during 3 days. The surface and subsoils contained respectively 4 and 3 % organic matter, 1.37 and 0.47 carbonate of lime and magnesia, 18 and 42 % clay, and 76 and 55 % sand.

V. A stiff clay soil which had been dressed at one time with burnt clay. Equal parts of surface and subsoil were mixed and left during 3 days in contact with a much weaker liquid manure (obtained from Mr. Mechi) than that used in the other four experiments. The surface and subsoils contained respectively 5 % organic matter, 2 and 1 % carbonate of lime, 78 and 75 % clay, and 11 and 9 % sand.

It will be observed in most instances, that the soils, when not too sandy, absorbed large quantities of ammonia, potash and phosphoric acid, but very little soda. On the other hand, most of the soils, again excepting the sandy one, gave up lime to the water, often in very considerable quantity and partly perhaps in the form of bicarbonate of lime, much of which exists in the original liquid manure. In general, more organic matter was dissolved out from the soil than was fixed by it, and this fact probably accounts for the removal of appreciable quantities of organic nitrogen from the soils by the water in several instances.

One imperial gallon of the Liquid Manure contained	I. Calcareous Soil. Before.	After.	II. Pasture Soil. Before.	After.	III. Infertile Sand. Before.	After.
Water and volatile matter	69,888.14	69,886.60	69,888.14	69,856.85	69,888.14	69,892.41
Organic matter	20.59	34.77	20.59	31.14	20.59	25.06
Ash ingredients	91.27	78.63	91.27	112.01	91.27	82.53
Ammonia, as carbonate and humate	35.58	20.81	35.58	20.83	35.58	33.15
Organic nitrogen	1.49	1.84	1.49	2.20	1.49	1.40
Soluble silica	2.34	0.70	2.34	3.06	2.34	5.10
Insoluble silica	—	2.55	—	2.97	—	1.39
Oxide of Iron	none	—	—	—	—	2.07
Lime	11.48	22.42	11.48	25.21	21.48	8.03
Magnesia	2.87	1.17	2.87	2.87	2.87	0.74
Potash	16.92	3.40	16.92	5.19	16.92	12.01
Chloride of potassium	2.74	none	2.74	4.88	2.74	none
Soda	—	—	—	—	—	0.45
Chloride of sodium	40.35	33.31	40.35	39.23	40.35	39.25
Phosphoric acid	4.83	0.60	4.83	1.74	4.83	1.92
Sulphuric acid	3.94	2.88	3.94	2.73	3.94	3.67
Carbonic acid and loss	5.80	11.60	5.80	24.13	5.80	7.90

One imperial gallon of the Liquid Manure contained	IV. Fertile Loam.		V. Very stiff Clay.	
	Before.	After.	Before.	After.
Water and volatile matter	69,888.14	69,871.03	69,970.81	69,954.92
Organic matter	20.59	35.52	7.70	5.46
Ash ingredients	91.27	93.45	21.49	39.62
Ammonia, as carbonate and humate	35.58	25.84	3.36	1.55
Organic nitrogen	1.49	0.84	0.52	0.20
Soluble silica	2.34	2.23	1.68	1.61
Insoluble silica	—	4.38	0.76	1.92
Oxide of Iron	—	—	—	—
Lime	11.48	16.50	4.43	7.80
Magnesia	2.87	2.37	1.78	2.87
Potash	16.92	10.96	1.91	3.90
Chloride of potassium	2.74	5.29	1.10	none
Soda	—	—	—	0.52
Chloride of sodium	40.35	39.11	5.46	9.12
Phosphoric acid	4.83	1.45	2.36	2.23
Sulphuric acid	3.94	5.18	2.15	5.59
Carbonic acid and loss	5.80	5.98	0.45	4.06

It is of interest to notice — in accordance with what has been said previously as to the limitations of the fixing power of soils — that none of the loams examined by Voelcker had the power of completely absorbing either ammonia, potash or phosphoric acid from the liquid during the 24 to 72 hours devoted to the experiments, though it is true, of course, that — as compared with the vast amount of earth in a field — only limited quantities of the soils were exposed to the action of the liquid manure.

In two of the soils above cited, and in other cases where liquid manure was brought into contact with soils rich in oxide of iron, appreciable quantities of this compound were dissolved out from the soil probably in combination with an organic acid, or with organic matters similar in character to those found in bog-iron ore. It is conceivable, as Voelcker has suggested, that this solution of iron may be injurious to vegetation, and possibly account for some instances where liquid manure has disappointed expectations.

In some of the examples above given, it is evident that phenomena of physical fixation were supplemented in some part by those of chemical absorption. Practically the several kinds of fixation must constantly act together, i. e. simultaneously and side by side, in the same soil.

But it is often desirable to hold the various conceptions apart, and to endeavor to distinguish between the cases where one or another kind of absorption would be likely to have a preponderating influence. Generally speaking, chemical absorption is thought to be more important than physical adhesion. There are at all events good reasons for believing that much of the potash, lime, magnesia, ammonia and soda, which plants take from the soil, existed there in the form of the hydrated double silicates or of the double humates above described, or that they were held loosely combined with colloid humates or silicates; and it is known, also, that small quantities of saline matters, such as plants need, may be held in the soil by force of mere adhesion.

The whole subject of the fixing power of soils has been well treated by Professor Johnson, in "How Crops Feed," p. 333. The student will there find judicious selections from the details of numerous experiments.

It may be well to remark yet again, that, while the power of sand to retain salts by adhesion has doubtless some slight influence in preventing the admixture of sea-water with the ground-water of land near the sea, it is in no sense the prime cause of the freshness of water in wells dug in sand near the shore, as has been already explained. Manifestly the physical absorptive power of a soil

will be greater in proportion as the soil is porous, and the power
of sand must always be comparatively feeble on this account,
since the particles of sand are solid and destitute of pores.

A Dry Soil may fix the Water of a Saline Solution rather than the Salt thereof.

Some mention should here be made of a curious phenomenon —
closely related to the general subject of the capillarity of saline solutions, mentioned in Chapter VII — which was experimented upon
by Schoenbein in his time, and more recently by several other
observers. Schoenbein noticed, when one end of a sheet of blotting-paper is dipped into a saline solution, that the solution is not
absorbed as such by the paper. On the contrary, some water from
the solution passes into the paper faster than the saline matter does;
and in the case of a mixed solution of several salts some of the salts
will be absorbed more quickly than others, for, as Graham has
shown, each and every substance has its own special rate of diffusi-
bility.

In view of the fact that the height to which saline matters rise in
paper is different for different salts, it might even be possible to
detect the presence of the several constituents of a mixture by placing a series of rolls of paper touching each other, end to end, one
above the other, in a glass tube set up in such wise that only the end
of the lowest roll shall be in actual contact with the solution. By
subsequently examining the several rolls, taken from different heights
above the solution, each of them will be found to contain a preponderating quantity of the salt which can most readily be lifted to that
particular height. (E. Fischer.)

As a matter of course, dry earth will act very much in the same
way as blotting-paper, and it has in fact been observed by Schloesing on pouring a solution of nitrate of lime upon a column of dry
earth — which had been washed free from the last trace of nitrates
before it was dried — that the solution of the nitrate became somewhat more concentrated as it passed down through the earth, because
a part of the water of the solution was abstracted, so to say, from its
combination with the salt, and was taken in as water by the dry
earth and firmly held. Thus it might happen perhaps that a saline
solution could become more concentrated in the soil, both by loss of
water evaporated into the air and by the fixation of a part of its
water by the soil.

CHAPTER IX.

MODES OF ACTION OF SPECIAL MANURES.

In passing to the consideration of different kinds of manures,
and the theory of the action of each special kind, it is a matter of
much indifference which particular fertilizers are first chosen as
subjects for study. It is necessary only that care should be taken
to discuss some of the simpler instances at the beginning, and to

proceed step by step to cases which are more complex. It needs to be insisted, however, at the start, that the word "simple" is here used merely as a term of comparison, for it is wellnigh impossible to conceive of simplicity of action on the part of any substance put in contact with a mixture so complex and variable as the soil is.

In point of fact, there is no manure so simple in its action that this action can be comprehended at a glance.

Gypsum, or Plaster of Paris.

As an example, gypsum may be taken, otherwise called "plaster," "land-plaster" or plaster of Paris, or sulphate of lime. This substance has been used as a fertilizer from time immemorial. Even the Greeks and Romans employed it in this sense. According to several French agricultural writers, considerable quantities of gypsum were exported from France to America during the last century, to be used for fertilizing purposes. At the present time, large quantities of it are brought to New England from Nova Scotia, and the material is abundant in some parts of the State of New York.

There is a story that Benjamin Franklin in his time strewed gypsum upon a clover-field, so that the words, "This has been plastered," were written in gypsum upon the middle of the field, and could be read there as long as the crop remained upon the land; i. e. the plastered clover grew more vigorously than the rest of the crop.

It was thought at one time, that the good effects of gypsum on clover are due solely to the lime in the gypsum, and even so acute an observer as Boussingault defended this proposition. He found in fact that clover, to which he applied gypsum for two years in succession, contained much more lime than similar clover which had not been treated with gypsum. But more recent observations have shown that this conclusion of Boussingault fails to explain all the facts which he himself observed, and that the mere taking up of an excess of lime by the clover-plant is not necessarily advantageous to it. Even if it were admitted that clover is "a lime plant," as has often been held, and if it were true that it habitually takes much lime from gypsum, the questions would still be left to answer, Why should gypsum be a better fertilizer for clover than lime itself, or than any other compound of lime? And, why should gypsum often do good service on soils already well charged with calcareous matter? Several acute observers have noticed that gypsum may sometimes give excellent results when applied to calcareous soils. (A. Young, Rieffel.) Gasparin found that it worked very well on soils that contained 20% and more of lime.

Another old idea was, that gypsum absorbs and fixes ammonia from the air, as will be explained directly. But these hypotheses failed wholly to clear up the well-known fact, that the action of gypsum as a fertilizer is exceedingly capricious, and that its behavior upon any untried soil could seldom be predicated with certainty. Many years ago Stoeckhardt wrote as follows: "The action of gypsum, perhaps more than that of any other manure, depends upon the kind of soil and crop, upon climate and other conditions, and is subject to manifold limitations." And yet, with the progress of knowledge, gypsum has now become a fit subject for an initial chapter on fertilizers because of the simplicity of its action.

Gypsum forces Potash from the Soil.

The fact is, that the experiments of several different observers, working independently of one another, have shown that gypsum exerts a powerful action in setting free potash which has been absorbed and fixed by the earth, that is to say, by double silicates in the earth.

It is found that the lime of the gypsum is fixed in the soil, while a corresponding quantity of sulphate of potash goes into solution.

$$\left.\begin{array}{l} Al_2O_3 \\ CaO \\ K_2O \\ H_2O \end{array}\right\} x\,SiO_2 + CaO,SO_3 = \left.\begin{array}{l} Al_2O_3 \\ CaO \\ CaO \\ H_2O \end{array}\right\} x\,SiO_2 + K_2O,SO_3$$

Thus it happens not only that gypsum can liberate potash (as well as magnesia and ammonia) for the use of the crop, but it may cause potash to be transferred from the upper to the lower layers of the soil, so that the roots can everywhere find a store of it.

There is no lack of evidence to show that gypsum really does act in the manner above stated. For example, Boussingault, many years ago, strewed gypsum on one part of a clover-field, and analyzed the ashes of the plants there gathered, as contrasted with the ashes of clover-plants from a contiguous part of the field that had received no gypsum.

It will be seen from the following statement of the analyses, that very much more potash, and magnesia also, were taken up by the plants that had been dressed with gypsum than by the others.

It might be argued, indeed, and with justice, that the more vigorous plants of the gypsum patch were able to take up more food than the others. But there will still remain abundant ground for the conviction that the gypsum must have acted upon the soil to loosen up its constituents.

Boussingault himself, having no inkling of the absorptive power of soils, which was not discovered until some years after his experiments, was particularly impressed by the large amount of lime in the ashes of the gypsum plants; but in the light of the wider experience of to-day, it is plain that the great preponderance of potash is the more important consideration. In the clover from a hectare were found the following quantities, in kilos, of the several ash ingredients : —

	1st year, 1841.		2d year, 1842.	
	Gypsum.	No Gypsum.	Gypsum.	No Gypsum.
Ashes, free from CO_2	270.0	113.0	280.0	97.0
Silica	28.1	22.7	104.0	12.7
Oxides of Iron, Manganese, and Alumina	2.7	1.4	?	0.6
Lime	79.4	32.2	102.8	32.2
Magnesia	18.1	8.6	28.5	7.1
Potash	95.6	26.7	97.2	28.6
Soda	2.4	1.4	0.8	2.8
Sulphuric Acid	9.2	4.4	9.0	3.0
Phosphoric Acid	24.2	11.0	22.9	7.0
Chlorine	10.3	4.6	8.4	3.0

One important bit of evidence is seen in the fact that sulphate of magnesia acts very much in the same way that gypsum does, both empirically as a fertilizer and in the laboratory, when used as a means of setting potash free from the hydrous silicates. Pincus harvested the following quantities of hay per Morgen (= 0.631 acre) from land treated as stated.

Meadow not manured	21.6 cwt.	
Meadow treated with gypsum	30.6	"
Meadow treated with sulphate of magnesia	32.4	"

And numerous trials of leaching loams, in great variety, with a solution of gypsum, have shown that much more potash, magnesia and soda can be extracted by this solvent than by mere water. Meanwhile, it is observed that a part of the lime of the gypsum is absorbed and fixed by the loams. Sulphate of soda also may be used instead of gypsum, as well as the magnesium sulphate. (Pierre.)

When to apply Gypsum.

In Germany, where enormous quantities of gypsum were formerly used upon red clover, it was thought at one time that the best season for applying the fertilizer is in the spring, when the plants are 3 or 4 inches high, and the earth is completely covered with the young leaves. And from the fact that gypsum acts with special vigor upon clover when strewn upon it in this way, it was supposēd by some observers that the clover absorbs the gypsum through its leaves as fast as it is dissolved by dew or rain. This idea is probably erroneous. But it is evident that the gypsum thus strewn upon clover-leaves is peculiarly well placed to enable it to act upon the soil about the roots of the plants. When dissolved by rain and heavy dew, the gypsum, or rather its solution, would flow down the stems of the plants, and be aborbed by the soil immediately around them, and would thus favor the development of roots at those spots [and of nodules on the roots (?)].

In case clover has been sown together with grain, there is an objection to the plan of strewing gypsum as soon as the young clover-plants have appeared, because this crop would be forced unduly at the expense of the grain crop. In such cases, gypsum may be applied after the grain has been harvested, and again perhaps in the following spring. Some writers have urged that it is well to strew gypsum upon clover after each mowing, in order to excite a new growth, while others argue that as a general rule the best time to strew gypsum is in the autumn, rather than after the crop has started, or than in the early spring even. This opinion appears to be now quite generally held, viz., that gypsum should be applied to the land some months before the growth of the crop for whose benefit it is used, in order that there may be time enough for it to act upon the matters in the soil.

Admitting that the chief value of gypsum depends on its power of setting free potash, it is plain that some little time will often be needed for the accomplishment of this purpose. There is no longer any difficulty, moreover, in explaining how it is that gypsum sometimes does its best service on fairly good soils, which have been well manured and kept in good heart, so that potash may have accumulated in them. Nor is there any difficulty in seeing why gypsum is apparently so capricious in its action; for upon soils that are tolerably rich in fixed potash it may do good service, while upon soils poor in potash it may not.

Gypsum has in fact often been found useful on new lands of certain kinds and qualities, and on old fields which have been cropped and fertilized in a way which was perhaps not wholly judicious. It is often of great use in regions where wheat is grown in alternation with clover, since by encouraging the growth of the clover it acts as a manure for the wheat. It was noticed very early, not only that gypsum is particularly well suited for use upon leguminous crops, such as clover and peas, but that much better crops of oats could often be grown after peas that had been dressed with gypsum than were got by putting gypsum directly upon the oat-field.

Gypsum Acts Indirectly.

But it is none the less true that gypsum is a fit manure neither for poor land nor for regions where high farming is practised. It has found place only in districts where the methods of farming were simple, and so to say backward, and is really a fertilizer of times that are past. The action of gypsum is too slow and too feeble to meet the requirements of modern agriculture, at least on farms where the soil is highly manured, and where complex systems of cropping are practised. Wherever there is profit to be got from high farming, gypsum would usually be found to be a much less efficient fertilizer than potassic manures, used either as such, or in conjunction with lime or with leached ashes.

In any event, gypsum is to be regarded as an excitant, rather than as a form of plant-food. That is to say, it is a manure of indirect action. An illustration of this fact may be seen in the following experiment of Heinrich. Gypsum was applied, in contrast with sulphate of potash, upon mixed clover and timothy grass on a poor, sandy soil, that had never previously borne clover within the memory of man. There was obtained per Morgen (= 0.631 acre) 1,400 lb. of dry crop from the unmanured land, 1,653 lb. from the gypsum plot, and 1,772 lb. from the plot dressed with sulphate of potash; and it was noticed that the growth of clover, rather than that of the true grass, was favored by the gypsum.

Of course, gypsum can, and does, supply plants with lime and sulphur in cases where the plants need more of these things than can be found already in the soil; but, considered as a manure of direct action, it has infinitely less significance than bone-meal, guano, superphosphate of lime, and the like, which actually give to the plant substances which are lacking in the soil.

With regard to the notion that clover is a lime plant, and that sulphate of lime is good for it on this account, Knop has remarked, that it is in one sense hardly fair to regard clover as a plant specially grateful for lime. It is a matter of observation, that all leaves contain a comparatively large proportion of lime; and, as clover is a leafy plant, a good deal of lime is taken from the soil by a crop of it. But it does not therefore follow that the need of the entire plant is especially lime. In other words, if there be applied to the clover-plant all the nitrogen, potash and phosphoric acid it can dispose of, the chances are, that, as soils go, it can usually get out of the earth all the lime it will need.

It is noteworthy that the chemical efficacy of gypsum depends as much upon the sulphuric acid contained in it as upon the lime. It is sulphate of potash that goes into solution when the gypsum acts upon the soil. It is sulphate of ammonia that is formed when moist gypsum acts upon carbonate of ammonia in manure or in the soil, or when gypsum acts upon humus or other porous component of the soil which has charged itself with ammonia by absorption.

Gypsum is an Uncertain Manure.

Gypsum is said to be more highly esteemed in moist than in dry climates, though it is taught that the soil on which it may be placed should be neither heavy nor wet. It is thought to be good practice to strew gypsum at a moist time; and it is plain, in any event, that the soil should be moist enough to permit and facilitate the action of the sulphate upon the potassic silicate. Moreover, the physical condition of the soil can hardly fail of having considerable influence upon this reaction, for the decomposing action of the sulphate will be more or less rapid and complete, not only according as the soil is wet or dry, but according as it is light or heavy, mellow or stiff. In soils not properly aerated and rich in organic matter, the sulphate will be reduced to calcium sulphide (CaS).

Although the fact that gypsum does good on some lands, while it is worthless upon others, was familiarly known long before the modern artificial fertilizers came into use, there may perhaps be something of truth in Heiden's suggestion, that the uncertainty which attends the use of gpysum may really be greater nowadays than it was formerly, because in all regions where superphosphates, rectified guano and other fertilizers rich in gypsum are used freely, as they have been in Europe during many years, so much of the farm-land must have become charged with gpysum that no good can be expected from the application of new portions of it. In corroboration of this view, Heiden insists that the records of scientific experiments show that

those trials in which gypsum has approved itself to be decidedly useful were made either before superphosphates had come into use, or
they were made upon land that had seldom or never been fertilized
in any way.

Gypsum favors Clover.

It is to be noted, however, that gypsum has always done its best
service in promoting the growth of clover and other leguminous
plants, and that it came long ago to be regarded in some sort as
a special manure for clover, just as potash compounds are nowadays, as will be shown on another page. It is a matter of common observation, that the application of gypsum to pastures and
mowing-fields favors the growth of white clover.

But it is notorious that clover is one of the most capricious of
crops — because of certain physiologic peculiarities which will be
insisted upon in the chapter on Symbiosis — and there can now be
little doubt that some part of the uncertainty of action of gypsum,
as observed by our forefathers, must really have been due to the
capriciousness of the clover to which the gypsum had been applied.
As Gasparin has said, if pulverized gypsum is spread upon a field
of lucern, red clover, or sainfoin, even at the rate of no more
than 175 or 260 lb. to the acre, the crop will not infrequently be
doubled; the leaves are more numerous, larger and of a deeper
green color, and the roots participate in the increase as well as the
other organs. It is remarkable, on the other hand, that gypsum
exerts little or no useful effect on the growth of the cereal grains
and other true grasses, although it greatly favors leguminous crops,
and helps many other plants, such as the cabbage, rape, turnip,
hemp, flax, buckwheat and maize.

In southern Europe, according to Gasparin, excellent crops of
lucern are often obtained, without manure, by simply applying
gypsum to the land; though in order to full success it is essential
that the field should never before have borne lucern, and that, no
matter how stony the soil may be, it shall be deep and mellow, and
at least fertile enough to produce mediocre crops of wheat or rye.
After the lucern has stood for several years, fine crops of grain
are grown upon the inverted sod without manuring. So, too, with
sainfoin; the agriculture of several districts in Europe, which had
previously been given over to long terms of fallow with the interpolation of an occasional crop of rye or oats, was revolutionized
by the introduction of this plant, which enabled the farmers to
keep cattle and so to obtain manure. At first, it was supposed

that the sainfoin could be grown only on calcareous soils, but afterwards it was discovered that by means of gypsum this plant could be made to grow on many other soils that were not naturally calcareous.

It is not yet known how the gypsum or the potash act in these cases, though the observed fact that applications of gypsum are apt to make pea-vines run to leaf, while the ripening of the seeds is retarded, points to the probable presence of a source of nitrogenous plant-food, and suggests the thought that the development of those micro-organisms on pea and clover roots which take nitrogen from the air may perhaps be favored. See the chapter on Symbiosis. It is in fact highly probable that these micro-organisms may prosper better in soils which are slightly alkaline than in those which are neutral or acid, and there is no difficulty in conceiving that the sulphate of potash which has been set free by gypsum from double silicates in the soil may be changed there to carbonate of potash, for it is a matter of familiar observation that gypsum, when in contact with moist humus which is undergoing fermentation, is easily reduced to the condition of sulphide of calcium,

$$CaSO_4 + 2C = 2CO_2 + CaS,$$

and that under slightly changed conditions the moist sulphide and the carbonic acid will reach upon each other to form sulphuretted hydrogen and carbonate of lime (or carbonate of potash when circumstances permit).

$$CaS + CO_2 + H_2O = CaCO_3 + H_2S.$$

The waters of many mineral springs are charged with sulphides, and with sulphuretted hydrogen, formed, no doubt, in a similar way, through the reduction of sulphates deep in the earth. So, too, a rotting pump-log or decaying leaves in a well of hard water, that is to say, of water charged with sulphate of lime, will soon convert the well into a veritable sulphur spring. The odor of sulphuretted hydrogen which exhales from the mud of salt marshes and docks is due to the action of carbonic acid from the air or from fermenting organic matters upon sulphide of calcium which has been formed by the reduction of sulphate of lime in the sea-water by organic matter in the mud.

In the case now under consideration it is a fair enough inference that some carbonate of potash may be formed in the soil, and that this soluble alkali will neutralize any acidity which the soil might otherwise have exhibited. Indeed, Spatzier long ago proved experimentally that carbonates may be formed in the soil readily enough as a result of the application of gypsum. Having strewn a quantity of gypsum in a garden on a bed of vegetable mould, which had been dressed with horse-dung and sprinkled with water when it was dry, he noticed at the beginning of the experiment that no trace of carbonates could be detected either in the bed or in the gypsum, while at the end of 3 weeks the soil was so highly charged with carbonates that it effervesced strongly on being treated with acids, even when taken from a depth of 6 inches. Much the larger part of the gypsum had been changed to carbonate of lime.

Other writers have urged that clover and some other broad-leaved crops may put to profit a certain amount of organic matter taken from the soil and used by them as food, and Dehérain has suggested that carbonate of potash may dissolve out this desirable organic matter from the humus of the soil, and bring it within reach of the clover roots. It is not impossible withal that the power of feeding upon organic matter, as here suggested, may be true of the micro-organisms which live upon the clover-roots, rather than of the plant itself.

It is remarkable that in his experiments, made in Germany, on high-lying moor-land (heaths), Fleischer noticed that on such land gypsum had a decidedly hurtful effect on the growth of clover and peas, and that the injurious action was still evident even in the 5th and 6th year after the application of the gypsum. No such injurious action was exerted by the gypsum on potatoes, rye and oats, grown on the moor-land, which seemed indeed to be helped by it somewhat when it was applied in small quantities.

It is a curious fact, to which attention was called many years ago, that, on trying to cook peas (or beans) grown on land which has been manured with gypsum, it often happens that they cannot be boiled soft. A similar difficulty is encountered on cooking peas in hard water which contains gypsum.

Action of Gypsum on Ammonium Carbonate.

So many statements are to be found in old works on agricultural chemistry relating to the power of gypsum to absorb and retain ammonia from the air, that this point deserves to be mentioned, although it can no longer be considered as of importance. It is now known that in ordinary air there is next to no ammonia to be absorbed. In horse-stables and sheep-stalls, it is true, the use of gypsum in this sense may sometimes be appropriate. But it is to be remembered that the gypsum must be moist in order that the desired reaction shall occur.

$$CaSO_4 + (NH_4)_2CO_2 = CaCO_3 + (NH_4)_2SO .$$

In case dry powdered gypsum and solid ammonium carbonate be stirred together, the odor of the ammonium salt will continue to be perceived. But if water be poured upon the mixture, the odor will cease if an excess of the gypsum is present, and on filtering the moist mass there will be found in the filtrate a quantity of non-volatile sulphate of ammonia, while carbonate of lime remains on the filter. It is evident, therefore, that gypsum must be moist if it is to be of use as an absorbent of ammonia in the soil or upon a dung-heap. Practically, it is not probable that the above-mentioned reaction between gypsum and ammonium carbonate is a thoroughly satisfactory one as it occurs in the dung-heap, for under favorable conditions and when carbonate of lime is in excess a precisely opposite reaction might occur; i. e. carbonate of lime may react upon sulphate of ammonia to set free the volatile carbonate of ammonia, especially when the materials are heated. Hence, in speaking of manure-heaps, it might well be argued that it must depend largely upon time, chance and circumstance, whether the one or the other reaction will occur. It might even happen that one of them could occur at one moment, and the other at another. In any event the second of the foregoing reactions would tend to hinder the first from being definite and complete. It is to be observed also that the old notion that the efficacy of gypsum was dependent upon its power of absorbing ammonia from the air is refuted by the fact that the crops specially benefited by applications of gypsum are precisely those which do not respond to dressings of ammoniacal fertilizers.

Gypsum may often do good upon some kinds of soils, such as clays, for example, in that, like other calcium compounds, it can act to improve their mechanical condition by causing the finer particles to flocculate or granulate, as will be explained under the heads of Lime, and of Common Salt. But for this particular purpose lime would usually be a better material to apply to the land than gypsum.

Gypsum may preserve Dung.

Several observers have noticed that, when gypsum is mixed with decaying organic matters, it acts as a preservative, and that the loss of nitrogen from the materials is lessened. Morren has observed, moreover, in experiments where 5% of gypsum was added to blood, bone-meal and horn-meal, that the decaying matters remained slightly acid and lost considerably less of their nitrogen than when they were allowed to ferment either by themselves or admixed with earth. In the absence of gypsum, the materials became alkaline and evidently fermented in a different way. Koenig and Kiesow, on the contrary, who stirred up bone-meal or flesh with gypsum and water to a pap, and allowed the materials to ferment, found that they became alkaline, and that, while considerable quantities of ammonia were formed and retained, the gypsum wholly prevented a loss of nitrogen.

As will be explained in a subsequent chapter, the chief points to be attended to in order to preserve manure are to keep it slightly moist and firmly packed together, in order to exclude air. If these points are attended to, the addition of gypsum or other chemicals is of little practical importance. Thus, Heinrich put fresh horse-dung — with and without addition of preservatives — into large glass vessels, and in some instances packed the manure firmly, while in others it was allowed to lie loose. In the table are given the loss in per cents of the dry matter of the fresh dung according as one or the other preservative had been added to it :—

		Loss of dry matter. per cent.
No preservative	Loose,	47.6
	Packed,	19.5
5% of gypsum	Loose,	38.5
	Packed,	18.1
5% acid sulphate of potash . .	Loose,	38.7
	Packed,	22.9
5% superphosphate of lime . .	Loose,	35.1
	Packed,	28.2

It has been insisted, none the less, by so good an observer as Heiden, and by several other chemists also, that waste phosphatic gypsum (see beyond) from superphosphate works is even more effective than ordinary gypsum for preserving manure. Heiden strewed the phosphatic gypsum, morning, noon and night, on the dung and in the troughs of a cow-stable at the rate of 2 lb. per diem for every 1,000 lb. live weight of the animals. From July to October, inclusive, there was produced 27,500 lb. of manure containing 5,650 lb. of dry matter, and after 15 weeks there was still found in the dung-heap 24,250 lb. of this manure and 4,675 lb.

of dry matter. The loss of moist manure was 12%, and the loss of dry matter 17.2%; while in a similar trial with manure to which no gypsum was added, but which had been carefully kept in compact heaps, the loss from the moist manure was 20½% and from the dry matter 36%. When ordinary land-plaster was used, the heap of fresh manure lost 6.7% of its weight in 15 weeks, and 21½% of its dry matter.

During the 15 weeks 22% of the original nitrogen was lost from the plain manure, while only 6% of that in the manure treated with the phosphatic gypsum disappeared. In other words, the phosphatic gypsum reduced the loss of dry matter one-half, and that of the nitrogen nearly four times. It was noticed that the temperature of the plastered dung-heap remained comparatively low, and this fact might of itself explain the small amount of decomposition.

In dung-liquor that had been mixed with the phosphatic gypsum the loss of nitrogen was 12⅓%, while from mere dung-liquor 66 and 70% of the nitrogen went to waste. It was manifest that the gypsum acted both to fix ammonia and to prevent decay of nitrogenous organic matters.

Troschke, on the other hand, noticed very considerable losses both of dry matter and of nitrogen in manure that was kept three months after having been treated with gypsum or with kainit. In the case of gypsum the loss amounted to 19% of the dry matter and 32% of the nitrogen; while with kainit the loss of dry matter was 20% and that of nitrogen 10%. A strong odor of sulphuretted hydrogen was given off from the heap that contained the gypsum. Krause also, on mixing cow's urine with quantities of gypsum varying from 0.5 to 5%, found that the fermentation of the urine proceeded rather more rapidly than when no gypsum was present, and that considerable quantities of nitrogen went to waste, especially when the proportion of gypsum was small. In any event, much ammonia was retained as sulphate, particularly when the supply of gypsum was ample. He argued that, in so far as the saving of nitrogen is concerned, there is no economic advantage in employing gypsum.

It would seem indeed that the use of gypsum for preserving manure must be subject to various limitations. The experience of practical men with regard to it points also to this conclusion, for in some instances it has served them an excellent purpose, while in others it has failed to justify itself. Christiani published years ago the results of experiments in which potatoes dressed with plastered manure gave a much better crop than was got from the same amount of manure which had not been treated with gypsum, and similar results have been reported by Eichhorn, Didieur, and other observers. But no very encouraging results were reached in trials that were made in Prussia some years since, by different persons, to test the practical utility of strewing gypsum on fresh cow-manure at the rate of 2 to 2½ lb. of land-plaster to 100 lb. of the fresh dung. It did not appear to the people who tried these experiments that there was any particular use in employing the gypsum in this way. For although it was noticed in several instances that the gypsum seemed to delay the fermentation of the dung, it was thought and argued that the farmer has already other methods of accomplishing this result which are cheaper than the use of gypsum.

As regards the loss of ammonia, this seldom, if ever, amounts to much in the case of old manure-heaps which are kept duly moist; and in general it may be said of manure which is moist and firmly trodden that it loses very little ammonia and decays but slowly. Under such conditions there is small need of adding any gypsum to the manure; although, as will be explained under Nitrification, it is not impossible, when the manure comes to be applied to the land, that the presence of gypsum may increase the activity of the manure. (Warington.) As Dehérain has suggested, it is well to remember that the reactions of gypsum in a manure-heap are highly complicated, and that they are by no means restricted merely to the conversion of volatile ammonium carbonate to non-volatile ammonium sulphate. It is well known that when sulphates are buried in a mass of moist fermenting dung (or other organic matter) the oxygen in them speedily combines with organic matters, so that the sulphates are reduced to sulphides, which in their turn may be converted more or less completely to carbonates by the action of carbonic acid set free by the fermenting materials. But as a result of this reaction, sulphuretted hydrogen-gas is evolved, and some free sulphur is deposited. Furthermore, gypsum when mixed with dung might react upon the carbonate of potash therein contained, as well as upon carbonate of ammonia, and change it to sulphate of potash, and one result of this change would be the destruction of the alkaline reaction natural to the manure, and which, in the absence of gypsum, enables the mixture of dung and straw to undergo useful fermentations. Hence, from the scientific as well as from the practical point of view, it may well be regarded as an open question whether the admixing of gypsum with manure is a commendable practice.

Strewing of Gypsum in Stables.

But though probably not to be recommended as a direct addition to the manure-heap, it is none the less true that gypsum scattered with a liberal hand on moist places in horse-stables and cow-stalls may do excellent service by checking the fermentation of the urine, and by absorbing some of the odors which arise from it. For this purpose it has been extensively used in many localities. Heiden has found, by direct experiment, that, on mixing 2 or 3% of gypsum with stable-manure that contained ammonium carbonate, much of the latter was arrested. Schulze used one-third of a pound of gypsum per head and per day. At Eldena, 8 lb. were used for 24 horses, and the odor of the stable was almost completely removed.

Muntz and Girard, on trying to prevent the waste of nitrogen, due to ammoniacal fermentation, which occurs in recently voided manure, as it lies in the stable under the feet of the animals, got no satisfactory results either from the use of gypsum, or lime, or carbonate of lime, or phosphate of lime, or sulphate of iron; for manure is so highly alkaline that a large quantity of the gypsum, or what not, has to be expended for mere purposes of neutralization, and its efficiency as a preservative is very much lessened. No economic advantage was gained by using it. To illustrate this point, Muntz and Girard have drawn up the following table to show how much sulphate of iron (copperas) would have to be used in order to prevent the loss of nitrogen from fresh manure, in case that substance were to be chosen as the preservative agent: —

Pounds of:	Horses.	Cattle.	Sheep.
Manure produced per head and year .	22,440	25,080	1,760
Nitrogen lost in the stable	28.38	101.64	15.18
Copperas required to fix this nitrogen	324.28	1,161.46	173.36
Copperas neutralized by the fixed alkali in the manure	121.44	365.86	30.14
Total copperas needed	445.72	1,527.46	203.50

(Compare Kainit, under Potash Compounds.)

Some Soils and Waters contain Gypsum.

It is to be observed that many soils, as in Boston and its immediate vicinity, naturally contain more or less gypsum. This natural gypsum is derived from several sources. Many rocks contain iron pyrites, and where this mineral comes in contact with air a part of it changes to soluble sulphate of iron, and the latter is in its turn decomposed by lime-salts in the soil, with formation of gypsum.

All those ingredients of plants and animals which contain sulphur give rise to the formation of sulphuric acid as they rot in the soil, or they form gaseous sulphuretted hydrogen, which is subsequently oxidized in the air to sulphuric acid, and the acid thus formed is carried down by rain to form sulphate of lime in the soil. So, too, with the sulphurous acid which results from the burning of coal. Thus it is that the yearly waste of the sulphate which goes to sea in the waters of brooks and rivers is in some part made good.

The "hard" water of very many wells in the vicinity of Boston owes its hardness to the fact that a large proportion of sulphate of lime is held dissolved in it. The "scale" which forms in steam-boilers and "water-backs" fed with such water is sulphate of lime, just as the scale of marine boilers is.

Beside the quarries of gypsum from which the chief supply of this fertilizer is drawn, there are several subordinate sources worth mentioning. When sea-water or the water of saline springs is evaporated to obtain common salt, considerable quantities of gypsum are deposited. Sometimes this deposit is raked from the vats and thrown away, and at other times it is sold as a manure. In the manufacture of soda-water and some other effervescing drinks, powdered marble is treated with sulphuric acid to set free carbonic-acid gas, but the residue is acidified gypsum, and it may be had of the apothecaries or makers of soda-water for the asking. So, too, the refuse of the workers in stucco and plaster of Paris, and of stereotypers, dentists, and other persons who make plaster-casts. In the aggregate, a very large quantity of this material is thrown away daily in a city like Boston. All stucco-work and the cornices around the interiors of rooms contain more or less plaster of Paris, and so does the mixture with which masons repair cracks in ordinary plastering. The spent lime of gas-works contains much gypsum, especially after the material has been allowed to weather; and so do the ashes of some kinds of peat and some kinds of bituminous coal, as well as wood-ashes, and even anthracite-ashes to a certain extent.

In Germany of late years large quantities of gypsum that contains traces of phosphate of lime have been as good as given away by the manufacturers of high-grade superphosphate of lime, in the preparation of which substance the gypsum is formed incidentally, as a waste product. In the Rhine region this waste gypsum is held to be worth no more than 25 cents the long ton, as it lies in heaps at the works, and less than twice this price when put upon railway-cars at the cost of the manufacturer.

Gypsum as an Oxidizing Agent.

There is yet another mode of action of gypsum which may properly be mentioned here, though there will be occasion to refer to it more particularly hereafter, viz. its oxidizing power. Sulphate of lime, $CaSO_4$, is a substance that contains a considerable amount of oxygen (almost half its weight), and it gives up this oxygen rather easily to many other substances. Hence it is by no means impossible that part of the good effect of gypsum, when employed as a fertilizer, may be due to this oxidizing power brought to bear upon nitrogenous and carbonaceous substances in the soil.

Gypsum is commonly used at the rate of 200 or 300 lb. to the acre, — about as much as a man can conveniently scatter from his hand in walking across the field.

CHAPTER X.

PHOSPHATIC FERTILIZERS.

PHOSPHATE of lime, a substance which has acquired great commercial importance in recent years, is a fertilizer of a very different order from gypsum, and one of much greater consequence. There are several varieties of this substance, for the term "phosphate of lime" includes such well-known fertilizers as bone-meal, bone-ash, bone-black, superphosphate of lime, phosphate rock, such as is found in South Carolina and Florida, and the neighboring states, as well as in Canada and in many foreign localities; and the phosphatic guanos, such as those of Baker's Island, Jarvis Island and Howland's Island in the Pacific, and Navassa, Sombrero, Aves, and the other guano-islands of the West Indies.

Bones.

It will be well first of all to consider bones, both as to their mechanical and their chemical composition. If a bone is soaked for some time in dilute muriatic acid, there will be left a tough, elastic mass of organic matter, of the same shape as the original bone. On the other hand, if a bone be burned thoroughly in the fire, there will be left a friable earthy substance, known as bone-ash, which, though free from any trace of the elastic matter, may also exhibit the original shape of the bone.

By the process of burning, all the carbonaceous or other "organic" portions of the bone have been converted into gaseous products, which disappear in the air; while by the action of the acid, in the previous experiment, the earthy portion of the bone simply went into solution. The bone-earth thus held dissolved may readily be recovered by neutralizing the acid solvent with an alkali, such as ammonia or lime.

It appears from the facts thus stated, that bones are composed of two distinct substances which interpenetrate one another. There is as it were a skeleton of the earthy matter, which is called phosphate of lime, or bone-earth, and a flesh of the organic matter, which is called ossein; sometimes, though less properly, it is called gelatine. The term "collagen" includes ossein, as well as other animal matters, which are capable of being converted into glue or gelatine by long-continued boiling with water. This organic matter amounts to from a quarter to a third of the weight of the original bone.

It should be said in passing that, although bone-earth consists for the most part of phosphate of lime, it is always admixed with some carbonate of lime and a little phosphate of magnesia. Heintz's analyses of clean, dry leg-bones of oxen and sheep gave 6 or 7% of carbonate of lime, 58 to 63% of phosphate of lime, 1 or 2% of phosphate of magnesia, and 25 to 30% of organic matter. Frerichs found in human bones from 50 to 60% of phosphate of lime, 10 or 12% of carbonate of lime and some 38% of organic matter. In the bones of a haddock, Duménil found 55% of phosphate of lime, 6% of carbonate of lime, and nearly 38% of organic matter.

Bone-ash.

If the ash of bone were to be applied as a fertilizer, some of the phosphoric acid in it would doubtless be taken up slowly through those rootlets of plants which might happen to come into contact with it, and the ash would be acted upon to a certain extent by micro-organisms in the soil and by chemical agents also, especially in case the soil contained much humus, and was adequately moist and well aerated. But excepting some particular instances, such as reclaimed bogs, for example, bone-ash is not a particularly efficient manure. It is not much esteemed, and is seldom or never used directly as a manure nowadays, since experience has taught that on most soils it is inferior to bone-meal, and to several other varieties of phosphatic fertilizers to be described directly. It is evident that the phosphoric acid in bone-ash is less readily assimilated by plants than that in several other fertilizers. Even if it be admitted that it might possibly be used with profit in certain localities on some kinds of soils, it would still remain true that there are other cheap phosphates which are superior to it. Some idea of its inferiority may be got from what will be said directly of the analogous material, bone-black.

Considerable quantities of bone-ash are imported into England to be used in the manufacture of superphosphate of lime, and small quantities have been received at New York also. It comes from South America principally, though a little is carried to England from the Danube. Bones make a hot fire, as was found long ago by the old navigators who wintered on Spitzbergen and Nova Zembla, and it appears that they are often used for fuel on the treeless plains of South America. Darwin, in his Narrative of the Voyage of the Beagle, in describing a locality on one of the Falkland Islands, says: "The valley was pretty well sheltered from the cold wind, but there was very little brush-wood for fuel. The Guachos, however, soon found what, to my great surprise, made nearly as hot a fire as coals; this was the skeleton of a bullock lately killed, from which the flesh had been picked by the carrion-hawks. They told me that in winter they often killed a beast, cleaned the flesh from the bones with their knives, and then with these same bones roasted the meat for their suppers." Inasmuch as it is much more compact and manageable than bones, — beside being more concentrated in the chemical sense, — bone-ash can be transported comparatively easily. That is to say, it can be brought on the backs of mules from places somewhat distant from tide-water, in regions where carriage is so difficult that it might cost more than the bones would be worth to bring them out as such.

As imported from South America, bone-ash contains from 60 to 80% of the phosphates of lime and magnesia. Good samples may be said to contain from 30 to 38% of phosphoric acid. It consists of fragments and splinters of burnt bone admixed with powdery ashes. Usually it needs to be ground before treating it with sulphuric acid. It contains also about 2% of carbonate of lime and 3 or 4% of lime which appears to be not in combination either with carbonic or phosphoric acids. Voelcker found that the ashes of pure bones of oxen and horses contain 40% of phosphoric acid, which corresponds with 87% of bone-phosphate of lime. They contain more carbonate of lime (7 or 8% in all) than the commercial ash, which is formed in presence of silica, and about 6% of free lime.

Bone-meal.

Bone-meal differs from bone-ash very materially, because of the ossein which it contains. This ossein is to all intents and purposes flesh. It is in fact a highly nitrogenized substance; and all that can be said of the nitrogenized manures will apply to it. When bone-meal is buried in moist earth, the flesh-like ossein soon putrefies, and yields ammonia or some other assimilable nitrogen compound, to the very great advantage of the crop, provided it be growing upon a soil that contains plenty of potash, and the other kinds of plant-food. But beside acting by virtue of its nitrogen, the ossein is valuable as an easily putrescible organic substance, which helps somewhat to dissolve the bone-earth, both by means of the carbonic acid which results from its decomposition, and by the solvent action of the other products that are formed from it.

Bone-meal is used particularly for turnips of all kinds, and for other roots, for tobacco, and for potatoes. Speaking in general terms, it is used for hoed crops rather than for grain, though good results have often been obtained by applying 200 lb. or so of bone-meal to the acre in late summer for winter grain, and reinforcing the nitrogen in it with light dressings of nitrate of soda, applied one-half in the autumn and one-half early the next spring. In some localities, bone-meal used in this way has a particularly useful effect on the clover which follows the grain. Used in connection with some potassic manure, bone-meal has often approved itself an excellent top-dressing for mowing-lands and pastures that are not too dry.

In the County of Cheshire, bone-meal was at one time highly esteemed for pastures, though in most other parts of England no very great success appears to have attended its use. It was for cold clays of inferior quality in a rainy region that the bone-meal had its highest repute as a permanent manure productive of sweet and luxuriant herbage, of which cattle were very fond. At first, clovers of several kinds were brought in, and when these plants disappeared, after 5, or 10, or 15 years, good varieties of grass replaced them. Bone-meal is said to have been applied to thousands of acres of poor clay-soil in

Cheshire, at the rate of from half a ton to a ton to the acre. Sometimes as much as a ton and a half was applied, but too heavy dressings were deprecated, because in some instances the change of herbage from poor grass to rich clover caused cattle to become hoven.

It has been said of Westmoreland also that "The application of bones to old cow-pastures is pretty sure to answer a good purpose, on strong, newly drained soils naturally producing heath, rushes or bent. Bones have been found to have a wonderful effect also in renovating old pastures where other top-dressings had failed. But they must not be used indiscriminately, lest they lead to costly failures and disappointments. On thin, light and gravelly soils, or on bare limestone-land, they have often little or no effect."

On the whole, however, as Lawes has said, "The application of bones to grass-land is not recommended for general adoption. They appear to be chiefly adapted to the exhausted pastures of certain localities, and not to be generally applicable to meadow-land, which is mown for hay." So, too, Voelcker, in reporting the results of numerous field experiments with fertilizers on permanent pastures, notes that bone-meal often does good service, and at other times does not. He says, "On some soils, more especially on poor, light pastures (in England), the effect of bone-dust on the herbage is truly marvellous; and hence it is that in certain countries bone-dust is justly held in the highest esteem as a means for renovating worn-out pasture-land; whilst in other localities bones do not show any marked effect upon meadow-land, and are seldom employed upon pasture. I have had brought under my notice, at one time or the other, many instances in which the expenditure of money for bone-dust as a means of improving pasture-land was almost entirely thrown away; and I would therefore strongly advise landlords and tenants to ascertain, by a field trial on a limited scale, whether or not bones really and materially improve the grass-land on a particular farm, before heavy expense is incurred in boning permanent pastures. On cold clay-soils money not infrequently is wasted by applying bone-dust to pastures. On such land, it has been found a much better plan to top-dress the pasture with a mixture of superphosphate, potash salts, and guano, or nitrate of soda, than to apply to it a heavy and more expensive dressing of bone-dust."

Bone-meal and Wood-ashes.

Many farmers living in New England have found that mixtures of bone-meal and wood-ashes serve them an excellent purpose when used as substitutes for farmyard manure. On good land, the materials are applied at the rate of 500 or 600 lb. of bone-meal to the acre, together with 15 to 25 or 30 bushels of the ashes, though sometimes on mowing-fields, especially such as are in urgent need of refreshment, as many as 40 bushels of ashes are used with the bone. Occasionally the bone-meal also is applied with a more liberal hand, even to the extent of 1,000 lb. to the acre. The mixing of these materials is easily accomplished by putting them in a "manure-spreader" wagon, layer by layer, taking care not to load into the wagon at any one time more of the two fertilizers than will be just sufficient to cover the land at the rate which has been determined upon beforehand. Sometimes the materials are thrown into heaps beforehand at the rate of 2 or 3 bushels of bone-meal to 5 or 6 bushels of wood-ashes. These heaps are moistened with water, and their contents are admixed by shovelling. The mixture may either be used at once, or allowed to stand for a few weeks, in order that fermentation may occur, as will be explained directly. Occasionally, potash salts are used with the bone-meal, instead of wood-ashes. As much as half a ton of bone to the acre, 300 or 400 lb. of muriate of potash, and from 100 to 150 lb. of nitrate of soda have been used with advantage.

In a somewhat similar sense, mixtures of wood-ashes and fish-scrap have often been found to be advantageous. I have myself grown heavy crops of barley on light, dry land manured with wood-ashes and fish-scrap, applied at the rates of 1,600 lb. and 1,100 lb. to the acre, respectively. Bush-beans did extremely well when thus manured, and rutabagas also.

Efficacy of Bone-meal.

According to Saxon experience, and Saxony has soils that are commonly not deficient in potash, a cwt. of fine bone-meal is worth as much as 25 or 30 cwt. of manure as obtained from cow-stables. It has often been found advantageous to use a small proportion of Peruvian guano at the same time with bone-meal, and an old French practice of causing bone-meal to ferment by keeping heaps of it moistened with urine was based on a kindred thought. Sometimes it has been found advantageous to mix bone-meal with superphosphate even. But the admixture with potassic fertilizers, in cases where the soil or the crop are in need of these materials, is clearly the better plan, in most instances.

European writers urge that bone-meal does its best service upon soils that are neither too light and dry, nor too close and wet; it is not of much use on any soil, unless the land is well drained and of free and open texture. Both air and moisture are necessary in order for the fermentation and solution of the bone-meal. It is esteemed to be a good and a lasting manure on non-calcareous, clayey loams that are not too stiff. But it often fails to be of much service on stiff clays, and as a rule appears to be better adapted to lighter soils, provided they are adequately supplied with moisture. "The action of bones depends very much upon the character of the soil to which they are applied. In heavy soils their action is very slow, and therefore the more lasting; but in light soils it is more rapid and less lasting." (Lawes.)

Generally speaking, bone-meal would doubtless answer a good purpose on land newly broken up, and rich in decomposing organic matters, provided the land were neither too stiff nor too dry. So, too, when other conditions are favorable, bone-meal will be likely to do better on land full of refuse from a previous crop, such as clover-stubble, for example, than on land that has been closely cropped, as by flax. It will naturally do well in conjunction with stable-manure used in smaller quantity than if it were not thus reinforced. In New England, it was recognized long ago, by practical men, that bone-meal should not be applied to dry soils. It is esteemed in this region, however, for light soils that are fairly moist. On the moist, peaty soil of the fens of Cambridgeshire, England, bone-meal at one time did excellent service both upon turnips and upon rape.

Varieties of Bone-meal.

Much might be said of the various kinds of bone-meal, and of the methods which are employed either for reducing bones to powder, or for preparing them to be powdered. The subject is an interesting one, and worthy of careful study; and it is well-nigh certain that the superphosphates which are now so prominent will never replace bone-meal for all cases, or drive it from the market. In spite of all that has been said and written in past years in favor of converting bones to the condition of superphosphate, there is hardly any doubt that bone-meal will continue to be used as a manure, for beside being cheaper than the superphosphate, it has its own peculiar characteristics and advantages, and the proper ways and places in which to employ it will no doubt be accurately formulated in the course of time. The old practice of bone-grinding is not only likely to persist, but to be greatly extended, and it will probably come to pass that all the bones procurable will be applied to the land in the form of a fine powder, and that superphosphate of lime will no longer be made from bones proper, but only from mineral phosphates and from bone-black.

At all densely populated places, great quantities of bones are continually collected; and the working of them over into oil, " ivory," bone-meal, bone-char, and sometimes gelatine, is a considerable branch of industry. I am told that in Boston the provision-dealers commonly get from one half to three quarters of a cent per pound for green bones, — the lower price being paid in case the renderers call for the bones at the meat-shop, and the higher price when the bones are delivered by the provision-dealer, either at the works or at some central point in the city.

The old method of crushing the bones to coarse fragments between steel rollers has no longer any particular interest, excepting in so far as it may still be employed as a preliminary movement to make the bones fit to be ground in mills. When thus crushed, it is perfectly possible to grind dry bones between millstones, as if they were grain. With raw bones the grinding is difficult, particularly if the bones are fresh, since in that event they lubricate the stones; but old, dry bones, even if they be raw, can be ground to a satisfactory powder between the hardest French buhr-stones; and bones that have been steamed can be ground between stones of almost any kind.

Stamps for Pulverizing Bones.

In Germany, formerly, in the days when railways had not yet been built, a common way of proceeding was to stamp the bones, as if they were so much ore of copper or of lead, i. e. pound them to powder beneath a set of stamps moved by water-power. The stamps consisted of a number of long wooden pestles shod with steel, which, by means of a sort of trip-hammer arrangement of cams, were made to play up and down in an iron trough which was the mortar, and into which the bones were thrown. At the sides of this trough there were numerous fine holes through which the bone-meal sifted as fast as it was produced. This process has merit on account of its extreme simplicity. The first cost of the establishment is small, and the stamps can be operated with but little oversight wherever there is a small fall of water. I have myself had opportunity, in the year 1856, to visit several of these little stamps, which were encouraged formerly by the local agricultural societies as a means of improving agriculture by bringing a new kind of manure to the farmer's door, and of suggesting to him the utility of using more fertilizing materials than could be obtained from his cattle. The cost of transporting any article so heavy as bones is of course large, and there was at one time a real advantage in having such local stamps. They led to the collection and use of many bones which would otherwise have been wasted, but nowadays the work of grinding bones can be better done in large establishments, excepting of course such bones as each farmer may find time to treat for himself, with alkalies, as will be described directly.

When the bones are raw it is not easy to stamp them completely to powder, for portions of the bone remain so tough and elastic that they cannot be broken. This difficulty may be obviated for the most part by steaming the bones strongly beforehand. Indeed, it has long been customary, in well-regulated establishments, to steam the bones before grinding or stamping them; or, in default of facilities for steaming, it helps matters somewhat to remove a part of the fat by merely boiling the bones in water. After the steaming, the bones need to get thoroughly dry before the grinding process is proceeded with. Meal which is free from dust can then be readily prepared from them.

Bones from different parts of an animal differ widely as to their hardness and toughness. It is said that ribs and heads may be ground with comparative ease, even when fresh, and they are so ground near Boston to be sold as food for poultry. But there is no use in trying to grind the tough leg and knee bones of oxen in the raw state. Such bones can be ground, it is true, but only slowly and with difficulty, and the product would hardly be worth the cost of making it. Hence the importance of steaming such bones to destroy their toughness.

Raw Bones and Steamed.

Contrary to what might be thought at first, and indeed contrary to what has often been taught, it appears that the meal from steamed bones, unless they have been very strongly steamed to extract the ossein, as happens in some processes of glue-making, is really better as a general rule for agricultural purposes than that from raw bones, or even that from bones which have been boiled.

The meal from raw bones has the demerit of containing the natural fat or oil. This fat is not only useless to the plant, but it may clog the meal, and hinder it from undergoing putrefaction and solution. It may even be true, perhaps, that the fat can combine with lime or iron in the soil to form an insoluble soap, which then incrusts the meal. Even in case a part of the fat has been removed, by boiling the bones at the ordinary pressure of the air, the unchanged ossein of the meal ferments but slowly, in northern countries, and the action of the manure is slow.

When, however, the bones are placed in a close boiler and subjected to steam-pressure,—i. e. to heat powerful enough to melt out all their fat and a portion of their ossein also, — then the bones not only become so friable that they can be cheaply reduced to fine powder, but the chemical character of the ossein left in them is changed. It is changed to such an extent that the meal decomposes readily in the earth, and acts as a quicker and more powerful manure than meal from raw bones which has been sifted through sieves of the same dimensions. As the German writers put it, the meal from steamed bones seems to be " of a finer nature" than the raw meal. It is true, that the quantity of nitrogen in bones that have been steamed in this way may be two or three per cent less than that in raw bone; but nevertheless the meal from steamed bones has practically proved itself to be better in temperate climates than that from ordinary bones. But in hot countries the difference between steamed and raw bone-meal is less marked. From numerous experiments made in Japan, Kellner has concluded that, as regards fertilizing power, there is no use in preparing steamed bone-meal, since fine meal from raw bones serves an equally good purpose. He finds that in countries where the climate is warm, and rains abundant, bone-meal is an extremely valuable manure, even when in the raw state, and that by applying it early in the season, or by means of a preparatory fermentation in the compost heap, it may do as good service as the much more costly superphosphate. Bone-meal does well in Japan on autumn-sown cereals, both in respect to its phosphoric acid and its nitrogen.

Kellner found that, thanks to decompositions which occurred in the soil, the phosphoric acid in raw bone-meal was readily assimilable by crops even in the third year after its application. Indeed it was then taken up by plants much more readily than phosphoric acid which had been applied at the same time with it in the form of a superphosphate. It was noteworthy in Kellner's experiments that the presence of much fat in the bone-meal was not disadvantageous. Like the ossein of the bone, the fat evidently was involved in certain fermentations which helped to dissolve the bone-earth and to promote its solution. In experiments made in Germany for the purpose of contrasting steamed bone with superphosphate made from bones, the steamed meal has often been found preferable to the superphosphate, account being

taken of the efficiency and the cost of the two kinds of fertilizers.
It may be said indeed that meal from steamed bone has gained
firm ground in European agriculture, both as against meal from
raw bone, and as a special manure of peculiar merit.

Cheapness of Bone-Meal.

From the very fact of its being a chemical product, superphosphate of lime will necessarily cost more than bone-meal.   In the
days when bone-meal was sold at some $40 or $45 the ton, the
price of a ton of bone-superphosphate was $50 or $60.   But the
bone-meal contains more phosphoric acid than the superphosphate,
because the gypsum which is formed in making the latter necessarily dilutes its phosphatic constituent.

In large establishments, both the fat and the glue obtained from
the bones are put to the ordinary technical uses for which these
substances are valuable, so that the cost of steaming is more than
offset; but in the case of small local mills, the glue is usually
neglected, or the solution of it is used directly as a manure upon
grass-land, or for the preparation of compost with peat.   Nowadays, before the bones are steamed, the fat is sometimes dissolved
out from them by means of naphtha, whereby a more complete
removal of the fat is accomplished without changing in any way
the ossein or the bone-earth.   Indeed the percentage proportion
of nitrogen and phosphoric acid is larger in bones that have been
leached with naphtha than it is in raw bones, in accordance with
the amount of fat which has been removed.

The fineness of the meal to which bones are ground is a very
important consideration.   Not so very many years ago it was the
custom to use crushed bones, and an article is still sold under this
name in Boston, though it is chiefly used for feeding to poultry
and milch-cows.   But there is no longer any question that fine
meal is greatly to be preferred to that which is coarse.   The finer
the meal, so much the more readily will it putrefy and dissolve in
the earth, so much the more quickly can the plants be fed by it,
and so much the sooner and the more surely will the value of the
crop be increased.

Slow-acting Fertilizers are objectionable.

As regards the endurance of the fertilizer, that is to say, the
continuance of its action through several years, it is questionable
whether even the finest bone-meal is not too enduring, or, in other
words, too slow of action.   The old notion, that those fertilizers

are best which make themselves felt through a long series of years, is now recognized to be an error. The adage that "one cannot eat the cake and have the cake," is conspicuously true in agriculture; and just as it is the part of prudence in household or maritime economy to abstain from laying in at any one time more provisions than can be properly disposed of in a year or during a voyage, so should the farmer refrain from bringing to the land an unnecessary excess of plant-food. Such food is liable to spoil withal in the soil, as well as other kinds of provisions that are kept too long in store. A just proportion of food, properly prepared, is the point to be aimed at always.

In general terms, it may be said that an enduring manure is enduring only in so far as it is inaccessible to the crops, excluding, of course, the case where so much manure has been applied that the crops cannot possibly consume the whole of it. In the words of Voelcker, "Greater permanency is no recommendation whatever, for the primary use of all manures is to enable us to grow not scanty, but heavy crops; not to deposit on the land fertilizers which may last for 3 or 4 years, but by prompt, efficacious action to render a quickly remunerative return from a moderate outlay."

It may be accepted as a truism, that, if the farmer will use artificial fertilizers successfully, he must be at pains to have them prepared properly and so to dispose them upon his fields that he may get back in the crops, in the shortest possible time, not only the interest of the money that has been expended in buying the fertilizers, but the principal itself. Indeed, most of the artificial fertilizers are so costly, that they need to be managed with care, good judgment, and knowledge, in order that due profit may be got from them. So clearly are the advantages of quick action now recognized, that the comparatively speaking soluble superphosphate of lime has come to be substituted to an enormous extent for bone-meal, as will be explained directly.

Floated Bone.

One idea was to reduce bones to an impalpable powder; and large quantities of bone-flour of extraordinary fineness — so fine indeed that it actually floated in the air — were prepared in Boston some years since by the patent pulverizing machinery of Mr. Whelpley. The process consisted in whirling the bones against one another so rapidly and forcibly that they were ground to the finest powder, somewhat on the same principle that stones are

rubbed down to sand or mud upon a shingle beach, except that
with the bones the friction occurred in the air, instead of in water,
and that there was hardly any limit to the degree of fineness which
was easily attainable, until the dust actually floated in the air.
This product was sold under the name of "floated bone," at very
high prices. It was prepared almost exclusively from raw bones,
in the belief, which may perhaps have been true enough in respect
to meal so fine, that it is better to retain in the meal all the nitrogen of the original bones.

This floated bone was a powerful manure well suited for greenhouse horticulture; but it was ill adapted for use in the field, since,
unless thoroughly admixed with damp loam before strewing it, a
large part of it blew far away, even if no more than a breath of
wind were stirring. Perhaps there are not half a dozen days in
the year calm enough to permit of this material being properly
scattered by itself. It is apt to float away into the air, like so
much smoke. The lesson is an instructive one, as teaching how
the fineness of bone-meal has to be limited to a point of greatest
convenience, all things considered. Bone-dust so fine as this is
exceedingly liable to putrefy. Fine flour of bone, from unsteamed
bones, has to be salted like so much flesh before it can be packed
in barrels. Indeed any unsalted meal from bones that have not
been strongly steamed putrefies so readily, especially in moist air,
that care has to be taken to keep in a dry place the barrels or
bags which contain it.

Many manufacturers of bone-meal do not hesitate to use salt as
a preservative, and some bone-grinders in this country are accustomed to mix a considerable proportion of salt-cake (or nitre-cake)
with their products instead of common salt. It is said that bones
so damp and soft — "wet," as the term is — that they could not
be handled or transported by themselves, may be brought into
merchantable shape by means of this admixture. Doubtless a
small proportion of the bone is corroded by the acid salt-cake,
with formation of a little superphosphate of lime at first and diphosphate of lime afterward. Hence it happens that a part of the
phosphoric acid in bone-meal which has been admixed with salt-
cake is rather more soluble than that in pure bone-meal. To
countervail this advantage, however, there is less phosphoric acid
and less nitrogen to the ton in the salt-cake specimens, simply
because the bone-meal has been diluted by the salt-cake.

Grades of Bone-meal.

S. W. Johnson has suggested that it may be well to distinguish several grades of fineness in bone-meal. All the meal that passes through a sieve the meshes of which measure one-fiftieth of an inch may be called "fine," and the nitrogen and phosphoric acid in it may be estimated to be worth $0.16 and $0.05 per pound, respectively. Whatever passes through meshes that are between one twenty-fifth and one-twelfth of an inch may be called "medium," and the nitrogen and phosphoric acid in it may be rated at $0.12 and $0.03 per lb., while in the intermediate grade, "fine medium," they may be rated at $0.15 and $0.04. The meal larger than one-sixth of an inch may be called "coarse," and its nitrogen and phosphoric acid may be rated at $0.07 and $0.02 per pound. It is found that, when bone-meal is adulterated or contaminated, the foreign matters are apt to be present in the state of fine powders which pass through the sieves with the finer portions of the meal, during the sifting process. This circumstance must be kept in mind and allowed for by the purchaser of bone-meal when examining samples.

Composition of Bone-meal.

Payen and Boussingault found $6\frac{1}{4}\%$ of nitrogen and 8% of water in raw bones; and $5\frac{1}{2}\%$ of nitrogen and 30% of water in steamed bones as they came from the rendering vats. When dry, the steamed bones contained 7% of nitrogen and $7\frac{1}{2}\%$ of water. Good bone-meal as prepared from bones steamed moderately under a pressure of about 1.5 atmospheres may contain something like 4% of nitrogen and 20% of phosphoric acid; while the meal from strongly steamed bones may contain 25% or even more of phosphoric acid and 3.5% of nitrogen. Contrary to what has sometimes been taught, the meal from bones which have been steamed thus strongly is of excellent quality, and is to be regarded as a fertilizer of high grade.

Analyses of commercial bone-meal show that when unadulterated it usually contains 3 or 4% of nitrogen and from 21 to 24% of phosphoric acid. Thus, as the average of numerous analyses made at the experiment station in Halle (Germany) during the four years 1874–77, the percentage of nitrogen in bone-meal was 3.7 and that of phosphoric acid 21.3. So, too, at the Connecticut Experiment Station it has been observed that good bone-meal naturally contains not far from 4% of nitrogen and about 21% of phosphoric acid. According to Holdefleiss, normal bone-meal from bones which have been steamed to remove fat, but not for making glue, should contain at least 4 % of nitrogen and 20 % of phosphoric acid; while Koenig urges that a distinction should be made between the more highly nitrogenous meal, which contains from 4 to 5.3 % of nitrogen and 19 to 22 % of phosphoric acid, and the meals which are less nitrogenous and carry no more than 3 or 4 % of nitrogen against 21 to 25 % of phosphoric acid.

Beside these standard meals, there is still another variety made from bones which have been steamed much more strongly, i. e. under higher pressure and for a longer time, for the sake of obtaining glue. Such meal, while containing from less than 1 % to 1.5 % of nitrogen, usually contains as much as 27 to 30 % of phosphoric acid. According to Otto, the meal from bones which have been extracted with benzine contains 4.75 to 5 % of nitrogen, 21 to 23 % of phosphoric acid, and generally speaking less than 2 % of fat. He maintains that samples containing less than 4 % of nitrogen and 20 % of phosphoric acid are not pure unsophisticated meal.

Impurities in Bone-meal.

It is to be observed, in any event, that the quality of bone-meal as it occurs in commerce is subject to considerable variations. Even bones themselves vary in composition according to the kind and age of the animal from which they came; and those obtainable in commerce are sometimes contaminated with as much as 10 or 12 % of sand, and some 8 % of water. The amount of phosphates in them may range from 44 to 60 %, and the nitrogen may vary considerably as to its value.

According to S. W. Johnson, the nitrogen in hard raw bone is considerably more soluble and decomposable than that in the mixture of soft bone, cartilage, muscular tissue, and grease which makes up " kitchen bone," so called; and as a rule the hard firm bones contain more nitrogen and more phosphoric acid than the softer kinds which are wet and greasy. Such damp, soft bones are often discarded by manufacturers of bone-black as unsuitable for their purposes, and subsequently converted into bone-meal admixed with plaster of Paris, or salt-cake, or some such material, which has been used either as a drier or preservative, or for both these purposes. " Kitchen bones," moreover, and all bones that have been gathered by bone-pickers, are apt to have sand or loam adhering to them, or lodged in their cavities; and at the mill itself it is customary occasionally to throw in inert matters of one kind or another, to clear the grinding surfaces.

Beside the driers and preservatives already mentioned, bone-meal often contains small quantities of ground oyster-shells, coal-ashes, waste lime, plaster of Paris, coal, or loam. From all of which it appears that the terms "ground bone" and "bone-meal" are applied properly enough to products which may vary to no inconsiderable extent both as to their composition and their value. There is a limit of tolerance, however, as regards these extraneous matters, and Prof. Johnson has urged that any bone-meal which contains less than 19% of phosphoric acid, or more than 5% of matters insoluble in strong acids, should be regarded as an adulterated article.

Adulterated Bone-meal.

Pains must be taken also to determine that the bone-meal has not been adulterated with phosphates or nitrogen compounds of inferior value to those contained naturally in bone-earth and in ossein. It would not be a difficult matter to mix with adulterated bone-meal enough ground phosphate-rock or horn-meal, or similar substances, to make the meal rich in phosphoric acid and nitrogen, though really inferior as a fertilizer to genuine bone-meal. Sometimes saw-dust, from the making of wooden buttons, has been used to adulterate bone-meal, and occasionally the meal of the palm-nut (Phytelephas macrocarpa), known as vegetable ivory, has been employed. Either of these adulterants would contain about 1% of nitrogen. It often happens withal that the feebly nitrogenous meal from bones which have been very strongly steamed is mixed with good bone-meal, or with enough flesh-meal or horn-meal, or the like, to bring the percentage of nitrogen in the mixture up to 4 and that of phosphoric acid down to 20. The following examples of adulterated bone-meal were analyzed by Voelcker: —

Name of the Adulterant.	The mixture contained per cent	
	of Nitrogen.	of Phosphoric Acid.
Vegetable ivory	2.41	17.09
Steamed bone	1.23	25.51

Valuation of the Phosphoric Acid in Bone-meal.

The price per pound which has to be paid for phosphoric acid as it exists in bone-earth is a simple commercial question which during many years depended primarily on the cost of bringing bone-ash from South America. But it is less easy to determine what value should be set upon the pound of phosphoric acid as it exists in bone-meal, because it is hard to say precisely what value should be allowed for the nitrogen which the bone-meal contains, and because the condition of the phosphate in the meal is somewhat peculiar, in that it is rather more readily soluble in water and in carbonic-acid water than the phosphoric acid in bone-ash.

It is safe enough, however, to allow for the pound of phosphoric acid in bone-meal a value somewhat higher than that for which the pound of phosphoric acid can be bought in the form of bone-ash or bone-black. As prices go, this assumption would make the phosphoric acid in bone-meal come to at least 5 cents the pound, and it is customary to allow as much as this for the pound of phosphoric acid in fine bone-meal.

Bone-meal, such as analysis has shown to carry 23% of phosphoric acid and 4% of nitrogen, can usually be bought for less than $40 the ton, and the price of the nitrogen in it will appear from the following calculation. There will be in the ton 460 lb. of phosphoric acid, worth (at $0.055) $25.30. But $40 — $25.30 = $14.70, as the cost of the 80 lb. of nitrogen, i. e. 18⅜ cents the pound, which is a not unreasonable price to pay for this kind of nitrogen.

If, on the other hand, the sample of bone-meal under consideration should contain no more than 17% of phosphoric acid and 2% of nitrogen, for example, the price per ton would have to be much less than $40 in order that the material should commend itself to the farmer; for although the 340 lb. of phosphoric acid to the ton of this meal may be worth $18.70, on the assumption of 5.5 cents to the pound, as before, the 40 lb. of nitrogen would be worth no more than $7.20, even if it were admitted that each pound of the nitrogen could be valued at 18 cents.

Many years ago Stoeckhardt found, on comparing all the field experiments on sugar-beets that had been published in the course of seven years, that bone-meal had given better crops than superphosphate in 17 experiments out of 32, and better than rape-cake in 15 out of 30; while superphosphate did better than rape-cake in 17 trials out of 25, though it is not in evidence that either of the fertilizers had been used under the conditions best suited to it.

Bone-black.

In connection with bone-meal, or rather with bone-ash, there is another product to be considered, viz. "bone-black," "bone-char" or bone-charcoal. This substance is prepared in enormous quantities for the use of the sugar refiners, and after it has served their purposes it may often be bought at a price which puts it within the reach of the farmer. In the vicinity of many large cities spent bone-black was at one time the cheapest source of phosphoric acid obtainable by the farmer.

When bones are strongly heated, under such circumstances that air has free access to them, they burn to mere white ashes (bone-ash). But when broken bones are put into iron cylinders, to the interiors of which the air has no access, and are there heated by fires beneath the cylinders, the bones are subjected, of course, not to a process of burning or combustion, but to "destructive distillation," and quantities of gas, water, tarry and oily matters, and ammoniacal products, are driven off from the bones, while black bone-charcoal is left in the cylinders. It is noticeable that the hardest bones — such as the shin and thigh bones of cattle — are esteemed more highly than soft, spongy bones, by the manufacturers of bone-black.

This bone-char consists of bone-earth most intimately admixed and covered with charcoal, which has resulted from the destruction of the ossein that was contained in the original bone. Fresh bone-charcoal is a very porous substance, well fitted for removing coloring matters from liquids; hence its use for clarifying brown sugar and many other chemical substances. After the bone-char has served the purposes of sugar-refiners, and become "spent," it is disposed of, at a low price, to the manufacturers of superphosphate of lime.

Composition of Bone-black.

According to Morfit, spent bone-black from sugar refineries contains 58% phosphate of lime (= 26½% phosphoric acid), 9% carbonate of lime, 19½% (?) carbon, and 4% sand. I have myself found, in a sample procured from a sugar refiner in Boston, 30% phosphoric acid, 6% carbon, and 2¾% sand. Wolff gives the average composition of it as 29% phosphoric acid, 8% organic matter, 10% sand, 8% water, and 0.7% nitrogen. Voelcker's analyses of spent bone-black show from 50 to 82% of the phosphates of lime and magnesia, 10 to 30% of moisture and organic matter, 6 to 14% of carbonate of lime, and from 2 to 6% of insoluble silica. Way found in spent bone-black from 65 to 75% of phosphate of lime, 10 to 12% of carbonate of lime, and about the same quantity of charcoal.

According to Wallace, fresh bone-black, as sold, generally contains about 10% of moisture, and traces of ammonia and of the sulphides of ammonium and of calcium. It contains from 8 to 10% of nitrogenous carbon, but the carbon in old bone-black contains less nitrogen than that in new, and the proportion of nitrogen constantly diminished as the black is revivified. Old bone-black should contain more carbon than new, because of the carbonization of the impurities which have been taken from the sugar. Monier contrasts fresh and spent black as follows : —

	Fresh.	Spent.
Phosphate of lime	81.0	75.5
Carbonate of lime	5.1	16.0
Nitrogenous carbon	10.5	4.0
Silica, etc.	3.4	4.5

Weber, in Germany, who analyzed some 30 samples, several of which were fresh, unused blacks, reports from 50 to 82% of terphosphate of lime, 5 to 10% of carbonate of lime, 1 to 6% of quicklime, $\frac{1}{4}$ to 2% of iron oxide, 9 to 26% of carbon and water, and 2 to 28% of sand, beside small quantities of sodium sulphate and sulphide, and occasionally gypsum and chloride of calcium. Some of these soluble impurities come manifestly from agents used abroad in processes of revivifying the char. In those samples of Weber's black which contained much sand, it seemed to have been added as an adulterant. Hoffmann, also, in Germany, found in 10 samples of spent bone-black, several of which were of very poor quality, from 11 to 34% of phosphoric acid, 5 to 25% of sand and inert matters, $1\frac{1}{2}$ to 6% of organic matter (? carbon), 0.08 to 0.91% of nitrogen. One sample contained 16% of carbonate of lime, and 0.3% of gypsum; and one was adulterated with powdered peat.

Beside its utility as an excellent material for making superphosphate of lime, no little interest attaches to bone-black because of its long-continued use as a fertilizer in Southwestern France, as described on a subsequent page.

Superphosphate of Lime.

The same kind of reasoning which led to the substitution of fine bone-meal for the coarsely crushed bones of former years has been pushed still further, with the result that a very important branch of chemical industry has grown up, viz. the manufacture of superphosphate of lime from the natural phosphates. In order to make bone-earth still finer than it exists in bone-meal, it became customary some years since in England to treat bones with sulphuric acid, so that a considerable portion of their phosphoric acid might be put into the earth in a condition in which it is soluble in water. Nowadays, not only bones are thus treated, but fossil phosphates of lime in great variety. Indeed, almost the whole of the enormous quantity of superphosphate now used is made, not from bones, but from the mineral phosphates.

It was especially in England and Scotland, where the whole system of farming in many districts was based upon the growing of turnips as cattle-food, that the use of superphosphate first became prevalent, and though this fertilizer usually does good when applied to grain-crops, it is upon turnips that its services are most conspicuous. It is admitted by everyone that on fairly good land turnips are more signally benefited by phosphates than by any other fertilizer, and that for this crop nothing is so well suited as the superphosphates to supplement farmyard manure or to make good a deficiency in the supply of dung. By folding sheep upon turnips as a preparation for grain, thousands of acres of outlying land on the chalk hills, which could never have been manured economically with the dung-cart, have been converted into fertile fields simply by the use of superphosphates as a means of obtaining the turnips.

Method of Manufacture.

Various methods of treating the finely powdered phosphatic materials with the acid have been employed. One common way is to stir the two together in iron pans, or, better, in a close vessel called the mixer. Sometimes the acid is heated expressly, to hasten its solvent action, though ordinarily the heat developed by the chemical reaction between the acid and the phosphate rock is sufficient for the manufacturer's purpose.

Close mixers, provided with suitable abduction flues to carry off the gases that are evolved, are specially convenient when phosphates that contain an unusually large proportion of fluorides are operated upon. Otherwise, the fumes of fluorine compounds that are given off would greatly inconvenience the workmen. Great quantities of carbonic acid gas also are given off in some cases, where the phosphate rock contains lime carbonate. Indeed, much carbonic acid is given off even from bone-ash and bone-black, when these substances are treated with acids.

One of the most interesting of the methods of dealing with phosphate rock which have fallen under my own observation may be

described as follows. A thin stream of the finely ground phos-
phate·rock is made to flow out from a hopper while a stream of
chamber sulphuric acid (i. e. acid of specific gravity 1.45 to 1.50,
such as can be made in the leaden chambers of sulphuric acid
works, and which, unlike the stronger acid of commerce, has never
had to bear any special expense for concentration by evaporating
off a part of its water in pans or other vessels heated by fire) flows
down beside it in such wise that both the streams fall together into
the top of a tolerably long cast-iron cylinder, that is set in a slant-
ing position and made to revolve constantly upon its long axis.
As they flow, or rather twist, down through this slowly revolving
cylinder, the acid and the powdered mineral become thoroughly
admixed, and they fall out from the lower end in the form of a
tolerably thick homogeneous pap, which is thrown into great heaps,
each of which contains several cart-loads of the material.

In these heaps, which are left to themselves for several days,
considerable heat is developed, thanks to the chemical action of
the acid upon the mineral; and a great deal of water is thus evaporated, whereby whatever acid has been left free in the mixture becomes concentrated, as well as hot, and better able to decompose
the rock-phosphate. Thus it happens that, towards the close of
the operation, a decidedly strong hot acid reacts upon the last,
undecomposed portions of the mineral, and the finished superphosphate is left dry and crumbly. It needs only to be crushed
to be ready for market.

The not very highly concentrated chamber acid may, of course,
be made to act in this way, no matter what mechanical method is
employed for mixing it with the powdered rock. It is only necessary that the heaps of mixed materials shall be tolerably large,
and shall be left long enough for them to become hot. The process is noticeably economical of fuel, both in respect to the concentration of the acid used at first, and to the bringing of hot,
strong acid to act at last on the most refractory portions of the
mineral.

No matter what the details of the process may be, the reaction
depends ultimately on the formation of a quantity of insoluble or
difficultly soluble gypsum by the union of the sulphuric acid with
a part of the lime in the phosphatic material. The reaction may
be written symbolically as follows : —

$$3\ CaO,\ P_2O_5 + 2\ (H_2O,SO_3) = 2\ (CaO,SO_3) + CaO,\ 2\ H_2O,P_2O_5$$

(Bone Phosp. of Lime.) (Sulph. Acid.)   (Gypsum.)   (Superphosp. of Lime.)

The gypsum, from the formation of which the soluble acid phosphate of lime has incidentally resulted, remains admixed with the soluble phosphate, as a mere diluent. It would be a considerable gain for all parties interested if some cheap and easy method could be devised for getting rid of this encumbrance; for, as compared with the value of the acid phosphate, the gypsum is of insignificant worth as a fertilizer, and the costs of transporting it are much larger than its worth. Of course, the gypsum thus admixed with the superphosphate may often do good service in the field by setting free potash from the soil for the use of the crop, and it has undoubtedly happened in a multitude of instances that superphosphates have on this account actually given better crops than would have been the case if no gypsum had been present. But where potash is thus needed, it would be much cheaper to apply it as such, or to buy gypsum on purpose, and strew it upon the land.

Highly concentrated Superphosphates.

Most of the gypsum in a superphosphate, as well as the other insoluble impurities, might be eliminated by leaching out the soluble acid phosphate with water, and then evaporating the solution to dryness. In this way, pure superphosphate of lime has been made that contained some 60% of soluble phosphoric acid, but the process is somewhat costly. There are cases, however, as where the fertilizer has to be transported to some distant and inaccessible locality, where it might be profitable to remove from it all useless ballast.

In like manner, a so-called "double superphosphate" is made at Wetzlar, in Germany, as follows: Rock phosphate, so highly charged with impurities that it is unfit to be used for making superphosphate in the ordinary way, is finely powdered and stirred up with an excess of highly dilute sulphuric acid. By means of filter-presses, the dissolved phosphoric acid which results from this treatment, together with the excess of sulphuric acid used, is separated from the gypsum and the insoluble impurities derived from the original rock, and the liquid is boiled down in great pans until it is strong enough to be used for treating the better kinds of rock phosphates instead of, or as an addition to, ordinary sulphuric acid. In this way, highly concentrated ("double") superphosphates are obtained. The gypsum, etc., that remains in the filter-press is washed with water and sold for a song; and, in order that no phosphoric acid shall be lost, the last washings from the gypsum are said to be used instead of pure water in the leaden chambers where the sulphuric acid is made. These double super-phosphates are made in Belgium also, and in England.

Not easy to make Superphosphate from Bone-meal.

It is noteworthy that it is more difficult to make a superphos-phate, rich in soluble phosphoric acid, by treating bone-meal with sulphuric acid, than it is to make it from spent bone-black, or from bone-ash, or even from some of the purer kinds of mineral phos-phates. According to Voelcker, as long as bones only were treated with sulphuric acid, a large proportion of the bone-earth was left unchanged in its chemical composition. Such partially dissolved bones seldom contained more than 8 or 10% of phosphate of lime that had been made soluble.

Sulphuric acid acts but slowly upon bones, unless they are very finely ground. The animal matter of the bone tends to protect the earthy portions from solution. In case the bones are "raw," as the term is, i. e., have not been boiled to remove fat, so much the worse for the superphosphate maker, for the fat, even more than the ossein, tends to prevent the acid from acting upon the bone-earth. Moreover, both the fat and the ossein tend to com-bine with and consume a considerable portion of the acid, and so add to the cost of the product; and, worst of all, they make the product slimy, and inconvenient of application to the land. On seeking to "dry" this sticky substance by mixing with it bone-black or wood-ashes, much of the phosphoric acid which had been made soluble undergoes change, and becomes insoluble in water. But, on the other hand, there is an advantage for the farmer, in that the superphosphate obtained from bone-meal contains a cer-tain proportion of nitrogen in the partially decomposed ossein, as well as some ammonia which has resulted from the total decompo-sition of the ossein.

Bone-superphosphate, as met with nowadays, differs essentially from the product formerly sold under this name. At the present time, nearly all the bone which is not used directly as "ivory," is converted either into bone-meal or into bone-black for refining sugar; though small quantities of bone-superphosphate are still prepared from bones which have been steamed under extremely high pressures, for the purpose of extracting ossein, in the process of glue making. The superphosphate obtained in this way contains but little nitrogen, though it is exceptionally rich in soluble phosphoric acid, of which it may contain as much as 20%. In Germany, such superphosphate is occasionally treated with fine bone-meal in such manner that a product containing 3% of nitrogen and about 20% of phosphoric acid is obtained. But, on the other hand, it is apt to be mixed with inferior nitrogenous matters, and sold as "prepared bone-meal," containing from 2 to 4.5% of nitrogen, and from 7 to 14% of soluble phosphoric acid.

Composition of Superphosphates.

The composition of really good ordinary plain superphosphates may be stated as follows : —

				Per cent
From Bone-black	{ Soluble phosphoric acid	. .	17.3
	{ Insoluble " "	. . .	0.1
" Navassa phosphatic guano	{ Soluble " "	. . .	11.0
	{ Insoluble " "	. . .	3.0
" Carolina rock	{ Soluble " "	. . .	11.0
	{ Insoluble " "	. . .	1.0
" Baker Island phosphatic guano	{ Soluble " "	. . .	20.0
	{ Insoluble " "	. . .	2.0
" Bone-meal	{ Soluble " "	. . .	16.0
	{ Insoluble " "	. . .	1.6
	{ Nitrogen		2.6

Superphosphates much more concentrated than the foregoing may be made by the process described above, or by making sulphuric acid act upon pure precipitated phosphate of lime; either such as may be prepared on purpose, or such as is obtained in Europe as an incidental product in the manufacture of gelatine. It is possible to get in this way superphosphates that contain 34 or 35% of soluble phosphoric acid. A certain amount of superphosphate of a grade as high as this, or even higher, is used in this country by the dealers in fertilizers, for mixing with other superphosphates to bring them up to a required standard, or for preparing mixtures of fertilizers, though as a general rule bone-black superphosphates seem to be used for these purposes of reinforcement.

It is to be remarked that in books published in England, the results of analyses of superphosphates are often reported in a somewhat different way from the foregoing. Instead of stating simply the percentage of soluble phosphoric acid, which has been found by analysis of the samples under examination, English writers are apt to state what proportion of the bone-phosphate in the original raw material has been dissolved during the process of manufacture. They say, "*phosphate made soluble*" or "*soluble phosphate*," meaning to express by these terms the amount of bone-phosphate ($3\,CaO, P_2O_5$) which has been fully decomposed, and converted to superphosphate ($CaO, 2\,H_2O, P_2O_5$). The figures of analyses stated in this way are necessarily rather high, for 310 pounds of bone-phosphate ($3\,CaO, P_2O_5$) contain 142 pounds of phosphoric acid (P_2O_5); or, in other words, 142 pounds of phosphoric acid correspond to 310 pounds of phosphate made soluble. It follows that a superphosphate containing 15% of soluble phosphoric acid may be said to contain 32.7% of "soluble phosphate," while a sample reported to contain 25% of "phosphate made soluble," really contains 11.5% of soluble phosphoric acid.

Mode of Action of Superphosphate.

When a superphosphate is applied to the soil, the first rainfall, or even the moisture of the soil, dissolves the soluble phosphoric acid, and causes it to soak into the earth. There it comes in contact with carbonate of lime, and with compounds of iron and alumina, and is arrested by these substances. That is to say, the phosphoric acid is precipitated in the earth, in the form of phosphate of lime for the most part at first, and of the still more difficultly soluble phosphates of iron and alumina. Unless, indeed, the soil is actually deficient in lime, it is not to be supposed that much if any of the soluble phosphoric acid can remain dissolved in the soil-water longer than a few days at the utmost.

It has been noticed by Ullik that, when freshly precipitated in the soil, much of the phosphoric acid can be dissolved out again rather easily by means of dilute acids, but that, after the lapse of some time, the precipitated phosphate becomes much less easily soluble; and similar results were obtained in experiments where phosphate of lime and phosphate of iron were precipitated out of contact with the soil. A marked diminution of the solubility of these compounds in acids occurred as they became more coherent through age, and the fact was specially noticeable in respect to phosphate of iron.

With regard to the ultimate conversion of precipitated phosphate of lime to the phosphates of iron or alumina, it is to be said that in the soil the change is usually a very gradual one; generally speaking, a long time would be required for its completion, though in laboratory experiments it is possible to obtain comparative rapid action. An experiment of P. Thenard illustrates this matter. He dissolved some phosphate of lime to saturation in carbonic-acid water, and put the liquid in a bottle with a small quantity of soil. After the mixture had stood three or four days, no trace of phosphoric acid could be detected in solution. The whole of it had been fixed by the earth. Similar results were obtained when the loam was replaced by alumina or oxide of iron. But since almost all soils contain an abundance of iron and alumina, it is no wonder that the phosphoric acid in manures is firmly fixed in the earth soon after its application.

A. Mayer digested 10 grm. of a superphosphate in 300 cc. of water, and added to the clear filtrate 45 grm. of precipitated carbonate of lime. The mixture was shaken frequently, and tested at intervals to determine how much phosphoric acid remained dissolved in the water. The following results were obtained. Three hundred cc. of water contained in solution

	Grm. of Phosph. Acid.
Before the carbonate of lime was added	1.26
6 hours after	1.16
24 hours after	1.01
8 days after	0.15
24 days after	0.03

Analogous results were obtained when a calcareous soil was mixed with the solution of a superphosphate. It appeared, in fact, as had been shown before by other chemists, that the phosphoric acid of a superphosphate is only slowly precipitated in the soil, even when the soil is calcareous. In other words, considerable time is allowed for the diffusion of the phosphoric acid in the soil before it is arrested. Schroeder made intimate mixtures of 5 grm. of dry superphosphate and 3 grm. of chalk, and, after having mixed them with enough water to form a thick paste, examined these mixtures after one day, after three days, and after twenty days. His results are given in the following table: —

There was contained in the	Phosphoric Acid		Of each 100 grm. of the original phosphoric acid there was now		
	Soluble in water %	Soluble in water and citrate %	Soluble in water %	Soluble in citrate %	Insoluble %
Original superphosphate,	21.32	21.86	96.5	2.4	1.1
Mixture at end of 1 day,	0.89	14.86	4.0	67.3	28.4
" " " " 3 days,	0.00	0.75	0.0	3.3	96.7
" " " " 20 "	0.00	0.00	0.0	0.0	100.0

But very different results were got when the superphosphate was mixed with loams to which some carbonate of lime had been added. Two grm. of superphosphate were mixed with 8 grm. of loam in each case, but the garden loam contained 0.215% of carbonate of lime, while that from the arable field contained 0.842%.

	Phosphoric Acid		Of each 100 grm. of the original phosphoric acid there was		
A. GARDEN LOAM :	Soluble in water	Soluble in water and citrate	Soluble in water	Soluble in citrate	Insoluble
There was contained in the	%	%	%	%	%
Superphosphate taken,	21.32	21.89	96.5	2.4	1.1
Mixture after 1 day,	19.32	21.54	87.4	10.1	2.5
" " 10 days,	10.55	12.48	47.7	8.7	43.6
" " 20 "	9.48	9.84	42.9	1.6	55.5
B. LOAM FROM ARABLE FIELD :					
There was contained in the					
Superphosphate taken,	21.32	21.89	96.5	2.4	1.1
Mixture after 1 day,	13.98	14.77	63.2	3.6	33.2
" " 10 days,	8.99	10.63	40.7	7.4	51.9
" " 20 "	8.49	9.70	38.4	5.5	56.1

The fixation of the phosphoric acid was extremely slow in both the loams, though in the beginning it was more rapid in the somewhat calcareous, sandy, arable loam that contained but little humus or clay. But at the end of three weeks nearly the same proportion of the phosphoric acid had become insoluble in both the loams, and the rapidity with which the precipitation proceeded in the garden loam during the last ten days of the experiment suggested the thought that it might subsequently have become more complete in that case than in the other.

Fixation of the Phosphates in Manure.

Voelcker, on filtering barn-yard liquor through loams of various kinds, found that most of the phosphoric acid in the liquid was speedily fixed by a moderate quantity of earth, even when the latter was poor in lime, though traces of phosphoric acid always remained in solution ; precisely as was the case with potash and ammonia, as has been already explained. When strong solutions of soluble phosphates were used instead of the weak dung-liquor, much more phosphoric acid was fixed by the loam in a given time than had previously been the case. When an alkaline carbonate, such as is contained in wood-ashes, stable-manure, or dung-liquor, is added to a solution of a superphosphate, Mayer found that from , to ⅜ of the phosphoric acid is speedily precipitated, while the rest remains dissolved as an alkaline phosphate, from which the phosphoric acid is slowly precipitated when the solution is put in contact with a calcareous soil. So, too, Petermann found, on mixing dung-liquor with a phosphatic chalk, which occurs abundantly in Belgium, that — far from any phosphoric acid being dissolved out of the mineral — the whole of that contained in the dung-liquor was precipitated in the form of terbasic phosphate of lime.

On adding ferric hydrate and hydrate of alumina to solutions of phosphate of lime in carbonic-acid water, Warington found, after some days, that 96 and 97 hundredths of the phosphoric acid had been abstracted from the solutions and deposited as phosphate of iron or of alumina, while the whole of the lime remained dissolved. So, too, Knox and Warington have found that phosphoric acid is fixed more rapidly and completely by soils to which alumina or oxide of iron has been added, and Gladding has shown, by direct experiments, that phosphoric acid is really fixed in soils in the form of phosphates of iron and of alumina, as well as in the form of phosphate of lime.

In spite of the tendency of phosphoric acid to come to rest in the soil in the form of phosphate of iron or of phosphate of alumina, it is none the less true that many cultivated soils, particularly those which have been repeatedly dressed with phosphates or with farm-yard manure, do contain considerable quantities of phosphate of lime. It has been found possible to dissolve out from such soils no inconsiderable quantities of phosphate of lime on leaching the soils with nitric acid. Acetic acid, also, and even solutions of citrate of ammonia, have been found capable of dissolving appreciable quantities of phosphate of lime from many good soils. Dehérain, who investigated this question in France, was led to the conclusion that soils in which all the phosphoric acid is in combination with iron or alumina, occur much more rarely than was at one time supposed.

In studying the fixing power of soils for phosphoric acid, Voelcker placed weighed quantities of six different kinds of loams in bottles, together with measured quantities of a solution of superphosphate of lime of known strength; and, after having shaken the mixtures repeatedly, he noted, from time to time, how much phosphoric acid still remained dissolved in the water. His results are given in the following table. By referring to the descriptions of the loams which succeed the tables, it will be seen that phosphoric acid is fixed with especial ease by those soils which contain a good store of calcareous matter. The power of clay soils to render soluble-phosphoric acid insoluble was far less than that of chalky soils.

Kind and Amount of Loam taken. Grains.	Soluble Phosp. Acid taken (stated in terms of bone earth, $3\ CaO, P_2O_5$). Grains.	Soluble Phosp. Acid (stated as before) that was retained by the Loam, After	Grains.
		24 hours	24.29
A. 5,250	40.67	8 days	31.49
		26 days	38.23
		24 hours	72.81
B. 10,500	81.17	8 days	80.31
		26 days	81.17
		24 hours	19.36
C. 5,250	40.67	8 days	27.66
		26 days	29.80
		24 hours	20.45
D. 5,000	41.15	8 days	24.95
		17 days	34.73
		24 hours	21.46
E. 5,000	40.93	8 days	23.92
		17 days	29.23
F. 16,000	79.43	7 days	77.30
		14 days	78.37

EXPERIMENT A, as given in the above table, was made upon a red loamy soil, deep and well suited for turnips, which contained 1.22 % carbonate of lime and 6 % oxides of iron and alumina. In this case, as the table shows, rather less than two-thirds of the phosphoric acid were fixed in the course of 24 hours by the limited quantity of loam that was employed. Three-quarters of the phosphoric acid had been absorbed at the end of a week; but even after 26 days, some of the acid still remained in solution. It will be noticed, however, that the purpose of these experiments was simply to compare the different kinds of loams, one with the others. No effort was made to absorb completely the phosphoric acid, and there is nothing surprising in the fact that a considerable proportion of the acid should have remained in solution when thus left in contact with a limited quantity of a non-calcareous loam. Indeed, this very evidence points to the conclusion that practically, in the field, superphosphates must be completely precipitated by most loams, because of the large amount of soil through which their solutions would have to pass. It is probably true of this particular soil (A), that if a heavy shower of rain were to fall in the course of 24 hours after the application of a concentrated superphosphate, it would simply distribute the fertilizer very effectively, though perhaps a little phosphoric acid might be carried into the subsoil, to be fixed there.

In actual field practice, dressings of superphosphate are always applied in very different proportions, as regards the amount of soil, from those of these experiments. Even in case very heavy dressings of 6 or 8 cwt. of concentrated superphosphate were added to a soil no more than 2 or 3 inches deep, it would still be true that the proportion which the earth in the field bears to such dressings is many hundred times greater than that which the pound or less of loam of the experiments bears to the amounts of soluble phosphoric acid that were added to it. In reality, i. e., when it is put in relation to 3 or 4 inches of surface soil, the quantity of soluble phosphoric acid contained in 6 or 8 cwt. of a rich superphosphate is so small that it is not easy to detect by analysis any difference in the amount of phosphoric acid present in the soil before and after the application of the fertilizer.

EXPERIMENT B was made upon a calcareous (chalky) soil, that contained 67.5 % carbonate of lime in a finely divided state. Here the soluble phosphoric acid was absorbed much more rapidly and completely than by the red loam; but the fixation was in no sense instantaneous, nor was it completed in a day. The same relative proportions of soil, water and superphosphate were employed in this experiment as in the preceding, and the results are strictly comparable.

EXPERIMENT C. A stiff clay subsoil which contained 1 % carbonate of lime and 17.38 % oxides of iron and alumina. Here the fixation of phosphoric acid was slow. At the end of 24 hours, more phosphoric acid remained in solution than had been fixed by the soil, and during the third stage of the experiment only 1.25 grains (of bone earth) were added to the soil.

EXPERIMENT D. A stiff clay surface soil, taken from above the preceding sub-soil (C). It contained 2 % carbonate of lime and nearly 8 % oxides of iron and alumina.

EXPERIMENT E. — A light sandy soil that contained but little clay or organic matter and no limestone gravel. Analysis showed only 0.15 % carbonate of lime and 12 % oxides of iron and alumina. The absorption was noticeably slow, particularly after the first day.

EXPERIMENT F. — A clay-marl which contained 12 % carbonate of lime and 10 % oxides of iron and alumina. Here nearly the whole of the phosphoric acid was absorbed in the course of a week, whence it appears that marly soils, like those which contain chalk, readily absorb soluble phosphoric acid.

Ritthausen has observed that the conversion of soluble phosphoric acid to the insoluble state is apt to be effected very much more slowly by the carbonate of lime in natural marls than it is by pure, finely divided carbonate of lime, as obtained by way of chemical precipitation. Thus, on shaking together fine precipitated carbonate of lime and a highly dilute solution of superphosphate of lime, it appeared that nearly all the phosphoric acid speedily became insoluble. When the mixture was shaken frequently, or when so large an excess of the carbonate of lime was used that the mixture was in the form of a thin paste, from 94 to 99 % of the soluble phosphoric acid was usually thrown down in the course of two or three days.

But when, instead of the pure carbonate, a compact marl was employed as the precipitant, the fixing of the phosphoric acid proceeded much more slowly. Even large quantities of the marl failed to precipitate much phosphoric acid in the course of a week from dilute solutions of superphosphates, though, subsequently, on passing a current of carbonic acid gas through the mixture, 20 % of the phosphoric acid was precipitated in the course of three days. On allowing the mixture of marl and superphosphate to stand for 2 months, with frequent shakings, 83 % of the phosphoric acid was precipitated, while 17 % still remained in solution.

On mixing a dry pulverulent superphosphate with much dry marl, and then adding water enough to make a thin paste, the conversion of the phosphoric acid to the insoluble state was rather more rapid, but even in this case a considerable amount of phosphoric acid remained in solution, even after several weeks. Only at the end of 6 weeks was the precipitation found to be well nigh complete. It is to be remembered, of course, that marls vary widely as to their condition of compactness, and that a similar remark will doubtless apply to the carbonate of lime, which occurs naturally in soils. Consequently the phosphoric acid of superphosphates may be fixed much more quickly in some soils than in others. In any event, the amount of earth with which a superphosphate comes into contact, when it is applied as a fertilizer, is so enormously large, as compared with the amount of soluble phosphoric acid, that the conditions can hardly fail to be favorable for the fixation of the phosphoric acid, even in cases where the carbonate of lime in the soil happens to be compact, and where no very large percentage of it is present.

An experiment of Heiden well illustrates the tendency of the phosphoric acid of phosphate of lime to pass into comparatively insoluble forms in the soil. To a plot of crude, rough, heavy granite land, he applied pure precipitated tri-phosphate of lime 6 times in the course of 10 years, each time at the rate of 477 lb. to the acre. Before the beginning of the experiment he found that the soil of the field contained 0.0754 of phosphoric acid that was soluble in muriatic acid, and 0.0449 that was soluble in sulphuric acid. At the close of the 10 years the soil contained no more than 0.1006 of phosphoric acid soluble in muriatic acid, and 0.0676 that was soluble in sulphuric acid. But since all the pure phosphate of lime which had been applied to the land during the experiment was readily soluble in acids, it is evident that a large part of it must have become fixed in the earth in a difficultly soluble form.

Superphosphates are Distributing Agents.

It is to be observed that, although the phosphoric acid which has been made soluble with toil and trouble is speedily reprecipitated in the earth, and that although some of the phosphoric acid may eventually be changed there to difficultly soluble forms, the precipitate is nevertheless exceedingly finely divided, and very thoroughly disseminated. It is far finer than the finest bone-dust; and, what is still more important, it is distributed everywhere in the soil. The roots of crops are thus provided with a continuous supply of phosphoric acid, and the microscopic organisms which prosper in soils where phosphates abound can everywhere find an abundance of this kind of food.

When bone-meal is applied to the soil, there will always be left numberless places where no bone-meal has fallen, no matter what pains may have been taken to reduce the meal to fine powder or to incorporate it thoroughly with the soil. But the dissolved phosphoric acid soaks into the earth in all directions around every point where a particle of the original superphosphate has come to rest, and there is thus obtained a dissemination of the manure infinitely more perfect than can be had by mere mechanical distribution.

It will be noticed that, in so far as mechanical dissemination goes, the bone-meal and the superphosphate are upon equal terms; either one of them can be mixed with the earth as well as the other; but the distribution by way of solution comes in as something additional and subsequent.

From what has been said above of the chemical character of superphosphate of lime, it follows that this fertilizer should generally be applied to the land long enough before seeds are sown or young plants set out to allow time for the soluble phosphoric acid to become fixed in the soil, so that its acidity may be annulled. Some plants are specially liable to be injured by this acidity. Thus Hellregel has noticed that while the cereal grains and some other plants, even some kinds of leguminous plants, have considerable resisting power, lupines suffer extremely; perhaps because the acid may destroy or cripple the useful bacterium which lives upon lupine roots and absorbs nitrogen from the air.

Generally speaking, it would not be well to mix superphosphate with loam before spreading it, lest some of the soluble phosphoric acid become fixed in this loam instead of in the soil proper. According to Voelcker, the more rapidly the soluble phosphoric acid in a superphosphate is precipitated and made insoluble in the soil, and the more uniformly this insoluble precipitate is distributed in that part of the surface soil which is just under the young turnip plants, the more energetic will be the fertilizing effect. In accordance with this fact, it is found that superphosphate acts more energetically when applied with the so-called liquid-drill than when applied dry; 2 cwt. applied with water have frequently produced as good crops as 3 or 4 cwt. used in the dry state, simply because a more equable distribution was procured.

Voelcker remarks that he has frequently picked up on fields bits of superphosphate a month or six weeks after the application of the fertilizer, and has found in them a considerable proportion of soluble phosphoric acid, in spite of the fact that some rain had fallen upon them. It follows that when applied in dry weather a part of the fertilizer might remain inactive in the soil at the very time when phosphates are needed by the young crop.

Whenever it is possible to disseminate fertilizers through every part of the soil, as can be done in the case of the superphosphates, it is not unreasonable to suppose that the roots of crops can grow continuously and rapidly, — much in the same way that they are seen to grow sometimes in house-drains, — without suffering any check or irregularity. But in the contrary case, where the roots have to pass through spaces of earth free from manure, the growth of the plant must necessarily be less regular and less rapid. In the one case, the free growth of the plant will be continuous and smooth, as it were, and in the other, it will be spasmodic and intermittent. With regard to the manner in which the phosphoric acid which has become fixed in the earth is made soluble again for the use of plants, it will be sufficient to say here, that, among the various means by which this result may be accomplished, the action of carbonic acid water and of the acid juices exuded by plant-roots are conspicuous. The subject will be referred to again hereafter.

Superphosphates may do Harm.

In using superphosphate, a certain amount of care should be exercised, as was said just now, lest this acid substance injure the seed or the young crop, or useful micro-organisms in the soil. It is well known that free mineral acids, even when highly diluted, are injurious to most plants. For example, sulphuric acid diluted even with a thousand parts of water has been used with advantage for killing grass and weeds in gravel walks made with flint or silicious sand. One or two applications of the acid will destroy the weeds and none will appear again for a long time. But if the walks contained any limestone gravel, the acid would be immediately neutralized and the weeds would suffer very little from the application of it. Voelcker noticed, in England, that when concentrated superphosphates are used in large quantities, say at the rate of 500 or 600 lb. to the acre, they may do positive harm to root-crops, because the soluble phosphoric acid is not all precipitated quickly enough. Even 200 or 300 lb. applied to land poor in lime may do harm in the same way. By good rights, there should be lime enough in the land to precipitate the phosphoric acid pretty quickly, and some time also must be allowed for the precipitation.

This corrosive power of the soluble phosphate is often useful no doubt in that many hurtful worms, insects and fungi are destroyed by it. Indeed the question may fairly be asked, both with regard to superphosphate of lime and to quicklime, whether, economically speaking, these substances may not really do almost as much good by acting as poisons as by increasing fertility. Care should always be taken, of course, so to apply them to the land that both kinds of service may be performed without hindering the growth of the crop proper.

There is the risk, of course, as was just now said, that soluble phosphoric acid may destroy useful micro-organisms in the soil or the manure, or check their development, as well as clear the land of insects and worms. It has been insisted, indeed, by Immendorf, that superphosphate of lime is highly effective as a preservative of manure in stables and yards. When applied for this purpose, in adequate quantities, he found the superphosphate much more efficient, both as a germicide and as a fixer of ammonia, than either gypsum, phosphatic gypsum or kainit. It may even be advisable, when a superphosphate is to be used in conjunction with farmyard manure, not to allow the soluble fertilizer to come into contact with the dung, lest some of the micro-organisms in the latter should be killed, but to apply the superphosphate to the land long enough before the manure is spread to allow for the complete precipitation of the soluble phosphoric acid.

From this point of view, it may sometimes be better policy to use precipitated phosphate of lime, together with dung, rather than to use a superphosphate. Some years since, Voelcker was surprised by the result of an experiment where less than 20 tons of Swedish turnips to the acre were harvested from a plot of land that had been dressed with 10 tons of farm-yard manure and 4 cwt. of superphosphate made from bone-ash, while an adjacent plot, manured with 20 tons of the dung, gave 22 tons of turnips; and another plot, which had received nothing but 4 cwt. of the superphosphate, gave 23 tons of the roots. For, in his experience, it often happened that 10 tons of manure and 1.5 cwt. of superphosphate gave as good, or nearly as good, crops of turnips as were got by using 20 tons of manure. It seems not improbable, in case the dung and the superphosphate were actually mixed in the cited instance, that they may have injured each other, i. e., useful micro-organisms in the dung may have been killed, while much of the soluble phosphoric acid may have been rendered insoluble by matters in the dung before it had any opportunity to soak into the land and become properly distributed.

Inasmuch as pure peat and pure sand can have little, if any, power to fix soluble phosphoric acid, heavy dressings of superphosphate may be quite out of place on many peaty and sandy soils, unless, indeed, these soils have been limed or marled. Indeed, it may possibly be true, as a general proposition, that precipitated phosphate of lime would be a better fertilizer than superphosphate for poor, sandy and peaty soils. On the other hand, superphosphate of lime, like any other acid salt, or any soluble salt of lime, for that matter, may sometimes tend to do good on clayey loams by acting to flocculate some of the fine particles of colloid clay, such as are apt to become puddled when rained upon.

Significance of Quick-acting Manures.

One of the best illustrations that can be given of the advantage of using manures that act quickly is drawn from the experience of English farmers with phosphate of lime in its various forms. A hundred or more years ago, when bones first began to be used in that country, they were applied either unbroken, or, somewhat later, in coarse fragments, at the rate of 10 or 12 cwt. to the acre. Afterwards, when bone-meal came to be manufactured, 6 or 7 cwt. of the meal per acre were deemed to be a sufficient dose; while later yet, 1 or 2 cwt. of superphosphate per acre were found to be sufficient to produce the same effect on some soils and crops. In other words, for a given sum of money, six or eight times as much land can be well fertilized with the improved manure as was possible before.

In many parts of England the use of bone-meal was soon superseded by that of superphosphate made from bone, and the effects produced by this manure were described as indeed wonderful. "Some parts of Norfolk," for example, "were naturally unkind for turnips. Formerly a good plant on such land was the exception, where now it is the invariable rule. Splendid crops of swedes are now grown with certainty where before only a tiny crop of white turnips was ever expected. On the lighter lands, too, the superphosphate has done wonders. In days gone by rape-cake was the only auxiliary the farmer could command. It was a good, sound fertilizer, but not well suited for the tender plant, although excellent for its later growth. Now a little superphosphate is used to start the plant and hurry it out of the way of the fly. By these means the weight of roots grown on the poor, light lands of Norfolk is wonderfully increased." (C. S. Read, 1858.) It is to be remarked that these Norfolk soils are highly calcareous.

Though specially esteemed for turnips and other roots, and for Indian corn, superphosphate has been applied not infrequently to wheat in this country, as will be set forth directly, and it is often applied to wheat in England, at the time of seeding in the autumn, at the rate of 225 lb. to the acre on land which has been half dressed with farm-yard manure. It is said to have been much used upon barley in England of late years, being applied at the time of sowing at the rate of 200 or 300 lb. to the acre. In the low-lying fen districts of Eastern England superphosphates have been applied with great advantage to oats also, in the spring. In some parts of Holland they are used more particularly upon clover. (A. Mayer.)

In experiments by Lawes and Gilbert where potatoes were grown continually during 12 years, the mean annual crop per acre was raised from barely 2 long tons, on unmanured land, to 3.75 tons by means of superphosphate of lime alone; and only a trifle more than 3.75 tons were got on using a mixed mineral manure which contained salts of potash, soda and magnesia in addition to the superphosphate. These experimenters remark that the benefit got by potatoes from mineral fertilizers are quite consistent with what has been noticed in respect to root crops having a comparatively shallow root development, and that in both cases nitrogen enough for the purposes of the crop may be derived from the store of it which is contained in the surface soil. They say that the beneficial effects of phosphates are observed generally with spring-sown crops, which have a short term of growth and a comparatively superficial rooting, and which are compelled to rely on the stores of food in the surface soil.

Superphosphates have approved themselves.

In the last analysis, it is of course always a matter of money value and of comparative efficiency whether the farmer shall use the large amount of crushed bone, as above stated, or the small amount of superphosphate. It was argued at one time, even as regards powdered phosphate rock that it might perhaps be better to apply a double dose of the raw material to the land than to pay for the cost of the acid, the labor, and the machinery involved in the preparation of the superphosphate.

The same amount of money, it was said, will probably do more lasting good to the land if it is applied in the form of a large quantity of the powdered mineral, than if the dressing be restricted to the smaller quantity of superphosphate which this sum of money is competent to buy; and it is doubtless true, as regards some kinds of soils, notably reclaimed marshes, moors, and bogs, that powdered phosphate rock may be a better manure, all things considered, than superphosphate of lime. This question was studied pretty thoroughly at one time on the poor granitic soils of the western coast of France, where powdered phosphatic nodules were used as a substitute for bone-black. In numerous instances highly satisfactory results were obtained from the natural phosphates when they were applied to newly broken pasture or moorland, i.e. to soils rich in organic matters of a somewhat sour character. Good crops of buckwheat in particular were got by means of the natural phosphate, applied at the rate of 250 to 350 lb. to the acre, i.e. rather more freely than bone-black, which was often used at the rate of 175 to 250 lb. It appeared, however, in numerous instances when the ground nodules were applied to fertile soils or to calcareous soils, that no appreciable gain was got from them; and it soon came to be recognized even in that locality, that superphosphates are much to be preferred on good land which has been for some time under cultivation. Indeed, as regards fertile European soils, the question was decided long ago adversely to the natural mineral. It has been decided by the long-continued experience of a multitude of farmers, and their conclusion has been plainly expressed by the ever-increasing demand for superphosphate.

There are cases, of course, as where a deposit of mineral phosphates of low grade might exist in the neighborhood of a farm together with running water wherewith to pulverize the materials, where it might possibly be best not to buy superphosphate of lime, but to make use of the home material; but an exception such as this is of small importance, and does but tend to strengthen the general argument in favor of buying the active fertilizer in most cases. There are withal special situations, soils, and crops, where an instructed farmer might find it more profitable to use a cheap insoluble phosphate, rather than the costly soluble product prepared from it. This point is one worthy of much consideration, though it relates to a mere question of detail that has not yet been adequately studied. According to Fleischer, experience in North Germany has shown that while powdered phosphate rock may be counted upon to do good service on moors of sour character, such phosphates may exert little if any useful effect on moorlands of the better class; or, at the least it may happen that no benefit will be derived from them until after the lapse of several years.

There was another question that used to be asked in all such speculations, viz., whether it would not be better economy to apply to the land a given money value of the raw material, plus a proper proportion of some nitrogenized or other manure, in place of an equivalent amount of the superphosphate. But this question would seem to have been answered long ago, in so far as good land is concerned, by the common English practice of using superphosphates — but not the phosphatic guanos with which the superphosphates were at one time in competition — in alternation with nitrogen compounds. According to Voelcker, experience has taught the English turnip-farmers that "mineral phosphates unaltered in chemical composition are of little more practical value to root-crops than sand, and that it is a waste of material to leave mineral phosphates in a turnip-manure in an insoluble condition." When superphosphates were first made from rock-phosphates the decomposition of the latter was far from being pushed to its utmost limit, and many complaints were made at one time in England on this account. But the manufacturers soon learned how to dissolve the rock-phosphate completely enough to enable the farmers to get good crops.

According to Kellner, who made experiments on a rotation of barley, millet, wheat and buckwheat on upland soils in Japan, the double superphosphates are in the beginning the most effective of phosphatic fertilizers. But after his first two crops had been gathered the superiority of this fertilizer was no longer manifest, and it was thought that the diphosphate, formed from it in the soil at first, must have changed to triphosphate and to other difficultly soluble compounds. Kellner argues from these facts, that the double superphosphate is best suited to quick-growing crops sown in the spring or summer on soils of medium absorptive power as regards phosphoric acid, and that it should be applied only a few days before sowing or transplanting.

Plain Superphosphates.

Plain superphosphates, made from "rock," or "ash," or "black," have the disadvantage as compared with bone-meal, that they do not contain the flesh-like nitrogenized substance which adds so much to the fertilizing value of the bone. Yet in spite of this fact, and of the cost of manufacturing them, the use of plain rock-superphosphates has steadily gained ground from year to year. The power of disseminating itself in the soil, and the consequent rapid action of the superphosphate, is a point of far greater significance than the cost of making the fertilizer, or than the absence of nitrogenized constituents. It is an easy matter always for the farmer to apply some kind of nitrogenized manure, such as nitrate of soda, or sulphate of ammonia, or fish-scrap, or meat-dust, or oil-cake to reinforce the superphosphate, as is often done in England. But not infrequently the humus of the field is all sufficient for supplying nitrogen to a turnip-crop. Voelcker wrote as follows, in 1862 : "Experiments extending over a period of 5 years have shown me that on the moderately tenacious, calcareous clay at Cirencester as large an increase in the produce of Swedish turnips may be obtained with bone-ash treated with sulphuric acid as by any other of the numerous fertilizing mixtures which I have employed in field-trials. My own experience is confirmed by the practice of many farmers who grow heavy crops of turnips on good calcareous clay-soils and on land that is moderately stiff and in good heart, with no other fertilizer than 3 or 4 cwt. of mineral superphosphate which contains neither organic matter nor ammonia. On light, sandy soils on the contrary, purely mineral superphosphates fail to produce good turnip-crops, and there is needed a reinforcement of dung."

Nitrogenized Superphosphates.

The American market has long been flooded with a great variety of so-called ammoniated or nitrogenized superphosphates, into which the nitrogen compound has been already put. In most of these products, the nitrogen exists in the form of fish-scrap; in other cases it is in the form of dried blood or tankage. Some specimens contain dried meat, as obtained from the offal of slaughter-houses. Formerly the scraps of flesh and gristle obtained as a residuum in the operation of rendering grease and tallow were sometimes employed; and at times a most improper use has been made of worthless torrefied leather for this purpose. Occasionally some of the nitrogen in these superphosphates is in the form of crystals of sulphate of ammonia, or of nitrate of soda, and in some of the earlier specimens Peruvian guano was detected. A few years since, when nitrate of soda happened to be exceptionally cheap, a good deal of this material was used for reinforcing phosphates. As a rule, these so-called ammoniated superphosphates are not to be commended. The chief reason why they continue to be made appears to be the ignorance of those farmers who know so little as to the modes of action of the chemical fertilizers that they do not feel competent to decide for themselves which they had better use.

When superphosphates were first made, bone-meal was the raw material. The farmers of those days thus became accustomed to a fertilizer which contained both phosphoric acid and nitrogen, and which could be used as a substitute for farmyard manure on many soils, such for example as were well charged with potash compounds. Hence when superphosphates began to be made from bone-black, bone-ash, and phosphate-rock, instead of from bone-meal, a feeling arose, not unnaturally, that some kind of nitrogenized matter should be added to the product, to compensate for the lost ossein; and the manufacturers were ready enough to add such materials, since several of them, notably guano and dried blood, serve extremely well as "dryers" to remove any excess of sulphuric acid with which a superphosphate may be charged. Moreover, some of the materials, such as fish-scrap and tankage, were formerly so cheap that no small profit could be gained by selling them in the form of a superphosphate. When Peruvian guano or sulphate of ammonia have been added to a superphosphate the product can truly be called "ammoniated," but this name is improperly applied to mixtures which contain only fish-scrap or blood or flesh-meal. With the advance of agricultural knowledge, superphosphates are nowadays much more generally regarded as distinctly phosphatic manures, and there is no longer any such justification for adding nitrogenous matters to them as there was at first.

Perhaps one explanation of the abundance of nitrogenized superphosphates in the markets of this country may be found in the character of some of the cotton-lands of the South. Many of them are said to be deep loams which have resulted from the disintegration of granite, gneiss, and other feldspathic rocks "in place," whereby soils have been formed which are rich in potash, and well adapted to withstand drought in many cases. As a rule, these soils do not run together or "bake" after heavy rains, and they are easily cultivated. But it would appear that they need additions of phosphoric acid and nitrogen, and that they respond quickly to dressings of nitrogenous superphosphate, which is for them a complete manure. It is said, however, that experience has taught that a superphosphate carrying 10% of soluble phosphoric acid should not contain more than 3% of nitrogen, for nitrogen tends to delay the ripening of the cotton, while the phosphate by itself hastens ripening.

Speaking in general terms, it may be said that for a long series of years very little knowledge and still less conscience were displayed in the manufacture of nitrogenized superphosphates in this country, while it was customary at that time to sell the products at exorbitant prices. Scientifically speaking, the fundamental idea of making such nitrogenized phosphates for sale is wrong, in so far as there cannot be much sense in carrying on at a manufactory any simple operation which the farmer can perform for himself just as well as the factory workmen, or better.

In this country the use of ammoniated superphosphates seems to have depended at one time largely upon the efforts of manufacturers to eke out the value of improperly prepared plain superphosphates by reinforcing them with another kind of manure. Subsequently, potash salts, as well as nitrogen compounds, were often added to low-grade fertilizers to improve them. Afterwards "special fertilizers" were prepared by the dealers from really good materials, and finally many farmers have learned that they can make such mixtures for themselves. It is not to be recommended, as a general rule, that the farmer should attempt to decompose either raw bones or rock-phosphates with sulphuric acid upon his farm. As was said before, the manufacture of superphosphate from bones, and from most kinds of rock-phosphates also, is a somewhat difficult operation, the successful conduct of which requires manufacturing appliances and chemical skill, i. e. trained workmen. But it can safely be asserted that the mixing of the finished superphosphate with a dry, harmless powder, like sulphate of ammonia, or with a friable substance, like dried ground-up fishes, is an operation not beyond the capacity of an ordinary farm-laborer. It is a mere matter of dumping the several fertilizers in separate heaps on a barn floor, and of spreading them together, layer by layer, with a shovel, into a bed which will finally be shovelled over, much in the same way that a compost-heap would be turned.

Some Fertilizers should not be Mixed.

It is to be observed, however, that some kinds of fertilizers should never be mixed one with the other, neither at the barn nor at the factory. Thus, if sulphate of ammonia or Peruvian guano were to be mixed with lime, or with wood-ashes, either "live" or leached, or with phosphatic slag, ammonia would be given off; and if nitrate of soda were mixed with a true superphosphate, some nitric acid might be expelled.

Home-made Mixtures.

A good example of home mixing is that reported by Mr. Webb, of Connecticut, as follows: Four tons of plain superphosphate, one ton of muriate of potash, and one ton of sulphate of ammonia, were purchased. A bag of the phosphate, weighing 200 lb., was emptied upon the barn floor, and the lumps beaten down with a shovel; 100 lb. of the muriate were poured upon the phosphate; then 200 lb. more of the phosphate were added, and finally 100 lb. of the sulphate of ammonia; the whole being mixed with shovels, sifted, and put into barrels for convenience. The mixture was found to be in excellent order for sowing, and gave great satisfaction in every way. The whole cost of the completed mixture was $36¼ the ton, and the value of it, as appraised from analysis, was $48¼ the ton. Other farmers have prepared still cheaper mixtures by using fish-scrap, bone-meal, tankage or cotton-seed meal in place of a part of the sulphate of ammonia. In Louisiana, a mixture of 1100 lb. superphosphate of lime, 700 lb. cotton-seed meal, and 200 lb. of kainit, applied at the rate of from 200 to 500 lb. to the acre, has been found useful on cotton. (Stubbs.)

The chief advantage to be derived from the home mixing is based upon the facts that nitrogenized manures, such as fish-scrap, oil-cake, and sulphate of ammonia, are, for the most part, cheap merchantable articles of peculiar appearance. Several of them are so well characterized, and so easily recognized, that it would be a comparatively difficult matter to adulterate them by themselves. But when once mixed with the superphosphate, the identity of the nitrogen compound is lost. Even chemical analysis can scarcely tell how much one of the current ammoniated superphosphates is worth, for there are many substances rich in nitrogen, such as leather-scraps, which have no value whatsoever as food for plants, and it is possible to incorporate these things into a nitrogenized superphosphate, so thoroughly that a mere estimation of the amount of nitrogen in the mixture might lead anyone to suppose that the material had a much higher value than can justly be put upon it. This remark applies, also, though with a trifle less force, to leather which has been steamed or roasted and then powdered, such as will be described hereafter.

Alternation of Fertilizers.

It is to be remembered, withal, that many good farmers would hold that it is best not to mix the nitrogenized compound with the superphosphate at all, but to apply the one this year to the grain crop, and the other to the same field, next year, for turnips or corn or potatoes; or to add one or the other of the materials to moderate dressings of farmyard manure. It would appear that the last-named plan must often be the best. In the case of corn or potatoes, for example, the superphosphate may be put in the hill; while fish-scrap, or oil-cake, or the like, could readily be admixed with the farm-manure by scattering it upon the layers of dung in a "manure-spreader" wagon as a part of the process of loading it.

The idea should be to reinforce the dung in one-sided ways, for on fairly good land there is naturally a large amount of plant-food available for crops, and there will be all the more after a light manuring with dung. But by adding to this general store a quantity of the particular kind of plant-food which the desired crop will be most grateful for, or would have most difficulty in obtaining, it will usually be easy to excite vigorous growth. It has been found, in England, that there are numerous soils which will give abundant crops of wheat or barley when dressed with nothing but an ammonium salt or nitrate of soda, and there is a still larger number of European soils which will give large grain crops when dressed with nitrate of soda and superphosphate of lime, since there is usually enough potash in those old lands to meet the wants of grain-crops. So, too, it is said that nitrate of soda alone will often give great crops of beets, and superphosphate alone large crops of turnips, while potash-salts alone may sometimes be profitably applied to clover-fields, or even occasionally to pastures.

Some experiments made long ago in England, by Mr. Pusey, for the sake of determining how large an amount of farmyard manure could be profitably applied to his land, well illustrate the significance of using superphosphate with dung : —

From the Acre of Land upon which had been put	He harvested Tons of Mangolds.	Increase over No Manure. Tons.
No manure	15½	—
13 tons of farmyard manure	27½	12
26 tons of farmyard manure	28½	13
13 tons of farmyard manure, together with 2 cwt. of superphosphate	36	20½

In England it is said that from 4 to 6 cwt. of superphosphate are often used nowadays upon potatoes, in addition to farmyard manure; or, as an addition to nitrogenized manures and potash salts. If no dung is to be used, 150 lb. of nitrate of soda and

200 lb. of kainit have been recommended as a proper addition to the superphosphate, both for potatoes and for mangolds. When used by itself on turnips, as much as 4 or 5 cwt. of superphosphate are sometimes applied with advantage, though for most soils smaller quantities of this fertilizer are commonly preferred. (See beyond.)

Superphosphates help young Crops.

Superphosphate of lime has often been found to be an effective manure for spring-sown grain, notably for barley, especially when used in connection with active nitrogenous fertilizers or upon land already well charged with useful nitrogen. In England, it has been used especially for turnips, as has been said, and not to any great extent upon winter-wheat. It is said to be no uncommon thing for a dressing of 200 lb. of superphosphate to the acre to yield an increase of five tons of turnips. It is held in England, that, although superphosphates are useful for the turnip-crop at every stage of its development, they are specially valuable at an early period of growth, when, by urging on the young plants, the fertilizer enables them to get beyond the reach of the turnip-fly. It is not that the superphosphate causes seeds to germinate rapidly, — on the contrary, it is liable to retard germination and to injure seeds, — but that, when once fairly up, plants manured with superphosphate grow much more vigorously than those not thus manured, and are soon twice as large as the latter. (Voelcker.) Herein is seen one great advantage which the superphosphates have over certain other phosphatic fertilizers which act more slowly. It may readily happen that a crop can gain comparatively little advantage from a slow acting mineral phosphate, simply because the latter does not give up its components soon enough. It is a matter of the utmost importance that a young crop shall be enabled to obtain an abundant supply of phosphatic food at the critical moment of its greatest need. Aitken found, in his field experiments, that land manured with superphosphate was always cleaner than that to which pulverized insoluble phosphates were applied. He says, "This was probably due to the rapid early growth of the crop, which discouraged the growth of weeds."

Lawes and Gilbert, in seeking to account for the fact that certain crops of potatoes, manured with nothing but superphosphate, had taken up large quantities of potash from the soil, have said,

"It is well known that one special effect of superphosphate of lime, applied to spring-sown crops, is greatly to increase the development of feeding-roots within the surface soil." The case has been reported in England of an old, sour cow-pasture — with a stiff clay subsoil resting on limestone — which, on being drained and top-dressed at the rate of 6 cwt. to the acre, with superphosphate made from bone-meal, speedily became covered with a profusion of white clover and fine grasses. On another part of the same field, where lime was applied as a top-dressing, the improvement of the herbage was much slower and less emphatic. Other experimenters have observed that not super-phosphates alone, but all kinds of assimilable phosphates may cause young plants to grow rapidly. In Germany, Maercker has noticed that on new fields, which have not often been dressed with phosphates, the growth of young sugar-beet plants is apt to be greatly promoted by application of phosphatic fertilizers, while on old fields, already surcharged with phosphates, no noticeable forc-ing effect is produced by new applications.

When certain sour, astringent heaths were brought under culti-vation in France, it was found not only that bone-black was an excellent fertilizer for such land, but that when very small quan-tities (no more than 5 bushels to the acre) of the powdered black were made to adhere to moistened seed-wheat at the time of sowing, good crops could be grown on land where the seed-wheat would not have reproduced itself without such addition, and where applica-tions of lime gave much smaller crops than the bone-black did. (Gasparin.) As bearing somewhat upon this question, it should be said that Petermann has found that plants fertilized with pre-cipitated diphosphate of lime are "earlier," i. e. they vegetate more rapidly than those not manured with a phosphate. In his experiments, spring wheat fed with the diphosphate, and with nitrogen, formed ears and blossomed several days sooner than plants to which nitrogen alone had been applied, or than those which were not manured. He noticed also that sugar-beets manured with the diphosphate vegetated rapidly; and he has urged that the use either of superphosphate of lime, or of the precipitated diphosphate, is an excellent method of preventing any bad effect which might be exerted upon the ripening of sugar-beets by heavy dressings of nitrogenous fertilizers.

In general, phosphatic manures promote the early maturity of

crops, and to this end superphosphates are often applied with
excellent effect to sugar-beets when the seed is drilled in. Since
ripe beets contain more sugar than those which are unripe, one
consequence of the early ripening is that the sugar manufacturer
can the sooner obtain a highly saccharine juice, and it has become
customary in some districts to apply specially heavy dressings of
phosphatic manures to those fields of beets from which the crop
is to be soonest harvested. Conversely, but little of the phosphate
is put upon the fields from which the beets are to be harvested
late in the season. It is because of these results that beet-grow-
ers often say that "phosphates make sugar." (Maercker.) It
is said that something analogous occurs with potatoes also, i. e.
it seems as if potatoes are specially rich in starch when grown on
fields heavily dressed with phosphates; the explanation being
that the crop ripens early and thoroughly.

According to Lawes, "The most prominent effect of superphosphate of lime, when applied to a root-crop, is to cause a
great development of root-fibres, thus enabling the plant to
gather up much more of other food from the soil. It therefore
serves to increase the immediate effect of other manures supplied
with it; also to turn to account accumulations of nitrogen within the
soil, which, if not taken up, would be liable to loss by drainage."
It is to be remarked, however, that Voelcker has observed that
soluble saline matters, such as potash salts and common salt, often
cause Swedish turnips to run to leaf, "though not in all seasons,"
and that this growth of tops at the expense of bulbs occurs
sometimes even when a superphosphate is used in conjunction
with a potash salt.

Phosphates assist Nature.

Voelcker has called attention to the fact that the seeds of plants
naturally contain much phosphoric acid, while soil usually contains very little of it. By putting phosphates within reach of the
young plant, we simply act upon a hint which has been given "by
Nature in the care she takes to provide plants in their earliest
periods of existence with a constituent which possesses so
remarkable an effect in pushing on the young plant." To this
thought may be added the remark of Loew, that inasmuch as
phosphoric acid is a constituent part of the substance (nuclein) of
which the very kernel or nucleus of each plant-cell consists, it is
not strange that phosphates should be stored up in seeds, where

they are essential for the development of the embryo, and for the making of the nuclein which is needed for the formation of cells in the new plant.

On growing the filamentous alga spirogyra — which is a plant of very simple form — in a solution which contained no phosphoric acid, Loew noticed that the cells were crippled, they were in fact much shorter than those grown in solutions which contained phosphates. But according to Klebs such abnormal growth depends on inadequate nourishment of the nuclei of the cells.

In this country, where superphosphates are used for cotton, corn, wheat, and potatoes, they are reputed to do their best service in hastening the growth of young plants. This effect is said to be specially noteworthy in the case of Indian corn, though wheat and potatoes are thought to be somewhat benefited in the same way. In respect to potatoes, it had often been claimed that tubers grown by the use of superphosphate or other artificial fertilizers are fairer and smoother, and less apt to be marred by scabs and scars than those grown on land that has been dressed with farmyard manure. The inference was that worms, insects, or fungi, harbored by the manure, attacked and injured the potatoes. It now appears that this idea is well founded. Scientific experiments have shown that the potato scab is caused by a fungus which may remain in the soil from one year to another, and in manure also, so that the "prejudice" in favor of using artificials for potatoes is really founded in truth. It is now well known that farmyard manure will cause scabby potatoes in case it has come from animals that have been fed with materials charged with the scab-fungus; and it is known that carbonate of lime favors the growth of the fungus. The trouble may be avoided, on new land at least, by washing the seed-tubers with a solution of corrosive sublimate and dressing the land with appropriate artificial fertilizers. Voelcker observed long ago that on light land, mixtures of superphosphate, kainit, and an assimilable nitrogen compound give excellent crops of potatoes.

Superphosphate on Turnips.

The great merit of superphosphate for turnips has been repeatedly illustrated by the experiments of Voelcker. Thus in one instance, on land in high condition which yielded 18 tons of Swedish turnips to the acre without any manure, 4 cwt. of a plain superphosphate made from bone-ash gave 23 tons of roots, i.e. an increase of 5 tons, and this increase was larger than that (4 tons) got by using farmyard manure at the rate of 20 long tons to the acre. Voelcker remarks that, " Having found repeatedly in other experiments that on land in a high state of cultivation mineral superphosphate, rich in soluble phosphate of lime, produced a better root-crop than a heavy dressing of dung, this result did not surprise me."

As regards mangolds, on the other hand, Voelcker has said that " Mineral superphosphate alone appears not to be the kind of manure that should be employed for mangolds on light land." He found, in fact, on rich land which gave 22 tons of mangolds to the acre, without any manure, that 3 cwt. of plain superphosphate brought an increase of less than 2 tons of roots, while a contiguous plot manured with 3 cwt. of the superphosphate and 2 cwt. of kainit bore a crop of more than 29 tons of roots, i. e. there was an increase of 7 tons ; and a mixture of 3 cwt. of the phosphate, 2 cwt. of kainit and 1 cwt. nitrate of soda gave nearly 32 tons of mangolds, which was a better crop than was obtained by means of 20 tons of well-rotted manure.

Very heavy dressings of superphosphate are not infrequently applied to turnips in England ; as much, for example, as 5 to 7 cwt. to the acre. But when used in conjunction with farmyard manure, 3 or 4 cwt. of the fertilizer are there thought to be enough. According to Voelcker, "5 cwt. of good superphosphate appear to be a sufficient dressing for Swedes on rich, light land. Consequently it is a waste of money to apply such large dressings as 8 or 10 cwt." In this country much smaller quantities than the foregoing have often been used, such, for example, as 150 or 200 lb. to the acre ; though latterly larger quantities are not infrequently employed. 500 lb. of superphosphate and 15 to 25 bushels of wood-ashes to the acre have been recommended for potatoes. The superphosphate to be sown in the furrows and the ashes broadcast.

Superphosphates should be applied liberally on good Land.

As a lesson learned through much observation in a fertile district in Germany, Maercker urges that superphosphates should not be administered in homœopathic doses. He holds that quantities smaller than 26 lb. of soluble phosphoric acid to the acre should never be applied, and that, ordinarily, as much as 30 or 40 lb. should be used. For crops like sugar-beets, which need to be highly manured, 50 lb. of soluble phosphoric acid to the acre is a proper and a usual application. But it is to be remembered that heavy dressings of artificials have given their best results on good

land well charged with moisture, i. e. under conditions particularly
favorable for the growth of the crop. Thus in the moist climate
of Scotland, where 50 long tons of Swedes to the acre are harvested
not infrequently, superphosphates are applied much more liberally
than they are at the south of England where nothing like so large
a crop of turnips as is usual in Scotland can be grown in the
generality of years. Even for mangolds, 300 lb. of superphosphate, together with some nitrate of soda, is thought to be an appropriate dressing in Southern England, on land that has not been
dunged very heavily.

Heiden recommends that, in applying superphosphate, it will
be well to maintain a just relation between the amount of phosphoric acid used and that of the nitrogen which is applied, either
in the form of farm-manure or as a commercial fertilizer. Thus,
according to the kind of crop and the condition of the land, he
would apply either 2, 3, 4 or 5 lb. of phosphoric acid for each
and every lb. of nitrogen used.

Superphosphate for Grain.

In some parts of England it has been found that late-sown
barley, or barley grown on land that is out of condition, is much
improved by superphosphate, or better yet by a mixture of equal
parts of superphosphate and guano, applied as a top-dressing, at
the rate of 3 or 4 cwt. to the acre; and an opinion prevails that
barley is much more improved by superphosphate than wheat or
oats are. Voelcker thinks that the fact that barley is often sown
late in the season, and later than the other grains, has some connection with the observation that on late-sown barley superphosphate, applied at the rate of 3 cwt. to the acre, has a strikingly
beneficial effect. He says, the later the barley-crop is put into
the soil, the more beneficial will the application of the superphosphate be found.

According to Mr. Harris, superphosphate is sown quite generally on winter-wheat in Western New York, and also on barley
and oats in the spring, while its use is not so common there upon
maize and potatoes. He is in doubt as to how much this difference in practice may depend upon the superphosphate's giving a
more marked increase in the yield per acre with grain, or upon
the fact that a given weight of increase of grain will sell for more
money than the same weight of Indian corn; but he inclines to the
belief that one prominent reason for the difference may be that

the cost of applying the fertilizer to the grain-land is merely nominal, while it is by no means so easy to apply it to the hilled crops. The drill from which the grain is sown has an attachment for distributing the superphosphate at the same time as the grain. Though not actually mixed with the seeds, the fertilizer drops into the same tubes which deliver the seed, and is sown in the same drill-mark, so that it is deposited where the roots of the young plants can readily find it; whereas, when maize and potatoes are planted in hills, the superphosphate has to be dropped into the hill by hand, and that at a very busy season.

The winter-wheat is sown early in September at the rate of $1\frac{1}{2}$ to $2\frac{1}{4}$ bushels to the acre, together with about 200 lb. (say \$3 worth) of the superphosphate, and if the fertilizer gives an increase of no more than 5 bushels of wheat to the acre, the farmer has usually good reason to be satisfied. Practically, the increase is said to be often much more than 5 bushels.

Here again, with wheat, it is thought that the superphosphate does good service by enabling the young-crop to get a fair start, notably by promoting a vigorous growth of roots in early autumn, so that the plants are better able to find moisture and food than they would have been if less fully equipped, and better fitted to survive a hard winter. By thus saving a crop, which but for the fertilizer would have perished, a couple of hundred pounds of superphosphate may do an amount of good out of all proportion greater than the cost of the material. An impression gains ground withal, that the presence of good phosphates in the soil specially favors the fermentations which convert the inert nitrogen of humus into assimilable plant-food. It is noteworthy, that as used for turnips on the light and shallow chalky and gravelly soils of England, superphosphate of lime may be said to help the crop to assimilate nitrogen from the soil. In the four-course rotation usual upon such land, wheat is sown upon clover-stubble which has been dressed with farmyard manure, so that the turnips which follow the wheat have access to very considerable amounts of nitrogenous vegetable matter which is slowly undergoing decomposition. It is found as a matter of experience that the addition of a phosphatic fertilizer enables the turnips to put the organic nitrogen to better use than they could have done otherwise.

In experiments made by Thorne and Hickman in Ohio, on a drained clay soil, it appeared that plain bone-black superphos-

phate, used by itself, had a marked effect in stimulating an early
and heavy growth of straw. When the superphosphate was used
in conjunction with nitrate of soda, the wheat lodged badly in
rainy seasons, and it seemed as if the superphosphate exerted as
much influence as the nitrate to throw the crop down. When the
nitrate was used by itself and the superphosphate by itself, the
tendency to lodge was not so great; and the crops stood up fairly
well in experiments where nitrate of soda was used at the same
time as powdered phosphate-rock or ground phosphatic slag.

Home-made Superphosphates.

Superphosphate of lime may be made at the farm without difficulty, from bone-black or from bone-ash, but not from bone-
meal. The trouble with the last is, that, when treated with acid,
it forms a sticky, unmanageable mass that can neither be handled
nor spread upon the land. In order to do anything with it, much
trouble has to be taken in mixing the slimy product with dry
earth, or coal-ashes, or gypsum, "to dry it"; but, with the
exception of the gypsum, either of these substances would do
harm in the chemical sense by "fixing" some part of the phosphate
that had been made soluble by the acid. It is said that practically not more than one-third of the phosphoric acid in raw bones
can be dissolved by means of sulphuric acid without making the
product too sticky for convenience.

The following method has been commended as giving perhaps
the best approximation to good results: Pour 50 lb. of oil of vitriol into a volume of water equal to that of the acid, stirring the
water meanwhile with a stick. Pour this diluted acid upon 100
lb. of bone-meal that is contained in a wooden trough, and stir
the meal slowly and carefully with a hoe. The product obtained
in this way admits of being dried, after a fashion, by stirring it
up with earth or with gypsum; but if a larger proportion of acid
were used, the mass would be apt to become so very adhesive as
to be unmanageable.

By using bone-black, however, no such trouble is met with, and
many farmers have prepared excellent superphosphate, with great
economy, by mixing spent bone-black and sulphuric acid, even in
a mere hole in the ground, as has been set forth, for example, in
the Bussey Bulletin, Vol. I, p. 187. Prof. Johnson reports a
similar instance where 100 parts by weight of the bone-black,
having been spread on a mortar-bed and moistened with 42 parts

of water, were treated with 55 parts of strong oil of vitriol, and thoroughly stirred with a hoe. There must have been an unpleasantly tumultuous effervescence in this case, but the product was found to contain 13 % of soluble phosphoric acid after it had been left to itself for a week.

A more methodical and agreeable method of procedure has been formulated by J. R. Nichols, as follows: First make a tank of pine planks, four feet square and one foot deep, and line it with sheet lead. There is no trouble in doing this, for a roll of sheet lead of these dimensions, or a trifle larger, may be bought at the lead-works, and the sheet may be pressed down into the tank-frame, and the metal be allowed to crinkle to suit itself at the corners. Into the finished tank ten gallons of water are poured, and then slowly the contents of a carboy of oil of vitriol (165 lb.), while the contents of the tank are stirred with a stick. Into the acid thus diluted throw gradually from a shovel 380 lb. of spent bone-black from the sugar-refinery. There will be a tolerably violent effervescence, due to the escape of carbonic acid from the carbonate of lime that was contained as an impurity in the bone-black. After the mixture has been left to itself for a couple of hours, it will be dry and fit for use.

This process could be used perfectly well for decomposing bone-ash, and powdered phosphatic guano, or even for finely ground rock-phosphates of good quality. It is to be remembered that bone-ash contains several per cent of carbonate of lime also, which would naturally cause a considerable amount of frothing, as is the case with the bone-black.

Bone-black Superphosphate.

It is as true of the factory as of the farm, that it is particularly easy to make good superphosphates from bone-black. The product has the advantage, moreover, that, when well made, it can be kept indefinitely without undergoing detriment. It was these essential merits of bone-black superphosphates, doubtless, that long ago led many farmers to prefer them to products made from the rock-phosphates. Indeed, it is a well-known fact that, at a time when the making and selling of superphosphates was ill-understood in this country, one or two manufacturers were able to establish a high reputation by simply persisting in using nothing but bone-black as their raw material. They became in some sort masters of the situation, because they could turn out products of constant composition and assured quality, while their competitors were unable to do so. Hence, latterly, the name "dissolved bone-black" has been used to describe this form of superphosphate. Hence, also, the fact that, in some sections of the country, purchasers much prefer to buy black or dark-colored superphosphates, — a prejudice which has sometimes been gratified by the addition of soot or lamp-black to light-colored superphosphates during the process of manufacture. In like manner, spent bone-black is so much more highly esteemed by the manufacturers of fertilizers in this country, than most kinds of rock-phosphate are, that it is said to be sometimes adulterated, before it is sold to them, with inferior kinds of phosphate-rock suitably ground and blackened.

Latterly, it appears to have been somewhat customary for the manufacturers of fertilizers to employ bone-black (or bone-ash) to reinforce their inferior superphosphates made from rock. Probably one way of proceeding is first to treat a quantity of powdered phosphatic rock with an excess of sulphuric acid, in order to render soluble the largest possible amount of the phosphates contained in it, and then to add enough bone-black to neutralize the excess of acid, and to make the product dry and merchantable. Perhaps the good bone-black superphosphates are sometimes mixed directly with superphosphates of inferior quality, in order to bring the latter up to a salable standard of quality, in the same way that the high-grade foreign superphosphates are said to be used. It was reported, at all events, a few years ago, at a time when a depression in business caused many sugar-refiners in this country to suspend their operations, that so little spent bone-black was then procurable that some manufacturers of superphospates had considerable difficulty in maintaining their products in marketable condition.

Waste Acid for making Superphosphates.

It is an interesting circumstance bearing upon the cost, odor, and appearance of many American superphosphates, that they are sometimes made with acid that has already been used for purifying petroleum to fit it for being burned in lamps. When strong sulphuric acid is made to act on partially rectified petroleum, it combines with certain impurities therein contained to form a dense tar-like or pitchy product, called "sludge," which settles beneath the purified oil. If water is added to this sludge after it has been run off from the petroleum, the tarry compounds are decomposed, and much of the sulphuric acid is set free again. A weak, impure sulphuric acid, smelling strongly of petroleum products, is thus obtained, which, under the name of "sludge acid," is used for making superphosphates. Since the sludge acid costs next to nothing, and can hardly be used for any other purpose because of its vile smell, some manufacturers of fertilizers have found their advantage in making use of it. Some part of the peculiar odor of the petroleum products naturally remains attached to the finished fertilizers.

Phosphate and Carbonate of Lime are somewhat Incompatible.

In some cases it may happen that the presence of carbonate of lime in a phosphatic fertilizer, as in bone-ash or bone-black, tends to impair the efficiency of the fertilizer; for carbonate of lime is more soluble than phosphate of lime in carbonic-acid water and dilute acids, and it might protect the phosphate from solution so long as there was any of it left to use up, or, so to say, neutralize the solvent. Warington found that a very small amount of the calcic carbonate, comparatively speaking, was sufficient to prevent the solution of the phosphate. From a mixture of the two substances, carbonic-acid water at first dissolved the carbonate accompanied by only a trace of phosphate; and it was only after the carbonate had been gradually removed that the phosphate freely entered into solution.

The older French writers were accustomed to insist that neither bone-black nor any other phosphate should be applied to fields which had recently been limed. They urged that bone-black is found to be comparatively useless on soils that are naturally calcareous, and argued, as was just now said, that the lime carbonate, by absorbing carbonic acid and the other acids in the soil, will hinder, or even prevent, these solvents from acting upon the phosphates. In point of fact, it has been demonstrated by experiments made in several laboratories, that from a mixture of carbonate and phosphate of lime carbonic acid will dissolve the carbonate of lime first, and will not much act upon the phosphate of lime so long as there is any of the carbonate present. It is to be observed, however, that, in the light of the better knowledge of to-day, these views of the earlier French chemists must be considerably qualified. It is now known that the roots of plants coming in contact with phosphates, even in a limestone soil, can absorb phosphoric acid from them. It is to be presumed, therefore, that, although an actual admixture of carbonate and phosphate of lime, as in bone-black, may be disadvantageous, that is no reason why the farmer should not apply appropriate phosphatic fertilizers to limestone soils for the purpose of charging those soils in all their parts with finely divided phosphate.

In fact, it is a matter of common experience that, on some of the light, chalky soils of England, the effect of superphosphate of lime upon turnips is well-nigh magical. In many localities where it had been thought to be impossible to grow turnips, the introduction of superphosphate enabled the farmers to count upon this crop almost with certainty. There are methodical experiments by Voelcker, and others, which leave no doubt as to this fact. Bone-meal, also, was formerly used very extensively upon chalk-land in England, for all kinds of roots, though superphosphate appears to have superseded it.

It is to be presumed withal, that, while the carbonate of lime, in a calcareous soil, might interfere, to no inconsiderable extent, with the action of bone-black, or bone-ash, or ground rock-phosphate, there could hardly be any such serious interference in the case where superphosphate of lime is put upon a calcareous soil, or upon land which has recently been limed or marled. For into such soils the soluble phosphoric acid of the superphosphate soaks in all directions, and is fixed (and disseminated) as diphosphate of lime, upon which the roots of plants act readily. Indeed, several of the French agricultural chemists of to-day insist — with regard to the application of both phosphate and carbonate of lime — that a great deal depends on the order in which the two fertilizers are put upon the land. They point to the fact that practical experience in the matter of reclaiming sour soils shows that it is best to apply the phosphate to the newly broken land a year before the land is limed, in order to allow time for the organic matter of the soil to react upon the phosphate. They say that, in case the lime were applied before the phosphates, or even at the same time as the phosphate, the acidity of the humus would be so quickly neutralized that there could be very little opportunity for the phosphate to be acted upon. They admit, however, that some farmers are accustomed to apply light dressings of lime soon after the phosphate has been distributed. (Muntz & Girard.)

Phosphate of Lime of the Gelatine-Makers.

In Europe, large quantities of bones are treated every year with muriatic acid for the purpose of obtaining their ossein, as a preliminary step in the manufacture of gelatine. In this case the earthy matter of the bones is actually dissolved out from the ossein by means of weak muriatic acid. The method is applied particularly to horn-piths, and to other bones which expose a large surface for the action of the acid, — notably to the thin waste slices of bone from which buttons have been cut.

To the clear solution of phosphate of lime in muriatic acid thus obtained, enough milk of lime is added to neutralize the acid and precipitate the phosphate of lime. This precipitate, which consists of bone-earth in the form of an exceedingly fine powder, might of course be applied to the land directly, as if it were bone-ash. According to Wolff, it contains on the average, as sold, 19.5 % of phosphoric acid, about 28 % of water, and 1.5 % of nitrogen. But it is an interesting bit of evidence in favor of the use of superphosphates, that the precipitate in question is everywhere treated with sulphuric acid, and so converted into superphosphate before it is sent into commerce.

Enormous quantities of gelatine are made by this method in Europe at the alkali-works, where weak muriatic acid is a drug upon the manufacturers' hands, so that no small quantity of bone-earth is thus dissolved. But I found, some years ago, on visiting many chemical works in Europe, that everywhere in England, France, and Germany the reprecipitated bone-earth was converted into superphosphate, as a matter of course, before it was offered for sale, so thoroughly convinced were the European farmers of the value of soluble phosphoric acid.

Variable Composition of Superphosphates.

The simple fact that milk of lime is used to precipitate the bone-earth from its solution in muriatic acid, as above mentioned, would of itself be sufficient to suggest that the precipitate may vary considerably in composition, according as more or less of the lime-milk is added. Hence, a certain liability to variation in the composition of superphosphates made from such material even.

But this point is as nothing in comparison with the impurity of many of the mineral phosphates from which most superphosphates are now made. In not a few localities there are found considerable quantities of impure phosphate of lime in the form of nodules or concretions, which were at one time called "coprolites," from a supposed resemblance to fossil dung. Occasionally, these nodules may contain as much as 80 % of calcic phosphate, and at other times no more than 10 % ; 30, 40, 50, and 60 % are common proportions. Samples of nodules from the sandstone of the Connecticut River, examined by the late Dr. Dana of Lowell, contained 40 % of phosphates; and specimens from Canada have been found to contain from 40 to 50 %.

As found, however, in the form of the minerals apatite and phosphorite, the proportion of phosphate of lime in pure specimens may amount to 90 %, or even more. Canadian apatite, as sent into commerce, contains some 80 to 86 % of calcic phosphate. This mineral is very compact, however, and hard to grind, and is said to give off much hydrofluoric acid when treated with oil of vitriol.

Inexhaustible beds of phosphorite occur in Spain and Portugal, and those in the province of Estramadura have long been famous. As obtained by the manufacturers of fertilizers, these phosphates contain some 70 to 85 % of phosphate of lime, and they are esteemed because they are comparatively free from compounds of iron and alumina. Phosphate rock from Norway also contains 70 to 90 % of calcic phosphate.

The Nassau phosphorite, which occurs in beds or nests, contains about 65 % of phosphate of lime, or rather from 60 to 70 %, though some samples contain as much as 80 or 90 %. That from South Carolina is said to contain 57 to 60 % as exported. It is easily acted upon by the acid, though rather hard to grind. There are several varieties of Florida phosphate, notably: I. Land or river "pebbles," which contain as exported some 60 or 70 %, occasionally even 80% of phosphate of lime. II. "Rock phosphate," containing 75 to 80 %, of phosphate of lime; and III. Soft phosphate, which sometimes contains as much as 70% of phosphate of lime, but which is apt to be so much contaminated with earthy matters that the percentage of phosphate is not larger than 60 to 65 %. Some samples of Florida phosphates contain much alumina and oxide of iron, though the pebbles ordinarily contain no more than 2 % of these ingredients, while the rock phosphate often contains 6 % or more, and the soft phosphate from 3 to 7 %.

Phosphatic Guanos.

There are certain islands in the Pacific Ocean and in the Caribbean Sea, exposed to abundant rains, where the dung of sea-fowls has accumulated under such conditions that all readily soluble matters have been washed away, while phosphate of lime has been left, sometimes in a state of tolerable purity. In some instances the bird-dung has reacted upon the coral-rock, or other rock of the island, to form masses of stony hardness; in other cases the phosphate has become admixed with much sulphate of lime from the sea-water, and occasionally the material is badly contaminated with compounds of alumina and iron derived from the rocks with which it has been in contact. Generally speaking, these phosphatic guanos, as they are termed, are easily acted upon by acids, and several of them were well-fitted for making high-grade superphosphates. The supply of the best of the phosphatic guanos has been practically exhausted; but at one time, before the invention of double superphosphates, these guanos were important as sources of the best superphosphates then obtainable. Baker Island guano, for example, contained some 65 to 85 % of phosphate of lime (i. e., from 30 to nearly 40 % of P_2O^5), and hardly more than traces of iron and alumina. It seems to have been formed by the reaction of bird-dung on moist coral-sand. So, too, the phosphate from Howland's Island is said to have been nearly as good as that from Baker's. Voelcker's analyses showed 73 to 76 %. An analogous product from Jarvis Island was also good, though it contained more gypsum than that from Baker's. It is said to have contained some 45 to 52 % of phosphate of lime.

On the other hand, the phosphatic guano from Sombrero, in the West Indies, though equally rich in phosphates with that from Jarvis Island, or even richer (for it may contain 70% or more), is less valuable, because it is contaminated with iron and alumina compounds. The Navassa phosphate, also, from an island on the coast of Hayti, which has been a good deal used in this country, is much contaminated with the harmful alumina and iron compounds, although it is often rich in phosphates. It contains sometimes as much as 30 to 35% of phosphoric acid.

Redonda phosphate contains from 20 to 38% of phosphoric acid, or as much as would amount to from 42 to 84% of phosphate of lime, though in reality there is but little lime in this material, the phosphoric acid being combined with alumina.

Mejillones guano contains some 65 to 75 % of phosphate of lime, some of it in the form of diphosphate, and nearly one per cent of nitrogen, and that from Patagonia some 20 or 30% of phosphates and 4½.% of nitrogen. Curaçao guano contains 65 to 73 % of phosphates.

Chemical Analysis essential for discriminating between Super-
phosphates.

The statements given above, as to the varying composition of superphosphates, indicate clearly how important it must be for the farmer who may wish to buy a quantity of this fertilizer, to know beforehand what the chemical composition of the samples submitted to him really is. As a matter of course, all the solid impurities and inert matters that are contained either in the bone or the rock-phosphate used for the manufacture of a superphosphate are left admixed with the finished product, in addition to the gypsum which is necessarily formed by the action of the sulphuric acid. And beside these differences, dependent on the varying composition of the raw materials, the amount of soluble phosphoric acid in the superphosphate is apt to vary widely, according as more or less care and skill have been devoted by the manufacturer to the treatment of the original substance. Even the earliest superphosphates made from bones were found to differ from one another in composition and value, according to the mode of manufacture.

It is, consequently, an absolute necessity that superphosphates must be bought and sold according to their contents of fertilizing matters, as shown by chemical analysis. There is simply no foreshadowing of a suggestion in the external appearance or character of the material as to what may be its real worth, or whether, indeed, it be worth anything. There can be no question that every ton of superphosphate sold in open market should be accompanied with a chemist's certificate of analysis, just as is done when soda-ash, bleaching-powder, and saltpetre are sold.

Moreover, it is the bounden duty of the manufacturers of superphosphate to employ competent analysts to keep the run of the article as manufactured, so that no samples inferior to the standard shall be thrown upon the market.

As matters now stand here in America, there is a wide range, both as to quality and price; and although there have been very great improvements in recent years, there are even now none too many preparations that can be cordially commended. There have been procurable, it is true, for many years, superphosphates made from bone-black that contained from 13 to 16% or more of soluble phosphoric acid, and these products were really excellent. They are still to be had, under the name of dissolved bone-black, or bone-black superphosphate, and there are likewise procurable, nowadays, other products of approved excellence; but, for a long term of years, the general rule in this country seems to have been to add a quantity of cheap fish-scrap to a miserably prepared superphosphate, and to demand a high price for the mixture.

It has always been interesting to observe the absence, in very many cases, of any visible relation between the prices of these so-called superphosphates and the amounts of soluble phosphoric acid contained in them. There are numerous instances on record where products of extremely low value have been sold at specially high rates. It has frequently been noticeable, withal, that some of the very best of the superphosphates, notably those made from bone-black, were offered to the farmers at exceptionally low prices. Apparently, the same conscience and good judgment that led the manufacturer to produce a superior article made him merciful in respect to his desire for pecuniary profit.

Even at the present time, the lack of relation between value and price is sometimes very conspicuous. For example, two specimens of bone-black superphosphate, from different makers but of almost precisely the same composition, analyzed at New Haven some years since, contained respectively —

	A.	B.
Soluble phosphoric acid	17.13	17.29
Insoluble " "	0.09	0.11

But the price at which A was sold was $34½ the ton, while the price of B was $26.

It is absolutely necessary that the buyer shall have some kind of guaranty as to the chemical composition of superphosphates, and of late years it has become somewhat customary in this country to enact special laws for controlling the sale of fertilizers, and to appoint State inspectors of fertilizers, to whom farmers may appeal. This system is still on trial, though open to grave criticism. One fundamental trouble is, that the matters to be inspected are too complex; the subject itself is too occult to be safely given over to a clique of political appointees. It is not here, as it is with the inspection of fish, or lime, or lumber, or potash, where the things to be passed upon are so familiar that there could readily be found, in every community really interested in the subject, scores of people who would be perfectly competent to criticise the doings of the inspector; and, besides, a simpler and a much more equitable way of overcoming the difficulty lies ready at hand. If the large consumers of superphosphates, and the reputable retailers of it, would but refuse to buy except on the strength of a certificate from a responsible chemist; and if the agricultural societies would but pursue any dealer, or any so-called chemist, who plays their members false, a much healthier condition of things than now prevails might doubtless soon be brought about.

The best way to buy fertilizers is by large quantities, and, in order to do that, it will usually be necessary for a number of farmers to combine. It is not essential for the success of a club of this kind, that its members should be neighbors. All is, they must constitute for the moment one of their number "Agent and Treasurer," and let him deal with the manufacturers and sellers of fertilizers, and with the analysts also.

Each member of the club will submit a statement of the number of tons of fertilizers he wishes to buy, and the agent will make the necessary inquiries as to the best place to buy. In order to get this information, he will not only compare prices and samples, but will have analyses made of the samples that attract him.

He will buy large lots of the best manures he can find; that is to say, amounts equal to the sums of all the separate lots which the members of his club have asked for; and he will have the materials sent from the manufactory to the persons who have asked for them. Of course, there will have to be a clear understanding that the fertilizers shall have such and such composition. After they have come into the possession of the club, samples would naturally be drawn by lot, here and there, and subjected to analysis in order to make sure that the matters are what they purport to be, and that there may be no chance for fraud.

A system similar to this was at one time not unusual in England, and it has, indeed, often been put in practice in this country for the purpose of bringing cargoes of lime, or ashes, or leached ashes, or grain, to a township, either by ship or by rail; but our farmers have hitherto known so little of chemistry, that they have lacked that confidence in themselves, and in one another, which would be necessary if they were to deal in superphosphates successfully in this way.

Reverted Phosphate.

There are three different phosphates of lime familiarly known to agricultural chemists; viz., the triphosphate, such as is found in bones and in phosphatic minerals; the monophosphate, or soluble phosphate, or superphosphate, above described; and, intermediate between the two, there is a third kind, called biphosphate of lime, or dicalcic phosphate. The differences in composition between these three phosphates will appear from the following table.

| Name | Symbol. | Composition in Terms of Molecular Weights. | | | | Per Cent. | | |
		Lime.	Water.	Phosp. Acid.	Total.	Lime.	Water.	Phosp. Acid.
Tri- or bone phosphate	$3\,CaO, P_2O_5$	168	0	142	310	54.19	0.00	45.81
Bi- or di-phosphate	$2\,CaO, H_2O, P_2O_5$	112	18	142	272	41.18	6.61	52.21
Mono- or super-phosphate	$CaO, 2\,H_2O, P_2O_5$	56	36	142	234	23.93	15.39	60.68

One great trouble in respect to superphosphates is, that most of them cannot be kept for any great length of time without suffering deterioration. The soluble phosphoric acid contained in them is liable to "go back," as the term is, or to "revert," as is sometimes said, to an insoluble state.

The causes of this reversion are twofold. First, in making a superphosphate, it is hard to hit the precise point where the whole of the bone phosphate ($3\,CaO, P_2O_5$) has been converted to soluble phosphate ($CaO, 2\,H_2O, P_2O_5$) without using an excess of the sulphuric acid. But the presence of an excess of sulphuric acid is objectionable on many accounts, so that practically the manufacturers lean to the other alternative, and take care to use a little less sulphuric acid than would be needed to decompose every particle of the bone phosphate. Or, in cases where it is advisable to employ an excess of the sulphuric acid at first, they are at pains to "dry" the product, as the term is, by adding to it bone-black, or bone-ash, or the precipitated phosphate of the gelatine makers, either of which would use up the free sulphuric acid. Thus it happens that the soluble phosphate, which has been formed at first by the action of the sulphuric acid, finds itself in presence of a certain quantity of undecomposed bone-phosphate of lime, and in the course of time the two phosphates react upon each other, with formation of the intermediate compound, the so-called bi- or di-phosphate of lime :—

$$3\,CaO, P_2O_5 + CaO, 2\,H_2O, P_2O_5 = 2\,(2\,CaO, H_2O, P_2O_5).$$

That is to say, for every molecule of bone-phosphate that has been left undecomposed, one molecule of the soluble phosphate is made to revert to an insoluble state.

In case the original materials are tolerably pure, as when bone-ash, or bone-black, or a first-rate rock phosphate, such as Baker Island guano, have been used for making the superphosphate, there is no inherent necessity that the reversion of the soluble phosphoric acid should amount to much. Of course there may be trouble if the manufacturer is careless or ignorant. If he fails to decompose the chief part of the bone-phosphate which he has treated with sulphuric acid, the subsequent reversion will be large, and the depreciation in the value of the fertilizer will be serious. But if pains be taken to decompose the bone phosphate pretty thoroughly in the first instance, the subsequent reversion cannot be large. As was said just now, each molecule of the undecomposed bone-phosphate can only decompose one molecule of the soluble phosphate, and when that has been done the action ceases. Manifestly, if but little bone phosphate has been left undecomposed by the manufacturer, there will be but little reversion of the soluble product. All this applies, however, only to the case where pure materials have been operated upon.

Impurities may cause Reversion.

There is another cause of reversion, far less simple in theory and much more serious in its effects, which depends upon the presence of impurities, such as compounds of iron and alumina, in the natural phosphatic rocks, from which superphosphates are chiefly prepared nowadays. The difficulty here is that so long as the manufacturer uses the impure materials for making superphosphate in the ordinary way, he cannot avoid the reversion, no matter how careful or skilful he may be.

Just what the reactions are which are produced by the iron and alumina compounds has never been made out very clearly. But some idea of them may be gained from the following suggestions, which were thrown out by Patterson. Suppose the sulphuric acid has dissolved a quantity of iron or alumina, then we may have the reaction —

$$Fe_2O_3, 3SO_3 + CaO, 2H_2O, P_2O_5 = Fe_2O_3, P_2O_5 + CaO, SO_3 + 2(H_2O, SO_3),$$

and the free acid thus formed would proceed to dissolve more iron or alumina from the rock that had previously escaped decomposition, and the reaction here formulated would occur again and again. Here we have a cumulative process continually increasing the quantity of insoluble Fe_2O_3, P_2O_5, and diminishing in the same proportion the soluble P_2O_5. Again, we might have simply

$$2 Fe_2O_3 + 3 (CaO, 2 H_2O, P_2O_5) = 2 (Fe_2O_3, P_2O_5) + 3 CaO, P_2O_5;$$

where 3 molecules of the soluble phosphoric acid are made to revert to the insoluble state at one blow.

In case the iron in the original rock were in the state of ferrous oxide, perhaps the following reaction might occur : —

$$4 (FeO, SO_3) + 2 O + CaO, 2 H_2O, P_2O_5 + 3 CaO, P_2O_5 =$$
$$2 (Fe_2O_3, P_2O_5) + 4 (CaO, SO_3).$$

In all these equations, except the last, alumina would serve as well as oxide of iron.

The bone phosphate of lime precipitated in the second of the foregoing equations would manifestly react in its turn upon a new molecule of the soluble phosphate in the manner described before.

But even supposing no biphosphate of lime $(2 CaO, H_2O, P_2O_5)$ were formed, but only Fe_2O_3, P_2O_5 or Al_2O_3, P_2O_5, these last would still represent reversion of soluble phosphoric acid, and reversion of the worst kind, for the alumina and the iron phosphates are notoriously insoluble, and they are worth less than biphosphate of lime when applied as fertilizers. There is a kind of phosphatic-guano or phosphate-rock from the West Indies, called Redonda phosphate, that contains naturally a large proportion of phosphate of alumina, but for many years this material was reputed to be worthless for agricultural purposes. No doubt it could be used in many situations, but it is none the less true that it is on the whole inferior to phosphate of lime.

Valuation of Reverted Phosphoric Acid.

It may here be said, that many disputes have arisen among chemists as to what value should be allowed for the reverted phosphoric acid in superphosphates, as compared with that of the soluble phosphoric acid and that of the original undecomposed bone-phosphate. According to Ritthausen and others, this same reverted phosphate of lime is the substance which is formed in the soil when the phosphoric acid of a superphosphate is fixed there; and it is a well-known fact that the reverted or biphosphate $(2 CaO, H_2O, P_2O_5)$, though well-nigh insoluble in water, is considerably more soluble in carbonic-acid water and in saline solutions than ordinary bone-phosphate is. There can be no question that it is an easily assimilable fertilizer. On the other hand, Lawes and Gilbert have observed that the best action of a superphosphate is to be got in the first year of its application, and that the compounds left by it in the soil have comparatively little effect after they have lain in contact with the earth during several years. Thus, in their experiments on potatoes, where superphosphate of lime and barnyard manure were applied together during 7 years, crops of 5 tons and 12 cwt. of tubers were harvested per year and per acre during 6 years, on the average. But on ceasing to apply the superphosphate, while the dressings of dung were continued, the average crop of potatoes was reduced to 4 tons and 5 cwt. as the average of 5 years, whence they conclude that " the residue of the superphosphate had comparatively little effect; and that, in fact, it remained within the soil in a condition only slowly available."

In view of the undoubted value of the biphosphate when properly managed by itself, it has been argued by some chemists that, in estimating the merchantable value of a superphosphate, any reverted phosphate which may be found in it should not be classed in the same category with the undecomposed triphosphate, but that a somewhat higher value should be allowed for it. The dealers in fertilizers generally stand by one another in maintaining that a price intermediate between the prices of soluble phosphoric acid and of insoluble bone-phosphate should be allowed for the reerted phosphate. Thus, when soluble phosphoric acid was held to be worth 13 cents per pound, and the acid in insoluble bone-ash phosphate to be worth 5 cents, they claimed that the reverted phosphoric acid was worth 8 or 9 cents per pound.

There are several methods, it should be said, of estimating the quantity of the reverted phosphoric acid in a superphosphate. One of the commonest of these methods is as follows: After the soluble phosphoric acid has been dissolved out from the superphosphate by means of cold water, the residue is treated with a solution of ammonium citrate, which dissolves the reverted phosphate; and, finally, the residue from the citrate leaching is treated with a strong acid, such as muriatic acid, in order to obtain that portion of the phosphoric acid which was neither soluble in water nor in the citrate of ammonium.

On looking at the matter, however, from the point of view of an instructed farmer, it is not easy to find any real and permanent basis for the assumption that the price paid for reverted phosphoric acid in a superphosphate should be much if any higher than the price ordinarily paid for insoluble phosphoric acid in the form of bone-meal.

It would have been difficult, in fact, to find evidence that the price of 8 or 9 cents a pound, so often allowed formerly for the reverted phosphoric acid in a superphosphate, had any justification whatsoever. There is but one criterion by which to appraise any chemical fertilizer, and that is by asking and answering the simple commercial question, What can this particular chemical substance be bought for in its cheapest form?

Now, as for biphosphate of lime, that is to say, reverted phosphate of lime, this substance is prepared in Europe, in a condition of almost absolute purity, and it could undoubtedly be imported, either from England or from the Continent, at small cost. In Europe, the price of this precipitated phosphate is controlled by the price of bone-ash, and the market value of a pound of phosphoric acid, in the form of the precipitated phosphate, is very nearly the same that it is when taken in the form of bone-ash. As was said before, a somewhat less pure form of precipitated phosphate of lime has, for many years past, been made in England, France and Germany in no inconsiderable quantities, as a product incidental to the manufacture of gelatine from bones; which is a branch of industry of whose importance, particularly to the wine-growing regions, few Americans have any just idea.

This precipitated phosphate of the gelatine makers is bought by the manufacturers of superphosphate as a substitute for bone-ash, and of course for an analogous price. When properly made, i. e., when it has been prepared with due precautions, and has been washed free from adhering acid and calcium chloride, this precipitated phosphate has undoubtedly an intrinsic agricultural value of its own. It might be applied directly to the soil, and would produce useful effects in many instances when so applied. It has, in fact, been tried in this way often enough in Europe, especially in the early days when fertilizers were less abundant than they are now, and the very fact that it is no longer bought by the farmers, but by superphosphate makers, shows that for general use it has been unable to compete with superphosphate of lime. The story is the same as that of bone-ash, bone-black, and the phosphatic guanos; each of these substances has been beaten in the race which they held long ago against the superphosphates.

It appears to have been proved conclusively, by practical experience, that neither of these substances has so wide a range of
applicability as the superphosphates. No one of them can be
profitably applied to so many kinds of soils, and to so great a
variety of crops, as the superphosphates; though, as has been repeatedly urged already, there are doubtless special cases and situations, notably on sandy and peaty soils, where one or another
of them should be preferred to the more costly soluble product.

Diphosphate of Lime is Valuable.

It must be freely admitted that on some soils the precipitated
dicalcic phosphate has approved itself to be an excellent fertilizer,
and instances are not wanting where it has done better service than
superphosphate. These facts have been illustrated by the experiments of many different chemists. For example, Petermann grew
oats in pots, some of which were filled with a poor, sandy soil,
and others with a good, sandy-clay loam, and in both instances
got as much grain, and as much straw, when precipitated diphosphate of lime was used as a fertilizer, as when superphosphate
was used. Similar results were obtained when peas and barley
were grown in the loam. On repeating the experiments, with both
kinds of soils, with spring wheat, and adding sulphate of ammonia to each of the pots, in order to supply an abundance of nitrogenous food, as good crops were got from pure precipitated phosphates of lime, iron, and alumina, as from superphosphate of
lime. All the phosphate crops in these experiments were better
than those got from unmanured soil, or from soils fertilized with
nothing but sulphate of ammonia.

It should be said, however, that these results were naturally to
have been expected, in view of the highly favorable conditions in
respect to thorough distribution of the fertilizers, and to abundant
waterings. For that matter, the results do not differ materially
from those obtained by other observers who have experimented in
a similar way with rock-phosphates. Horse-beans, grown by Petermann in a garden, and in a field of sandy-clay loam, gave as
good crops, when dressed with precipitated diphosphate of lime,
as when dressed with superphosphate. In both cases, the cro p
were decidedly better than those obtained from adjoining land, to
which no phosphate had been added.

Dehérain has remarked, with much truth, that, for non-calcareous soils which have long been highly cultivated, precipitated

phosphate, or even powdered phosphatic slag, may be a better fertilizer than superphosphate; while in regions of highly cultivated calcareous soils, superphosphates are much to be preferred to any other kind of phosphatic fertilizer. On such soils, true superphosphate may be used to good advantage in connection with barnyard manure, especially where the soils contain but a small proportion of phosphates naturally.

On the other hand, Petermann has argued that, on calcareous soils, precipitated diphosphate of lime will be likely to do better service than a superphosphate, because the diphosphate, when incorporated with the soil, will remain there undecomposed for a long time, while much of the soluble phosphoric acid of the superphosphate will be precipitated in the form of triphosphate of lime on coming in contact with the great excess of carbonate of lime in the soil. But triphosphate of lime is less soluble than the diphosphate, and is presumably less readily assimilated by plants.

Petermann has even gone so far as to suggest that on some kinds of clayey and sandy soils, poor in lime, but rich in active compounds of alumina and oxide of iron, diphosphate of lime worked into the land may remain there undecomposed for a long while, comparatively speaking, and may act powerfully as a fertilizer, where the soluble phosphoric acid of a superphosphate would quickly be converted to insoluble phosphates of iron and alumina. Hence the importance of testing upon many farms, and on different fields, the question whether a superphosphate or the diphosphate is the better fertilizer for use in each particular locality.

Kellner has studied this question in Japan, both in respect to rice grown on low-lying irrigated land, and as regards a succession of upland crops, viz., barley, millet, wheat and buckwheat, grown on a soil that did not suffer from any lack of water. The soil consisted in both cases of sand admixed with volcanic ashes. It was a light ferruginous loam, of dark-brown color, rich in humus. Though readily permeable, the capacity of the soil to hold water was high. It contained very little lime and had a slight acid reaction, but was unusually rich in silicates of iron and alumina that were easily soluble in acids, hence its power to fix soluble phosphoric acid was very great. On applying superphosphates to this land, so much of the soluble phosphoric acid was speedily absorbed and rendered inactive that the fertilizer did its best service only in the first year. It did not exhibit much endurance, and soon fell to the same level as raw bone-meal. Yet it appeared that a precipitated phosphate which consisted chiefly of diphosphate of lime was a less active fertilizer than superphosphate, evidently because its distribution in the soil was less complete. On the low land indeed the precipitated phosphate helped the rice-crop more than superphosphate did, even in the first year. It was remarked, however, that in tilling the rice-land all the fertilizers were mixed very intimately with the muddy soil and that the precipitated phosphate was here much more evenly distributed than was possible with the dry upland soil.

The following table gives the results obtained by Kellner and his pupils in experiments made to test the merit of various phosphatic fertilizers as applied to rice. Each of the plots received sulphate of ammonia and carbonate of potash in addition to the phosphate : —

Kind of Phosphate.	Increase of crop in two years for each 100 grm. of P_2O_5 Grm.	Relative increase of the rice-crop.	Relative amts. of P_2O_5 taken up by the crop.	Relative fertilizing value.
Double superphosphate . . .	7044	100	100	100
Precipitated phosphate . . .	7758	110.7	115.2	113
Steamed bone-meal	5388	76.5	70.6	74
Raw bone-meal	5228	74.2	73.0	74
Phosphatic slag	5025	71.2	72.0	72
Peru guano	3845	54.6	50.2	52
Bone-ash	2309	32.6	33.7	33
Phosphorit (rock phosphate) floats	1394	18.3	13.6	16

For the experiments with the upland crops, the soil received additions of carbonate of lime, sulphate of potash and sulphate of ammonia, beside the several phosphates. Here, the double superphosphate gave better results than the precipitated phosphate. The results obtained with the first crop (winter barley) were as follows : —

Kind of Phosphate.	Relative increase of the barley crop.	Relative amts. of P_2O_5 taken up by the crop.	Relative fertilising value.
Double superphosphate	100	100	100
Steamed bone-meal	80	77	79
Precipitated phosphate	60	64	62
Raw bone-meal (freed from fat) . .	55	58	56
Raw crushed bones	54	59	56
Phosphatic slag	49	61	55
Bone-ash	20	23	21

On the crops which followed the barley, each of the several

kinds of phosphates exerted an appreciable influence, though their fertilizing power depreciated gradually after the second crop. As to the rate or rapidity of the depreciation, no great differences were observed, and the several phosphates continued to bear very nearly the same relations to each other that were exhibited at the beginning. It was noticed, however, that the after-effect of the raw bone was decidedly stronger than that of the other fertilizers, thanks no doubt to the fact that the raw bone must long have remained subject to processes of decay and putrefaction in the soil. When all four crops were taken into the account, it appeared that raw crushed bone gave a higher total effect than either of the bone-meals, and that in this point of view the steamed bone-meal was inferior to the raw meal.

It was intimated long ago by Voelcker that precipitated phosphate may be a better fertilizer than superphosphate or than bone-meal in certain cases. He urged as a fact of observation, that on sandy soils in England, and on all soils deficient in lime, heavy dressings of superphosphates rich in soluble phosphoric acid do not produce on root-crops effects nearly so beneficial as are produced by them on soils that are somewhat strongly calcareous, or on soils which contain even a moderate proportion of lime. When applied to root-crops upon sandy soils greatly deficient in lime, a concentrated superphosphate may produce a smaller crop than a fertilizer containing only a quarter as much soluble phosphoric acid. The experience of light-land farmers in England, he says, in districts were the soil is deficient in lime, goes to prove that on land of that description it is better to apply to root-crops bone-dust, or precipitated phosphate, or phosphatic manures containing no soluble phosphoric acid. But, since the nitrogen in bone-meal is notoriously inefficient on dry, light land, it may perhaps be true that upon such land the precipitated phosphate, used in conjunction with dung, will serve as good a fertilizing purpose as bone-meal, or possibly do better than bone-meal, while it would practically be preferable to bone-meal because its first cost is less. So too on reclaimed bogs and moorland, the precipitated phosphate, especially when in the form of cheap phosphatic slag might well be preferable to any other kind. It is not improbable, indeed, that as a general rule pure precipitated phosphate may really be a better fertilizer than superphosphate on sandy soils and on moorland.

Precipitated Phosphate cheaper than Superphosphate.

So long as the prominent processes of chemical manufacturing industry remain as they are now, there will always be one fundamental reason why phosphoric acid in the form of precipitated (i. e. reverted) phosphate of lime must necessarily be cheaper than phosphoric acid in the form of superphosphate. For the dilute muriatic acid which collects as an incidental waste product at the great alkali works in Europe can readily be employed for preparing precipitated phosphate of lime from inferior rock phosphates which are so poor and impure that they could not economically be used directly for making superphosphate. If need were, the precipitated phosphate could doubtless be profitably prepared in this way, and sold at a price but little if any higher than the cost of bone-ash.

Not only by the use of waste muriatic acid, but in several other ways, has it been proposed in Europe to prepare pure precipitated phosphate of lime in unlimited quantities from phosphatic rocks that are so impure that they cannot profitably be used directly for making superphosphates, and some of the methods suggested are so manifestly judicious that they must eventually be put in practice, even if they have not come into use already (as seems probable), so that there need be no difficulty in getting all the reverted phosphate any one may wish for, in a state of purity and at a low price. Moreover, very abundant supplies of extremely cheap, impure, reverted phosphate are obtainable in the form of a phosphatic slag which forms in the manufacture of steel from certain kinds of pig-iron, as will be explained directly.

Means of making Reverted Phosphate.

Indeed, there are several ready methods by means of which any one could make the precipitated phosphate in case he should wish to do so for purposes of experiment or comparison. Thus, if a true superphosphate be mixed with slaked lime, or wood ashes, or leached ashes, or, better yet, with bone-black or bone-ash, the soluble phosphoric acid will be made to revert, and the cost of each pound of the product will be small in case bone-black or bone-ash has been used as the precipitant.

Each man must decide for himself as to whether this method of procedure seems to him judicious. The superphosphate has been prepared with toil and trouble, and the proposition is, that it shall be destroyed without ever giving it opportunity to do the work for which it was especially fitted.

There is still another way of looking at the matter, viz., the presence of either reverted or insoluble phosphoric acid in a superphosphate is, from the farmer's point of view, a mere impertinence. He has no use for either of these substances in this particular connection. They are merely in his way; they tend to interfere with his plans and calculations, and the selling of them thus admixed with soluble phosphoric acid is a practice that should be discouraged on many accounts.

Soluble phosphoric acid has its own peculiar part to play; the superphosphate is bought in order to get the soluble phosphoric acid that is contained in it, and the farmer has no use for any more insoluble phosphoric acid of any kind in this particular case than is supplied by the decomposition of the superphosphate in the soil.

But why is it, if the reverted or biphosphate of lime has some fertilizing power, that the presence of it in a superphosphate is undesirable? This point is well worthy of being considered in some detail. As has been said already, the evidence which has been accumulated by chemical investigators indicates clearly that soluble compounds of phosphoric acid change to insoluble forms after they have soaked into the earth. The only reason why phosphoric acid is ever used in the soluble form is to insure its thorough distribution in the soil, so that, after the precipitation of the phosphate, the roots of plants may everywhere find a little of their phosphatic food.

It is just as easy to scatter a superphosphate upon the land in the first place, as has already been insisted, as it is to scatter bone-meal; and the same remark will apply to the processes of tillage by which the fertilizers are incorporated with the earth. So far as mere mechanical distribution goes, the farmer can do as well with bone-meal as with a superphosphate, and with a superphosphate as with bone-meal. It is after the mechanical distribution has been completed that the distribution which depends upon the solubility of the soluble phosphoric acid of the superphosphate comes into play; and that this supplementary chemical distribution is real, and highly efficient, has been proved by the experiments of many chemists.

It is plain that, at the points where the solid particles of a superphosphate have actually touched the earth, there will be some phosphoric acid left in any event. Some phosphoric acid will remain there in the insoluble form, anyway, and the chances are that a good deal more will be left there than will be left in those other parts of the soil to which the acid has been carried only by way of solution.

At the points where the superphosphate fell upon the earth during its mechanical distribution, some phosphoric acid will be fixed — as it would be in any other part of the soil — by means of compounds of lime, iron, and alumina, with which the fertilizer comes into contact there; and since there is a larger quantity of phosphoric acid "in action" at these points than at any other place, the chances are that more of the acid will be fixed there than anywhere else.

But there is another and a very important matter to be considered in this connection, and that is the insoluble phosphoric acid originally present in the superphosphate. Since superphosphates are never absolutely pure, it must always happen that the soil, wherever the particles of superphosphate fall, will receive this amount of insoluble phosphoric acid also, in addition to what is fixed there by chemical action.

Now if, perchance, it should happen that a crop could put to profit more phosphoric acid, at these points of mechanical contact, than it actually finds there, the inference is plain that this crop would undoubtedly have made good use of more phosphoric acid in all parts of the soil than it got; whence the final conclusion that the application of soluble phosphoric acid should have been larger.

But, on the other hand, if it were really desirable to increase the amount of phosphoric acid at the points of mechanical contact, i. e. at the surface of the soil, that could be done readily enough by mechanical means. This result could be accomplished by scattering, in addition to the true superphosphate, some bone-meal by itself, or some of the precipitated phosphate of the gelatine makers, that had been bought as such, or some phosphatic slag.

So far as this particular point is concerned, there would assuredly be no sense in the farmer's paying for the labor and skill, and other costs of manufacture, that must of necessity be expended in the preparation of a superphosphate, when the purpose he has in view can be accomplished by simpler means. Just so much of his purpose as can be accomplished by the simpler means should be so accomplished, as a matter of course. If, by using a certain proportion of bone-meal, or of the cheap precipitated phosphate, he can do away with the need of buying a large amount of super-phosphate, well; but let him not delude himself with the thought that his purpose can be more cheaply accomplished by means of a poor reverted superphosphate.

In view of these considerations, it is not easy to escape the con-viction that the precipitated phosphoric acid in a superphosphate is worth no more to the farmer than the same amount of the acid would be in the form of bone-meal, or of precipitated phosphate of lime, or even in that of ground phosphatic slag.

Whether it is ever worth the farmer's while to use any precipi-tated or other insoluble form of phosphoric acid in connection with a superphosphate, is a question that can only be determined by long-continued intelligent observation and experimentation in the field. As bearing upon this question, it is to be noted that it was at one time customary, in some English localities, for farmers to mix moistened crushed bones with freshly prepared mineral super-phosphate, in order to obtain a substitute for the "bone-super-phosphate" of former days, for use upon turnips. Heaps of the mixture were allowed to "ferment" during several months before the product was applied to the land. Other farmers, who were at one time accustomed to dress permanent pastures every fourth year with 7 or 8 cwt. of boiled bones to the acre, found that good results were obtained by mixing the bone with mineral super-phosphate.

It may be accepted as a fact, that the reverted phosphate is more readily soluble in carbonic-acid water than bone-ash is; and it is probably true that the reverted phosphate will be dissolved by the acids of plant roots that come in contact with it much more readily than powdered phosphate-rock would be dissolved. But all this is no reason why the stuff should be bought at a high price in a su-perphosphate, when it can be procured on more reasonable terms elsewhere.

Reverted Phosphate in some Iron Slags.

Of late years, the discussion of the question, What price should be put upon reverted phosphoric acid? has lost a part of its former interest since vast quantities of an impure variety of this com-pound have been made accessible to the farmer, at very cheap rates, in the form of phosphatic slag. There is, indeed, nowa-days, no justification whatsoever for putting a high valuation upon the reverted phosphate in a superphosphate, for in recent years enormous quantities of it are found in the slags which are obtained as a product incidental to the purification of pig-iron by the so-called basic process invented by Thomas. It is a matter of old experience that many iron-ores contain small proportions of phosphates. In Great Britain, for example, about 85% of the known deposits of iron ore are contaminated with more than one part of phosphorus to every thousand parts of iron. When these ores are smelted, practically the whole of the phosphorus of the ore remains in the pig-iron, and it was long a matter of no little difficulty to convert such iron to steel. It was not easy to remove the phosphorus by the old methods of procedure, and it was inadmissible to leave phosphorus in steel, for phosphoric steel is brittle, or, as the technical term is, " cold short."

Nowadays, phosphoric pig-iron can readily be converted into excellent steel and ingot iron by means of the Thomas process. To this end, a quantity of melted pig-iron is run into a "converter," which has been lined with strongly ignited magnesian limestone, and a powerful blast of air is forced into and through the molten metal. At the beginning of the "blow," as much lime as will amount to 15 or 20% of the weight of the iron is thrown into the converter, together with a certain amount of iron ore (oxide of iron). The oxygen of the air acts to oxidize the impurities of the pig-iron. All the silicon, for example, in the iron is speedily changed to silica, while four-fifths of the phosphorus are oxidized to phosphoric acid, and these products unite with the lime to form a slag, or cinder, which floats upon the melted steel.

Beside phosphate of lime and silicate of lime, the "Thomas-slag" naturally contains much quicklime, since a large excess of this substance was thrown in upon the iron. Hence the name "basic cinder," which is sometimes applied to it. In addition to the lime, it contains ferrous and ferric oxides, and fragments of iron and steel. Those portions of the slag which flow off from the molten iron at the beginning of the "blow" are apt to contain a particularly large proportion of uncombined lime; and this highly alkaline product quickly slakes, and falls to a coarse powder when it is left in contact with the air. But, towards the close of the operation, the slag contains more phosphate and silicate of lime than at first, and does not so readily undergo change when left in the air. In any event, the slag has to be freed from particles of steel by processes of sifting and grinding. That which has slaked in the air might be applied directly, without being ground, to land in the vicinity of the works where it is made, especially to sour land, and to land that stands in need of being limed, though it might be well in some places to allow time for the oxidation of ferrous compounds in the slag before sowing seeds after the application of it to the land. But, ordinarily, it is best to use the slag only after it has been ground to a fine powder.

The slag is unfit for making merchantable superphosphate, because of the large amount of iron-oxide which it contains. A superphosphate made by treating the slag directly with sulphuric acid would speedily "revert;" though perhaps there may be cases where it would be advantageous to drench the powdered slag with sulphuric acid at the farm, and to apply the mixture to the land as soon as it was dry enough. Stocklasa has, in fact, obtained good results by operating in this way. Several schemes have been proposed for treating the slag in such wise that pure phosphate of lime or alkaline phosphates may be obtained from it, though it is doubtful whether these products might not be obtained more cheaply from other materials.

The slag is liable to vary considerably as to its composition, according to the amount of phosphorus in the iron operated upon, and to the methods of treatment. Ordinarily, nearly 50% of lime may be counted upon, and about 20% of phosphoric acid.

Occasionally only a small part of the phosphoric acid in the slag is soluble in ammonium citrate, and sometimes none at all, though usually as much as one-half, or even the whole, of the phosphoric acid dissolves in the ammonium citrate. The slag usually contains some 20% of the oxides of iron and manganese, as well as 6 or 8% of silica, beside other matters. Ordinarily, it contains from 19 to 20-odd per cent of phosphoric acid, though quantities of this constituent, varying from 12% to more than 20%, have been found in different samples of the unadulterated material. But it is said in Europe, that, after having been ground to powder, the slag is often sophisticated by the admixture of Redonda-phosphate (phosphate of alumina), or of ground phosphate-rock, and these adulterated samples not infrequently show a high percentage of phosphoric acid on analysis.

Cheapness of Phosphatic Slag.

The amount of phosphoric acid now obtainable in the form of this slag is something enormous, for the process of purification has been applied not only to the treatment of ordinary pig-iron, but has led to the smelting of vast quantities of phosphatic iron-ore, such as was formerly well-nigh worthless, but is now held in high esteem. In 1889, more than 2,200,000 tons of steel were made yearly by this process in Europe, and there were produced some 700,000 tons of slag, containing as much phosphoric acid as would amount to about 36% of bone-phosphate of lime. In Germany and Austria, nearly one and a half million tons of steel were made in this way in 1889; and on the supposition that the pig-iron contained 1.5% of phosphorus, there would result a hundred millions of pounds of phosphoric acid. At a single factory, where one hundred and seventy-six million pounds of iron were worked, the product of phosphoric acid in the slag was rated at twelve million pounds. As long ago as 1886, Meyer estimated that some 45,000 cwt. of phosphoric acid a month were produced in Germany, in the form of phosphatic slag. In 1889, Thoms asserted that almost one-third of the phosphoric acid needed in German agriculture was even then supplied in the form of phosphatic slag.

When ground to an extremely fine powder, the slag is often found to give useful results in field-practice; much better results, for example, than have ordinarly been obtained by using ground rock-phosphates. It may even be said, now that the cheap phosphatic slag can be procured in abundance, that the old question whether ground phosphate-rock (floats) should sometimes be applied directly to the soil has lost much of its significance. Cases must still occur, occasionally, where it will be well to use the powdered rock from South Carolina and Florida, because of its extreme cheapness; but, as a general rule, it is to be presumed that the finely powdered slag will be able to do better service than the floats. There are numberless experiments which point to this conclusion. The importance of thorough pulverization is illustrated by experiments of Wagner, who is said to have found that if the benefit got from superphosphate is rated as equal to 100, that from finely powdered slag was 61, while that from ground slag was 58, and that from crushed slag only 13.

The slag may be regarded as a useful fertilizer on soils which are benefited by the better kinds of phosphatic fertilizers, especially, perhaps, upon those which are somewhat sour, and which would be helped by being limed; but usually it will be well to apply it in rather large quantities,—perhaps twice as large as the amounts of superphosphate which are ordinarily used. In order to avoid annoyance from dust, when the finely powdered slag is strewn, it may be sprinkled beforehand with water, applied by means of a gardener's watering-pot, at the rate of something like a gallon of water to each hundredweight of the slag. Since the slag is very heavy, it is not easy to strew it evenly unless it has been mixed with dry earth or some other diluent.

On drained moorland, in Germany, highly remunerative results have been obtained by employing a mixture of kainit and phosphatic slag upon fields of mixed grass and clover. The directions are, to apply 5 cwt. of kainit and 2 cwt. of the phosphatic slag, in the first year, to each Morgen of land, and subsequently to apply at least 3 cwt. of kainit and 0.75 cwt. of the powdered slag per annum. Under this treatment, the hay-crops obtain an abundance of nitrogen from the soil of the moor.

From the results of pot-experiments on wheat, barley, and flax, Wagner, in Germany, has drawn up a scale of assimilability of phosphoric acid as applied in different forms; and several of the figures of this scale have been signally confirmed by the results of experiments on rice made in Japan, by Kellner and his pupils, as will be seen in the following table: —

Kind of Phosphate.	Wagner's Scale.	Kellner's Results.
Superphospate	100	100
Phosphatic slag	50	53
Peru guano	30	34
Steamed bone-meal	10	56 [1]
Coprolite meal	9	9

It is to be remarked that, although the ground slag did half as well as the superphosphate upon the first crop in Kellner's rotation, it failed to exhibit the excellent after-effects observed by Wagner. Kellner's soil was a light ferruginous upland loam, rich in humus, and there was a copious rainfall. It should be said, moreover, that Wagner's conclusion, that the phosphoric acid in Thomas-slag is more readily available for plants than that in bone-meal, has been called in question by Marek and Holdefleiss, and other observers, some of whom have argued that Wagner must have employed, in his experiments, bone-meal of poor quality. It is to be remarked, withal, that Wagner's dictum as to bone-meal is plainly not in accord with common experience, which has

---

[1] Kellner argues that bone-meal is a vastly more efficient manure in hot climates than it is in northern Europe.

proved, beyond cavil, that bone-meal, when applied under proper
conditions, is one of the surest and most effective of fertilizers.
It is to be noted, furthermore, that although Maercker found, in a
series of experiments carried on during three years, that as much
straw could be got by applying heavy dressings of phosphatic slag
as was got by using superphosphate, he did not in a single instance
obtain so large a crop of grain, by means of the slag, as were
those grown with the superphosphate, not even when more than
twice as much of the slag as of the superphosphate was applied
to the land, or when a larger sum of money was expended for the
slag than for the superphosphate.

From the results of experiments made in Japan on a light ferruginous upland loam with a rotation of barley, millet, wheat and
buckwheat, Kellner has drawn up the following table of the relative fertilizing power of the phosphates named : —

	First crop.	Average of 1st and 2d crops.	Average of 1st, 2d and 3d crops.	Average of all four crops.
Double superphosphate . . .	100	100	100	100
Steamed bone-meal	79	78	82	81
Precipitated phosphate . . .	62	68	75	75
Raw bone-meal	56	69	108	113
Crushed bones, raw	56	64	113	122
Phosphatic slag	55	46	48	48
Bone-ash	21	24	38	39

Dyer, in England, has argued that, speaking broadly and with
some reservations, it may be laid down as a general rule, that
while superphosphates are most economical and efficient on soils
that contain a fairly abundant quantity of lime, bone-meal, floats
and phosphatic slag are to be specially recommended for soils
which are decidedly deficient in lime, — which would include of
course many moorlands and bogs.

Phosphatic Guanos as compared with "Slag."

It may be said of all the phosphatic guanos which have been
formed from bird-dung in rainy regions, that, although the nitrogen
compounds and the potash of the original dung have been almost
completely washed away, the phosphate itself is in a very different
state from that in many of the rock-phosphates proper, such as
Canadian apatite, for example.   Much of the phosphoric acid in
the phosphatic guanos could be dissolved tolerably easily by plant-
roots, and by carbonic-acid water in the soil.   There can be no
question that the phosphatic guanos, used as a fine powder, at the

rate of 500 or 600 lb. to the acre, might be applied directly to the land in many situations. Most of them would probably do as good service as bone-black or bone-ash, or even better, on soils rich in humus, such as reclaimed bogs, or on cranberry beds or moist grass-lands, or even for turnip and buckwheat fields. The powdered material might be incorporated with composts also, or with manure when the heaps are established, or when they are forked over, though the practical interest in this inquiry has been as good as destroyed in recent years by the introduction of phosphatic slag, which will be found to be in most localities a cheaper and a better fertilizer than either of the phosphatic guanos.

But for the easily obtainable slag, it might still be urged that the fact of the phosphatic guanos having been tried years ago, and found wanting when put in direct competition, on upland soils and for all kinds of crops, with farmyard manure, Peruvian guano, and superphosphates made from fresh bones, should not in the least deter any farmer who may happen to have easy access to these materials from using them in conjunction with other kinds of fertilizers, and in those particular positions which are suited to their character and to their real power.

According to Voelcker, " The invariable presence of nitrogenous organic matters yielding, on an average, from 0.5 to 0.75 % of nitrogen, and the fine powdery condition of all true phosphatic guanos, plainly indicate their origin and mode of production. . . Generally speaking, guanos from which nearly the whole of the nitrogenous and saline constituents have been removed by rain and other atmospheric agencies contain the phosphatic elements in a finely divided condition; and although their efficacy as manures is no doubt much enhanced by treatment with acids, they may in virtue of their fine condition be applied to the land with more or less advantage in their natural state."

" On the other hand, it appears to be objectionable to give the name of ' rock-guano' to Sombrero and Curaçao rock, or to Alta Vela, Redonda, and other phosphatic minerals the origin of which is shrouded in mystery, and which are found in nature in the shape of rocks or stones. These rock-phosphates frequently contain little or no trace of organic matter, and their phosphatic constituents are in a completely mineralized state. Generally speaking, they cannot be applied to the land with advantage unless they have been subjected to chemical treatment. . . They differ essentially in physical characters from Mejillones, Malden Island, Starbuck Island, Lacepede and other phosphatic guanos."

It may be said in general of the mineral phosphates, that the softer kinds, such as are obtained in Florida and elsewhere, would be much more likely to be useful when applied directly to the land than the hard, rock-like masses which were formerly called coprolites, or than the crystalline apatite of Canada or the phosphorite of Spain. Nowadays, there are so many of the softer varieties of phosphates procurable that the harder rocks need not engage the farmer's attention in the least, until after they have been subjected to treatment with acids. But, as was just now said, the direct use of any of these natural materials has been greatly discredited by the introduction of the phosphatic slag, which will usually be found to be a cheaper and a better fertilizer than either floats or phosphatic guano, in spite of the results obtained by many scientific experimenters which show clearly enough that plant-roots which are abundantly supplied with nitrogenous and potassic food, and with moisture, can readily obtain phosphoric acid from powdered phosphatic guano, and even from powdered rock-phosphates; and of those of other observers who have noticed that some of the softer kinds of natural phosphates may be slightly acted upon in compost-heaps.

Field Experiments with Rock Phosphates.

Many field experiments have been made in recent years to test the fertilizing value of finely ground phosphatic rocks, with the result that, although by no means absolutely worthless, the natural phosphates have usually been found to be very much inferior to superphosphates and to phosphatic slag. Some of the results obtained by Voelcker may here be cited as examples of the kind of evidence which has been accumulated by means of field experiments. One set of trials was made with rutabagas on a rather strong turnip-loam which consisted to the depth of 18 inches of a fair admixture of sharp sand and clay, together with 1 % of carbonate of lime, and rested on a retentive clay subsoil. The yield of roots on unmanured plots was 18 cwt. to the acre. Applications of 6.33 cwt. of ground coprolites gave an increase of 3.5 tons of roots to the acre, while 10 cwt. of finely ground Redonda phosphate (phosphate of alumina and iron), gave an increase of 5.5 tons of roots. Five cwt. of superphosphate made from coprolites produced nearly twice as much increase in clean topped and tailed roots as was produced by the same money value of finely ground coprolites (= 6.5 cwt.). On the other hand, the addition of 6.5 cwt. of coprolite powder to 10 tons of rotten dung gave if anything a larger increase (7.33 tons) than the same quantity of dung and 5 cwt. of coprolite-superphosphate. Twenty tons of rotten dung gave no larger crop than 10 tons of dung and 6.5 cwt. of ground coprolites.

The largest increase in these experiments (nearly 9 tons of roots) was obtained by means of a mixture of 3 cwt. of coprolite-superphosphate and 2.5 cwt. of Peruvian guano. Four and a half cwt. of precipitated phosphate of lime from the gelatine makers gave an increase of 5.33 tons of roots, which was almost as large as that produced by 3.5 cwt. of superphosphate made from bone-meal. Three cwt. of raw bone-meal gave little more than 1.5 ton increase.

In the following year, similar experiments with rutabagas were made on a light and deep sandy soil, which contained but little lime and alumina and a good deal of oxide of iron, especially in the subsoil. Here the yield of roots on unmanured land was 19.5 tons to the acre. Applications of 5 cwt. of ground coprolites gave an increase of 6 tons of roots; 5 cwt. of ground Redonda phosphate gave 7 tons increase; 4 cwt. of precipitated phosphate of lime gave only 2 tons increase, and 3 cwt. of bone-meal gave 5.5 tons increase, while 5 cwt. of superphosphate, made from coprolites, gave 7.75 tons increase, 3 cwt. of bone superphosphate gave 7 tons increase, and 3 cwt. of coprolite-phosphate, mixed with 2.5 cwt. of guano, gave 7.5 tons increase. Petermann has insisted strongly that no profit is to be gained by using in this way rock-phosphates which are contaminated with carbonate of lime.

Other Methods of Decomposing Bones.

It must not be forgotten that other ways of decomposing bones have been resorted to beside the ordinary method with sulphuric acid. Long before the introduction of superphosphates it was the practice of some European farmers to ferment their bone-meal before applying it to the land. To this end, the meal was left for a time in heaps, which were kept moist with water or with urine, or with barnyard liquor. Sometimes the bone-meal was fermented in heaps of moist earth alone, or better yet with moist sawdust, in the proportion of 2 or 3 parts of the earth to one of bone-meal, and sometimes it was commingled with a mixture of earth and wood-ashes, and then kept moist with water or with barnyard liquor during several months. For grass-land 30 or 40 bushels of the product obtained from these processes of fermentation were thought to be a sufficient dressing; and upon ploughed land they were used at the rate of 20 to 25 bushels.

Even bones that have been broken into rough pieces at the farm with sledge-hammers may be reduced to a finer state of division and converted into a highly efficacious manure for root-, crops, by fermenting them in heaps with earth and dung-liquor, or water, as above stated. (Voelcker). An English farmer named Dixon, who cultivated a poor, chalky and flinty soil in Surrey, was accustomed long ago to make little heaps of ground bone and coal-ashes, by mixing 8 bushels of the bone with 24 bushels of the ashes, and to keep these heaps moist by throwing house slops upon them. After 2 or 3 months' time the heaps were allowed to dry out, or they were spread for a day or two, to render their contents dry enough to be sown from a drill. The mixture was then drilled in for turnips with the seed. Each heap contained enough material to fertilize an acre of land, and it was found to be a much more effective manure than ground bone by itself, which was, indeed, comparatively speaking, useless upon that land.

Experiments made by Pusey also show that fermentation is a cheap and easy way of obtaining a quick-acting manure from crushed bones. He found that "when crushed bones and moist peat-ashes are thrown in a heap together, the mixture heats violently, and the bones in a few days almost disappear, while their strength as manure is greatly increased." Next, wishing to prove that the foregoing statement does not depend upon anything peculiar to peat-ashes, he compared three separate compost-heaps, as follows: For the first heap, a cartload of crushed bone was wet and mixed with two cartloads of peat-ashes; for the second heap, a load of the bone was wet and mixed with two loads of coal-ashes; and for the third heap, a load of the bone was wet and mixed with two loads of sterile sand, dug up from a pit. The heaps all heated equally in the course of a few days, and became so hot at their centres that the hand could not be held there. After a few more days the bones disappeared in each heap equally, excepting at the outsides of the heaps, to a depth of 5 or 6 inches, where they remained unchanged, because the heat was insufficient. Some few corroded fragments of bone were found at the centres of the heaps also.

It is necessary, of course, in order that hot fermentation shall occur, that a considerable bulk of bones, etc., should be contained in the heap, and both the bone and the materials mixed with it should be wetted, in case they are dry. The fertilizing powers of the bones fermented as above were tested upon turnips, with the result that the crops produced by each mixture were equally good.

The next year, experiments were made to test the action of fermented bone, in comparison with that of plain bone and of bone-superphosphate. A wagon-load of crushed bone having been wet and mixed with half a wagon-load of sand, the heap heated violently and became fit for use in the course of a few days. During the fermentation the heap sank one foot in four, and it was argued that there would be more than two bushels of bones in three bushels of the mixture. The material was applied to turnips in contrast with other fertilizers, as stated in the following table: —

Bushels of Manure to the Acre.	Cost of the Manure.	Weight of Crop. Tons and Cwt.	
No manure	$0.00	5	0
17.00 Crushed bone	11.25	13	5
25.50 " "	16.80	14	5
8.50 Composted bone	5.00	13	5
12.75 " "	7.40	17	1
4.25 Bone superphosphate	5.50	14	5
7.50 " "	7.40	14	5

Another year, the following results were obtained with late-sown turnips: —

5.25 Bone superphosphate	8.90	16	13
8.00 Composted bone	5.25	13	14
No manure		1	0

The composted bones in this case were from a small heap, and were not well decomposed. On two other lots, where the bones had lain in a large heap and had been better fermented, the yield was equal to that from superphosphate. Thus: —

Bush.		Cost.	Tons. Cwt.	
5.25	Bone superphosphate . . .	$8.90	15	14
8.00	Composted bone	5.25	15	12

A neighboring farmer, who, at Mr. Pusey's suggestion, composted bones with coal-ashes, found that 16 bushels of unprepared (crushed) bones, 4 bushels of composted bones, and 2 bushels of bone-super-phosphate, gave each the same yield of Swedish turnips. Mr. Pusey concluded that, practically, the fertilizing power of his crushed bones was increased from 3 to 4 fold by the fermentation, and that the labor of preparation was but trifling. He says that, when applied to turnips at the rate of from 5 to 8 bushels of bone to the acre, the compost did not produce, at first, so lively an effect on the young plants as bones that had been treated with sulphuric acid. "The super-phosphate always pushes on the turnips faster at first, and therefore is best for late-sown turnips." The lot which gave the best result, as stated in the first of the above tables, looked worse, during many weeks, than the superphosphate plants adjacent to it. It would often be easier to prepare such compost upon the field itself, and to use earth taken from the field instead of sand or coal-ashes.

In other experiments, Pusey "mixed crushed bones with peat-ashes, coal-ashes, sand, vegetable mould and sawdust. The fermen-tation was equal where the size of the heap was the same; but a small heap, unless carefully enclosed and covered, will not decompose so thoroughly as a large one, perhaps not even then. Whatever the sub-stance employed, it should be in a free, pulverized state; should be moistened, and the bones thoroughly drenched. Finely-ground bones decay more than coarsely ground. Boiled bones did not heat so well, nor fall to pieces so much, as raw bones. Bulk of the heap is a de-cided advantage. Four cartloads in one heap heated much better than four cartloads in separate heaps. As the heat does not main-tain itself well within a foot of the surface, it is useful to give the heap an external covering of the same material employed in the mix-ture. The quantity of coal-ashes or sand may be reduced, I believe, to one-half the quantity of bone. A bone-merchant has told me that, having made up a large heap, he turned it and watered it afresh at the end of a fortnight, and that, at the close of a month, very few whole bones remained."

One effective method of fermentation is to mix wool-waste with fragments of bone in moist heaps.

Loss of Ammonia during the Fermentation.

There is no doubt that these processes are effective, in that they make the bone-meal act quickly as a manure, but the fermentation is of course liable to destroy a considerable proportion of the ni-trogen in the bone. This point has been studied with care by Ulbricht. He mixed 550 lb. of fine bone-meal with 100 lb. of barnyard liquor, and incorporated the whole thoroughly with 1,000 lb. of earth. The mixture was shaken out into a heap some eight inches high, and left to ferment. At the beginning, the tempera-ture of the heap was 63° F., but in the course of 24 hours it went up to 117°, while ammonia and water vapor were given off freely, and at the end of 48 hours it had risen to 129°. After that, the heap gradually cooled, and at the end of a week the odor of ammonia ceased to be apparent.

Ulbricht analyzed the various components of the heap in the beginning, and he determined the amounts of nitrogen, etc., at different stages of the fermentation. It appeared that 16% of the nitrogen in the original bone-meal went to waste in the course of the first two days of the fermentation, but that afterwards the loss was very small. The loss of nitrogen could probably be very much lessened by making the fermentation less rapid, as could be done by mixing the meal with a larger proportion of earth or with peat, as will appear when the preparation of composts is described. Kuester, a German farmer, has proposed to save the ammonia by covering the fermenting heap with a layer of superphosphate, but by so doing some soluble phosphoric acid would be changed to the insoluble condition.

A German receipt for fermenting whole bones with horse-manure is as follows: Soak the bones in water for several days, then pack them in a dung-pit, layer by layer, with horse-manure, taking care to moisten each layer with the water in which the bones have soaked, and with other water as well. Each layer of bone should be about 3 inches thick, and the layers of horse-manure 12 inches thick. The heap is topped with loam. At the end of ten months the bones will be reduced and the mixture fit for use. In Norfolk (England), it was customary, at one time, to increase the solubility of bone-meal by fermenting it with manure. Alternate layers of bone-meal and of fresh farmyard manure were built up to a conical heap, which was covered with earth, to prevent loss of ammonia and to exclude rain. (Voelcker.)

Bones and Alkalies.

Several receipts for decomposing bones by means of wood-ashes have been published from time to time, especially in this country. More than a century ago, Hunter said: "I have found it a judicious practice to mix ashes with bones. A cartload of ashes may be put to 30 or 40 bushels of bones (crushed?), and when they have heated for 24 hours, which may be known by the smoking of the heap, the whole should be turned. After lying 10 days longer, this most excellent dressing will be fit for use." In cases where few bones are to be had, the commonest plan seems

to be to pack them, layer by layer, with wood-ashes, in an old hogs-
head or barrel, and to keep the. mixture well moistened during
several months.   But a better plan, particularly where only small
quantities of bones are to be treated, will be to boil them in lye,
prepared either by dissolving potashes in water, or by leaching
wood-ashes.   There are many farms where the small quantities
of bones obtainable might readily be reduced in this way at very
small expense.

I am informed by Mr. W. M. Stone, of Washington, Pa., formerly a student at the Bussey Institution, that he has boiled bones
with success in lye obtained by simply leaching wood-ashes with
water (without any use of lime.)   At first, the kettle was filled with
the moderately dilute leachings of the ashes, but the liquor naturally became concentrated by the boiling.   Whole bones were thus
treated.   "Even a horse's head was reduced in this way."   In this
case, the liquid or muddy product was poured out upon enough
wood ashes to "dry" it, and the mixture was used for manuring
Indian corn.   Probably it would be better to pour the alkaline product upon heaps of weeds to kill their seeds, and to ferment the
vegetable matter, or to use it for fermenting peat or sods, as will
be explained under the head of Composts.

Action of Potash on Bone.

A solution of caustic potash would be even more effective than
the carbonate for this purpose.   According to Ilienkoff, a ten per
cent solution of caustic potash acts so strongly on bones that,
when a mixture of the two substances is left to stand for a week
and is then treated with water, there will be obtained an emul-
sion consisting of an alkaline solution of ossein with bone-earth
suspended in it in a finely divided condition.   Similar results may
be obtained by means of a mixture of carbonate of potash, caustic
lime, and water.   Seeking to reduce these laboratory experiments
to farm practice, Engelhardt procured 4,000 lb. of bones, 4,000
lb. of wood ashes, 600 lb. of quicklime, and 4,500 lb. of water.
He dug a couple of trenches 2 feet deep, and lined them with
boards, and, having slaked the lime with a part of the water,
mixed the powdery product with the ashes.   Into one of these
trenches he put half the bones, viz. 2,000 lb., layer by layer with
the mixture of lime and ashes, taking care to wet the materials.

The mixture was left to itself, with occasional moistenings,
until the bones had become so soft that they could be rubbed

down between the fingers. 3,600 lb. of water were used in this trench, beside that employed for slaking the lime. When the contents of the first trench had become soft, they were spread layer by layer in the second trench with the remaining 2,000 lb. of fresh bones, and the whole was well worked together and then left to ferment until the bones were softened. The mass was then shovelled out and mixed with 4,000 lb. of dry loam or peat to make it manageable. The dry product should contain altogether some 880 lb. of phosphoric acid, 340 lb. of potash, and 160 lb. of nitrogen. In this country, where labor is so costly, it would certainly be well to omit the operations conducted in the second trench of this experiment.

Probably a better plan in many cases will be to use crude American potashes at once, instead of wood-ashes and lime. Several farmers have reported their successful use of this material. In one case the hard mass of potashes was broken into small lumps with a sledge-hammer, and a strong solution prepared by throwing the lumps into a large kettle of boiling water. This lye was poured upon coarse bone-meal that had been spread upon the floor of a barn-cellar, in the proportion of 1 lb. potashes to 4 or 5 lb. of the bone. Much heat is developed at first by the action of the lye on the bone. During the course of the next two or three weeks the mixture is turned over occasionally, and is then fit for use.

The disintegration of the bone produced in this way is said to be so complete, that any large pieces of bone which may happen to be present will be found to be so friable after the action of the potashes that they can be crushed with the fingers. Bone-meal thus treated has been used with success for fertilizing strawberries, cabbages, grape-vines, and pear-trees. Mr. W. H. Hunt, of Concord, Mass., reports that he has used as much as a ton of potashes in a year upon bone-meal in this way, and that the fertilizer obtained is excellent.

Although the process is troublesome because of the care which has to be taken in handling the corrosive potashes and the lye prepared from them, he finds the use of this material for reducing bone cheaper than that of sulphuric acid, while the product is much more valuable for his purposes than superphosphates such as he had bought in previous years. Mr. Hunt is accustomed to strew gypsum on the mixture of bone-meal and lye, at the time when heat is evolved from it, and when the mixture is worked over also; but, as Hilgard has pointed out, such use of gypsum is hardly to be commended, since reactions might occur between this substance and the carbonate of potash, which would tend to weaken the solvent action of the potashes on the bone. A modification of the foregoing method is to put bone-meal in a pit, to pour the solution of potash upon it, and to cover the mixture with 2 feet of loam.

Where only small quantities of the material are procurable, it would probably be best simply to boil the unbroken bones in the solution of potashes, and to pour the solution upon peat or weeds, as was said. This method deserves to be carefully studied, at all events, since it promises to be easily applicable to the bones, hoofs, and horn-piths procurable upon a farm or in any country village.

As regards bone-meal, however, when used in considerable quantities, the method of drenching heaps or layers of it with the hot lye will probably be most commendable. Bone-meal is quickly acted upon by wet wood-ashes also, and some writers have urged, perhaps rather too hastily, that only a few hours are required to reduce the bone-meal sufficiently in this way. One method of procedure is to mix a barrel of raw bone-meal and three barrels of dry wood-ashes to a heap on the barn floor, and to add gradually to the mixture 10 gallons of water, while stirring constantly with a hoe. According to J. R. Nichols, 5 barrels of this mixture to the acre is a cheap and effective dressing for almost any crop. He advises that the mixture should be used in the hill on land where half an ordinary dressing of farm-yard manure has been ploughed or harrowed in. Another receipt directs that 5 barrels of fine bone-meal should be mixed with 5 barrels of wood-ashes, that water enough to moisten the heap should be added, and the whole be covered with loam. The heap is left to ferment for 3 weeks, and a little water is to be added meanwhile, in case the mixture should seem to be nearly dry on examining it. (Darling.) When whole bones are composted with wood-ashes, considerable time is needed in order thoroughly to soften them, though the process is nevertheless said to be an economical one under some circumstances.

The following method, taken from a German source, is said to have originated in Russia. In a trench 3 or 4 feet deep, wood-

ashes and whole bones are piled in alternate layers, each about 6
inches thick. The lowest and the uppermost layers are of ashes,
and each layer of ashes is saturated with water as soon as it has
been laid.   In the beginning, upright stakes are set in the trench
at intervals of about 3 feet, and they are withdrawn after 8 or
10 days' time.   Into the holes which the stakes have left enough
water is poured to saturate anew the ashes.   At the end of two
months, when the bones have become considerably softened, the
heap should be thrown over, moistened, and allowed to ferment
anew ; and this process is repeated at intervals, as often as may
be needed.   Five months in all, and perhaps three forkings over,
will be sufficient to reduce the bones so completely that only some
fragments will remain of the largest head and thigh bones. These
rejections will naturally be laid aside, to be thrown into the next
heap that is made.

Field Experiments with Fermented Bone.

The following experiments by J. Lehmann relate to the fertilizing action of bone-meal that had been fermented with alkali.
Grain was grown during four successive years, but the fertilizers
were all applied at the beginning of the first year. Hence the
crops of the later years indicate the powers of endurance both of
the bone-meal and of the reinforcements that were added with it.
In all the experiments, excepting the one where the material was
converted to superphosphate, the bone-meal, after having been
thoroughly mixed with the reinforcing fertilizer, was moistened
with as much concentrated lye as was needed in order that the
meal should " ball" when squeezed in the hand and slowly fall
asunder again after the pressure of the hand was removed.   The
mixture was then left to ferment during several days before it was
worked into the soil.

The figures of the following table are given in pounds, and they
relate to a German acre : —

YIELD OF GRAIN.

Year.	Crop.	No Manure.	10 cwt. of the Bone-meal.	10 cwt. Bone-meal and 2 cwt. Sulphuric Acid.	10 cwt. Bone-meal and 4 cwt. Nitrate of Soda.	10 cwt Bone-meal and 5 cwt. Sawdust.	10 cwt. Bone-meal and 5 cwt. 40 lb. Peruv. Guano.
1858	Rye	880	1,240	2,380	2,680	3,000	3,080
1859	Rye	1,980	2,420	2,620	2,440	2,640	3,040
1860	Oats	1,900	2,460	3,200	3,560	3,480	3,800
1861	Barley	1,840	2,360	2,360	2,160	2,176	2,280
Sum		6,600	8,480	10,560	10,840	11,296	12,200

STRAW AND CHAFF.

1858	Rye	5,700	6,780	7,780	6,680	7,400	7,240
1859	Rye	5,420	6,380	7,420	7,520	7,440	8,000
1860	Oats	2,980	3,420	4,100	4,360	4,200	4,560
1861	Barley	2,900	3,360	3,040	3,200	3,240	3,240
	Sum	17,000	19,940	22,340	21,760	22,280	23,040

MONEY PROFIT FROM THE CROPS OF THE FOUR YEARS.

$108	$123	$153	$144	$171	$168

The influence of the fertilizers is plainly marked, both in respect to the production of grain and of straw. It will be noticed, also, that larger crops were obtained on adding active nitrogenous fertilizers. Even sawdust shows conspicuous merit as a cheap means of hastening the action of the bone. The first year happened to be very dry, and the effects of this drought are shown plainly in the small crops of rye on the unmanured land and on that which got nothing but bone-meal.

According to Voelcker, one of the best manures known for growing turnips on light land is made by putting alternate layers of dung and bone-meal in a heap, 3 or 4 months before the time when turnip-sowing begins, and allowing the heap to ferment. On several farms in Norfolk County this mixture has been used in preference to all other manures with most signal benefit. To prepare the mixture, a heap of bone-meal — calculating 6 or 8 bushels to the acre — is deposited in a corner of the field where the dung-heap is to be, and when a thick layer of the dung has been laid down, a thin sprinkling of the bone-meal is thrown upon it, then a layer of dung and again a sprinkling of bone-meal, until layer by layer the heap has been built up. About a month before sowing the turnips, the heap is turned over; and it is found finally at the time when the manure is applied to the land, that the bone-meal has been disintegrated and dissolved to such an extent that nearly the whole of it has become decomposed and amalgamated with the dung.

For light lands, deficient in organic matter, such as could not properly be manured with superphosphate alone, or bone-meal alone, this mixture is regarded as an economical and effective way of applying a phosphatic manure to the turnip-crop. In default of such a mixture as the foregoing, it is customary in England when turnips are to be grown on light land, to apply either a fair dressing of well-rotted dung, or half a dressing of the dung, and afterwards, when the seed is drilled in, 2 or 3 cwt. of guano and 2 or 3 cwt. of superphosphate. It is held that bone-meal, partially dissolved by sulphuric acid, is a better manure for turnips on light land than a plain superphosphate made from rock, and that a mixture of equal parts of guano, and a plain superphosphate, will do better service than either of the two manures would do by itself.

Disintegration of Bones with Lime.

Efforts have been made in Germany to decompose bones by means of the alkali quicklime instead of potash. For example, Walderdorff has recommended the following method: Ordinary bones which have been neither boiled nor broken are spread out in a layer six inches deep, and covered first with a layer of quick-lime of equal depth, and then with a layer of loam. Other similar layers are piled above the first series until the heap has been built up to a convenient size, when it is covered with a thick layer of earth. Holes are then pierced in the heap, and water poured in to slake the lime. As much lime is taken as will amount to about twice the bulk of the bones.

A heap of this sort which contained some 8,000 lb. of all sorts of bones remained very hot for eight weeks, and in active fermentation; the heat coming not only from the action of the water upon the lime, but from the action of the lime upon the bones. When the fermentation ceases, the bones are said to be found in a brittle, friable condition, and the heap is finally shovelled over in order to mix the materials.

Peters reported, some years since, that he obtained good results by composting bones with a mixture of quicklime and sulphate of potash. The whole subject of reducing bones with quicklime and Stassfurt potash salts, notably the muriate of potash, deserves to be studied at the farm.

Phosphates occur in all Soils.

Although phosphoric acid is universally acknowledged to be one of the most important of manures, and, after nitrogen, and in some places potash, the one of which ordinary soils stand in greatest need, it must always be borne in mind that minute quantities of phosphates occur in almost every kind of rock, and consequently in the soils which result from the disintegration of the rocks.

This fact has been thoroughly established by pot-experiments, in which plants were grown in soils composed of crushed rocks, the amount of phosphoric acid in the seed sown and in the plants harvested having been carefully determined in each case. The difference between the two quantities indicated, of course, the amount of phosphoric acid that had been taken from the rock. For that matter, the presence of traces of phosphoric acid in most rocks is proved by the fact that wild plants are found growing everywhere in the soils which rocks have produced. But though widely diffused in nature, phosphoric acid is seldom really abundant in any rock or soil. It is one of the ingredients of soils which is most likely to be exhausted by cropping, and it must be regarded as one of the rarest kinds of plant-food.

In this country, Hilgard has observed that the percentage of phosphoric acid in a soil, taken in connection with that of lime, seems to govern most commonly the productiveness of the virgin soils of the Southern and Western States. Even in California and the adjacent regions, where summer rains are infrequent, the soils contain comparatively little phosphoric acid, although they are exceptionally rich as regards potash, lime and magnesia. "The forecast that for most Californian soils, fertilization with phosphates is of exceptional importance, has been abundantly confirmed by experience." (Hilgard.) Generally speaking by far the larger number of cultivable soils throughout the world contain less assimilable phosphoric acid than crops need, and in some soils the deficiency is very marked, though in fertile regions soils are occasionally met with that contain so large a proportion of easily assimilable phosphates, that no profit is gained by using special phosphatic manures upon them.

According to Hilgard, the average of many analyses of good American soils shows 0.113% of phosphoric acid in the humid regions and 0.117% in the arid regions. Similarly, it is admitted by chemists in Europe that good arable land may ordinarily contain from 0.1 to 0.2% of phosphoric acid, which would amount to some 3500 to 7000 lb. to the acre. Having in view the virgin soils of our Southern and Western States, Hilgard urges that in sandy loams 0.1% of phosphoric acid, when accompanied by a fair supply of lime, secures fair productiveness for 8 to 15 years; though when lime is deficient twice this percentage of phosphoric acid will only serve for a similar time.

Ordinarily, it is not to be supposed that the whole of the phosphoric acid exhibited by analysis in a soil is in a condition fit to be immediately assimilated by plants, since the economic value of it will naturally depend largely upon whether it can or can not dissolve readily in the soil-water or be acted upon easily by the roots of crops. I have myself observed, in field experiments made at the Bussey Institution in 1871, that phosphatic fertilizers did little or no good on a dry soil which contained 0.25% of phosphoric acid, and Dehérain has noticed the same fact upon a soil which contained 0.127% of phosphoric acid; while Corenwinder and Contamine found that the application of superphosphate increased the crop on land, with which they experimented, that contained 0.12% of phosphoric acid.

A test for the Availability of Soil-phosphates.

Dehérain has sought to distinguish those soils which contain easily assimilable phosphates by determining how large an amount of phosphoric acid can be dissolved out from them by means of boiling acetic acid. This solvent would naturally dissolve di-phosphate of lime, bone-phosphate, and the better kinds of mineral phosphates as well as considerable portions of the more refractory rock-phosphates, while it would have little or no action on the phosphates of iron and alumina. By applying this test to a variety of soils, on which farmers had got no good from the use of special phosphatic fertilizers, he found that from 0.03 to 0.09% of phosphoric acid could be dissolved out from them by the hot acetic acid, i.e. from 1000 to more than 3000 lb. per acre. From a sample of Nile-mud, hot acetic acid dissolved out 0.065% of phosphoric acid. On the other hand, by experiments on a soil containing about 0.1% of total phosphoric acid, but from which hot acetic acid dissolved no more than a trace of phosphate, it appeared that the wheat-crop could be trebled by applying super-phosphate. It is to be remembered in any such discussion as this, that phosphoric acid is an important component of the dung of animals, of barnyard manure, and of many other commercial fertilizers beside those already described.

In seeking to make practical application of the foregoing data, Dehérain has argued that, in regions where artificial fertilizers can be used at all, phosphates may probably be applied with advantage to soils which contain less than 0.1% of total phosphoric acid; and to soils which, though they contain more than 0.1% of total phosphoric acid, give up less than 0.02% of this substance to hot acetic acid. For the sake of including in the rule even those soils which are so thin that they weigh less than the conventional 3,500,000 lb. to the acre, he says briefly that phosphatic fertilizers are indicated for all soils which contain no more than 450 lb. to the acre of phosphoric acid soluble in hot acetic acid.

On the other hand, he does not recommend that phosphoric acid should be applied to soils which contain more than 0.1% of total phosphoric acid and more than from 0.02 to 0.03% of phosphoric acid that is soluble in acetic acid. It being presupposed that the soil is thick enough that there shall be contained in an acre of it as much as 800 or 900 lb. of phosphoric acid, soluble in acetic acid. He argues furthermore that on good land to which abundant and frequent dressings of barnyard manure are applied, much of the phosphoric acid in the soil will be kept in an easily assimilable condition, thanks to the action of the soluble alkaline carbonates in the manure; but that where no farm-manure is used, so much of the phosphoric acid may pass into a non-assimilable condition that the application of phosphatic fertilizers might be profitable. It follows that in many instances where phosphates would yield a profit when used in conjunction with other artificial fertilizers, no advantage might be got by applying them together with farm-manure.

Dyer, in England, who has studied the question in a similar way, i. e. by noting how much phosphoric acid can be dissolved out from a soil by means of weak citric acid, has concluded that phosphatic fertilizers are needed by any and every soil which gives up no more than 0.01% of phosphoric acid when treated with dilute citric acid containing one per cent of the crystallized acid.

It is to be remarked that in Hilgard's method of analysis the soil is digested on a water-bath for 5 days in hydrochloric acid of about 1.115 sp. gr. The maximum percentage of phosphoric acid found by him in this way in any upland soil, is about 0.25% in the splendid table-land of West Tennessee and Mississippi. In the best bottom-lands of Mississippi he found 0.3%, and in the soil of a black Texan prairie, 0.46%. In Dyer's practice any carbonate of lime which the soil may contain is removed by means of an equivalent quantity of citric acid before applying the one-per-cent acid.

Beside phosphates, properly so called, there is in many if not in most soils a certain small proportion of phosphorus combined with organic matter. Several chemists have noticed on treating moor-earth with strong acids, that less phosphoric acid is dissolved than can be got from the earth by first burning it to ashes, and then treating the ashes with the solvent. There are good reasons for believing that this insoluble phosphorus is contained in albuminoid matters analogous to the difficultly digestible "nuclein" which occurs in the cells of plants and animals, and contains several per cent of phosphorus.

In rocks the phosphoric acid is supposed to exist ordinarily in the form of phosphate of lime, though it sometimes occurs as phosphate of alumina or as phosphate of iron. As will be shown, the rock phosphate of lime is not absolutely insoluble in pure water; it is sparingly soluble in water charged with carbonic acid, and in water containing various neutral salts and organic matters. The carbonated and silicated alkalies, in particular, help to dissolve it. But in the soil the tendency often is that the phosphate of lime shall be changed to the even more insoluble phosphate of iron. Hence the solubility of the iron phosphate becomes a matter of no little interest. As regards this matter, Pierre showed long ago that phosphate of iron is appreciably soluble in carbonic-acid water; and more recently Peters has observed that reactions occur between the humus of the soil and ferric phosphate, which greatly promote the solution of the phosphate. While the ferric phosphate is reduced to ferrous phosphate by the humus, the latter is oxidized to the state of an acid product which acts as a solvent of the phosphates. Peters corroborates, moreover, the old observation, that the presence of neutral and alkaline salts in the soil promotes the solution of the phosphates.

Phosphates in Sea- and River-Water.

It is to be remembered always, that, since the phosphate of lime of bones dissolves comparatively easily in the earth, there is far less reason and profit in treating bones with acid than there is in acting upon the fossil phosphates.

At the worst, however, the phosphates are not so insoluble but that quantities of them — small by comparison with the amount of water, but enormous in the aggregate —are constantly poured into the sea by every brook and river. In the ocean, they serve to nourish the aquatic plants and animals, and thence some small portion of them is recovered nowadays in the form of fish-scrap, sea-weeds, and guano.

The sea is in fact an inexhaustible reservoir of phosphoric acid, from which any amount of manure may be drawn; the only question is how to reduce this manure to a transportable form. The preparation of guano by the sea-fowl was one way of reaching this result. The saving of fish-refuse of various kinds is another way of utilizing the marine phosphoric acid, etc.; and this industry might easily assume large proportions in case high farming should ever again become highly remunerative in any civilized country. The use of sea-weeds in agriculture will be described in due course. It will be enough to say here that through them it has long been customary to recover large quantities of ash-ingredients and of nitrogen from the water of the ocean. In like manner, it was customary in some parts of Holland, long ago, to rake out duck-weed (Lemna) from the ponds in August or September, to leave it in heaps during the winter, to spread the rotted material an inch thick on the land in the spring, and to sow peas and beans upon it. The seeds germinated quickly and grew remarkably well.

It has even been suggested in Europe that the so-called water-pest (Elodea Canadensis), the American weed of the English, may sometimes serve a useful purpose in brooks as a means of collecting phosphoric acid and other kinds of plant-food which would otherwise escape into the sea. The idea was that the weed might be collected and composted, or burned to ashes, according to circumstances. In most brooks where the current is slow the water-pest and various other aquatic plants grow freely on the bottom, and materially retard the flow of the water — sometimes even to the extent of one-half of what it might be if the course were clear. Consequently it is customary in Europe to cut the weeds in canals and in small navigable rivers of low velocity, two or three times a year; and pains are taken to drag the weeds on shore with rakes lest they float down the stream to accumulate in bends and quiet places to form nuclei for shoals and other obstructions. In this country where mowing-machines are used to cut the weeds that grow under water on the bottoms and inside banks of canals, some farmers are doubtless so situated that they might avail themselves of the material thus obtained.

European experience has shown that the water-pest ploughed under as green manure has a quick but ephemeral action. The use of it has been found to be remunerative in some cases where it had been thrown up on the shore by the action of winds and waves, though it did not pay to pull or cut it up from beneath the surface of the water. According to Fittbogen, the fresh plant contains 0.4% of nitrogen, 0.43% of potash, and 0.14% of phosphoric acid. He found in it 77% of water and nearly 18% of organic matter. Hoffmeister found 12% of dry matter in the fresh plant, and in the pure ashes he found 17 to 19% of potash, 6 to 9% of phosphoric acid, and 22% of lime. When taken from the water, his specimens were covered with a thin coating of sediment which could not be washed off, and in consequence of this coating the plants left a large amount of ashes on being burnt. As much as one-fifth the weight of the dry matter of these plants consisted of ashes, though it is to be supposed that the amount and character of the adhering sediment might vary in different brooks. When the water-pest is offered to neat cattle they eat it greedily, and since it resembles red clover in composition, the plant may perhaps be worthy of attention, in some places, as a foddering material. It may here be said that phosphoric acid is one of the things that tends most strongly to accumulate in the seeds of plants. It passes rapidly from the leaves and stem into or towards the fruit, through all the stages of growth from first to last.

Curiously enough, another instance in which marine phosphoric acid has become available for agriculture, is to be seen in the phosphatic slag just now described. There is good reason to believe, namely, that the phosphorus in the iron ores of the lias and the coal-measures was assimilated from sea-water by organized beings of low forms, at an early period in the history of the globe. Myriads of these organisms were buried in ferruginous mud at the bottom of the sea which served as their feeding-place, and the phosphorus they derived from the water now reappears in the pig-iron obtained by smelting ores which have formed in sediments where the remains of these prehistoric creatures were embalmed. (Bell.) It is to be presumed withal, that many of the deposits of mineral phosphates which are mined for making superphosphates, have been derived from the remains of marine animals or plants. In some instances it is believed that they have come from beds of guano.

Price of Phosphoric Acid.

A few words more need to be said concerning the price which has to be paid for phosphoric acid when bought in the form of one or another of the various kinds of phosphates above described. In this country the pound of useful phosphoric acid can generally be bought for the least money in the form of finely powdered phosphate rock, such as is sold under the trade name of "floats." In some situations farmers would probably find an advantage in using this material, either directly upon soils surcharged with humus, or perhaps in composts, as well as by treating it with sulphuric acid in the manner described on a previous page. Next in order comes phosphatic slag, which is sold at a low price at the iron-works where it is produced. It is a bulky, incidental product, which needs to be put out of the way of the workmen speedily. Bone-ash also is an article of commerce, the price of which is usually low, and not subject to wide fluctuation. The market price of this material may well serve as a starting point. In Boston it was at one time convenient to take the price of spent bone-black from the sugar-refiners as a basis from which to compute the value of phosphoric acid in all its forms. For if this bone-black cost the farmer, say $27 the ton, or 1^1 cents per lb., each pound of the phosphoric acid contained in it could be rated at 4½ cents (very nearly), since the black contains nearly 30 % of phosphoric acid.

The value of a pound of phosphoric acid in a superphosphate followed from the price that had to be paid for it in bone-black or bone-ash; for as has been shown above, and as has been set forth in detail in the first volume of the Bussey Bulletin, it is easy for the farmer to make superphosphate for himself from bone-black. In Mr. Saltonstall's experience, as cited in the Bussey Bulletin, the pound of soluble phosphoric acid cost about 18 cents in 1873.

At the time this computation was made, it was found by actual trial that the pound of soluble phosphoric acid could be imported in small lots into Boston from either England or Germany, in the form of superphosphate, for the same price; viz., 13 cents. Subsequently the price was reduced to 10 cents the lb., and latterly it has fallen to 6 cents. Several years ago the cost of making a quantity of reverted phosphoric acid, for an experiment, was calculated as follows, taking the then current price of bone-ash ($24 the ton) and of bone-black superphosphate ($32 the ton) as reported at the time in New York agricultural papers. The ash was assumed to contain 70% of bone-phosphate, i. e. 1400 lb. to the ton, and the superphosphate to have 16% of soluble phosphoric acid, which would mean 320 lb. of soluble phosphoric acid (or a little more than 527 lb. of monocalcic phosphate) to the ton. There action would occur between 155 lb. of $3\ CaO, P_2O_5$, costing at that time $2.66, and 117 lb. of $CaO, 2\ H_2O,P_2O_5$, costing $7.10; and there would result 272 lb. of $2\ CaO, H_2O, P_2O_5$, costing $9.76.

But in the 272 pounds of the diphosphate of lime thus produced there are 142 lb. of phosphoric acid; hence the pound of such phosphoric acid would have cost a little less than $0.07. Assuming that the cost of labor in making 1,000 lb. of the material would be $1, twenty-five cents must be added to the cost of the 272 lb. of diphosphate on this account, which will bring the price per pound fully up to 7 cents. If the bone-phosphate for this experiment had been bought in the form of bone-black, the final cost of the diphosphate would have been a little more than 7 cents the pound; but if it had been bought in the form of ground phosphate rock, the cost would have been a little less.

Other kinds of Soluble Phosphates, beside Superphosphate.

Efforts have been made in Germany to induce farmers to use phosphate of potash and phosphate of ammonia instead of superphosphate of lime. A preparation warranted to contain 36 to 38% of soluble P_2O_5 and 26 to 28% of soluble K_2O, has been put upon the market at a reasonable price. Other samples have been described as containing 25% of soluble P_2O_5 and 25% K_2O and 10% N respectively. They are said to be strongly acid. While there can be little doubt that pure products such as these will eventually take the place in many instances of the comparatively crude mixture of fertilizers now in use, it is none the less true that the soluble alkaline phosphates may be unfit for application to soils capable of fixing phosphoric acid very quickly. Kellner has noticed in his experiments on an irrigated volcanic soil rich in silicates of iron and alumina which were easily soluble in acids, that phosphate of soda was decidedly inferior as a fertilizer, to precipitated diphosphate of lime and to superphosphate. The sodium phosphate gave a smaller increase of crop than the lime phosphates gave, and less of its phosphoric acid was taken up by the plants. Moreover the sodium phosphate did less good when it was put upon the land as a solution than when it was applied as a powder. The trouble appeared to be that the soluble phosphoric acid was too quickly fixed in the soil in the form of difficultly soluble phosphates of iron and alumina.

Amounts of Phosphates sold off from Farms.

Highly interesting computations have been made by several German writers, notably Crusius and Heiden, as to the amounts of phosphoric acid that had been removed in crops, or added in the form of manure, in the cases of certain special farms where a careful system of bookkeeping permitted such calculations. Every agricultural student will do well to study in detail the examples given by Heiden in his book entitled "Statik des Landbaues." From lack of space, only rough outlines of one or two of the published examples can here be given.

Crusius tells of a farm that consisted of 670 Saxon acres of good arable loam overlying gravel, — by which it was well drained, — and 120 Saxon acres of good permanent meadow. The arable land was subjected to a rotation consisting of, 1. Rape, 2. Wheat, 3. Peas, 4. Rye, 5. Potatoes, 6. Barley, 7. Clover, 8. Rye, 9. Oats, 10. Turnips, 11. Rye, 12. Barley, 13. Clover, 14. Rye,

15. Oats, 16. White Clover, and was manured with farmyard manure four times during the 16 years, at the rate of 80 to 95 loads of 1,650 lb. each.

Accurate accounts were kept as to income and outgo of products during two full courses of the rotation, and when these results came to be stated in terms of five-year periods, it appeared that, although the total product of the farm had increased, grain and straw had not increased in the same proportion, for the proportion of straw was appreciably larger in the later years. This fact may readily be seen from the following table, which relates to the rye crop : —

Years.	No. of Shocks of Sheaves.	100 Shocks of Sheaves gave Bushels of Grain when threshed.
1826–30	4,250	166
1831–35	5,379	170
1836–40	5,363	154
1841–45	6,857	140
1846–50	8,417	156
1851–55	7,082	121
1856–60	7,881	125

During the last 16 years, i. e. from 1845 to 1860, it appeared that 985.67 cwt. of phosphoric acid had been sold off the arable land, and that only 408.33 cwt. of phosphoric acid were returned to it, so that the fields had been deprived of this constituent to the extent of 577.34 cwt., a fact which may perhaps explain the gradual diminution in the yield of grain.

Another interesting example is that of an estate at Waldau, where, as it appeared, both phosphoric acid and potash were continually added to the arable land in larger amounts than they were taken off, thanks to the fact that the estate comprised an unusually large proportion of permanent meadow. Beside patches of garden, woodland, etc., the estate consisted of 1,030 Morgen (1 M. = 0.631 acre) of arable, 773 M. of meadow, and 113 M. of pasture. The following table gives the outgo and income of phosphoric acid in German pounds for three years.

OUTGO OF PHOSPHORIC ACID (P_2O_5).

	1860–61. lb.	1861–62. lb.	1862–63. lb.
From sale of crops	1,040	1,176	797
Through cattle : —			
A. Sale of animals	132	287	790
B. Sale of milk	87	115	137
C. Sale of wool	1	1	1
Sum of the outgo	1,260	1,579	1,725

Income of Phosphoric Acid (P_2O_5).

	1860-61. lb.	1861-62. lb.	1862-63. lb.
Through purchase of fodder	898	463	468
Through hay from the meadow	2,685	2,757	1,790
Through purchase of fertilizers	1,405	2,181	. . .
Sum of the income	4,988	5,401	2,258
The income consequently exceeded the outgo to the extent of	3,728	3,822	533

Many similar computations might be cited from European experience. It is to be regretted that there are no American observations of this sort to discuss.

Use of Bone-black in France.

It is worthy of remark that for a considerable period of time, spent bone-black, as it came from the sugar refineries, played a very important part in the development of French agriculture, notably on the western seaboard in the region about Nantes, where enormous quantities of the material were used much in the same way that bone-meal and afterwards superphosphate of lime were used in England during the same period. The sources whence the French farmers were supplied with this fertilizer were not by any means confined to their own sugar-houses, for during many years spent bone-black was regularly imported into France both from America and from Russia, to be used directly for agricultural purposes.

This prejudice of the French farmers in favor of using bone-black rather than bone-meal was peculiar. At first sight their practice seems to have been not wholly intelligent, though something may no doubt be said in favor of it. Unquestionably, in the beginning, when spent bone-black of super-excellent quality could be had from their own refineries almost for the asking, the French did well to use that substance freely. The only point questionable is the propriety of their afterwards using an inferior kind of bone-black, and continuing to use it so long as they did, instead of bone-meal or super-phosphate.

Still, it should be said that bone-black was used in France, not for high farming, such as in England justified the use of the more costly bone-meal and bone-superphosphates, but chiefly for the production of buckwheat, which is a crop of very low value, comparatively and commercially speaking. Moreover, the bone-black was used chiefly upon soils which were naturally poor and sour, i. e., under conditions well suited for utilizing its phosphoric acid; and it is not altogether improbable that for the crop, the locality, and the time in question spent bone-black may have been better, all things considered, than either bone-meal or superphosphates. Now that plain superphosphates are to be had at cheap rates in France, they are said to be largely used by the buckwheat farmers. Experiments have been reported withal which go to show that even ground phosphate rock might sometimes do fairly good service on these poor French soils. The student of agriculture will still find much of interest in the accounts of the old methods of using bone-black in that country, as given in the books of Bobierre and Malaguti.

Bone-charcoal, when freshly prepared, contains some 8 or 10 % of carbon, which retains about one-tenth its weight of nitrogen as an essential constituent; but although some ammonia is evolved when red-hot bone-charcoal is quenched with water, it is to be presumed — as is true also of the somewhat similar cases of coke and coal — that a compound so inert and refractory as this nitrogenous carbon cannot be of any direct use for feeding plants. Fresh bone-black would be valuable as a manure only because of the bone-ash which is contained in it. As in bone-ash proper, so in bone-black, the bone-earth is so open and porous that it may be regarded as finely divided and apt for the solvent action of plant-roots, or of chemical substances in the soil-water. But as with bone-ash, so here the absence of the easily putrescible flesh-like ossein makes the material less soluble and less valuable as a manure.

But the bone-black used in French agriculture was not the freshly prepared charcoal. On the contrary, it consisted of various residual products obtained at the sugar-houses after the bone-charcoal had served its purpose of clarifying and decolorizing syrup. These products differed considerably both from the original charcoal and from one another, accordingly as blood had or had not been used by the refiners as an adjunct to their processes of clarification. Where blood was used, the spent bone-black, admixed with the coagulum of the blood, might contain as much as 8 or 10, or even 14 % of nitrogen, though generally speaking the proportion of nitrogen was no more than perhaps a third of these amounts. Such materials as these were manifestly fit to be put into competition with bone-meal.

Nowadays the sugar refiners prefer to use bone-charcoal in a rather coarse condition, like fine gravel; but formerly it was much more finely powdered, and was consequently more valuable for agricultural use. There can still be obtained from sugar refineries small quantities of coagulated blood, admixed with various impurities derived from the raw sugar, together with a little bone-black. This substance is a powerful and valuable nitrogenized manure, well worthy the attention of farmers in the immediate vicinity of the refinery; but the amount of it is small, and it must not be confounded with the spent black of former days, such as is now under consideration.

In any event, even when no blood is mixed with the syrup, bone-black absorbs a certain quantity of mucilaginous nitrogenized matters from the solution of brown sugar, and the French farmers could formerly buy black in this condition as well as that which was more highly nitrogenized. It is noteworthy that, beside coloring matters and certain slimy albuminous and mucilaginous compounds, bone-black absorbs from the sugar solution a quantity of lime and of compounds of lime which occasionally come, in some part, from hard water used to dissolve the sugar, but which ordinarily are referable to the milk of lime which is employed to neutralize the acidity of sugar solutions and which is added for this purpose both to the cane-juice immediately after its expression and to the solution of crude sugar also before it is subjected to the action of bone-charcoal.

According to Malaguti, writing in 1857, the spent bone-black from the refineries of Nantes generally contained some 2 or 3 % of nitrogen,

from 54 to 60 % of phosphate of lime, and 4 or 5% of carbonate of
lime.   It was in the form of a fine powder. The Russian and American blacks, as sold in Nantes at that period, contained hardly as
much as 1 % of nitrogen, but they contained 70 or 80 % of phosphate
of lime, and 8 or 10 % of carbonate of lime.

Spent Bone-black is now practically Non-nitrogenous.

It is a long while since those varieties of spent bone-black that
were admixed with nitrogenous matters could be obtained in large
quantities, as for many years it has been the custom of sugar refiners to "revivify" the spent black, as the term is, and so use it over
and over again.   To this end, the spent black, after thorough washing, is put again into the iron cylinders, and redistilled, as if it were
the fresh bone.   Since beet-juice contains a much larger proportion
of impurities than cane-juice does it has to be "limed" more heavily
in the process of purification, whence it follows that the bone-black
used for purifying beet-sugar becomes heavily charged with foreign
matters, and that special pains have to be taken in revivifying it.
Usually, the spent black is soaked in dilute muriatic acid to remove
lime and carbonate of lime, one result of the action of the acid being
to remove a certain amount of bone-earth and to make the coal more
porous. After the calcium chloride and the excess of acid have been
washed out, the bone-black is subjected to a process of fermentation,
to loosen or destroy albuminoid matters, and is then boiled in a solution of caustic soda or carbonate of soda to dissolve out albuminoid
matters, as well as gypsum which tends to accumulate in the pores of
the coal and to clog them.

Finally, after having been washed clean with water, the bone-
black is redistilled. The main purpose of the fermentation and of
the alkaline solutions is to remove organic matters which, if left until
the moment of redistillation, would be converted into useless carbon
in the pores of the bone-black and diminish its decolorizing power.
It is because of this clogging of its pores by extraneous carbon that
the value of bone-black tends to diminish the oftener it is revivified.
In any event, the distilled product is sifted and the finest powder is
discarded to be sold for agricultural use.   Sometimes dry muriatic
acid gas has been made to act directly upon the hot-coal, and the
calcium chloride has subsequently been removed by washing; but in
cane-sugar refineries the general rule is simply to redistil the spent
coal and separate the finest powder by sifting.

It is this fine, practically non-nitrogenous powder that constitutes
the spent bone-black which is procurable nowadays. When of good
quality, it may contain some 30 % or so of phosphoric acid, as has
been said. The foreign blacks analyzed by Malaguti, as above
stated, had perhaps been revivified, or used without any addition of
blood, while the French blacks appear at that time not to have been
revivified at all, so quick was the demand for the spent material
among the farmers of the neighborhood. Probably the practice of
revivifying bone-black was not adopted by the sugar refiners at
Nantes so early or so generally as it was in other countries. Since,
looking from the sugar-boiler's point of view, bone-black suffers a

certain amount of deterioration every time it is revivified, the refiners formerly were probably not unwilling to sell the material after it had been redistilled a certain number of times, particularly in cases where there was a good demand for the spent black to be used as a manure. But in large manfacturing establishments it is so important to have all the processes of manufacture systematized and methodized to the utmost, that the practice has finally become general to use the bone charcoal over and over again so long as it can be used, with repeated revivifications, and to discard only that which has become utterly worn out, viz. the fine siftings.

In the French practice it was the fine nitrogenized black above described that was found to be especially effective for the growth of buckwheat, and it was for the cultivation of this grain that almost the whole of the bone-black sold at Nantes was used. On the poor granitic soil of Brittany, buckwheat sown on freshly broken land is said to serve extremely well as a preparatory crop for wheat. It smothers weeds and leaves the soil in fit mechanical condition for the wheat-plants.

French writers recommend that the coarse varieties, which contain little or no nitrogen, should be applied to land newly broken up; the argument being that the carbonic acid and other acid products resulting from the decomposition of the vegetable matter will dissolve the phosphate of lime. Malaguti even laid stress upon the action of the sugar which the French spent black held in its pores. According to this chemist, and his argument is perfectly reasonable, a mixture of phosphate of lime and of dried blood will not produce so good a result when used as a manure as a quantity of spent bone-black equally rich in phosphate of lime and nitrogen, for the small quantity of sugar in the spent black will ferment in the soil, and produce acetic and lactic acids, and the like, by which the phosphate of lime will be made soluble, and available as plant-food.

Bone-black, even more emphatically than bone-meal, was regarded as a lasting manure. The good effects of the application of it could be seen and felt for several years. But as has been said already when speaking of bone-meal, this slowness of action is in one sense an objection to the use of any manure. It is not well for the farmer to have his capital lying dead in the earth for several years. When a high-priced fertilizer is applied to the soil, it is in some sort a necessity of the case that a quick profit must be returned.

Hence it happened in England, and in the other countries where agriculture is well advanced, that bone-black was never much esteemed, and that even bone-meal fell at one time into comparative disuse. It is on this account that even in France bone-black is no longer used to any great extent. It has been superseded in good part by superphosphates, which are now regarded in that country as almost a specific for buckwheat.

Beside the sugar refineries, there is another very subordinate source of bone-black at some iron founderies, where ground bone is used for case-hardening small castings. The bone being distilled in the process, bone-black is left, which is often thrown away or to be had at a low price.

Solubility of Phosphates.

The solubility of pure precipitated terbasic phosphate of lime in carbonic-acid water, as determined by Warington, is 1 part of the phosphate in 1,789 parts of the liquid at about 50° F. and a mean barometric pressure of 29.535 inches. In one instance only did he obtain a rate of solubility as high as 1 in 1,540. He states that the solution of tricalcic phosphate in carbonic-acid water has a slight acid reaction.

Earlier and less elaborate experiments by Bischof gave the solubility as 1 part of the moist precipitated phosphate in 1,102 parts of carbonic-acid water, and Lassaigne gave it as 1 in 1,333 parts of carbonic-acid water, at 50' F. and the ordinary pressure of the air.

Other experiments by Warington are given in the following table: —

EXPERIMENTS ON MOIST PRECIPITATED TRICALCIC PHOSPHATE.

Materials tested.	Solvent employed.	Barometic Pressure in Inches.	° F.	Parts Liquid to 1 Part Phosphate.
Tricalcic phosphate, pure precipitated	Boiled water		44.5	89,449
The same . . .	1 % chloride of ammonium in boiled water		50.0	19,629
The same . . .	10 % chloride of ammonium in boiled water		62.5	4,325
The same . . .	Water saturated with carbonic acid	29.585	50.0	1,789
The same . . .	1 % chloride of ammonium in water saturated with carbonic acid	29.348	53.5	1,352
Same plus carbonate of lime . .	Water saturated with carbonic acid	29.776	69.8	42,314
Same as above . .	1 % chloride of ammonium in water saturated with carbonic acid	29.378	60.8	18,552
Carbonate of lime alone	Water saturated with carbonic acid	29.463	70.0	1,016
The same . . .	1 % chloride of ammonium in water saturated with carbonic acid	29.425	55.5	950

The phosphates which occur in nature are all much less soluble in carbonic-acid water and other solvents than is the pure precipitated phosphate, as prepared in the laboratory. Thus, according to Warington, 1 part of the phosphate of lime in bone-ash dissolves in 6,788 parts of water saturated with carbonic acid. He found that the magnesium phosphate of the bone dissolved before the calcic phosphate; and that, in general, more phosphate is dissolved by the first portions of the solvent that are applied to the bone-ash than by the succeeding portions.

According to Voelcker, 1 part of recently precipitated and still moist terphosphate of magnesia dissolves in 4,888 parts of water, while 1 part of terphosphate of lime in a similar fresh state dissolves in

12,591 parts of water. After the precipitates have been dried and ignited, they dissolve in 9,943 and 31,818 parts of water respectively.

Action of Carbonic Acid under pressure.

At temperatures somewhat higher than that at which water boils, the action of carbonic acid on terphosphate of lime is much more emphatic than it is at the temperature of the air, and Seybold and Heeder have published a process for putting this reaction to practical use. Finely ground phosphate rock is moistened with water and spread out in a close oven, which is gradually heated to about 250° F., while a current of carbonic-acid gas and steam is made to pass through the chamber. The carbonic acid acts upon the terphosphate to form carbonate of lime, while superphosphate and diphosphate of lime are also formed. In case the powdered rock were to be moistened with a solution of carbonate of soda or carbonate of potash, instead of the water, an alkaline phosphate would be formed together with the carbonate of lime. One advantage of this process would be the freedom of the products from the gypsum with which superphosphate made in the usual way is always contaminated.

According to Muntz and Girard, terphosphate of lime is much less soluble in a solution of bicarbonate of lime than in carbonic-acid water. Thus, in an instance where a litre of carbonic-acid water dissolved 0.13 grm. of the phosphate, a litre of carbonic-acid water charged with carbonate of lime dissolved no more than 0.04 grm. of the phosphate.

In saline solutions that contained one per cent of the salt, one part of moist, precipitated terphosphate of lime dissolved as follows, viz.: —

In 3,217 parts of a solution of chloride of ammonium.
In 6,206 " " " carbonate of ammonium.
In 15,766[1] " " " chloride of sodium.
In 10,174 " " " nitrate of soda.

After digestion in water for a week, the following quantities of terphosphate of lime were found dissolved in 100 litres of the liquid obtained from —

Grm.

Pure bone-ash (from the very hard shin-bone of a horse) 0.168
American bone-ash 0.268
Peruvian guano 0.359
Kooria Mooria guano 0.188
Sombrero phosphatic guano 0.120
Monk's Island phosphatic guano 0.142
Suffolk County coprolites 0.090
Cambridgeshire coprolites 0.085
Estramadura phosphate 0.014
Norwegian apatite 0.063

Some of the same kinds of phosphates digested with 1 % solutions of ammonium salts gave the following results. The figures represent the number of grams of terphosphate of lime that were contained in 100 litres of the solutions: —

---

[1] The precipitated phosphate used in this experiment had been kept some time, and had become less gelatinous and more dense than the samples tested with pure water and with the solution of nitrate of soda.

Pure bone-ash with chloride of ammonium 0.445
American bone-ash with chloride of ammonium (3 days' digestion) 0.137
The same (12 days' digestion) 0.536
Cambridge coprolites 0.216
The same with carbonate of ammonia 0.228
Suffolk coprolites with carbonate of ammonia 0.249
The same with chloride of ammonium 0.160

It will be noticed that, in presence of the ammonium salts, the phosphate of lime in each of the materials dissolved more freely than it had done in mere water. But it was found that solutions of nitrate of soda and of common salt, of various strengths, dissolved no more phosphate of lime than distilled water did.

Solubility of Bone-meal.

Voelcker has determined the solubility of various kinds of bone-meal, in water, as stated in the following table. It appears that there are wide variations as to solubility among different kinds of bone-meal. The phosphate in meal from hard bones, even when very fine, is less soluble than that from porous, spongy bones. The fat of raw bones hinders their solution, and their decomposition also. Putrefying bone-meal is more soluble than that which is fresh. As has long been known, certain soluble organic matters and ammonium salts that are formed during the decay of bone-meal promote the solubility of the phosphates that are contained in it.

When water was made to act upon the various samples of meal, there were found dissolved in each 10,000 grams of the water the specified amounts of phosphate of lime and of nitrogen.

	Terphosphate of Lime.	Nitrogen.
	grm.	grm.
Very fine meal from very hard bones that were raw and contained some fat, first extract	0.090	1.298
Same, second extract	0.100	0.200
Coarser meal, chiefly from hard bones (raw as before), first extract	0.351	1.891
Same, second extract	0.301	0.783
Very fine meal from softer bones (raw as before), first extract	0.399	0.898
Same, second extract	0.299	0.299
Same, third extract	0.399	0.100
Half-inch spongy bone, free from fat, first extract . .	0.800	3.893
Same, second extract	0.349	0.620
Steamed bone-meal, first extract	1.297	1.000
Same, second extract	0.400	0.500
Same, third extract	0.242	0.449
Ivory meal, first extract	0.648	0.978
Same, second extract	0.349	0.489
Bones that had been strongly boiled, residue from glue-making, first extract	0.598	2.495
Same, second extract	0.299	0.299
Same, third extract	0.306	0.254
Putrefying bone-meal, first extract	2.895	4.092
Same, second extract	1.497	0.700
Same, third extract	0.898	0.499

Various Phosphates.

According to Fleischer, 1,000 parts of water at the ordinary temperature dissolve 0.0563 part of phosphoric acid from pure precipitated diphosphate of lime. (See beyond, also.) He states that the diphosphate dissolves as such both in water and in carbonic acid water, its solubility in the latter being much larger than in pure water. In presence of sodium bicarbonate the solubility of the diphosphate is greater than in mere water, though the second molecule of carbonic acid in the sodium salt does not dissolve so much of the phosphate as a molecule of free carbonic acid would. The presence of lime-salts or chloride of sodium, or of the matters which water can extract from some moor-earths, hinders the solubility of the diphosphate in water.

When bone-meal is treated with water, much more carbonate of lime than of phosphate of lime goes into solution. Moreover, fine bone-meal gives up more phosphoric acid to water and to carbonic-acid water than coarse meal does, and steamed meal more than raw meal of the same degree of fineness.

Dehérain has noticed that the solubility of the powder of some kinds of phosphatic nodules in carbonic-acid water is greatly increased by exposing the powder to the air. From 10 grm. of powder which was digested at once in carbonic-acid water there was dissolved enough phosphoric acid to amount to 0.04 grm. of magnesium pyrophosphate, while on subjecting to the same treatment 10 grm. of powder which had been kept for three months in store, 0.30 grm. of the pyrophosphate was obtained.

In another set of experiments, the powder was subjected to the action of weak acetic acid, through which a current of carbonic-acid gas was made to pass, and there was obtained 0.44 and 0.88 grm. of the pyrophosphate from the fresh powder and the exposed powder respectively. These results were attributed to changes in the state of oxidation of silicates of iron in the nodules. The passage of the original ferrous compound to the ferric condition disaggregated the mineral, and laid the phosphate open to the action of solvents.

Action of Ammonium Citrate.

A common method of testing the solubility of different varieties of phosphate of lime is to digest the materials in an aqueous solution of ammonium citrate, which dissolves diphosphate of lime completely and rock-phosphates not at all. That bone-meal is soluble to no inconsiderable extent in the slightly acidulated solvent will appear from the following table, which gives the results of Otto's experiments: —

Meal from bones which had been leached with benzine to remove fat.	Composition of the bone-meal. Phosp. Acid. Per cent.	Nitrogen. Per cent.	Mesh of the sieve. Millimeters.	Per cent of Phosp. Acid soluble in the Ammonium Citrate. Per cent of the bone.	Per cent of Phosp. Acid in the bone.
I. Fine meal { a .	22.2	4.75	1.5	8.05	38.28
{ b .	22.2	4.75	1.0	9.15	41.20
II. Coarser meal, from stamps	19.0	5.10	1.0	7.40	38.94

Dyer, having found that an alkaline solution of ammonium citrate is not well suited for determining the solubility of rock-phosphates, tested a variety of the minerals with diluted citric acid of such strength that it contained either 0.25, 0.5 or 1 % of the crystallized acid. **He** urges that good results may be obtained by using citric acid of 1 %, and taking 200 parts of the liquid for 1 part of the mineral that is to be tested.

Rock Phosphates.

Water and carbonic-acid water dissolve out from crude Mejillones guano no inconsiderable quantity of phosphoric acid, because of the presence in this guano of diphosphate of lime and phosphate of magnesia. No appreciable quantity of phosphoric acid was dissolved from powdered Lahn phosphorite by water, while from another phosphorite, from Grosshütten, water dissolved considerable quantities of it, although the material was largely contaminated with carbonate of lime. From precipitated ferric phosphate, water dissolved an appreciable quantity of phosphoric acid, apparently with decomposition of the precipitate, but from precipitated phosphate of alumina much less phosphoric acid was dissolved by water. (Fleischer.)

According to Pierre, 1 part of ferric phosphate dissolves in 12,500 parts of carbonic-acid water that contains rather more than one volume of the gas, while for dissolving 1 part of ferrous phosphate no more than 1,000 parts of the carbonic-acid water are needed. When the carbonic-acid water was mixed with $\frac{1}{100}$ part of ordinary acetic acid, 560 parts of the mixture dissolved one part of ferrous phosphate. But when 9 % of a concentrated solution of acetate of ammonia was added to the carbonic-acid water, then 1,666 parts of the liquid were needed in order to dissolve 1 part of the ferrous phosphate.

According to Nessler, the following amounts of phosphoric acid were dissolved out by 600 cc. carbonic-acid water in one day from 100 grams of the materials enumerated: —

	Grm.
From precipitated terphosphate of lime that was still moist	0.228[1]
From precipitated terphosphate of lime that had been dried	0.308
From precipitated terphosphate of lime that had been ignited	0.428[1]
From finely powdered Sombrero phosphate	0.000

On adding 2 grm. of ammonium carbonate to the carbonic-acid water, 0.64 grm. of phosphoric acid was dissolved from the moist precipitate.

Karmrodt caused carbonic-acid gas to pass during 5 or 6 weeks through layers of coarsely powdered phosphates that were kept moist by drops of water which fell at intervals. He noticed that more lime was dissolved out than is contained in terphosphate of lime. At first, less phosphoric acid went into solution than was the case after the action of the carbonic acid had been longer continued.

From a sample of yellowish-gray phosphorite that contained 32 % of phosphoric acid, 1 part of phosphoric acid was dissolved by 8,300 parts of the carbonic-acid water.

From a sample of phosphorite, very red from the presence of oxide of iron, that contained 26 % of phosphoric acid, one part of the phosphoric acid dissolved in 10,400 parts of the carbonic-acid water.

From bone-ash, with 34 % of phosphoric acid, 1 part of the latter

---
[1] These figures should probably be transposed.

dissolved in 4,380 parts of the carbonic-acid water; and from raw bone-meal, with 20½ % of phosphoric acid, 1 part of the acid dissolved in 5,267 parts of the carbonic-acid water. In the time specified, there was dissolved: —

	Per Cent of the Material.	Per Cent of the Phosphoric Acid in the Material.
From the 1st phosphorite	3.06	9.57
From the 2d phosphorite	2.39	9.20
From the bone-ash	5.49	16.13
From the bone-meal	4.63	22.60

From the bone-meals, phosphate of magnesia dissolved in the carbonic-acid water before the phosphate of lime.

To test the comparative solubility of various phosphates in water and in carbonic-acid water, Bretschneider charged large bottles with the phosphates, covered the latter with the solvent, and shook the mixtures frequently at 64° F. during 24 hours. The carbonic-acid water was not quite saturated, but was $\frac{97}{100}$ of the full strength. The first column of figures in the following table gives the number of parts of water, and the second column the number of parts of carbonic-acid water, by which one part of phosphoric acid was dissolved in the several instances: —

	Parts of Water	Parts of Carbonic-acid Water.
Precipitated terphosphate of lime, fresh .	87,832	13,181
" " " ignited,	159,532	13,324
Precipitated diphosphate of lime, fresh .	29,350	8,916
Phosphate of magnesia and ammonia . .	21,967	1,969
Ferric phosphate, freshly precipitated . .	160,625	146,570
" " ignited	732,958	732,958
Finely powdered bone-black	. . . .	249,480

According to Moser, one part of the phosphoric acid in finely powdered Mejillones guano dissolved in 24 hours' time in 55,800 parts of pure water, and in 13,084 parts of water that was saturated with carbonic acid. In another trial where carbonic-acid gas was made to pass during an hour each day for ten days through a mixture of water and the powdered mineral, one part of phosphoric acid dissolved in 8,542 parts of the water.

Williams suspended several powdered phosphates in water through which a current of carbonic-acid gas was made to flow during fifty hours at a temperature of 60° to 70° F. His results are as follows:

One part of the calcic phosphate (3 CaO,P O₅)
in Canadian apatite dissolved in	222,222	parts of the CO_2 water.	
In same, very finely ground	140,840	"	" "
In fine raw bone-meal	5,698	"	" "
In bone-ash	8,029	"	" ..
In South Carolina phosphate	6,983	"	" "
" " " finely powdered	6,544	"	" "
In Orchilla phosphatic guano	8,009	"	" "

Bischof had stated previously that 1 part of apatite dissolves in 393,000 parts of water saturated with carbonic acid, 1 part of fresh shavings of ox-bone in 4,610 parts, and 1 part of precipitated phosphate of lime in 1,102 parts (Lassaigne says 1,333 parts).

Dietrich and Koenig acted upon various phosphates with carbonic-acid water applied in such manner that the minerals were soaked in a half-saturated solution of it for 48 hours, and the residue from this treatment was digested in saturated carbonic-acid water for 12 weeks.

Material.	Per cent of Phosp. Acid contained in the Material.	After 48 Hours' action of ½ Saturated CO₂ Water, 1 Part Phosp. Acid dissolved in Parts of the Liquid.	After 12 Weeks with Saturated CO₂ Water 1 Part P₂O₅ dissolved in Parts of the Liquid.
Estramadura phosphorite	37.20	90,900	90,900
Lahn phosphorite	14.80	60,100	60,100
Same	34.32	53,000	39,000
Sombrero phosp. guano	38.81	48,000	48,000
Baker Island guano	41.74	19,000	8,330
Peruvian guano	13.70	2,440	1,230
Raw bone-meal	16.63	18,800	5,980
Steamed bone-meal	21.79	21,100	5,630
Bone-ash	37.57	25,250	7,350
Precipitated terphosphate of lime (ignited)	39.60	13,900	4,250
Ditto, dried at 212° F.	42.99	13,500	3,630
Precipitated diphosphate of lime, sample No. I.	46.45	5,430	2,250
Ditto, sample No. II.	41.83	5,480	2,440
Ditto, sample No. III.	41.92	6,130	5,900

The most remarkable fact brought out by this series of observations is the ready solubility of the precipitated diphosphate of lime in carbonic-acid water. Excepting Peruvian guano, none of the other materials were anything like as soluble.

Action of Acetic Acid.

Many experiments have been made also to determine the solubility of phosphates in weak acetic acid. Voelcker's remark that "weak vinegar readily redissolves precipitated bone-phosphates, but has hardly any effect upon even fine bone-dust," is manifestly too emphatic, as will appear from the following experiments of Dietrich and Koenig, who used a 10 % solution of the acid, and allowed it to act upon the minerals during 24 hours, at the end of which time a sample of the liquid was drawn off for analysis, while the remainder was left to digest during 12 weeks. The results of these trials are given in the following table. The composition of the materials has been given above in the table relating to carbonic acid.

	1 Litre of the Dilute Acid dissolved in 24 Hours grm. of Phosp. Acid.	1 Litre of the Dilute Acid dissolved in 12 Weeks grm. of Phosp. Acid.	Percentage of the Phosp. Acid in the Material that was dissolved.
Estramadura phosphorite	0.260	0.317	8.5
Lahn phosphorite, inferior.	0.260	0.336	22.7
Same, better	0.400	0.587	16.8
Sombrero guano	1.122	2.170	56.0
Baker Island guano	1.177	1.865	44.7
Peruvian guano.	1.122	2.875	100.0
Raw bone-meal.	1.392	1.632	98.0
Steamed bone-meal	1.936	3.859	100.0
Bone-ash	1.884	2.869	76.0

Precipitated terphosphate of lime dried at 212° F. . . .	3.232	....	100.0
Same, ignited	2.489	3.718	86.0
Precipitated diphosphate of lime, No. I.	3.348		100.0
Same, No. II.	6.265 [1]	....	100.0
Same, No. III.	3.997	....	100.0

Krocker caused the finely powdered materials to be digested for 24 hours, at a temperature of 68° F., in dilute acetic acid that contained 12½% of the anhydrous acid. It was found that there had been dissolved by 1,000 parts of the solvent, from

Lahn phosphate rock	0.200 parts of phosp. acid.
Spanish phosphorite	0.200 " " "
Coprolites	0.310 " " "
Bone charcoal	0.310 " " ..
Baker Island guano	2.660 " "
Bone-meal	3.720 " " "
Precipitated phosphate of lime	5.456 " "
Same, slightly ignited	0.496 " "
Lahn phosphorite with ammonium sulphate	0.370 " " "

Whence it appears that the solubility of precipitated phosphate of lime in the weak acid is 27 times larger, and that of bone-meal 18 or 19 times larger, than the solubility of the phosphate in some kinds of phosphate-rock. The comparatively easy solubility in acids of a good phosphatic guano, like that from Baker's Island, is noteworthy.

In the experiments of Albert, 100 cc. of a mixture of 1 part acetic acid and 9 parts of water were made to act during three periods each of 4 days, upon one and the same gram of the finely powdered phosphatic material.

	In 1 Gram of the Phosphate there was of Phosp. Acid.	100 Grams of the Dilute Acid dissolved of the Phosp. Acid in			Total dissolved by Dilute Acetic Acid in 12 Days.	
		1st 4 Days.	2d 4 Days.	3d 4 Days.		
	grm.	grm.	grm.	grm.	grm.	%
Steamed bone-meal .	0.232	0.229	....	....	0.229	99
Raw bone-meal . . .	0.221	0.066	0.053	0.040	0.159	71
Peruvian guano . . .	0.114	0.107	0.004	....	0.111	97
Baker Island guano .	0.381	0.221	0.065	0.060	0.346	91
Bone-charcoal . . .	0.346	0.239	0.057	0.024	0.320	92
Precipitated phosphate of lime (hot dried) .	0.339	0.304	0.002	....	0.306	90
Sombrero phosphatic guano.	0.348	0.208	0.024	0.057	0.289	62
English coprolites . .	0.266	0.059	0.057	0.041	0.157	55
Estramadura phosphorite	0.387	0.056	0.025	0.016	0.097	25
Lahn phosphorite . .	0.259	0.025	0.008	0.003	0.036	14
Same, ignited	0.264	0.025	0.002	0.016	0.063	31
Same, boiled with potash lye	0.259	0.040	0.018	0.016	0.074	28
Navassa phosphatic guano	0.002	....	....	....	0.002	¼
Leached superphosphate, made from phosphorite . . .	0.088	0.043	0.009	0.008	0.060	68
The same	0.170	0.071	0.021	0.016	0.108	62

[1] An excess of the material was added purposely.

The ready solubility of the steamed bone-meal is noteworthy, and so is the hindrance to solution caused by the fat in the raw bone. In general the bone products dissolve more readily than the rocks, though the latter are still soluble enough to suggest the belief that appreciable quantities of them will dissolve in the course of time in the soil by the action of humic acid, carbonic acid, saline solutions, and plant-roots. The easy solubility of the phosphate in guano and in Baker Island guano will be noticed.

Influence of Pulverization.

The question as to how much influence on the solubility of a mineral phosphate may be exerted by extremely fine pulverization has occupied the attention of several French chemists. The following table contains the results obtained by Vivien on subjecting powdered nodules from several localities to the action of acetic acid and ammonium oxalate. The character of each of the powders is indicated by the proportion of it which passed through the sieve: —

Locality from which the phosphatic mineral was obtained.		Of each 100 parts of of phosp. acid in the mineral there was dissolved,		From 100 parts of the mineral there passed through a sieve the meshes of which measured 0.15 millimetre.
		by Acetic acid. Parts.	by Ammonium oxalate. Parts.	Parts.
Somme	I.	15.95	52.10	60.20
	II.	11.55	42.91	52.00
	III.	5.75	36.10	35.84
Ciply	I.	7.87	45.52	91.40
	II.	6.35	34.55	53.60
Meuse.	I.	13.02	61.31	84.80
	II.	15.47	42.59	62.40
Quievy	I.	98.24	81.72	100.00
	II.	6.40	68.07	79.20

Solvent action of Humus.

Several investigators have tested the solubility of rock phosphate in humic acids, and in humate of ammonia, in the belief that the sparing solubility of phosphates in carbonic-acid water does not fully explain the good effects sometimes produced by such phosphates on peaty or moorland soils; and it has been shown that the humic acids have really a considerable solvent power for phosphates.

Dietrich mixed 50 grm. of finely powdered phosphorite (of 50 %) with 50 grm. of powdered peat, and left the moistened mixture exposed to the air. He leached the mixture with water at intervals during ten months, with the result, that in 1,000 grm. of the water used to leach the mixture there was dissolved 0.4688 grm. of phosphoric acid. But, as Dietrich has remarked, a dressing of phosphorite applied in field-practice would find itself in presence of a much larger proportion of humus than was the case in his experiments. In another trial, where the peat was treated with a small amount of ammonia, rather less phosphoric acid was dissolved from the phosphorite, viz. .03769 grm. in 1,000 grm. of water.

Ten years after Dietrich, Fleischer, Koenig, and Kissling studied the question anew, and arrived at the conclusion that many kinds of peats and moor-earths exert a more or less pronounced decomposing and solving action upon the so-called insoluble phosphates. It was found that pure precipitated diphosphate of lime was acted upon comparatively easily, and that precipitated terphosphate of lime also was strongly attacked, though very much less readily after it had been ignited than when fresh. Fine bone-meal was more readily acted upon than coarse, and bone-ash was considerably less soluble than bone-meal of the same degree of fineness. Precipitated phosphate of alumina was more strongly acted upon by the moor-earth than precipitated phosphate of iron, and it was noticed that these phosphates could be decomposed by humate of lime in the moor-earth with formation of phosphate of lime. Powdered phosphorites were less readily attacked than the substances above enumerated, though they were still acted upon to a noticeable degree.

Fleischer argues that there can hardly be a doubt that the free humic acids of the peat act to decompose the phosphates by combining with their lime or other base. He states that neither the precipitated nor the rock phosphates were much acted upon by moor-earths which contained no free humic acids; but that, on the contrary, even the solvent action of mere water upon the phosphates was hindered by the presence of such earths, apparently because of the humate of lime which is contained in them.

Peats derived from moss, such as contain specially little inorganic matter, were found to act particularly forcibly upon the phosphates. Moreover, on adding lime or carbonate of lime to the moor-earths which acted most freely upon the phosphates, their action ceased. So too, when moorland is cultivated, and the free humic acids in it are thereby neutralized to some extent, its power of dissolving the insoluble phosphates is materially lessened, and the more completely in proportion as the land has been more thoroughly manured. Nevertheless, it was found that even those moorlands which are most thoroughly cultivated still have the power to dissolve considerable quantities of the precipitated and rock phosphates. Moorland that has been burned for the sake of rendering it cultivable has its power of dissolving phosphates lessened, since considerable quantities of humic acids are destroyed by the combustion. For example, while 100 parts of air-dried peat derived from moss dissolved 0.4317 part of phosphoric acid, 100 parts of peat taken from cultivated fields dissolved on the average no more than 0.1944 part of phosphoric acid.

In general, the larger the quantity of the moor-earth which was made to act upon a given weight of a phosphate, the more of the latter was decomposed, though the amount of phosphoric acid dissolved was not strictly proportional to the amount of moor-earth used, since that intimate contact between the earth and the phosphate which is needed to insure chemical action cannot be so well secured when large quantities of the earth are employed. As a rule, more points of contact between the phosphate and the earth can be secured, and more phosphoric acid dissolved, by applying large quantities of phosphate to the land, although, in case the phosphate happens to be contaminated with carbonate of lime, the solvent action of the earth will be diminished in so far as humic acids are neutralized by the lime-carbonate. In presence of sulphate of potash the solvent action of the moor-earth upon phosphates was decidedly increased. Kainit also, muriate of potash, and even nitrate of soda, helped the solvent action somewhat; but gypsum, chloride of calcium, and especially carbonate of potash, hindered it very decidedly, apparently by neutralizing humic acids.

Holdefleiss, as the result of numerous and careful experiments on composting rock-phosphates, concluded that they are really very little acted upon by humus, no matter whether it is sour or undergoing decay, excepting always such moor-earth as contains free sulphuric acid.

Koenig and Kiesow digested various phosphates with solutions of humate of ammonia that had been prepared with considerable care. Five grm. quantities of phosphorite, for example, were warmed upon a water-bath, with varying quantities of the humate solution. The results were that 1,000 grm. of water dissolved the following amounts of phosphoric acid respectively from

| | When digested with Humate of Ammonia. | | | |
	50 cc. grm.	100 cc. grm.	200 cc. grm.	300 cc. grm.
Powdered phosphorite that contained 31¼ % of phosphoric acid	0.051	0.064	0.071	. . . .
Recently precipitated terphosphate of lime	0.199	0.222	0.234	0.323
Recently precipitated ferric phosphate	0.160	0.121	0.182	0.213
Recently precipitated aluminum phosphate	0.070	0.146	0.182	0.272

Pitsch also observed that solutions of humate of ammonia dissolve appreciable quantities of precipitated di- and tri-phosphate of lime, of precipitated ferric phosphate, and of Curaçao guano. He even compared the solvent action of the humate of ammonia with that of citrate of ammonia.

CHAPTER XI.

NITRATES.

It has long been known that the growth of many kinds of plants is greatly promoted by the presence of nitrates in the soil; such as the nitrates of potash, lime, soda, and ammonia. "I firmly believe," said Evelyn, writing in 1675, "that were salt-petre (I mean factitious nitre) to be obtained in plenty, we should need but little other composts to meliorate our ground." And Davy, in his turn, near the beginning of this century, wrote as follows : —

"The vague ancient opinion of the use of nitre and of nitrous salts in vegetation seems to have been one of the principal specu-lative reasons for the defence of summer fallows. Nitrous salts are produced during the exposure of soils containing vegetable and animal remains, and in greatest abundance in hot weather, and it is probably by the combination of nitrogen from these remains with oxygen in the atmosphere that the acid is formed."

The justice of this view has been exemplified by the experiments of Lawes and Gilbert, in which from 34 to 60 lb. of nitrate-nitrogen to the acre have been found in the uppermost 27 inches of soils of fields that had lain fallow during the spring and summer months. The smallest quantity (34 lb.) was taken from a field which had received no manure for 27 years, and had borne wheat and lain fallow on alternate years during this period. The largest quantities were from manured fields which were occasionally left fallow. On adding the quantities of nitrate-nitrogen thus found in the soil to those carried out in the drainage waters, it appeared, in some years, that as much as 87 lb., or even 90 lb., of nitrogen had been nitrified per acre during the 14 or 15 months that the land had lain fallow. The magnitude of these quantities will be made evident by the remark that they correspond respectively to 553 lb. and 572 lb. of commercial nitrate of soda to the acre. It is to be said, moreover, that much larger quantities of nitrate will be produced on rich or highly manured soils than are found on fallow land.

But in spite of their clear views, neither Evelyn nor Davy was fully informed as to the real value of nitrates, and it is only comparatively recently that their paramount importance has been established by observation and experiment. It is now known, that for many crops the nitrates are capable of supplying all the nitrogen which is needed; and that they are perhaps, on the whole, better adapted than any other one substance for supplying nitrogen to plants. The experiment of Boussingault, described on a previous page, well illustrates this point. In experiments made by way of water-culture, also, nitrates are relied upon as the best source of nitrogen. Generally speaking, they have been found to be more manageable, and at the same time more certain to promote the growth of plants, than ammonium salts or any other of the compounds of nitrogen.

Long-continued observations and many experiments have proved that, beside the inorganic or ash ingredients of plants, nitrogen in some available form must also be present, in order that a crop shall attain to any considerable development. The growth of many kinds of wild or uncultivated plants is really no exception to this rule. It is certain that plants must be supplied with nitrogen in some useful form if there is to be abundant vegetation, and there are numerous instances in which the influence of nitrates upon the growth of wild plants, and of weeds in particular, is very clearly marked. For some crops, such as wheat and the other cereal grains, it is all-important that nitrates should be present in the soil, in order that the crop may grow freely, and it is a familiar observation that the leaves of grain-plants fed with nitrates take on a peculiarly intense green color.

The significance of nitrates as plant-food is well shown by some experiments of Wolff, who grew oats, by way of water-culture, in solutions charged with varying amounts of nitrates, but containing, in every instance, an abundant supply of all necessary ash-ingredients. As will be seen from the following table, the increase of crop was well marked, according as the supply of nitrate was increased. The solutions employed contained 0.3 grm. of saline matters to 1,000 grm. of water : —

The (1,600 c. c.) solution contained Nitrogen, grm.	Weight of Dry Crop. Grain.	Total.	No. of Seeds.	Per cent of Nitrogen in dry crop.
. . . .	1,190	3,361	54	0.61
0.052	3,275	9,314	133	0.87
0.104	4,400	13,988	179	0.77
0.156	5,500	17,433	227	0.74
0.208	5,324	19,777	215	1.01
0.260	6,451	21,190	257	1.06

It will be noticed that the larger amounts of nitrogen favored the production of straw rather than that of grain, a result which is constantly observed in farm practice. It is to be observed, also, that, in order that the plants might grow, they needed to accumulate as much nitrogen as should amount to at least 0.6 or 0.7% of their (dry) weight. It was only when the plants could take in an amount of nitrogen equal to 1% of their dry matter that vigorous growth was assured.

It needs to be said, however, that some kinds of plants get comparatively little benefit from nitrates. As will be explained directly, leguminous plants, such as clover, peas and beans, obtain a large part of their nitrogenous food in a different way from the cereals, and it would not be advisable to apply any large quantity of a nitrate for fertilizing such crops.

Sources of Nitrates.

Thus far, only nitrate of soda and nitrate of lime, more particularly the former, can be obtained cheaply enough to be used as manures. Large quantities of nitrate of soda are constantly imported from Chili, to be used both in agriculture and in the chemical arts. Crude nitrate of soda is found there incrusting the soil of a desert.

Nitrate of lime, mixed with small quantities of the nitrates of potash, soda, and magnesia, might be prepared, if need were, by establishing saltpetre plantations like those which were formerly worked in Europe in the interest of gunpowder-making. These "nitre-beds" have already been alluded to as illustrating certain processes, the results of which may be detected in almost any good porous soil; and it has been suggested, by a German chemist, that farmers might perhaps find their advantage in some cases, even nowadays, in working saltpetre-beds up to the point of obtaining an earth highly charged with nitrate of lime. This earth could then be spread upon the land like any other ripe compost. In any event, saltpetre plantations may be regarded as little more than compost-heaps methodized and exaggerated. It is doubtless true, that in almost every very old compost-heap more or less saltpetre may be generated. Perhaps one of the advantages of keeping manure until it is very old, and of forking it over repeatedly, may depend upon the fact that nitrates form with especial ease in such manure when it is applied to the land after active fermentation and putrefaction have ceased. It is in the field itself that the instructed farmer should strive to encourage the formation of the lime-nitrate.

One question not yet accurately studied is, whether nitrate of lime may not be a better fertilizer, in some cases and for some kinds of crops, than nitrate of soda is. The fact that plants may be acted upon very differently by the two nitrates has been shown clearly enough by means of experiments [1] made in pots filled with sand, or loam, or calcined loam. I am ignorant as to whether any one has put upon record observations upon this point made in field-culture.

Saltpetre Waste.

In addition to the above-mentioned nitrates, some slight allusion may be made to certain residues or waste products left in the process of refining East Indian saltpetre, which are occasionally sold as a fertilizer, and to old plastering taken from damp and dirty

---

[1] See Bulletin of the Bussey Institution, vols. I and II, *passim*.

houses. The saltpetre residues now in question are often obtainable at powder-mills, as well as at some kinds of chemical works. They consist of varying quantities of the sulphates and chlorides of potassium and sodium, together with some nitrate of potash or of soda, say from 5 to 10%. There are doubtless a number of localities in this country where small quantities of the saltpetre waste may be obtained at cheap rates, since the material is of no use whatsoever excepting as a manure. It would be well, however, to have the substance analyzed before buying it, since its value depends almost wholly upon the nitrogen and the potash which are contained in it, and the proportion of these ingredients may sometimes be very small.

Old plastering, particularly that from the walls of damp and filthy rooms in cellars or basements, has long been esteemed valuable as a manure; though the European experience which applies to very old, very dirty, and very damp houses has comparatively little meaning in America. Lime plastering is made by mixing cow's hair with mortar, and through the decay of this hair, as well as of filth which the plastering may have absorbed, nitrates are formed. Scrapings from the limestone walls of cellars, particularly from those of barns and stables, are likewise valuable. In both cases it is the nitrate of lime which has formed as the result of changes undergone by the nitrogenous matter, when in contact with air and limestone, that gives special value to the plastering or to the porous stone. In the same category with these last should be placed the saltpetre-earth of the Mammoth Cave, and of various other caves in the Middle and Western States. Wherever such nitrous earth can be obtained cheaply, it deserves the farmer's careful attention.

Nitrate of Soda.

Nitrate of soda is employed in very large quantities as a fertilizer in some parts of Europe, especially upon grain-crops, as a supplement to farmyard manure. It is said to do better service, on the whole, on heavy land than on light land; and in many parts of England it is believed that nitrate of soda may always be applied with advantage to wheat on strong, clayey soils, unless, indeed, the land has already received very heavy applications of farmyard manure. On land already fairly well fertilized, the nitrate is usually strewn in the spring as a top-dressing, at the rate of 100 to 150 lb. to the acre, when the young wheat-plants are well above ground.

If larger quantities than these were to be applied, there would be a risk that the wheat might grow too rank, and finally lodge; though in the case of strong clays, which have been inadequately manured from the farmyard, as much as 200 lb. of the nitrate to the acre are sometimes applied. It is said that the liability of the wheat to suffer from over-rank growth may be very much lessened by applying the nitrate in successive small instalments, at intervals of a week or two, instead of all at once. In this event, no more than 50 or 60 lb. would be put upon the land at any one time; but care would naturally be taken not to apply any of this soluble nitrogenous fertilizer too late in the season, lest the crop should be led to run too much to leaf at a time when the leaf-making stage of growth should by good rights have been completed. It is noticeable, on the other hand, that experience has taught that very often no great economic advantage has been gained by applying nitrate of soda in the autumn to winter wheat or to winter rye.

To insure the even distribution of the above-mentioned small quantities of the fertilizer, it is well to mix the nitrate crystals with 3 or 4 parts of loam. First of all, however, any lumps or agglomerations of crystals which may be found should be picked out and broken down with a maul or rammer. Sometimes these lumps are very hard. Experiments made by Voelcker in England, in different years, on top-dressing winter wheat, gave the following results. The soil was a calcareous clay. The fertilizers were mixed with ten parts of loam, and strewn broadcast in late March or early April, when the wheat had fairly started.

Fertilizer on Acre.	Crop of 1859.	
	Grain. Bushels of 60 lb.	Straw, etc. Long Tons.
1.75 cwt. nitrate of soda	38	1.2
2.5 cwt. Peruvian guano (15 % N)	40.1	1.14
180 lb. nitrate of soda and 1.5 cwt. common salt	40.6	1.2
4 tons chalk marl	27	.8
No manure	27	.8

	Crop of 1860.		Crop of 1861.	
	Grain.	Straw.	Grain.	Straw.
1.5 cwt. of nitrate of soda	44.17	1.8	45.2	1.5
2 cwt. sulphate of ammonia	44	2	44.33	1.33
2.5 cwt. Peruvian guano (of 15 % N). . .	46.1	1.8	40.5	1.25
1.5 cwt. nitrate of soda, with 3 cwt. common salt	47.5	2	45.5	1.5
3 cwt. common salt	35.25	1.14	37.86	1.1
32 bushels of soot	41.66	1.6	. . . .	
No manure	34	1.33	31	1

| | Crop of 1862. | |
	Grain.	Straw.
2 cwt. nitrate of soda	44.5	1.5
2 cwt. nitrate of soda with 4 cwt. common salt	44.75	1.5
1.5 cwt. nitrate of soda with 3 cwt. common salt	41.5	1.5
1 cwt. nitrate of soda with 2 cwt. common salt	38.75	1.33
3 cwt. of common salt alone	38.75	1.2
2 cwt. Peruvian guano (of 15 % N)	43	1.5
2 cwt. Peruvian guano with 2 cwt. common salt	43.5	1.33
No manure	29	1

It is noticeable in 1859 that $8 worth of nitrate of soda gave 11 bushels of wheat and 6.25 cwt. of straw over and above the crop from unmanured land; and that in some instances the addition of salt to the nitrate was beneficial. After several years experience Voelcker urged that, "On soils in good condition, a top-dressing of 1.5 cwt. of nitrate of soda and 3 cwt. of salt, applied in the spring, is one of the best manures for wheat that can be employed. . . When the price of wheat is high, a liberal outlay in the purchase of nitrogenized top-dressings is attended with great profit." He dwells on the speedy action of the nitrate of soda, even as compared with that of the guano.

In 1859, the effects of the nitrate became visible four days after the application of the fertilizer, and in the course of a week the dark-green color of the nitrated wheat was unmistakable. The action of the guano first became visible on the eighth day and was plainly observable at the end of a fortnight. While admitting that guano may on the whole be preferable to nitrate of soda for top-dressing wheat, Voelcker urges that the nitrate is excellent for producing a rapid improvement in sickly-looking wheat on clay soils, and in general on all land which is productive under good cultivation. It is not to be recommended for poor land— i. e. land the poverty of which is caused by a deficiency of mineral food—but in many situations where, as on the brows of hilly fields, young wheat is apt to turn yellow and sickly in dry spring weather, a slight sprinkling of nitrate of soda or of nitrate of soda and salt will cause a marvellous improvement.

Upon light loams the nitrate is applied in rather smaller quantities than to clays, i. e. at the rate of something like 100 lb. to the acre, though it is generally speaking highly esteemed on such land, in England, as a means of forcing grain crops. As long ago as 1858, it was reported of the light chalky soils of Norfolk, England, that, "In the spring it is a common practice to top-dress the wheat with nitrate of soda and salt; and as this custom has become general, it is a proof that it is successful." Upon soils of this character, that are not too dry, nitrate of soda often does excellent service, and it is especially efficacious upon warm, deep, mellow loams.

It has been suggested indeed that there is a certain amount of risk in using the nitrate on cold, backward land, lest the ripening of the grain be too long delayed, and several observers have remarked that stiff clay land does not respond to applications of the nitrate so freely as land of a lighter character. An instance has even been cited of a tract of cold clay-land in South Durham, England, where nitrate of soda is less highly esteemed than sulphate of ammonia.

As applied to winter wheat in the spring, nitrate of soda is strewn as a top-dressing, as has been said; but in the case of barley, or other spring-sown grain, it is best to harrow in the fertilizer lightly before sowing the seed. That is to say, as is true of all the other saline fertilizers, it is well, when possible, to incorporate the nitrate thoroughly with the soil rather than to leave it strewn upon the surface; for by mixing it with the earth, the seeds or young plants are protected in some measure from actual contact with the nitrate, a more perfect dissemination of the fertilizer is assured, and the risk that it may help to encrust the surface of the soil is very much lessened. It is said that the best time to apply the nitrate is after the heaviest spring rains have fallen, but before these rains have ceased. It is well also to strew it, or to harrow it in, at times when showers are expected.

Shall Nitrates be exhibited by Instalments?

It was supposed at one time that if it were possible to apply the easily soluble nitrates by successive instalments it might always be best to do so, but it is now recognized that this idea is subject to limitations. It is known that if nitrate of soda were to be used by successive portions it would be necessary to scatter very small quantities at each of the sowings, and in respect to grain at least, care would have to be taken that none of the fertilizer was applied too late in the season; for, as was just now said, after the grain-plant has attained a certain development the addition of any easily assimilable nitrogenous fertilizer would be apt to interfere with the production of grain and to make the plants run to leaf. In no event, should nitrates be applied to grain-plants which have attained any considerable size. Care should always be taken in using nitrate of soda upon grain to guard against the risk of the crop's lodging.

It is recommended by European writers that grain, and especially summer grain, which is to be dressed with the nitrate, should be sown very thinly and in wide drills, so that a sufficiency of light may gain access to the plants. Otherwise, the crowded stalks would be blanched and feeble. As a general rule, it would not be well to apply very large quantities of nitrate of soda to the land. According to Heiden's experience useful results may be obtained by applying from 50 to 250 lb. to the acre, but only in exceptional cases should more than 275 lb. to the acre be used. It is true, however, that when used in conjunction with heavy dressings of phosphates on land not over charged with farmyard manure, nitrate of soda may be applied with comparative freedom, because the phosphates tend to make a crop ripen off rather than to run to leaf. This idea is illustrated by the following experiment. A field of winter rye grown in Germany on land rich in potash and phosphoric acid, which received its last dressing of farmyard manure in 1887, for roots, and had borne oats in 1888, and peas in 1889 — was dressed with varying quantities of nitrate of soda in May, 1890, and there was harvested per hectare the following amounts of grain and of straw : —

Fertilizer, per hectare.	Double Centners of Grain.	Straw.
No manure	26.91	103.89
15 kilos nitrogen	29.04	106.25
30 " "	30.10	107.05
45 " "	34.78	105.75

Contrary to ordinary experience, which goes to show that nitrate of soda favors the growth of straw rather than of grain, the formation of grain was distinctly promoted by the nitrate in this instance, and the grain was heavy as well as abundant. According to Maercker, from 60 to 80 lb. of nitrate of soda applied to light lands in early spring, or from 60 to 110 lb. on soils of better quality, are customary dressings for grain in Germany. He urges that a top-dressing of the nitrate, applied in early spring to winter grain which was manured with bone-meal at the time of sowing, often does extremely good service.

Nitrates not fit for poor, dry Land.

It has been observed in Germany that nitrate of soda is not a proper application for grain, upon poor, sandy soils, which are liable to drought in late spring or early summer. So long as there is plenty of moisture in the soil, crops fed with the nitrate grow freely; but, when drought sets in, such succulent plants suffer much more severely than plants which have never been pampered. So, too, instances have been reported in England where nitrate of soda, applied to wheat on poor, dry land, produced its best results in those years which were so wet that throughout the kingdom the wheat crop was very poor. Voelcker urged that, while nitrate of soda, either by itself or admixed with salt, is extremely well adapted for top-dressing wheat on stiffish soils in good condition, a specially prepared mixture of mineral and nitrogenous fertilizers is to be preferred for lighter soils, and soils which are naturally poor. For light land, he recommended, many years ago, the following mixture: 1.5 cwt. nitrate of soda, 3 cwt. common salt, 2 cwt. Peruvian guano, and 40 bushels of soot.

The following experiments with rye were made in 1885, by Rimpau, in North Germany, on light, sandy, upland soils in a region of moors. In the autumn of 1884, before the rye was sown, all the land was manured with kainit and superphosphate at the rate of 3 centners of kainit and 20 lb. of phosphoric acid to the Morgen. Next spring, some plots were top-dressed with 100 lb. nitrate of soda to the Morgen, and some with 50 lb., while other plots received none of the nitrate. The kinds of crops previously grown upon the fields, and the increase of rye brought by the use of nitrate of soda, are given in the following table: —

Previous Crop.	Lb. Nitrate of Soda used.	Rye Crop, in lb. per Morgen.		Lb. increase, per Morgen, due to Nitrate.	
		Grain.	Straw.	Grain.	Straw.
White Lupines . .	0	675	1555	. . .	. . .
" " . .	50	795	1905	120	350
" " . .	100	1125	2715	450	1160
Red Clover . . .	0	680	1340	. . .	. . .
" " . - .	50	820	1540	140	200
" " . . .	100	970	2010	290	670
Red Clover . . .	0	636	1260	. . .	. . .
" " . .	50	700	1420	64	160
" " . . .	100	960	1960	324	700
Crimson Clover, for	0	610	1940	. . .	. . .
seed	100	860	2040	250	100
Clover and Grass,	0	402	718	. . .	. . .
pastured . . .	50	614	1266	212	548
" . . .	100	885	1814	483	1096

Previous Crop.	Lb. Nitrate of Soda used.	Rye Crop, in lb. per Morgen.		Lb. increase, per Morgen, due to Nitrate.	
		Grain.	Straw.	Grain.	Straw.
Potatoes, heavily	0	390	850	...	...
manured . . .	50	550	1150	160	300
" . . .	100	760	1760	370	910
" . . .	0	680	1320	...	...
" . . .	50	750	1810	70	490
" . . .	100	820	2300	140	980
" . . .	0	500	1100	...	...
" . . .	50	672	1408	172	308
" . . .	100	1062	1658	562	558
" . . .	0	756	1364	...	...
" . . .	100	1087	2013	331	649

In the cases where rye was grown after potatoes, the land was specially poor. Two of the potato-fields were situated in one locality and two in another, while the land which had borne lupines, etc., was in yet another locality, and was of rather better quality.

Some striking experiments were made long ago, by Pusey, on land which had been " exhausted " by growing five grain-crops upon it in succession. The idea was to compare the action of nitrate of soda upon wheat with the action of superphosphate of lime. The results are given in the following table : —

	Wheat Grain, bu. to the acre.
No manure	7.33
170 lb. nitrate of soda	19.30
6 cwt. peat charcoal	8.75
6 " " " and 170 lb. nitrate of soda . .	18.00
4 " superphosphate	7.00
4 " " and 170 lb. nitrate of soda . .	19.33

Pearlash applied to this land, at the rate of 7 cwt. to the acre, gave no appreciable increase of crop.

Nitrate of Soda is good for Beets.

Nitrate of soda may be used to force root-crops as well as grain. In Europe, it is employed largely both upon mangolds and sugar-beets. One common plan is to dress the beet-land with farm-manure and superphosphate in the autumn, and to apply nitrate of soda the next spring. But it is recognized that upon sugar-beets the nitrate needs to be used with care, and in not too large quantities, lest the quality of the beet-juice should be impaired. Indeed, great, overgrown beets are apt to be rather poor in sugar, and are not specially esteemed for sugar-making. Hence, when nitrate of soda is used as a fertilizer, it is customary to make the beets stand rather close together, in order that they may not become unduly large.

It is said that sugar-beets should never be top-dressed with the nitrate, but that half of the proposed dressing should be ploughed under deeply in the autumn, and that the other half should be strewn in the spring together with a superphosphate, before the land is prepared for seeding. According to Maercker a suitable dressing for sugar-beets on the rich loams near Magdeburg, is 110 lb. of the nitrate applied to the Morgen of land in the autumn together with farmyard manure, and 165 lb. of the nitrate in the spring together with 30 or 40 lb. of soluble phosphoric acid.

With mangolds — where a large crop is the chief desideratum — nitrate of soda may be used more freely than upon sugar-beets; 300 or 400 lb. to the acre are often used in England, in conjunction with farmyard manure, or with phosphate and potash salts. Even on land heavily dressed with farmyard manure, 225 lb. of the nitrate are sometimes applied to ensure a maximum crop of mangolds. According to Dyer, 4 cwt. of nitrate of soda may be used with a moderate dressing of dung, while with half a dressing of dung the 4 cwt. of nitrate should be supplemented with some phosphatic fertilizer. He urges that the risk of running to tops may be avoided by putting on the nitrate in successive doses — 1 cwt. before the seed is sown, 1 cwt. at the time the young plants are thinned out, and the remaining 2 cwt. in two applications, a month apart, the nitrate being simply strewn by hand between the rows of beets.

In this country, market-gardeners have often found it advantageous to work into the soil of their onion-beds enough nitrate of soda to give the crop a start whenever the slow growth or unhealthy appearance of the plants indicates that they stand in need of a stimulant. As a rule it would be better to apply the nitrate after a crop has come up than to strew it upon a seed-bed where it might sometimes do harm by helping to form a crust at the surface of the soil, as will be explained directly.

Nitrate of Soda for Potatoes.

Potatoes respond freely to dressings of nitrate of soda, though it is to be remembered that in years which are damp and muggy, and so favorable for the development of the fungus which causes the potato-rot, the rank-growing nitrate-fed vines will be specially liable to the attacks of the fungus. It was noticeable in Ireland in 1845, that luxuriant beds of potatoes that had been manured with guano were the first to be destroyed by the rot-fungus, and the observation is now familiar that potatoes fed with easily as-similable nitrogen compounds are particularly liable to suffer from the rot. For this reason, no very large amounts of the nitrate should be applied to potatoes. Heiden says from 50 to 100 lb., in addition to stable-manure. Or, in case artificial fertilizers are used, and no dung has been recently applied to the land, as much as from 130 to 250 lb. of the nitrate may be applied, according to the condition of the land.

Nitrates for Tobacco.

Tobacco is a plant which can bear to be heavily manured, and which yields little or nothing when not well fed; and it is found that reinforcements of nitrate of soda (or better yet nitrate of potash), used in addition to stable-manure, are advantageous for this crop. The nitrate brings a heavier crop and the tobacco burns better, and as a general rule it is stronger, i. e. the leaves are richer in nicotin.

As regards color, A. Mayer has urged as a general proposition, especially true of young leaves, that the less nicotin there is in tobacco the lighter will be its color when dry, and the more nicotin the darker the color. But he has noticed that the uncured leaves of tobacco which has been manured with nitrate of soda are often spotted, manifestly because the leaves of any plant which has been fed with nitrates are apt to ripen slowly and irregularly, as has often been noticed in respect to wheat and other kinds of plants. Thus it happens that many spots upon a leaf may remain alive and green at the time of harvest after the adjoining parts of the leaf have dried. It has been claimed, however, that this irregular coloration may be corrected during the process of fer-mentation to which tobacco is subjected after it has been har-vested.

In general it may be said that the color of merchantable tobacco is largely a matter of fashion, and dependent upon the process of curing as much or even more than upon either soil or manure. The color of crude tobacco may be changed materially according to the duration and the kind of fermentation to which it is sub-jected and according as the fermentation is interrupted by drying at one or another stage. According to Kosutany, tobacco which has been manured with farmyard manure plus ammonia tends to be of a reddish tinge, while that which has received nitrate of soda is apt to have a green tint.

Nitrate of Soda for Grass.

On good, sound, sweet pastures, in Europe, nitrate of soda, applied at the rate of from 50 to 100 lb. to the acre, has often done good service, especially when used in conjunction with compost. In England, particularly good results have been obtained by strewing the nitrate on spots where cattle have neglected to feed. Upon clover the effect of the nitrate is said to be particularly well marked, as well as upon Italian ray-grass and the aftermath of meadows. It will be seen below — and in the chapter on hay-fields also — that nitrate of soda gave good results when applied as a top-dressing to grass-land, in the experiments of Lawes and Gilbert.

Efficiency of Nitrate of Soda.

When used as a nitrogenous addition for reinforcing stable-manure, a given weight of the nitrate has sometimes been estimated in England to act at least one quarter better than the same weight of the best Peruvian guano. An experiment of Mr. Hope will illustrate this point. In the month of April, he sowed nitrate of soda (mixed with salt) and guano upon parts of a field of winter wheat of unpromising appearance, which had followed potatoes on a dry, gravelly loam. The nitrate plots soon took the lead and kept it. The amounts of fertilizers used upon the acre of land and of crops harvested therefrom were as follows:—

Fertilizers used.	Bushels of wheat.	Cwt. of straw.
Nothing	39	33
3 cwt. guano	49	36
1 cwt. nitrate of soda and 1 cwt. salt	53	38

Others have held that one cwt. of nitrate of soda will give a more certain return of wheat than 50 times its weight of farmyard manure, and that it can be carried to the land and spread there at less than one-fiftieth the labor. There can be little doubt that the application of nitrate of soda to wheat on fertile, well-manured soils in Europe must often enough have been of the nature of insurance, for in case cold weather were to persist in the spring, or if dry weather should set in at a time when the grain-plants needed to be growing rapidly, the nitrification of the farmyard manure in the soil would proceed much too slowly for the best results, and the presence of a little nitrate of soda, which had been added as such, might obviate the risk of the crop's failing. In any event, a small addition of nitrate of soda in the spring, as a reinforcement of farmyard manure, would ensure the timely starting of the crop. Of course the best action of such a manure can only be had on rich soils, which contain all the other ingredients necessary for plants, and on soils moist enough to maintain prosperous crops. The soda saltpetre, like any other merely nitrogenous fertilizer, acts by exciting the plant to grow. It is not alone that the nitrate supplies the plant with food, but that it makes the plant vigorous enough to collect food for itself from the soil and the soil-water.

Forcing Effect of Nitrates.

As practical men know well, nitrate of soda — like some other manures which contain easily assimilable nitrogen, notably ammonium salts, guano, blood and night-soil — tends to exhaust poor land when applied to it injudiciously. The nitrate forces, as it were, the crops to use up, with undue rapidity, the small store of potash and phosphoric acid which the soil contains, and there is risk that the condition of the land may be seriously injured. In general, nitrates should not be applied to poor, sandy soils, unless, indeed, other kinds of fertilizers are used to supplement them.

It has, in fact, been shown by A. Mayer that, under the impulse given by nitrate of soda, grain-plants can make better use of the rather inert phosphates naturally contained in poor soils than they could in the absence of any " forcing action," such as the nitrate gives. Discretion must always be exercised when using this fertilizer, lest it cause the plants to run too much to leaf, and become too rank. It was recognized long ago in England, that, in the event of the spring and summer happening to be wet, nitrate of soda tends to produce blight upon wheat, and a weak, bent straw, which may lodge before the ears have had time to fill well. This result would be sure to happen in case too much of the nitrate were sown upon land already richly manured.

Methodical experiments by Hannam have shown that dressings of nitrates applied to oats and barley have a tendency to increase the straw in a greater ratio than the grain, to render the straw soft and bulky, and to retard slightly the ripening of the crop. It need hardly be said, therefore, that it would be improper to put nitrate of soda upon land already highly charged with available nitrogen compounds. It was noticed very early in England, that on land in high condition the nitrate does harm, in that it makes crops grow rank, and causes grain to lodge. It is upon land which, though naturally fertile, happens to be "out of condition," and upon fields which, from the previous course of cropping, may stand in need of a nitrogenous reinforcement that nitrate of soda does its best work.

The forcing effect of the nitrate is well shown by the results of some experiments by Pusey, where nitrate of soda was used as a top-dressing in the spring upon winter wheat which had been fertilized with blood-meal or rape-dust or guano the previous autumn. The land was a sandy loam, which had borne three consecutive grain-crops before the time of the experiment. The fertilizers, as specified in the following table, were drilled in with the wheat in the autumn, and one-half of each plot was twice top-dressed in the spring with a mixture of nitrate of soda (90 lb. to the acre) and common salt. It is stated that the autumn and winter were unusually rainy : —

No. of turns of the drill.	Amount of fertilizer.	Bushels of Grain from	
		Plots not top-dressed.	Top-dressed plots.
10	3 cwt. guano	6.25	13.00
10	3 cwt. blood-meal	6.75	12.50
10	3 cwt. rape-dust	4.50	11.75
10	3 cwt. nitrate of soda	5.12	11.25
2	Nothing	1.00	2.75
5 acres		28.63	51.25

Waste of Nitrates by Leaching.

The risk of losing much of the nitrate, when large quantities of it are applied, is illustrated by the following experiments of Lawes and Gilbert : When 550 lb. of nitrate of soda were applied, year after year, to wheat in March, together with ash-ingredients, the drain-water from March to May contained 48.4 parts of the nitrate to 1,000,000 parts of water, while the drainage from unmanured land and from land fertilized with ash-ingredients contained only 1.7 parts to the million, and that from land dressed with 200 lb. of ammonium salts and ash-ingredients contained 8.1 parts. From June to August, the numbers of parts of nitrate in 1,000,000 parts of water were 9.1, 0.1 and 0.7 respectively; while taking the whole year, the quantities were 12.3, 3.7 and 5.0 respectively. In any event, the liability to loss by leaching, during the spring months, is larger in the case of nitrate of soda than in that of sulphate of ammonia, for the ammonia of the latter is fixed by the soil, and held there for a time, while it is undergoing nitrification. Lawes and Gilbert have remarked that it is a striking evidence of the excellence of the nitrate as a manure, that, notwithstanding the greater losses it suffers during the spring months, it should, on the average of seasons, give a larger produce than ammonium salts for the same amount of nitrogen supplied.

Nitrates may Encrust the Land.

According to Heiden and to Maercker, large dressings of nitrate of soda may do harm on some soils by causing hard, compact crusts to form at the surface of the land, which hinder air from passing into the soil, and check the growth of seedling crops, such as sugar-beets. In one instance, Maercker observed that the coming up of young beet-plants was delayed 5 or 6 days when 2.5 centners of nitrate of soda were applied to the Morgen of land, and to the extent of 8 or 10 days when 5 centners of the nitrate were applied. Moreover, the beet-plants came up irregularly, and some little time elapsed before the land was well covered by the crop. Maercker urges that it is not well to apply as much as 2 centners of the nitrate all at once to the Morgen of land just before seeding. A better plan is to put on one-half the dressing before the seeds are sown, and the other half at the time of the first or the second hoeing of the crop. In case as much as 3 centners of the nitrate are to be used, one-third of it might be applied before seeding, one-third at the time of the first hoeing, and one-third at the second hoeing. This advice he holds to be specially sound in case potash salts are to be applied in addition to the nitrate of soda.

This tendency to encrust the land is shared to a certain extent by other saline fertilizers beside nitrate of soda, and is said to be specially noticeable on soils that are somewhat heavy, while sandy loams are free from it. The crusts may of course be broken by hoeing or "cultivating" the land frequently. Hence a feeling has arisen in some localities that upon heavy land large dressings of nitrate of soda can be applied only to such crops as are subjected to frequent cultivation, such as beets and potatoes, or grain that has been sown in rows wide enough to permit the cultivator to pass between them. It has even been hinted that the successful use of nitrate of soda in England may have depended in some part upon the fact that grain is often sown there in wide drills and cultivated as a hoed crop. Upon fields of winter grain that have been sown broadcast, it would probably be easy to destroy such crusts by dragging a smoothing-harrow over the field at a dry

time when the crop is young. But, it is safe to say, as regards
grain, that no harmful encrusting of the land is likely to occur in
actual practice, because of the fact that upon grain nitrate of soda
is habitually used as a mere reinforcement, i. e. in quantities so
small that no very material change in the physical condition of the
soil could be produced by them.

Nitrates may improve Tilth.

A remarkable instance of the power of nitrate of soda to change
the texture of soils has been reported by Maercker. Seeking to
determine how large a quantity of nitrate of soda can be supported
by a potato-crop, he applied the nitrate in the spring to plots, each
of one Morgen area, which were adjacent to plots of similar size
that received none of the fertilizer. The nitrate was used in quantities ranging from 1 to 5 cwt. to the Morgen. The soil was a
calcareous (Loess) loam, and it was noticed after the potatoes had
been harvested in the autumn, that the character of the soil had
been so much changed by the nitrate that the field looked like a
checker-board. After several falls of rain it became evident that
while the plots which had received none of the nitrate had the usual
appearance of porous loam of medium quality, the nitrated plots
were highly charged with moisture, and the more so in proportion
as more of the nitrate had been applied. Indeed, the plot which
had been dressed with 5 cwt. of the nitrate is said to have looked
like a swamp.

Evidently, the tilth of the land had been materially changed by
the action of the nitrate of soda, and the inference is that the capacity of the soil to hold water had been largely increased. According to Maercker, it is a common observation that in places
where considerable quantities of nitrate of soda have been spilled
upon the land, as where bags of the fertilizer have been opened
or handled carelessly, moist spots may be seen for years.

Lawes and Gilbert had noticed in their experiments — which
were made upon a rather heavy loam resting on a clay subsoil
which reposed on chalk — that " wherever nitrate of soda is employed year after year, on the same plot of arable land, the difference in the appearance and texture of the soil is very great and is
discernible at a considerable distance." The effect of the nitrate
is to improve the condition of the clay subsoil and to make it better able to hold water. The nitrated soil, " apparently retains
very much more moisture, and may indeed become agglutinated

and so sticky compared with that of adjoining plots under equal
conditions of weather as to be with difficulty worked at the same
time, and never brought to the same tilth without the expenditure
of extra labor upon it."

During a severe drought, in 1870, a vastly better crop of hay
was obtained from an old mowing-field which had long been dressed
with nitrate of soda and mineral fertilizers than was got from contiguous fields which had received farmyard manure, or mixed fertilizers that contained ammonium salts. So striking was the difference in the effect of the drought on plots of grass growing side
by side, that it was decided, on the removal of the hay-crop, to determine how much water existed in the soil at depths lower than
the deepest roots could be traced. For this purpose samples of soil
were taken on July 25 and 26, from three different plots, to the
depth of 54 inches, the grass-roots having been traced to within
a few inches of this depth in the land fertilized with nitrate of soda.

The following table gives the moisture, in per cents, which was
expelled from the earth (on drying it at 212° F.) taken from three
different plots, at the depths stated.

Depth in inches from which the earth was taken.	Unmanured Land. Moisture %.	Manured with Ammonium Salts and Minerals. Moisture %	Manured with Nitrate of Soda and Minerals. Moisture %
First 9 inches	10.83	13.00	12.16
Second 9 inches	13.34	10.18	11.80
Third 9 inches	19.23	16.46	15.65
Fourth 9 inches	22.71	18.96	16.30
Fifth 9 inches	24.28	20.54	17.18
Sixth 9 inches	25.07	21.34	18.06
Mean	19.24	16.75	15.19
Yield of hay to the acre in the droughty year, 1870, lb.	644	3,306	6,300
Average annual yield of hay during 20 years, lb.	2,383	5,711	6,406

It will be noticed that, while the drought caused an enormous
diminution in the crop of hay obtained from the unmanured land,
and a very considerable diminution in the case where ammonium
salts had been used, there was comparatively little decrease on the
nitrated land. Yet, on the assumption that the acre of land
weighs 18,000,000 lb., to the depth stated in the table, the nitrated land contained 325 long tons less water than the unmanured
land, and the ammoniated land contained 200 tons less than the

unmanured,—quantities which correspond to 3.25 and to 2 inches respectively, of rainfall. From all of which it appears that the heavy crops of grass on the manured land had pumped out more water from the lower layers of soil than had been taken by the feeble crop on the unmanured land, and the superiority of the crop obtained from the nitrated plot must have been due, in part, to the excellent capillary condition of the soil, induced by the action of the nitrate, and in part to the better development of roots in this land, occasioned by the thorough diffusion of the nitrate, whereby the soil was made both fertile and porous.

In one word, the tilth of the nitrated soil was such that the crop grown in it could obtain ample supplies of water from the sub-soil, even during a long-continued drought. For the better understanding of the table, it needs to be said that the amount of water found in the surface layer of soil depended, in some part, on the fact that nearly an inch of rain fell between the time when the hay-crop was removed and that when the samples of soil were collected. In these experiments, Lawes and Gilbert noticed as a remarkable fact, when nitrate of soda was strewn, year after year, on an old grass-field, that the growth of meadow-foxtail (Alopecurus pratensis) and of Poa trivialis were greatly encouraged. But, as is well known, these grasses grow by preference in moist places, and soon disappear, for the most part, from dry fields.

In their experiments, also, on the continuous growth of barley, it was noticed that where large quantities of nitrate of soda had once been applied, the crops tended to increase rather than to decrease, and to be less troubled by droughts than were the crops which had been dressed with ammonium salts. They suggest the question, "whether the explanation be not that where the excessive amount of nitrate of soda was applied in the earlier years of the experiment, the subsoil was so acted upon, disintegrated, and rendered more porous, that it offered a greater surface for the retention of the otherwise easily washed-out nitrate; a greater surface for the retention of moisture, and greater permeability to the roots; thus increasing the store, both of available food and available moisture at command of the plant, and facilitating the penetration of the roots in search of them."

Reactions of Nitrate of Soda in the Soil.

According to Sachsse and Becker, the cause of the incrusting action of nitrate of soda, as above described, is to be attributed to the formation of carbonate of soda in the soil, through the decomposition of the nitrate, both by its reacting with carbonate of lime to form nitrate of lime and (bi)carbonate of soda, and by the action of plant-roots which take from it nitrogen and give off carbonic acid to unite with the soda. The action of alkaline carbonates to agglutinate soils is well known, and will be described under the head of Potassic Manures and of Alkali Soils.

. Since the first action of nitrate of soda — like that of other saline compounds — is to flocculate clay rather than to agglutinate it, it might be inferred that, for a time at least, before the decomposition of the nitrate in the soil, the fertilizer might act in a different way from that above described, which is really closely analogous to the action of wood-ashes; but M. Whitney has noticed, in laboratory experiments, that, on adding to a soil successive portions of a solution of nitrate of soda, the rate of percolation decreased very remarkably, and that the soil soon became almost impervious to water.

Nitrate of Soda may kill Insects and Worms.

One merit of the nitrate is that it tends to destroy slugs and cut-worms. In cases where young wheat was suffering from the attacks of the wire-worm, applications of nitrate of soda have been found to be specially beneficial, though the operators were uncertain whether the nitrate actually killed the worms or merely made them forsake the young plants. Other observers have testified that nitrate of soda will kill earth-worms, within half an hour from the time it is sown, in a very surprising way. The nitrate has been used with advantage, also, on young onions that were suffering from the attacks of a maggot, and upon cauliflowers.

It is a wise precaution to pay some attention to the condition of emptied bags in which nitrate of soda has been kept, for, unlike the potash salt, nitrate of soda is hygroscopic. It absorbs moisture rather easily from damp air, and the cloth of the bags in which it is usually transported may readily become saturated with the salt, especially if they have been stored in a damp place. But a heap of cloths thus impregnated with the nitrate might take fire spontaneously if it were left undisturbed for some time in a hot, damp place.

Nitrate of Potash sometimes used.

Pure nitrate of soda contains about 63 % of nitric acid, regarded as "real," as the commercial term is, i. e. anhydrous, and 37 % of soda. Theoretically, this comparatively large proportion of soda would seem to be an objection to the use of the salt, for plants have little or no need of sodium. It would seem, consequently, as if it would be much more appropriate to use as manure some substance like nitrate of potash, both ingredients of which are useful. But up to the present time the cost of nitrate of potash has been too great to admit of that salt's being used with much freedom in agriculture.

It is somewhat used of late for horticultural purposes, and in some special and peculiar cases in agriculture proper; but ordinarily the farmer contents himself with using mixtures of nitrate of soda and a potash salt, whereby the two constituents of nitrate of potash are brought to the land. No doubt it happens usually that some of the nitrate of soda applied to the land by itself soon changes there to nitrate of lime and nitrate of potash.

As met with in commerce, nitrate of soda is not quite pure, though usually very nearly so. It contains, on the average, some 94 or 95 % of the pure salt, or say 15¼ % of nitrogen. Of late years, a mixed potash-soda nitrate has been carried to Europe from a particular locality in the South American desert whence nitrate of soda is derived. This mixed nitrate is of somewhat variable composition, but usually contains about 16 % of potash and 15 % of nitrogen. The proportion of nitrate of soda in it ranges from 55 to 68 %, and that of nitrate of potash from 31 to 42 %. The sum of the two nitrates ranges from 90 to 95 %.

Nitrification.

During many years, chemists were greatly perplexed in trying to explain the manner in which nitrates form in a saltpetre bed and in cultivated fields. For more than a century, indeed, experiments had been made continually, in the hope of discovering a satisfactory theory of nitrification, as the process is termed. Several of the facts of nitrification are familiar and conspicuous. For instance, it has long been known that, when animal and vegetable matters containing nitrogen decay in the air, in contact with earth charged with limestone, or with wood-ashes, the nitrates of lime and of potash are formed. On the other hand, there are numerous localities, particularly in warm climates, where the soil is highly charged with nitrates. This remark is true, not only of the East Indies, but of Egypt, Poland, Hungary, and Italy. In each of these countries, earths occur which are rich enough in saltpetre to pay the cost of working.

In all these places, the nitrate of potash appears to have resulted from the decomposition of organic remains. In Egypt, for example, the nitrate comes from heaps of refuse thrown out by the earlier inhabitants, and in Poland from tumuli or hillocks, which are really the remains of former habitations. " In several parts of Hungary, saltpetre is produced in considerable quantities from the soil on which the flocks and herds have been long feeding." (R. Bright.) At the time of the American Revolution, when enough gunpowder and saltpetre to attract attention were exported from Russia, it was reported that the inhabitants of the Ukraine were accustomed to spread wood-ashes upon the sites of old encampments for the purpose of " attracting saltpetre," which could thereafter easily be separated.

Even in Bengal, which produces a large proportion of the saltpetre of commerce, the nitrate is leached from earth obtained in and around the mud walls which enclose the huts and cow-sheds of the inhabitants. (Palmer.) At certain seasons, saline efflorescences appear at the surface of the ground, which are scraped up and lixiviated. It is said that the best earths are found where the soil is calcareous, and where the ground-water does not lie within 20 feet of the surface. Under these conditions, the nitre forms most rapidly during the rainy season ; and the process of nitrification is favored by the custom of the inhabitants of throwing wood-ashes outside their dwellings.

Out of contact with carbonate of lime, or other alkali, a quantity of nitrate of ammonia is formed when nitrogenized matters decompose in the soil. This fact has been proved by careful experiments, but may be verified any day by testing the water of wells in old and crowded cities. Such water will almost always be found to contain nitrate of ammonia, often in large quantity, when the well happens to be near a leaky cesspool. The putrid contents of the cesspool ooze out into the soil, and are there brought into contact with enough air to convert a part of the ammonia in the filth into nitrate of ammonia, and since this substance is readily soluble in water, it passes into the wells into which the water of the soil flows. Warington has found that in a solution of ammonium carbonate, nitrification will proceed until one-half of the ammonia is oxidized, and will then stop, because all the ammonia has been converted either into ammonium nitrite or ammonium nitrate, and all the available base is exhausted.

For the same reason, nitrification ceases in diluted urine when one-half of the nitrogen is oxidized. For the complete nitrification of the nitrogen of ammonium salts, some salifiable base must be present. Ordinarily there is enough carbonate of lime in soils to supply this need. According to Warington, a soil which contains little or no available base is sure to be very deficient in fertility, and to be greatly benefited by dressings of chalk or lime.

In the light of what is known to-day, it is a fair inference that almost all the nitrates found in nature have been derived from the oxidation of ammonium compounds, for these last are formed in abundance during the earlier stages of the putrefaction and decay of organic matters, and when once they have been formed, they change readily to nitrates, under fit conditions. Schloesing found that a quantity of ammonia put upon moist loam changed completely to a nitrate in the course of a fortnight; and Dehérain, on applying 0.02 grm. of ammonia-nitrogen to moist garden-loam, found that 0.0194 grm. of nitrate-nitrogen was produced from it in the course of five weeks.

The Nitrifying Ferments.

It is now known that the formation of nitrates in the earth, from ammonia or from other nitrogenous matters, is not a process of chemical oxidation pure and simple, such as might occur if the nitrogen compounds were to be treated in the laboratory with powerful oxidizing agents. It is not a plain chemical reaction, such as is obtained when caustic ammonia is boiled with potassium permanganate or subjected to the action of peroxide of hydrogen. It appears, on the contrary, that the intervention of certain microscopic organized "ferments" is necessary, in order that nitrites and nitrates may be formed. Precisely how these ferments act is not yet known. But it has been clearly made out that they are minute microscopic plants, analogous to yeast, which, under favoring conditions of warmth, moisture, and darkness, prosper in ordinary loams, with the result that nitrites and nitrates are formed there. Not to force the analogy, it might be said that the production of nitrites and nitrates by the agency of living things is somewhat akin to the production of carbonic acid by men and animals; for animals always live in localities that supply carbonaceous food and air, and it was noticed very early that carbon is in some way oxidized to carbonic acid in the places which animals frequent.

It is of no little interest to recall the fact that some very old receipts for making saltpetre enjoined most explicitly that, in making a new nitre-bed, it should be "seeded" by commingling with it a certain amount of earth taken from an old bed. This practice was of course akin to the use of leaven in the making of bread; for just as leaven contains numberless yeast-plants, so does the earth of an old nitre-bed swarm with micro-organisms

There is a Nitrous and a Nitric Ferment.

According to Warington and to Winogradsky, two kinds of ferments are necessary for the completion of the process of nitrification. The first species of ferment changes ammonia (or the like) to a nitrite, and the second species changes nitrites to nitrates. In reality, three kinds of micro-organisms must be needed in most cases, one kind to set free ammonia by acting upon organic matters, a second to change this ammonia to a nitrite, and the third to convert the nitrite to a nitrate. In ordinary speech, however, nitrification is spoken of as if it represented but a single step. In this sense it may be said that the process is favored by tolerably high temperatures. Experiments have shown that nitrification is feeble below 40° F., though it does not absolutely cease in solutions kept at a mean temperature of 37° to 39°. The formation of nitrates becames really active at 54° and increases rapidly as the temperature rises above that point. Just below 100° (at 98° or 99°), nitrification is at its maximum. Experimenters have obtained results in the course of a few days, when operating at 98°, that would in our climate have required months or years in ordinary outdoor experience. Above 100° the formation of nitrates decreases rapidly as the temperature rises. According to Schloesing and Muntz nitrates form less readily at 113° than they do at 59°; at 122° only very small quantities are formed, and above 131° no trace of the formation of nitrates could be detected. Under favorable conditions, other things being equal, ten times as much saltpetre can be obtained at 99° as at 57°. Warington, on the other hand, failed to start nitrification in a solution kept at a temperature of 104° F. But it is evident enough that it is during hot summer weather that nitrification is most active in the field, and to this fact should be attributed the popular opinion that many plants have the power to digest particularly large quantities of manure during the warmer season. As has been said, a proper proportion of moisture promotes nitrification, but drought is wellnigh fatal to the process. Indeed, in absolutely dry air the ferment perishes, and mere dryness, as ordinarily understood, stops the action of the ferment as long as the condition of dryness lasts. But nitrification does not occur in soils so completely saturated with water that air cannot penetrate them.

Nitrification of Ordinary Loams.

Dehérain has found by pot-experiments that large quantities of nitrates may be produced from the organic matters naturally contained in soils, provided the earth is made permeable to air and is methodically watered. 100 grm. of a soil that contained 0.26% of nitrogen yielded in six months' time 88 milligrams of nitric acid, which would be equal to more than 600 lb. to the acre in a year, a much larger amount namely than has been found sufficient for the growth of maximum crops. In laboratory experiments so arranged that the air above the nitrifying earth could be kept saturated with aqueous vapor, Dehérain found that nitrification could be induced when there was no more than 5% of water in the earth, and that 10 or 15% were sufficient for good results. No advantage was gained by adding more than 15% of water to the earth so long as evaporation was prevented by keeping the air above the earth saturated with moisture.

The Ferments need Food.

Naturally enough, all kinds of food necessary for the growth of the microscopic organisms which cause nitrites and nitrates to be formed must be present in order to the success of the process. Phosphates, for example, are indispensable, and small quantities of the other ash ingredients of plants are needed, as well as some compound of nitrogen, and of carbon. It has been discovered, however, by Winogradsky, and confirmed by other observers, that although the nitrous ferment can apparently feed upon organic matter, the presence of such matter is not necessary for the production of nitrates, since both of the nitrifying organisms can readily assimilate the carbon of carbonic acid, and obtain in this way all the carbon they need. The nitrous ferment has the power to form nitrites from ammonium salts and carbonates (or, better yet, bi-carbonates) without causing any evolution of oxygen, for while the carbon of the carbonic acid goes to form the cells of the ferment organism, its oxygen is put to immediate use in forming a nitrite from the nitrogen of the ammonia.

Organic Matter is not Necessary.

According to Warington, an endless series of generations of the nitrous ferment may be reared in solutions of ammonium salts and carbonates (and phosphates) which contain no organic substance whatsoever. He finds that bi-carbonate of soda, bi-carbonate of lime and acetate of soda are well suited for feeding the nitrous ferment, but that the presence of simple carbonate of soda hinders nitrification. Godlewski has suggested that the force developed during the oxidation of the ammonia is sufficient to account for that needed to decompose the carbonic acid and to build up the cells of the ferment organism. The nitric ferment also, as well as the nitrous ferment, develops freely in solutions to which no organic matter has been added, and its development is favored by the presence of the acid carbonates of calcium or sodium; but although under fit conditions it quickly oxidizes nitrites, it appears to have no action on ammonia, and the presence of any considerable quantity of ammonium carbonate hinders its development and prevents it from acting upon nitrites.

Oxygen is Essential.

That the presence of oxygen is essential for nitrification has been well known to saltpetre boilers time out of mind. Pallas, writing in 1772 of his travels in Siberia, mentions as a fact familiarly known that nitre forms only near the surface of the soil. He cites an instance where, through ignorance of this circumstance, the discoverer of a saltpetre cave, instead of contenting himself with leaching the surface soil, which was highly charged with nitre and yielded much profit, excavated the earth to a considerable depth, and consequently suffered great pecuniary loss. In the soil of Lawes and Gilbert's fields — which overlies a clay subsoil reposing on chalk — the ferment was found invariably in a state of high activity at all depths down to 9 inches from the surface. But in the clay subsoil the nitrifying organism was "small in quantity or feeble in condition," and there was no question that nearly the whole of the nitrification in the heavy land at Rothamsted was in the surface soil, though it was admitted that in a sandier soil nitrification would probably occur at greater depths. It was found on studying the clay subsoil that the presence of gypsum in the test solutions was helpful; when it was added, the ferment could be detected in almost every trial to depths of 3 feet, but below this point the number of failures to detect the presence of the ferment increased. At 6 feet half the trials made with the clay subsoil were failures, and at 8 feet in the clay none of the ferment organism could ever be found. Several trials made at a depth of 5 feet from the surface, in the chalk subsoil, failed to detect any of the ferment. It is to be noted, however, that in permeable soils, well aerated by tillage or by tile drains, the conditions might be somewhat more favorable for nitrification in the subsoil; and especially where a deep-rooted crop pumps so much water from the subsoil that the pores thereof are opened for the admission of air.

Moisture is of Great Importance.

Here in Massachusetts, in upland fields, it is probable that the conditions best suited for nitrification are seldom to be found unless it be once in a while for brief periods, for when the soil is thoroughly wet, there will not be air enough in it for the support of the ferments, and on the other hand when the surface soil becomes too dry the activity of the ferments will be impaired. One merit of low-lying land adequately supplied with moisture is that nitrification readily occurs there. As bearing on the importance of tillage, it may be said that beside acting to aerate the soil the mere mechanical stirring of the particles of earth may promote nitrification by distributing the nitrifying organisms anew and bringing them into contact with fresh supplies of food.

It has been noticed that the nitrifying ferments do not prosper very well in a strong light. Darkness is favorable for their development. Indeed, it was said by Lord Bacon in his day that, "the way to hasten the breeding of saltpetre is to forbid the Sunne and the growth of vegetables. And therefore, if you make a large hovell thatched, over some quantity of ground; nay if you doe but planck the ground over, it will breed saltpetre."

The Ferments are Easily Poisoned.

The nitrifying ferments are killed easily by poisons, notably by acids, by chloroform, coal-tar, the spent lime of gas-works, ferrous sulphate, and by large quantities of saline matters, though, as Schloesing and Muntz have shown, the presence of small quantities of saline matters does not hinder nitrification. On adding various salts to soils in quantities not exceeding 485 parts per million, no apparent effect was produced on the rate of nitrification. But Dehérain, using larger proportions, found that common salt began to be harmful when it exceeded one-thousandth of the weight of the soil, and with larger quantities nitrification almost ceased. Even additions of nitrate of soda may stop nitrification for a time, though it recommences afterward. Maercker reports that no nitrates could be detected in a moor-earth that contained . as much ferrous sulphate as would be equivalent to $1\frac{1}{2}\%$ of ferrous oxide, and only very small quantities of nitrates could be found in other parts of the moor that contained about a quarter as much of the sulphate. But nitrates were abundant in a contiguous part of the moor that was free from the ferrous salt. An acre of the moorland taken to the depth of $39\frac{1}{2}$ inches contained, where no ferrous sulphate was present, as much as 980 lb. of N_2O_5; where there was as much ferrous sulphate as would amount to 0.298% and 0.395% of ferrous oxide there were found 90 lb. and 147 lb. respectively of N_2O_5 to the acre, but where the ferrous sulphate amounted to 1.349% of ferrous oxide there was no nitrate whatsoever.

Inasmuch as an excess of saline matters would be apt to kill the nitrifying ferments, it would not be wise to apply any very large quantity of common salt or muriate of potash, or superphosphate even, to places where nitrification is active. Even a great excess of nitrate of soda might do harm. Dehérain found that nitrification did not set in until after the lapse of four weeks in a pot containing 100 grm. of loam with which 0.06 grm. of nitrate of soda had been mixed; but that afterward nitrates were gradually formed when the ferment organisms had adapted themselves to the untoward conditions. He found in fact that 0.009 grm. of nitrogen had been nitrified in the course of 105 days. A still stronger dose of nitrate of soda, amounting to 0.6 grm., in 100 grm. of loam, arrested nitrification, as before; but after a while it set in again, though more feebly than in the previous experiment. He found also that while nitrification ceased when quantities of common salt amounting to from 0.4 to 1 grm. were mixed with 100 grm. of loam, there was formed in five weeks' time, in a moist loam which contained one-thousandth of common salt, 0.024 grm. of nitric acid. But inasmuch as no more than 0.032 grm. was formed in twelve weeks it seemed as if the activity of the nitrification was slowly diminishing. On mixing 0.25 grm. of salt with 100 grm. of loam, tolerably active nitrification was noticed at the end of six weeks, but during the next six weeks very little nitre was formed, and it appeared that, instead of becoming wonted to the new conditions, the ferment organisms had perished.

Practically, a risk that nitrification might be hindered by the presence of chlorides or nitrates that had been applied as fertilizers would arise when, through long continued dry weather, these saline matters had been brought up by capillary action and concentrated near the surface of the soil. It is evident enough that heavy applications of saline fertilizers, or of gas lime, or of sulphocyanide of ammonium, or of mud charged with sulphuretted hydrogen, or with sulphides, or with ferrous sulphate, might sometimes do much harm to a field or to a compost heap.

The facility with which ammonia may be changed to nitrates within the soil by ferment action is illustrated by the following experiment of Knop. A quantity of sandy loam was exposed to the vapor of ammonia for three days. It was then spread out in a thin layer, moistened with water, and kept sheltered from rain until it had dried. Finally the amount of nitrates contained in it was determined. At the beginning of the experiment there were found 52 parts of nitric acid in 1,000,000 parts of the earth, but at the close there were 591 parts of nitric acid in every million parts of the earth,— more than eleven times as much as at the start. It was noticed in this experiment that the ammonia absorbed by the soil suffered no change so long as the soil was kept dry. It was only after the soil was moistened that the nitric ferment could act to oxidize the ammonia.

Nitrates from the Dust of the Air.

Doubtless a minute proportion of the nitrates which are formed in soils may be derived from ammonia that has come from the air; but the quantity of ammonia in the air is ordinarily so extremely small that there is no probability that any considerable amount of nitrates can be formed in this way. Another source of nitrates is the organic matters in the dust of the air. It is known that ammonia is apt to be formed, through the decomposition of this organic matter, upon the surfaces of all substances upon which atmospheric dust is deposited, and that nitrates are formed from the ammonia in due course. It is a very old observation that the outer layers of beds of marls and limestones often contain more or less nitrate of lime, and recent investigations have shown that nitrates and ammonium compounds are usually present upon the surfaces not only of limestones, but of all kinds of rocks, soils and other materials.

It is not improbable, withal, that the formation of ammonia and of nitrates upon the surfaces of solid bodies may be aided by the presence of microscopic organisms capable of obtaining nitrogen from the air, as will be explained in another chapter. One familiar fact which seems to point to this conclusion, is the habitual occurrence of ammonia in iron rust, as has been observed by several generations of chemists. However this may be, it is instructive to observe how rapidly polished iron may become tarnished when exposed to the dust of the air. American housekeepers are familiar with the fact that articles of polished steel or iron, such as knives, pokers, tongs, fire-shovels, grate-bars and blowers for grates are apt to become rusty during the summer months, when they are out of use. In order to prevent this rusting, careful housewives are accustomed to wrap up each particular article in paper, so that no dust shall come to the steel. So, too, before plated steel came into use, it was customary to roll up spare sets of table-knives in flannel, or to keep the knives in little bags, in order to avoid rust. The explanation of the matter appears to be that when dust and germs from the air are left in repose upon steel, ammonium compounds and nitrates are speedily formed, particularly in summer weather, and that the nitrates corrode the metal. It is in order to avoid such damage that pains are habitually taken to cover steel articles, to exclude the dust. One reason why copper, bronze and brass are not thus corroded appears to be that copper salts are poisonous for micro-organisms.

The Ferments as Disintegrators.

Muntz has suggested that there is good reason to believe that the organisms which cause nitrification must play an important part in the superficial disintegration of rocks. He has detected the presence of the nitrifying ferments in large numbers on the bare surfaces of many rocks — calcareous, feldspathic, micaceous, schistose and others — even at the summits of mountains in the Pyrenees, Alps and Vosges. He finds that these ferments are not killed by the lowest temperatures of the Alps, that they penetrate to a considerable depth in the cracks of the rocks, and are specially abundant on surfaces where disintegration is most clearly marked.

It was noticed long ago, by geologists, that many rocks contain small quantities of organic matter, and Muntz has suggested that the presence of this organic matter in disintegrated rock may depend upon the activity of the organisms now in question, though it seems more probable that such humus is produced by certain other micro-organisms, such as have been noticed by Berthelot, as will be explained on a subsequent page. It is evident that the corrosion of rocks may be promoted both by the mechanical action of micro-organisms and by their secretions, as well as by the nitrates which are formed incidentally.

Nitrites can be formed directly from Organic Substances.

Although it is to be presumed, in the generality of cases where nitrates are seen to have been derived from organic matters, that ammonium was first formed, and that it was acted upon by the ferment organisms, it is true, none the less, that the intervention of ammonia is not strictly necessary, since nitrites are sometimes formed directly from organic compounds. Munro and Warington have found that nitrites may be formed directly by the action of the nitrous ferment on albumin, gelatin, asparagin, urea, ethylamin and thiocyanates, and from milk and urine also; and it is known that nitrites thus formed are readily converted to nitrates by the action of micro-organisms in the soil. Indeed, it has been shown by Muntz that the oxidizing action of the ferments is not confined to organic matter, for even as nitrites are oxidized to nitrates, so are metallic iodides changed to hypoiodates and iodates, and bromides to hypobromites and bromates.

Putrefaction adverse to Nitrification.

It is to be observed that the formation of nitrates from organic matters can occur only during the slow decay of the organic matter, under circumstances which admit the presence of a large excess of oxygen. Kellner has shown that nitrification does not occur in the rice-swamps of Japan. A soil fully saturated with water is unfit for nitrification, not only because air is excluded from it by the water, but because, in warm weather, the constituents of such a soil are apt to enter into putrefactive decomposition, and, as has long been known, no nitrates are formed in putrefying materials. On the contrary, any nitrates which might be present in the fermenting mass would soon be reduced and destroyed. Thus it has been noticed that, by the putrefaction of the white of egg, nitrate of potash that had been mixed with it was destroyed, and ammonia formed.

This matter has been studied by adding small quantities of sewage, or of chicken broth, or some other easily putrescible substance, to a mixture of nitrate of potash and sugar-water. It is found that the liquid speedily becomes charged with micro-organisms,

under the influence of which the nitrate is reduced to a nitrite or
to some other lower oxide of nitrogen, and in some part even to
the condition of free nitrogen. (Garnier.) The most common
form of action is a reduction to nitrite, which afterward remains
unchanged. Several well-known bacteria possess, in a high degree, the power of reducing nitrate of potash to the nitrite; but
among the reducing bacteria there are some which carry the reduction further, and produce nitric oxide, nitrous oxide, or even nitrogen gas. In the manufacture of sugar from the beet-root, a
fermentation, accompanied by evolution of "red fumes," is apt
to occur in molasses which is not kept sufficiently acid.

In order to get an idea as to what may happen when manure is
applied to fields where nitrification is active, Leone filled a large
box with garden loam that contained 0.025 % of nitrates, and
mixed hen-dung intimately with this loam in the proportion of
300 grm. hen-dung to 10 kilos of loam, taking care so to arrange
matters that air could pass freely through the particles of earth.
After 48 hours, less nitrate was found in the loam than it had
contained at first, and at the end of a week the amount of nitrate
had still furthur diminished, while nitrites could be detected.
After the lapse of a fortnight, both nitrates and nitrites had disappeared totally, and the earth was found to be highly charged
with ammonia. The formation of ammonia reached its maximum
at the end of a month, and then remained constant for 5 or 6
days. But on the 35th day nitrates again began to be formed,
and after the lapse of 3 months only nitrates could be detected in
the earth. In another box, filled only with the loam, without any
admixture of hen-manure, nitrification suffered no interruption,
but ran its course naturally from the very first. From all of which
it follows that a very heavy manuring might destroy the nitrate in
a soil, while light dressings of manure can hardly do more than
reduce small portions of nitrates, here and there, in spots, as it
were.

Mere exclusion of oxygen from a moist soil is sufficient to induce actions which destroy nitrates. Thus, Schloesing found that
nitrates quickly disappeared from a moist soil rich in humus which
he placed in an atmosphere of nitrogen gas, and the same denitri-
fying action occurred when only a small and limited amount of
air was present.

More than a hundred years ago a couple of French inspectors

of saltpetre, Gavinet and Chevrand, called attention to the fact that the hog-pen is not of the nature of a nitre-bed; while, on the contrary, large quantities of saltpetre commonly form in stables where sheep or goats are kept. The hog, as they put it, reduces the earth and manure in his pen to the state of a thick moist paste, which is not at all favorable for the formation of nitrates; while in the sheep stalls the dung is spread about and kept moderately warm, and it is only occasionally moistened by the urine of the animals, in such wise that nitrates form there in large quantities. At the period when these observations were made, i. e. at a time when nitre-beds were still cultivated on the continent of Europe, an Italian named Lorgna stated most explicitly, that, " although quite beyond our limit of vision, it is none the less a fact that the act of nitrification is the last term of putrefaction." " It is well known," he says, " that putrescible matters do not become fit for the production of nitre unless they can undergo complete putrefaction, and it often happens that not an atom of nitre will form in a great mass of putrescible matters, not even when they have been kept for a long time, unless these matters have been divided and dispersed among porous substances and distributed in small parcels, so that their fermentation may not be hindered, and that putrefaction may freely attain its highest point."

Not only in the hog-pen, but in all non-aerated, boggy places — notably on flooded rice-fields (as Kellner has shown) — are nitrogenous organic matters protected from nitrification. If nitrates were put upon wet bog-land they would soon be deoxidized, for in such situations processes of reduction occur, such as produce ammonia and marsh-gas. According to Boussingault, Schloesing, and others, even the vegetable mould of woodland is apt to contain only very small amounts of nitrates, probably because the kinds of decay which occur in such humus are to be classed among processes of reduction rather than of oxidation or nitrification.

Carbonate of Lime aids Nitrification.

A certain slight degree of alkalinity in the soil has been found to favor the growth of the nitrifying ferments, a result which is in harmony with the old belief that the presence of a certain amount of lime carbonate is necessary for the success of a nitre-bed. Touvenal, who experimented long ago with a variety of earths and chemicals, found that among them all chalk and pure carbonate of lime most constantly favored the formation of nitrates. He urged that it is to the presence of the lime carbonate that must be attributed the fact that nitrates are found more abundantly in calcareous soils than in those which have resulted from the decomposition of rocks other than limestones. In calcareous soils, he says, nitrates form even in the open air, though to a much smaller extent than in covered places, and in caves or huts or sheds that are inhabited.

Quicklime he found, on the contrary, to be much less useful than the carbonate for promoting the formation of nitre ; and this difference was so strongly marked that he was led to question whether lime can ever by mere exposure to the air regain the whole amount of carbonic acid needed to neutralize it. This suggestion is one of some importance from the agricultural point of view, as teaching that air-slaked lime can perhaps never be a complete substitute for leached ashes, for example.

Touvenal's observation has been corroborated by experiments made by Boussingault, who found that nitrification ceased in garden-loam when caustic lime was present. He even remarked that quicklime seemed to help to destroy nitrates which had been contained in the soil before the lime was added. On the other hand, the lime, by acting on inert nitrogen-compounds in the soil, caused a constant slow formation of ammonia. Two months after the earth of his experiments had been mixed with lime it contained no more nitrates (but sometimes less) than had been found at the beginning ; although in parallel experiments an abundance of nitrates formed in similar earths to which no lime had been added. In respect to ammonia, the results obtained were of a totally different character, much more ammonia being found, constantly, in the limed earths than in those which received no lime.

For each of the experiments in question, two parallel series of large glass globes were charged with the earth to be tested. In all cases, the earths were adequately moistened with pure water, and they were kept under similar conditions favorable for nitrification. But the earth in one series of the globes was left in its natural condition, while that in the other series was mixed with varying quantities of hydrate of lime. Some of the results obtained by Boussingault are given in the following tables.

I. A fertile, sandy loam, very rich in organic matter, from an old kitchen-garden.

During the times stated, there was produced in each kilo of air-dried earth : —

		Limed Series. Grams of		No Lime Series. Grams of	
		Ammonia.	Nitric Acid.	Ammonia.	Nitric Asid.
During 6 days.	With 0.3 grm. lime	0.012	Not det.	....	....
" 10 "	" 2.0 " "	0.007	0.005	....	....
" 2 "	" 18.9 " "	0.084	Not det.	....	....
" 1 month	" " " "	0.076	0.009	0.005	0.233
" 2 "	" " " "	0.079	—0.003	0.010	0.226
At the beginning of the experiment the natural earth contained 0.21% of organic nitrogen and				0.009	0.067

II. A good clayey loam taken from a tobacco-field on a farm, in another locality : —

		Limed Series. Grams of		No Lime Series. Grams of	
		Ammonia.	Nitric Acid.	Ammonia.	Nitric Acid.
After 6 days.	With 0.3 grm. lime	0.007	Not det.	....	....
" 10 "	" 2.0 " "	0.010	0.008	....	....
" 1 month	" 10.0 " "	0.046	—0.020	—0.002	0.187
" 2 "	" " " "	0.036	0.034	—0.002	0.176
At the beginning of the experiment the natural earth contained 0.14% of organic nitrogen, and				0.011	0.042

In this case, where the loam contained comparatively little organic matter, it appeared that the action of the caustic lime was exhausted, as regards the formation of ammonia, in the course of the first month; though but little nitrification occurred even in the second month.

III. A very fertile sandy loam.

During the times stated there was produced in each kilo of air-dried earth : —

		Limed Series. Grams of		No Lime Series. Grams of	
		Ammonia.	Nitric Acid.	Ammonia.	Nitric Acid.
During 14 days	With 10 grm. lime,	0.018	—0.018	....	....
" 5 weeks	" " " "	0.020	—0.022	0.001	0.010
At the beginning of the experiment, the natural earth contained 0.09% of organic nitrogen and				0.012	0.022

In other experiments, made with loam (No. I.), from the old kitchen-garden, the idea was to compare the action of lime, marl, and wood-ashes with the effects obtained by leaving the loam fallow as it were, after mixing it with sand. His results were as follows : —

Grammes of the loam.	Mixed with grm.	Left during months.	Gained grammes of Ammonia.	Nitric Acid.
1,000	850 of sand	8	0.012	0.482
1,000	5500 of sand	3. 5	0.035	0.545
1,000	500 of marl	8	0.002	0.360
1,000	2 of carb. of potash	8	0.015	0.290
1,000	200 of slaked lime	8	0.303	0.099

Here again the lime, when employed in such large quantity that the mixture could be compared with a compost-heap rather than

with a limed field, distinctly hindered nitrification, while it produced much more ammonia than either of the other materials. It
appeared, however, in spite of the great increase of ammonia, that
no more assimilable nitrogen was got from the loam by means of
the lime than was obtained in the form of nitrates by leaving the
loam fallow. It will be noticed that the carbonate of potash in
Boussingault's experiment hindered nitrification, and it is now
known to be true in general that, while a slight degree of alkalinity promotes nitrification, any large proportion of alkali should
be avoided, since it does harm to the nitric ferment. Indeed,
when much lime or other strong alkali is mixed with moist earth,
rich in humus, processes of putrefactive fermentation set in, whereby nitrates are speedily reduced to ammonia. Warington also
has observed that the alkalinity of lime-water is about twice as
great as the maximum beyond which nitrification will not occur,
and that a heavy dose of lime put upon a soil may for a time suspend nitrification in the surface soil.

According to Hilgard, the process of nitrification is peculiarly
favored in California and in other warm, dry countries where summer rains are infrequent. Such regions are moderately moistened
by the winter rains, though not enough water falls to wash away
the nitrates, and there is almost always an adequate supply of carbonate of lime, considerable quantities of which are formed every
year in such soils through the decomposition of silicates of lime.

Alkalinity favors Nitrification.

Instead of the lime carbonate, very dilute solutions of carbonate
of potash or carbonate of soda have been found to favor nitrification; but if such solutions are more concentrated than 2 or 3
thousandths they check the action of the ferment. So it is with
carbonate of ammonia also. Solutions of it that are above a certain moderate strength will check nitrification as effectually as
solutions of carbonate of soda. Warington has urged that the
presence of undue quantities of the ammonium carbonate, either
that formed naturally, as when the urine of sheep ferments on dry
land, or that added expressly as a test, will greatly hinder the
process of nitrification. It is because of this action of concentrated carbonate of ammonia that urine does not nitrify, unless it
has been diluted with water, or admixed with much earth. Herein
also lies one justification of the practical rule that liquid manures
should be applied to crops in a highly diluted condition. Waring-

ton argues that, if gypsum were mixed with strong solutions of urine, so that the carbonate of ammonia should be converted to sulphate, and the excessive alkalinity of the liquid be thus annulled, they could be nitrified easily enough.

In spite of the fact that the presence of carbonate of lime or even of wood-ashes in a nitre-bed may be highly important, practically speaking, it is still true that nitrates will form when neither of the stronger bases, such as lime, potash, or soda, are present, since in their absence a part of the ammonia remains unoxidized, and serves as a base to hold the nitric acid which is formed : —

$$2\,NH_4 + 5\,O = NH_4\,NO_3 + 2\,H_2O.$$

But if lime or potash be present, then either nitrate of lime or nitrate of potash will be formed, as the case may be, and the whole of the ammonia, perhaps, may be changed to a nitrate. In any ordinary soil this result would be likely to occur, since nitrate of ammonia, on soaking into the soil, would be decomposed by compounds of lime, potash, and soda which the soil contains. It is to the absorption and change of gaseous carbonate of ammonia that the formation of saltpetre on cellar walls must be attributed in many cases, though a part of the nitre is doubtless derived from filth thrown against the wall, or sucked up into it from the earth by capillary attraction. Indeed, there is in most soils, according to Muntz, a special micro-organism which causes the nitrogen of organic matters to change to ammonia, which substance is in its turn speedily converted to a nitrite, and this again in due course to a nitrate by means of special ferments.

Reduction of Nitrates.

The easy reduction of nitrates by putrefying organic matters, as above set forth, fully justified the assertion of Kuhlman that nitrates are often deoxidized in the lower layers of soils which are not thoroughly aerated. It has since been shown indeed by several different observers that in some cases nitrates may be so completely reduced by soils rich in humus that nitrogen gas is set free. As Angus Smith has said, it is " a peculiar putrefactive condition [which] produces a deoxidation of nitrates. In some conditions nitrogen is eliminated as gas, the oxygen going to the carbon in whole or in part. In weak solutions containing water enough to absorb the carbonic acid (probably), nearly pure nitrogen may be obtained with considerable rapidity."

It is to be expected as a matter of course that deoxidation of nitrates will occur in undrained bogs and similar situations, as it does in manure-heaps, and it is evident also that even in fertile soils the conditions may sometimes be such that deoxidation will be favored, although normally they may be well fitted for nitrification. Processes of reduction might prevail, for example, when a soil was water-soaked, and remained for some time in such condition that no air could enter its pores. Hence the inference that the reduction of nitrates would occur most readily in heavy, compact undrained soils, and that those operations of tillage which tend to aerate soils and to make them sweet and mellow may really act to preserve nitrates as well as to promote their formation, though it has been remarked by Grouven that soils fit for the cultivation of ordinary crops are usually too porous to permit the deoxidation of nitrates.

It has often been observed that soils which are exceptionally rich in organic matters may contain no nitrates, or as good as none. In specimens of the somewhat famous " black earth," from a fertile region in Russia, that contained respectively 7 and 9% of humus, Knop found only 0.0002 and 0.0006 part of nitric acid in 100 parts of earth. Boussingault had found 0.0004%. A remarkably rich alluvial soil from the banks of the Amazon, examined by Boussingault, contained no trace of nitrates, but as much as 0.05% of ammonia. This soil was composed of alternate layers of sand and decaying leaves, and contained some 40% of the latter. As was just now said, woodland soils usually contain only slight traces of nitrates, and it is evident that the conditions which obtain in such soils are rarely favorable for nitrification. According to Bréal, there is an aerobic ferment which occurs on straw, and doubtless on other kinds of vegetable refuse, which reduces nitrates in a very energetic way when in presence of water, with evolution of free nitrogen. He argues that the destruction of nitrates by this particular organism can hardly amount to much in ordinary tilled land because of its freedom from water, but that in low-lying meadows and in moist woodland humus, its development would be favored, and that the absence of nitrates from woodland humus is explained by this fact.

According to Pichard, the presence of an excess of nitrogenized organic matter in a nitre-bed hinders nitrification. He found, in fact, that a mixture of materials which contained 3 % of organic nitrogen yielded a smaller quantity of nitrates than a mixture that contained only 1 %. Hence he argues that, in establishing a nitre-bed, or a compost for the production of nitrates, it will be well not to have more than 1 % of organic nitrogen in the mixture. According to Laurent, nitrates are reduced to nitrites, in the absence of oxygen, by bacteria, yeasts and moulds, and by the filamentous algæ. He noticed, also, that when oxygen is lacking, nitrates are reduced to nitrites during the germination of seeds, and that the reduction may occur inside of growing plants (of high orders) that are watered with a solution of nitrate of potash.

Warington, also, has noticed that when fresh soil is added to diluted urine, which has begun to nitrify, a destruction of the nitrates already present precedes the formation of new quantities of nitrates. The liquid always becomes turbid during this reduction of the nitrates, which is completed in a few days' time. It has been argued, in this case, that the bacteria which cause the reduction of nitrates multiply very rapidly for a time, and run their course before the bacterium which causes nitrification has become active.

"Endurance" of Nitrates.

As illustrating one practical consequence of the reduction of nitrates in the soil, the fact may be mentioned, that in field experiments made at the Bussey Institution, I have noticed several times that, in spite of the easy solubility of nitrate of soda, the fertilizing effect of this substance is not wholly exhausted in the first year of its application, but is seen to make itself felt somewhat in subsequent years. The same thing is shown in some of the field experiments of Lawes and Gilbert. Thus a patch devoted to barley, which had been dressed annually during 5 years with nitrate of soda, at the rate of 550 lb. to the acre, subsequently received every year 275 lb. of the nitrate during 14 years, while an adjacent plot received 275 lb. of the nitrate during the whole period, or, rather, for 19 years. But the first plot not only gave larger crops than the second plot during the earlier years, when it was more heavily manured, but it continued to yield more grain and more straw than the second plot during the final 14 years after the cessation of the heavier dressings of the nitrate. There was manifestly a somewhat lasting effect, due to the extra amount of nitrate applied in the earlier years.

Apparently, there must have been a considerable accumulation in the soil of nitrogen supplied by the earlier manurings, and neither recovered in the increase of the crops nor leached out of the soil in the drainage-water. I have myself been inclined to attribute this after-effect to the fixation in the soil of some nitrogenous compound resulting from the reduction of the nitrate, or, possibly, to the formation of Knop's basic nitrates of iron and alumina. Lawes and Gilbert have suggested that the nitrogen left in the roots and stubble of the crops that have been dressed with nitrates or with ammonium salts, may be the chief, if not the sole, remnant of the artificial fertilizer that abides in the soil for the benefit of subsequent crops. Their suggestion seems to me wholly inadequate to explain the appearances noticed by myself.

Berthelot has in part found, by direct experiment, that nitrates may be reduced in the soil to the condition of nitrogenous organic matters. Thus, a pot which contained 48.3 kilos of loam (reckoned as dry) and 361.5 grm. of nitrate of potash, was kept without vegetation, and protected from rain, from April 15 to September 25, and then subjected to analysis. At the beginning of the experiment, the loam contained 1.669 grm. of organic nitrogen to the kilo of earth, or, in all, 72.3 grm.; but at the close of the experiment, after the loam had been washed until no more saltpetre could be removed from it, it was found to contain 2.0467 grm. of organic nitrogen to the kilo. That is to say, there had been a gain of 0.3777 grm. to the kilo, or, in all, 16.4 grm. of organic nitrogen, equal to nearly one-quarter of the original amount. In a parallel experiment, made under like conditions, a pot of earth carried 11 plants of Amaranthus pyramidalis, but in this case it did not appear that the plants took up much of the saltpetre with which the soil had been charged, and there was found in the soil 2.0646 grm. of organic nitrogen to the kilo, i. e., very nearly as much as had been found in the other pot of soil in which no plants were growing.

It is slow decay, such as is seen in very old manure or compost heaps, that have been turned over repeatedly, that favors the formation of nitrates. Thus much is known, and there is good reason to believe, nowadays, that the active ferments find fit refuge and feeding-grounds in the well-rotted manure. So, too, manure which has been buried, not too deeply, in the soil, or even spread upon the surface of the ground, is fit to be changed to nitrates. In this sense, the practice of top-dressing the land with manure in the autumn, and leaving it uncovered during winter, is probably not ill-suited to warm climates, like those of many parts of Continental Europe, for a part of the manure soaks into the porous earth, and the nitrogen of it is there converted into nitrates in due season. But this mild commendation can hardly apply to a custom, which prevails in some parts of New England, of spreading manure upon frozen ground, there to be swept and leached by the winter rains.

Oxidation by Ferric Compounds, etc.

It has not yet been clearly made out what influence upon the formation of nitrates is exerted by substances in the soil, such as the oxides of iron (Fe_2O_3) and manganese (MnO_2), or sulphates of one kind or another (MSO_4), which are known to be capable of acting as oxidizing agents. The fact, familiar to chemists, that the black oxide of manganese, as found in nature, is apt to contain small amounts of nitrates, would of itself indicate that this compound may in some way promote the formation of nitrates; and Hünefeld and Reichart have reported experiments in which the presence of the higher oxides of manganese favored the formation of nitrites and nitrates.

The power of ferric oxide to convey oxygen from the air to organic matters is a familiar fact, seen in the holes around rusty nails in old shingles or boards, and in the wood of iron-fastened ships, and there are experiments of Knop and of Thenard which seem to show that ammonia itself may be oxidized by manganic and ferric oxides. The true explanation of the experiments of these chemists, however, would seem to be, that certain nitrogenous matters in the soil were oxidized and changed by these agents to ammonia in the first place, and that this ammonia was changed to a nitrate in due course by ferment action.

It has been noticed as a fact of very general applicability in localities where red-colored soils prevail that they are apt to be fertile and to be esteemed by farmers, whence the inference that ferric compounds, and especially ferric hydrate, when finely diffused throughout the soil, must exert some important influence, either physical or chemical. This view is supported by the fact that such soils often contain a very considerable proportion of the iron oxide. From numerous observations made in the Southern States of this country, Hilgard finds that highly colored "red lands" contain from 7 to 12% of ferric oxide, and occasionally from 12 to 20% and more. Ordinary, ferruginous loams may

contain from 3.5 to 7%, while soils that are but little tinted often
contain as much as from 1.5 to 4% of it. Naturally enough the
presence of ferric compounds in heavy clays will facilitate tillage,
and the color of the red soils tends to keep them warm in that it
favors the absorption of the sun's heat. The iron oxide will
naturally promote the oxidation of organic matters in the soil, and
it is a fact of familiar observation that soils which are strongly ferruginous seldom contain a high percentage of humus. The ferric
oxide acts to destroy humus by carrying to it oxygen from the
air. In other words, the iron oxide "burns out" the humus.

Pichard has shown that the presence of ferric oxide in the soil
may materially promote nitrification both by acting to supply
oxygen and by its power of fixing and holding the ammonia, derived from the decay of organic matters, long enough for the
nitrifying ferments to act upon it. This power of temporarily
holding ammonia is noticeable in clay as well as in ferric oxide,
and it may often hinder ammonia from going to waste. Beside
all this the ferric hydrate helps to keep the soil moist by virtue of
its well known power of absorbing the vapor of water and other
gaseous matters. Hilgard has in fact noticed that the hygroscopic
power of soils is increased by the presence of ferric hydrate, and
he has observed also in actual farm-practice that red soils resist
drought better than soils of similar character in which the ferric
hydrate is lacking.

Sulphates as Oxidizing Agents.

As regards the sulphates, it has long been known that they act
as oxidizing agents upon carbonaceous matters in the soil, as has
been explained already under Gypsum, and it is not wholly improbable that they can help to oxidize nitrogen compounds as well.
Indeed it would appear from the researches of Pagel and Oswald
on moor-earth, that ammonia, at least, may be formed by the
oxidizing action of sulphates on nitrogenized organic matters in
the soil. It is to the oxidizing action of sulphates, which results
of course in their own reduction, that is to be attributed the formation of the black earth which is found between the bricks of sidewalks and the stones of pavements in city streets, and particularly
between the bricks or stones of the yards of city houses. So, too,
the black color of the soil of privies and of stagnating sewers and
house-drains is often due to a similar cause, viz. the formation of
black sulphide of iron through the reduction of sulphates in the

soil. On being exposed to the air these black earths soon lose their deep color, for the ferrous sulphide is quickly oxidized, with formation of red oxide of iron.

Generally speaking, the experiments which have been made to test the influence of gypsum on nitrification have given negative results. Thus Wolff, on leaving cubic-foot portions of cow-manure to rot during 15 months in a north room, found that a much smaller proportion of nitrates had been formed in the box which contained gypsum than in those which contained mere ma-nure, or mixtures of manure and lime or charcoal; though it might perhaps be urged in this case that the materials were too dry. Fittbogen also in his experiments on the nitrification of peat found that the mixing of gypsum with the peat had little if any influence in promoting the formation of nitrates. Experiments made by Dehérain gave in like manner only negative results. Pichard on the other hand having noticed that the nitrification of organic matters in sterile soil seemed to be promoted by the presence of the sulphates of potash, soda, and lime, but especially by the last, i. e. by gypsum, has sought to explain the fact by arguing that gypsum may perhaps sometimes favor nitrification by acting to fix and hold ammonia as a sulphate, as fast as it forms, i. e. by preventing it from escaping by way of evaporation, before the nitrifying ferment has had opportunity to act upon it. Under conditions favorable for nitrification, the ammonium sulphate will naturally be oxidized in due course by the ferments. This view is justified by an experiment of Spatzier, who found long ago on strewing gypsum on a garden-bed composed of fresh horse manure and loam that a large part of the gypsum soon changed to carbon-ate of lime, while a considerable quantity of ammonia was held in the form of sulphate.

Pichard found that gypsum was more favorable for nitrification than sulphate of iron. But it is not to be supposed that the pres-ence of gypsum can be helpful for nitrification unless the soil is thoroughly aerated; and it was noticed by Pichard of clay that it seemed to fix ammonia so firmly, or perhaps change it so radically, that nitrification was hindered. In a subsequent communication, Pichard remarks that nitrification may be interfered with by gypsum in cases where an abundance of humus is present under conditions favorable for the reduction of the humus to calcium sulphide, which is poisonous for the nitrifying organisms.

Hilgard, in California, who has found that gypsum is an excellent corrective for many alkali soils, speaks of "the energetic action of gypsum in favoring nitrification," as of a known fact. But as Warington has set forth, it is to be presumed that the beneficial influence of gypsum on nitrification really depends on its acting to annul the alkalinity of alkali carbonates in cases where they are present in undue quantity. Nitrification is impossible in concentrated dung-liquor, in putrid urine, in an alkali soil, or in any other substance which contains a considerable amount of an alkali carbonate; but by means of gypsum it is easy to change the alkali carbonate to a sulphate, while carbonate of lime is also formed, and nitrification thus becomes not only possible but easy. For example, it has been found that urine diluted with an equal bulk of water becomes nitrifiable when admixed with a sufficient quantity of gypsum.

Nitrates formed in Plants.

According to Berthelot and André, nitrate of potash is continually formed within the stalks and roots of plants, by the action of certain cells of the plant. The argument is, that these cells act in a manner analogous to those of the true ferment which causes nitrification in the earth; and that one prime purpose of the cells in the interior of plants is to promote processes of oxidation, such as give rise to the formation, not only of nitrates, but of compounds of carbonic, oxalic, tartaric, malic, citric, and other oxygenated acids. This action of the plant-cells is similar to that of the cells in certain fruits, which, as Lechartier observed, can excite alcoholic fermentation much as if they were ordinary yeast.

It has been noticed that plants must be vigorous rather than sickly, in order that nitrification may occur in their stems, and that nitrates tend to disappear from the leaves of plants. That is to say, in the leafy, green parts of the plant reducing actions prevail, instead of those which cause oxidation. It is there that carbonic acid from the air is reduced, with evolution of oxygen, and that nitrates also are transformed to amids and albuminoids.

Light, which favors the activity of the chlorophyl grains, appears to accelerate the decomposition of the nitrates, i. e. their transformation to amids; while darkness, as in the roots of plants, may be favorable for nitrification in the plant, as it is for the action of the ordinary nitric ferment in the soil. To show the analogy between the nitrifying plant-cells and the ordinary nitric ferment,

Berthelot and André leached a quantity of garden-loam with water to remove nitrates, and heated the leached loam strongly in order to kill any organisms which might have been contained in it. They then put pieces of the stems of amaranth plants in the loam thus washed and sterilized, and it appeared that this vegetable matter was really capable of acting as a ferment; for after a while notable quantities of saltpetre were detected in the loam thus treated, although none was found in similar samples of loam to which none of the amaranth-cells had been added. It is to be said, however, that several observers have denied the fact that nitrates can be formed by the action of the cells in ordinary plants. They urge that — excepting the case of bacteria — the nitrates found in plants have always originated outside the plant and have been taken in as such.

Nitrates may be formed by purely Chemical Reactions.

Although the action of living cells, either those of the microscopic "ferment," or those within ordinary plants, seem to be essential for the conversion of ammonia or other nitrogen compounds to nitrates at the ordinary temperature of the air, it is to be remembered that it is not difficult to oxidize ammonia in the laboratory, so that it shall be converted into nitrous acid, nitric acid, and water. There are several ways of effecting this result, just as there are several ways of reducing nitrates to the condition of ammonia. For example, ammonia gas may be oxidized by passing a mixture of it and air over platinum sponge heated to 570° F., or even by thrusting a red-hot platinum wire into a mixture of the two gases:

$$2\ NH_3 + 7\ O = N_2O_4 + 3\ H_2O.$$

So, too, a vivid reaction is obtained on passing the vapor of chloride of ammonium and oxygen gas over hot platinum sponge:

$$2\ NH_4Cl + 7\ O = N_2O_4 + 3\ H_2O + 2\ HCl.$$

Conversely, nitric acid may be reduced by passing the vapor of it, together with hydrogen gas, over hot platinum sponge:

$$N_2O_5 + 16\ H = 2\ NH_3 + 5\ H_2O;$$

or by treating zinc or iron, or certain other metals, with a mixture of dilute nitric and hydrochloric acids:

$$HNO_3 + 8\ H = NH_3 + 3\ H_2O.$$

It was thought at one time that ozone could combine with the free nitrogen of the air, and that nitric acid was continually being formed in this way. But it is now known that this supposition was

erroneous, and that ozone has no such power, although it can oxidize both ammonia and nitrites readily enough.

Formation of Nitrates in the Air.

It was observed long ago that small portions of the nitrogen and
oxygen of the air may be made to combine by passing electric
sparks through the air, or even by means of silent discharges of
electricity; and it is now known that nitrogen is actually a com-
bustible gas at very high temperatures, such as can be produced
readily by means of powerful currents of electricity. At these
temperatures, nitrogen burns in the air with a visible flame, and a
strong odor of nitrous acid is manifested. By operating in a
closed glass globe, red nitrous fumes are seen to be formed. But
the kindling point of nitrogen is higher than the temperature produced by the combustion of nitrogen, so that the flame of burning
nitrogen cannot set fire to the whole air, and the combination of
nitrogen with oxygen is restricted to the place where intense heat
has been produced by special appliances. There can be no doubt
however, that small quantities of nitric acid are incessantly produced in nature in this way, as an accompaniment of flashes of
lightning. Minute quantities of nitrous and nitric acids may be
formed also in various processes of combustion, as when hydrogen, coal-gas, alcohol or the like are burned in air which contains
ammonia. It is easy to detect the presence of nitrates in rooms
where gas-lamps are habitually burned, by rinsing with water the
wall of the room, or any object which has stood for some time in
the room, and testing this water with appropriate reagents.

One of the most interesting examples of the oxidation of atmospheric nitrogen is seen in the familiar fact that nitrites and nitrates
are formed during the slow oxidation of phosphorus at the ordinary temperature of the air; for it is a fair inference that, if nitrites
are thus formed during the slow oxidation of one substance, they
may be during the slow oxidation of some other substances, perhaps of many other substances. Berthelot has in fact shown that
minute quantities of nitrates are formed from the nitrogen of the
air during the slow oxidation, at the ordinary temperature, of ether,
aldehyde, oleic acid and various other analogous liquids.

Nitrites are not fit Food for Plants.

It needs to be said that nitrites are not capable of taking the place
of nitrates as a means of supplying nitrogen to crops. Far from
being classed among compounds which are fit for feeding plants,

the nitrites must be regarded as actually poisonous in respect to plants of the higher orders, for the roots of such plants contain acids which would decompose any nitrite which might come in contact with them and would set free nitrous acid, which is extremely poisonous. It has been found in fact that the roots of agricultural plants are quickly killed by nitrites, and that these compounds can be supported only by those plants (algae, etc.) which have non-acid, neutral juices. Even these plants, like all other living cells, are speedily destroyed when they are brought into contact with highly dilute solutions of free nitrous acid.

How is the World's Store of Nitrates maintained ?

It is to be observed that in the combustion experiments above cited, the absolute amount of nitrites formed in any one particular experiment is extremely small. But, the fact that any nitrite is thus formed is one of very great importance, because of its bearings on the questions: How was it that the first plants in the world got any nitrogenous food? and, how is it that wild and uncultivated plants grow in the world as we find it now? and because of the hope held out by these reactions that all the nitrates which an improved agriculture may need will ultimately be manufactured artificially by purely technical processes. For although nitrites are not of themselves capable of supplying nitrogen to plants, they are so readily changed to nitrates that they must be regarded as valuable. By the action of ozone, for example, they are readily changed to nitrates, as happens to some of those formed during the slow oxidation of phosphorus.

Inasmuch as the development of vegetable and animal life upon the surface of the globe is dependent on supplies of assimilable nitrogen, it is plain on the face of the matter, that somewhere and somehow very considerable quantities of free nitrogen, such as is found in the air, must be converted into nitrates or ammonium compounds, or some other combination fit for feeding plants. If this were not so, the amount of vegetable and animal life on the globe would necessarily diminish from hour to hour; for it must often happen, in some forms of decay, as well as when vegetable or animal matters are burned, that a part of the combined nitrogen which was contained in them will escape into the air, as free nitrogen gas, and thus be lost, so to say, to vegetation.

Several observers have noticed that, through the action of certain micro-organisms, some nitrogen gas may be lost during the decay of organic matters, and it is well known that much nitrogen is liberated during the combustion and distillation of wood and coal and other organic substances. For example, the nitrogen exhaled from volcanoes, and from many hot springs, is supposed to be derived not infrequently from the decomposition of organic matters deep in the earth. Bischof found, by experiment, that when wood burns, most of the nitrogen that was contained in it separates in the free state. He found also, that the gases evolved during the progressive decomposition of bituminous coal are accompanied by free nitrogen, which had previously been contained in combination in the coal. But there is no evidence of any general diminution of vegetable or animal life from year to year, and the conviction is consequently forced upon us that the plants and animals which now exist upon the globe cannot wholly be supported by the great reservoir of humus which has been handed down to us from an earlier period. Those portions of the nitrates and ammonium salts contained in the soil and in the waters of the earth, which have resulted from the oxidation of this old humus, could hardly be sufficient for the maintenance of all the living things which are now seen to prosper, and there is need of looking elsewhere for other sources of supply which shall furnish enough combined nitrogen to compensate for the waste that is known to occur in processes of decay and putrefaction.

This matter will be explained at some length in the chapter on Symbiosis. But it may here be said that, geologically speaking, it is to be accepted as proved, that some part of the constant new supply of combined nitrogen, so necessary for the maintenance of life of all kinds, must have come from the aforesaid union of nitrogen and oxygen, as an incident to electrical discharges and to processes of combustion. It has been argued, indeed, by some writers, that much more nitrogen was probably thus oxidized in earlier geological epochs than now, but there can be no manner of doubt that some nitrogenous plant-food continues to be supplied to the world in this way. The only trouble is, that the amount of nitrates, etc., brought to the land in a year is not large enough to compensate for the quantities carried off in minimum crops, or even for those that are leached out from the soil by the rain-water that drains away from it. It would be an enormous gain for agriculture if cheap and effective methods of producing such combination of nitrogen and oxygen at will could be discovered.

It has often been urged by political economists, that the rate of agricultural production is not likely ever to keep pace with the increase of population, since, as they say, no great or striking improvements in agriculture can be expected. No such improvement, they mean, as would double or treble the present rate of production. But in point of fact, the discovery of a cheap and easy method of making nitrates from the air would enormously increase the food-producing capacity of the earth. Indeed, the probabilities are that the mere discovery of what appears to be the true theory of nitrification, viz., the ferment theory, just now alluded to, will ultimately greatly increase the production of food. Not only will farmers soon learn to make composts, and to apply manure in a more rational manner than was possible before, but they will take pains to foster and protect the ferment germs, and to sow them, as it were, and cultivate them in fit places.

Applications of the Ferment Theory.

Already the ferment theory of nitrification has thrown much light upon several agricultural problems which were formerly extremely obscure. For example, this theory goes far to explain why it was that European farmers so long persisted in leaving their land fallow, as a preparation for growing wheat, for wherever nitrification has been active during the summer months, when soaking rains are rare and no crop has been growing upon the land to consume the nitrates, a very considerable amount of this active form of nitrogen will accumulate in the soil and be put to profit by a grain-crop that is sown in the autumn. It seems, easy, moreover, to understand nowadays why Indian corn is found to differ so widely from wheat and barley in respect to the kinds of fertilizers it requires. Generally speaking, American farmers have found no great advantage in applying to their corn-crops either nitrates or ammonium salts, although these fertilizers are regarded almost as specifics for wheat and barley in countries where the art of agriculture is somewhat advanced. The fact is, that the growth of Indian corn occurs at a different time and season from the growth of the smaller grains.

The growth of the cereal grains takes place either in the autumn, or in the spring and early summer, and these crops need nitrogenous food first in the autumn, after the wheat has sprouted, and again in the early spring, when the store of nitrates natural to the soil has been reduced to its lowest terms by the leaching rains of winter and spring, and when only comparatively small quantities of nitrates are in process of formation, because of the coolness of the soil.

But Indian corn grows most freely in the hottest weather of midsummer, at the very time when nitrates are formed most rapidly from the humus of the soil. It is to be remembered, withal, that in the spring the corn finds as large an amount of nitrates in the soil as the cereals can find at this season, and that afterwards it is continually supplied with this form of plant-food at times when the cereal crops have become so nearly ripe that they can no longer make any use of it.

It may perhaps be true also that nitrates are formed somewhat more readily beneath broad-leaved crops, like beets, turnips, clover, or Indian corn, than on land covered with a grain crop, for it is not unlikely that the nitrifying organisms may prosper particularly well beneath the leafier plants in the deeper shade and more abundant surface moisture which exist there.

Influence of Ozone and Peroxide of Hydrogen.

It has not yet been clearly made out what influence for the formation of nitrates may be exerted by the ozone and the peroxide of hydrogen which are contained in small amounts in atmospheric air. It is not probable that either of these substances occurs naturally in sufficient quantity at any one spot to destroy the ferment microdemes, while there is good reason to believe that they may act to form nitrates in some cases, either directly by oxidizing organic matters, or more probably, perhaps, by oxidizing organic matter to ammonia, which is afterwards changed to nitrates by the ferment. It is known, withal, that both ozone and peroxide of hydrogen can oxidize ammonia to nitrates.

Peroxide of hydrogen is often brought to the ground in appreciable quantities by summer showers, and the peculiarly rapid formation of rust sometimes noticed on iron articles which have been wet by such rains, is probably due to the presence of this substance.

As for the ozone in the air, there is never very much of it in any one place. Indeed, the quantity is exceedingly minute, amounting to no more, perhaps, than one part in several million parts of air. But, taken in the aggregate, the amount of ozone is by no means small, and it is not improbable that it may have considerable influence in the formation of nitrates. It is known, for example, that ozone acts rapidly upon many kinds of organic matters. For the reactions of ozone have repeatedly been detected in the air on the windward side of manure-heaps, when no trace of it was indicated in the air to leeward of the heap. It has often been noticed, also, that little or no ozone can be detected in the air of cities at times when it is abundant in the air of the neighboring country. Sometimes it is abundant on the windward side of a city, and as good as absent from the air immediately to leeward; the inference being that it has been consumed in oxidizing organic matters. Interesting observations upon this point have been made by Dietrich and Mohl at Cassel, in Germany.

It is to be said, however, that experiments made in the laboratory of Lawes and Gilbert go to show that organic matters subjected to the action of ozone in certain stages of decay do not yield nitrates. In these trials it appeared, in harmony with what has been said already, that the best conditions for the formation of nitrates are found when the organic matters have been converted into the condition of old, slowly decaying humus.

Quantity of Nitrates in Soils.

One question of much interest is to determine how large an amount of nitrates is contained in ordinary soils, and in general the deportment of nitrates towards the soil. Voelcker remarked long ago, "I never examined soil that had been well penetrated by air, without finding large quantities of nitrates present." Indeed, for the sake of the argument, it might be assumed that the nearer the farmer can bring the soil of his field to the condition of a saltpetre-yard, the more fertile will it be. But let him do his best, he can never accumulate a very large proportion of nitrates in his field, for the soil has comparatively little power permanently to retain these substances. Not only do these extremely soluble, mobile, crystalloid compounds diffuse rapidly in all directions into the moisture which the soil contains, but every rainfall must dissolve the nitrates which have formed in the upper layers of the soil and carry them down into or towards the lower layers, and in case the rain should happen to be abundant and long continued, it may even wash the nitrates utterly out of the soil. The double silicates and double humates, which serve so well to arrest potash and ammonia, have no power to stop the waste of nitrates. One prime condition for the success of saltpetre-making in the old plantations was the avoidance of the leaching action of rain. The

heap of materials was either sheltered by means of a roof, or there
were reservoirs below the heap in which to receive any liquid that
might flow from it. Numerous experiments by Lawes and Gilbert
have shown that, in wet seasons, large quantities of nitrates pass
downward through arable soils which are in good agricultural condition, and that a great deal of nitrate-nitrogen is thus lost with
the drainage waters. They urge that, under certain circumstances,
there may be larger quantities of nitrates in the soil at depths of
2 or 3 feet than at the surface of the land.

That the yearly loss of nitrates by leaching from bare soils may
be very large, is shown by experiments made by Lawes and Gilbert on the waters that percolated through their three great drain-
gauges, respectively 20, 40, and 60 inches deep. The soils of
these gauges were left without manure and without crops for 13
years, and during the last 6 years enough nitric acid was found in
the drainage waters to amount, on the average, to 40.2 lb. of nitrogen per year and per acre. The minimum amount of nitrates
in the drainage water was in the spring, while the maximum was
found in July, or in the first month after July, when rain enough
fell to pass through the gauges.

In the soils of three fields at Rothamsted, that were in fair agricultural condition, and had been cultivated as bare fallow since
the barley harvests of the previous years, there were found, in
September and October, 56.5, 58.8, and 59.9 lb. of nitrogen to
the acre, in the form of nitrates, taking the soil to a depth of 27
inches.   In one of these good soils, there was 49 lb. of the nitrate-
nitrogen in the uppermost 18 inches of earth; but that this result
was in some part due to the richness of the soil in nitrifiable matters was shown by the fact that two other soils, in low agricultural condition, which had been cultivated as bare fallow, contained to the depth of 18 inches only 33.7 and 36.3 lb. to the
acre of nitrate-nitrogen.   In exhausted land, left uncropped for
4 years, after beans, there was found only very small quantities
of nitrates, comparatively speaking.   When no excess of rain fell
during the summer months, it was found that most of the nitrates
in a fallow soil remain in the uppermost 9 inches of earth, where
nitrification mainly occurs; but in case much rain should fall during the later summer months, the nitrates will be found at lower
levels, and a part of them will have passed below the depth of 27
inches.

On allowing for the amount of nitrates lost by leaching, Lawes and Gilbert were led to the conclusion that on the Rothamsted soils, which were in good agricultural condition and cultivated as bare fallow, something like 80 lb. of nitrogen to the acre, in the form of nitrates, were produced during the 14 or 15 months which elapsed between the removal of the previous crop and the time when the samples of earth were collected. Even on soils which were in an exhausted condition, they estimated that the annual production of nitrate-nitrogen must be equal to 30 lb. to the acre. They remark that they have as yet no experience as to the quantity of nitrates produced in extremely dry seasons.

The foregoing results have been confirmed by Warington, at Rothamsted, and by Dehérain, in the vicinity of Paris. The latter operated on lighter land and in a warmer climate than his predecessors, and noticed that the waste of nitrate-nitrogen was even larger than in the experiments of the English chemists. Tests made by Dehérain in the years 1889–90, on large pots of earth from a field that had not been manured since 1875, but which had borne a variety of crops, showed a waste of 82 lb. of nitrate-nitrogen per year and per acre. From a pot filled with earth which had been regularly cropped and manured, the waste of nitrate-nitrogen was at the rate of 121 lb. per year and per acre, while in earth from a field on which legumes and grass had been grown since 1879, the waste of nitrate-nitrogen was at the rate of 91 lb. per year and per acre. Evidently the waste of nitrates must vary widely on different fields, according as more or less rain falls, as nitrification is more or less active, as the soil is more or less retentive of moisture, and as the drainage is perfect or restrained.

The following experiments of Boussingault forcibly illustrate the fact that nitrates are continually formed in cultivated soils during the summer months. Boussingault placed twenty-two pounds of sifted earth upon a stone slab under a glass roof, and moistened the heap from time to time with pure water. The proportion of nitric acid in the soil was determined at the start, and afterwards at intervals during the course of the summer, with the following results : —

1857.	Percent of Nitrate of Potash.	Pounds of Nitrate of Potash per Acre.
5th August	0.001	35
17th "	0.006	210
2d September	0.018	630
17th "	0.022	770
2d October	0.021	735

During the hot weather the formation of nitrates from the organic matter in the soil was rapid, but it appears to have received a check with the advent of cooler weather in the autumn. The soil experimented upon by Boussingault was from an old garden; it was porous and sandy, and had been heavily manured time out of mind. These experiments are in full accord with universal experience, that the formation of nitrates is most rapid in hot climates and in hot weather, provided the soil is adequately moist as well as warm.

The ready nitrification of humus and of manure in the fields is manifestly a result much to be desired. Indeed the power of a soil to supply nitrates continually to crops is a prime condition of fertility, though it must be admitted that in northern countries where the ground long remains cold in the spring, the farmers are at a disadvantage because of the sluggishness of the nitrifying ferments at that season. It would be a great gain for the wheat-fields in cold countries if the ferment organisms could but become active sooner than they do, and work to supply food for the young crop, for it is precisely at this season that the soil contains the smallest amount of nitrates because of the leaching action of the winter's rains. It is to the inability of the micro-organisms to do their whole duty when the ground is cold that is to be attributed the advantage gained by English farmers on applying nitrate of soda to their young grain-crops. It is a great merit of calcareous soils that the nitric ferments prosper upon them, provided the other conditions necessary for their activity are favorable. On the other hand, one fatal objection to the growing of crops on undrained, sour, soggy bog-land is that nitrification can hardly if ever occur upon it.

The following determinations, by Boussingault, show the amount of saltpetre found in fertile soils taken respectively from two kitchen-gardens, from a wheat-field (strong clayey loam), and from a grass-field (ferruginous loam) : 0.153 %, 0.018 %, 0.002 %, and 0.005 %. The soil of a field which had been dressed with shell-marl contained 0.0054 % of the nitrate. In soils taken from hop-gardens he found 0.003 and 0.06 %. Generally speaking he found but little of the nitrate in land on which crops were growing, such as grass (and pasturage), clover, wheat, beets, turnips, maize and grape-vines. One field of Jerusalem artichokes showed 0.01 % of saltpetre, but other fields bearing this crop contained less than 0.0003 %. A tobacco and a hemp field each showed 0.003 %. Soils taken from woodland contained but little salt-petre. Of eight different specimens of woodland soil only one contained as much as 0.0004%, and several contained no nitrates whatever. A specimen of black sandy soil from a heath contained 0.0009 % of saltpetre, but after having been left under a shed for a year it contained 0.03 %.

Wolf determined in 6 different soils how many kilos of nitrogen were contained to the hectare of land taken to a depth of 8 inches, in the form of organic nitrogen, ammonia-nitrogen and nitrate-nitrogen, respectively, as is stated in the following table. It will be noticed how very little ammonia-nitrogen was contained in these soils, how much nitrate-nitrogen was present in most of them, and what very large quantities of organic nitrogen there were to keep up the supply of nitrates.

Rocks from which the soil came.	Condition of the Land.	Organic Nitrogen. Kilo.	Ammonia-Nitrogen. Kilo.	Nitrate-Nitrogen. Kilo.
Clay slate . . .	Good and fertile . .	5602	26.2	272
Conglomerate .	Lightly manured . .	4235	19.2	435
Gneiss	Fallow land . . .	5755	27.3	468
Gneiss	Poor and sterile . .	7426	6.3	82
Greenstone . .	Friable and fertile .	6264	89.0	522
Rothliegendes .	Heavy loam cropped with potatoes for 8 years, without any manure.	4509	27.9	553

In experiments upon soils made in laboratories, where all the conditions were favorable for nitrification, very considerable quantities of nitrates have been obtained even in the course of a few days. Thus, Schloesing having mixed some ammonium sulphate with a soil containing 19 % of water and rich in organic matter, found that during 12 days nitrogen was oxidized at the rate of 56 parts per day and per million parts of the dry soil, i. e. for every 100 grm. of dry soil, 0.0056 grm. of nitrogen was oxidized per diem. Admitting that the surface soil on an acre taken to the depth of 4 inches weighs about 1,000,000 lb., the nitrifying of 56 lb. of nitrogen, as above, would be equivalent to the production of 340 lb. of nitrate of soda.

Warington, working with soils taken from the upper 9 inches of ordinary arable fields at Rothamsted, found that about 70 parts of nitrogen per million parts of the air-dried soil were nitrified in 119 days, i. e. 0.588 part per day. Similar soils supplied with

ammonium chloride nitrified about 110 parts per million in the
same space of time, i. e. 0.924 part per diem. In each case the
powdered soil was loosely placed in a percolator and was nearly
saturated with water at starting, but afterward it remained untouched during the 119 days. In other experiments made by
Lawes and Gilbert at a higher temperature and on much richer
soils, from Manitoba, average daily rates of nitrification of 0.7
part of nitrogen per million during 335 days were noted. During
the earlier part of this period the daily rates of nitrification were
as high as 1.03 to 1.72 parts per million. The largest proportion
of nitrogen nitrified in 335 days was 5.4% of that orginally present in the soil. Dehérain working with a soil that contained
0.16 % of nitrogen obtained daily rates of nitrification varying
from 0.71 to 1.09 parts per million in 90 days. In his most successful experiment about 6% of the soil-nitrogen was nitrified in
100 days. In the case of a highly manured soil that contained
0.261% of nitrogen he obtained a maximum daily rate of nitrification during 40 days of 1.48 parts of nitrogen per 1,000,000 parts
of soil. When the soil was exposed to alternate drying and watering the daily rate of nitrification was increased to 1.8 part per
million during 104 days. During the first month, the rate was
2.4 part per million. It has been generally noticed in experiments of this kind that the rate of nitrification in a soil diminishes
rapidly as the trial proceeds; the easily nitrifiable matter being
first oxidized the subsequent action is comparatively slow. The
rate of nitrification increases somewhat with the proportion of
water in the soil provided the soil still remains porous, but when
the pores are closed and oxygen excluded denitrification sets in.
Boussingault noticed that soils with 60% of water lost the greater
part of their nitrates in a few weeks. (Warington).

Some old observations made by Touvenal, in France, may here
be cited. In temperate climates, he says, the spontaneous nitrification of arable fields varies very much according to the kind of
soil and the term of its exposure to the air. It is evident enough
that a substance so variable in texture and character as humus is
might sometimes be readily attacked by the ferment-organisms
while at other times it would resist their action. Looking from
the point of view of a saltpetre-boiler in search of nitrous earth,
the amount of nitrates formed in the fields is, generally speaking,
inconsiderable. Even at times when there has been no rain for a

considerable interval, saltpetre can seldom be extracted economically anywhere in France from those cultivated soils that are either very sandy or very clayey. Soils composed of mixtures of sandy, clayey, and calcareous loams, such as are common in France, rarely yield more than an ounce or an ounce and a half of saline matters to the quintal. Very chalky, fine, light soils, like those of Champagne, sometimes yield a little more, while the soils of kitchen-gardens that are carefully tilled often yield considerably larger quantities. As much as four ounces of saline matters, consisting of a mixture of nitrates and chlorides, especially of lime and soda, have been extracted from each quintal of earth taken in spring, after two months of warm dry weather, from the garden of the Tuileries. One and a half ounces of saline matter to the quintal of earth amounts to almost 0.1 %, or nearly 3300 lb. to an acre of land one foot deep. Four ounces to the quintal is equal to 0.25 %, or 8750 lb. to the acre. Four ounces was the largest amount obtained by Touvenal from the soils of gardens or fields where the earth was unsheltered and uncovered. But he remarks that such earth is as rich as perhaps half the nitrous earth that is taken from houses and cellars to be worked by the saltpetre boilers, or even as much of the earth which has been cultivated for nitre expressly in the artificial nitre-beds.

According to Boussingault, the officials charged with the superintendence of gunpowder works and the making of saltpetre, reported in 1777, that in some French provinces, nitrous earths yielding as much as 0.12 % of saltpetre occur naturally, while from the artificial nitre-beds there was obtained usually 0.85 %, or 1.0 % when the beds were well established. In exceptional instances, even as much as 3.0 % of saltpetre was obtained from the artificial nitre-beds. Bauer, in his description of the nitre-beds formerly worked in Sweden, says that nitrous earth of ordinary quality yields from 0.165 to 0.22 %, while the richest earths yield 0.6, or 0.7 %. At Malta, Demasis reported that nitrified calcareous earths, when mixed with one-fifth their weight of wood-ashes, yield 0.352 % of saltpetre. It has long been known that nitrification is peculiarly rapid in calcareous soils in warm climates, and it is recognized nowadays, that the humus in such soils is mild and mellow, and fit to be acted upon by the nitric ferment.

In searching for a soil favorable for the nitrification of organic nitrogenous matters, Muntz and Girard found a light, calcareous

soil from Jourville, which was well suited to their purpose; while
a chalky soil from Champagne was somewhat inferior because it
was less permeable to air. They found that organic nitrogen
compounds, such as dried blood and bone-meal, nitrified rapidly
in garden-loam, while they were hardly at all nitrified in a very
heavy calcareous soil. In this soil there was an abundant formation of ammonia from the buried materials, instead of any nitrification, though nitrification set in when the soil was loosened by
means of bulky, coarse materials, such as farmyard manure and
green manures. In a sour soil from a moor, no nitrification
occurred, but only formation of ammonia, until the soil was made
alkaline by the addition of stable-manure or of lime.

Nitrates Sink and Rise with the Ground-water.

The leaching action of rain was well shown long ago by one of
Boussingault's experiments. In view of the fact that sugar-beets,
and certain other plants, grown in an old kitchen-garden, which
had formerly belonged to a monastery, were apt to contain no inconsiderable quantities of nitrates, he took occasion to test the
soil at intervals and obtained the following results. A sample of
the soil collected on August 9, 1856, after a fortnight of hot, dry
weather, contained, when dried, as much nitric acid (N_2O_5) as
would amount to 0.0211% of nitrate of potash or, say, 940 lb. of
saltpetre to the acre. After three weeks of rainy weather, during
which time 2 inches of rain fell, another sample of earth was
taken from the garden, on August 29, immediately after rain had
ceased falling, and there was found in it less than 0.001% of nitrate of potash; in fact barely 31 lb. to the acre. In the course
of the month of September, there were 15 rainy days during which
four inches and a fifth of rain fell. But on October 10, after a
fortnight of dry, windy weather, the soil of the garden had become
so dry that it needed to be watered, and there was then found in
it nearly 0.03% of nitrate of potash, or 1040 lb. to the acre. The
soil of this garden was light and gravelly and non-retentive of
moisture. It had long been heavily manured and frequently
spaded. It is to be observed that, agriculturally speaking, some
of the foregoing quantities of the nitrate are large. In field practice 200 lb. of nitrate of soda to the acre is esteemed to be a good
dressing.

This rapid accumulation of nitrates in the upper layers of the
soil after a few weeks of dry weather is a point to be specially in-

sisted upon. Doubtless a very considerable part of these nitrates has been brought up from lower layers of the soil, and returned to the surface by means of the upward movements of the soil-water that are induced by the capillary action of the soil, the evaporation of water at the surface of the soil, and the exhalation of water from the leaves of plants. Precisely the same phenomenon is witnessed in some saltpetre-soils of the East Indies, where the surface of the earth becomes incrusted with nitrates during the dry season.

Nitrates are not Leached from Soils Rapidly.

The matter is instructive as illustrating the slowness with which nitrates must usually be washed out from the land during the summer months. Common observation and methodical experiments alike teach that the water of most summer rains does not soak into the earth to any great extent, and that its movements within the soil are slow. Most soils, moreover, have the power to absorb and hold larger quantities of water than a single moderate rain can bring to them, so that a large proportion of the nitrates which are carried into the soil by rain while crops are growing is still kept within reach of the crops by means of the upward capillary movement which sets in when the downward movement of the rain-water has ceased. Practically speaking, it is probable, for the great majority of cases, that nitrate of soda applied to crops in the spring is not washed out of the land to any very serious extent before the autumnal rains; though farmers who use this fertilizer will do well to consider carefully the character of the soils to which they apply it, both as regards their situation and their capacity for holding water.

It has been found that a much smaller amount of nitrates leaches out from the soil of fields that are covered with vegetation than from land which is bare. On land constantly covered with a thick growth of grass, for example, the nitrates are so completely taken up by the plants that only a very small proportion of them goes off in the drain-water, while the drain-water that flows out from fallow fields is apt to contain nitrates in comparatively large quantities. Lawes and Gilbert found that in late spring and early summer, nitrates disappear wellnigh completely from land covered with crops. For instance, only very small quantities of nitrates remain, at the end of June, in the uppermost 27 inches of soil where wheat or barley are growing, provided no excess of nitrogenous manure has been put upon the land, simply because these crops assimilate nitrates very rapidly. They remark that, as the development of the wheat-crop proceeds, the assimilation of nitrates by the growing plant becomes so active that in summer nitrates are not found in the drainage-waters of many of the plots in their experimental wheat-field, and go on to say: "The quantity of nitrates which disappears from the soil in early summer is in some cases truly astonishing. In the case of plots receiving in the spring a dressing of ammonium-salts, it may apparently amount to more than the quantity of nitrogen found in the crop at harvest. It must be recollected, however, that the crop as harvested does not represent the whole plant — the roots, stubble, some of the lower leaves, and shed grain being left behind in the soil. We must also take into account the presence of weeds, which doubtless actively assimilate the nitrates of the soil." They noticed, also, that the power of plants to use up the nitrates in the soil is appreciably less whenever available inorganic food, especially potash and phosphoric acid, is lacking.

Leaching occurs in the Rainy Season.

It is chiefly in times of continuous, heavy rains — as in late autumn and early spring — when new quantities of water are constantly falling upon the land and soaking downward through the soil, that this fresh water displaces, as the chemical term is, and pushes before it the solution of nitrates and other saline matters with which the soil is naturally charged. Samples of soils collected by Lawes and Gilbert in March and April, i. e. after the autumnal and winter rains, seldom contained large quantities of nitrates near the surface, and the amounts found in the subsoils also were singularly small. It seemed probable that a part of the nitrates formed near the surface of the soil must have suffered reduction in the subsoil. They remark that at Rothamsted nitrates continue to be produced slowly throughout the winter, and are consequently always to be found in the soil, notwithstanding the loss through drainage. Reckoning the year from April to March, the largest quantity of nitrate discharged from the soil in any one year in the drain-waters (21.66 inches), collected at a depth of 20 inches on land which for many years had been left unmanured, untilled, and bare of all vegetation, was equivalent to 54.2 lb. of nitrogen per acre, while the smallest quantity was 20.9 lb. in 8.96 inches of drainage.

The average quantity of nitrogen discharged as nitrate during 13 years at a depth of 20 inches was 87.3 lb., at 40 inches, 32.6 lb., and at 60 inches, 35.6 lb., equivalent respectively to 239, 209, and 228 lb. of nitrate of soda. The average annual drainage through this bare uncropped soil during 13 years was about 15 inches, or one-half of the rainfall, though the drainage bore no fixed proportion to the rainfall. It was estimated that an amount of nitrate equal to at least 60 % of that found in the soils of their wheat-field in October had passed into the subsoil below the level of the drain-pipes (2.5 feet) by the end of January. The following tables show the waste of nitrates from plots on Lawes and Gilbert's wheat-field, and emphasize the excessive waste which may occur when soluble nitrogenous fertilizers are applied in the autumn, or in extremely large quantities : —

When the nitrogenous fertilizers were applied in March.	Parts of nitrate-nitrogen in 1,000,000 parts of drain-water.				
	March to end of May.	June to harvest.	Harvest to autumn sowing.	Autumn sowing to March.	The whole year.
No manure	1.7	0.1	5.6	3.9	3.5
Ash ingredients	1.7	0.2	5.6	4.5	3.9
Ash ingredients and 200 lb. ammonium salts to the acre	8.1	0.7	7.3	4.8	5.0
Ash ingredients and 400 lb. ammonium salts	16.3	1.4	8.3	5.2	6.4
Ash ingredients and 600 lb. ammonium salts	21.5	4.0	14.7	7.3	9.3
Ash ingredients and 550 lb. nitrate of soda	48.4	9.1	14.3	6.8	12.3
400 lb. ammonium salts, and nothing else	28.6	11.4	11.5	6.3	9.9
Superphosphate of lime and 400 lb. ammonium salts	19.5	5.8	9.2	7.1	8.5

But when the nitrogenous manures were applied in October, the waste of nitrates was as follows : —

Ash ingredients and 400 lb. ammonium salts	5.7	2.9	7.4	26.4	19.4
1700 lb. rape-cake	4.7	0.5	8.2	12.5	10.1
14 tons farmyard manure	2.7	1.4	7.4	7.3	5.6

On comparing the two plots, each of which received 400 lb. of ammonium salts and a mixture of mineral fertilizers, the waste by leaching in the autumn will be seen very clearly; this loss of nitrates was reflected in the crops, which, on the average of years, were decidedly smaller on the plot which received the ammonium salt in the autumn than on the one which was dressed in the spring; but whenever a wet winter was followed by a dry spring and summer, so much of the nitrate which had been washed from this plot into the subsoil below the level of the drain-pipes came up again toward the surface, that the crop was decidedly improved, and gave better results at harvest than had been expected. The comparatively small quantities of nitrates lost from the rape-cake and the farmyard manure illustrate the comparative fitness of organic manures for autumn application.

It may here be said that Prevost has shown that growing crops prevent other kinds of plant-food, as well as nitrates, from passing out of the soil in the drain-water. He found, as others have done, that considerably less water escapes through the drains of fields on which crops are growing than goes out through the drains of bare fallow land; and, in addition to this, he found that absolutely less plant-food—notably less potash, lime, magnesia, phosphoric acid, sulphuric acid and nitrates — passes out through the drains on land which carries crops than escapes through the drains of bare land.

Some idea of the waste of fertilizing matters by drainage may be got from the experiments of Lawes and Gilbert, in which it was observed — as the mean of 10 analyses, and admitting an average drainage of 10 inches of water— that the annual loss of lime and magnesia from an acre of unmanured land was 223 lb. ; from land dressed with superphosphate, etc. (supplying about 86 lb. of lime to the acre), the loss of lime and magnesia was 297 lb. ; from land dressed with nitrate of soda, etc., the loss was 284 lb. ; from land dressed with ammonium salts alone the loss of lime and magnesia was 389 lb. ; and when superphosphate was applied with the ammonium salt, the loss was 443 lb. When ammonium salts, superphosphate and sulphate of potash were used together, the loss of lime and magnesia was 485 lb. to the acre. It is noticeable that, where nitrate of soda was applied, no such loss of lime occurred as was caused by applications of ammonium salts, which decompose the carbonate of lime in the soil. The losses of potash and phosphoric acid in the drain-waters were naturally very small. On land that received no potash, 3.6 lb. went out in the 10 inches of drainage, and where potash salts were applied, 9.5 lb. of potash were leached out per year and per acre. The mean loss of phosphoric acid was 2.1 lb. per acre.

Waste of Nitrates by Leaching.

Agriculturally speaking, all cultivated soils, with some rare exceptions, contain an appreciable quantity of nitrates. According to Knop, small quantities of nitric acid are even held in the insoluble condition in soils, in the form of highly basic nitrates of alumina and iron. These compounds alone among all the nitrates are insoluble in water. With this trifling exception, it is easy to wash every trace of nitrates out of a soil by means of water. In point of fact, enormous quantities of nitrates are incessantly being washed out of the soil and carried to sea. The water of field-drains, brooks, rivers, lakes and wells always contains more or less of the compounds of nitric acid, the proportion being largest, as a general rule, in populous and highly cultivated localities. Boussingault found 0.0042 to 0.0086 grm. nitric acid to the litre in water taken from the river Seine, and the waters of many other streams examined by him were found to be equally rich. In Rhine water he found 0.0008 to 0.001 grm. to the litre.

From the results of experiments made by Lawes and Gilbert, it has been estimated that, in England, the annual loss to the soil, by removal of nitrates in the ground-water, probably amounts, on an average, to as much as 8 lb. of nitrogen to the acre. Meanwhile, it is to be remembered that there is, in the aggregate, a vast quantity of nitrates held in store in the soil, in the ground-water. It has been observed in England, as the result of numberless analyses, that the waters of uncontaminated wells contain, on the average, some 4 to 4.5 parts of nitrate-nitrogen to every million parts of the water. (Warington.)

It is the inability of the soil to retain nitrates permanently which suggests the thought that nitrate of soda might be applied to the land in successive portions, and there are published experiments that go to show the benefit of this course, as regards certain crops which are to be mown green for forage, though, as has been said, a risk is encountered that the grain-crop may be made to run too much to leaf, and that the fungi which cause blight may be attracted to the luxuriant plants. For the same reason, nitrate of soda should be applied in the spring rather than in autumn. For the same reason, again, it may often be better policy to apply nitrate-forming manures rather than nitrates themselves.

Inasmuch as all kinds of nitrogenous fertilizers, including the organic matter of dung and of decaying plants, change more or less rapidly in the soil to nitrates, and thus become liable to be carried away in the drainage waters, while phosphates, potash, lime, and the other mineral fertilizers, remain fixed in the surface soil, it follows that many old agricultural soils may contain an excess of these mineral constituents in available condition as compared with the amount of available nitrogen. Herein lies one explanation of the observed fact that many soils are specially grateful for applications of nitrate of soda and other kinds of active nitrogenous manure.

In his elaborate investigation of the composition of the waters of land-drainage, Voelcker found that the moisture which circulates in agricultural soils invariably contains some traces of nitrates at all seasons of the year, that the water which passes out from the land through drains always contains a larger proportion of nitrates than rain-water, and that nitrates are so readily washed out from the soil by water that it is an easy matter to lose much of the nitrate of soda which is applied as a manure. When, for example, a liberal dressing of the nitrate is applied in England in autumn, and there is much wet weather during the succeeding winter, a great deal of the nitrate will be removed from the land by the percolating rain-water, and so lost. By far the larger proportion of the drainage takes place, of course, during the autumn, winter, and early spring, but even when the nitrate is applied in the spring to winter wheat, a considerable part of it may be lost in case the weather should continue to be wet, i. e. if there should be heavy and continuous rains after the sowing of the nitrate. But if the spring is not unduly wet, the growing wheat will take up so much of the nitrate that no very large amount of it can escape in the drainage-water.

It is to be observed that the reason why the effect of nitrate of soda sown in the spring upon growing wheat is seen so immediately after a good shower of rain has fallen, is that the dissolved nitrate circulates and diffuses freely in the soil-water, and supplies the crop at once with an excess of nitrogenous food. In one instance, Voelcker detected nearly 6 parts of nitrogen in 100,000 parts of drain-water flowing in April from land which had been heavily dressed in March with nitrate of soda, and this amount would be equivalent to a loss of about 13 lb. of nitrogen per acre for every inch of rain then passing through the soil.

In consonance with the statement already made that the waste of nitrates from any given field depends primarily on the amount of water which percolates through the soil, it is noticeable that nitrates leach out much more readily from light and open soils than from those which are compact. It is said to be a matter of experience in France that light, calcareous soils are specially liable to become impoverished simply because they are leachy, while nitrification is rapid and well nigh constant in such soils. Hence it happens that farm-manure, humus and organic matters of any kind rapidly go to waste on those lands. From heavy, clayey soils on the contrary, the waste of nitrates is less rapid, both because such soils are little permeable to water, and because nitrification in not specially rapid upon them.

Nitrates in City Wells.

The tendency of nitrates to flow out from the soil with the water, as well as the fact of the rapid formation of nitrates in the soil under favorable conditions, is capitally illustrated in the wells of crowded cities, as was just now said. As much as one part of saltpetre in five hundred parts of water has been detected in the wells of the older part of Paris, and it is easy to find well-waters highly charged with nitrates in almost any city. Many years ago, I prepared a quantity of distilled water from the water of a well that had long been left unused in the cellar of University Hall in the College yard at Cambridge. But the distillate was so highly charged with nitrous salts of ammonia that it was wholly useless for analytical purposes. There was at that time a large privy-vault some forty or fifty feet from the well.

It is often well to keep Land covered with Vegetation.

The fact that living plants can put to use the nitrates and other fertilizing matters which might otherwise go to waste, is one point to be counted in favor of a method of culture which has been commended by several American writers. The idea is to keep the ground covered with vegetation all the time, or as constantly covered as may be possible, in order to smother weeds and to prevent the land from being baked by the sun or washed by rain. Thus, for example, if a crop of Indian corn were upon the ground, rye might be sown among it in August, at the time when the corn is last cultivated. Since the surface soil is shielded by the maize and kept somewhat moist by dew and vapor that come from its great leaves, the rye will germinate and grow slowly under the corn in spite of the shade until the crop is harvested, when, if the season is at all favorable, the rye will take a start and cover the ground before winter. The next spring the rye will begin to grow long before the weeds, and will soon cover the ground with a mat which will be more or less dense according to circumstances. Consequently, when the spring work of the farm begins, and the question arises what shall be done with the old corn-field, it is not a bare field that is to be dealt with, but a rye-field which has been established at the cost of scarcely any trouble, and which probably did very little injury to the corn-crop.

Manifestly, the rye can either be left to grow, to be harvested as hay or as grain, in due season; or the young rye might be pastured in the spring and early summer, and the cropped sod be ploughed under for turnips or for Hungarian grass; or the growth of rye could be treated as green manure, pure and simple, and ploughed under for potatoes or for corn. The practice above described, though akin in one sense, is really different from some other instances of keeping land covered; as, for example, when rye is sown immediately after a grain-crop, or on fields whence a crop of early potatoes or of sweet corn has been taken, and where, instead of leaving stubble, or a bare field, to itself, oats or barley or mustard or rape, or the seeds of some other quick-growing plant are sown with the view of pasturing the young growth or mowing it for forage, and ploughing under the green stubble late in the autumn. The peculiarity of the corn case is, that the interpolated crop uses the surface water, viz. that which dribbles as dew from the corn, or which is exhaled as vapor from it. It is noteworthy that in earlier days, when large quantities of rye were grown in New England, for bread, it was the usual practice in many localities to sow the (winter) rye in July in the corn-fields, at the time of the last hoeing. The practice was given up because of the liability of the young rye-plants to rust during the hot, muggy weather of August. (E. Hersey.)

Not only rye but wheat may be sown among Indian corn early in autumn, long before the corn-crop is harvested. It is said, indeed, that in Michigan the corn-stalks are often left standing until the next spring, that they may hold snow and serve in some measure to protect the wheat from the high winds of winter. How important the saving of nitrates by growing crops may be in some instances is shown by the experiments of Lawes and Gilbert, just now cited, which exhibited in the drain-waters flowing from a poor unmanured arable soil, that was kept bare of vegetation, as much nitrate-nitrogen as was equivalent to an annual loss of 2 cwt. of nitrate of soda. Dehérain, in France (see beyond), observed in

October, 1889, that the loss of nitrates from a field at Grignon, under conditions favorable for leaching, amounted to 72 kilo. of nitrate-nitrogen to the hectare, which would be equivalent to 450 kilo. of nitrate of soda to the hectare. Although the waste of nitrates in this case was known to be unusually large, it is evident, that for the sake of insuring against the risk of such loss, it might often be well to put one's self to considerable trouble in growing autumnal crops, even such as would not be directly remunerative.

Saving of Nitrates by Catch-crops.

In the following table are given the results obtained by Dehérain, on determining the amounts of nitrate-nitrogen in the drainage waters from fields, some of which had been left fallow after the summer's crops had been removed, while others had been sown with catch-crops, as stated: —

The summer crop was	After the summer crop, the land had upon it.	Kilos of nitrate-nitrogen that went out from a hectare of land, in Nov. 1888, in the drainage water.
Beets	Nothing	7.500
Fodder maize	Nothing	14.500
Oats	Field cabbage	0.370
Hemp.	Nothing	10.500
Peas	Rape	0.510
Ray-grass	Ray-grass.	0.380
Clover	Clover	1.100

That is to say a hectare of bare land lost on the average 10.8 kilos of nitrate-nitrogen, while there was lost no more than 0.4 to 0.5 of a kilo from the land that bore rape and colza, or about as much as was lost from a grass-field. Dehérain determined furthermore the loss of nitrate-nitrogen in the drainage waters from bare fields of permeable soil in which nitrification was active. As will be seen from the figures which follow, very different amounts of nitrates were lost in different years, according to the weather. But he found between the time of harvesting the crops in late summer September), and that of ploughing the land in November in preparation for the new crops, there was lost from the hectare of land, —

In the year 1889	72.2 kilos of nitrogen.
" " 1890	10.2 " "
" " 1891	42.5 " "
Mean of the three years	41.6 " "

But 41.6 kilos of nitrogen is the amount contained in 260 kilos of nitrate of soda, which would represent an application of 230 lb.

of nitrate of soda to an acre of land. The success of any plant sown in summer to hinder the waste of nitrates will naturally depend very much upon the weather. In seasons when rain was abundant Dehérain found that the plants started well, and that sometimes the young crops transpired so much water that there was no longer any flow of water from the tile-drains beneath the plots on which the cro p were growing. Even in cases where there was more rain than the plants could use, and there was a flow of water from the drains, next to no nitrates went off in the water, so completely had they been taken up by the growing plants.

In the year 1891, vetches sown after hemp grew so well that they stopped the flow of water from the drains, so that of course no nitrates were washed out from that land. In the same year, mustard sown after oats on drained land did not catch well, but clover enough grew spontaneously in its place to keep down the loss of nitrate-nitrogen to 0.808 kilos per hectare. On several parcels of undrained land, mustard sown early in August at the rate of 12 to 15 lb. of seed to the acre, grew well, however, and it was observed that the green plants weighed on the average, at the time when the crop was ploughed under, 4770 kilos to the hectare. The green plants contained 26.64% of dry matter and 1.75% of nitrogen, so that there must have been put into the soil, when the crop was buried, 83.47 kilos of nitrogen to the hectare. On comparing this result with the amount of nitrate-nitrogen lost from bare land, as previously stated, it appears that the green crop not only prevented 42.5 kilos of nitrogen per hectare from being washed out from the land during the autumn, but that the plants had taken up an additional 40 kilos of nitrogen which might perhaps have been washed out by the rains of winter.

Vetches did not always succeed in Dehérain's experiments, his crops having varied between 8833 kilos, to the hectare, and 12,780 kilos, as weighed at the time when the plants were to be ploughed under. The green plants contained 20.75% of dry matter and 1.31% of nitrogen. Hence if the average crop be taken as weighing 10,806 kilos, there would be ploughed under in it 141.6 kilos of nitrogen. It is evident in this case that a considerable amount of nitrogen had been collected from the air by the fungi which live upon the roots of the vetch plants.

Summer Fallows may have Merit also.

In spite of the propriety of thus growing crops in autumn and spring to prevent loss of nitrates by leaching, it is none the less true, in view of what is now known of nitrification, that much more than has hitherto been customary may be urged in favor of summer fallows as a preparation for winter grain. It is known that, as a general rule, bare land is both warmer and moister than land on which crops are growing, and that these conditions are specially favorable for nitrification. As has been said already, Lawes and Gilbert found towards the end of summer from 34 to 55 lb. of nitrogen in the form of nitrates to the acre of fallow land; from which result they argue that the accumulation of nitrates would probably enable the soil to produce twice as much wheat as it could have done without the fallow, provided the season has been fairly dry, and that the rains have not been heavy enough to wash away the nitrates before the autumn wheat-plants could put them to profit. It would seem probable from this consideration, that a not too rainy climate is requisite in order that fallows shall have their best success.

Gasparin long ago illustrated the merit of fallow fields, considered as a device for cultivating much land without the aid of manure, by stating how favorably the amount and the value of grain produced on the average of seasons on dry soils in the valley of the Rhone, compared with the amount and value of grain produced in that locality by means of manure. He contrasted in this way both wheat grown on dry soils consisting of good clay or mellow humus, and rye as grown on sandy land.

As a matter of course it will be necessary in all such cases to study anew the economic question whether the given fields might not be managed more profitably by the application of fertilizers or the interpolation of green crops. Thus Lawes and Gilbert in one of their field-experiments grew wheat in alternation with bare fallow, but without any manure, during a term of 30 years, and it appeared that the total product of wheat after fallow was to wheat after wheat (on adjacent land) as 150 is to 100 during the first 15 years of the experiment, and as 129 is to 100 during the second 15 years. It was noticed also that the fertility of the fallow land declined more quickly than that of adjacent unmanured land which was continuously cropped with wheat, and analysis showed that the nitrogen of the soil fell away most rapidly in those cases where the land was subjected to spring and summer tillage. It was only in some of the earliest years that the wheat after fallow amounted to the double product, which should result from a double supply of nitrates. But it will be noticed that in actual farming there would seldom or never be any need of considering any other years than those corresponding to the earliest years of Lawes and Gilbert.

It is noticeable that fallow fields are often so foul with weeds that the nitrates formed there may be taken up by the weeds. In case, for example, stubble land is not ploughed until the spring, the loss of nitrates by leaching during the autumn and winter will be much smaller than if the land were kept clean. When rain follows the grain-harvest, and especially if the land be ploughed, a considerable formation of nitrates may then occur.

It sometimes happens that land which is naturally very fertile cannot safely be fallowed as a preparation for winter wheat, because of the large quantities of nitrates which are formed in it. More than 100 years ago it was found that wheat could not be grown after a summer fallow on certain deep rich loams in Norfolk (England), because "the wheat-crop was invariably spoilt through an over-rankness." The trouble became all the greater when these soils were marled.

Nitrates in Air and Rain.

From what has been said already of the formation of nitrates by electric sparks and as an incident to combustion, and from the action of ozone on ammonium compounds, it follows that there must be more or less nitric acid in the air. It has in fact been proved to exist there by direct experiment. Not only can nitrates be detected in rain-water, in snow, hail, dew, and fogs, but by causing large quantities of air to bubble through alkaline solutions it is possible to collect enough of the atmospheric nitrate to prove its existence. Naturally enough, it is easier to detect nitric acid in rain-water, that is to say, in water that has fallen through air, than in the air itself, for the water in question collects nitrates from the enormous quantity of air through which it falls.

Detailed statements of many observers as to the quantity of nitrates brought down by rain may be found in the works of Knop and Boussingault, and in Professor Johnson's "How Crops Feed," p. 86. In any event, the amount of nitric acid (N_2O_5) brought down by rains, dews, etc., in the course of a year is extremely small in temperate climates. Warington found that 0.84 lb. per acre per annum was thus brought to the land at Rothamsted, England, and he notes that 1.00 lb. was observed at Lincoln, New Zealand, and 2.84 lb. at Barbadoes, all as the average of 3 years.

With comparatively rare exceptions, there is more than enough ammonia in the air to neutralize the nitric acid. It is to be presumed, therefore, that the atmospheric nitric acid exists in the form of nitrate of ammonia. There are exceptions to the rule, however, for free nitric acid has occasionally been detected in the air and particularly in hailstones. Indeed, one or two instances have been recorded where hailstones have actually tasted sour.

Since nitrate of ammonia is not appreciably volatile at ordinary temperatures, it is to be inferred that that which exists in the air is held there in mechanical suspension, just as the dust that is seen in the sunbeam is held suspended. There are many things thus perpetually floating in the air. It is a fact, for example, that there is so much salt dust in the air, brought inland by winds from the sea, that it may easily be detected at any time by testing the air for sodium with the spectroscope. On evaporating large quantities of rain-water to dryness, chemists have frequently found appreciable quantities of the nitrates of lime and soda in the residue left by the evaporation. Manifestly, the bases in question have been derived from dust in the air.

CHAPTER XII.

AMMONIUM COMPOUNDS.

LIKE the nitrates, ammonium salts, when applied to the soil, exert a marked influence upon the growth of many plants.

Most crops that are fed with ammonia soon acquire that deep green foliage which is so indicative of health and vigor. Both the absolute amount of the foliage and the proportion of nitrogen contained in it are distinctly increased by their use.

There can be no question as to the great value of ammonia and its compounds considered as fertilizing agents. This fact may readily be illustrated by watering almost any plant, standing in loam, with a highly dilute solution of an ammonium salt, and comparing the growth of this plant with that of another similarly

situated, but watered only with water. In the words of Schattenmann, "Ammoniacal salts appear to exert an extraordinary influence on wheat. In my experiments, the crop acquired the deep
green color, which is a sure sign of great vegetative energy, one
week after the fertilizer had been applied to the land."

The widely extended use of Peruvian guano and of sulphate of
ammonia, in Europe, shows the esteem in which ammonium compounds are there held by practical farmers. Indeed, until a comparatively recent period, many chemical writers were accustomed
to regard ammonium compounds as the sole source from which
plants could derive nitrogen. It was taught that not only the
ossein of bones, but even the nitrogenized constituents of barnyard manure, must change to ammonia in order to be assimilated
by plants.

It is now known, much as still earlier writers supposed, that
nitrates are on the whole better fitted than ammonium compounds
for exciting vegetable growth; and it has been proved, as will be
seen hereafter, that several other compounds of nitrogen, beside
nitrates and ammonium salts, are directly assimilable by plants.
But the fact that certain ammonium compounds are obtained
cheaply and rather abundantly, as incidental products, which result
from the manufacture of other and more valuable substances, puts
it in the farmer's power to procure them if he so pleases.

Comparative Merit of Nitrates and Ammonia.

So far from ammonium salts being better than nitrates as plant-
food, the tendency of modern investigation has been to show that
the ammonium compounds are, generally speaking, inferior, and
many observers have noticed that plants are much more likely to
be injured by neutral solutions of ammonium salts — unless these
solutions are extremely dilute — than by solutions of nitrates.
Either free ammonia, or carbonate of ammonia or diphosphate of
ammonia — which may readily be formed from neutral ammonium
salts when the latter react upon the juices in the plant — may
exert a distinctly poisonous action upon plants, for unless the
solutions are highly dilute they are apt to react injuriously on the
protoplasm in the cells.

As regards plants of the lower orders, it is known with certainty that ammonium salts are well adapted for feeding many
micro-organisms, while nitrates are much less suitable for this
purpose. Pasteur and Naegeli and numerous other observers have

shown that the microscopic fungi can obtain the nitrogen necessary for their support from ammonium salts as well, or nearly as
well, as they can obtain it from albuminoid matters, while but
few of them can feed on nitrate-nitrogen. According to Loew,
beer-yeast can support for a long time, without injury, a 10%
solution of ammonium chloride even when the liquor is heated to
104° F.; though it has no such power of resisting carbonate of
ammonia, which acts upon it even more quickly than carbonate of
soda would. Neither bacteria nor moulds are easily affected by
solutions of neutral ammonium salts, though some kinds of algae
are somewhat susceptible. Loew has seen Spirogyra suffer in
solutions of neutral ammonium salts that contained no more than
1 part of the salt to 1000 parts of water. He remarks on the
curious fact that, unlike the ammonium salts, neutral salts of the
ammonium bases are not poisonous to the lower orders of plants.
Algae will live for weeks in a 0.2% solution of tetraethyl ammonium chloride, and neurin is an excellent food for moulds. The
observed injurious action of ammonium salts on algae probably
depends on too great concentration, for Bineau and others have
stated that algae speedily consume any ammonia which may have
been put in the water in which they are living. It has been said,
however, by other observers that algae prefer nitrates to ammonium salts.

Practically, for feeding plants of the higher orders, such as are
grown as agricultural crops, nitrates have as a rule been found
more useful than ammonium salts. But, as will be set forth on
another page, Loew maintains, as a highly probable hypothesis,
that it is really from ammonia that the plant-cells build up albumen and the like, and that the nitrates which enter a plant as
such must be changed to ammonia before their nitrogen can be
put to use. According to Loew, the reason why ammonium salts
have been found practically to be somewhat less useful fertilizers
than the nitrates, must depend upon the fact, well known to physiologists, that ammonia and carbonate of ammonia are apt to act
injuriously on the protoplasm in the cells of plants. Unless the
ammonia is extremely dilute it causes the protoplasm to granulate
and seriously impairs its activity. Hence the importance of having ammonia supplied to the cells little by little, as happens when
a nitrate is reduced by cell-action within the plant.

The question was broached occasionally, not many years ago,

whether quantities of ammonium compounds and of nitrates that are
chemically equivalent have the same value for the plant, as sources
of nitrogenous food.   The significance of the inquiry will appear,
in some part, on comparing the composition and the molecular
weights of nitric acid and ammonia, as here set forth : —

Ammonia.		Ammonium.		H	1	Nitric Acid.	
N	14	N	14	N	14	N_2	28
H_3	3	H_4	4	O_3	48	O_5	80
NH_3	17	NH_4	18	HNO_3	63	N_2O_5	108 [÷ 2 = 54]

If it is the nitrogen alone of these substances which is of value as
plant-food, and if one or the other of them is competent to give
up its nitrogen to the plant with equal facility, then 17 lb. of ammonia (NH_3) would do as much good as 54 lb. of anhydrous nitric acid (N_2O_5), such as may be supposed to exist in the nitrates.

In favor of the view of the equivalency of the two substances,
were the familiar facts that ammonium compounds and nitrates are
rather easily transformed one into the other within the soil, and
that ammoniacal manures, as well as those which contain nitrates,
do, on many kinds of soils, give excellent results in farm practice.
It is true, moreover, that both ammonium compounds and nitrates
occur habitually within the plant.   Hosäus has shown that appreciable quantities both of ammonium compounds and of nitrates
are contained in living plants, although the amounts of both these
substances are subject to wide variations, according to the stage
of development of the plant.   In grain plants, he found that both
ammonia and nitrates are most abundant in the spring, when vegetation begins, and that they are least abundant when the plants
are in blossom.   After the time of flowering, the amount of these
constituents gradually increased again.   Usually, there was more
nitrogen in the form of ammonia in the plants than in the form of
nitrates, though in half-ripe wheat he found nitrates to be more
abundant than ammonium compounds.

Berthelot and André, on the other hand, who confined their attention to the nitrates, found that nitrate of potash became more
and more abundant, in the plants they examined, from the moment
when the seed germinated until just before the time of flowering.
Subsequently, while flowers and fruit were being formed, the percentage proportion of the nitrate in the plants diminished; but it
increased again when the process of fruition had wellnigh run its

course, until the withering and death of the vegetable matter put a stop to the formation of nitrates by the plant cells.

This diminution of the nitrate during the period of reproduction is due to the using up of the nitrate-nitrogen for the formation of amids and albuminoids that are needed for the making of flowers and fruit. There is no evidence, however, that nitrates are not really formed within the plant as freely at the time of fruition as before.

As has been stated in the previous chapter, nitrate of potash was found to be most abundant in the stems of plants, while the roots also contained considerable quantities of it. In other words, the nitrate was most abundant in those parts of the plant where most of it is formed. There was much less of it found in the rootlets and flowers, and especially in the leaves. Moreover, less of the nitrate was found in plants that were " forced " in such manner that they " ran to leaf," than in plants that developed normally; manifestly, because in leaves, nitrates as well as other things suffer reduction. It is believed that the oxygen of the nitrates may act upon sugar, or some other carbohydrate, to form an organic acid, as well as carbonic acid and water, while the nitrogen of the nitrate combines with hydrogen to form ammonia, which serves, in its turn, to form albuminoids.

Somewhat akin to this view is the idea of Berthelot and André (and others), who have noticed that considerable quantities of oxalic acid are formed in the leaves of some kinds of plants, apparently as a product of the incomplete reduction of carbonic acid taken in from the air. They urge that oxalic acid is more abundant in leaves than in any other part of plants, and that leaves are rich in albuminoids also, though poor in nitrates; and they make the suggestion that oxalic acid and hydrogen might be generated from formic aldehyde, COH_2 (mentioned on page 26), and water, according to the reaction—

$$2\,COH_2 + 2\,H_2O = C_2H_2O_4 + H_4,$$

and that this hydrogen might serve for the production of albuminoids, i. e. of substances which contain more hydrogen than the carbohydrates.

The constant presence of ammonia in plants at all stages of their development, as observed by Hosäus, certainly seemed to be good evidence of the importance of ammonia-nitrogen for vegetable growth. But on the other hand, numerous experiments made in pots with artificial soils, and experiments made by way of water-culture also, have, with some few exceptions, resulted decidedly in favor of the nitrates, and adversely to the doctrine of equivalency. Speaking in general terms, it may be said that, while many experiments have shown clearly enough that nitrates are competent to supply many kinds of plants with all the nitrogen they need, it has been extremely difficult, if not impossible, to make some kinds of plants grow in solutions that were charged with ammonium salts instead of nitrates, as the source of nitrogen. Moreover it has been observed in field practice that on some soils sulphate of ammonia or chloride of ammonium produce very little fertilizing effect unless they are used in conjunction with some alkaline manure, such as wood-ashes, leached ashes, lime or farmyard manure.

It was thought at one time that the chief trouble with the ammonium salts, in the water-culture experiments, lay in their acids, which, as has already been stated, are apt to be set free when the ammonia of the salt is taken up by the plant. These acids would naturally corrode or poison the plant-roots, in the absence of any soil to absorb and retain and neutralize them. But it is now recognized that conditions unfavorable for nitrification are usually inimical to the best action of the ammonium salts.

Some Kinds of Plants prefer Nitrates, others prefer Ammonia.

From a general review of all the experiments, it is hard to escape the conviction that some kinds of plants may need or prefer ammonia at one stage of their growth, and nitrates at another stage. It is not all unlikely, indeed, that at still other stages of growth plants may prefer still another form of nitrogenous food, different from either the nitrates or the ammonium salts. It follows therefore, that, agriculturally speaking, nitrogen in the form of a nitrate (nitrate-nitrogen) may have a very different practical value from nitrogen which exists in the form of an ammonium salt (ammonia-nitrogen) or from that which is in the form of an organic compound (organic-nitrogen). Though as regards plants, such as rice, which grow in swamps where nitrates cannot exist, the superiority of ammonia can hardly be open to question. (Kellner.)

As will be seen directly some physiologists believe that in the last analysis ammonia-nitrogen is really a better plant-food than nitrate-nitrogen, but that it is useful only when highly diluted or when supplied to the plant very gradually, since the contents of the cells of plants are liable to suffer injury when even moderately strong solutions of ammonium salts come in contact with them.

The Experiments of Lehmann.

One of the earliest series of experiments made expressly to test the question whether nitrates or ammonia salts are best suited to supply plants with nitrogen are those of Julius Lehmann. He grew a number of buckwheat and of maize plants, by way of water culture, in solutions which were all of one and the same composition in respects to their inorganic constituents, but which differed from one another in that some of the solutions contained nitrate of lime while others contained sulphate of ammonia. There were two rows of jars, each row containing eight jars, and to one row nitrate of lime was given, while the other got sulphate of ammonia.

The buckwheat-plants grew very well in the solutions that contained the nitrate,— as well indeed as they would have grown in a garden,— but they grew very badly in the solutions that contained the ammonia salt. The two best buckwheat-plants grown in the nitrate jars were 130 and 140 cm. high (i. e. 50 and more inches); they bore 288 and 174 seeds, and weighed (air-dried) 29 and 27 grams.

Many investigators have grown luxuriant buckwheat-plants in solutions, and in sand, that contained nitrates as the only nitrogenous food; and experiments made by S. W. Johnson, as long ago as 1861 ("How Crops Feed," p. 302), plainly indicated the inferiority of ammonium compounds as compared with nitrates, for this particular crop.

In the case of Indian corn the results obtained by Lehmann were very different from those got with buckwheat. Maize-plants that had already germinated were placed in the jars on the 19th of June, and at the end of a week it was seen that those in the nitrate jars exhibited all the signs of starvation, while those in the ammonia jars were in a highly prosperous condition. At the start, the ammonia plants began to grow most luxuriantly, and exhibited convincing evidence that they were abundantly fed with the right kind of food.

After the experiment had lasted six weeks, the appearance of all the plants, both those in the nitrate jars and those that were fed with ammonia, suddenly changed. The nitrate plants became green all at once, although no change had occurred in respect to the outward conditions under which they were growing; and from this time forth the nitrate plants grew rapidly and well.

But with the ammonia plants precisely the reverse of all this occurred at the very same time. The leaves of the ammonia plants lost their healthy color, and the plants themselves presented an unhealthy appearance. While the nitrate plants grew continually and developed normally until the 15th of September, the ammonia plants did not increase, but remained standing in a most miserable condition. Moreover, the weight of the nitrate plants when harvested attested their normal development.

On changing some of the sickly nitrate plants, during the first period, into jars that contained the ammoniacal food, they revived immediately and took on a lively green color in two days' time; and so, conversely, on putting some of the healthy ammonia plants into a solution that contained nitrate of soda, they became at once pale and sickly.

So too, during the second period, when it appeared that the maize-plants had need of nitrogen in the form of a nitrate, such shifting of the plants from one kind of a jar to another immediately exhibited the advantage of this kind of food. Lehmann tried this changing of some of his plants repeatedly, and found that he had it completely in his power to make the plants pale and sickly, or green and healthy, as he might will.

From these experiments with maize, it would appear that this plant has need of ammonia when young, and of nitrates when more mature. But manifestly, if this apparent fact be really true, the whole theory and practice of manuring Indian corn will need to be revised. It should here be said that earlier experiments upon maize, as cited in "How Crops Feed," pp. 303, 304, though seemingly somewhat conflicting, do none the less point to the conclusion that this plant can be supported by ammonia during certain stages of its growth. One experimenter found, for example, that maize could be grown with ammonia, while oats invariably failed. But on the other hand, it is true also that normal maize-plants have been grown by way of water-culture by means of nitrates and ash-ingredients without any addition of ammonia. Moreover, Dehérain, in field experiments made in 1876, '77, '78 and '79, on a light, slightly calcareous soil at Grignon, in France, got better results in growing fodder-corn with nitrate of soda than were obtained when sulphate of ammonia was used, as will appear from the following table:

Fertilizers used.	Average crop of the 4 years. Tons of green fodder to the hectare.
No manure	49.3
Farm-manure	79.9
400 kilos nitrate of soda	59.6
1200 kilos nitrate of soda, applied in 1876, '77, '78, but not in 1879	56.7
400 kilos sulphate of ammonia	53.4
1200 kilos sulphate of ammonia, applied in 1876, '77, '78, but not in 1879	49.6

Lehmann next proceeded to experiment with tobacco. But in this case he grew the plants in quartz sand instead of by way of water-culture. He supplied the plants, as before, with all the mineral matters they needed, and to some of the plants he gave, in addition, nitrate of soda, while to others he gave sulphate of ammonia.

Here, with the tobacco, the plants that were fed with ammonia were healthy and sound from first to last; the stalks and leaves were always succulent and green, and the plants grew normally all the while. The nitrate plants, on the contrary, remained far behind the ammonia plants during the first half of the experiment, and, being of pale color, had a sickly appearance. But during the last half of the experiment the nitrate plants exhibited a strong tendency to improve. They became green, and their growth was evidently stronger than before. In spite of this improvement, the final weight of the nitrate plants was comparatively small. It turned out that the crop of ammonia plants was six times, and the crop of nitrate plants three times, as heavy as a crop grown in sand without any addition of nitrogen.

Here it would seem as if ammoniacal manures, rather than the nitrates, were "indicated" for the tobacco plant. With buckwheat, it will be remembered, the fact was just the other way. The buckwheat plants prospered with nitrates from first to last, just as Boussingault's small sunflower prospered.

The fact that the tobacco-plants got some good from the nitrate during the second stage of their growth supports in some sort the results that were obtained with the maize, for the maize-plants when mature put the nitrate to good use. As Lehmann suggests, it may be that all his tobacco-plants really fed upon nitrates during the last half of their life; for it might easily have happened that the ammonia salt was changed to a nitrate, and this oxidation would be more likely to have occurred in the sand-jars than in those used for water-culture, since in the latter the solutions were frequently changed.

It may here be said that Harz also found in his experiments that for tobacco, sulphate of ammonia was a better fertilizer than nitrate of soda. But in the fields, as Schloesing has remarked, sulphate of ammonia may nitrify with extraordinary rapidity under favorable conditions.

The readiness with which ammonium compounds change to nitrates in such experiments has often been remarked upon, both in respect to sand culture and water culture. Indeed, this liability to change constitutes one of the many difficulties which make the question of the comparative merits of ammonia and nitrates so hard to solve. In field experiments, for example, with ammonium salts, it might always be argued that, since ammonia changes readily to nitrates in porous soils during the growing season, in presence of the nitric ferment, it may, after all, be nitrates, and not ammonia, that feed the crops.

Curiously enough, it has been noticed in some experiments in water-culture with ammonium salts, that, after long-continued sickly growth, the plants have suddenly thrown out new shoots, and have begun to grow vigorously. Examination of the solutions has then shown that a large part of the ammonia had really been changed to nitrates, and the inference was plain that the new growth must have been due to the formation of the nitrates.

In view of the foregoing facts, there is little difficulty in admitting that in numberless instances the useful fertilizing effects obtained by means of sulphate of ammonia, in field practice, may really have been due to nitrates which have been formed in the soil from the ammonium salt. By the same reasoning, it would appear that nitrate of soda should be applied in preference to sulphate of ammonia to cold, sour land, and to land which contains but little calcareous matter, since the process of nitrification can hardly ever be rapid upon such soils.

It should here be said that, in field practice, nitrates have approved themselves a very good manure for tobacco. Moreover, field experiments by A. Mayer, in which nitrates and ammonia were carefully contrasted on three different kinds of soils, which had all been dressed with farmyard manure, showed that well-fed tobacco-plants grow more luxuriantly when supplied with nitrates than when supplied with ammonia. Generally speaking, Mayer's tobacco-plants contained more nitrogen than those fed with ammonia, and they were always rich in nicotin, also. But in some instances, plants which had received ammonia, in addition to farmyard-manure, contained an exceptionally large proportion of nicotin, though no such result was obtained in the absence of stable-manure as when the tobacco-plants were fed with mixtures of ammonia and other artificial fertilizers. The poverty of Mayer's unmanured tobacco-plants, in respect to nitrogen and to nicotin, was remarkable. So too was the enormous increase of both these constituents in plants that were richly fed.

In connection with his other tests, Lehmann experimented with the yellow lupine, which is a plant that contains a great deal of nitrogen, but which nevertheless grows upon extremely sterile land. The lupine had been found to succeed perfectly upon the sandy heaths of Germany, where hardly anything else will grow, and it had long been a very mysterious question as to how and where it gets its nitrogen.

Lehmann grew his lupine-plants in quartz-sand; he fed them all with the necessary ash-ingredients, and to some he gave no nitrogenous food, to others he gave nitrate of soda, and to others sulphate of ammonia. To all outward appearance the lupines that got nitrate of soda grew best of all. Compared with the other plants, they were stronger, and they were developed more symmetrically. But at the time of harvest it appeared that the seeds of the nitrate plants weighed less than those from the ammonia jars. In a word, the nitrate of soda produced a good deal of leaf, but comparatively little seed. Long after Lehmann's experiments, Budin observed very much the same thing on applying nitrates to lupines. Six weeks after the seeds were sown the plants fed with the nitrate were luxuriant, but in spite of this early promise the crops finally obtained by the use of the nitrate were no larger than those got without using any nitrogenous fertilizer. The question arose whether the nitrate plants might not have run through the several steps of life too rapidly, and the practical conclusion was that the nitrate is not at all to be commended as a means of increasing the lupine crop.

Lehmann's lupines fed with sulphate of ammonia began to look miserably as soon as they had developed three or four leaves. The leaves were crumpled and yellow; several of the plants died after a short time, and the remainder were crippled and feeble, until in July a change came over them. They began to grow vigorously, and developed many flowers, from which seeds ripened in due course, in a perfectly normal way.

As for the lupine-plants that got no nitrogenous food, they held way, during the first week or two, with the nitrate plants; during the next ten weeks, they fell behind somewhat, but caught up again afterwards to such an extent that only a slight difference could be detected on comparing the best plants of the two lots, although there were many more good plants to be found among the nitrate jars than in the no-nitrogen jars. Still, at the time of harvest, the no-nitrogen crop gave a larger yield of seeds than the nitrate crop or the ammonia crop. The weights of the seeds were, with

No Nitrogen.	Ammonium Sulphate.	Sodium Nitrate.
143 grams.	133 grams.	128 grams.

Since these experiments were made, it has been discovered that the lupine (as well as the pea, the bean, and various clovers) habitually obtains nitrogen from the air through the intervention of parasitic organisms which live upon its roots, and that — although capable of using nitrates to a certain extent — the lupine plant does not thrive in the absence of this parasite. It is to be presumed that in Lehmann's experiment spores of the parasite came to one or more of his plants, from the air, and not to the others, and that much of the ammonium salt was changed to a nitrate also.

In a classical research on the sources whence leguminous plants obtain their nitrogenous food, Hellriegel has shown conclusively that although nitrates are readily assimilated and put to profit by peas, clovers, serradella, etc., and to a certain extent even by lupines, it is none the less true that leguminous plants ordinarily obtain so large a proportion of their nitrogenous food from the air — by the help of micro-organisms living upon their roots — that the presence of nitrates in the soil is far less important for the legumes than it is for the cereal grains and for most other crops. Wolff and Kreuzhage also found in numerous experiments that while the growth of oats was always greatly promoted by applications of nitrates, and while this crop could not be grown with success unless it was supplied with an abundance of nitrate-nitrogen, a very different rule obtained in respect to most leguminous crops.

It appeared in their experiments that nitrates have practically comparatively little influence on the development of red clover, horse-beans, peas and most other legumes, simply because the action of the root-fungus is of paramount importance. So long as the clover (etc.) plants were young their growth was evidently promoted by nitrates, but this influence tended to disappear as the plants became mature. The first clipping of clover, for example, was appreciably larger in those cases where the plants were fertilized with nitrates than in those where the sand had been mixed with nothing but ash-ingredients, but even at the time of the second clipping the difference in yield was small, and in subsequent clippings the differences diminished to such an extent that they were sometimes hardly noticeable. In the case of serradella, however, nitrates manifestly served a useful purpose. On attempting to grow this crop without nitrates the plants developed with extreme slowness, though they eventually yielded as much dry substance as plants which had received a light dressing of nitrate-nitrogen. But on applying an abundance of the nitrate the serradella grew rapidly and yielded a crop which was very much larger than those grown without nitrates or with but little of the nitrate.

It is to be observed that these results, with clover, etc., are not inconsistent with those of Lawes and Gilbert, who found in actual field practice that horse-beans and clover of various kinds assimilate large quantities of nitrates. Thus, manured land on which beans were growing was found to contain only 20.5 lb. of nitrate-nitrogen to the acre, to a depth of 18 inches, while contiguous bare land contained nearly 49 lb., and on other plots fertilized with nothing but superphosphate, the bean-land contained about 11 lb. of nitrate-nitrogen, while the corresponding bare fallow contained more than 36 lb. The soil of a red-clover plot (manured), taken to a depth of 27 inches, contained 19.6 lb. of nitrate-nitrogen, while there was nearly 60 lb. in the soil of a corresponding bare fallow. The soil of a white-clover plot which had been dressed with mineral manures contained 26.3 lb. of nitrate-nitrogen, to a depth of 54 inches, while a corresponding plot covered with a heavy growth of the coarse free-growing Bokhara clover contained only 8.5 lb. In the first 27 inches of depth, the white-clover soil contained 13.5 lb. of nitrate-nitrogen, and the Bokhara-clover soil only 5 lb. In the second 27 inches the white-clover soil contained 12.8 lb., or nearly as much as the first, and the Bokhara-clover soil only 3.5 lb. "It is obvious that the Bokhara-clover had withdrawn nitrates to the full depth examined, and it had doubtless done so to a lower depth still."

Heiden remarks that the foregoing result is confirmed by field experiments made by himself with lupines on a sandy soil, for 2,275 seeds sown upon unmanured land gave 617 plants, 5,686 grm. of air-dried seeds, and a total crop that weighed 84,110 grm. when fresh; while a plot fertilized with sulphate of ammonia, and similarly sown, gave only 200 plants, 1,332 grm. of air-dried seeds, and 27,040 grm. of total green crop.

Budin found that the growth of lupines may be specially promoted by means of earth taken from fields where leguminous plants have grown, and by means of compost made by drenching with urine heaps of mixed weeds, street-sweepings, and other refuse. The crops obtained by using this compost yielded four and a half times as much seed, and nearly three times as much total crop, as were got without fertilization.

In corroboration of Lehmann's experiments on tobacco and maize, Kellner has found that swamp-rice can be fed either with ammonia or with nitrates, but that the ammoniacal food does the most good when the rice-plants are young, while in later stages of growth, nitrates are better food than ammonia. It seems, indeed, that the rice-plant, in the later stages of its growth, has no little difficulty in making use of ammonia-nitrogen. In the farm practice of Japan, the rice-fields are kept under water during the first half of the term of growth of the crop, so that nitrification is as good as excluded. So far from nitrates being formed in the soil of the flowed rice-fields, it is known that processes of reduction occur there, and that ammonia and marsh-gas are continually produced. Moreover, the fields are habitually manured with green plants, or bean-cake, fish-scrap, night-soil, or the like, i. e. with substances that need to be in presence of an excess of oxygen if nitrates are to be formed from them. But careful experiments have shown that the swamp-rice puts these fertilizers to good use, or, rather, that it makes use of the ammonia which is formed by their decay; and that dressings either of sulphate of ammonia or of night-soil are fit fertilizers for rice.

In pot-experiments made by way of water-culture, Kellner grew rice in solutions that were alike as to ash-ingredients, but different in that some jars got nitrate of potash, others a mixture of nitrate of potash and nitrate of lime, others phosphate of ammonia, and others mixtures of nitrates and the ammonium salt. At first, the ammonia plants were superior to those fed with nitrates; they were taller, and seemed to be healthier. But later, the nitrate plants recovered their vigor, while the ammonia plants suddenly came to a standstill. As the condition of the ammonia plants failed to improve, nitrate of potash was given to a number of them, after some time, with the result that they began to grow again, although those which had no other source of nitrogen than ammonia remained somewhat crippled to the end of their lives, and failed to yield so good a crop as the nitrate plants. It was noticed, however, that although the organs of the ammonia plants were not well developed, these plants had neverthless taken up a larger proportion of nitrogen and of ash-ingredients than the others. As regards the plants fed with nitrates alone, they were backward at first, and developed but slowly at the very time when the ammonia plants were growing rapidly; but after a time the nitrate plants became vigorous, and they grew normally thenceforth, while the ammonia plants fell behind, as has been said, and suffered visibly. Rice-plants fed with a mixture of ammonia and nitrates, as well as ash-ingredients, grew well from first to last, and did better, in fact, than any of the plants which were supplied with only one form of nitrogen. It will be noticed that the foregoing refers to swamp-rice, which is grown on flooded land free from nitrates, and manured with substances which supply to it ammonia. Kellner has said of this kind of rice, that it prefers ammonia-nitrogen, and does not thrive when irrigated if it is supplied wholly with nitrates. But there is another kind of rice, common in Japan, which cannot habitually get ammonia, since it is grown on upland soils where nitrification is active.

In some field experiments, the original purpose of which was to find out how to make crude, new land fruitful, two kinds of soils were tested, the one light and sandy and the other a heavy clay. Excellent crops of oats and rye were constantly obtained upon the clay-land by means of sulphate of ammonia. But upon the sandy soil the rye-crop thus fertilized suffered severely, and remained much inferior to rye grown upon plots that had received no manure whatever. At the same time, some plots of the sandy soil which had been dressed successively with sulphate of ammo-

nia, ash-ingredients, and lime, gave excellent crops of rye; and
on analyzing the several soils, it appeared that the favorable development of the crops was coincident with the formation of nitrates from the ammonium salt. Both upon the clay and upon the
limed sandy soil, nitrification had occurred at a time when the
sandy plot that had been dressed with sulphate of ammonia contained no nitrates. (Heiden.)

In field experiments with oats, Heiden found that nitrate of
soda, applied as a top-dressing to the young plants, gave rather
better results than sulphate of ammonia that had been worked into
the soil a short time before sowing the seed. On a soil formed
through the disintegration of granite, he found that a dressing of
30 or 40 lb. of soluble phosphoric acid, and from 7 to 14 lb. of
nitrogen (i. e. 53 to 100 lb. of nitrate of soda) to the acre, gave
profitable returns with oats.

Wein grew oats, peas, horse-beans, and soy-beans in mixtures
of pure humus (prepared by acting upon sugar with hydrochloric
acid) and ash-ingredients, with additions of one or another form
of nitrogen. All the plants grew well with nitrate of soda; but
sulphate of ammonia hindered their early development, and many
of the plants were killed by it. After a time, however, those
plants which still remained alive were able to put the ammonium
salt to use; perhaps when some of it had changed to a nitrate?
Similar results were obtained by Wein with soy-beans grown in a
calcareous sandy soil, rich in humus. Plots between 3 and 4
square metres in area were dressed with 120 grams of a plain superphosphate of 27 %. To plot No. I no nitrogenous fertilizer
was added, while No. II got 20 grams of nitrogen in the form of
nitrate of soda (121½ grams), and No. III got 20 grams of nitrogen in the form of sulphate of ammonia (94.3 grams). The
weights of the crops harvested were as follows: —

Plot.	Fertilizer.	Weight in Grams of			Total Dry Crop.	Total Albumi-noid Matters.
		Grain.	Shells.	Straw.		
I.	No nitrogen . . .	381.3	233.0	806.5	1,242.8	202
II.	Nitrate of soda . .	1,185.2	478.1	2,102.0	3,332.4	670
III.	Sulphate of ammonia	944.6	382.0	1,621.0	2,603.3	574

In this case, both of the nitrogenous fertilizers did good work,
but especially the nitrate of soda. The plants that received the
sulphate of ammonia were backward during the earlier period of
their development, but they recovered themselves afterward. But
it is questionable whether this recovery may not have been due to

the growth of bacteria upon the roots of the plants, and not at all to the presence of the ammonium salt. (See the Chapter on Symbiosis.)

Baeyer had previously failed repeatedly in persistent efforts to grow oats with ammonium salts by way of water-culture. The ammonium compounds distressed the young plants, and it was proved in these trials that it was only after some of the ammonia had changed to a nitrate that the oats prospered. In England, it was recognized long ago that dressings of nitrate of soda are of the greatest service to oats. The straw grows large and strong, and the yield of grain is increased. Pusey noticed, in his turn, that while nitrate of soda is an excellent top-dressing for oat-fields, sulphate of ammonia sometimes does no good.

Hässelbarth grew barley in pots of sand admixed with needful amounts of ash-ingredients, which were supplemented in some cases with nitrates, and in others with ammonium salts. The results of all his trials went to show that, while the nitrates were proper food for this crop, the barley-plant could not supply itself with nitrogen directly from the ammonium salt. When the conditions were favorable for the nitrification of the ammonium compounds, the barley grew with more or less luxuriance, according as the nitrification was more or less rapid. Similar results were obtained by Hellriegel, in his elaborate experiments on the growth of barley and other cereals. He found that nitrates were put to profit by these plants under all circumstances, and that, when other kinds of food were present, and so long as no excess of the nitrate was used, the crops obtained were proportional to the amounts of nitrate applied to the land. He deems it probable that no other form of nitrogen is of any direct use to the cereals.

In field experiments with barley and with wheat, Lawes and Gilbert found that larger amounts both of grain and of straw were obtained, especially in dry seasons, from a given amount of nitrogen applied in the spring in the form of nitrate of soda, than were got from an equal amount of nitrogen applied as an ammonium salt. Moreover, when ammonium salts were applied to wheat in the autumn, a much smaller proportion of their nitrogen was recovered in the increase of the crop than when they were applied in the spring to barley or oats. They say: "Although there is often a strong prejudice against the use of nitrate of soda (upon wheat), it is evident that, when judiciously applied (in conjunc-

tion with mineral fertilizers), its properties as a manure are much
higher than those of salts of ammonia. . . . According to the experiments at Rothamsted, it would appear that, at equivalent
prices, a given amount of nitrogen, as nitrate of soda, may, in
the long run, be more effective than an equal amount as ammonia;
for, contrary to the current opinion, the full effect of the nitrate
was not obtained until it had been used for some years on the
same plot.''

Experiments on Grass, etc.

On hay-fields, on land overlying chalk, ammonium salts, used
in conjunction with mineral fertilizers, gave as much, or even
more, hay during several years than nitrate of soda similarly reinforced; but in later years the nitrate mixture yielded considerably
larger crops than the ammonia mixture. It appeared, however,
that, by the continued application of the nitrate, the soil became
saturated with nitrogen to a considerable depth; that the texture
of the soil was improved by the nitrate, and that the growth of
deep-rooted kinds of grasses was encouraged, so that the hay-crop
obtained a good command of sub-soil moisture. After 20 years'
experience, Lawes and Gilbert have concluded "that a given
amount of nitrogen applied as nitrate of soda gave more produce
than the same amount applied as ammonia-salts, whether these nitrogenous manures were respectively used alone or in conjunction
with a mixed mineral manure supplying in excess all the mineral
constituents of the hay-crop."

Since the action of an ammonium salt on grass-land differs in
some respects from that of nitrate of soda, there is still room for
believing that on some soils it may occasionally be advisable to
apply sulphate of ammonia to grass-land, rather than nitrate of
soda, especially in cases where it is desired to smother the Canada
thistle, white-weed, rib-grass, dandelions, or the like. The experiments of Lawes and Gilbert go to show, however, that sorrel
flourishes under the influence of ammonium salts, and also, though
to a less extent, under that of nitrate of soda, though its development is restricted when the conditions are favorable for the
luxuriant growth of the grasses. It was noticed, also, that the
growth of June-grass and orchard-grass was favored by ammonium salts used in conjunction with potash and other mineral fertilizers, while neither of these grasses became prominent on plots
to which nitrate of soda was applied. On the other hand, the ni-

trate encouraged the growth of the meadow Poa (P. trivialis), which declined markedly on the plots dressed with ammonium salts, and of the meadow fox-tail, which was helped by ammonia also. I have myself observed repeatedly that sulphate of ammonia is a capital fertilizer for grass-fields, and Bréal has maintained that grasses grown by way of water-culture do as well when fed with ammonium salts as when fed with nitrates.

In field experiments on cabbages made by Dyer in England, sulphate of ammonia gave but poor results as compared with equivalent dressings of nitrate of soda, though it was questioned whether this result may not have been influenced by continued dry weather. In this country, nitrate of soda has sometimes been found to be a profitable fertilizer for tomatoes, on light soils.

In field trials, during three years on sugar-cane, made by Harrison at Barbadoes, a large increase in the weight of the canes was obtained by means of mixtures of readily available nitrogenous fertilizers and mineral manures, though excessive dressings of the nitrogen compounds caused a marked decrease in the richness and purity of the juice. In these trials, nitrate of soda was decidedly inferior to sulphate of ammonia as a source of nitrogen, and somewhat similar results have been obtained in Louisiana by Prof. Stubbs. Earlier statements relating to Demerara are to the effect that "Ammoniacal salts have been largely tried as a manure for sugar-cane; the result being the rapid growth of the canes and the production of a juice poor in sugar."

Alkaloids formed from both kinds of Nitrogen.

A very striking experiment has been made by Dietrich to test the comparative efficacy of ammonium salts and nitrates in producing morphine in poppy plants. The plants were grown on a sandy soil that contained very little nitrogen. When no manure was used, the opium produced contained no more than $\frac{1}{2}$% of morphine. But there were 3 or 4 times as much morphine in the opium from plants fertilized with nitrate of soda, and 13 times as much in that from plants fertilized with sulphate of ammonia. Analogous experiments by Broughton on cinchona plants manured with sulphate of ammonia, guano, and farmyard manure, go to show that, at different stages of growth, one or another kind of nitrogen may be best fitted to promote the formation of alkaloids.

Hosäus grew onions by way of water-culture in solutions that contained, beside ferric phosphate, in No. I, sulphate of potash, sulphate of magnesia, and chloride of ammonium; in No. II, the nitrates of lime and of potash, and sulphate of magnesia; and in No. III, a mixture of equal parts of Nos. I and II. At first the plants grew equally well in all the jars, but subsequently those in the ammonia jars fell behind, and several of them died, though no difference was noticed between the plants in the other two jars. At the end of six weeks, analysis showed the presence of nitrates in the roots and bulbs of all the plants, but not in the leaves. In the plants that had been fed with nitrates alone, it was only in the roots that any great amount of nitrates was discovered. Ammonia, on the contrary, was contained in all parts of those plants which had been fed with the ammonium salt, though it was as good as absent from the plants which were fed with nitrates alone. Hence the inference that living plants have power to convert ammonium compounds into nitrates; while, as regards the case now in question, there was no evidence of any power in the plant to change nitrates to ammonia.

It was noticed by Hosäus, moreover, in other experiments, that the bulbs of onions, as well as those of leeks and the sword-lily, contained no nitrates in October, although they contained no inconsiderable quantity of nitrates in June.

Nitrates are best for Potatoes.

As regards potatoes, Wagner concluded from field experiments that ammonium salts do harm rather than good. He found that ammonia hindered the vegetation of the crop, and made the plants sickly and of a yellowish color. In a case where the conditions as to soil and temperature were such that the ammonia could not readily change to a nitrate, dressings of 40 kilos of nitrogen to the hectare, applied in the form of sulphate of ammonia, gave no increase of the potato crop; while, under similar conditions, dressings of 40 kilos of nitrogen in the form of nitrate of soda gave an increase of crop amounting to 28%. Baessler also, in a set of field experiments with potatoes made on a fertile, sandy loam, manured with superphosphate, found that sulphate of ammonia hardly paid for itself, either when used alone or in conjunction with nitrate of soda, while good economic results were got from nitrate of soda, when applied at the rate of 90 lb. to the acre. When used at the rate of 180 lb. to the acre, the increase of crop brought by the nitrate was not commensurate with the increased cost of the fertilizer. It is noteworthy that sulphate of ammonia had given Baessler good results in previous years when used upon barley and oats, in comparison with nitrate of soda.

In experiments made by way of sand-culture, Wolff and Kreuzhage observed that nitrates were excellent food for potatoes, though it was evident that a tolerably large quantity of the nitrate-nitrogen was required. They found, for example, that small quantities of nitrate of potash had very little influence upon the growth of potatoes, although similar quantities of the nitrate had a highly beneficial action upon oats.

The numerous field experiments of Grouven, to be mentioned in Volume II, when treating of the peculiar merit of dung, tended to show that, on the whole, nitrate of soda did rather better service upon potatoes than sulphate of ammonia. But Voelcker, as the result of numerous field experiments with potatoes, was led to conclude that on light, sandy soils, in dry seasons, nitrate of soda used in conjunction with superphosphate and potash salts has a less beneficial effect than sulphate of ammonia similarly used.. That is to say, the nitrate, although it did a considerable amount of good, did not answer quite so well as an equal weight of the sulphate. On stiffish soils containing a fair proportion of clay, neither sulphate of ammonia nor nitrate of soda, added to the superphosphate and potash salts, materially increased the yield of potatoes.

Maercker in his field experiments with potatoes found no great difference between nitrate of soda, sulphate of ammonia, and Peruvian guano, when used by themselves or in conjunction with plain superphosphate. A notable increase in the yield of potatoes was obtained by the use of either of these nitrogenous fertilizers, almost always, even when they were applied by themselves, but light dressings of the nitrate gave comparatively larger yields than heavy dressings. No useful effects were derived from nitrogenous fertilizers of organic origin applied to potatoes in the spring, either by themselves or with superphosphate; and no appreciable increase of crop was obtained when superphosphate was used by itself. But when the superphosphate was applied in conjunction with an active nitrogenous fertilizer, much better results were obtained than could be got by the nitrogen compounds alone, provided the superphosphate was used in large quantity.

When no dung was used, the best results were got from mixtures of nitrate of soda and a large quantity of superphosphate. i. e. 350 lb. to the acre of Baker Island superphosphate, such as contains 18 or 20 % of soluble phosphoric acid. Where no farmyard-manure is to be used, Maercker suggests as a normal dressing for potatoes 350 lb. to the acre of Baker Island superphosphate and 175 lb. of nitrate of soda.

In another set of experiments, Maercker found that nitrate of soda was a useful addition to farmyard-manure, and for this purpose it proved to be superior to sulphate of ammonia, which plainly did harm, though, unless the nitrate was applied at or shortly after the time of planting, it did harm and diminished the crop of potatoes both as to quantity and quality. Here again nitrogenous fertilizers of organic origin, though used in conjunction with farmyard-manure, did no good.

Plain superphosphate used as an addition to farmyard-manure gave a very considerable increase in the yield of potatoes, and such addition was found to be highly satisfactory in many instances. But the largest crops of all were obtained by using stable-manure, superphosphate, and nitrate of soda together. In this case much smaller quantities of superphosphate were sufficient than when it was used without the dung. 175 lb. of Baker Island superphosphate, and from 80 to 125 lb. of the nitrate, are deemed to be fit additions to a dressing of fresh farmyard-manure.

Dreschler also, in very elaborate farm experiments on potatoes in Germany, found that nitrate of soda used with superphosphate almost invariably gave good results, and that, with few exceptions, the advantage was in getting increased yields of large tubers. Lawes and Gilbert in their experiments on growing potatoes continuously noticed the very remarkable fact that this crop responds less readily than some others to applications of easily assimilable nitrogen compounds. There was less increase of crop when the land was dressed with nothing but nitrate of soda, or with ammonium salts, than when — no nitrogen being put upon it — it received a mixture of potash salts, superphosphate of lime and others mineral fertilizers. It will be noticed that, although the soil of their fields is somewhat calcareous, nitrate of soda alone proved to be a somewhat better fertilizer for potatoes than ammonium salts alone. The following table shows the average annual crops of potatoes harvested during 12 consecutive years :

Kinds of Fertilisers.	Weights of the crops, in long tons and cwt.
No manure	2.0
Ammonium salts alone [1]	2.6
Nitrate of soda alone [1]	2.13
Mixed mineral manure [2]	3.15
Superphosphate of lime alone	3.14
Ammonium salts and the mixed minerals	6.15
Nitrate of soda and the mixed minerals	6.13
14 tons farmyard manure (for 6 years)	2.6
Ditto and superphosphate of lime (for 7 years)	5.12
Ditto, ditto and nitrate of soda (for 6 years)	7.2

It will be noticed that the gain got by means of ammonium salts alone was only 6 cwt., and that with nitrate of soda the gain was 13 cwt. They say, "the better result by nitrate of soda is doubtless due to the nitrogen being more immediately available and more rapidly distributed within the soil, and so inducing a more extended development of feeding-roots. The negative results by the nitrogenous manures alone, confirm the conclusion that, by the continuous growth of potatoes on this land, it was the available supply of mineral constituents within the root-range of the plant, more than that of nitrogen, that became deficient."

It was observed also that the unmanured land, and that dressed with ammonium salts alone, and with nitrate of soda alone, yielded smaller crops during the second term of 4 years, and still less during the final term of 4 years, than were harvested during the first four years. On the land dressed with superphosphate alone, with the mixed minerals, and with the mineral and nitrogenous fertilizers together, there was more produce over the second 4 years than over the first four. But there was a marked reduction during the last term of 4 years; the conclusion being that by the continuous growth of potatoes without manure or with nitrogenous manures alone the available supplies of mineral food became relatively deficient. Nevertheless, it will be noticed that the very satisfactory yield of more than 6.5 long tons of tubers was obtained annually, on the average of the whole term of 12 years, by the means of mixed mineral and nitrogenous fertilizers. The merit of nitrate of soda (as well as that of superphosphate of lime) was exhibited also in an experiment where the land was dressed during 6 consecutive years with farmyard manure, superphosphate of

---

[1] Supplying 86 lb. of nitrogen per year and per acre.
[2] Containing superphosphate of lime and salts of potash, soda and magnesia.

lime and nitrate of soda; and thereafter, for another term of 6
years, it got farmyard manure alone. The average crops of tubers
per year and per acre were 7 tons and 2 cwt. during the first 6
years, and only 4 tons during the last 6 years.

It may here be remarked that there is a somewhat serious objection to the use of large quantities of any active nitrogenous
fertilizer on potatoes, since succulent, over-luxuriant vines are
specially open to the attacks of the fungus which causes the disease known as the potato-rot. So long ago as when this rot first
caused serious trouble in Ireland, it was noticed there that fields
which had been heavily manured with guano were quickly ruined,
and Lawes and Gilbert found that although the amount of the
disease was not enhanced at Rothamsted by the continuous growth
of the crop year after year on the same land, there was unmistakable evidence that (excepting dry seasons) the highest manuring and the most luxuriant growth brought a much higher proportion of diseased tubers than was observed in those crops where
the growth of the vines had been less rank. Without manure,
and with purely mineral manures, the proportion of diseased tubers
was much less than where nitrogenous manures were applied; and
it was less where the nitrogenous manures had been applied by
themselves than where they were used in conjunction with mineral
manures, and where the crops had been consequently the most
luxuriant.

Nitrates are best for Beets.

Beets are known to be greatly benefited by nitrates applied in
the earlier stages of the growth of the crop, and by seasonable
tillage, which promotes nitrification in the soil, though in the later
stages of growth the beet-crop is apt to take up nitrates uselessly,
to the detriment of the leaves in case they are to be used as fodder, and to the injury of the juice when sugar is to be made from
it. Sulphate of ammonia, on the contrary, when used under conditions unfavorable for nitrification, is not only inferior to the nitrates as a fertilizer for beets, but it has sometimes been observed
that extremely large dressings of it may do positive injury to the
land, as will be explained on another page.

Maercker states emphatically that, as a general rule, sulphate of
ammonia is not a proper source of nitrogen for mangolds and
sugar-beets. Much better crops of beets can be grown by means
of nitrate of soda, he says, than by using sulphate of ammonia.

Thus, in comparative experiments made in Saxony, 1 cwt. of nitrate of soda, applied in the spring, gave an average increase of beet-roots of from 25 to 30 cwt., while the increase got by means of the same weight of nitrogen applied in the spring, in the form of sulphate of ammonia (0.75 cwt.), amounted to no more than 15 to 20 cwt.; though when the ammonium salt was applied in the autumn, almost as good crops were obtained as those got by means of nitrate of soda. In like manner, Stocklaza, operating on granitic and sandstone soils, found that nitrate of soda was a much better fertilizer than sulphate of ammonia taken by itself, for sugar-beets, though the sulphate gave as good crops as the nitrate when it was used in conjunction with carbonate of lime.

P. Wagner also found that the nitrification of sulphate of ammonia is so much promoted, on some soils, by the addition of carbonate of lime, that the sulphate may then be used well enough for manuring root crops. In comparative experiments made with sulphate of ammonia and nitrate of soda, on summer turnips, on peaty and loamy soils — some plots of which had been marled, while others had not — he found that on unmarled peat the ammonia-nitrogen had no more than 28 % of the efficiency of the nitrate-nitrogen, and that it did 90 % as much good as the nitrate-nitrogen on the peat that had been marled. The loamy soil, on the contrary, was naturally more favorable for nitrification than the peat, and it may perhaps have already contained lime enough to neutralize the sulphuric acid in the ammonium sulphate; at all events, the addition of lime to this soil had no appreciable influence on the action of the ammonia. Here the ammonia-nitrogen was 89 % as efficient as the nitrate-nitrogen on the unmarled peat, and 90 % as efficient as the nitrate-nitrogen on the peat that had been marled.

The foregoing results consist with those obtained by Voelcker, long ago, in his field experiments upon mangolds. "On light land," he says, "a moderate amount of an ammoniacal salt or of nitrate of soda, added to a manure composed of available phosphates and salts of potash, appeared to be very useful. I have repeatedly observed that a small quantity of nitrate of soda helps on the mangold plants in a striking manner, provided other fertilizers are used at the same time, or the land is in a high agricultural condition."

In the year 1858, Voelcker concluded, from the results of his field experiments, that sulphate of ammonia, when used alone and applied in the spring, had an injurious effect upon Swedish turnips, even when used in small quantities. When employed in conjunction with a superphosphate, the ammonium salt did very little good; and in general it had much less effect than nitrate of soda had on the growth of turnips. Sometimes, as he says, turnips have done better with fish-scrap or other animal refuse than with nitrates or ammonium salts. At another time he remarked that there are clay-soils in some parts of England on which the application of ammonium salts to root-crops often diminishes the crop, and at the best is of no benefit whatever to turnips or rutabagas.

Stoeckhardt, on comparing the results of all the field experiments upon sugar-beets that had been published in the course of several years preceding 1862, found that nitrate of soda gave better crops than ammonium salts in 7 experiments out of 11; than bone-meal, in 14 out of 22; than superphosphate, in 20 out of 29; than rapecake, in 15 out of 20; but that Peruvian guano did better than nitrate of soda in 11 experiments out of 22; and better than ammonium salts in 9 out of 10. In general, it appeared from the experiments of seven years, made in 23 different localities, that of the 100 largest crops, 96 were obtained by the use of easily soluble nitrogen compounds, and only 4 when these fertilizers were absent. 77 of the largest crops had received phosphates (usually superphosphate) and 23 of them had not. According to Bineau, the lower forms of plants that have chlorophyl grains — such as the algæ — can be supported as well by ammonium compounds as by nitrates.

One fact to be remembered is, that nitrates, at least in warm and temperate climates, appear to be naturally supplied to plants much more freely than compounds of ammonia are. Most soils contain appreciable quantities of nitrates, and many soils contain them in very considerable quantities. But very few soils contain at any one time more than faint traces of ammonium compounds, as will be explained directly, though it may still be true that small quantities of ammonia are continually formed in the soil.

Desmarest has noticed that several plants apt to accumulate nitrates, such, for example, as borage, sunflower, and pellitory, remain dwarfed and stunted unless nitrates are added to the soil in which they are standing, or unless the conditions are favorable for nitrification there.

Plants prefer one or another form of Nitrogen.

The upshot of all these experiments is, that, while there are some plants that feed upon nitrates during their entire life, there are other plants that can feed upon nitrates only when they are mature; and that, while there are some plants that are benefited exceedingly by ammonia when young, there are others which get no good from it in the earlier stages of their development. On the other hand, the fact that nitrates do not form readily in woodland soils would seem to indicate that forest-trees must get their nitrogenous food either from ammonium compounds, or from humus, or from the air, by the intervention of fungi living upon their roots. (See the chapter on Symbiosis.)

As Lehmann has remarked, the varying behavior of crops as regards nitrates and ammonium salts has evidently some connection with the observations of practical men, that some kinds of crops may be grown with advantage on land that has just been dressed with fresh dung, while other crops had better be fed with well-rotted manure. The remark of Gilbert may here be cited, to the effect that nitrate of soda has been found in the field experiments of Lawes and himself to act much more favorably than sulphate of ammonia upon the growth of highly nitrogenous leguminous crops, such as peas, beans, and clover. On the other hand, long experience in farming practice has shown that the ammonium salts are extremely well fitted for manuring wheat and barley; and Lawes and Gilbert have found that, when spread upon a lawn, they encourage the growth of the true grasses, as distinguished from clover and weeds.

A noteworthy example of the preferences exhibited by some kinds of plants for particular forms of food is to be seen in the growth of several familiar weeds, such as the thorn-apple (Datura) on dung-heaps, and hog-weed (Amarantus) and barn-yard grass about pools and drains in farmyards. It is evident enough that these gross-feeding weeds can endure certain kinds of nitrogenous compounds, peculiar to dung-heaps, which are hurtful to ordinary crops, and that they can put these nitrogen compounds to profit and prosper by feeding upon them. An analogous instance of preference for a special kind of nitrogenous food is seen in the power of leguminous plants to feed upon nitrogen compounds which have been derived from the air by micro-organisms which live upon the roots of these plants, as will be explained in due course.

Ammonium Salts change readily to Nitrates in the Soil.

Although, as has been said, the study of the question is complicated not a little by the easy conversion of ammonium salts, under fit conditions, to nitrates in the soil, the very fact of such conversion makes the question one of less practical importance than might at first be supposed; for in most cases where ammonium salts are employed as fertilizers, some part of them is soon changed to nitrates in the soil. And the nitrates are known to be useful in most cases, and to mature plants. It is the cases in which ammonium compounds particularly favor the growth of young plants that need to be specially studied, and allowed for in field practice. It is noteworthy that in the great majority of instances where sulphate of ammonia has proved to be useful it has been applied to soils naturally more or less calcareous, and been used in conjunction with farmyard manure under conditions favorable for nitrification. Maercker in particular has called attention to the fact that sulphate of ammonia is specially esteemed as a fertilizer in regions of calcareous soils, i. e. in situations where the ammonia would most readily change to a nitrate. To a deficiency of lime in the soil, and consequent tardy nitrification, he refers the unsatisfactory results obtained in his own experiments in which potatoes were dressed heavily with dung together with an ammonium salt. It will be remembered that on using nitrate of soda as an addition to the dung the crop of potatoes was increased. According to Warington, the first action which occurs when sulphate or chloride of ammonium is put upon a fertile soil is purely chemical. The ammonium salt reacts on carbonate of lime in the soil, and the decomposition is greatly aided by the fact that the resulting ammonium carbonate is fixed and held by humates, silicates, etc., as fast as it forms, while the soluble calcium salt tends to pass off with the drainage water. After its fixation, the ammonia immediately begins to nitrify, and only a comparatively short time is required for the conversion of the whole of it to a nitrate, but meanwhile a very much larger proportion of chloride of calcium or sulphate of lime than of nitrate is found in the drainage waters until the moment when the calcium salt has been completely washed out from the soil. The change of ammonium compounds to nitrates in the soil is usually so nearly complete in temperate climates, that it is hard to find more than a mere trace of ammonia in the earth at a depth of six feet, and there is small reason to doubt that, when a field is manured with ammonium salts in warm climates, a very large proportion of the nitrogen taken by plants from that field will be taken in the form of nitrates. Voelcker insisted long ago that, other circumstances being equal, ammonium salts may be used with much greater propriety and more largely in a warm climate or a good season than in a colder country or in an ungenial season.

The following experiments, made in France by Schloesing, illustrate the rapidity with which the change from ammonia to a nitrate may occur. Two samples of loam, each weighing 500 grm., were mixed with ammonium chloride and tested as stated in the table:—

No. of the experiment.	There were found milligrams of		At beginning of the trial.	At close of the trial.
I.	{ Ammonia	. . . .	55.65	5.95
	{ Nitric Acid	. . . .	0.00	186.50
II.	{ Ammonia	. . . .	57.00	6.80
	{ Nitric Acid	. . . .	0.00	206.50

So, too, on the experimental wheat-plot of Lawes and Gilbert to which 200 lb. of ammonium salts were applied in the spring together with an abundance of the ash-ingredients of crops, so small a proportion of nitrates could be detected in the drainage waters at the end of August, that there was " no reason to suppose that any nitrates derived from the ammonium salt remained unused in the soil at harvest time." Similar results were obtained when 400 lb. of ammonium salts were used in conjunction with ash-ingredients. But when 400 lb. of ammonium salts were applied in the spring to land which had received no ash-ingredients during 31 years, the wheat-plants were unable to assimilate the whole of the nitrates formed from the ammonium salts and considerable quantities of unused nitrates were detected in the soil after the harvest, especially in dry seasons.

In the following experiments of Heiden, made at an earlier period than those just now cited, where sulphate of ammonia was found to be a profitable manure for grain though not for leguminous plants, there is good reason to believe that much of the ammonium salt was changed to a nitrate before it was used by the crops. In the case of the oats grown in 1869, for example, on land that had received the ammonium salt in 1868, there must have been ample time for the formation of much nitrate, and the fact that in 1870 the plot that had been fertilized in 1868 gave no better crop than the unmanured land goes to show, not only that nitrates had been formed, but that they had subsequently been washed out of the soil in the course of the two years. So also with the rye of 1875.

The results given in the table refer to plots of land of 18.44 square metres, which received respectively either one kilogram of sulphate of ammonia at the stated dates, or nothing at all : —

Year of Growth.	Kind of Crop.	Sulphate of Ammonia applied in	Crop from the Fertilized Plots. Grain, Grams.	Straw and Chaff.	Crop from the Unmanured Plots. Grain, Grams.	Straw and Chaff.
1869	Oats	1868	3,090	5,885	820	2,090
1870	Oats	1868	89	322	89	320
1871	Oats	1871	5,267	9,185	167	523
1872	Vetches	1872	2,233	7,214	1,666	6,391
1873	Rye	1873	4,298	13,523	825	2,525
1874	Clover	1873	20,511	3,942	584	12,472
1875	Rye	1873	1,190	2,643	1,220	2,917
1876	Peas	1876	2,035	6,700	4,220	7,000
1877	. Rye	1877	8,380	10,608	970	1,902
1878	Potatoes	1878	34,360	2,800	9,730	460

The following experiments by Heiden (2d edition, 2, pp. 559, 571) contrast the action of ammonia-nitrogen and nitrate-nitrogen as applied to field-crops of oats.

I. OATS WITH SULPHATE OF AMMONIA. The plants were grown upon a granitic soil, on plots each of which measured one-quarter hectare, i. e. rather more than 0.6 acre. These oats had been preceded by potatoes which were dressed with farmyard manure at the rate of 15 tons to the acre.

Kind of fertilizer.	Kilos of crop harvested. Grain.	Straw, etc.	Total.	Increase over no nitrogen. Grain.	Straw.	Total.
20 lb. soluble phosp. acid.	559.91	850.42	1,410.33	....	....	....
Ditto plus 4 lb. nitrogen in form of sulphate of ammonia.	653.48	979.23	1,632.71	93.57	128.81	222.38
20 lb. soluble phosp. acid and 8 lb. of the nitrogen.	676.28	1,000.42	1,676.70	116.37	150.00	266.37

II. OATS WITH SULPHATE OF AMMONIA grown after potatoes on a rather heavy loam. The potatoes had been dressed with dung. The plots in these cases were each 0.3 hectare.

Kind of fertilizer.	Kilos of crop harvested. Grain.	Straw, etc.	Total.	Increase over no nitrogen. Grain.	Straw.	Total.
24 lb. soluble phosp. acid.	366.43	1,064.20	1,430.63	....	....	....
Ditto and 4.8 lb. nitrogen in form of sulphate of ammonia.	653.52	1,288.90	1,942.42	287.09	224.70	511.79
24 lb. soluble phosp. acid and 9.6 lb. of the nitrogen.	821.04	1,463.71	2,284.75	454.61	399.51	854.12

III. Oats with Nitrate of Soda grown broadcast on a moderately heavy granitic soil, on plots of 0.25 hectare. The preceding course of crops had been oats, meslin (oats and vetches), rye, and potatoes. The potatoes has been dressed with farmyard manure, 15 tons to the acre. The nitrate was strewn broadcast on the young oats.

Kind of fertiliser.	Kilos of crop harvested.			Increase over no nitrogen.		
	Grain.	Straw, etc.	Total.	Grain.	Straw.	Total.
20 lb. soluble phosp. acid.	559.9	850.4	1,410.0	....	....	....
Ditto and 4 lb. nitrogen in form of nitrate of soda.	701.7	1,025.0	1,726.7	141.8	174.6	316.4
20 lb. soluble phosp. acid and 8 lb. of the nitrogen.	680.3	1,008.4	1,688.7	120.4	158.0	278.4

IV. Oats with Nitrate of Soda, grown on plots of 0.3 hectare. The preceding course of crops had been oats (dressed with ammoniated superphosphate), meslin, without any manure, wheat dressed with bone-meal and sulphate of ammonia, and potatoes (dunged).

Kind of fertiliser.	Kilos of crop harvested.			Increase over no nitrogen.		
	Grain.	Straw, etc.	Total.	Grain.	Straw.	Total.
24 lb. soluble phosp. acid.	366.4	1,064.2	1,430.6	....	....	....
Ditto and 4.8 lb. nitrogen in form of nitrate of soda applied as top dressing.	609.6	1,291.5	1,901.1	243.1	227.3	470.4
24 lb. soluble phosp. acid and 4.8 lb. of the nitrogen, harrowed in.	622.5	1,343.0	1,965.5	256.0	278.8	534.8
24 lb. soluble phosp. acid and 9.6 lb. of the nitrogen as a top dressing.	855.1	1,532.4	2,387.5	488.7	468.7	956.9
24 lb. soluble phosp. acid and 9.6 lb. of the nitrogen harrowed in.	812.8	1,508.2	2,321.0	446.4	444.0	890.4

Rye with Sulphate of Ammonia, grown in 1878–79 upon moderately heavy land, on plots of 0.25 hectare. The preceding course of crops had been potatoes with dung in 1876, oats in 1877, and (meslin) oats and vetches in 1878, when the soil was dressed lightly with bone-meal.

Kind of fertiliser.	Kilos of crop harvested.			Increase over no nitrogen.		
	Grain.	Straw, etc.	Total.	Grain.	Straw.	Total.
10 lb. soluble phosp. acid.	536.75	960.10	1,496.85	....	....	....
Ditto and 4 lb. nitrogen in form of sulphate of ammonia.	635.65	1,084.15	1,719.80	98.90	124.05	222.95
10 lb. soluble phosp. acid and 8 lb. of the nitrogen.	652.65	1,142.60	1,795.25	115.90	182.50	298.40

Rye with Nitrate of Soda on soil and plots similar to those of the preceding experiment. The nitra e was applied as a top dressing, one-half in the autumn and the other half in the spring.

Kind of fertiliser.	Kilos of crop harvested.			Increase over no nitrogen.		
	Grain.	Straw, etc.	Total.	Grain.	Straw.	Total,
10 lb. soluble phosp. acid.	536.8	960.1	1,496.9	....	....	....
Ditto and 4 lb. nitrogen in form of nitrate of soda.	652.9	1,169.1	1,822.0	116.1	209.0	325.1
10 lb. soluble phosp. acid and 8 lb. of the nitrogen.	574.0	1,057.6	1,631.6	37.2	97.6	134.8

The bad effect of too much nitrate-nitrogen is well shown in the last of these experiments. In general, it appeared that while the application of 4 lb. nitrogen, of either kind, to the moderately heavy loam of the experimental plots did good service, and was distinctly remunerative, the double dose of nitrogen was not profitable, although it usually gave a considerable increase of crop.

Plants contain Ammonium-compounds.

It cannot be said, however, that ammonia is never taken in as such by plants, for, as has been set forth already, Hosäus has found an abundance of ammonia, as well as of nitrates, in a great variety of plants, in all parts of the plants, and at all stages of development. Indeed, it would appear from his researches that ammonium compounds are more universally present than nitrates in the juices of plants; for in some plants, at certain seasons, he was not able to detect nitrates, though ammonia was exhibited in abundance. It seems probable, withal, that in extremely cold countries nitrates from the soil must naturally play a very subordinate part in the nourishment of plants, simply because the activity of the nitrifying ferments must necessarily be comparatively feeble where the ground is cold, and because the time suitable for any action may be very short in some localities; though it needs to be said that the nitrifying ferments act at a lower temperature than is necessary for the activity of most micro-organisms. The experience of Lawes and Gilbert teaches that nitrification occurs freely in the fields in England during ordinary winters, and it was observed in laboratory experiments that nitrification by no means ceased in solutions the mean temperature of which was between 37 and 39° F.

A. Mayer found noteworthy amounts of ammonia in the fresh leaves of tobacco-plants. Some 12 or 13 % of the total nitrogen was always in the form of ammonia-nitrogen. He noticed, too, that — unlike the proportion of nitrates, which is subject to wide variations, according to the kind of manuring — the proportion of ammonia was remarkably constant, no matter how the plants were fed. Even when ammonia-water was applied to the soil in which the plants were growing, the leaves contained no more ammonia than usual, or than those of plants which had been fed with nitrate of potash.

Plants can use Ammonia.

Direct proof that ammonia can be taken in and put to use by various crops is afforded by the experiments, already alluded to, where gaseous ammonia was supplied to the leaves of plants. A. Mayer also grew wheat, and various other plants, in pots provided with tight covers, so that the soil was cut off from contact with the air, and from time to time he moistened the leaves of certain chosen plants with a highly dilute solution of carbonate of ammonia, while certain other plants got none of the ammoniacal solution. Not only did the plants thus fed with ammonia grow better than the others, and produce more dry matter, but, on subjecting all the plants to analysis, more nitrogenous matter was found in those which had been treated with the ammonium salt.

In experiments, reported by Pitsch, upon oats, barley, wheat and horse-beans, which were grown in sterilized earth, i. e. in loam which had been strongly heated for the purpose of killing all microscopic organisms, and especially all germs of the nitrifying ferments, it appeared that plants which were deprived of nitrates and fed with sulphate of ammonia, did not grow nearly so well as those which got nitrates. The plants fed with ammonia were healthy, though somewhat less robust than those fed with nitrates; early in their growth they came to a standstill for a short time, but after a short period of rest they grew again normally. It was evident enough that grain-plants can obtain nitrogenous food from the ammonium salt, and can produce large quantities of organic matter and of albuminoids when thus fed, but that their development is less vigorous than that of plants similarly situated which have access to nitrates. The nitrate plants develop normally at the time when the ammonia plants are suffering.

Muntz, also, has made similar experiments, and has found that ammonia-nitrogen is readily taken in and put to use by Indian corn, beans, horse-beans and hemp, and to a certain extent by barley, i. e. by all the plants which he tested. In these experiments the soil was freed from nitrates by washing, then dressed with sulphate of ammonia and sterilized by heating to 212°. The seeds were dipped in boiling water before they were sown, the pots were watered with boiled water free from nitrates, and both soil and plants were shielded from the air in such wise that no germs could gain access to them. All the plants grew normally during several months, and several of them were more than a yard high when harvested. Analysis showed that the plants had taken in large quantities of nitrogen, and that there were no nitrates in the soil.

How Ammonia may do Harm.

According to Loew and Bokorny, the reason why ammonium salts ordinarily have a less beneficial action than nitrates, when employed as manure, is due to the fact that ammonia, like other bases, is apt to granulate the protoplasm in the cells of plants. These observers maintain that an ammonium salt does no harm so long as the amount of it which has passed into a plant-cell is no larger than can be changed immediately to albumen.

They urge that when more ammonia is brought into a cell than can immediately be changed to albumen, it is liable to cause co-agulation, and to exert a highly injurious action, though in case the excess of ammonia is small, the plant may still be able to bear it. On the other hand, when plants are fed with nitrates, the re-duction of the latter to the form of ammonia is usually so slow that no very great accumulation of ammonia can occur. In re-spect to those plants which thrive when fed with ammonium salts, it is suggested that their cells may perhaps decompose these salts particularly slowly, or that the fact of their being highly charged with soluble carbohydrates may promote the rapid conversion of ammonia to albumen.

As the result of still further study and research, Loew argues that, while both nitrates and ammonium compounds may serve for the production of albuminoids in plants, the nitrates must first be reduced to ammonia before the nitrogen in them can be put to this use. He urges that the ammonia thus derived from nitrates must be used up at once by the plant-cells as fast as it is formed, since plants cannot bear any large accumulation of ammonia within them. This reduction of nitrates (and sulphates) for forming albuminoids may be conceived of as incidental to the oxidation of organic mat-ters, such as glucose, in the plant-cells, at the expense of the oxy-gen of the nitrate (or sulphate), whereby water, carbonic acid, oxalic acid, and other acids are formed, while the nitrogen of the nitrates and hydrogen from the organic matter combine to form ammonia, which is speedily converted to an albuminoid. To illustrate the readiness with which a nitrate may thus be reduced to ammonia, Loew dissolved 3 grm. of glucose and 1 grm. nitrate of potash in 200 grm. of water, and added 110 grm. of platinum black to the liquid, which he heated to 140 or 158° F. for six hours. He then found that almost 46 % of the nitrogen of the nitrate had been changed to ammonia, while the solution had become acid through the formation of saccharic and gluconic acids and another unknown acid, i. e. products of the oxidation of the glucose by the oxygen in the nitrate of potash, aided, doubtless, by oxygen from the air.

Albumen is formed from Ammonia.

From his experiments on bean-plants, Emmerling concluded that nitrates taken up through the roots from the soil are changed to organic nitrogen compounds (amids) in the green parts of plants, especially in the leaves, and that these amids subsequently change to albuminoids. It was found, at all events, that while the roots and stems of the bean-plants contained appreciable quantities of nitrates, no more than minute traces of nitrates could be detected in the leaves and buds, or in the flowers or fruit. Conversely, the proportion of amids was largest in the fresh new parts of the plants, where life was most vigorous and the formation of new matter most abundant, as other investigators had previously noticed, and as Berthelot has insisted since then.

It is thought by many physiologists that, in order to the formation of albuminoids in the active cells of plants, there must be present an amid, such as asparagin, a carbohydrate, such as sugar or soluble starch, and the minute quantities of sulphur and phosphorus which are essential to the existence of albuminoids. The fact that albuminoids do not ordinarily form in plants that are kept in the dark seems to depend on the absence of the necessary carbohydrate which, as is well known, is formed in the leaves by the action of light, for Loew has found, in experiments on fungi, that light is not necessary for the formation of albumen and does not promote its formation.

Emmerling had argued that ammonia probably plays a subordinate part, as compared with nitrates, in forming amids in the (bean) plant, since he found more ammonia in the leaves than in the stems, whereas, if ammonia were really used up in the leaves with any rapidity, it would be difficult to detect any of it there; but as was just now said, Loew maintains that there is much evidence tending to show that albuminoids are formed from ammonia and not from nitrates, unless indeed the nitrates have first been reduced to ammonia. Compounds of cyanogen, for example, such as ferro-cyanide of potassium, nourish only those bacteria which can split up these compounds with formation of ammonia; they are not fit food either for yeasts or for moulds. He insists that nitrates must first be changed to ammonia before the nitrogen in them can serve for making albumen, and argues that the oxygen of nitrates and of sulphates is practically transferred in the plant-cells to organic matters, such as sugar, whereby organic acids, such as oxalic acid, are formed, as well as carbonic acid and water, while at the same time some of the hydrogen of the decomposed organic matter unites with the nitrogen of the nitrate or with the sulphur of the sulphate to form ammonia and hydrogen-sulphide, which are immediately put to use for the formation of albumen. The more abundant formation of amids in the leaves of plants he attributes to the specially active respiration which occurs there and to the consequently greater vitality of the cells in those organs. In order to explain the circumstance that solutions of ammonium compounds often serve less well than solutions of nitrates for feeding plants, Loew insists, not that the ammonia is actually poisonous, but that it is a fact of familiar observation that ammonia and salts of ammonia readily bring about changes in the state of aggregation of the plasma in plant-cells which are inimical to its activity. He finds that hydroxylamin and diamid, unlike ammonia, are intensely poisonous to plants.

In the field, either the Nitrate or the Ammonium Salt may be used for grain if the price of the nitrogen be low enough.

Looking from the scientific point of view, it is evident from the foregoing statements that nitrate of soda is a better fertilizer on the whole than sulphate of ammonia, and it seems to have been used in farm practice of late years more freely than sulphate of ammonia, because the nitrogen in the nitrate can be bought for less money nowadays than that in the sulphate, as will be explained directly. But, as Maercker has urged, the superiority of the nitrate in the field — some 10 or 15 %, as regards wheat and barley — is really so small that whenever the price of sulphate of ammonia is low enough it may well be used for these crops instead of the nitrate. On good calcareous loams, at all events, that are carefully cultivated, sulphate of ammonia has approved itself a safe and useful fertilizer. The question is simply whether the desired effect shall be produced by using a somewhat larger quantity of ammonium sulphate or a smaller amount of nitrate of soda. That is to say, when a given sum of money will buy enough nitrogen in the form of ammonium sulphate to do the required work, it will be as well to use the sulphate as to spend the same amount of money in buying the nitrate. In general, the sulphate may be used instead of the nitrate, according to Maercker, whenever ammonia-nitrogen costs one-quarter less than nitrate-nitrogen.

On collecting a large number of field experiments, made by different observers in various parts of Germany, in which wheat was dressed in the autumn either with sulphate of ammonia or with nitrate of soda, used in such quantities that equal weights of nitrogen were applied to the land, it appeared that on the Morgen of land the average increase of grain due to sulphate of ammonia was 295 lb., and that due to nitrate of soda was 344 lb., over and above what was got from contiguous fields to which no nitrogen was applied. The increase of straw and chaff due to the use of the two fertilizers was 790 and 914 lb. respectively. In other words, the increase of grain in the two cases was about as 3 is to 3.5; and the increase of straw was as 3 to 3.49. Hence, 87.5 lb. of sulphate of ammonia, containing 17.9 lb. of nitrogen (see beyond) are as efficient as 100 lb. of nitrate of soda, containing 15.5 lb. of nitrogen. But at the time and place of Maercker's writing sulphate of ammonia was sold at so cheap a rate that the price of the 17.9 lb. of ammonia-nitrogen was about one-eighth lower than that of the 15.5 lb. of nitrate-nitrogen. In Lawes and Gilbert's experiments on wheat also it appeared that if the increase due to nitrate of soda be called 100, the increase due to sulphate of ammonia was 88.56 as regards grain, and 80 as regards straw and chaff.

As regards barley, many German experiments show that the increase brought by the two fertilizers is as 3 to 3.74, for grain, and as 3 to 6 for straw and chaff. Here again it would have been well to use sulphate of ammonia, at the price noted by Maercker. It will be noticed that the production of barley-straw is increased much more by nitrate of soda than by sulphate of ammonia. The fact is a general one which has been corroborated by many observers. In another experiment, cited by Maercker, where the increase of barley-grain obtained by using nitrate of soda or sulphate of ammonia was as 3 to 3.36, while the price of the nitrogen was as 3 to 4, it would still have been profitable to use the sulphate.

In Lawes and Gilbert's experiments, where barley was grown for 16 years on heavy loam, if the mean increase due to nitrate of soda be called 100, the mean increase of grain due to sulphate of ammonia was 90.74 and that of straw and chaff was 79.64. In Voelcker's experiments on barley the corresponding figures were 91.85 and 76.9.

Lime with Ammonium Salts.

To test the question whether lime might not exert a beneficial influence upon the ammonium salt, Maercker added finely powdered lime, at the rate of 10 centner to the Morgen, to fields which had been dressed with sulphate of ammonia, and he ploughed this lime under with a shallow furrow. He obtained the following amounts of increase per hectare over and above the quantities harvested from fields fertilized with sulphate ammonia, without any lime : —

Barley, grain	373 kilos.
Oat, "	440 "
Wheat, "	60 "
Potatoes, tubers	812 "
Sugar-beets, roots	481 "

Only in the case of mangolds did he get a better crop without lime than with it.

P. Wagner, on studying the question, how completely can the nitrogen of ammonia salts be changed to nitrates in the field? has concluded that under favorable conditions — as when light dressings of the ammonia salt have been put upon a warm, loose, marled soil, rich in humus — every 100 parts of the ammonia-nitrogen will yield 90 parts of nitrate-nitrogen, and that the fertilizing effect of sulphate of ammonia may be reckoned as equal to 90% of the fertilizing effect of nitrate of soda. On some soils, he finds that the nitrification of sulphate of ammonia may be materially hastened by adding lime or carbonate of lime to the soil.

Generally speaking, it is seen to be true that whenever the price of nitrate of soda is so low that each lb. of the nitrogen in it can be bought for less money than the lb. of nitrogen in sulphate of ammonia, the nitrate is used in farm practice more freely than the sulphate.   But it was said some years ago in England that much sulphate of ammonia continued to be used there at a time when the nitrogen in it cost more than that in the nitrate, and it has been taught in that country, that, while nitrate of soda does best in a dry season, sulphate of ammonia is to be preferred in a wet one.

It may be a merit of sulphate of ammonia, in some cases, that it acts more slowly than nitrate of soda. But either of these fertilizers would naturally produce its chief effect upon the one crop to which it has been applied.   Practically speaking, no gain can be expected from either of them in the second year even. They have no "endurance," such as is almost always counted upon when farmyard manure is used.

Nitrates often accumulate in Plants.

It has long been known that very considerable quantities of nitrates do sometimes collect in various kinds of plants that have grown on rich soils.   Lorgna, for example, noticed " a prodigious quantity of nitre " in sunflower-plants that had grown on compost heaps, and none, or next to none, in those that had grown in the open fields.   I have myself seen purslane, taken from a garden border, so full of nitrates that, when dried, the plant burned like touch-paper.   Several of the earlier chemists, notably Lemery, John, and Baumé, and likewise Vannes and Granit, insisted strongly upon this point; and long lists of plants have been made out from which considerable quantities of nitrates may not infrequently be extracted.   Strong-growing, gross-feeding plants are thought to be specially liable to contain nitrates, and those that grow about walls and refuse heaps.   The sunflower, borage, fumitory, pepper-grass, henbane, thorn-apple, tobacco, beets, and many other plants, have been mentioned as rich in saltpetre.

The fact that large quantities of nitrates can be stored in plants in this way, accidentally as it were, is a very curious one, for it would seem at first sight as if the plants would, if they could, make immediate use of this form of nitrogen, and build up by means of it the various albuminoid constituents which are so essential for the life and growth of all kinds of plants.   It has not yet been determined what connection, if any, exists between the storage of nitrates by various plants, as above described, and the preferences of plants for nitrates rather than for ammonium salts.

Leaves can absorb Ammonia and Carbonate of Ammonia.

It is a very interesting fact, that ammonia gas and the vapor of carbonate of ammonia can be absorbed by the leaves of plants. As has been stated already, it was observed some years since that the growth of plants in conservatories may be promoted by placing lumps of carbonate of ammonia upon the steam-pipes, so that the air with which the plants are bathed shall be charged slightly with the vapor of the salt. Or, instead of the carbonate, a mixture of sal-ammoniac and slaked lime might be used. It is only necessary to keep the proportion of ammonia in the air so low that no more than four ten-thousandths of the salt be present in the air at any one time. Otherwise, some of the more tender plants might be injured. It does not appear that sunlight has any influence upon this absorption of ammonia through the leaves. It is not improbable, on the contrary, that the ammoniacal vapors may be seized and held by the acid juices of the plant.

The tendency of nitrogenized manures to increase the growth of foliage, rather than of seeds or fruit, may be remarkably illustrated by exposing a plant to the vapor of carbonate of ammonia at that moment of its development when the growth of leaves and branches ceases and that of the flowers begins. The development of the flowers will usually be checked at once, — or, even in case the flower is formed, it will be sterile and will yield no seed, — while the stem and the leaves take a new lease of life and proceed to grow vigorously.

Ammonia of the Air.

In spite of all that has just been said, the power of plants to absorb ammonia from the air is practically less important than might be thought at first sight. The proportion of ammonia naturally present in the air is so insignificant that it cannot be supposed to have much influence on the growth of vegetation, and in point of fact it has none or next to none. It is only on the supposition that the atmospheric ammonia might perhaps accumulate continually in the soil, and be "fixed" there when brought thither by rains and dews, that the question becomes one of interest. But in that case it would be the roots of plants and not their leaves that would have to do with the ammonia, and as will be seen directly, the quantity of ammonia thus brought to the soil is still too small to be of any practical importance. It is noticeable withal that the proportion of ammonia naturally present in the air and in soils is so small that it must be of wholly subordinate importance for the support of plants as compared with the nitrates naturally found in the soil.

Sulphate of Ammonia.

Of the various salts of ammonia, the sulphate specially interests the agricultural student. It is particularly important, since, with the possible exception of Peruvian guano, it is the only commercial source of ammonia within the farmer's reach. The original guano, that was imported formerly from Peru, contained much ammonia combined with uric, oxalic, and phosphoric acids, as will be explained in due course.

Sulphate of ammonia is prepared in very large quantities from the ammoniacal water which is obtained incidentally in the manufacture of illuminating gas from coal. Bituminous coal, like peat, humus, wood and all kinds of organized matter, contains a certain small proportion of nitrogen; and when either of these substances is subjected to destructive distillation, ammonia is given off from it, together with aqueous vapor, illuminating and other gases, and a variety of tarry and oily products. On cooling these products of distillation, the water and the ammonia condense together to form the so-called ammoniacal liquor.

Gas-liquor.

This gas liquor varies widely as to the proportion of ammonia contained in it, both according to the kinds of coal used at the works, and to the methods employed for purifying the gas. Speaking in very general terms, it may be said to contain on the average about 1% of real ammonia (NH_3) : that is to say, the proportion of ammonia is too small to admit of the liquor's being transported to any considerable distance.

The ammoniacal liquor might well be used for making compost on some farms near gas-works, but it would not be safe to apply the undiluted liquor directly to growing crops, because it is apt to be contaminated with several substances which are poisonous to plants. Moreover, though too weak to bear the cost of transportation, the ammonia in the liquor is too strong to be applied to growing plants. That is to say, the carbonate of ammonia in it might by itself kill plants unless the liquor were mixed with some 10 or 12 times its bulk of water before applying it. Cases are on record where a mixture of one part of the ammoniacal liquor with no more than three parts of brook-water was found to be injurious to a variety of crops. Other experiments have shown, however, that when put upon the land in moderate quantities at appropriate times and seasons it may largely increase the yield of some kinds of crops. It is true, moreover, that if gas-liquor (or carbonate of ammonia) could but be obtained cheaply enough, it might sometimes be well to actually drench the land with it for the purpose of destroying earth-worms and grubs and other larvæ of insects. To this end it would naturally be applied to bare land some little time before seeding or planting.

Sulphate of ammonia is prepared by driving out the volatile ammonium compounds (carbonate, sulphide, and sulphocyanide) from the gas-liquor by means of heat, and collecting them in sulphuric acid, where the sulphate is deposited in the form of small, gray, sand-like crystals. As thus obtained, sulphate of ammonia has been used by thousands of tons in European agriculture, and it was formerly sometimes used in this country also for reinforcing a few of the better kinds of ammoniated superphosphates. It appears to be used in this way to-day as an addition to inferior cargoes of guano.

Practical Use of Ammonium Sulphate.

So far as the results of field practice are concerned, it was a not unnatural inference that sulphate of ammonia commonly acts directly as plant-food. It increases the vigor of the plants, and enables them to take up more of other kinds of food in a given time than they could take up if they were not thus excited. Of course, the sulphate, applied alone, is far enough from being a complete manure. But it is none the less useful as an adjunct to slow-acting manures, or as one term among the manures in a judicious course of rotation. It has been found, moreover, to answer an excellent purpose upon many European soils, in which, through long-continued, injudicious, ignorant, rule-of-thumb cultivation, some kinds of plant-food have accumulated to an unnecessary extent.

It is important that sulphate of ammonia should be prepared in such manner that it shall not be contaminated with any large amount of sulphocyanide of ammonium, — a substance which forms during the distillation of coal, and which exerts a highly pernicious action on vegetation. The sulphocyanide is, in fact, a powerful poison as regards many plants, and Voelcker found reasons for believing that as little as 10 lb. of it to the acre applied in a top-dressing of sulphate of ammonia might injuriously affect young wheat and barley plants.   Not many years ago, samples of dark, brown-colored sulphate of ammonia which were contaminated with the sulphocyanide found their way into commerce, but with the discovery of its harmful character this grade of the sulphate has been generally discredited.

From the field experiments of Wollny, it appears that different kinds of crops are affected in very different degrees by the sulphocyanide.   Grass can bear but little of it, and potatoes and maize are specially sensitive.   As much as 18 lb. to the acre was applied to a field of winter rye without doing any appreciable harm, but when more than 9 lb. to the acre were applied to rape, peas and mangolds, these crops began to suffer.

The Field Experiments of Lawes and Gilbert.

In illustration of the very great practical merit of ammonium sulphate, some of the celebrated field experiments of Lawes and Gilbert may here be cited.   These experimenters manured a large plot of land, during many consecutive years, with nothing but ammonium salts, and they found that the crop of wheat taken from the plot thus manured was every year considerably larger than that taken from a similar and adjacent plot which received no manure; though, naturally enough, the yearly increase of crop diminished as time went on.   During the first 9 years the increase due to the ammonium salt was rather more than 9 bushels to the acre, while during the next 10 years the increase averaged only 7¼ bushels per annum.

By the same set of experiments it was found that the application of soluble mineral manures alone to wheat upon that land produced little or no useful effect, unless an ammonium salt or some other source of active nitrogen was used in conjunction with the minerals.   Upon the land in question, a complex mineral manure, which supplied annually more of potash, magnesia, lime, phosphoric acid, and sulphuric acid than were taken off in the crops, gave, during the first 8 years, an annual increase of only about 3 bushels over the land that received no manure whatsoever; during the next 8 years there was less than 2 bushels of annual increase.   As compared with farmyard manure, the minerals produced annually 15 bushels less during the first 8 years, and 20.5 bushels less during the next 8 years; and these results are the more noteworthy, in view of the fact that the manure was applied to

land which had been previously enriched during several years by
the accumulation of unexhausted residues from ammoniacal and
mineral manurings.

The largest crops were obtained when mineral manures and nitrogenized manures were employed together; the yield being then
in some instances decidedly larger than that obtained by the use
of farmyard manure. Similar results were obtained with barley,
also, as will be seen in the chapter relating to this crop. But the
point to be specially insisted upon now is, that, since the ammonium salts alone increased the produce of the field very much more
than the mineral manures alone, and continued to do so for a long
series of years, it is obvious that that soil contained a considerable
excess of available mineral matters over and above its available
supply of nitrogen.

Nitrogenized additions to good, old land.

In many parts of Europe, the soil, through long-continued cultivation and the abundant application of dung and straw, is apt to
become charged with an excess of the ash-ingredients of plants, —
just as was the case with the experimental plots of Lawes and
Gilbert. Hence the advantage of applying a certain proportion
of easily assimilable nitrogenized manure to the land, in order that
the plants may be incited to feed close, as it were, and utilize fully
the manure which is within their reach. It hardly needs to be said
that this remark can be true only of good strong land, for the very
fact that the easily assimilable nitrogen compounds act as they
do, i. e. as " forcing manures," leads to the exhausting from land
to which they are applied of the store of ash-ingredients which
serve as plant-food.

In illustration of this point may be cited the experience of
Heiden, who, in studying the question how best to render fertile
a new field of crude, heavy loam, had occasion to manure one part
of it 7 times in the course of 10 years with sulphate of ammonia,
with the result that good crops were got in each instance by means
of the ammonium salt. But subsequently, i. e. in the 11th year,
and the four following years, when the entire field was manured
in one and the same way, it appeared that the crops which grew
on that part of the field to which the ammonium salt had formerly
been applied were noticeably poorer than the rest. Indeed, the
crops on this, so to say, ammoniated land became poorer and
poorer during each of the five years that comparisons were made,

although, like the rest of the field, this land was now well manured. For example, in the 4th and 5th years, the land was fertilized at the rate of 100 kilo nitrogen, 200 kilo phosphoric acid,
and 300 kilo potash to the hectare, yet, as the following table
shows, the crop of barley grown in the fifth year, on the plot that
had been dressed with sulphate of ammonia at intervals during the
earlier 10 years, was distinctly inferior to that grown upon the
plot that had received no manure whatsoever during the 10-year
period : —

| The barley crop yielded kilo of | On the plot that had received during the 10-year period | | Difference in favor of no manure. |
	No Manure.	Sulph. of Ammonia.	
Grain	3310.6	1556.8	1753.8
Straw and chaff . . .	5957.6	2273.2	3684.4
Totals	9268.2	3830.0	5438.2

The necessity that an abundant supply of ash-ingredients should
be present in the soil, in order that the nitrogen of ammonium
salts shall fully be put to use by crops, is made evident by the
great waste of nitrogen in the drainage waters, which occurs when
ammonium salts are put upon land which is inadequately charged
with ash-ingredients. Thus, in 1,000,000 parts of drain-water
flowing out from experimental plots on Lawes and Gilbert's wheat-
field, which had been fertilized as stated in the table, there was
found, on the average of 5 years, the stated numbers of parts of nitrogen which were washed out from the land in the form of nitrates : —

| Fertilizers applied in March. Lb. to the acre. | Parts of nitrate-nitrogen in 1,000,000 parts of drain-water. | | | | |
	March to end of May.	June to Harvest.	Harvest to Autumn Sowing.	Autumn Sowing to March.	The whole year.
400 lb. ammonium salts and no other fertilizer . . .	28.6	11.4	11.5	6.3	9.9
400 lb. ammonium salts and superphosphate of lime .	19.5	5.8	9.2	7.1	8.5
400 lb. ammonium salts and all kinds of ash-ingredients	16.3	1.4	8.3	5.2	6.4

Manner of using Sulphate of Ammonia.

The usual method of applying sulphate of ammonia is at the rate
of 100 or 125 lb. to the acre on land which has previously been
richly dressed with farmyard manure. It may either be used for
top-dressing, or be worked in lightly just before seeding. In order
to secure the even distribution of the small quantities usually employed, it is said to be well to mix the salt with 3 or 4 times as
much loam. It is applied to grain-crops in particular, and almost
always, as one may say, as an addition to other manures. In

England, it is said to have been used especially upon strong, heavy, clayey soils, such as are well suited for producing frequent crops of wheat, though they are less well adapted than lighter lands for growing roots as a means of procuring dung.

Practically speaking, sulphate of ammonia is seldom or never used alone, not even when in a course of rotation it follows a phosphatic manure. But experience teaches, none the less, that ammonium sulphate should neither be mixed with farm manure nor applied to the land at the same time as the manure, — probably because ammonia does not change so rapidly to a nitrate when in presence of putrid organic matter as when mixed with mere loam.

It is not well to apply very large quantities of sulphate of ammonia, not even when it is used in conjunction with mineral fertilizers. In experiments made by Lawes and Gilbert, on land which received every year an ample supply of mixed mineral fertilizers, the application of 200 lb. of ammonium salts per annum (i. e. 43 lb. of nitrogen) gave an average annual increase of 9 bushels of wheat to the acre, during 32 years, over the crops obtained from land which was manured with minerals alone; and twice this quantity of the ammonium salts gave a further annual increase of between 8 and 9 bushels. But on applying thrice as much of the ammonium salts (i. e. 129 lb. of nitrogen to the acre), there was obtained only 3.5 bushels more, and it was evident that nitrogen was now being applied to the land in larger quantity than the crop could use. Even in an exceptionally good year for wheat-growing, when the plot that got 86 lb. of nitrogen (400 lb. of ammonium salts) yielded 53.5 bushels of wheat, the plot that got 129 lb. of nitrogen (600 lb. of ammonium salts) only yielded 2 bushels more.

The best use of sulphate of ammonia seems to be upon grain crops when they are well above the ground in the spring, though, as is the case with all easily soluble saline fertilizers, it should never be sown together with the seed lest germination be hindered and the young plants destroyed by the strong solution of the salt which is formed when the latter is first dissolved by the moisture of the soil. According to P. Wagner, sulphate of ammonia is no more hurtful in this respect than nitrate of soda. On the whole he found that when unfavorable conditions, as to the weather or the soil, caused crops to suffer from heavy dressings of saline fertilizers, they were apt to suffer rather more from nitrate of soda than they did from correspondingly heavy dressings of sulphate of ammonia. On soils that are adequately calcareous, light dressings of ammonium sulphate might sometimes be used on the very best mowing-fields after growth is well started in early spring, and again, perhaps, after mowing, in order to keep down weeds and other inferior plants by insuring a vigorous and enduring growth of the true grasses. Mr. Gregory says that he sometimes uses sulphate of ammonia " to hurry along crops of onions that are rather backward. I spread 200 lb. of the sulphate per acre just before the onions begin to bottom and work it into the soil with a slide hoe."

Lime and Carbonate of Lime decompose Ammonium Salts.

Boussingault, Voelcker and others have called attention to the risk that on calcareous soils much ammonia may be lost through the reaction of the lime carbonate in the soil upon the sulphate (or any other salt) of ammonia when it is applied to the land. It is urged that ready formed ammonia should not be applied to calcareous soils, because lime displaces the volatile ammonia from its salts. "Some years ago," Voelcker says, "we used sulphate of ammonia on several thin, stony calcareous soils, and portions of the fields were left undressed in order to observe any difference in the crop ; but not any difference could be seen. The smell of ammonia on the land on which sulphate of ammonia was employed was very strong indeed, and I have little doubt that almost all the ammonia contained in the salt had been driven off by the lime in the soil, and that for this reason no effect on the appearance of the crop was observed." He recommends that for such soils nitrate of soda is to be preferred to an ammonium salt, and that in using farmyard manure, even, it will be well to apply it in the fresh condition rather than after ammonia has been formed in it through fermentation. Similar observations and statements have been published in England by T. Brown. On mixing a few pounds of the calcareous soil with half a handful of sulphate of ammonia, a strong smell of ammonia will soon be perceived and will become powerful in the course of half an hour.

Dehérain has made the further objection that on applying sulphate of ammonia to calcareous soils, the causticity of the carbonate of ammonia which forms may have, under some circumstances, a decidedly hurtful effect upon the crop. Thus in case sugar-beets were to be sown on such land and a heavy dressing of the sulphate were applied just before seeding, or immediately afterward, the crop might be greatly damaged. If the sulphate were to be used at all on beets, it should not be applied until the plants are well started and should even then be drilled in between the rows of beets rather than be strewn broadcast.

Harm from Ammonium Sulphate.

Dehérain urges in general that sulphate of ammonia is not a fertilizer that can be applied safely to all kinds of soils, in large quantities, at any season. On the contrary, he would restrict its use to stiff land and would not apply more than 140 to 175 lb. to the acre. He has observed at Grignon, in France, when sulphate of ammonia is applied to a light, calcareous soil, that as soon as dry weather sets in the land speedily becomes covered with an efflorescence of sulphate of lime which has been formed by the re-action of the sulphate of ammonia on the carbonate of lime naturally contained in the land. Meanwhile, the soil becomes hard and smooth and the clay in it is coagulated so that it no longer forms a plastic paste with water. It seemed as if the harm natu-rally due to the drying out of this light land had been exaggerated through the action of the ammonium salt. It was noticed more-over that the bad effects thus produced lasted during several years. Nitrate of soda on the other hand did good service on this light soil when applied in moderate quantities. In the following table are given the results obtained on growing sugar-beets on the light soil now in question :—

Quantity of Fertilizers applied to the Hectare.	Kilos of Beets from the Hectare.		
	1876.	1877.	1877.[1]
No Manure	17,400	30,600	46,600
Farm-yard Manure	. . . .	44,000	70,400
400 kilos Nitrate of Soda	19,000	34,600	57,300
400 " ditto and 400 Superphosphate	21,400	. . . .	. . . .
1200 " Nitrate of Soda	21,400	29,800	56,400
400 " Sulphate of Ammonia . . .	16,400	29,400	49,100
400 " ditto and 400 Superphosphate	16,400	. . . .	. . . .
1200 " Sulphate of Ammonia . . .	14,600	20,000	37,200

The harm done by the heavy dressings of the ammonium salt was even felt in subsequent years. The beets of 1876-77 were followed by fodder corn in 1878, and then by sainfoin in 1879, '80 and '81. The quantities of sainfoin hay obtained are given in the following table :—

---

[1] Another variety of beet.

Fertilizers used.	Average No. of tons of Hay from the Hectare.
No Manure in either year	5.860
Farm Manure in 1875, '76, '77, '78	8.269
400 kilos Nitrate of Soda in 1876, '77, '78 and '79	6.300
1200 " Nitrate of Soda in 1876, '77 and '79	6.815
400 " Sulphate of Ammonia in 1876, '77 and 78	5.827
1200 " ditto in 1876 and 1877	4.295

The enduring harm done to the light Grignon soil by the ammonium salt is shown also by the wheat crops of 1880 to '83, which were grown without fertilization on fields which had previously borne potatoes, 1875 to '79, which had been fertilized as stated in the following table :—

Fertilization.	Mean Metric Quintals of Wheat.
No Manure at all	18.75
Farm Manure in 1875 to '79, nothing since	24.71
400 kilos Nitrate of Soda, 1875 to '79, nothing since	21.09
1200 " " " 1875 to '77, " "	20.57
400 " Sulphate of Ammonia, 1875 to '79, nothing since . .	19.45
1200 " " " 1875 to '77 " " - -	17.77

Lawes and Gilbert's Experiments.

The increase of produce obtained in the experiments of Lawes and Gilbert by combining the mineral and the ammoniacal manure was remarkable.

The same amount of mineral manure which by itself gave scarcely any increase, and the same amount of ammonium salts (400 lb. to the acre) which when taken alone was less efficient than farmyard manure, and which diminished in efficiency from year to year, gave when employed together an average annual increase, during 20 years, of about 21 bushels of wheat to the acre and 23 cwt. of straw over the unmanured plot, or about 1 bushel of wheat and 3 cwt. of straw over the plot treated with farmyard manure. As was just now stated, other experiments, in which the proportion of ammonium salts to that of the mineral manure was somewhat larger, gave still larger amounts of increase, though at a very much diminished rate in proportion to the quantity of ammonia employed.

Nitrate of soda, taken in such quantity (550 lb.) that the land should receive about as much nitrogen as is contained in 400 lb. of the ammonium salts, and used in conjunction with the same mineral manure as before, gave decidedly more wheat than was got by means of the ammonium salts and minerals, and more than

was got with farmyard manure.   At first, the nitrate gave rather
smaller crops of wheat than the ammonium salts, and it was not
until after the experiment had been carried on for 8 years that the
nitrate began to show its superiority.   Nevertheless, during a
period of 32 years the nitrate gave a yearly increase over the salts
of ammonium of not quite 4 bushels to the acre; and the produce
of grain (36.25 bushels) obtained by an amount of nitrate of soda
(550 lb.) that supplied 86 lb. of nitrogen to the acre was exactly
equal, on the average of 32 years, to that got from salts of ammonia that supplied 129 lb. of nitrogen.   Moreover, this amount
of the nitrate gave more straw than the cited amount of ammonium
salts.   It was noticed that when used continuously upon wheat,
for 32 years, in conjunction with mineral fertilizers, the power of
the nitrate to produce growth appeared to increase rather than
to diminish.

Lawes and Gilbert have stated, both in respect to wheat and to
grass that, although, during the earlier years of their experiments,
mixtures of mineral fertilizers and ammonium salts gave more
produce than mixtures of minerals and nitrate of soda, the general result in later years has been that the nitrate-mixtures have
given larger crops than the ammonia-mixtures, and sometimes
crops that were considerably larger, especially as regards straw.
They think that this improved action may be due to the more
rapid and more extended distribution of the nitrate of soda, or of
products of its decomposition, within the soil and subsoil, to the
greater power of the soil to lift and hold moisture after nitrate of
soda has acted upon it, and to more active development and
thorough distribution of roots in the soil charged with and changed
by the nitrate.   In other experiments they found that more increase of crop was got from a given quantity of nitrate of soda
applied to barley in the spring than from winter wheat which had
been similarly manured.

How much Wheat may be got from a Pound of Ammonia?

Lawes and Gilbert have endeavored to predict roughly how much
wheat, over and above that to be obtained from the soil alone, can
be got by the application to a good English soil of a given weight
of ammonia.   They conclude that, great as is the difference of
effect of a given quantity of ammonia, according to the amount
applied per acre, and according to the mineral condition of the
soil and to the season, still, when only moderate quantities are

used, and when there is present a sufficient supply of mineral constituents, it appears that the farmer may assume, for practical purposes, that on the average of seasons he will get one bushel of wheat and its proportion of straw, beyond the produce of the soil and season, for each 5 lb. of ammonia applied as manure for the crop.

Recapitulation.

The results of Lawes and Gilbert may again be stated, briefly, as follows : —

On a soil of not more than average wheat-producing quality, according to the English view, which was taken for the experiments after it had supported a course of five crops subsequent to the application of any manure, wheat was grown successfully for more than 40 years in succession, — on some plots without any manure, and on other plots with manures of different descriptions.

Without manure, the yield of dressed wheat was, in the first year, 15 bushels per acre; in the 20th year, 17¼ bushels; on the average of the 20 years, 16¼ bushels; and on the average of 40 years, 14 bushels.

Mineral manures alone, though applied in the soluble form, scarcely increased the produce. They did not, to any material degree, enable the plant to assimilate more carbon and nitrogen from atmospheric sources than it assimilated when grown upon the unmanured land. Taking the average of the crops of 32 years, it appeared that the minerals were only competent to increase the yield by 1.25 bushels per year and per acre.

Nitrogenized manures taken alone increased the yield of grain very considerably for many years in succession; whence it appeared that the soil subjected to the experiment was relatively much richer in available mineral constituents than in available nitrogen.

With farmyard manure, applied every year, the yield was, in the first year, 20.5 bushels; in the 20th year, 44 bushels; on the average of 32 years, 33.5 bushels; and on the average of 40 years, 32.4 bushels.

The highest produce obtained by means of mixed mineral and nitrogenous artificial manures, in the first year, was 24.25 bushels; in the twentieth year it was 55.75 bushels. Taking the average of 32 years, some of the plots yielded 36.25 bushels annually.

Of course it is not claimed that the artificial manures were applied in the very best proportions in this most interesting and valuable set of experiments. For that matter, it is not likely that the proportions were anywhere near the best. As Mr. Donald Mitchell has put it: Any bumpkin may rear a crop which shall keep him from starving. But to develop the utmost economic capacity of a given soil by fertilizing appliances, or by those of tillage, is the work of a wiser man than belongs to our day.

Experiments with rye, oats, wheat, and barley, made on a variety of soils in different parts of Prussia, at the instigation of the Central Bureau of Agriculture, gave results very much like those of Lawes and Gilbert. Nitrate of soda used by itself usually gave a considerable increase both of grain and straw. But, on the other hand, mixtures of the ash-ingredients of crops used without any addition of nitrogen generally gave no increase worth mentioning.

It is to be observed, however, that the use of easily assimilable nitrogen compounds for stimulating the growth of grain, as in the foregoing experiments, is subject to many limitations. Unless the land is naturally fertile, and well supplied with capillary water, continued stimulation would be improper. On light, thin, dry soils, no such favorable results could be hoped for as were got by Lawes and Gilbert on their good, strong loam. In case light, dry land were continually "forced" with nitrogen compounds it would be apt soon to fall out of condition. In order to maintain such land in good heart, applications of farmyard manure are necessary, and the occasional interpolation of ameliorating crops.

Indirect Action of Ammonium Salts.

Beside its action as plant-food, sulphate of ammonia plays an important part in the soil as a chemical agent. Like gypsum and other saline manures, it acts upon the soil in such manner that some of the plant-food therein stored up is set free and made available for the plant. It acts upon the double silicates of alumina and lime, or magnesia, or potash, in the soil, converting them in part into silicate of alumina and ammonia, while corresponding quantities of the sulphates of lime, or of magnesia, or of potash, go into solution. Voelcker found that the application of ammonium salts to wheat-fields increased the proportion of mineral constituents in the drainage-water, and that, as a rule, more mineral matters were found in the water that drained out from those fields which had been heavily dressed with ammonium salts than from fields manured with more moderate quantities. So, too, Lawes and Gilbert found 450, 542 and 615 parts of solid matter in each million parts of the drainage-waters from plots of land that had received respectively 200, 400 and 600 lb. of ammonium salts to the acre, in addition to a mixture of mineral fertilizers, while only 380 parts of solid matter in a million parts of water were found where the land had been manured with minerals alone. The matters removed by the action of the ammonium salts were chiefly sulphate, chloride and nitrate of calcium, and the 400 lb. of ammonium salts would be able to remove annually in this way from the soil some 172 lb. of lime.

Price per Pound of Ammonia Nitrogen.

Gray sulphate of ammonia as sold by the cask or ton costs some 3.5 or 4 cents the pound; and the question presents itself, how much does nitrogen cost per pound when bought in this form? The formula of the pure salt is $(NH_4)_2SO_4$; from which, as a starting point, the percentage of nitrogen may be ascertained by a very simple sum in proportion. The atomic weights of the several elements which compose sulphate of ammonia are as follows: $N = 14$; $H = 1$; $S = 32$; and $O = 16$. Hence the molecular weight (132) of the compound, which is the sum of the weights of all the atoms contained in it, may readily be obtained by addition as follows: —

$$N_2 = 28$$
$$H_8 = 8$$
$$S = 32$$
$$O_4 = 64$$
$$\overline{132}$$

But as the molecular weight of the salt is to the weight of all the nitrogen which is contained in it, so is 100 to the percentage of nitrogen. That is to say,

$$132 : 28 :: 100 : (x = 21.2).$$

These figures refer, of course, to the perfectly pure salt. But as found in commerce, sulphate of ammonia varies somewhat in quality, according as more or less moisture or other impurities are present. On the average, it contains about $20\frac{1}{4}\%$ of nitrogen; or, speaking in round numbers, it may be said that every 5 lb. of the crude sulphate contain 1 lb. of nitrogen.

The result is thus reached, that each pound of nitrogen bought in the form of sulphate of ammonia will cost 17.5 or 20 cents, according as 3.5 or 4 cents per pound is paid for the sulphate. It is to be noted that the price of sulphate of ammonia has fallen very materially in recent years, so that this form of nitrogen may be obtained at much cheaper rates than were formerly usual. At one time nitrogen of analogous quality could be obtained at better advantage by buying Peruvian guano; and the price of sulphate of ammonia was dependent for many years upon the price of guano. It is still true, to a certain extent, that the price of guano regulates that of the sulphate; if the price of guano were to rise, that of the ammonium salt might rise also. A somewhat similar remark will apply to the cost of nitrogen in the form of nitrate of soda, though of late years this kind of nitrogen can usually be had at a lower price than that in sulphate of ammonia.

Price of the Pound of Nitrogen when bought in Nitrate of Soda.

The composition of nitrate of soda is as follows. The formula of the salt is written $NaNO_3$, and the atomic weight of sodium (Na) is 23. Hence,

$$\begin{aligned} Na &= 23 \\ N &= 14 \\ O_3 &= 48 \\ \hline &85 \end{aligned}$$

and $\qquad 85 : 14 :: 100 : (x = 16.47)$.

The commercial salt is seldom or never perfectly pure. Usually, however, it contains about 97 % of pure nitrate of soda — beside a little common salt and some moisture — and it is commonly warranted to contain 96 %. Hence,

$$100 : 96 :: 16.47 : (x = 15.81).$$

That is to say, the commercial salt will contain 15.8 % of nitrogen, and to get a pound of nitrogen 6¼ lb. of the salt will be needed, for

$$15.81 : 100 :: 1 : (x = 6.33).$$

If the pound of nitrate of soda costs 2½ cents, the pound of nitrogen in this form will come at a little less than 16 cents; and if the lb. of nitrate costs 2 cents, the lb. of nitrogen will cost almost 13 cents.

Beside nitrate of soda and sulphate of ammonia, there are several other fairly good sources of nitrogen at the farmer's command, notably bone-meal, fish-scrap, oil-cake, and slaughter-house refuse, as will be explained directly; and in these forms nitrogen may be procured at somewhat lower cost than it can be bought in sulphate of ammonia. But it is still true that there is no fertilizer which, in a given weight, can supply more nitrogen to crops than sulphate of ammonia, and that there are few sources of nitrogen that can be handled and transported to great distances so conveniently, so safely, and so cheaply, or which work so assuredly in field practice.

As bought by the cask of responsible dealers, gray sulphate of ammonia is ordinarily very nearly pure. Sometimes, however, the sulphate is contaminated with reddish brown sulphocyanide of ammonia, which, as has been said, is poisonous to many plants, and it has occasionally been found to be adulterated with salt, sand, and Epsom salt. An instance is on record where common copperas (sulphate of iron), in fine crystals, has been sold as sulphate of ammonia. In another instance, a sample of the sulphate was found to be contaminated with 16 % of free sulphuric acid. The average amount of nitrogen found in commercial samples of sulphate of ammonia has been stated as 20.39%, the least amount found as 15.29 %, and the highest 21.12 %. (Petermann.)

Other Salts of Ammonia.

Beside the sulphate, the salts of ammonia that specially interest the agriculturist are the carbonate and the humate. The carbonate is formed abundantly during the putrefaction of nitrogenized substances of vegetable or animal origin, and is consequently a constituent of many kinds of manure. It is a substance of pungent odor, which, when perceived in horse-stables and cow-stalls, is commonly called "ammonia," for short.

When a solution of carbonate of ammonia is brought into contact with loam it tends to make the loam muddy and sticky, as do the other alkaline carbonates, whence the inference that manures which contain ammonium carbonate may sometimes exert no small influence upon the texture of soils, by puddling them, as it were. But, as a general rule, carbonate of ammonia is readily converted into humate of ammonia by contact with vegetable mould, or with the humic acid which is formed during the slow fermentation of barnyard manure; whence it follows that humate of ammonia, rather than the carbonate, may be actually concerned sometimes in the business of supplying plants with food.

Carbonate of ammonia is formed in processes of distillation, as well as in those of putrefactive fermentation. It is by distilling the nitrogenized substances coal and bone, that the commercial compounds of ammonia, excepting Peruvian guano and some small parcels of carbonate and sulphate from putrid urine, are obtained. Even the chloride of ammonium, often found about volcanoes, seems to be derived from the distillation of organic matters in the soil. The original "sal-ammoniac" came from the distillation of camel's dung. The ammoniacal liquor of the gas-works contains carbonate of ammonia chiefly, as well as some sulphide and sulphocyanide; and so does the much more concentrated distillate from bones, which is obtained as a product incidental to the manufacture of bone-black.

Since chloride of ammonium is more costly than the sulphate, it has comparatively little interest from the farmer's point of view. Moreover, it appears to be intrinsically somewhat inferior to the sulphate when considered as a fertilizer. It nitrifies less readily than the sulphate, and the chloride of calcium formed by its reacting on carbonate of lime in the soil would be more apt than sulphate of lime to injure plants. Nevertheless, if chloride of ammonium were but cheap enough, it would have merit as a fertilizer. In Schloesing's experiments with ammonium chloride, 111.3 and 114 parts of ammonia were added in solution to 1,000,000 parts of soil, and 89.3 and 88.1 % respectively of the ammonia disappeared in 18 days, while nitric acid equivalent to 105.5 and 114.1 % of the ammonia were produced, the excess having been derived from nitrification of some of the soil nitrogen. In another experiment, in which ten times as much of the ammonium chloride was employed, viz. 1,136 parts of ammonia to 1,000,000 parts of soil, but little nitrification occurred during the first 14 days, but during the next 32 days the formation of nitrates was very active. At the end of 57 days it appeared that 85.6 % of the ammonia had disappeared, while an amount of nitric acid equivalent to 83.7 % of the ammonia had heen formed.

Warington noticed that nitrification was somewhat retarded in presence of ammonium chloride. Two equal masses of moist, powdered soil having been selected, one received ammonium chloride equivalent to 70 parts of ammonia per 1,000,000 parts of air-dried soil, while the other received no ammonia. After 119 days 97.6 % of the ammonia had disappeared, while the nitrification of soil-nitrogen amounted to only 83.6 % of that occurring in the absence of the ammonium salt.

With sulphate of ammonia Schloesing obtained a more rapid nitrification than with the chloride. Using 694 parts of ammonia
to 1,000,000 parts of soil, active nitrification began in 2 days and
lasted 8 days. At the end of 22 days 98.6 % of the ammonia had
disappeared, and the nitric acid produced was equal to 96.4 % of
the ammonia. In experiments with carbonate of ammonia 526,
1,271, and 2,251 parts of ammonia were added each to 1,000,000
parts of soil, and the duration of the nitrification was respectively
28, 37 and 86 days. The ammonia which disappeared amounted
to 97.7, 99.2 and 97.6 % of that taken, but in the case of the largest amount of ammonia 8.7 % of it were lost in the form of free
nitrogen, and with the intermediate quantity the free nitrogen was
3.4 % of the ammonia.

It is worth noticing that, as regards coal, distillation is the only
known means of rendering the nitrogen available for plant-food.
Neither fermentation nor composting, nor treatment with acids or
alkalies, has any effect upon this most refractory form of nitrogen.
It is different as regards the nitrogen in bones, and in fish or flesh,
which can readily be changed by fermentation.   So too in respect
to vegetable matters and peat, fermentation is a valuable means for
improving the nitrogen that is contained in them.   These substances, and the changes they undergo when they decay in the soil
or in a compost heap, will be treated of hereafter. Peruvian guano
also, which is an important source of ammonia, will need to be discussed by itself.

Phosphate of Ammonia and Magnesia.

Another compound of ammonia that has a certain interest for
the agricultural student is the phosphate of ammonia and magnesia.
This difficultly soluble compound is actually employed sometimes
as a manure, for it must often be formed during the fermentation
of dung and urine, and, for that matter, within the soil.   Large
crystals of it, an inch or two long, have in fact been found in the
soil of some of the old German cities, where the contents of privies
had been allowed to soak into the soil for centuries.

This double phosphate is especially interesting to the chemist,
since it offers one of the few known means of bringing ammonia
into the insoluble condition.   At the same time, it enables the
analyst to collect phosphoric acid from exceedingly dilute solutions,
such as sewage water. Several chemists have urged that a good part
of the phosphoric acid and ammonia in the urine which now runs

to waste from cities might be saved by precipitating it with some cheap magnesium salt. Unfortunately, however, in order to gain any advantage in this way, the urine must be putrid; and this condition is manifestly inadmissible in densely populated places. If sulphate of magnesia, for example, is added to fresh urine, there is no precipitate, and no apparent reaction of any kind. It is only after the mixture has stood for several days, until fermentation and the formation of ammonia have set in, that the liquid becomes cloudy through separation of the insoluble double phosphate of magnesia and ammonia. Once formed, this precipitate has great fertilizing power, as has been shown by numerous experiments on a comparatively large scale.

Amount of Ammonia in the Air.

Much labor has been expended in past years on experiments relating to the amount of ammonia in atmospheric air. A great deal has been written upon the subject, moreover, and it was at one time held by some chemists that plants derive nearly all their nitrogen from this source. But with the increase of knowledge, the subject has lost much of its interest. It is now known that the amount of ammonia in the atmosphere is exceedingly minute. It is in fact far too small to have much influence upon the growth of plants. About one part of ammonia in fifty million parts of air may be assumed to represent the average proportion, though the amount is liable to large fluctuations.

Many wrong notions regarding the amount of ammonia in the air have obtained currency through the false interpretation of experiments made upon the air in and about houses and cities. The very first observations that were made forcibly illustrate this point. Thus, Scheele, towards the close of the last century, argued that there must be ammonia in the air because a coating of some salt of it was formed around the mouths of bottles containing acids which were kept in his house. Not many years later, De Saussure noticed that crystals of ammonia alum separated from a dish of sulphate of alumina that had been left uncovered; whence he too immediately inferred the presence of ammonia in the air.

These observations, it will be noticed, were strictly correct. There was ammonia in the air in both these cases, but there is no longer any reason to doubt that there were local emanations of the gas which produced the observed effects; and a precisely similar remark will apply to many later experiments, where no sufficient

care was taken to allow for and avoid special or accidental sources
of ammonia.

At first thought, it would seem as if a great deal of ammonia must
necessarily be contained in the atmosphere.   For carbonate of ammonia is not only rather easily volatile of itself, but it is readily
taken up with the aqueous vapor formed by the evaporation of
water, and may so be carried into the air.   It is noteworthy that
in the evaporation of water, as in the distillation of water, any carbonate of ammonia which may have been held dissolved escapes in
the gaseous form with the first portions of the aqueous vapor.   In
recovering ammonia for manufacturing purposes from its solution
in water, it is noticed that practically the whole of it goes forward
in the first fifth of the distillate.   Brustlein kept a soil that contained 0.067 % of ammonia 43 days in a dry place, with but trifling
loss of the gas.   But on moistening and drying some of the same
earth three times, half its ammonia evaporated.

Moreover, carbonate of ammonia is generated incessantly upon
the surface of the earth.   Wherever vegetable or animal remains
decay, in the quick way, there carbonate of ammonia is set free.
It is to be presumed that many a decaying leaf or worm may con-
tribute its share of ammonia to the sum total, as well as the bodies
of the larger beasts that sometimes offend our nostrils.   It is true
indeed, as has been shown by Angus Smith and others, that minute
quantities of ammonia are found adhering to the surfaces of almost
all bodies, notably to the walls of houses and to all manner of objects
and implements in houses, and in some degree also to sticks and
stones in country fields far from human habitations.   Traces of
nitrates and nitrites occur, together with the ammonia, upon the
surfaces of most things, at least in places occupied by men or
animals, and it is supposed that this ammonia is formed by the
decay of organic matters and that much of it speedily changes to a
nitrate through the intervention of the nitrifying ferments.   It is
known, too, that a great deal of ammonia must be thrown into the
air during the combustion of nitrogenized substances, such as wood
and peat and coal; for such combustion is ordinarily greatly complicated by processes of distillation.   But, upon the other hand,
most soils have the capacity of absorbing ammonia freely and
readily, and of holding it rather forcibly.   Hence the gas generated in processes of decay or putrefaction has usually but little
chance of escaping into the air; and since carbonate of ammonia is

readily soluble in water, some part at least of that in the atmosphere must necessarily be washed out from the air into the soil by every fog, dew or rain. It is absorbed by the leaves of plants also, as has been said, so that, if any large amount of it were to escape from the restraining influences of the soil and the atmospheric waters, it would soon be removed from the air by the action of foliage.

A moment's consideration of these facts teaches that the question of atmospheric ammonia differs materially from that of carbonic acid. In the case of carbonic acid, a comparatively large proportion of the gas is maintained in the atmosphere by virtue of constant and abundant supplies through processes of decay, combustion, and animal respiration. But as regards ammonia, the forces which absorb and withdraw the gas are in excess of those which produce it. Methodical experiments by several observers have shown that that fraction of the yearly rainfall which passes out from the soil, as drain-water, carries away, in the form of nitrates, considerably more nitrogen than is brought to the land, as ammonia, in all the rain which falls upon it.

Direct experiments by Boussingault, which have been corroborated by numberless observers, showed conclusively that atmospheric ammonia has practically no influence on the growth of plants kept beneath a glass roof so as to be sheltered from rain and dew, and this fact is now familiar to investigators occupied with experiments in sand or water culture.

Amount of Ammonia in Rain.

The amount of ammonia brought down by rain, however, is often large enough to be of some scientific interest. Fresh rain-water may contain from one to three millionths of its weight of ammonia; fog and dew, from two to six millionths; and snow and hail, about as much as rain on the average.

Those portions of rain that fall at the beginning of a storm or shower generally contain a larger proportion of ammonia than those which fall subsequently. The first portions of water wash the layer of atmosphere between the cloud and the earth, and collect almost the whole of the ammonia that was contained in it. The rain that falls afterward merely dilutes the ammoniacal solution first obtained. Towards the close of a long-continued rain the water that falls is wellnigh absolutely free from ammonia.

The rain-water collected in cities contains far more ammonia than that which falls in the country : as much as thirty parts of ammonia in a million parts of water have been observed. It has sometimes been noticed, also, that the amount of ammonia in rain may be comparatively large when the rainfall occurs after long-continued dry weather.

In the year 1855 Lawes erected a large rain-gauge at Rothamsted, having a surface of $\frac{1}{1000}$ of an acre, and the waters collected in it have been analyzed from year to year, and even from day to day at times. Warington has reported that the average amount of ammonia-nitrogen in the water of this rain-gauge is about 0.3 part in 1,000,000 parts of water. But the quantity of ammonia varies widely in the waters of different showers, so that the amount of ammonia-nitrogen ranges from 0.043 to 5.491 parts to the million.

Warington computes that about $2\frac{1}{2}$ lb. of nitrogen in the form of ammonia fall upon an acre of land in one year at the locality in question. In addition to the ammonia nitrogen, nearly one pound falls as nitric acid and another pound in organic combination, making all together about $4\frac{1}{2}$ lb. of nitrogen to the acre.

Earlier observations, obtained by rather less accurate methods of analysis, gave larger amounts of ammonia. Thus Way, in 1855, found 7 lb. of ammonia to the acre, and, in 1856, $9\frac{1}{4}$ lb., in the waters of the Rothamsted gauge, which amounted to rather more than 600,000 gallons each year. German observers obtained in their turn $6\frac{1}{2}$ lb. and $9\frac{3}{4}$ lb. of ammonia in yearly rainfalls of 400,000 and 500,000 gallons. Goppelsroeder at Basel got $7\frac{1}{2}$ lb.

How Important for Crops is the Ammonia of the Air?

It is a matter of no little interest to compare the quantity of assimilable nitrogen brought down in the course of a year to an acre of land in the atmospheric waters with the quantities of nitrogen habitually taken off from an acre of land in various kinds of crops. Thus, Lawes and Gilbert concluded at one time that, at Rothamsted, as much as 4 or 5 lb. of total nitrogen were supplied per acre in the annual rainfall. But on the other hand, Boussingault, who weighed and analyzed all the crop from a five years' rotation, found that the following quantities of nitrogen were taken from each acre of land : —

Year.	Crop.	Pounds Nitrogen taken from the Acre of Land.	
1st	Potatoes	41	
2d	Wheat grain	23	} 31
	Wheat straw	8	
3d	Clover	75	
4th	Wheat grain	29	
	Wheat straw	10	} 50
	Turnips	11	
5th	Oat grain	21	} 26
	Oat straw	5	
Sum of the five years		223	
Average of each year, almost		45	

Whence it appears that, under this system of cultivation, nearly 45 lb. of nitrogen were taken off the land each year in the crops, or nine times as much as ordinarily comes to the acre of land in the rain.

On the other hand, if the nitrogen of the rains and snows and dews is contrasted with the amounts of nitrogen contained in those quantities of various fertilizers which practice has proved to be sufficient to insure a good crop upon an acre of land, it will seem at first sight as if the atmospheric supply were not wholly insignificant. Thus, as Johnson has urged, Chincha Island guano and nitrate of soda each contain about 15 % of nitrogen. Hence 33 lb. of either of these fertilizers would contain 5 lb. of nitrogen, or, as was just now said, as much as falls upon an acre of land in a year. But a dressing of 112 lb. of nitrate of soda to the acre has been known in England to double the grass-crop, and the application at a favorable moment of 30 or 40 lb. of either of the fertilizers here cited would be expected in many cases to produce a visible effect upon a crop of grain or grass. Nevertheless, it must be remembered that a large proportion of the atmospheric ammonia, etc. is brought down during the winter months. The experiments of Lawes and Gilbert relate to the entire year. But only that portion of the nitrogen which is retained by the soil or the crop can be accounted useful; and during the winter months little if any of it can be thus retained in our climate. Hence, in the last analysis it appears that the amount of assimilable nitrogen derived from atmospheric ammonia and nitrates is wholly insufficient for the growth of crops.

Most Plants are supplied with Nitrogen from the Humus of the Soil.

Excepting the case of leguminous crops, in which supplies of nitrogen are habitually procured from the air, as will be explained hereafter, it is from the soil that plants obtain their nitrogenous food as well as all other kinds of plant-food excepting carbonic acid, and, in some part, oxygen.   In point of fact the humus of the soil contains much nitrogen, though it is true enough that by far the larger portion of this soil-nitrogen occurs in insoluble and inert forms, which have never been accurately studied.   They will be discussed more in detail in another place.

There is usually a small amount of nitrogen in the soil in the form of nitrates, as was stated in the preceding chapter, and a still smaller proportion is found to be in the condition of ammonium compounds.   Generally speaking, no more than a minute proportion of ammonium compounds can be detected in ordinary soils, but the fact that any ammonia can be found there is important, and many experiments have been made to determine how widely the proportion of it may vary at different times and in different soils.

Contrary to an old belief, which was founded on imperfect experiments, it is now known that ordinary soils usually contain no more than 0.0002 to 0.0008%, say 0.0006% on the average, of ammonia.   Rich garden soils may contain some 0.002%, while rich alluvial tropical soils have shown 0.004 to 0.009%.   In a sample of peat, Boussingault found 0.018% of ammonia, and in leaf-mould from South America 0.05%, as was previously stated.

The Soil may absorb Gaseous Ammonia.

It seems strange at first, in view of all the ammonia which may be formed in the soil by processes of decay and fermentation, that so little of it is commonly found there; and the more especially since, with the exception of mere sands, most soils can absorb and hold considerable quantities of ammonia both by mechanical and by chemical means.   It has long been known that ammonia gas and the vapor of carbonate of ammonia can be absorbed physically by soils and other porous substances, notably by charcoal and peat, by mere force of adhesive attraction, and that the ammonia thus absorbed can slowly enter into chemical combinations in the soil.   Schloesing has been inclined to attach much importance to this fact, which he has illustrated by numerous experiments.   He found that moist soils freely exposed to the air took up nitrogen at the rate of about 38 lb. per year and per acre, and subsoils somewhat less.   He argues that ammonia was the prin-

cipal substance absorbed, though in moist soils the gain of nitrogen appeared in the form of nitrates.　Berthelot has noticed,
furthermore, that small quantities of free nitrogen from the air are
continually, though slowly, fixed by dead vegetable matters in the
soil, under the influence of feeble, silent electrical discharges such
as occur constantly everywhere upon the earth's surface.

Reversion of Ammonia-Nitrogen to Inert Forms.

There are at least two reasons why ammonium compounds do
not accumulate in the soil; viz. their easy conversion to nitrates,
as has been explained; and, secondly, their conversion into organic substances such as exist in humus.　It is known that some
of the ammonia in ammonium salts, such as the sulphate for example, can combine with the hydrated double silicate of alumina
and lime, and so be "fixed" in the soil in a difficultly soluble condition, much in the same way that potash, magnesia, lime, and
other bases can be fixed.　When a dilute solution of sulphate, carbonate, chloride, or even nitrate of ammonia, is allowed to percolate through a column of loam, it will be found that much of the
ammonia is retained in the earth in a manner analogous to that in
which potash is retained when potassium salts are thus filtered
through earth, or lime when lime salts are thus treated.

In addition to the hydrated silicates which take part in the fixa-
tions just described, there are various organic substances in the
soil, such as, in default of any precise knowledge as to their
chemical composition, are commonly classed together as "humic
acids," and with these compounds ammonia as well as other bases,
such as potash, lime, magnesia, soda, and oxide of iron, or the
like, can enter into combination to form double humates which are
well-nigh insoluble in water.　Simple humate of potash, or humate
of soda, or humate of ammonia, is readily soluble in water.　But
the double humates of potash and lime or iron oxide (or some other
base), or of ammonia and lime, or other base, are hardly at all
soluble.　It will be noticed that this power of the double humates
to fix soluble bases is a general fact, almost as important in its
bearings as the analogous power of the double silicates.

It might be thought at first sight that ammonia, when once fixed
in the form of a double humate or double silicate, would be held
in store permanently in the soil, as potash is, and so be available
for the use of crops.　It appears on the contrary that the complex
compounds of humic acid, ammonia, and metallic oxides which

result from this kind of fixation, slowly undergo such changes in the earth that the ammonia in them ceases to exist as such, and is converted into a nitrogenous substance, or substances, which are insoluble in water, and of comparatively little direct value for feeding plants. It has been noticed moreover that, beside ammonia, various other nitrogen compounds — such as strychnine, nicotin, and the toxines which result from the vital action of some kinds of bacteria — undergo changes of this sort in the soil. (Falk.) The poisonous properties of the alkaloids are destroyed on mixing solutions of them with humus or (less readily) with sandy loam. As yet, the inert nitrogen compounds which result from this destruction of ammonia are not to be distinguished from those naturally contained in humus. They will be considered more particularly in connection with humus. It may be said here, however, that there are to-day few agricultural problems of more importance than the question how to devise ways and means of making the inert nitrogen compounds of the soil readily available for the support of crops.

Action of Ammonia on Carbohydrates.

It should be said, moreover, that several laboratory experiments have been tried by chemists, by means of which ammonia may be made to undergo changes analogous to those just suggested. Thus, when ammonia-water is strongly heated in contact with starch, or grape-sugar, or dextrin, or when it is left to act for a long time on cane-sugar at the ordinary temperature of the air, the ammonia appears to be destroyed or decomposed, while several new substances, rich in nitrogen, are formed by the union of some of the constituents of the ammonia with some of those of the starch or sugar.

Moreover, there can be no question that ammonia is constantly changed to organic nitrogen compounds in many processes of fermentation and decay, simply from the fact that many of the microorganisms which cause fermentations feed upon compounds of ammonia and put to use the nitrogen in them for building up their own bodies. From the time of Pasteur's earliest investigations it has been customary for experimenters to cultivate micro-organisms in mixed solutions of pure chemical substances, such as phosphates and the like, in which the nitrogenous element of food is represented by tartrate of ammonia or some other compound of ammonia and an organic acid.

There is consequently nothing forced in the supposition that either ammonia or carbonate of ammonia in the soil, or ammonia which has been fixed there as a silicate or a humate, may be radically changed by long-continued contact with the organic matters in the soil; and experiments made by Knop have shown, in fact, that when ammonia is kept during several summer months in closed vessels in contact with peat or with soils rich in humus, the ammonia actually disappears either wholly or in good part. And since, in these experiments, there was not enough air in the vessels to supply as much oxygen as would be needed for changing the ammonia to nitrates, the inference is that the ammonia was changed to some kind of an organic substance analogous to those ordinarily contained in humus.

The Fertilizing Effect of Ammonium Salts is Ephemeral.

Lawes and Gilbert, in their experiments on wheat and barley, observed that a part of the nitrogen applied in the form of ammonium salts remains in some form in the soil, and that when once fixed in this way it is only very slowly and partially recovered in the increase of crops grown after the use of ammonia or other nitrogenous fertilizers has ceased. They observed also when large quantities of ammonium salts were put upon the land, that a considerable part of the nitrogen thus applied could not be found again either in the crops or in the nitrates of the drainage waters, and that the amount of nitrogen unaccounted for was the larger in proportion as more of the ammonium salt had been applied. Far from arguing, however, that much of the nitrogen of the ammonia is retained in the soil in the form of inert nitrogen compounds, they incline to believe that the source of what little fertilizing power is exhibited by soils in the years that succeed an ammoniacal manuring must be sought for in the roots and stubble left upon the land by the crop that received the manure.

In evidence of the small endurance of ammonium salts they cite the results obtained on certain plots of wheat-land which were manured alternately with a mixture of minerals and with 400 lb. of ammonium salts, equal to 86 lb. of nitrogen. Each year one set of the plots received minerals while the other set received ammonium salts, and the next year the first set got ammonium salts while the other set got minerals, so that during the 32 years of the experiment, each plot received 16 applications of mineral manures and 16 applications of ammonium salts. The following table gives.the average crops obtained in periods of 8 years, according as ammonium salts or as minerals were applied. For the sake of comparison, the yield of another plot is given to which nothing but minerals were applied year after year : —

	Minerals every year. Wheat, Bush.	When only minerals were applied. Wheat, Bush.	When only ammonia was applied. Wheat, Bush.	Minerals every year. Wheat and straw, lb.	When only minerals were applied. Wheat and straw, lb.	When only ammonia was applied. Wheat and straw, lb.
8 years, 1852-'59	19.0	18.9	32.4	3191	3235	5938
8 years, 1860-'67	15.3	16.5	31.3	2450	2696	5297
8 years, 1868-'75	14.9	15.0	28.5	2144	2404	4781
8 years, 1876-'83	12.6	12.3	27.8	1899	1869	4930
32 years, 1852-'83	15.3	15.6	30.0	2421	2551	5237

It will be observed that no better crops were obtained in the years when no ammonia was applied to the land than were got from the plot that never received any ammonia. Each year when ammonia was used the land gave good crops, but the ammonia exhibited no endurance. Although it exerted a highly beneficial influence at first, this influence ceased to be appreciable in the very next year, i. e. in those years when the mixture of minerals was applied.

Even when very large quantities of ammonium salts were used the fertilizing influence did not long endure. Thus, to some plots of land there was applied every year, during 13 successive years, a mixture of mineral manures and 800 lb. of ammonium salts (equal to 172 lb. of nitrogen), and the land was afterwards continually cropped with wheat during 19 years without receiving any further addition of fertilizers. During the last two years of the period of manuring there were harvested 56 and 51 bushels of wheat. But the crop of the first year without manure was 32 bushels, against 14 bushels on an adjacent plot of land that had long been unmanured, and that of the second year was 17 against 13.

During the next two years the crops on the land in question were 5 bushels in excess of those on the permanently unmanured land; but in the years that followed the produce on the two kinds of land was almost identical, though it was not until 12 years after the last application of the fertilizers that all influence due to them ceased. It is known, however, that much of this influence must be attributed to the action of the mineral fertilizers, formerly applied, which promote nitrification of the nitrogen in the humus of the soil. It was computed that during the 13 years when am-

monium salts were applied at the rate of 800 lb. to the acre, more
than 1000 lb. of the nitrogen, which had been put upon the land,
were not recovered in the crops, while not more than 60 lb. of nitrogen were contained in the excess of produce obtained during
the next 10 years, over that got from permanently unmanured
land.   .

Little or no Ammonia in Well-water.

It is a curious fact that, because of the power of the soil to absorb and fix ammonia, and because of the easy conversion of ammonium compounds to nitrates, hardly a trace of ammonia can be
detected, ordinarily, in the soil below the depths reached by the
ploughshare.   It is not ammonium salts that are found in the
waters of country wells and field-drains, but the nitrates of lime
or soda into which the ammonium salts have been converted by
oxidation through ferment action.   At the worst, as in city wells,
a nitrate of ammonia will be found, and not chloride or sulphate
of ammonium. It is in the form of nitrates, and not as ammonium
salts, that the assimilable nitrogen of soils is washed out.   Even
in water flowing through tile-drains from land to which large quantities of ammonium salts have been applied, Voelcker found mere
traces of ammonia, while nitrates were always present in abundance.

It is not to be understood, however, that the compounds first
formed by the combination of ammonia or ammonium salts with
the constituents of the soil are totally insoluble in water.   On the
contrary, it has been shown repeatedly, by experiment, that most
of the ammonia absorbed by a given small sample of soil may be
washed out again by water if the water be applied speedily.   Much
water is required, it is true, and the washings must be many times
repeated.   In other words, the compounds of ammonia formed at
first in the soil are not absolutely insoluble, although they are very
difficultly soluble.   It is of interest to know that in the beginning
they are soluble enough to be fed upon by plants.

But, after all, the washing out of ammonia from a soil is possible only as a laboratory experiment.   It could hardly be done in
a field, for, by experiments made in fields, it appears that the proportion of ammonia removed by several washings is small as compared with that retained by the soil; and that the power of soils
to absorb ammonia from solutions of its salts is greater than the
power of water to redissolve it.   Hence the farmer need have no

fear that heavy showers of rain will remove much ammonia from his land, not even when he has just been strewing guano or sulphate of ammonia. With nitrate of soda the case is different. Here there would be risk of loss if the rain were long continued; and no matter what form of nitrogenized fertilizer has been applied to the land, a small proportion of it will be found leaching away all the while in the soil-water or the drain-water, in the form of nitrates.

Loss of Ammonia from the Soil by Nitrification.

The oxidation of ammonium salts in porous soils, that is to say, the conversion of a good part of the ammonia to nitrates, was shown very clearly, some years ago, by the experiments of Voelcker, Frankland, and others, on the composition of the waters of field-drains. It was then found that whenever ammonium salts are left in contact with soils that are permeated by air, they are slowly but steadily decomposed with formation of nitrates, considerable quantities of which appear in the drainage-waters whenever rain enough has fallen to make the drains run. Samples of drain-water collected in December always contained more nitrates in proportion as the quantity of ammonium salts applied to the land in the previous spring had been larger. In other words, with each increase in the amount of nitrogen applied in the form of ammonium salts, there was an increased loss of nitrogen in the form of nitrates carried away in the drain-water.

Voelcker insisted that considerable quantities of nitrogen might be lost in this way during mild, wet winters, such as frequently occur in England, whenever liberal dressings of ammonium salts have been applied in the autumn to winter grain. His analyses show that 100,000 parts of drain-water, from land manured in autumn with enough ammonium salts to supply 82 lb. of nitrogen to the acre, may contain as much as 2.5 to 3.75 parts of nitrogen. But since one part of nitrogen in 100,000 parts of drain-water means a loss of 2.25 lb. of nitrogen per acre for each inch of rain which thus passes out from the soil, it follows that 3.75 parts of nitrogen would be equivalent to a loss of 8.5 lb. of this element from an acre of land for every inch of water of percolation. Frankland has observed as much as 7.841 of nitrogen in 100,000 parts of drain-water collected in winter after an application of ammonium salts in the autumn, at the rate of 600 lb. to the acre, and in this case nearly 18 lb. of nitrogen per acre would be carried away by an inch of percolating rain-water.

Voelcker concluded that, as a rule, ammoniacal manures should not be applied in the autumn, though they may be put upon the land in the spring earlier than nitrate of soda, with less risk that their nitrogen will be washed out of the soil. Drain-water collected in May, from wheat fields which had been highly manured in March with ammonium salts, contained only small quantities of nitrates, while large amounts of nitrates were always present in drain-waters that were collected in winter from wheat-fields on which ammonium salts had been plowed in and harrowed in before the wheat was sown in the autumn. It appeared that in the winter, when no crop was growing, nitrates escaped from the soil rather easily, but that this waste was checked as soon as active growth set in in the spring.

Not all the Nitrogen in Manures applied is recovered in the Crops grown.

Experiments made in England to determine how much of the nitrogen which has been applied as manure can be recovered again in the increase of the crop which the manure brings, have indicated that, under the conditions of the trials, no more than from a third to a half of the nitrogen applied to the land was recovered in the increase of the first crop. It appeared, indeed, that the whole of the nitrogen was not recovered in the increase of many succeeding crops. It is to be remembered, of course, that crops as harvested do not represent the whole amount of vegetable matter which is produced in a field, for there is usually left upon the land a quantity of roots, stubble and weeds, as well as many fallen leaves, and often some scattered seeds. It is known, moreover, that a good part of the observed waste depends upon the incessant leaching away of soluble nitrates, into which the ammonium compounds or other nitrogenized fertilizers have been converted by fermentation and oxidation, while another part of the nitrogen is retained in the soil in some insoluble form. Analysis of soils showed Lawes and Gilbert that, even to a depth of 27 inches, there was a considerable accumulation of nitrogen from the manure which had not been recovered in the increase of the crop.

With nitrate of soda, sown in the spring, the loss of nitrogen by drainage was larger than with ammonium salts sown at that season; but it was still larger from ammonium salts sown in the autumn. As was just now said, whenever large amounts of ammonium salts were put upon wheat-land in the autumn, large quantities of nitrates went to waste in the waters of field-drains during the winter, though this waste was considerably checked as soon as the crop began to grow again in the spring. It was noticed, moreover, that much smaller proportions of the nitrogen of ammonia salts were recovered in the increase of crop when they were applied in the autumn to wheat than when they were sown in the spring for barley or for oats.

In case there was any lack of available potash and phosphoric acid in the soil, the loss of nitrogen in the drain-water was larger than it was where the crops had access to abundant supplies of mineral fertilizers. On plots dressed with similar amounts of ammonium salts and mixtures of mineral fertilizers there was obtained the maximum amount of nitrogen per acre in the crop and the minimum amount in the drainage; but on plots dressed with the ammonium salts without the mineral manure, there was the minimum amount of nitrogen in the crop and the maximum amount in the drainage.

Amount of Ammonia obtainable from Coal.

As has been said, the ammonium compounds procurable in commerce have, with hardly an exception, been derived from coal. But the amount of nitrogen in coal is very small. It varies from a mere trace to perhaps a little more than two per cent in exceptional cases. Probably it does not exceed three-quarters of one per cent on the average; and even of this small proportion only about a third passes off in the form of ammonia when the coal is distilled. Nevertheless, the manufacture of gas is conducted on so vast a scale that very large quantities of ammonia are obtained in it. For example, considerably more than a million tons of coal are distilled every year for gas in London; and it has been computed that, if the ammonia due to one-third of the nitrogen in this amount of coal were converted into chloride of ammonium, as much as 10,000 tons of this salt could be got every year from the gas-works of that single city.

It has been estimated that, in the year 1883, 6,500,000 tons of coal were distilled in England, and that more than 745,000 tons of ammoniacal liquor were produced, from which 60,000 tons of ammonium sulphate might have been made. Much coal is distilled in France also, and in Belgium, and special care seems to be taken in Belgium to save the ammonium products. In Germany, in 1883, 1,516,000 tons of coal were distilled at gas-works, and some 152,000 tons of ammoniacal liquor were produced.

Ammonium salts, prepared from gas-liquor are necessarily somewhat costly, because of the labor and fuel which have to be expended in order to bring the contents of the liquor into merchantable shape. Hence, no little thought has been given at one time or another to the discovery of new sources of ammonia, as well as to the possibility of manufacturing ammonia from atmospheric nitrogen.

There are several sources of waste of ammonia, which may one day be checked. In countries where bituminous coal is abundant vast quantities of the coal are distilled simply for the sake of the coke which is left as the residual product of the distillation. This coke is used for generating steam, for smelting metals, and in general as an excellent kind of fuel. But until comparatively recently, enormous amounts of ammonia were allowed to go to waste from the coke-ovens, together with the other products of the distillation. In 1885, Maercker computed that from the 13,000 coke furnaces in Germany, which used daily some 32,000 tons of coal, as much as 6,400 centners of sulphate of ammonia might be got daily, or, in a year, $2\frac{1}{4}$ million centners.

So also, enormous quantities of ammonia are lost in the refuse of cities. A noticeable quantity of ammonia that had already been manufactured has been lost in the making of ammonia alum also.

Efforts have been made from time to time to diminish the waste from these sources, and as regards the coke-furnaces these efforts appear to have been fairly successful. Indeed, in processes recently invented in Europe, bituminous coal (or shale) is subjected to distillations so regulated in respect to the admission of air and superheated steam that an exceptionally large proportion of the nitrogen in the coal is converted into ammonia.

Some kinds of coal admit of being used directly for smelting ores of iron, and even from the gases evolved in this industry no inconsiderable quantities of ammonium sulphate have been manufactured. In the year 1889 the English inspector of alkali works reported that the production of sulphate of ammonia in that country was gradually increasing. Reckoning the value of it at $60 the ton, he stated that the yearly output had risen to the amount of $7,500,000, and he believed that this quantity might be increased ten-fold. Small amounts of ammonium products are made also from the refuse of some European cities, where the lack of an abundant supply of water prevents the use of water-closets, and permits, or rather compels, the collection of human excrements. A practicable method of working this material for ammonia will be described under Night-Soil.

Soot.

The soot deposited in chimneys leading from fires where bituminous coal or wood is burned, contains small quantities of ammonium and potassium compounds and phosphates, and has long been esteemed in England as an excellent top-dressing for young wheat in the spring, particularly on heavy soils, and for grass. It is applied in calm, showery weather, very early in the season, at the rate of 20 to 40 or even 60 bushels to the acre. It is said to increase the quantity and improve the quality of wheat without forcing an undue quantity of straw. Or, as others have said, it brings on the wheat gradually up to the time of harvest, while guano tends to keep the plants green and growing too late in the season. Sometimes it has been used for manuring potatoes.

It is said to be well to mix soot with loam before strewing it, and to throw the mixture to leeward from a wagon at a time when but little wind is stirring. At the best, the strewing of soot by hand is a very disagreeable operation, and implements have been invented in England by means of which this fertilizer may be applied " with some degree of comfort to the laborer."

It will be noted that soot contains a much smaller proportion of nitrogen than nitrate of soda does, and that a considerable bulk of it must be applied to the land, in order to produce the wished-for effect. When applied to cold, stiff clays soot is thought to do good, particularly in backward seasons, in that it absorbs the sun's heat by virtue of its dark color and so warms the land. Conversely, it has been said that soot is objectionable on thin uplands because of its liability to burn off young crops in dry weather. In general, little or no good is got from soot that has been sown late on wheat, in case continuous dry weather should set in. "If sown late, and no rain falls to wash it, it is thought to be injurious rather than beneficial to wheat, and if it be sown early and the frost catch it, its strength is thereby lowered. In any case, it is not found to be of much if any service to the crop of barley which follows the wheat." (Marshall.)

Beside acting as a stimulant to excite the growth of the plants, soot is said to destroy slugs and worms, and to be obnoxious to rabbits and other vermin. It has been recommended also for protecting germinating peas, in which case it is to be strewn as a top-dressing, either by itself or admixed with saw-dust.

Payen and Boussingault found 1.35% of nitrogen in coal soot and 1.15% in wood soot. Breunlin found 1.31%, 2.05%, and 2.46% of nitrogen respectively in soot from wood fires, coal fires, and fires of mixed wood and coal. He found also 23.80, 24.77, and 24.75% of ashes in the soots. These ashes contained fine clay, ashes that had been drawn up the chimneys, and traces of gypsum. He found neither phosphoric acid nor alkalies in the soot from the wood fire. In London soot, known to be genuine, Hutton found 1.75% of ammonia, 0.20% of potash, 2.08% phosphate of lime and alumina, 14.40% of sand, 53.2% of carbon and 18.00 of tar and oil, beside other matters. In Glasgow soot, probably adulterated, he found 2.8% of ammonia, 0.30% of potash, 3.20% phosphate of lime and alumina, 25.7% of sand, 35.7% of carbon, 15% of tar and oil, etc. He says that not more than 500 tons of soot are collected in Glasgow in a year, and that the value of it never exceeds $5,000 per annum. He adds that a considerable quantity of soot is shipped from Great Britain to the West Indies for fertilizing the sugar-cane. Many years ago, Braconnot reported 0.2% of acetate of ammonia, 4.46% of acetate and chloride of potassium, and 1.50% of phosphate of lime in soft soot from wood fires. Voelcker found $3\frac{1}{2}$% of ammonia, $2\frac{3}{4}$% of alkali salts, 11% of carbonate of lime, and 2% of carbonate of magnesia, in a sample of commercial soot. In other samples he found respectively 2.35, 3.63 and 5.04% of nitrogen. In coal-soot, Koenig found 0.6% of nitrogen, 0.5% of phosphoric acid, 0.9% of potash, more than 3% of lime, and 42% of ashes. According to Wolff coal-soot may contain 2.5% of nitrogen, 0.1% of potash, 4% of lime and 25% of ashes. For wood-soot he gives the following figures: nitrogen 1.3%, potash 2.4%, lime 10%, ashes 23%.

A sample of Belgian soot gave Petermann $2\frac{1}{2}$% of nitrogen in the form of ammonium salts, and $\frac{3}{4}$ of one per cent of phosphoric acid. Pavesi found in Italian soots $1\frac{1}{4}$ to 2% of nitrogen, and 1 to $1\frac{1}{2}$% of carbonate of potash. Both these observers remark on the difficulty of obtaining pure soot that has not been mixed with earth or with coal ashes. According to A. Mayer, soot from peat fires is more highly esteemed than any other kind. He reports that he found in it, on one occasion, as much as 2.8% of nitrogen in the form of ammonia. Laktine noticed in peat-soot 26.4% of ashes, and his analysis of wood-soot showed 1.2% of water, 28.4% charcoal, 5.1% of ashes insoluble in acid, and 65.4% of matters easily soluble in water and dilute hydrochloric acid. In 100 parts of the soluble matter there was contained 21% of lime, 2% of alumina and iron oxide, 16% of potash, 1% of soda, 3% of magnesia, 3% of phosphoric acid, 11% of sulphuric acid and 1.5% of silicic acid.

Ammonia from Leather, etc.

It is to be noted that, by means of reducing agents, ammonia could be made from nitrates and nitrites in case these substances should ever become much cheaper than they are now. Ammonia could be made also very cheaply from organic matters rich in nitrogen, such as leather or peat, by heating them strongly in retorts together with a mixture of caustic soda and quicklime, or with a mixture of slaked lime and carbonate or sulphate of soda. (S. W. Johnson.) It is a very old observation, that when an organic substance which contains no nitrogen, such as starch or sugar, for example, is ignited with an excess of the hydroxide of an alkali-metal, the carbon of the organic matter unites with the oxygen of the hydroxide to form carbonic acid, while much hydrogen is set free. A similar reaction occurs when nitrogenous organic matters are ignited with the alkali hydroxides, only that in this case the nitrogen combines with enough of the hydrogen, at the moment of its liberation, to form ammonia, which can readily be collected and put to use. As a means of detecting and estimating nitrogen, this reaction has long been familiar in the analytical laboratory, where — for the sake of convenience — a mixture of caustic soda and lime, known as soda-lime, is used. L'Hote has proposed to manufacture ammonia in this way by soaking leather scraps in soda-lye, stirring into the mass enough slaked lime to make a stiff paste, and distilling this mixture in retorts. All the nitrogen in the leather is converted into ammonia, which is swept out of the retort by the gases (hydrogen and carburetted hydrogen), which are set free at the same time with it.

Another analogous method is to heat leather scraps in a retort supplied with regulated quantities of air and steam under such conditions that large quantities of ammonia shall be formed. (C. E. Avery.) So far from ammonia becoming more costly in the future, it is probable that the methods of manufacturing it will continually be improved, and that the price at which it can be sold will become lower and lower.

CHAPTER XIII.

OTHER ASSIMILABLE NITROGEN COMPOUNDS BESIDE AMMONIA AND NITRATES.

THE question will naturally be asked, What other chemical substances beside ammonium salts and nitrates are capable of supplying nitrogen to plants? The answer is, that while many substances that contain nitrogen — such as cyanogen compounds, nitro-substitution compounds, and alkaloids, such as caffein, cinchonin, quinin and morphin — appear to be incapable of feeding plants, even when they are not actually poisonous to the plants, experimenters have been able to grow plants of the higher orders by means of urea, uric acid, leucin, tyrosin, glycocoll, hippuric acid, guanin, creatin, asparagin, and acetamid. Several of these substances, it is true, are mere chemical rarities, but others are of great agricultural importance, since they occur in urine and in the dung of birds. An account of them will be found in "How Crops Feed," page 293. It is to be noted that small quantities of asparagin and its congeners are found in most plants, that leucin and tyrosin are often produced during the decay of albuminoid bodies, and that glycocoll is a product of the decomposition of hippuric acid.

It is known that fungi can assimilate the nitrogen of organic matters, such as the albuminoids, and that in ammonium salts, nitrils, amido-acids, amins, ureas, guanidins, some alkaloids, nitrates, and in some cases even that in nitrites. As Loew has said: "Not only salts of ammonia and nitrates, but also organic compounds of the most different structure may serve; thus, amins, amids, derivatives of urea and of guanidin, amido-acids, and organic cyanides, — for example, methylamin, acetamid, hydantoin, creatin, glycocoll, leucin, asparagin, methylcyanide. Of inorganic combinations, ferrocyanide of potassium is but a poor source of nitrogen, while hydroxylamin and diamid are entirely unfit for use, being very poisonous. Nitrites are less favorable sources than nitrates, and the nitrates are more quickly reduced to ammonia than the somewhat poisonous nitrites."

It has been urged, at one time and another, in respect to several of the complex nitrogenous substances above-mentioned, that perhaps they might have been converted into ammonia or nitrates in the soil before the plant consumed them; and there may be something of truth in this suggestion, since it is known that there are micro-organisms in ordinary loams which are capable of decomposing asparagin, leucin, tyrosin, and albumin, with production of ammonia. But as regards urea, at least, it has been proved that this substance does not readily decompose in the soil, either to form ammonia or nitrates. It has been found, in fact, unchanged in plants that have been fed with it. Uric acid, also, is a substance not easily decomposed. It is known, moreover, that urine may be kept fresh for a month or more by mixing it with clay. The clay seems to absorb and remove the substances that ordinarily occasion the fermentation and putrefaction of urine, and the destruction of the urea which it contains. Hence the suggestion that urea may sometimes remain undecomposed in the soil for an appreciable period.

As against the supposition that the substances now in question are changed to ammonia or to nitrates, it is to be remembered that the experimenters who have most carefully examined the subject were themselves convinced that plants can be nourished directly by several of these compounds, particularly by urea, uric acid, guanin, and creatin.

Importance of Urea and Urates.

The practical significance of the inquiry is very great. New light has been thrown upon a mass of farm experience by the evidence thus presented that urine may as well be used as a manure when fresh as after it has been fermented, and that the uric acid in guano acts directly as plant-food. Formerly it was thought by some persons that fresh urine is of little or no use as a fertilizer. They maintained that the nitrogen in urine is incompetent to feed plants before the urea has fermented, and so changed to carbonate of ammonia. It is plain enough now, however, that it may often be good practice to add preservative agents and germicides to urine, with the view of keeping its urea intact. It is an old custom, in some parts of Switzerland, to add copperas (sulphate of iron) to the pits or cisterns in which dung-liquor collects, and it has been proved by Schattenmann, in France, that the practice has considerable merit. This custom has often been explained as if the sole object of it were to change the volatile carbonate of ammonia to the non-volatile sulphate, but it is not improbable that the copperas actually preserves the urine, and enables the peasants to bring a good deal of urea directly to their fields.

It is to be observed, however, that fresh urine is so concentrated a material that a certain amount of care needs to be exercised in applying it. In China and Japan it is a matter of old observation that plants are liable to wilt when watered with fresh human urine that has been diluted with an equal bulk of water; but, as Kellner has shown, the trouble is that, even when thus diluted, the solution contains more urea than plants can readily support. Since the original urine may contain some 2% of urea, the diluted liquor would contain 1%, while all experience teaches that it is best not to employ solutions of fertilizers that are stronger than 1 : 1000. Hence it appears that the partially diluted urine which sometimes causes plants to wilt is really a ten times stronger solution than can safely be applied. Indeed, Kellner maintains that agricultural plants grow best when watered with solutions that contain no more than from 0.25 to 0.5 part of nutrients to 1000 parts of water.

One peculiarity of urea, as contrasted with the carbonate of ammonia into which it changes when fermented, needs to be kept in mind; viz., that urea is not absorbed and fixed by the soil as the ammonium compounds are, and that it soaks into the land in all directions to the very great advantage of the plants that are growing there. For aught that is now known to the contrary, it is barely possible that in times of prolonged rain some urea may even be washed out of the soil, and go to waste with the excess of the ground-water, as the nitrates do, though in most cases the urea would doubtless be changed to a nitrate before passing off in this way.

Kellner has shown that at the surface of the soil (in summer weather) urea is speedily changed to carbonate of ammonia, by the action of aerobic ferments which live in the surface soil; but that no such change occurs in the subsoil. In soils taken from the depth of one foot the conversion of urea to carbonate of ammonia was so slow that the process was hardly completed at the end of two months, while even porous soils taken from depths greater than two feet were powerless to cause such conversion. As was just now intimated, as regards urea, it is true of this substance and its derivatives, as it is of guanidin also and methylguanidin, that — like the ammonium salts — they are poisonous when used in strong solutions. That is to say, neither animals nor plants of the higher orders can support them unless they are dilute. A one-thousandth solution of urea will kill algae, though fungi can support it well enough.

Peruvian Guano.

Next in order comes the consideration of various substances, used as manures, which are capable, sooner or later, of supplying nitrates, ammonía, urates, or some other easily assimilable compound of nitrogen. First among them is guano, a substance which has exerted a marked influence upon the development of scientific agriculture.

True guano is a substance found upon certain rainless islands off the coast of Peru, which has resulted from the slow decomposition of the dung and other refuse of sea-fowls. As first imported to Europe and this country, some years since, it consisted to the extent of almost one-half its weight of soluble ammonium salts, viz. urate, oxalate, carbonate and phosphate, together with a little sulphate and chloride of ammonium, and compounds of ammonia and fatty acids. It is to these fatty acids rather than to ammonia that the peculiar odor of guano is to be attributed.

The percentage of nitrogen in Chincha Island guano ranged from 10 or 11% in the lower grades to 16 or 17% in the best kinds, say 12 to 13% in guano of average quality. Nearly one-quarter of the weight of the guano was phosphate of lime, equivalent to some 10 or 12% of phosphoric acid; and beside these ingredients there were small quantities of potash salts, a little sand, and organic matters. All this (and much of what follows also) refers to guano from the Chinchas, which has now become in some sort historic, since the supply has been practically exhausted. The Peruvian guano which is procurable nowadays comes from other groups of islands, and is distinctly inferior to that which was formerly exported.

Composition of Guano.

Several years ago, Wolff gave the average percentage composition of the guanos then procurable, as follows, excluding non-essential matters : —

	Water.	Organic and Volatile Matter.	Nitrogen.	Phosp. Acid.	Potash.	Lime.
"Peruvian" . . .	15.0	42.0	7.0	14.0	3.3	12.6
Guanape	21.6	36.3	9.3	13.4	3.7	11.3
Ballestas	22.9	42.0	12.2	13.1	2.8	10.5
					And soda.	
Pabillon de Pica . .	6.2	48.8	9.2	13.5	8.4	13.7
Punta de Lobos . .	14.3	42.8	8.3	13.4	7.3	12.8
Huanillos	10.0	40.9	8.0	15.0	6.8	14.6
					Potash.	
Saldanha Bay . . .	12.2	35.5	9.0	9.2	1.3	7.6
Ichaboe, recent . .	16.0	29.5	8.0	11.3	0.8	21.0

As tested at the New Haven laboratory in recent years, the composition of guano, as procurable in New York, may be set down at nearly 8% of nitrogen, 12 to 15% of phosphoric acid, and 2 or 3% of potash. It is to be noted, however, that not infrequently, nowadays, more or less sulphate of ammonia is added to many cargoes of guano in order to increase the proportion of nitrogen in the material. That is to say, when a cargo of guano happens to contain less nitrogen than is contained in that recognized in the market as a standard article, a certain proportion of sulphate of ammonia is admixed with it in order to make up the deficiency. This practice is hardly to be commended. In view of its liability to such re-enforcement it cannot be said of the guano now procurable that it possesses the same peculiarities and excellences which characterized the guano of thirty years since. It is not only a weaker, but it may be a sophisticated material, the price of which is out of proportion higher than that of the guano which was formerly so much esteemed.

Nitrogen is the most important Constituent of Guano.

It is to the nitrogenized compounds in guano that its value is to be chiefly attributed. Of course the phosphate of lime has a certain significance, and it is a real significance. Were it not for this ingredient, guano could never have been used as it so often was, as a general manure. As it is, guano contains both the ingredients, viz. nitrogen and phosphoric acid (not to mention the small amount of potash), which are most needed by good soils. Land of fair quality, such as is found in many parts of Europe, may be perfectly well manured with guano alone year after year, just as it could be manured with farmyard manure. As long ago as when guano was first imported into Europe, it was noticed that it served an admirable purpose on strong clay soils.

But it is important to avoid a prejudice, at one time not uncommon, that phosphate of lime is the chief ingredient of guano. If this had been so, the cheap phosphatic guanos of Baker, Jarvis, and Howland Islands, from which almost everything but phosphate of lime has been washed out by rains, would have been more valuable than the guano of Peru; whereas, as a matter of fact, after some years of practical experience, the phosphatic guanos came to be used solely for making superphosphate, and were finally never applied directly to the land except perchance occasionally for the purpose of repeating some old experiment. The phosphatic guanos could be bought for $18 or $20 the ton at a time when Peruvian guano was sold at $50 or $60, or more.

The fact that guano may often do good service as a general manure, because it contains both nitrogen and phosphoric acid, together with a little potash, is well illustrated by the following statement of Boussingault. He observed along a great extent of the coast of Peru, that the soil, which consists of quartzose sand admixed with clay and is perfectly barren of itself, is rendered fertile, and made to yield abundant crops, by the application of guano, and irrigation. He says that the change produced there by such manuring is immediate and very remarkable.

Like nitrate of soda and sulphate of ammonia, guano is a manure of quick action, tending to develop rapid growth of the leafy parts of plants. Hence it is commonly used in small quantities, and as an adjunct to barnyard-manure. All that has been said of the good effects of ammonia or nitrate of soda, upon lands that have long been tilled, will apply to guano with equal or even greater force, for in guano we have not a single salt, but a mixture of several salts; it contains phosphate, urate, carbonate, and oxalate of ammonia, beside free uric acid, a little guanin, and often traces of nitrates, though the amount of nitrogen in this form rarely exceeds 0.3 or 0.4 %.

Guano on Young Grain.

One merit of guano, that it assures a good start to the seedling crop, has often been insisted upon. Not only is a strong and vigorous young plant better able to withstand drought and bad weather, but it will, as a rule, suffer less from the attacks of insects, and will the sooner be able to gather within itself a store of food fit to carry it happily forward through the subsequent stages of development. Light top-dressings of guano have often been found to do much good upon grain-fields that had suffered during hard winters. Guano may be used also in this way to bring forward any patches of grain or grass which are more backward in early spring than the rest of the field, and although, as has been said, it is somewhat slower of action than nitrate of soda, in so far as nitrogen is concerned, guano has one advantage, in that it remains longer in the land than the nitrate. It supplies phosphates, also, and some potash.

Starting with land which is in good heart, the efficiency of guano, as compared with that of barnyard-manure of good quality, is estimated by Stoeckhardt to be in the proportion of 1 cwt. of guano to 65 or 70 cwt. of the barnyard-manure. Manifestly, the difference in the time and labor required for handling the two kinds of material is a point worth considering.

Formerly, 200 lb. of the original guano to the acre was an ordinary dose. 400 lb. were thought a large application, even when no other manure was used, though quantities larger than this were sometimes applied. If more than 500 lb. to the acre of such guano had been used, the vegetation would probably have been too coarse and luxuriant. Grass or grain thus heavily guanoed would have been almost sure to " lodge." It is said that when guano was first carried to England it was often applied with too free a hand, with the result, in the case of wheat, that the plants grew rank and coarse, and produced a large crop of soft, dingy straw, and a small yield of lean, dark-colored grain. Turnips, also, that were liberally dressed with guano, were apt to grow so rapidly that they became hollow-hearted, and subject to speedy decay. In a case recorded by Norton, 8 cwt. of the best guano were applied to an acre of turnips; the plants all grew to tops, and produced no bulbs, and even the succeeding crop of wheat was so rank that the grain was miserable.

The guano of to-day is said to be used in England at the rate of from 3 to 5 cwt. to the acre, but twice these quantities are said to be sometimes used hereabouts by market gardeners. In general, the best way of using guano appears to be at the rate of 2 or 3 cwt. to the acre, together with half the usual quantity of barnyard-manure. In the damp, cold climate of Scotland, guano has been found to do good service upon turnips, and on strong land as much as 3 to 5 cwt. of it are often used there upon early turnips and upon other roots, without any other manure. But for late-sown turnips, such large dressings of guano are thought to be too stimulating; they are apt to make the crop run to leaf, so that for this case superphosphate is preferred to guano. When used for winter grain, it is said to be well to apply one hundredweight of guano when the seed is sown, and two hundredweight in the spring, at the time when the field would naturally be gone over with a smoothing-harrow to break the crust.

It is well to bury Guano.

Several experimenters have urged that guano should be ploughed under, or harrowed in deeply, as soon as may be practicable after spreading it, and the need of so doing points clearly to two of the modes of action of guano; viz., that it helps to ferment the humus of the soil, and that the urate of ammonia in it is peculiarly useful for feeding plants. But if this urate were left at the surface of the land, it would quickly change to carbonate, and some of this carbonate would exhale. On the other hand, if the guano were but slightly buried, its nitrogenous constituents might speedily be converted to nitrate, and this change is not wholly desirable, as will be shown in another place.

According to Hellriegel, while it is undoubtedly of great importance, in dry years, that guano should be ploughed under in order that its best action may be assured, there is no need of burying it deeply in wet years. Indeed, in years when moisture is abundant, guano may do better service when it has merely been worked into the soil than if deeply buried. Stoeckhardt's experiments upon the burying of guano are given in the following table. The figures relate to the weight in pounds of the sheaves obtained from one square rod (Saxon). The guano was applied at the rate of 1.5 cwt. to the Morgen (= 0.631 acre): —

	Winter Wheat.	Winter Rye.	Oats.
Harrowed in with the seed	7¼	6¼	21
Ploughed in to depth of 2 to 4 inches	7¼	6¼	21
Ploughed in to depth of 4 to 6 inches	11¾	5¾	22¼
Ploughed in to depth of 6 to 8 inches	13¼	7¼	23

After-effect noticed in a second year: —

	Oats.	Winter Rye.	Winter Barley
Harrowed in with seed	11¼	9¼	3
Ploughed in to depth of 2 to 4 inches	10¼	10	4¾
Ploughed in to depth of 4 to 6 inches	13¾	11	6
Ploughed in to depth of 6 to 8 inches	14¼	12	8¼

Heiden, who tried experiments with barley on a sandy loam, found that 1 cwt. of guano plowed under did as much good as 1½ cwt. applied as a top-dressing. His results are given in the table below: —

	Guano on Morgen (= 0.631 Acre).	Crop on Morgen. Grain.	Straw and Chaff.
No manure	...	500	847
As a top-dressing	1 cwt.	545	873
Ploughed in	1 "	669	980
As a top-dressing	1½ "	570	976
Ploughed in	1½ "	685	1257

Guano fails on Dry Land.

Of course, the supposition is in all cases that the land to which guano is to be applied is adequately supplied with water. If there is a lack of moisture, the components of the guano will not dissolve, ferment action cannot occur, and comparatively little effect will be produced by the manure. In dry seasons, guano is apt to disappoint expectations, and in this country there is a certain prejudice against it on that account. It is in rainy countries, or in wet seasons, that guano is specially efficacious. Nowhere has it been more highly esteemed than in the west of Scotland and in the rainy western counties of England, at the very time when it was superseded in great measure by superphosphates in the drier eastern counties. (Voelcker.) "It is well known that Peruvian guano is a capital manure for potatoes, especially on light soils, yet in a dry season it produces but an inconsiderable increase in potatoes on light land." (Voelcker.) From the first, European experience has taught that guano is not so supremely excellent on light soils as on clays and on good moist loams. In order to see what guano will do when the conditions are really favorable, we have only to look at the results which are obtained with it every day by greenhouse men upon their potted plants. Any one who has systematically fertilized plants with guano admixed with water, i. e. who has applied it frequently by small portions, in presence of an abundance of moisture, knows what an admirable fertilizer it really is.

Voelcker found that about one-half the weight of the original guano was soluble in water; and that by far the larger portion of the nitrogen contained in the organic matter of the guano is soluble in water, and consequently in a condition readily accessible to plants. In field culture, the most decided effect of guano will be seen in the first year, if the season is at all favorable; but after the second year its effect is hardly perceptible.

Care necessary in applying Guano.

Before scattering guano upon the land, it is well to mix it with 2 or 3 times its bulk of earth, some say with 5 or 10 times its bulk of earth. The earth should be freshly dug, so that it may be somewhat moist, and the guano, which has previously been reduced to a homogeneous powder by sifting and threshing the lumps upon a barn floor, should be thoroughly mixed with the earth by shovelling the mass over and over repeatedly. The purpose of the admixture with earth is not only to insure an even distribution of the fertilizer upon the land, and to check the volatilization of ammonia, but to prevent the possibility of the guano's injuring any of the young plants or seeds. Guano is so rich in ammoniacal salts that it might burn and destroy the roots of young plants if much of it were brought into immediate contact with them, especially if the ground happened to be dry.

For the same reason, it is well enough to strew the mixture of guano and earth two or three days before planting, and to plough or harrow it in; or the land may be rolled when the guano is sown, and the seed be harrowed in afterwards in due course. It is well, also, to apply guano during or just before rain, that is to say, at a time when heavy showers or a succession of wet days may confidently be expected. According to Voelcker, a comparatively small quantity of water, corresponding to a passing shower of rain, applied to a field recently manured with guano, appears to have a different effect on its constituents from that exerted by a large downfall. In the case of potatoes to be planted in hills, a handful of a mixture of guano and much earth may be thrown into the hill at the moment of planting, or, perhaps better, the ordinary mixture may be distributed along the furrow in which the hills are to be made.

These particulars were formerly much insisted upon, because of the corrosive character of this essentially chemical manure, and of the prejudice which, singularly enough, existed against it.

Guano may Spoil in Damp Air.

It is to be observed that, although guano suffers but little loss so long as it is kept dry and away from the air, it may rapidly depreciate by keeping in damp air. Krocker has noticed that guano may lose from $\frac{1}{3}$ to $\frac{1}{4}$ of its ammonia during a single winter when moist air is allowed to have access to it. The moistened urate of ammonia changes to carbonate, and the latter exhales. Indeed, moistened guano rapidly passes into a condition of active fermentation, and the nitrogen in its organic constituents is changed to carbonate of ammonia. So, too, the admixing of guano with earth, as above described, may hinder, but does not wholly prevent, the volatilization of the ammonia. The escape of the latter is still readily perceptible when guano is mixed with 5, 10, 20, or 50 parts of loam. According to Nesbit, even 1,000 parts of earth do not wholly prevent the volatilization. It may be questioned, however, whether in this experiment the peculiar odor of guano may not have been mistaken for the odor of ammonia. Voelcker drenched a couple of ounces of genuine Peruvian guano with dilute sulphuric acid in such manner that all the ammonia in the guano must have been changed to a non-volatile sulphate. But the characteristic smell of the guano was not removed, nor even weakened, and on drying down the mixture upon a water-bath, for 5 or 6 hours, the strong, peculiar odor which characterizes guano was constantly given off. When dry, the mixture still smelt strongly, though less so than when wet.

The loss of ammonia from guano is analogous to the results obtained by Brustlein in methodical experiments on the removal of ammonia from soils by means of currents of air and by the evaporation of water. Brustlein found, for example, that much of the ammonia which had been absorbed by a soil from ammonia-water escaped again easily when the soil was exposed to the air, and especially when the soil was repeatedly moistened and allowed to dry. He found, also, on passing a current of mixed ammonia gas and air through a considerable amount of earth, that although most of the ammonia was absorbed by the soil, yet on passing a stream of pure air through the soil thus charged with ammonia most of the latter left the soil and passed off with the air.

Guano and Common Salt.

When guano first came into use, it was a not uncommon practice to mix it with common salt before applying it to the land, and it has been thought that, by giving more weight to the guano, the salt enables the sower to distribute it more evenly, while the loss of dust which might escape from mere guano is prevented. But the excellent crops often obtained on using such mixtures have seemed to point to some specific action of the salt. (Compare Sodium Compounds.) For example, Heiden mixed some high-grade guano, which contained 14 % nitrogen and 13 % phosphoric acid, with an equal weight of salt, and manured therewith a sandy loam that had not been manured for six years, upon which he grew barley. His results are here given : —

	Crop on a Morgen (= 0.631 Acre).		Increase over no Manure.	
	Grain.	Straw, &c.	Grain.	Straw, &c.
No manure	500	846	. . .	. . .
110 lb. guano	669	980	169	134
110 lb. guano and 110 lb. salt .	752	1281	262	434

It was thought at one time that the salt acted to fix ammonia and prevent it from volatilizing. But it is now known that this supposition was erroneous, and that no ammonia is fixed by the salt, in a strictly chemical sense. So far from fixing the ammonia of guano, salt rather tends to liberate it in the earth and to disseminate through the soil that which would naturally become fixed there by the double silicates. (Voelcker.) Perhaps the salt may act also as an antiseptic to hinder the decomposition of urate of ammonia in the guano, so that more of the urate is available as such for crops when salt is used.

Genuine Guano could be bought formerly.

Another point to be noted is that the manner in which guano was imported into this country, and sold here, long afforded an excellent guaranty of its genuineness. In several of the Atlantic cities there were responsible agents of the Peruvian government from whom guano could be purchased in full confidence that the fertilizer received was what it purported to be.

For many years Peruvian guano was the cheapest source of active nitrogen at the farmer's command, and until a comparatively recent period the price of nitrogen in guano remained practically in accord with its price as contained in sulphate of ammonia and even in nitrate of soda. For example, a sample of Peruvian guano examined some years since by Prof. Johnson at New Haven was found to contain 8¾% of nitrogen and 14% of phosphoric acid. The price of this guano was $70 the ton. In a ton of the material there were 175 lb. of nitrogen and 280 lb. of phosphoric acid. The phosphoric acid was at that time regarded as worth 6 cents a pound. Hence there was 6 × 280 = $16.80 worth of this constituent in the ton, and by subtracting this value from $70, the price of the ton of guano, there is obtained $53.20 as the price of the 175 lb. of nitrogen in the ton. But $53.20 ÷ 175 = $0.30, as the price of the pound of nitrogen, and this was precisely the rate at which nitrogen could be bought in the form of sulphate of ammonia, at the time the analysis in question was made.

There was really, however, a slight advantage in favor of the guano, for it will be observed that in the foregoing estimate the 2% of potash that was contained in the guano has been neglected. The 40 lb. of potash in the ton at 4½ cents the pound would be equal to $1.80, and if this sum be brought into the account we will have $70 — (16.80 + 1.80) = $51.40, as the price of the 175 lb. of nitrogen. But $51.40 ÷ 175 = 29 cents, as the price of the pound of nitrogen.

When guano was first introduced to European agriculture the price at which it was sold was not based on any accurate estimate of its composition, but depended directly on the cost of mining, shipping and selling the substance, and on the profit which farmers could get by using it; but with the advance of chemical knowledge more accurate conceptions have prevailed, and it is no longer true that guano is sold at cheap rates, as compared with other fertilizers. Of late years nitrate of soda has been sold at very low prices, and the price of sulphate of ammonia has sympathized with that of the nitrate, while the price of guano has been fixed by the Chilian government at comparatively high figures. In the spring of 1885 guano that contained 7⅜ % of nitrogen, 12 % of phosphoric acid, and 2 % of potash, was held at $65 the ton in New York by the agent of the Chilian government, although nitrogen in the form of nitrate of soda and of sulphate of ammonia could then be had at rather less than 18 cents the pound.

In Europe it has been customary to neglect the potash when estimating the value of guano, for the alleged reason that most soils good enough to bear the application of guano already contain considerable quantities of potash. Besides, a good deal of potash is supplied to the land in the barnyard-manure that is usually employed in conjunction with guano. Perhaps the fairest way of considering the potash is as something " thrown in " and " given to boot," which shall lead the farmer sometimes to give the preference to guano rather than to sulphate of ammonia, in case the price of nitrogen were the same in both. A somewhat similar remark will apply to the 2 or 3% of soluble phosphoric acid usually present in guano. For since soluble phosphoric acid may be estimated to be worth about twice as much as ordinary insoluble phosphoric acid, it is not fair to allow only six cents a pound for the whole of the phosphoric acid of the guano. Whence it again appears, in respect to the guano above mentioned, that at $70 the ton it was a cheaper source of nitrogen than sulphate of ammonia at 6 cents the pound, or than nitrate of soda at 4½ cents.

Dung of Poultry.

The dung of fowls is a manure somewhat analogous to guano, though far less valuable than guano weight for weight. To begin with, the food of hens, of pigeons, and even of turkeys, except in grasshopper season, is of vegetable rather than of animal origin, while the sea-fowl that produced the guano lived upon fish, and consequently voided a more highly nitrogenized excrement; and moreover the guano has become highly concentrated by the peculiar processes of slow decay to which it has long been subjected. But it is none the less true, as a general proposition, that the excrements of birds (and reptiles) contain uric acid and thereby differ essentially from the excrements of quadrupeds, which contain none of this form of nitrogenous plant-food, or as good as none. Uric acid is a very valuable fertilizer, being directly assimilable by plants and easily converted into oxalate of ammonia by putrefaction. To the presence of urates in Peruvian guano the peculiar merit of this substance may fairly be attributed. Hence the presumption that while guano for certain purposes is one of the cheapest manures the farmer can buy, it would ill become him wholly to neglect the droppings of his hen-roosts. Analyses show that the following percentages of substances are contained in the fresh dung of

	Fowls.	Pigeons.	Ducks.	Geese.
Water	56.00	52.00	56.60	77.10
Organic matter . .	25.50	31.00	26.20	13.40
Nitrogen	{ 0.80–2.00 say 1.60	1.25–2.50 say 1.75 }	1.00	0.55
Phosphoric acid . .	1.50–2.00	1.50–2.00	1.40	0.54
Potash	0.80–0.90	1.00–1.25	0.62	0.95
Lime	2.00–2.50	1.50–2.00	1.70	0.84
Magnesia	0.75	0.50	0.35	0.20

Voelcker found in dung taken from a henhouse 44 % of water, 2.34 % of nitrogen, 5.37 % of phosphate of lime, and 4.18 % of carbonate of lime and alkali salts. In another sample from a poultry-farm he found only 0.89 % of nitrogen and 2.31 % of phosphate of lime. This sample contained 40 % of silicious matter, insoluble in acid, while the other sample contained less than 7 %. A sample analyzed by Koenig, taken from a poultry-farm, contained 13.64% water, 73.45% organic matter, 12.91% ash, 4.01% nitrogen, 2.78% phosphoric acid, 0.58% potash, 3.18% lime and 0.25 % magnesia. Pigeon-dung ground to meal, as sold in Riga, gave Knieriem 19.58 % of sand, 3.19 % of nitrogen (most of it in the form of uric acid), and 1.86 % of phosphoric acid. A good sample of pigeon-dung, containing but little foreign matter, analyzed at New Haven in 1890, contained among other things

9.55 % water, 62.38 % organic and volatile matter, 18.12 % sand
and silica, 3.9 % phosphoric acid, 1.07 % potash, and 2.12 % of
lime. The organic nitrogen amounted to 3.43 %, and there was
0.47 % of ammonia-nitrogen.

Many analyses made in different years by Thoms, in Riga,
showed from 2.5 to 3 % nitrogen, 1.6 to 2 % phosphoric acid,
and from 0.8 to 1.12 % potash; or, on the average, 2.84 % nitrogen, 1.8 % phosphoric acid, and 0.96 % potash. A quantity
of pigeon-dung, imported into England from Egypt some years
ago, contained 6¾ % of water, 60 % of organic matter, 21½ % of
sand, 3¼ % of nitrogen in organic combination, 1½ % of ammonia, 8 % of phosphates of lime and magnesia, and ½ % of alkali
salts. Wein found in pigeon-dung taken from a church-steeple
11 % of water and 89 % of dry matter. The dry matter contained
56 % of organic and volatile matters, and 33 % of ashes, 2¼ % of
nitrogen, 2 % of phosphoric acid, and 5½ % of potash. Boussingault found in a specimen of dry pigeon-dung 8¼ % of nitrogen.
It contained 9¹ % of water also (see below). A Belgian farmer
has computed that a pigeon yields about 6 lb. avoirdupois of dung
in a year, a hen about 12 lb., a turkey or a goose about 25 lb.
each, and a duck 18 lb.

Allowing 18 cents for the pound of nitrogen in this form, 6 cents
for the pound of phosphoric acid, and 5 cents for the pound of potash, 100 lb. of hen-manure will be worth some 30 or 40 cents.
An experienced farmer, living near Boston, tells me that he is glad
to buy the dung of hens at $0.75 the barrel. He says that this
manure, when dry and granular, weighs about 30 lb. to the
bushel.

Hen-manure is applied to the land in comparatively small quantities, and is particularly esteemed for dressing strawberry-beds,
and as an excitant upon Indian corn, to ensure that the crop shall
be well started. An approved method of procedure is to mix the
hen-manure with an equal bulk of wood-ashes — together with
some peat or loam, to hinder the escape of ammonia — to throw
the mixture into little heaps, and to moisten them by sprinkling
with a watering-pot. In this way, the uric acid is made ready to
act immediately as a powerful forcing-manure. (E. Hersey.) Hen-
manure is apt to be sticky when fresh, and lumpy when dry, and it is
not easy to make it fine enough to be sown from a drill. Its lightness
also hinders it from running freely through the tubes. Hence it

is better suited for the gardener and the small-way farmer, who can distribute it by hand, than for field operations. But there can be no question as to its value when properly managed.

Pigeon-Dung formerly Important.

Pigeon-dung, and the dung of other domestic birds, played an important part in Roman husbandry,[1] and in that of several Eastern nations, notably Persia and Egypt. Until a comparatively recent period, it was much thought of by European agriculturists also. It was an old practice, for example, in England, on heavy, undrained land, to dress in the spring the chilled wheat-crop near the water-furrows with pigeon's dung. (Pusey.) Previous to the French Revolution, great dove-cotes were attached to the establishments of all large land-owners. It may be said of it emphatically that it is a manure of historic importance. Since the discovery of guano and the diffusion of correct information concerning the use of nitrates and of ammonium salts, the dung of land-birds is no longer of much economic importance, but the old use of it may still serve to teach a valuable lesson as to the significance of active nitrogenous fertilizers, while it illustrates the conspicuous merit of uric acid almost as well as guano does, although, as was said, the dung of fowls and pigeons really differs very considerably from guano, in that it has never been concentrated, and, so to say, purified, by the slow processes of fermentation to which the guano-beds have been subjected. Pigeon-dung continues to be used in Egypt and Persia to the present day, as travellers tell us.

The dung of poultry is liable to suffer much injury from fermentation and from becoming flyblown (see Bussey Bulletin, I, 24). Pigeon-dung, in particular, often consists largely of inert matters, such as the husks of oats. I have noticed samples of pigeon-dung that must have been wellnigh valueless because they were composed almost wholly of broken cherry-stones (Bussey Bulletin, II, 324).

Dung of Bats.

In many hot countries the dung of bats collects in caves in such considerable quantities, often to a depth of many feet, that attention has repeatedly been called to it as a source of fertilizing matters. This bat-guano varies widely, both as to appearance and chemical composition, according as it is more or less contaminated

[1] See, for example, the references given by Heiden in his Düngerlehre, II, 243.

with dirt and has been more or less exposed to oxidation and chemical action.   Voelcker and other analysts have found that it may contain of moisture, 7 to 64 %; organic matter and ammonium salts, 6 to 65 %; phosphoric acid, $1\frac{1}{4}$ to 25 %; nitrogen, $\frac{1}{4}$ to 9 %. It often contains nitrates, even as many as would represent 2 or 3 % of nitric acid (N_2O_5).

Guano gave a great Impulse to Agriculture.

There are several points of general interest with regard to guano that bear so closely upon the laws of political economy and of social progress that they deserve to be taken to heart.   From what has been said of the price of guano as compared with that of other manures, something may be inferred as to the enormous influence which this price has exerted, and still exerts, in regulating the price of all kinds of fertilizers.   But this point is a trifle in comparison with other considerations, for the bringing of guano into the markets of the world, even more than the introduction of crushed bones, gave a very powerful impetus to the progress of intelligent agriculture.

Before the introduction of these concentrated manures, the farmer had little or no freedom of action.   He was almost wholly dependent upon his barnyard for supplies of plant-food, and in all old countries, at least, he was tied hand and foot by a more or less complicated course of rotation of his crops.   If he had money enough, he could indeed buy food for cattle, and so increase his stock of manure; and he could also employ ameliorating agents, such as lime and marl and gypsum, or he could buy a little ashes or soot on occasion.   But all these things were bulky and difficult of transportation.   Much labor had to be expended in handling them.   It was wellnigh impossible for the European farmer to act upon the maxim of the nimble penny, which is so characteristic of modern civilization, or to carry on his estate as if it were a manufactory.   In case he had forecast a market, as a merchant would, the farmer was wellnigh powerless either to grow or to force a special crop to meet this market.   If, for example, he saw evidence that barley would be in demand next year, he could not profit by this knowledge, nor by any special sagacity of this kind, unless, indeed, he should leave his legitimate business and become a trader, that is to say, a speculator in the produce of his neighbors.

By means of guano and tile-drains this state of things was completely changed, and the so-called high farming became possible in Europe. There was developed an enlightened system of agriculture, which prospered during many years in England, Scotland, and Germany, — a system of agriculture, namely, which was governed by business rules and habits of thought, and which depended on capital as well as upon labor. Very soon after the introduction of guano into those countries, it was found, as Stoeckhardt has formulated the matter, —

I. That, by means of this manure, the most fruitful fields might be excited to yield still larger crops;

II. That the regular courses of rotation might be broken in upon without harm on an emergency, and that consequently a much larger proportion of land could be given over to the growth of any crop for which a special demand was anticipated than was possible before;

III. That any field which might happen to fall behindhand, as regards its fertility, could quickly be brought up to its normal condition; and

IV. That growing crops, or patches of crops, that had suffered from drought or from cold could often be saved by a timely application of it;

V. That new fields could soon be brought to a high degree of fertility; and

VI. That the number of cattle kept upon a farm could either be diminished, in case the conditions were favorable for such diminution, or largely increased by virtue of the increased yield of forage due to the use of guano. Of course, where the stock of cattle was thus increased, the yield of stable-manure was increased in a like proportion.

But when the farmers had learned that through the use of guano all these things were possible, it was but natural that they should be ready and eager to welcome other concentrated manures. Hence the easy introduction of nitrate of soda, of sulphate of ammonia, of the superphosphates, and more recently of fish-scrap, flesh-refuse, and potash-salts. So too with regard to the desire for knowledge as to the action and the management of the concentrated manures.

Peruvian guano is no longer the only artificial manure (so called), nor the most important; but it is none the less a fact that the influence exerted upon human activity and intelligence by the introduction of guano into commerce has not been confined to the farm alone. This influence is felt to-day wherever agriculture is taught. It is to be seen in the schools and colleges, as well as in the books and newspapers that relate to husbandry. Singularly enough, the influence of guano is felt also in the conduct of those municipal and domestic affairs which bear upon the health and comfort of large populations. It is safe to say, that, were it not for Peruvian guano and the lessons it has taught, the whole modern system of cleansing cities by means of water-closets and quick-flowing sewers could never have become so general as it now is.

Under the head of Sewage, it will be seen how it is that cheap guano, and the other concentrated manures which have succeeded it, have in some sense compelled the cities to wash their filth into the sea. That is to say, the commercial fertilizers have as good as destroyed the old agricultural demand for the comparatively costly and less efficient night-soil.

As an example of the kind of feeling which was excited by the use of guano in Europe soon after its introduction to that country, may be cited the argument offered by Lord George Bentinck at a debate on the repeal of the corn-law, held in the English House of Commons in the year 1846. According to Lord George, 2 cwt. of Peruvian guano applied to an acre of wheat-land give an average increase of rather more than 9 bushels of the grain, at which rate a hundred thousand tons, or two million cwt. of this fertilizer, would add more than nine million bushels to the crop, or bread enough for the support of a million of people for a year. Or, for the sake of being perfectly sure, he would allow 3 cwt. of guano to the acre as necessary to produce the extra 9 bushels of wheat.

In like manner, as regards turnips, experience, he argued, had shown that 2 cwt. of guano will add 10 tons per acre to the crop. Or, if we say 3 cwt. guano, then 2,000,000 cwt. of the fertilizer would add 6,666,660 tons to the natural unmanured product of the English turnip-fields. But a ton of Swedish turnips, he maintained, will last 20 sheep 3 weeks, and each sheep should gain half a pound of meat a week, or a pound and a half in three weeks, so that the 20 sheep would make 30 lb. of mutton; and by multiplying this factor into the sum total, he naturally suggests an enormous amount of meat.

The foregoing figures, as regards wheat, differ so little from those proposed by Mr. Lawes (5 lb. NH$_3$ for 1 bushel of wheat), that it seems not improbable that one of the two computations may be merely a modification of, or perhaps a refinement upon, the other.

Rectified Guano.

In recent years a very considerable part of all the guano that is sold has been treated with sulphuric acid before reaching the consumer. The idea originated on treating some cargoes of guano that had been damaged by long-continued contact with sea-water, with the view of selling the product as superphosphate of lime. But the fertilizer thus prepared gave such excellent results in the fields, that much first-class guano has ever since been similarly treated with the acid. It is said also that Guanape guano in its natural condition is frequently far too damp and sticky for application to the land, and that there is a decided advantage in treating it with acid so that it may be sold in the form of a fine, dry powder. Moreover, the importers appear to be glad of the opportunity, which this process of manufacture affords, of mixing cargoes of high-grade guano with those of low grade. They are thus enabled to sell always a product of one and the same standard character and composition. Sometimes, indeed, they appear to add more or less sulphate of ammonia to increase the percentage of nitrogen. In this country, guano which has been thus treated with sulphuric acid is known as "rectified guano." It is usually guaranteed to contain 10% of ammonia (NH_3), say 160 lb. N to the ton; 10% of soluble phosphoric acid, say 200 lb. P_2O_5 to the ton; 2% of potash, say 40 lb. K_2O to the ton. At 20, 10, and 4½ cents respectively, these constituents would be worth $32, $20, and $1.80; or, all together, nearly $54 for the ton.

Other Forms of Nitrogen will be Studied in Subsequent Chapters.

In connection with the fossil bird-dung called guano, it might be well on some accounts to study the fresh excrements of men and animals, since these materials are conspicuous sources of urea and some other of the organic nitrogen compounds, just now mentioned, which are capable of serving directly as plant-food. Fresh urine and night-soil, in particular, are valuable forcing-manures, because they bring to the land very considerable quantities of easily assimilable nitrogen. But it will be more convenient on the whole, at this stage of proceedings, to consider several varieties of organic matters, available as fertilizers, which are capable of supplying ammonia or nitrates indirectly when they decay, although in themselves they may not contain either ammonia, nitrates, or any other form of nitrogen which is directly assimilable by the higher orders of plants.

Hence, the discussion of the value of animal excrements will be deferred to a special chapter which will treat of ordinary manure, as obtained from farmyards and stables, which is a material that differs not a little, generally speaking, from fresh excrements, both because of the straw or other litter with which the excrement is admixed and of changes which the mixture may have undergone in the process of decay. Most prominent among the useful, merchantable organic fertilizers are refuse fish, flesh and blood, and some kinds of oil-cake.

END OF VOL. I.